The Editor

Stephen H. A. Shepherd is Assistant Professor of English at Southern Methodist University. He received his doctorate from the University of Oxford. His honors include fellowships to the Huntington Library and the Bibliographical Society of America. He is the author of several articles on Middle English romances and editor of the Middle English *Pseudo-Turpin Chronicle* (forthcoming).

MIDDLE ENGLISH ROMANCES

AUTHORITATIVE TEXTS
SOURCES AND BACKGROUNDS
CRITICISM

A NORTON CRITICAL EDITION

MIDDLE ENGLISH ROMANCES

AUTHORITATIVE TEXTS

SOURCES AND BACKGROUNDS

CRITICISM

Selected and Edited by

STEPHEN H. A. SHEPHERD

SOUTHERN METHODIST UNIVERSITY

W • W • NORTON & COMPANY • *New York* • *London*

The text of this book is composed in Electra
with the display set in Bernhard Modern
Composition by PennSet, Inc.
Manufacturing by Courier Westford

Library of Congress Cataloging-in-Publication Data
Middle English romances : authoritative texts, sources and
backgrounds, criticism / selected and edited by Stephen H.A. Shepherd.
p.   cm. —(A Norton critical edition)
Includes bibliographical references (p.   ).
1. English literature—Middle English, 1100–1500—History and
criticism. 2. English literature—Middle English, 1100–1500.
3. Arthurian romances—History and criticism. 4. Romances, English—
History and criticism. 5. Arthurian romances. 6. Romances,
English.   I. Shepherd, Stephen H. A.
PR321.M45   1995
821′.030901—dc20   94–36710

ISBN 0–393–96607–0

W. W. Norton & Company, Inc., 500 Fifth Avenue, New York, N.Y. 10110
W. W. Norton & Company Ltd., 10 Coptic Street, London WC1A 1PU
1 2 3 4 5 6 7 8 9 0

Contents

Criticism

for J. F.

Preface

I was reading a sign high on the wall behind the bar:

ONLY GENUINE PRE-WAR AMERICAN AND
BRITISH WHISKEYS SERVED HERE

I was trying to count how many *lies* could be found in those nine words, and had reached four, with promise of more, when one of my confederates . . . cleared his throat with the noise of a gasoline engine's backfire.[1]

I would encourage anyone picking up *Middle English Romances* to follow the lead of Hammett's Continental Op and distinguish in its wholly traditional title a clutch of lies. That the majority of texts in this volume are written in *Middle English* is perhaps the closest thing to a truth suggested by the title—though *Havelok*, about 700 years old, can be considered an example of "Early Middle" English, and the *Capystranus*, printed in the reign of Henry VIII, is arguably an example of "Early Modern" English.

That the seven principal texts are *English*, in the sense of having an exclusive origin in England, is certainly a lie. As the Sources and Backgrounds section is intended to illustrate, all in one way or another have continental, Anglo-Norman, or Celtic antecedents; for some, the link is made through Middle English intermediaries; and others may bear an even fainter impress of dependence as composites of tradition and motif rather than as translations and adaptations of identifiable texts; but none exists in splendid isolation. This is not to say that there is nothing uniquely English about them—to the contrary, they have been selected largely because they have no peer—but responsibly to speak of them as English texts presupposes a sensitivity to that which they inherit from other places, and times. It is for this reason that, in taking advantage of the special format of the Norton Critical Editions, I have given over more space than is usual to sources and analogues, against reprinted criticism. In so doing, I have endeavored to supply nearly all of the relevant texts in as complete a form as possible; besides those self-contained passages which, like the Havelok episode in Gaimar or the selections from the *Gesta Romanorum*, have been excised in contiguous

1. Dashiell Hammett, "The Golden Horseshoe," in *The Continental Op* (New York, 1974), p. 69 (I refer to the most common edition, though the short story was first published in 1924).

xi

form, the only real exception to the practice is the sampling of Chrétien's *Yvain*, which poem is otherwise prohibitively long and of which several good translations are readily available.

That the principal texts of the collection are *Romances* is perhaps the most obvious lie of all. For some time it has been a commonplace for editors of Middle English "romances" to remark upon the inadequacy of inclusive definitions for the ostensible genre; the one hundred or more[2] so-called romances in Middle English present an extraordinary variety of form and theme to which no single critical paradigm is usefully equal. Indeed, an abiding sense of generic *distinction* is surely to be encouraged in the apprehension of these texts. It is to this end that I indicate in the table of contents an arrangement of the selected poems according to four different categories. So to replace one generalizing term with yet others may of course be to replace one set of lies with others—and it is not difficult to see, for instance, that all of the selected texts have their fair share of "trial and ordeal," that the impressionable Charlemagne of *The Sege off Melayne* is subjected to some rough "nurture and correction" at the hands of Turpin, that Havelok (with cross on chest) engages in a kind of "holy war" against Godard and Godrich, and so on. Such distinctions as are suggested, then, are intended only as distinctions of a perceived emphasis. And the standard against which the emphasis is measured (arbitrary though the standard itself may be) reflects fairly well-established ideas of the kind advanced in the first two critical essays printed in the back of this volume, especially those advanced by Erich Auerbach. Auerbach finds the hero's process to "self-realization" or "personal perfection" as the essential action of the ideal romance (pp. 420–22). The categories of the table of contents thus suggest how the selected texts represent gradations away from an interest in that kind of action. I trust that the categories will in the main be taken as polemical, though I hasten to add that it is doubtful whether any Middle English "romance" conforms satisfactorily to the Auerbachian paradigm—compare the essay by John Finlayson.

Each of the seven principal texts needs no introduction—each has been edited before and each has in its own right continued to attract scholarly attention—and I think it safe to say that each represents the work of confident, spirited, and intelligent minds. Whether, as a group, and given their evident variety, the poems are sufficiently representative of what French and Hale called "the first large body of English fiction"[3] is hard to say; but most, together with the related Sources and Backgrounds material, at the very least have the advantage of shedding light on other works which students of medieval English literature are likely

2. A useful guide to the number and content of the Middle English texts commonly identified as romances is to be found in the first volume of *A Manual of the Writings in Middle English*, J. Burke Severs, general ed. (New Haven, 1967).
3. Walter Hoyt French and Charles Brockway Hale, eds., *Middle English Metrical Romances* (New York, 1930), 2 vols., I, v.

to encounter. *Ywain and Gawain*, *The Awntyrs off Arthure*, and *The Weddyng of Syr Gawen*, for instance, can provide an invaluable sense of context for students of the *Gawain* poet, and possibly also of Malory. The *Weddyng* has further attractions for those wishing to improve their understanding of the peculiar genius of Chaucer's Wife of Bath's Tale, and the first part of *The Awntyrs* warrants comparison with sections of *Piers Plowman*; it is also worth noting that the *Weddyng* and the *Awntyrs* are analogues to one another. *Havelok* and *The Sege off Melayne* can be studied as the heirs, in differing ways perhaps, of more distant heroic traditions manifest in such texts as *Beowulf* and *The Battle of Maldon*. *Sir Orfeo* and *Sir Launfal*, as "Breton lays," can make invaluable complements to a reading of Chaucer's Franklin's Tale.

Each of the Sources and Backgrounds sections corresponding to the seven principal texts is prefaced with an introductory headnote. The headnotes are intended to establish the relevance of the sources or analogues printed thereafter; they aim to give a practical account of what is currently known about the principal text's provenance and to suggest ways in which comparison with the relevant sources and analogues might reveal something about the author's (or translator's or adaptor's) intentions. I must stress that the headnotes are not intended to provide an account of the state of the critical art as it applies to any other aspects of the texts in question; the Selected Bibliography will provide a start for students wishing to explore such matters further, and no doubt instructors will wish anyway to assign other readings according to their own preferences.

As an additional practical help to those interested in the circumstances generally of these texts' composition and their circulation, I have included essays by A. C. Baugh and Gisela Guddat-Figge. Baugh's essay provides a very helpful introduction to the nature of oral-formulaic composition and its influence on written texts; among other things, the essay will help students to see how the conventionalities of a Middle English text are not signs of incompetence (let alone plagiarism) but rather are valued constituents of meaning. Guddat-Figge's essay should assist those with questions about the relationship between the oral and literary manifestations of the (so-called) romances; I hope also that the essay will allow students to begin to see the relevance of manuscript studies to the understanding of texts which they otherwise only ever meet through printed editions.

All editions of Middle English texts in this volume are mine and have been prepared from manuscript or photographic reproductions thereof. The characters þ and ȝ have been modernized (the former to *th* and the latter to *gh*, *y*, or *z*), as has the use of *u* and *v*, *i* and *j* (and the first-person pronoun is rendered as *I* where manuscripts have Y); manuscript abbreviations are expanded silently. Otherwise, and excepting the correction of obvious scribal errors (notably in the case of damaged rhyme),[4] the orthography of the base manuscripts has not been excessively regularized; in cases where this may present difficulties, I have employed marginal glosses or explanatory footnotes. Word division, punctuation, and capitalization are editorial. Where possible, I have followed the base manuscripts in matters of paragraphing and the distinction of larger divisions of text. I have identified within square brackets editorial emendations to the base text only where I diverge from the usual practice of the standard scholarly editions; readings incorporated from a manuscript other than that of the base text are, however, always set within brackets and the source manuscript identified. Where the exigencies of Middle English prosody may present special problems for beginning students— as in the cases of unfamiliar word order, shifts of tense within one sentence, omission of verbs and relative pronouns, and multiple negatives—I hope to have erred on the side of caution in the quantity of explanatory apparatus. Persistently difficult words and phrases, and potential "false friends" (such as *in-fere*, "together"), are reglossed roughly every one hundred lines.

I am grateful to several libraries for permission to transcribe from their manuscripts; the specific contributions of each library are acknowledged in the titular footnotes to each edition. I am also grateful to several people who have made it possible to improve this volume in ways that I could not have envisioned alone; in particular I am grateful to Carrie Copeland, Lee Gibson, Douglas Gray, M. L. Lawhon, D. B. Lenck, Maldwyn Mills, Roger Pensom, and Helen Phillips. To Carol Bemis, my editor at W. W. Norton, go innumerable thanks for her care over this project since its inception. Above all, I must thank my mother for her inspired and well-timed encouragement as the hours of editing went by.

---

4. What to modern eyes may appear to be only approximate rhyme has, however, been retained. For a helpful study of the rhyming practices of medieval English poets, see E. G. Stanley, "Rhymes in English Medieval Verse: From Old English to Middle English," in *Medieval English Studies Presented to George Kane*, E. D. Kennedy, R. Waldron, and J. S. Wittig, eds. (Cambridge, 1988), pp. 19–54.

Reading Middle English[†]

The chief difficulty with Middle English for the modern reader is caused
not by its inflections so much as by its spelling, which may be described
as a rough-and-ready phonetic system, and by the fact that it is not a
single standardized language but consists of a number of regional dialects
each with its own peculiarities of sound and its own systems for representing sounds in writing. The Midland dialect—the dialect of London
and of *Sir Launfal, The Weddyng of Syr Gawen and Dame Ragnell,*
and (to a lesser extent) *Havelok,* which is the ancestor of our own standard
speech—differs greatly from the dialect spoken in the west of England
(*Sir Orfeo* appears originally to have been written in a southwestern
dialect), from that of the northwest (*The Awntyrs off Arthure*), and from
that of the north (*Ywain and Gawain, The Sege off Melayne*), and these
dialects differ from one another. The remarks that follow apply chiefly
to Midland English; non-Midland dialectal variations are regularly
glossed in the editions where they appear.

I. The Sounds of Middle English: General Rules

Though preserved for us only in written form, most of the Middle
English texts in this volume show signs of having been circulated orally
at some time in their history, and a number make appeals to a listening
audience. Such appeals may, of course, reflect only the artifice of convention, but the inherent drama of the rhetorical flourishes and frequent
exchanges of direct discourse which characteristically imbue these pieces
in any case makes for poetry which is at its best when read aloud. The
following general analysis of the sounds of Middle English will enable
the reader who has not time for detailed study to read Middle English
aloud so as to preserve some of its most essential characteristics, without,
however, giving heed to many important details. The next section,
"Detailed Analysis," is designed for the reader who wishes to go more
deeply into the pronunciation of Middle English. Middle English differs
from Modern English in three principal respects: (1) the pronunciation
of the long vowels *a, e, i* (or *y*), *o,* and *u* (spelled *ou, ow*); (2) the fact

---

† This section is reprinted and adapted from M. H. Abrams et al., eds., *The Norton Anthology
of English Literature,* 6th ed. (New York, 1993), 2 vols., I, 10–14, with permission of W.
W. Norton & Company, New York.

that Middle English final *e* is often sounded; and (3) the fact that all Middle English consonants are sounded.

1. LONG VOWELS

Middle English vowels are long when they are doubled (*aa, ee, oo*) or when they are terminal (*he, to, holy*); *a, e,* and *o* are long when followed by a single consonant plus a vowel (*name, mete, note*). Middle English vowels are short when they are followed by two consonants.

Long *a* is sounded like the *a* in Modern English "father": *maken, waast* (waist).

Long *e* may be sounded like the *a* in Modern English "name" (ignoring the distinction between the close and open vowel): *be, fleen* (flee).

Long *i* (or *y*) is sounded like the *i* in Modern English "machine": *lif, whit; myn, holy.*

Long *o* may be sounded like the *o* in Modern English "note" (again ignoring the distinction between the close and open vowel): *do, sone* (soon).

Long *u* (spelled *ou, ow*) is sounded like the *oo* in Modern English "goose": *obout* (about), *rownde.*

Note that in general Middle English long vowels are pronounced like long vowels in modern languages other than English. Short vowels and diphthongs, however, may be pronounced as in Modern English.

2. FINAL *E*

In Middle English syllabic verse, final *e* is sounded like the *a* in "sofa" to provide a needed unstressed syllable: *Blessed be that ilkë thrawë / That thou hire toke in Godes lawë*! (*Havelok*, ll. 1215–16). But final *e* is suppressed when not needed for the meter (cf. *hire* in the example). It is commonly silent before words beginning with a vowel or *h*.

3. CONSONANTS

Middle English consonants are pronounced separately in all combinations—*gnat: g-nat; knave: k-nave; write: w-rite; folk: fol-k.* In a simplified system of pronunciation the combination *gh* as in *night* or *thought* may be treated as if it were silent.

II. The Sounds of Middle English: Detailed Analysis

1. SIMPLE VOWELS

Sound	Pronunciation	Example
long *a* (spelled *a, aa*)	*a* in "father"	*maken, waast*
short *a*	*o* in "hot"	*swapped*
long *e* close (spelled *e, ee*)	*a* in "name"	*be, sweete*

Sound	Pronunciation	Example
long *e* open (spelled *e, ee*)	*e* in "there"	*mete, eeres*
short *e*	*e* in "set"	*hem*
final *e*	*a* in "sofa"	*ilke*
long *i* (spelled *i, y*)	*i* in "machine"	I, *ride*
short *i*	*i* in "in"	*in*
long *o* close (spelled *o, oo*)	*o* in "note"	*sone, goode*
long *o* open (spelled *o, oo*)	*oa* in "broad"	*go, foos*
short *o*	*o* in "oft"	*of*
long *u* when spelled *ou, ow*	*oo* in "goose"	*hous, flowre*
long *u* when spelled *u*	*u* in "pure"	*vertu*
short *u* (spelled *u, o*)	*u* in "full"	*ful, love*

Doubled vowels and terminal vowels are always long, whereas single vowels before two consonants other than *th* and *ch* are always short. The vowels *a*, *e*, and *o* are long before a single consonant followed by a vowel: *nāë, sēkë* (sick), *hōly*. In general, words that have descended into Modern English reflect their original Middle English quantity: *līven* (to live), but *līf* (life).

The close and open sounds of long *e* and long *o* may often be identified by the Modern English spellings of the words in which they appear. Original long close *e* is generally represented in Modern English by *ee*: "sweet," "knee," "teeth," "see" have close *e* in Middle English, but so does "be"; original long open *e* is generally represented in Modern English by *ea*: "meat," "heath," "sea," "great," "breath" have open *e* in Middle English. Similarly, original long close *o* is now generally represented by *oo*: "soon," "food," "good," but also "do," "to"; original long open *o* is represented either by *oa* or by *o*: "coat," "boat," "moan," but also "go," "bone," "foe," "home." Notice that original close *o* is now almost always pronounced like the *oo* in goose, but that original open *o* is almost never so pronounced; thus it is often possible to identify the Middle English vowels through Modern English sounds.

The nonphonetic Middle English spelling of *o* for short *u* has been preserved in a number of Modern English words ("love," "son," "come"), but in others *u* has been restored: "sun" (*sonne*), "run" (*ronne*).

For the treatment of final *e*, see under "General Rules" above.

2. DIPHTHONGS

Sound	Pronunciation	Example
ai, ay, ei, ay	between *ai* in "aisle" and *ay* in "day"	*saide, seid, day, preye*
au, aw	*ou* in "out"	*chaunge, utlawes*
eu, ew	*ew* in "few"	*newe*
oi, oy	*oy* in "joy"	*joye, point*
ou, ow	*ou* in "thought"	*thought, lowe*

Note that in words with *ou* and *ow* that in Modern English are sounded with the *ou* of "about," the combination indicates not the diphthong but the simple vowel long *u* (see "1. Simple Vowels" above).

3. CONSONANTS

In general, all consonants except *h* were always sounded in Middle English, including consonants that have become silent in Modern English such as the *g* in "gnaw," the *k* in "knight," the *l* in "folk," and the *w* in "write." In noninitial *gn*, however, the *g* was silent, as in Modern English "sign." Initial *h* was silent in short common English words and in words borrowed from French and may have been almost silent in all words. The combination *gh* as in "night" or "thought" was sounded like the *ch* of German *ich* or *nach*. Note that Middle English *gg* represents both the hard sound of "dagger" and the soft sound of "bridge."

III. Parts of Speech and Grammar

1. NOUNS

The plural and possessive of nouns end in *es*, formed by adding *s* or *es* to the singular: *knight, knightes; roote, rootes*; a final consonant is frequently doubled before *es*: *bed, beddes*. A common irregular plural is *eyen* (spelled variously, including *eyn, eghne, eyghen*—"eyes").

2. PRONOUNS

Where they appear, the chief differences from Modern English are as follows:

Modern English	Middle English
I	I, *Ich*
you (singular)	*thou* (subjective); *the(e)* (objective)
her	*hir(e)*, *her(e)*
its	*his*
you (plural)	*ye* (subjective); *you* (objective)
their	*her(e)*
them	*hem*

In formal speech, the second person plural is often used for the singular. The possessive adjectives *my* and *thy* take *n* before a word beginning with a vowel or *h*: *thyne oth, myn herte*.

3. ADJECTIVES

Adjectives ending in a consonant sometimes (though not consistently) add final *e* when they stand before the noun they modify and after another modifying word such as *the, this,* or *that* or nouns or pronouns in the possessive: *a good hors,* but *the (this, my, the kinges) goode hors.* They also may add *e* when standing before and modifying a plural noun, a noun in the vocative, or any proper noun.

Adjectives are compared by adding *er(e)* for the comparative, *est(e)* for the superlative. Sometimes the stem vowel is shortened or altered in the process: *sweete, swettere, swettest; long, lenger, lengest.*

Sometimes an adjective is used as a noun or "absolute adjective": *at Carlele shal that comly be crowned* (at Carlisle will that attractive man be crowned).

4. ADVERBS

Adverbs are formed from adjectives by adding *e, ly,* or *liche* (or *like);* the adjective *fair* thus yields *faire, fairly, fairliche.*

5. VERBS

Middle English verbs, like Modern English verbs, are either "weak" or "strong." Weak verbs form their preterites and past participles with a *t* or *d* suffix and preserve the same stem vowel throughout their systems, although it is sometimes shortened in the preterite and past participle: *love, loved; bend, bent; hear, heard; meet, met.* Strong verbs do not use the *t* or *d* suffix, but vary their stem vowel in the preterite and past participle: *take, took, taken; begin, began, begun; find, found, found.*

The inflectional endings are the same for Middle English strong verbs and weak verbs except in the preterite singular and the imperative singular. In the following paradigms, the weak verbs *loven* (to love) and *heeren* (to hear) and the strong verbs *taken* (to take) and *ginnen* (to begin) serve as models.

	Present Indicative	Preterite Indicative
I	*love, heere*	*loved(e), herde*
	take, ginne	*took, gan*
thou	*lovest, heerest*	*lovedest, herdest*
	takest, ginnest	*tooke, gonne*
he, she, it	*loveth, heereth*	*loved(e), herde*
	taketh, ginneth	*took, gan*
we, ye, they	*love(n) (th), heere(n) (th)*	*loved(e) (en), herde(n)*
	take(n) (th), ginne(n) (th)	*tooke(n), gonne(n)*

The present plural ending *eth* is southern, whereas the *e(n)* ending is Midland. In the north, *s* may appear as the ending of all persons of the present. In the weak preterite, when the ending *e* gave a verb three or more syllables, it was frequently dropped. Note that in certain strong verbs like *ginnen* there are two distinct stem vowels in the preterite; however, by the late fourteenth century one of these had begun to replace the other, and some texts occasionally use *gan* for all persons of the preterite.

	Present Subjunctive	Preterite Subjunctive
Singular	*love, heere*	*lovede, herde*
Plural	*take, ginne*	*tooke, gonne*
	love(n), heere(n)	*lovede(n), herde(n)*
	take(n), ginne(n)	*tooke(n), gonne(n)*

In verbs like *ginnen*, which have two stem vowels in the indicative preterite, it is the vowel of the plural and of the second person singular that is used for the preterite subjunctive.

The imperative singular of most weak verbs is *e: (thou) love,* but of some weak verbs and all strong verbs, the imperative singular is without termination: *(thou) heer, taak, gin.* The imperative plural of all verbs is either *e* or *eth: (ye) love(th), heere(th), take(th), ginne(th).*

The infinitive of verbs is *e* or *en: love(n), heere(n), take(n), ginne(n).*

The past participle of weak verbs is the same as the preterite without inflectional ending: *loved, herd.* In strong verbs the ending is either *e* or *en: take(n), gonne(n).* The prefix *y-* or *i-* often appears on past participles: *y-founde, i-maked, y-sette.*

Abbreviations

The following are the principal abbreviations used in the footnotes and headnotes:

c. *circa*
cf. *compare*
esp. *especially*
ff. *and following* (or *folios* in descriptions of manuscripts)
l. *line*
ll. *lines*
lit. *literally*
ME *Middle English*
MS *manuscript*
MSS *manuscripts*
n. *(foot)note*
no. *number*
nos. *numbers*
p. *page*
pp. *pages*
r *recto*
v *verso*

MIDDLE ENGLISH
ROMANCES

Nurture and Correction

Havelok†

Incipit vita Havelok, quondam Rex Anglie et Denemarchie[1]

Herknet° to me, gode° men—	*Hearken / good, worthy*
Wives, maydnes,° and alle men—	*maidens*
Of a tale that Ich° you wile° telle,	*I / will*
Wo-so° it wile here° and ther-to duelle.°	*Whosoever / hear / dwell, attend*
5 The tale is of Havelok i-maked:	
Wil he was litel he yede ful naked;[2]	
Havelok was a ful god° gome°—	*good, worthy / (grown) man*
He was ful god in everi trome;°	*company*
He was the wicteste man at nede[3]	
10 That thurte° riden on ani stede.°	*might / steed, war-horse*
(That° ye mowen° nou° y-here°	*(So) that / may / now / hear*
And the tale ye mowen y-lere,°	*learn*
At the biginning of ure° tale	*our*
Fil me a cuppe of ful god ale,	
15 And wile drinken, her I spelle,[4]	
That Crist us shilde° alle fro° helle:	*protect / from*
Krist° late° us hevere° so for to do	*(May) Christ / let / ever, always*
That we moten° comen Him to,	*may*
And, wit that it mote ben so,	

---

† Text of Bodleian Library MS Laud Misc. 108, ff. 204ʳ–219ᵛ, printed with the permission of the Bodleian Library, Oxford. This portion of the manuscript dates from the early fourteenth century; the poem's date of composition is held to be between 1295 and 1310 (cf. the notes to ll. 139, 1178, 2559). Paragraphing follows that of the MS; lines thought to be missing (marked in the edition by "[. . .]") are occasionally left unnumbered in order to maintain consistency of line-numbering with the most common scholarly edition of the poem, by W. W. Skeat and K. Sisam (see the Selected Bibliography for details of this and other chief editions).

    The poem is written in nominally four-stress couplets (but cf. ll. 87–105, where the extended rhyme is reminiscent of the continuous assonant rhyme of much Old French poetry).

1. (Here) begins the life (story) of Havelok, sometime King of England and Denmark. (*Vita* usually signifies the more obviously pietistic kind of tale known as the Saint's Life, of which there are several genuine examples in this manuscript; the attribution ought not, however, to be dismissed on those grounds and ought instead to be taken as evidence that at least one medieval manuscript compiler saw in the progress of the poem's hero some form of exemplary instruction.)

2. While he was little he went about completely naked. (I.e., in youth he was destitute.)

3. He was the most courageous man in a time of need.

4. And I will drink (to a prayer) before I tell the tale.

3

20 *Benedicamus Domino!*)[5]
Here I schal biginnen a rym°—   *rhyme, poem*
Krist us yeve° wel god fyn.°   *give/ending*
The rym is maked of Havelok,
A stalworthi° man in a flok;°   *stalwart, strong/company*
25 He was the stalwortheste man at nede
That may riden on ani stede.

    It was a King bi are-dawes,
That in his time were gode lawes
He dede maken an ful wel holden.[6]
30 Hym lovede yung, him lovede holde—[7]
Erl and barun, dreng° and thayn,°   *landholder/lesser landholder*
Knict,° bondeman,° and swain,°   *Knight/peasant/swain, youth*
Wydues, maydnes, prestes, and clerkes—[8]
And al for hise° gode werkes.°   *his/works, deeds*
35 He lovede God with al his micth,°   *might*
And Holi Kirke,° and soth° ant° ricth.°   *Church/truth/and/justice*
Ricthwise° men he lovede alle,   *Righteous, Just*
And overal made hem for-to calle.[9]
Wreieres and wrobberes made he falle,[1]
40 And hated hem° so° man doth° galle.°   *them/as/does/poison*
Utlawes and theves made he bynde°—   *bound, tied up*
Alle that he michthe° fynde—   *could*
And heye° hengen° on galwe-tre;°   *high/hanged/gallows tree*
For hem ne yede° gold ne° fe.°   *availed/nor/property*
45 In that time, a man that bore
[. . .]
Of red gold upon hiis bac,[2]
In a male, with or blac,[3]
Ne funde° he non° that him misseyde°   *found/none/insulted*
50 Ne with ivele on hond leyde.[4]
Thanne micthe chapmen° fare°   *chapmen, peddlers/fare, go*
Thuruth° Englond wit° here° ware,°   *Throughout/with/their/wares*
And baldelike° beye° and sellen   *boldly, openly/buy*
Overal ther he wilen dwellen;[5]
55 In gode burwes° and ther-fram°   *towns/(away) from them*

5. And, in order that it may be so, "let us bless the Lord!" (The Latin quotation is a versicle, a short sentence declaimed by a priest during the Mass.)
6. There was a king in days of yore, in whose time there were good laws which he caused to be made and very well kept. (So begins an extensive account of an exemplary king, Athelwold, named below; the values he represents are those to which the poem will constantly return.)
7. He was loved by young, he was loved by old.
8. Widows, maidens, priests, and clerics.
9. And had them summoned from all over.
1. He had inciters and agitators deposed.
2. Of red gold (i.e., gold alloyed with copper) upon his back.
3. In a bag, white or black (i.e., of any kind).
4. Nor malevolently laid a hand on him.
5. Wherever they would stop.

Ne funden he non that dede hem sham,
That he ne weren sone to sorwe brouth[6]
An° povere° maked and browt° to nouth.°   *And / poor / brought / nothing*
Thanne° was Engelond at hayse;°   *Then / ease*
60 Michel° was suich° a king to preyse°   *Much, Greatly / such / be praised*
That held so Englond in grith°—   *peace*
Krist of hevene° was him with;   *heaven*
He was Engelondes blome.°   *bloom, flower*
Was non so bold, lond to rome,
65 That durste upon his bringhe[7]
Hunger ne here,° wicke° thinghe.   *invasion / wicked, evil*
Hwan° he felede° hise foos,°   *When / put to flight / foes*
He made hem lurken° and crepen° in wros;°   *hide / creep / corners*
Thei hidden hem° alle and helden hem stille,°   *themselves / still, quiet*
70 And diden al his herte wille.[8]
Ricth° he lovede of alle thinge;   *Right, Justice*
To wronge micht° him no man bringe—   *might, could*
Ne for silver, ne for gold—
So was he his soule hold.[9]
75 To the faderles° was he rath;°   *fatherless / (a) guide*
Wo-so dede hem wrong or lath,°   *harm*
Were it clerc or were it knicth,
He dede hem sone to haven ricth.[1]
And wo dide widuen° wrong,   *widows*
80 Were he nevre knicth so strong
That he ne made him sone kesten
And in feteres ful faste festen.[2]
And wo-so dide maydne shame
Of hire bodi, or brouth in blame
85 (Bute it were bi hire wille),
He made him sone of limes spille.[3]
He was te° beste knith° at nede   *the / knight*
That hevere micthe riden on stede,
Or wepne wagge, or folc ut-lede.[4]
90 Of knith ne havede° he nevere drede,°   *had / dread, fear*
That he ne sprong° forth so° sparke of glede°   *sprang, leaped / like / ember*
And lete him shewe, of hise hand-dede,[5]

6. They found no one who assaulted them such that they (the assailants) were not soon brought
   to grief.
7. There was no one so bold, who intended to possess land, who dared bring upon his (land)
   (i.e., upon Athelwold's land).
8. And did according to his heart's desire.
9. To his soul loyal. (I.e., he assured the salvation of his soul.)
1. Whether cleric or knight, he soon caused them to receive justice.
2. There was never (such) a knight who was so strong that he did not have him forthwith thrown
   and bound fast in chains.
3. And whoever violated the body of a woman, or brought her into disrepute (unless it were by
   her consent), he soon had him castrated (*lit.* deprived of his members).
4. Or brandish a weapon, or lead an army to war.
5. And let him see, through his violence.

Hw° he couthe° with wepne spede;°   *How / could / succeed*
And other° he refte° him hors or wede,°   *either / deprived of / armor*
95 Or made him sone handes sprede[6]
And "Loverd,° merci!"° loude grede.°   *Lord / (have) mercy / cry*
He was large and no wicth gnede;[7]
Havede he non so° god brede,°   *such / roast meat*
Ne on his bord° non so god shrede,°   *(eating) table / morsel*
100 That he ne wolde thor-wit° fede°   *therewith / feed*
Povre° that on fote° yede,°   *Poor (people) / foot / went*
For-to haven of Him the mede
That for us wolde on rode blede—
Crist, that al kan wisse and rede
105 That evere woneth in ani thede.[8]

    The King was hoten° Athelwold.   *called*
Of word, of wepne, he was bold;
In Engeland was nevre knicth
That betere held the lond to ricth.
110 Of his bodi ne havede he eyr°   *heir*
Bute° a mayden, swithe° fayr,°   *But (for) / very / fair*
That was so yung that sho° ne couthe   *she*
Gon° on fote ne speke wit mouthe.   *Go, Walk*
Than him tok° an ivel° strong,   *took / illness*
115 That° he wel wiste° and underfong°   *(Such) that / knew / realized*
That his deth was comen him on,°   *upon*
And seyde,° "Crist, wat shal I don?°   *said / do*
Loverd, wat shal me to rede?[9]
I woth° ful wel Ich have mi mede;°   *know / (heavenly) reward*
120 Hw shal nou° mi douhter fare?   *now*
Of° hire have Ich michel kare;°   *For / concern, distress*
Sho is mikel° in mi thouth°—   *greatly / thought, mind*
Of meself is me rith nowt.[1]
No selcouth is thou me be wo;[2]
125 Sho ne kan° speke, ne sho kan go!°   *can / walk*
Yif scho couthe on horse ride,
And a thousande men bi hire syde,
And sho were comen intil helde,[3]
And Engelond sho couthe welde°   *govern*
130 And don of hem that hire were queme,[4]
An hire bodi couthe yeme,°   *take care of*

6. Or made him quickly spread out his hands (before him, in despair).
7. He was generous and not at all miserly.
8. To have the reward of He who would bleed on the Cross for us—Christ, who can guide and advise all who ever dwell in any nation.
9. I.e., what course of action should I follow?
1. I care nothing for myself.
2. It is no wonder that I am unhappy.
3. Come of age.
4. And do with them that which was pleasing to her.

Ne wolde me nevere ivele like—
Ne thou Ich were in hevene-riche."[5]

 Quanne° he havede this pleinte° maked   *When / complaint*
135 (Ther-after stronglike quaked)[6]
He sende writes° sone onon°   *writs, summonses / anon, forthwith*
After his erles, evere-ich° on,°   *every / one*
And after hise baruns, riche and poure,
Fro Rokesburw al into Dovere,[7]
140 That° he° shulden comen swithe°   *(Decreeing) that / they / quickly*
Til° him that was ful unblithe,°   *To / unhappy*
To that stede° ther° he lay   *place / there (where)*
In harde° bondes° nicth° and day.   *severe / constraints / night*
He was so faste wit yvel° fest°   *illness / constrained*
145 That he ne mouthe° haven no rest;   *could*
He ne mouthe no mete hete;°   *eat*
Ne he ne mouchte no lythe° gete,   *relief*
Ne non of his ivel that couthe red.[8]
Of° him ne was nouth buten° ded.°   *For / but / death*

150 Alle that the writes herden
Sorful° an sori° til him ferden.°   *Sorrowful / sad / went*
He° wrungen° hondes and wepen° sore,   *They / wrang / wept*
And yerne° preyden° Cristes hore°— *eagerly / prayed (for) / mercy*
That He wolde turnen° him   *lead*
155 Ut° of that yvel that was so grim.   *Out*
Thanne he weren comen alle
Bifor the King, into the halle
At Winchestre ther he lay,
"Welcome," he seyde, "be ye ay.°   *always*
160 Ful michel thank kan I yow[9]
That ye aren comen to me now."

 Quanne he weren alle set
And the King aveden° i-gret,°   *had / greeted*
He greten and gouleden and goven hem ille.[1]
165 And he bad° hem alle ben° stille   *bade / be*
And seyde that "greting° helpeth nouth,   *weeping*
For al to dede° am Ich brouth;°   *death / brought*
Bute nou° ye sen° that I shal deye,° *now (that) / see / die*

---

5. I would never be displeased—even though I were in the kingdom of heaven (i.e., even though I could not be with her).
6. (And) thereafter violently trembled (because of his illness).
7. From Roxburgh all (the way) to Dover. (I.e., the length of England. Though Roxburgh is essentially a Scottish town, it was for some years in English hands after 1295, during one of several occupations. This is one of a few details in the poem providing some sense of the date of the poem's composition; cf. ll. 1178, 2559.)
8. Nor (could he find) anyone who knew a remedy for his illness.
9. I express great thanks to you.
1. They wept and cried and were distressed.

Nou Ich wille you alle preye
170 Of° mi douther,° that shal be   *Concerning/daughter*
Yure° levedi° after me,   *Your/lady, governess*
Wo° may yemen° hire so longe—   *Who/look after*
Bothen hire° and Engelonde—   *her*
Til that she be wman° of helde°   *woman/age*
175 And that she mowe° hir° yemen and welde?"   *may/herself*
He ansuereden° and seyden° anon,   *answered/said*
Bi Crist and bi Seint Jon,
That therl Godrigh of Cornwayle[2]
Was trewe° man, wituten° faile,°   *loyal/without/doubt*
180 Wis° man of red,° wis man of dede,°   *Wise/counsel/deed*
And men haveden of him mikel drede—
"He may hire altherbest° yeme°   *best of all/look after*
Til that she mowe wel ben Quene."
The King was payed° of that rede.   *pleased*
185 A wol° fair cloth bringen he dede,°   *well, very/did, had*
And ther-on leyde the messe-bok,
The caliz and the pateyn ok,
The corporaus, the messe-gere;[3]
Ther-on he garte° the Erl suere°   *caused, had/(to) swear*
190 That he sholde yemen hire wel,
Withuten° lac,° wituten tel,°   *Without/fault/reproach*
Til that she were tuelf winter hold[4]
And of speche were bold,°   *confident*
And that she couthe of curteysye,°   *courtesy, courtly conduct*
195 Gon and speken of luve-drurye;[5]
And til that she loven mouthe
Wom-so hire to gode thoucte[6]
And that he shulde hire yeve°   *give*
The heste° man that micthe° live,   *highest/could*
200 The beste, fayreste, the strangest° ok—   *strongest*
That dede he him° sweren on the bok°—   *(Godrich)/book, missal*
And thanne shulde he Engelond
Al bitechen° into hire hond.   *hand over*

Quanne that was sworn on° this wise,°   *in/manner*
205 The King dede° the mayden arise,   *had*
And the Erl hire bitaucte[7]

---

2. That Godrich, the Earl of Cornwall. (On the possible significance of the choice of earldom, see l. 375, n.)
3. And laid thereon the missal (*lit.* "mass-book"), the chalice and the paten also, the cloth on which the consecrated bread of the Eucharist is placed, the (other) effects of the Mass. (The use of such effects secures the solemnity of the oath in question; cf. *Ywain and Gawain*, ll. 3907–20.)
4. Twelve winters old. (I.e., the earliest age at which she could be legally married.)
5. (And knew how to be) current and conversant in (the ways of) courtship.
6. And until she was able to love whoever to her seemed worthy.
7. And handed her over to the Earl.

And al the lond he evere awcte°—   *possessed*
Engelonde, everi del°—   *part*
And preide he shulde yeme hire wel.

210   The King ne mowcte don no more,
But yerne preyede Godes ore°   *mercy*
And dede him hoslen wel and shrive—[8]
I woth° fif° hundred sithes° and five—   *believe / five / times*
An ofte dede him sore swinge
215   And wit hondes smerte dinge,
So that the blod ran of his fleys
That tendre was and swithe neys.[9]
He made his quiste° swithe wel   *will*
And sone gaf° it, evere-il° del.   *gave, executed / every*
220   Wan it was goven, ne micte men finde
So mikel men micte him in winde
Of his, in arke ne in chiste
In Engelond, that no man wiste—
For al was yoven faire and wel
225   That him was leved no catel.[1]

       Thanne° he havede ben ofte swungen,°   *Then (when) / scourged*
Ofte shriven and ofte dungen,°   *beaten*
"*In manus tuas*"[2] loud he seyde.
Her that he the speche leyde,[3]
230   To Jesu Crist bigan° to calle,   *(he) began*
And deyede° biforn° his heymen° alle.   *died / before / nobles*
Than he was ded, there micte men se
The meste° sorwe° that micte be;   *most, greatest / sorrow*
Ther was sobbing, siking,° and sor,°   *sighing / pain, grief*
235   Handes wringing and drawing bi hor.[4]
Alle greten° swithe sore,°   *wept / sorely, bitterly*
Riche and poure that there wore.°   *were*
An mikel sorwe haveden alle,
Levedyes° in boure,° knictes in halle.   *Ladies / chamber*

240   Quan that sorwe was somdel° laten°   *somewhat / abated*
And he° haveden longe graten,°   *they / wept*

---

8. And had the sacrament fully administered to him and his confession heard.
9. And repeatedly had himself scourged and beaten painfully by hand, so that the blood ran from his flesh, which was tender and very soft. (Such mortification of the flesh was revered as a gesture of great piety; reminiscent of Christ's suffering on the Cross, it was seen as an affirmation of spiritual transcendence of the worldly and as a punishing of the sins of the body.)
1. When it was executed, throughout England men could not find in chest or coffer so much (as a sheet) of his in which they could shroud him, as far as any man knew—for all was so thoroughly given over that he was left with no property.
2. Into your hands. (From Christ's last words on the cross; Luke 23.46.: And when Jesus had cried with a loud voice, he said, "Father, into thy hands I commend my spirit.")
3. Before he gave up the power of speech.
4. Wringing of hands and pulling of hair.

Belles deden° he sone ringen,°   *had, caused / (to be) rung*
Monkes and prestes messe singen,
And sauteres° deden he manie° reden° *psalters / many / read*
245 That° God self° shulde his soule leden° *(So) that / himself / lead*
Into hevene biforn His Sone,°   *Son*
And ther wituten° hende° wone.° *without / end / dwell*
Than he was to the erthe brouth,
The riche Erl ne foryat nouth
250 That he ne dede al Engelond
Sone sayse intil his hond;[5]
And in the castels leth° he do° *allowed / to be placed*
The knictes he micte tristen to;[6]
And alle° the Englis° dede he swere *(to) all / English (people)*
255 That he shulden him ghod fey beren.[7]
He yaf alle men that god thoucte,
Liven and deyen til that he moucte,[8]
Til that the Kinges dowter° wore° *daughter / was*
Tuenti winter hold, and more.[9]

260 Thanne he havede taken° this oth *received*
Of° erles, baruns, lef and loth,[1]   *From*
Of knictes, cherles,° fre° and thewe,° *serfs / free(men) / slaves*
Justises dede he maken newe[2]
Al Engelond to faren° thorw,° *travel / through*
265 Fro Dovere into Rokesborw.[3]
Schireves he sette, bedels and greyves,
Grith-sergeans wit longe gleyves,[4]
To yemen wilde wodes° and pathes *woods*
Fro wicke° men that wolde don scathes°— *wicked / harmful deeds*
270 And for-to haven alle at his cri,° *command*
At his wille, at hise merci,
That non durste ben him ageyn,° *against*
Erl ne barun, knict ne sweyn.° *swain, youth*
Wislike, for soth, was him wel[5]
275 Of folc, of wepne, of catel;° *property*
Sothlike,° in a lite° thrawe° *Truly / little, brief / time*
Al Engelond of him stod awe°— *in fear*

---

5. I.e., the mighty Earl (Godrich) did not forget forthwith to take all England into his (legal) possession.
6. The knights in whom he could trust.
7. That they should bear good faith toward him.
8. I.e., he gave all men that which seemed good to him, for as long as they lived.
9. Twenty winters old, and more. (But presumably not twenty-one, at which age she would legally be able to take independent possession of the realm.)
1. Friend and foe (i.e., everyone).
2. He appointed new (itinerant) justices.
3. Cf. l. 139.
4. He appointed sheriffs, beadles (sheriff's assistants) and greives (town officials), peace-officers with long halberds.
5. Undoubtedly, in truth, he was well supplied.

Al Engelond was of him adrad°   afraid
So his the beste fro the gad.[6]

280   The Kinges douther bigan thrive
And wex° the fayrest wman on live.   grew (to be)
Of alle thewes° was she wis°   manners / wise, discerning
That gode weren and of pris.°   high esteem
The mayden Goldeboru was hoten°—   called
285   For hire was mani a ter° i-groten.°   tear / cried

Quanne the Erl Godrich him° herde   (for) himself
Of that mayden—hw wel she ferde,°   fared, did
Hw wis sho was, hw chaste, hw fayr,
And that sho was the rithe° eyr°   rightful / heir
290   Of Engelond, of al the rike°—   realm
Tho° bigan Godrich to sike,°   Then / sigh
And seyde, "Wether° she sholde be   is it possible that
Quen and levedi over me?
Hwether sho sholde al Engelond,
295   And me and mine, haven in hire hond?
Datheit hwo it hire thave—[7]
Shal sho it nevere more have!
Sholde Ic° yeve° a fol°—a therne!°—   I / give / fool / girl
Engelond, thou sho it yerne?°   desire
300   Datheit hwo it hire yeve
Evere more hwil° I live!   while
Sho is waxen° al to° prud°   grown / too / proud
For° gode metes° and noble shrud°   Because of / food / clothes
That Hic° have yoven° hire to offte;°   I / given / often
305   Hic have yemed° hire to softe.°   fostered / comfortably
Shal it nouth ben als sho thenkes°—   thinks, expects
Hope maketh fol man ofte blenkes.[8]
Ich have a sone, a ful fayr knave:°   boy
He shal Engelond al have;
310   He shal ben King; he shal ben sire,°   (feudal) lord
So brouke I evere mi blake swire."[9]

Hwan° this trayson° was al thouth,°   When / treason / thought up
Of his oth ne was him nouth.[1]
He let his oth al over-ga°—   go by, be deserted
315   Ther-of ne yaf° he nouth a stra,°   gave / straw
Bute sone dede° hire fete,°   had / fetched
Er° he wolde heten° ani mete,   Before / eat

6. As is the beast from the goad. (A striking contrast to the means by which Athelwold is said to
   have ruled; cf. ll. 59–61)
7. Cursed be he who would allow it to her.
8. Hope often plays tricks on the foolish man.
9. As I hope always to enjoy my pale neck (i.e., as I hope to live).
1. I.e., he thought nothing of his (former) oath.

Fro Winchestre ther° sho was,   *there (where)*
Al-so a wicke traytur Judas,
320 And dede leden hire to Dovre[2]
    That standeth on the seis° oure;°   *sea's / shore*
    And ther-hinne° dede hire fede°   *therein / rear, raise*
    Povrelike,° in feble° wede.°   *Poorly / inadequate / clothes*
    The castel dede he yemen° so   *keep*
325 That non° ne micte comen hire to   *none*
    Of hire frend,° with to speken,   *friends*
    That hevere° micte hire bale° wreken.°   *ever / suffering / avenge*

    Of Goldeborw shul° we nou° laten,°   *must / now / let be, leave off*
    That nouth° ne blinneth° for-to graten°   *not at all / ceases / weep*
330 Ther sho liggeth° in prisoun.   *lies*
    (Jhesu Crist, that Lazarun
    To live broucte fro dede-bondes,[3]
    He° lese° hire wit° hise hondes—   *(May) he / set free / with*
    And leve° sho mote° him° y-se°   *grant / may / (Godrich) / see*
335 Heye hangen on galwe-tre[4]
    That hire haved in sorwe° brouth,°   *sorrow, suffering / brought*
    So as sho ne misdede nouth!)[5]

    Say° we nou forth in hure° spelle.°   *Speak / our / tale*
    In that time, so it bifelle,°   *befell, happened*
340 Was° in the lond of Denemark   *(There) was*
    A riche King and swythe° stark.°   *very / mighty*
    The name of him was Birkabeyn;
    He havede mani knict° and sueyn.°   *(a) knight / swain, youth*
    He was fayr° man and wicth;°   *fair, just / courageous*
345 Of bodi he was the beste knicth
    That evere micte leden° uth° here,°   *lead / out / army*
    Or stede onne ride or handlen spere.[6]
    Thre children he havede bi his wif—
    He hem lovede so° his lif;   *as*
350 He havede a sone,° douhtres two—   *son*
    Swithe fayre, as fel it so.[7]
    He that wile non forbere,
    Riche ne poure, king ne kaysere—
    Deth—him tok than he best wolde

2. Like a wicked Judas of a traitor, and had her conducted to Dover. (The name of Judas—the apostle who betrayed Christ for thirty pieces of silver—is synonymous with treachery.)
3. Brought to life from bonds of death. (Lazarus was the friend Jesus raised from the dead; see John 11.1–44.)
4. Cf. l. 43.
5. Even though she had done no wrong.
6. Or ride on steed or handle spear. (Note the echoes in these lines with ll. 87–89 in the early description of Athelwold; so begins a sequence of such echoes which dramatize the near identity of evils wrought at once in England and Denmark.)
7. Very beautiful, as it so happened.

355 Liven; but hyse dayes were fulde[8]
    That° he ne moucte° no more live,   *(So) that/could*
    For gold ne silver, ne for no gyve.°   *gift, offering*

      Hwan he that wiste,° rathe° he sende°   *knew/quickly/sent*
    After prestes fer° an hende,°   *far/at hand, near*
360 Chanounes° gode and monkes bathe,°   *Canons (communal priests)/both*
    Him for-to wisse° and to rathe,°   *guide/advise*
    Him for-to hoslen an for-to shrive[9]
    Hwil his bodi were on live.

      Hwan he was hosled and shriven,
365 His quiste° maked and for him gyven,°   *will/given, executed*
    Hise knictes dede he alle site,°   *sit (in council)*
    For thorw° hem he wolde wite°   *through/know*
    Hwo° micte yeme° his children yunge   *Who/look after*
    Til that he° kouthen° speken wit° tunge, *they/could/with*
370 Speken and gangen,° on horse riden,   *go, walk*
    Knictes an sweynes° bi here° siden.   *swains, youths/their*
    He° spoken ther-offe, and chosen sone°   *They/quickly*
    A riche man that under mone
    Was the trewest—that he wende—[1]
375 Godard,[2] the Kinges oune° frende—   *own*
    And seyden he moucthe hem° best loke°   *them/look after*
    Yif° that he hem vndertoke,°   *If/took on, accepted*
    Til his sone mouthe° bere°   *could/bear*
    Helm on heved° and leden ut° here,   *head/out*
380 In his hand a spere stark,
    And King ben maked of Denemark.
    He wel trowede° that° he° seyde,   *trusted in/that (which)/they*
    And on Godard handes leyde
    And seyde, "Here biteche° I the°   *hand over/(to) thee*
385 Mine children, alle thre,
    Al Denemark, and al mi fe,°   *property*
    Til that mi sone of helde° be—   *age*
    But that Ich wille that thou suere,[3]
    On auter° and on messe-gere,°   *altar/effects of the Mass*

8. He who will spare no one, rich nor poor, king nor emperor—Death—took him then when he most desired to live; but his days were completed.
9. Cf. l. 212.
1. A powerful man, who was the most loyal under the moon (i.e., on earth)—as they believed.
2. It is surely no coincidence that the name is close to that of the other villain, Godrich. As Professor Smithers has observed, moreover, the two names combine to form "Richard" once "God" is removed. This, linked with the fact that Godrich is styled the Earl of Cornwall (l. 176)—a title not to be expected from one who dwells at Lincoln (see ll. 880–885)—recalls the historical Richard of Cornwall (1209–1272, Earl of Cornwall from 1227), the younger brother of King Henry III (1207–72). Between 1227 and 1238 he sided (inconstantly) with the barons of the realm against the King in various attempts to limit royal power; his rebelliousness, and his inconstancy therein, earned him disrespect from all sides.
3. Except that I would that you swear.

390 On the belles that men ringes,
    On messe-bok° the prest° on singes, — *missal / priest*
    That thou mine children shalt wel yeme
    That hire kin be ful wel queme,[4]
    Til mi sone mowe° ben knicth. — *may*
395 Thanne biteche him tho° his ricth,° — *then / rightful (legal) claim*
    Denemark, and that ther-til° longes,° — *thereto, to it / belongs*
    Casteles and tunes,° wodes° and wonges." — *towns / woods / fields*

    Godard stirt up an swor° al that — *swore (to)*
    The King him bad,° and sithen° sat — *bade, asked / then*
400 Bi the knictes that ther ware°— — *were*
    That wepen° alle swithe° sare° — *wept / very / sorely, bitterly*
    For the King, that deide° sone.° — *died / soon, forthwith*
    (Jesu Crist, that makede mone° — *(the) moon*
    On the mirke° nith° to shine, — *dark / night*
405 Wite° his soule fro helle-pine,° — *Protect / torment of hell*
    And leve° that it mote wone° — *grant / dwell*
    In heveneriche° with Godes Sone.)° — *the kingdom of heaven / Son*

    Hwan° Birkabeyn was leyd° in grave, — *When / laid*
    The Erl dede sone take the knave,° — *boy*
410 Havelok, that was the eir,° — *heir*
    Swanborow, his sister, Helfled, the tother,° — *other*
    And in the castel dede he hem do;° — *put*
    Ther non ne micte hem comen to
    Of here° kyn; ther thei sperd° were; — *their / locked up*
415 Ther he greten° ofte sore, — *wept*
    Bothe for hunger and for kold—
    Or° he° weren thre winter hold!° — *Before / they / old*
    Feblelike° he gaf hem clothes— — *Inadequately*
    He ne yaf° a note° of° hise othes°— — *gave / nut / for / oaths*
420 He hem clothede rith° ne fedde, — *right, properly*
    Ne hem ne dede richelike° be-bedde.° — *richly / furnish with bedding*
    Thanne Godard was, sikerlike,° — *truly*
    Under God the moste° swike° — *greatest / traitor*
    That evre in° erthe shaped° was— — *on / formed, created*
425 Withuten° on:° the wike Judas.[5] — *Except for / one*
    (Have he° the malisun° today — *(may) he / malediction, curse*
    Of alle that evre speken may—
    Of patriark° and of pope, — *patriarch, bishop*
    And of prest with loken kope,[6]
430 Of monekes and hermites bothe
    [. . .]

4. Such that to their kinsmen it will be wholly pleasing.
5. Cf. l. 319, 320, n.
6. And of priest in fastened cloak (i.e., formally dressed).

And of the leve° holi Rode°   *dear/Rood, Cross*
That God himselve ran on blode.[7]
Crist warie° him with His mouth!   *curse*
Waried wrthe° he of north and suth,°   *let be/south*
435 Offe alle men that speken kunne,°   *can*
Of Crist that maude° mone and sunne!)   *made*
Thanne° he havede of al the lond   *Then (when)*
Al the folk tilled° intil° his hond,°   *brought/into/hand*
And alle haveden sworen him oth,
440 Riche and poure, lef and loth,[8]
That he° sholden hise wille freme°   *they/do*
And that he° shulde him nouth° greme,°   *they/not/annoy, cross*
He thouthe° a ful strong trechery,   *thought up*
A trayson and a felony[9]
445 Of° the children for-to make—   *Against*
The devel of helle him sone take!

    Hwan that was thouth, onon° he ferde°   *anon, forthwith/went*
To the tour ther he° woren° sperde,   *they (the children)/were*
Ther he greten for hunger and cold.
450 The knave, that was sumdel° bold,   *somewhat, quite*
Kam° him ageyn;° on knes° him sette,   *Came/towards/knees*
And Godard ful feyre° he ther grette;°   *fairly, courteously/greeted*
And Godard seyde, "Wat is yw?[1]
Hwi° grete° ye and goulen° nou?"°   *Why/weep/cry/now*
455 "For us hungreth swithe sore,"[2]
Seyden he, "we wolden° more;   *desire*
We ne have to hete°—ne we ne have   *eat*
Her-inne° neyther° knith ne knave   *Herein/neither*
That yeveth° us drinken ne no mete°—   *gives/food*
460 Halvendel° that we moun° ete!   *Half of/must, need to*
Wo° is us that we weren born!   *Woe*
Weilawei! Nis it no korn,

7. On which God himself shed His blood.
8. Cf. l. 261.
9. *Felony*, as a legal term, may well refer to the specific and serious charge of having violated the most solemn bond between feudal lord and vassal. The essence of feudalism—a pervasive institution in western Europe from about the ninth to the fifteenth centuries—concerns the management of large estates, provinces, even nations. According to the system, chief land-owning lords ("liege" lords, including the king) granted a portion of their land (known variously as a "feoff," "fief," "feud," or land held "in fee") to a tenant ("vassal") in return for "fealty" —sworn loyal service, including the payment of various taxes and rents and the provision of military service on demand (such as that later demanded by Godrich, ll. 2548–73). The swearing of an oath of fealty was part of a most important feudal ritual. Performed annually, the ritual involved first the act of homage (*manrede* in *Havelok*), in which the vassal would, kneeling, place his hands between those of the lord; he would then swear the oath of fealty. Glimpses of the act of homage and echoes of the oath are found throughout *Havelok* (see. ll. 254–55, 487–90, 2263–70, 2307–11, 2772–87, 2814–16, and 2850–55).
1. What is wrong with you?
2. Because we grow bitterly hungry.

That men micte maken of bred?
Us hungreth—we aren ney ded!"[3]

465   Godard herde here wa;°   *woe*
Ther-offe° yaf he nouth a stra,°   *Thereof, For that / straw*
But tok the maydnes bothe samen,°   *together*
Al-so it were upon hiis gamen—
Al-so he wolde with hem leyke—[4]
470 That° weren for hunger grene° and bleike;°   *Who / green, sickly / pale*
Of bothen he karf° on° two here throtes,°   *cut / in / throats*
And sithen° hem° al to grotes.°   *then / (cut) them / pieces*
Ther was sorwe,° wo-so° it sawe,   *sorrow / (for) whosoever*
Hwan the children bi the wawe°   *wall*
475 Leyen and sprauleden° in the blod!   *sprawled*
Havelok it saw and ther bi-stod;°   *stood by*
Ful sori° was that seli° knave.   *distressed / innocent*
Mikel dred he mouthe° have,   *could*
For at his hert he saw a knif
480 For-to° reven° him hise lyf;   *Intended to / deprive*
But the knave, that litel was,
He knelede bifor that Judas,[5]
And seyde, "Loverd,° merci° nou!   *Lord / (have) mercy*
Manrede,° loverd, biddi° you!   *Homage / bid I, I offer*
485 Al Denemark I wile you yeve
To that forward thu late me live.[6]
Here Hi° wile on boke° swere   *I / book, Bible*
That nevremore ne shal I bere°   *bear, carry*
Ayen° the,° loverd, sheld° ne spere,   *Against / thee / shield*
490 Ne other wepne° bere that may you dere.°   *weapon / harm*
Loverd, have merci of me!
Today I wile fro Denemark fle,°   *flee*
Ne neveremore comen ageyn;
Sweren I wole that Bircabein
495 Nevere yete me ne gat!"[7]
Hwan the devel herde that,
Sumdel bigan him for-to rewe;°   *rue, feel pity*
With-drow° the knif that was lewe°   *(He) withdrew / warm*
Of the seli children° blod—   *children's*
500 Ther was miracle fair and god,
That he the knave nouth ne slou,°   *slew*
But for rewnesse° him wit-drow!   *pity*

3. Woe is me! Is there no corn (grain) from which people could make bread? We grow
   hungry—we are nearly dead!
4. As if it were for his sport—as if he would play with them.
5. Cf. l. 319, 320, n.
6. On the condition that you let me live.
7. I will swear that Bircabein never begot me!

Of Avelok° rewede° him ful sore—   *Havelok / pitied*
And thoucte he wolde that he ded wore,
505 But on that he nouth wit his hend
Ne drepe him nouth—that fule fend!⁸
Thoucte he, als he him bi-stod,
Starinde° als° he were wod,°   *Staring / as if / mad*
"Yif I late him lives° go,   *alive*
510 He micte me wirchen° michel° wo—   *work, do / great*
Grith° ne get I neveremo;°   *Peace / never*
He may me waiten for-to slo—
And yf he were brouct of live,⁹
And mine children wolden thrive,
515 Loverdinges° after me   *Lords*
Of al Denemark micten he° be.   *they*
God it wite,¹ he shal ben ded—
Wile I taken non other red!²
I shal do casten him in the she;°   *sea*
520 Ther I wile that he drenth° be,   *drowned*
Abouten his hals° an anker° god   *neck / anchor*
That° he ne flete° in the flod."°   *(So) that / float / water*
Ther anon he dede sende
After a fishere° that he wende°   *fisherman / knew*
525 That wolde al his wille do,
And sone° anon he seyde him to,   *soon*
"Grim, thou wost° thu° art mi thral;°   *know / thou, you / servant*
Wilte° don mi wille al   *Will you*
That I wile bidden° the?°   *bid, ask / thee*
530 Tomorwen° shal I maken the fre   *Tomorrow*
And aucte° the yeven° and riche make—   *property / give*
With than thu wilt this child take
And leden him with the tonicht,
Than thou sest the mone lith,
535 In to the se, and don him ther-inne;
Al wile taken on me the sinne."³
Grim tok the child and bond° him faste°   *bound / fast, securely*
Hwil° the bondes micte laste   *While, For as long as*
That weren° of ful strong line.   *were (made)*
540 Tho° was Havelok in ful strong pine;°   *Then / pain, affliction*
Wiste he nevere her wat was wo!

---

8. And (still) thought that he wished the boy dead, except only that he could not kill him with
   his (own) hands—that foul fiend!
9. I.e., and if he were killed.
1. Let God know it.
2. I.e., I will follow no other plan.
3. Provided that you will take this child and conduct him with you tonight, when you see the
   moonlight, to the sea, and throw him in; I will take the sin entirely upon myself (i.e., I will
   accept all responsibility).

(Jesu Crist, that makede to go
The halte, and the doumbe speken,
Havelok, the of Godard wreken!)[4]

545   Hwan Grim him havede faste bounden—
And sithen in an eld° cloth wnden°   *old / wound, wrapped up*
A kevel of clutes ful unwraste,[5]
That° he mouthe° speke ne fnaste°   *(So) that / could / breathe*
Hwere° he wolde him bere or lede—   *Wherever*
550   Hwan° he havede don that dede,   *When, After*
Als the swike° him bad,° he yede°   *traitor / bade / went*
That he shulde him° forth lede   *(Havelok)*
And him drinchen° in the se   *drown*
(That forwarde makeden he).[6]
555   In a poke° ful and blac°   *bag / dirty*
Sone he caste him on his bac,
Ant bar° him hom° to hise cleve,°   *bore / home / lodging*
And bitaucte him dame Leve,[7]
And seyde, "Wite° thou this knave,°   *Look after / boy*
560   Al-so° thou wilt mi life save.   *If*
I shal dreinchen him in the se;
For him shole° we ben maked fre,   *shall*
Gold haven ynou° and other fe°—   *enough, in plenty / property*
That havet° mi loverd bihoten° me!"   *has / promised*

565   Hwan dame Leve herde that,
Up she stirte,° and nouth° ne sat,   *started / not at all*
And caste the knave so harde adoun°   *down*
That he crakede ther his croune°   *crown, head*
Ageyn° a gret ston ther° it lay.   *Against / there (where)*
570   Tho Havelok micte sei, "Weilawei
That evere was I kinges° bern°—   *(a) king's / child*
That him ne havede grip or ern,
Leoun or wlf, wlvine or bere,
Or other best that wolde him dere!"[8]
575   So lay that child to° middel-nicht,°   *until / midnight*
That° Grim bad Leve bringen lict°   *(Such) that / light*
For to don° on his clothes: *put*

4. He had never beforehand known what misery was! (May Jesus Christ, who caused the lame to walk and the dumb to speak, take vengeance on Godard for you, Havelok!)
5. A very unkempt gag of rags. (The account of the gag as it stands describes its preparation and only implies its being thrust into Havelok's mouth. Before the equivalent of this line in the Cambridge fragments of the poem—about which see n. 2 of the Sources and Backgrounds headnote, p. 315—is the line *He thriste in his muth wel faste*. That line is later echoed at l. 638 of the Laud text, thus suggesting that the Cambridge line is closer to an original reading; editors often consequently insert the line at this point, at the expense of disturbing the couplet sequence of the rhyme.)
6. (After) they had made that agreement.
7. And handed him over to dame ("madam") Leve.
8. (Alas) that a vulture or an eagle did not take him (Grim), lion or wolf, wolverine or bear, or (any) other beast that would harm him!

"Ne thenkeste nowt of mine othes
That Ich have mi loverd sworen?⁹
580   Ne wile I nouth be forloren!°   *lost, destroyed*
      I shal beren° him to the se—   *bear*
      Thou wost that bihoves me—¹
      And I shal drenchen him ther-inne.
      Ris up swithe° an° go thu binne°   *quickly / and / inside*
585   And blou° the fir° and lith° a kandel."   *blow, fan / fire / light*
      Als she shulde° hise clothes handel°   *was about to / handle, take up*
      On for-to don, and blawe the fir,
      She saw ther-inne a lith ful shir,°   *brilliant*
      Al-so brith° so° it were day,   *bright / as if*
590   Aboute the knave ther he lay.
      Of° hise mouth it stod° a stem,°   *From / issued (as) / beam*
      Als it were a sunne-bem.
      Al-so lith° was it ther-inne   *bright*
      So ther brenden cerges inne.²
595   "Jesu Crist!" wat° dame Leve,   *said*
      "Hwat is that lith in ure° cleve?   *our*
      Ris up, Grim, and loke° wat it menes!°   *see, find out / means*
      Hwat is the lith, as thou wenes?"³
      He stirten bothe up to the knave
600   (For man shal god wille have),⁴
      Unkeveleden° him and swithe unbounden,   *Ungagged*
      And sone anon upon him funden,°   *found*
      Als he tirveden° of° his serk,°   *stripped / off / shirt*
      On hise rith shuldre a kynemerk—⁵
605   A swithe brith,° a swithe fair.   *bright (one)*
      "Goddot!"° quath° Grim, "this is ure eir   *God knows / said*
      That shal ben loverd of Denemark!
      He shal ben King, strong and stark;°   *powerful*
      He shal haven in his hand
610   Al Denemark and Engeland;⁶
      He shal do Godard ful wo;

9. (Are you) not mindful of the oaths that I have sworn to my lord?
1. You know it behooves me to do that.
2. As if candles burned therein.
3. What is the light, do you think?
4. I.e., for it is in the nature of a man to have goodwill.
5. On his right shoulder a (royal) birthmark. (See ll. 1262–63 and 2139–47 for further details
   about the mark. The mark, along with the light which issues from the boy's mouth, confirms
   Havelok's divine right to rule; and the subsequent reaction of Grim and Leve to their discovery
   demonstrates the attendant understanding that to harm the rightful heir is to defy God. Havelok
   and Goldeboru also have a certain presence which suggests to others that they are somehow
   extraordinary; cf. l. 1707, n.)
6. Although it may just have been possible for Grim to deduce from the two manifestations of
   Havelok's royalty that the boy will eventually rule two nations, it is unclear how he could
   have known that England would be the second nation; the poet has either made a clumsy
   attempt at further stressing the exalted destiny of Havelok's experience, or simply recalled the
   right details in the wrong place (cf. ll. 725–26 and 1265–72, where the prediction is handled
   better).

He shal him hangen or quik° flo,°   *quick, alive/flay*
Or he shal him al quic grave;°   *bury*
Of° him shal he no merci have."   *For*
615   Thus seide Grim, and sore° gret,°   *sorely, bitterly/wept*
And sone fel him to the fet,[7]
And seide, "Loverd, have merci
Of me, and Leve that is me bi!°   *by, with*
Loverd, we aren bothe thine—
620   Thine cherles,° thine hine.°   *serfs/servants*
Lowerd, we sholen the wel fede°   *nurture*
Til that thu cone° riden on stede,°   *can/steed, war-horse*
Til that thu cone ful wel bere
Helm on heved,° sheld and spere;   *head*
625   He ne shal nevere wite,° sikerlike°—   *know/truly*
Godard—that fule° swike!   *foul*
Thoru other man, loverd, than thoru the
Sal I nevere freman be;[8]
Thou shalt me, loverd, fre maken,
630   For I shal yemen° the and waken°—   *look after/watch over*
Thoru the wile I fredom have!"
Tho was Haveloc a blithe knave!°   *boy*
He sat him up and cravede° bred,   *begged for*
And seide, "Ich° am ney° ded,   *I/nearly*
635   Hwat for hunger, wat for bondes
That thu leidest° on min hondes—   *laid, set*
And for the kevel, at the laste,[9]
That in my mouth was thrist faste;
I was ther-with so harde prangled°   *constricted*
640   That I was ther-with ney strangled!"
"Wel is me that thu mayth hete;[1]
Goddoth," quath Leve, "I shal the fete°   *fetch*
Bred an chese, butere and milk,
Pastees° and flaunes°—al with suilk°   *Pasties, Meat pies/flans/such*
645   Shole we sone the wel fede,
Loverd, in this mikel° nede;°   *great/(time of) need*
Soth° it is that men seyt° and suereth:°   *True/say/swear*
Ther God wile helpen, nouth ne dereth!"[2]

    Thanne° sho havede brouth° the mete,   *Then (when)/brought*
650   Haveloc anon bigan to ete
Grundlike,° and was ful blithe.   *Heartily*

---

7. I.e., and immediately fell at Havelok's feet.
8. I shall never be made a freeman by any other man except you. (Grim thus renounces the pact offered him by Godard, ll. 527–36.)
9. I.e., and, finally, for the gag.
1. I am pleased that you can eat.
2. There where God will help, nothing can do harm!

Couthe° he nouth his hunger mithe°— *Could / hide*
A lof° he het,° I woth,° and more, *loaf / ate / know*
For him hungrede swithe sore;
655 Thre dayes ther-biforn,° I wene,° *before that / believe*
Et he no mete—that was wel sene!³
Hwan he havede eten and was fed,
Grim dede maken a ful fayr bed,
Unclothede him, and dede° him ther-inne, *put*
660 And seyde, "Slep, sone, with muchel° winne,° *great / happiness*
Slep wel faste, and dred° the nouth— *fear*
Fro° sorwe to joie art thu brouth!" *From*
Sone so it was lith° of day, *light*
Grim it undertok° the wey° *took / way*
665 To the wicke° traitour Godard *wicked*
That was of Denemark Stiward,⁴
And seyde, "Loverd,° don° Ich have *Lord / done*
That thou me bede of° the knave: *concerning*
He is drenched in the flod,
670 Abouten his hals an anker god;
He is witerlike° ded; *assuredly*
Eteth° he neveremore bred— *Eats*
He lith° drenched in the se. *lies*
Yif° me gold and other fe *Give*
675 That I mowe° riche be, *may*
And with thi chartre° make fre— *charter (of manumission)*
For thu° ful wel bihetet° me *thou / promised*
Thanne° I last spak° with the." *Then (when) / spoke*
Godard stod and lokede° on him *looked*
680 Thoruthlike,° with eyne° grim, *Penetratingly / eyes*
And seyde, "Wiltu° ben erl?° *wilt thou / (an) earl*
Go hom swithe,° fule° drit-cherl!° *forthwith / foul / dirty slave*
Go hethen° and be everemore *from here*
Thral and cherl, als thou er° wore!° *before / were*
685 Shaltu° have non other mede;° *Shalt thou / reward*
For litel I do the lede
To the galues, so God me rede—⁵
For thou haves don a wicke dede!
Thou mait° stonden° her to° longe, *may / stand, stay / too*
690 Bute° thou swithe hethen gonge!"° *But, Unless / go*

Grim thoucte to late⁶ that he ran
Fro that traytour, that wicke man,
And thoucte, "Wat shal me to rathe?

---

3. I.e., that was obvious enough!
4. On the occupation of steward, see the note to *Ywain and Gawain*, l. 1209.
5. For little (provocation) will I have you led to the gallows, so help me God!
6. I.e., Grim thought it not soon enough.

Wite he him on live, he wile us bathe

695 Heye hangen on galwe-tre.[7]

Betere us is of londe to fle[8]

And berwen° bothen ure lives,   save

And mine children° and mine wives."°   children's/ wife's

Grim solde sone al his corn,

700 Shep° wit° wolle,° neth° wit horn,   Sheep/ with/ wool/ cattle

Hors and swin, geet° wit berd,°   goats/ beard

The gees, the hennes of the yerd°—   (farm)yard

Al he solde that outh° douthe,°   anything/ was worth

That he evre selle moucte,°   might, could

705 And al he to the peni drou.[9]

Hise ship he greythede° wel inow;°   fitted out/ enough, adequately

He dede it tere° and ful wel pike°   tar/ (seal with) pitch

That it ne doutede° sond° ne krike;°   feared/ sand, beach/ creek

Ther-inne dide° a ful god mast,   (he) placed

710 Stronge kables and ful fast,°   fast, secure

Ores° gode, an° ful god° seyl°—   Oars/ and/ good/ sail

Ther-inne wantede° nouth a nayl°   lacked/ nail

That evre he sholde ther-inne do.[1]

Hwan he havedet° greythed so,   had

715 Havelok the yunge he dede ther-inne,

Him and his wif, hise sones thrinne,°   three

And hise two doutres that faire wore;°   were

And sone dede he leyn° in° an ore,   place/ in (the water)

And drou° him to the heye° se,   drew, betook/ high

720 There he mith° altherbest° fle.   could/ best of all

Fro londe woren° he° bote° a mile,   were/ they/ but

Ne were° nevere but ane hwile°   was (it)/ (little) while

That it ne bigan a wind to rise

Out of the north (men calleth "bise"),[2]

725 And drof° hem intil Engelond   drove

(That al was sithen in his hond,

His that Havelok was the name;[3]

But or,° he havede michel° shame,   before (that)/ great

Michel sorwe, and michel tene°—   affliction

730 And yete he gat° it, al bidene!°—   got possession of/ completely

Als ye shulen nou forthward° here,°   henceforth/ hear

Yf that ye wilen ther-to here).°   listen

In Humber° Grim bigan to lende,°   Humberside/ dwell

---

7. What course of action shall I take? If he learns that Havelok is alive he will hang us both high on the gallows tree.
8. It is better for us to flee the country.
9. I.e., and he turned all into cash.
1. That he should ever fit therein.
2. (A wind that) men call "bise." (Possibly from Old French bise, "north wind.")
3. All of which afterward came into his possession, his whose name was Havelok.

In Lindeseye, rith at the north ende.[4]
735 Ther sat is° ship upon the sond,   *his*
But Grim it drou° up to the lond,   *dragged*
And there he made a litel cote°   *cottage*
To° him and to hise flote.°   *For/group*
Bigan he, there for-to erthe,°   *settle*
740 A litel hus to maken of erthe,°   *earth*
So that he wel thore were
Of here herboru herborwed there.[5]
And, for that Grim that place aute,°   *possessed*
The stede° of Grim the name laute,°   *place/received*
745 So that Grimesbi it calle
That ther-offe speken alle—[6]
And so shulen men callen it ay,°   *always*
Bituene this° and Domesday.   *this (day)*

    Grim was fishere° swithe° god,   *fisherman/very*
750 And mikel couthe on the flod.[7]
Mani god fish ther-inne he tok,
Bothe with neth° and with hok;°   *net/hook*
He tok the sturgiun and the qual,°   *jellyfish*
And the turbut and lax° withal;   *salmon*
755 He tok the sele° and the hwel°—   *seal/whale*
He spedde° ofte swithe wel;   *succeeded*
Keling° he tok, and tumberel,°   *Cod/porpoise*
Hering, and the makerel,
The butte,° the schulle,° the thornebake.°   *halibut/plaice/skate*
760 Gode paniers° dede he make,   *panniers, baskets*
On til him, and other thrinne
Til hise sones, to beren fishe inne[8]
Up o° londe, to selle and fonge.°   *on/exchange*
Forbar° he neyther tun° ne gronge°   *Omitted/town/grange, farm*
765 That he ne to-yede° with his ware;°   *went to, visited/wares*
Kam he nevere hom hand-bare°   *empty-handed*
That he ne broucte bred and sowel°   *anything eaten with bread*
In his shirte or in his covel,°   *cloak*
In his poke° benes° and korn°—   *bag/beans/grain*
770 Hise swink° ne havede he nowt forlorn.°   *work, effort/wasted*
And hwan he tok the grete laumprei,°   *lamprey*
Ful wel he couthe° the rithe° wei°   *knew/right/way, route*
To Lincolne, the gode boru;°   *borough, town*
Ofte he yede it thoru and thoru,
775 Til he havede wol wel sold

4. In (the district of) Lindsey, right at the northern end.
5. So that they were well sheltered there by their lodging.
6. So that all who speak thereof call it Grimsby.
7. I.e., and very capable on the sea.
8. One for him, and three others for his sons, in which to carry fish.

And ther-fore the penies told.[9]
Thanne° he com,° thenne he° were blithe;   *Then (when) / came (back) / they*
For hom he brouthe fele° sithe°   *many / times*
Wastels, simenels with the horn,[1]
780 Hise pokes fulle of mele an korn,
Netes° flesh, shepes and swines,   *Cattle's*
And hemp to maken of gode lines,
And stronge ropes to° hise netes;°   *for / nets*
In the se-weres° he ofte setes.°   *sea-weirs, channels / set them*

785   Thus-gate Grim him fayre ledde;[2]
Him and his genge° wel he fedde   *group*
Wel twelf° winter other° more.   *twelve / or*
Havelok was war that Grim swank° sore   *worked*
For his mete, and he° lay at hom;   *(Havelok)*
790 Thouth he, "Ich am nou no grom°—   *boy*
Ich am wel waxen,° and wel may eten°   *grown / eat*
More than evere Grim may geten°—   *get*
Ich ete more, bi God on live,[3]
Than Grim an hise children five!
795 It ne may nouth° ben° thus longe;°   *not / be / longer*
Goddot,° I wile with them gange°   *God knows / go*
For-to leren° sum god° to gete.   *learn (how) / profit*
Swinken° Ich wolde for mi mete;   *Work*
It is no shame for-to swinken.
800 The man that may wel eten and drinken
That nouth ne have but on swink long—
To liggen at hom it is ful strong.[4]
God yelde° him, ther° I ne may,   *reward / there (where)*
That haveth me fed to this day!
805 Gladlike° I wile the paniers bere°—   *Gladly / bear, carry*
Ich woth° ne shal it me nouth dere,°   *know / harm*
They ther be inne a birthene gret
Al-so hevi als a neth.[5]
Shal Ich nevere lengere° dwelle°—   *longer / delay*
810 Tomorwen shal Ich forth pelle!"°   *hurry*

On the morwen,° hwan it was day,   *morning*
He stirt° up sone and nouth° ne lay,   *started / (did) not*
And cast a panier on his bac
With fish giveled° als a stac   *piled up*

9. Often he went throughout it (the town) until he had sold profitably and thus counted up the
  pennies.
1. Fine cakes and simnels (loaves of crisp bread made from fine flour) with cusped (?) crusts.
2. In this way Grim conducted himself well.
3. By God alive.
4. The man who would eat and drink well should have what he wants only in proportion to his
  work—to lie at home is wholly shameful.
5. Though therein is a great burden as heavy as an ox.

815　(Al-so michel he bar him one,
　　So he foure, bi mine mone!)[6]
　　Wel he it bar and solde it wel;
　　The silver he brouthe hom il° del,°   *every/piece*
　　Al that he ther-fore tok—
820　With-held he nouth a ferthinges° nok.°   *farthing's/fragment*
　　So yede he forth ilke day
　　That he nevere at home lay,
　　So wolde he his mester° lere.°   *business/learn*
　　Bifel° it so a strong dere°   *Befell, Happened/dearth*
825　Bigan to rise of korn of° bred,   *for*
　　That° Grim ne couthe no god red°   *(Such) that/plan*
　　Hw° he sholde his meiné° fede.   *How/household*
　　Of° Havelok havede he michel drede,°   *For/fear*
　　For he was strong and wel mouthe° ete   *could*
830　More thanne hevere° mouthe be gete;°   *ever/got*
　　Ne he ne mouthe on the se take
　　Neyther lenge° ne thornbake,   *ling*
　　Ne non other fish that douthe°   *was of value*
　　His meyné feden with he mouthe.
835　Of Havelok he havede kare,°   *concern, distress*
　　Hwil-gat° that he micthe° fare—   *(About) how/could*
　　Of his children was him nouth;[7]
　　On Havelok was al hise thouth°—   *thought, mind*
　　And seyde, "Havelok, dere° sone,°   *dear/son, boy*
840　I wene° that we deye mone°   *believe/must*
　　For hunger, this dere° is so strong,   *dearth*
　　And hure° mete is uten° long.   *our/exhausted, gone*
　　Betere is that thu henne° gonge°   *hence/go*
　　Than thu here dwelle longe;
845　Hethen° thou mayt gangen° to° late.   *From here/go/too*
　　Thou canst° ful wel the ricthe° gate°   *know/right/way, road*
　　To Lincolne, the gode borw—
　　Thou havest it gon ful ofte thoru.°   *along*
　　Of me ne is me nouth a slo;[8]
850　Betere is that thu thider° go,   *thither*
　　For ther is mani god man inne—
　　Ther thou mayt thi mete winne.°   *earn*
　　But wo is me thou art so naked;
　　Of mi seyl I wolde the° were maked   *(for) thee*
855　A cloth° thou mithest° inne gongen,°   *piece of clothing/could/go*
　　Sone,° no cold that° thu ne fonge."°   *Son, Boy/(so) that/catch*

　　　He tok the sheres° of° the nayl°   *shears/off, from/nail, peg*

---

6. He carried as much alone as the four of them (together), by my reckoning!
7. I.e., he thought nothing of his children.
8. I.e., I am not worth a sloeberry.

And made him a covel° of the sayl,   *cloak*
And Havelok dide° it sone° on.   *put / soon, forthwith*
860   Havede° neyther hosen° ne shon,°   *(He) had / stockings / shoes*
Ne none kines° other wede;°   *kind (of) / clothing*
To Lincolne barfot° he yede.°   *barefoot / went*
Hwan he kam ther, he was ful wil,°   *at a loss*
Ne havede he no frend to gangen til.°   *to*
865   Two dayes ther fastinde° he yede,   *fasting*
That° non for his werk wolde him fede.   *(Since) that*
The thridde day herde he calle,
"Bermen,° bermen, hider° forth alle!"   *Porters / (come) hither*
[. . .]⁹
870   Sprongen° forth so° sparke on glede.°   *Sprang, Leaped / like / ember*
Havelok shof° dun° nyne or ten   *shoved, pushed / down*
Rith amidewarde° the fen,°   *amid / mud*
And stirte° forth to the kok°   *started / (Earl's) cook*
[. . .]¹
875   That he bouthe at the brigge.²
The bermen let he alle ligge,°   *lie*
And bar° the mete to the castel,   *bore*
And gat° him there a ferthing° wastel.°   *got / farthing, small / cake*

     Thet other day kepte he ok
880   Swithe yerne the Erles kok,³
Til that he say° him on the brigge,   *saw*
And bi him mani fishes ligge.
The Herles mete havede he bouth
Of Cornwalie, and kalde oft,⁴
885   "Bermen, bermen, hider swithe!"
Havelok it herde, and was ful blithe
That he herde "Bermen!" calle;
Alle made he hem dun° falle   *down*
That in his gate° yeden and stode°—   *way / stood*
890   Wel sixtene laddes° gode;   *young men*
Als he lep° the kok til,°   *leaped / to, toward*
He shof hem alle upon an hyl!⁵
Astirte° til him with his rippe°   *(He) started / basket*
And bigan the fish to kippe;°   *snatch up*
895   He bar° up wel a carte-lode   *bore, took*
Of segges,° laxes, of playces brode,°   *cuttlefish / broad*

9. The missing line would probably have had something of the sense of "then the porters who waited there (to be hired)."
1. Another missing line, probably having the sense of "and saw the food."
2. That he (the cook) bought at the bridge. (Presumably High Bridge in Lincoln crossing the river Witham, up which fish caught at sea would be brought for sale. The poet speaks of the bridge casually, as would a native of Lincoln; cf. ll. 2828–29.)
3. The next day he also very eagerly watched for the Earl's cook.
4. He had bought the Earl of Cornwall's food, and called often.
5. He shoved them all into a heap!

Of grete laumprees and of eles.° *eels*
Sparede he neyther tos° ne heles° *toes / heels*
Til that he to the castel cam,
900 That° men fro him his birthene° nam.° *(So) that / burden / took*
Than° men haveden holpen him doun *Then (when)*
With the birthene of his croun,° *crown, head*
The kok stod and on him low,° *laughed*
And thoute him stalworthe° *stalwart, strong*
    man ynow,° *enough, in plenty*
905 And seyde, "Wiltu° ben wit me? *Wilt thou*
Gladlike wile Ich feden° the— *feed*
Wel is set the mete thu etes
And the hire that thu getes!"[6]

    "Goddot!" quoth° he, "leve° sire, *said / dear*
910 Bidde° Ich you° non other hire° *Bid, Ask / (of) you / wage*
But yeveth° me inow° to ete; *(that you) give / enough*
Fir° and water I wile you fete,° *Fire / fetch*
The fir blowe an ful wel maken;
Stickes kan Ich breken° and kraken,° *break / crack, break*
915 And kindlen ful wel a fyr,
And maken it to brennen° shir;° *burn / brightly*
Ful wel kan Ich cleven° shides,° *split / kindling wood*
Eles to-turven of here hides;[7]
Ful wel kan Ich dishes swilen°— *wash*
920 And don al that ye evere wilen!"
Quoth the kok, "Wile I no more!
Go thu yunder and sit thore,° *there*
And I shal yeve the ful fair bred,
And make the broys° in the led.° *broth / caldron*
925 Sit now doun and et ful yerne°— *earnestly*
Datheit hwo the mete werne!"[8]

    Havelok sette him dun anon,
Al-so stille als a ston,
Til he havede ful wel eten;
930 Tho havede Havelok fayre geten.[9]
Hwan he havede eten inow,
He kam to the welle, water up-drow,° *drew up*
And filde ther a michel so°— *tub*
Bad he non ageyn him go,[1]
935 But bitwen° his hondes° he bar it in, *between / hands*
Al him one,[2] to the kichin.

6. Well-invested is the food you eat and the wage you earn!
7. Flay the skins of eels.
8. Cursed be he who would refuse the food!
9. I.e., then had Havelok provided for himself well.
1. He commanded no one to meet (i.e., assist) him.
2. Himself alone.

Bad he non him° water to fett,°   *(for) him/fetch*
Ne fro brigge to bere the mete;
He bar the turves, he bar the star;[3]
940   The wode° fro the brigge he bar,   *wood*
Al that evere shulden he° nytte;°   *(the cook)/use*
Al he drow° and al he citte°—   *drew (from the well)/cut*
Wolde he nevere haven rest
More than° he were a best.°   *than (if)/beast*
945   Of alle men was he mest° meke,°   *most/meek, humble*
Lauhwinde° ay° and blithe of speke—°   *Laughing/always/speech*
Evere he was glad and blithe;
His sorwe° he couthe° ful wel mithe.°   *sorrow/could/hide*
It ne was non so litel knave[4]
950   For-to leyken° ne for-to plawe,°   *romp/play*
That he ne wode with him pleye;
The children that yeden in the weie
Of him, he deden al here wille
And with him leykeden here fille.[5]
955   Him loveden alle, stille and bolde,[6]
Knictes, children, yunge and holde;°   *old*
Alle him loveden that him sowen,°   *saw*
Bothen heye° men and lowe.   *high(born)*
Of him ful wide the word sprong,
960   Hw° he was mike,° hw he was strong,   *How/meek, humble*
Hw fayr° man° God him havede maked—   *fair, handsome/(a) man*
But° on° that he was almest naked,   *Except/only*
For he ne havede nouth° to shride°   *nothing/wear*
But a kovel° ful unride°   *cloak/coarse*
965   That was ful° and swithe wicke;°   *foul, dirty/disgraceful*
Was it nouth° worth a fir-sticke.°   *not/stick of firewood*
The cok bigan of him to rewe,°   *have pity*
And bouthe him clothes al span-newe;°   *brand-new*
He bouthe him bothe hosen and shon,
970   And sone dide him dones° on.   *put them*
Hwan he was clothed, osed° and shod,   *hosed, stockinged*
Was non so fayr under God
That evere yete in erthe were,
Non that evere moder° bere.°   *mother/bore*
975   It was nevere man that yemede
In kinneriche that so wel semede
King or cayser for-to be,

3. He carried the strips of turf, he carried the sedge. (Dried sedge would have been used for kindling, the turf for burning.)
4. There was no boy so little.
5. The children who came that way did what they pleased with him and with him they had their fill of play.
6. Placid and bold (i.e., everyone).

Than he was shrid—so semede he;[7]
For thanne° he° weren alle samen°   *then (when)/they/together*
980 At Lincolne, at the gamen,°   *(civic) games*
And the Erles° men woren al thore,°   *Earl's/there*
Than was Havelok bi the shuldren° more°   *shoulders/broader*
Than the meste° that ther kam.°   *largest/came*
In armes him no man nam
985 That he doune sone ne caste.[8]
Havelok stod over hem als° a mast.   *like*
Als° he was heie,° als he was long,°   *As/high/tall*
He was bothe stark° and strong;   *mighty*
In Engelond was non hise per
990 Of strengthe that evere kam him ner.[9]
Als he was strong so was he softe;°   *gentle*
They° a man him misdede° ofte,   *Though/wronged, abused*
Neveremore he him° misseyde°   *(of) him/spoke ill*
Ne hond on him with yvele leyde.[1]
995 Of bodi was he mayden° clene:°   *virgin/clean, pure*
Nevere yete in game° ne in grene°   *play/lust*
Wit hire ne wolde leyke ne lye
No more than it were a strie.[2]
In that time al Hengelond°   *England*
1000 Therl° Godrich havede in his hond,   *The Earl*
And he gart° komen° into the tun°   *caused/(to) come/town*
Mani erl and mani barun;
And alle that lives° were   *alive*
In Englond thanne wer there
1005 That they haveden after sent[3]
To ben ther at the parlement.°   *parliament, colloquium*
With hem com mani chanbioun,°   *(a) champion, athlete*
Mani with ladde, blac and brown;[4]
An fel° it so that yungemen,°   *befell, happened/young men*
1010 Wel abouten nine° or ten,   *nine (years old)*
Bigunnen there for-to layke.°   *play*
Thider° komen bothe stronge and wayke;°   *Thither/weak*
Thider komen lesse and more
That in the borw° thanne weren thore—   *borough, town*

---

7. There was never a man who ruled a kingdom who seemed so fit to be a king or emperor when he was dressed—so he seemed. (We are thus reminded of Havelok's true royal status—and we are so reminded in the midst of what amounts to an extended paean to his superior capacity for the essential labors, kindnesses, pleasures, and strengths of common folk. The best kings, it is implied, must be equal to the dignities of their most humble subjects.)
8. No man took him in his arms (in wrestling) who Havelok did not soon throw down.
9. In England his equal in strength never approached him.
1. Cf. l. 50.
2. He would no more dally or lie with an attractive woman than if she were a witch.
3. Whom they had sent after.
4. Many a strong young man, fair and swarthy (i.e., of every kind).

1015	Chaunpiouns and starke laddes,	
	Bondemen° with here° gaddes°	*Peasants / their / goads*
	Als he comen fro the plow.	
	There was sembling° inow—	*assembly, gathering*
	For it ne was non horse-knave,	
1020	Tho thei sholden in honde have,	
	That he ne kam thider the leyk to se.[5]	
	Biforn° here fet° thanne lay a tre,°	*Before / feet / (boundary) beam*
	And putten° with a mikel° ston°	*put, cast / great / stone*
	The starke laddes, ful god won.[6]	
1025	The ston was mikel and ek° greth°	*also / great, massive*
	And al-so° hevi so° a neth;°	*as / as / ox*
	Grund-stalwrthe° man he sholde be	*Profoundly strong*
	That mouthe° liften it to his kne°—	*could / knee*
	Was ther neyther clerc° ne prest°	*cleric, scholar / priest*
1030	That mithe° liften it to his brest!	*could, knew how to*
	Ther-wit° putten the chaunpiouns	*Therewith, With that*
	That thider comen with the barouns.	
	Hwo-so° mithe putten thore	*Whosoever*
	Biforn° another an inch or more,	*Ahead of*
1035	Wore° he yung, wore he hold,	*Were*
	He was for a kempe told.[7]	
	Al-so they stoden an° ofte stareden,°	*and / stared*
	The chaunpiouns and ek the ladden,	
	And he maden mikel strout°	*contention*
1040	Abouten the altherbeste° but,°	*best / throw*
	Havelok stod and lokede ther-til;°	*thereto*
	And of puttingge he was ful wil;°	*at a loss, inexperienced*
	For nevere yete ne saw he or°	*before*
	Putten the ston, or thanne thor.°	*there*
1045	Hise mayster bad him gon ther-to,	
	Als he couthe ther-with do.[8]	
	Tho° hise mayster it him bad,	*When*
	He was of him sore° adrad;°	*sorely, bitterly / afraid*
	Ther-to he stirte° sone anon,	*started*
1050	And kipte° up that hevi ston	*picked, snatched*
	That he sholde puten withe.	
	He putte at the firste sithe°	*time*
	Over alle that ther wore[9]	
	Twelve fote,° and sumdel° more.	*feet / somewhat, rather*
1055	The chaunpiouns that put sowen;°	*saw*

5. For there was no horse-boy (i.e., groom), when they (all) should have been about their business, such that he did not come thither to see the sport.
6. With abundant force.
7. He was accounted a champion.
8. Therewith to do as (best) he could.
9. I.e., beyond all the other puts that were (made) there.

Shuldreden he ilc other and lowen—[1]
Wolden he° no more to putting gange,°   *they/go*
But seyde, "We dwellen° her° to° longe!"—   *tarry/here/too*
This selkouth° mithe nouth ben hyd;°   *wonder/hidden*
1060 Ful sone it was ful loude° kid°   *loudly/made known*
Of Havelok, hw he warp° the ston   *cast*
Over the laddes everilkon°—   *everyone*
Hw he was fayr, hw he was long,
Hw he was wiht,° hw he was strong!   *mighty*
1065 Thoruth° England yede° the speke,°   *Throughout/went/word*
Hw he was strong—and ek meke.
In the castel, up in the halle,
The knithes speken ther-of alle,
So that Godrich it herde wel,
1070 The speke of Havelok, everi del°—   *part*
Hw he was strong man and hey,°   *tall*
Hw he was strong and ek fri°—   *of noble disposition*
And, thouthte° Godrich, "thoru° this knave°   *thought/through/boy*
Shal Ich° Engelond al have,   *I*
1075 And mi sone° after me,   *son*
For so I wile° that it be.   *wish*
The King, Athelwald, me dide swere
Upon al the messe-gere
That I shude his douther yeve
1080 The hexte that mithe live,
The beste, the fairest, the strangest ok—[2]
That gart° he me sweren on the bok.°   *had/book, missal*
Hwere° mithe I finden ani so 'hey'°   *Where/high or tall*
So° Havelok is, or so sley?°   *As/skillful*
1085 Thou I southe hethen into Inde,
So fayr, so strong, ne mithe I finde—[3]
Havelok is that ilke° knave   *same, very*
That shal Goldeborw have!"
This thouthe° with trechery,   *thought (he)*
1090 With traysoun and wit felony;[4]
For he wende° that Havelok wore°   *believed/was*
Sum cherles° sone and no more,   *churl's, slave's*
Ne shulde he haven of Engellond
Onlepi° forw° in his hond   *A single/furrow (of earth)*

1. They shouldered (i.e., nudged) each other and laughed.
2. An accurate epitome of the circumstances and terms of the original oath (of ll. 185–201). Godrich is about to take advantage of the pun available in *hexte*—which ought to signify "of highest birth, most noble" but which can also simply be taken to mean "tallest"; a further irony of Godrich's duplicity, however, is that Havelok is indeed also of the "highest" birth. The pun has a precedent in one of the French antecedents of *Havelok*; see the Sources and Backgrounds section, p. 320, n. 7.
3. Though I searched from here to India, so handsome, so strong (a man), I could not find.
4. Cf. l. 444.

1095	With hire° that was ther-of eyr,°	*her/heir*
	That bothe was god and swithe fair.[5]	
	He wende that Havelok were a thral;°	*thrall, servant*
	Ther-thoru he wende haven al	*thereby*
	In Engelond that hire rith was.[6]	
1100	(He was werse° than Sathanas°	*worse/satan*
	That Jesu Crist in erthe shop—[7]	
	Hanged worthe° he on an hok!)°	*may be/hook*

	After Goldeborw sone° he sende,°	*soon, quickly/sent*
	That was bothe fayr and hende,°	*gracious*
1105	And dide hire to Lincolne bringe.	
	Belles dede he ageyn hire ringen,[8]	
	And joie° he made hire° swithe mikel.	*joy, celebration/(for) her*
	But netheles° he was ful swikel;°	*nonetheless/treacherous*
	He seyde that he sholde hire yeve°	*give*
1110	The fayreste man that mithe live.	
	She answerede and seyde anon,	
	Bi Crist and Seint Johan,	
	That hire sholde no man wedde	
	Ne no man bringen to hire bedde	
1115	But° he were king, or kinges eyr,	*Unless*
	Were he nevere man so fayr.[9]	

	Godrich the Erl was swithe wroth°	*angry*
	That she swor swilk° an oth,	*such*
	And seyde, "Hwor thou wilt be	
1120	Quen and levedi over me?[1]	
	Thou shalt haven a gadeling°—	*rascal*
	Ne shalt thou haven non other king!	
	The shal spusen° mi cokes° knave—	*espouse, marry/cook's*
	Ne shalt thou non other loverd° have!	*lord*
1125	Datheit° that the° other yeve	*Cursed be he/thee*
	Everemore hwil° I live!	*while*
	Tomorwe ye sholen ben weddeth	
	And, maugré thin, togidere beddeth!"[2]	
	Goldeborw gret and yaf hire ille;[3]	
1130	She wolde° ben° ded, bi hire wille.	*wished/to be*
	On the morwen, hwan day was sprungen,	

5. Who was both good and very beautiful.
6. Through that means he thought to obtain all that was her rightful claim in England. (Godrich here takes advantage of feudal law, according to which a thrall could not own property, and an aristocratic woman would forfeit her rights of ownership and inheritance if she were to marry a man of Havelok's apparent status.)
7. Whom Jesus Christ created on earth. (I.e., Satan, as a part of Creation, himself exists through God's agency; cf. l. 421–25 where Judas is so described—and recall Luke 22.3: "Then entered Satan into Judas surnamed Iscariot, being of the number of the twelve [apostles].")
8. He had bells rung against her coming (i.e., to receive her).
9. I.e., no matter how handsome he was.
1. Is it conceivable that you would be queen and (liege) lady over me?
2. And, in spite of you, bedded together!
3. Goldeborw wept and was distressed.

And day-belle° at kirke° rungen,   *morning bell / church*
After Havelok sente that Judas[4]
That werse° was thanne Sathanas,   *worse*
1135 And seyde, "Mayster, wilte° wif?"°   *would you have / (a) wife*
"Nay!" quoth° Havelok, "bi my lif,   *said*
Hwat° sholde Ich with wif do?   *What*
I ne may hire fede, ne clothe, ne sho.°   *provide with shoes*
Wider° sholde Ich wimman° bringe?   *Whither / (a) woman*
1140 I ne have none kines° thinge;   *kind of*
I ne have hws,° I ne have cote,°   *house / cottage*
Ne I ne have stikke,° I ne have sprote,°   *stick / sprout, twig*
I ne have neyther bred ne sowel,°   *anything eaten with bread*
Ne cloth but of an hold° with° covel.°   *old / white / cloak*
1145 This° clothes that Ich onne have   *These*
Aren the kokes°—and Ich° his knave!"   *cook's / I (am)*
Godrich stirt up and on him dong,°   *leveled blows*
[. . .]
And seyde, "But° thou hire take   *unless*
1150 That° I wole yeven the to° make,°   *Who / as / mate*
I shal hangen the ful heye,
Or I shal thristen° uth° thin heie!"°   *poke, put / out / eyes*
Havelok was one° and was odrat,°   *alone / afraid*
And grauntede° him al that he bad.°   *granted / bade, asked*
1155 Tho sende he after hire sone,
The fayrest wymman under mone,°   *moon*
And seyde til° hire (fals° and slike°   *to / treacherous / plausible*
That° wicke° thral, that foule swike),°   *(Was) that / wicked / traitor*
"But thu° this man understonde,°   *thou / receive*
1160 I shal flemen° the of° londe,°   *banish / from / (the) land*
Or thou shal to the galwes° renne,°   *gallows / run, hasten*
And ther thou shalt in a fir brenne!"°   *burn*
Sho was adrad, for he so thrette,°   *threatened*
And durste nouth° the spusing° lette;°   *not / marriage / hinder*
1165 But they hire likede swithe ille,
Thouthe it was Godes wille—[5]
God, that makes to growen the korn,
Formede° hire wimman to be born.   *Formed, Fashioned*
Hwan he° havede don° him,° for drede,   *(Godrich) / compelled / (Havelok)*
1170 That he sholde hire spusen and fede°   *nurture, support*
And that she sholde til him holde,°   *keep, be loyal*
Ther weren penies thicke tolde,
Mikel plenté, upon the bok;[6]
He ys hire° yaf° and she as° tok.   *(to) her / given / so*

4. Cf. l. 319, 320, n.
5. But though she was very displeased, she thought it was God's will.
6. Pennies were counted out (in a) thick (pile), (in) great plenty, upon the missal. (A reference,
   here perhaps ironic, to a custom in which, at the conclusion of the marriage vows, coins were
   placed on the missal to signify the couple's sharing of the dowry and other properties.)

1175	He° weren spused fayre and wel;	*They*
	The Messe° he° dede, everi del	*Mass / he*
	That fel° to spusing, an god° clerk°—	*pertained / good / cleric*
	The erchebishop uth of Yerk,[7]	
	That kam to the parlement	
1180	Als God him havede thider sent.	

	Hwan he weren togydere in Godes lawe,[8]	
	That° the folc° ful wel it sawe,	*(So) that / folk, people*
	He ne wisten hwat he mouthen	
	Ne he ne wisten wat hem douthe,	
1185	Ther to dwellen or thenne to gonge.[9]	
	Ther ne wolden he dwellen longe,	
	For he wisten, and ful wel sawe,	
	That Godrich hem hatede—the devel him hawe![1]	
	And yf he dwelleden ther outh°—	*at all*
1190	That fel Havelok ful wel on thouth—	
	Men sholde don his leman shame,	
	Or elles bringen in wicke blame,	
	That were him levere to ben ded.[2]	
	Forthi° he token another red,°	*Accordingly / course of action*
1195	That thei sholden thenne° fle°	*thence / flee*
	Til Grim, and til hise sones thre;°	*three*
	Ther wenden he altherbest to spede,[3]	
	Hem° for-to clothe and for-to fede.	*Them*
	The lond he token under fote—[4]	
1200	Ne wisten° he non other bote°—	*knew / remedy, help*
	And helden° ay° the rithe° sti°	*kept to / always / right / road*
	Til he komen to Grimesby.	
	Thanne° he komen there, thanne was Grim ded;	*Then (when)*
	Of him ne haveden he no red—[5]	
1205	But hise children, alle fyve,	
	Alle weren yet on live,	
	That ful fayre ayen hem neme	
	Hwan he wisten that he keme,[6]	
	And maden joie swithe mikel;	

7. The Archbishop of York. (Ironically, an appropriate figure to preside over the royal wedding which is in fact taking place [however unwitting of this its participants may be]. That the Archbishop is said in the next line to have attended the parliament at Lincoln seems to reflect an actual parliament at Lincoln, to which the real Archbishop was summoned in 1301.)
8. I.e., when they were married.
9. They did not know what they could do nor what was best for them, to stay or thence to go.
1. May the devil take him!
2. That fully occurred to Havelok—people would do violence to his mistress, or else bring her into disrepute, such that it would have been preferable to him to be dead.
3. They hoped there to prevail best of all.
4. I.e., they set off.
5. They had no help from him.
6. Who all courteously took themselves to greet them when they knew that they had come.

1210	Ne weren he nevere ayen° hem fikel.°	*toward / inconstant, disloyal*
	On knes° ful fayre he hem° setten	*knees / themselves*
	And Havelok swithe fayre gretten,°	*greeted*
	And seyden, "Welkome, loverd dere,[7]	
	And welkome be thi fayre fere°—	*companion*
1215	Blessed be that ilke° thrawe°	*same, very / occasion*
	That thou hire toke in Godes lawe!	
	Wel is hus we sen the on lyve;[8]	
	Thou mithe° us bothe selle and yeve,	*can*
	Thou mayt° us bothe yeve and selle,	*can*
1220	With° that thou wilt here dwelle!	*Provided*
	We haven, loverd, alle gode°—	*goods, possessions*
	Hors, and neth,° and ship on flode,°	*cattle / flood, sea*
	Gold and silver, and michel° auchte°—	*much / property*
	That Grim ure° fader° us bitawchte;°	*our / father / gave*
1225	Gold and silver and other fe°	*property*
	Bad he us bitaken° the.°	*give / (to) thee*
	We haven shep,° we haven swin;°	*sheep / swine*
	Bileve° her,° loverd, and al be thin!°	*Stay / here / thine*
	Thou shalt ben loverd,° thou shalt ben syre,°	*(feudal) lord*
1230	And we sholen serven the and hire°—	*her*
	And hure° sistres sholen do	*our*
	Al that evere biddes sho;°	*she*
	He sholen hire clothen° washen and wringen,°	*clothes / wring out*
	And to hondes° water bringen;	*hands*
1235	He° sholen bedden° hire and the,	*They / put to bed*
	For levedi° wile° we that she be."	*(liege) lady / wish*
	Hwan he this joie haveden maked,	
	Sithen° stikes broken and kraked	*Then*
	And the fir brouth on brenne.[9]	
1240	Ne was ther spared gos° ne henne,	*goose*
	Ne the hende° ne the drake;	*duck*
	Mete° he deden plenté° make—	*Food / plenty*
	Ne wantede° there no god mete.	*wanted, lacked*
	Wyn° and ale deden he fete°	*Wine / fetch*
1245	And made hem glade and blithe—	
	Wesseyl ledden he fele sithe.[1]	
	On° the nith,° als° Goldeborw lay,	*In / night / as, while*
	Sory and sorwful was she ay,°	*interminably*
	For she wende° she were biswike,°	*believed / betrayed*
1250	That she were yeven unkyndelike.[2]	

7. Dear lord. (Grim's children greet Havelok as would loyal followers of a king.)
8. We are pleased to see you alive.
9. I.e., and kindled the fire.
1. Many times they conducted a wassail (i.e., a toast, a drinking of one's health).
2. That she had been given (in marriage) against nature (i.e., beneath her innate social rank).

O° nith saw she ther-inne a lith,°   *In / light*
A swithe° fayr, a swithe bryth°—   *very / bright*
Al-so° brith, al-so shir,°   *As / brilliant*
So° it were a blase° of fir.   *As / blaze, flame*
1255 She lokede north and ek south,[3]
And saw it comen ut° of his mouth   *out*
That lay bi hire in the bed—
No ferlike° thou she were adred!°   *wonder / afraid*
Thouthe she, "Wat may this bimene?°   *mean, signify*
1260 He beth heyman yet, als I wene—
He beth heyman er he be ded!"[4]
On hise shuldre, of gold red,[5]
She saw a swithe noble croiz.°   *cross*
Of an angel she herde a voyz:°   *voice*

1265   "Goldeborw, lat° thi sorwe be!   *let*
For Havelok, that haveth spuset° the,   *espoused, married*
He is kinges sone and kinges eyr°—   *heir*
That bi-kenneth° that croiz so fayr.   *signifies*
It bi-kenneth more; that he shal
1270 Denemark haven and Englond al;
He shal ben King strong and stark°   *powerful*
Of Engelond and Denemark—
That shal thu wit° thin eyne° sen,°   *with / eyes / see*
And thou shalt Quen and levedi ben."

1275   Thanne she havede herd the stevene°   *voice*
Of the angel uth° of hevene,   *out*
She was so fele sithes blithe
That she ne mithe hire joie mythe,°   *conceal*
But Havelok sone anon she kiste°—   *kissed*
1280 And he slep° and nouth° ne wiste°   *slept / not at all / knew*
Hwat that aungel havede seyd.
Of his slep anon he brayd,°   *started*
And seide, "Lemman,° slepes thou?   *Beloved*
A selkuth° drem° dremede me nou!° *wondrous / dream / (just) now*

1285   Herkne nou hwat me haveth met.°   *dreamed*
Me thouthe° I was in Denemark set,°   *thought / situated*
But on on° the moste° hil°   *one (that is) / greatest / hill*
That evere yete kam° I til.°   *came / to*
It was so hey that I wel mouthe°   *could*
1290 Al the werd° se, als me thouthe.   *world*
Als I sat upon that lowe°   *hill*
I bigan Denemark for-to awe,°   *take possession of, seize*

---

3. I.e., in every direction.
4. He will be an exalted man yet, so I believe—he will be an exalted man before he is dead!
5. On "red gold," see l. 46, n.

The borwes° and the castles stronge;   *boroughs, towns*
And mine° armes weren so longe   *arms*
1295 That I fadmede° al at ones°   *embraced / once*
Denemark with mine longe bones.
And thanne° I wolde° mine armes drawe   *then (when) / wished*
Til me, and hom° for-to have;   *(at) home*
Al that evere in Denemark liveden°   *lived*
1300 On mine armes faste° clyveden,°   *fast, securely / clung*
And the stronge castles alle
On knes bigunnen° for-to falle—   *began*
The keyes° fellen at mine fet.°   *keys / feet*
Another drem dremede me ek,
1305 That Ich° fley° over the salte se°   *I / flew / sea*
Til Engeland, and al with me
That evere was in Denemark lyves,°   *alive*
But° bondemen° and here° wives,   *Except / peasants / their*
And that Ich kom° til Engelond,   *came*
1310 Al closede° it intil° min° hond—   *enclosed / within / my*
And, Goldeborw, I gaf° it the.°   *gave / (to) thee*
Deus!° lemman! hwat may this be?"   *God*
Sho answerede, and seyde sone,
"Jesu Crist, that made mone,
1315 Thine dremes turne to joye!⁶
      [. . .]
      [. . .]
That wite° thw° that sittes in trone!°   *know / thou / throne*
Ne non strong king, ne caysere°   *emperor*
So° thou° shalt be, for thou shalt bere   *As / (Havelok)*
In Engelond corune° yet.   *crown*
1320 Denemark shal knele to° thi fete;   *at*
Alle the castles that aren° ther-inne   *are*
Shaltow,° lemman, ful wel winne—   *Shalt thou*
I woth so wel so Ich it sowe!⁷
To the shole comen heye° and lowe   *high(born)*
1325 And alle that in Denemark wone°—   *dwell*
Em° and brother, fader and sone,   *Uncle*
Erl and baroun, dreng and thayn,⁸
Knithes and burgeys° and sweyn°—   *burgess / swain, youth*
And make the King heyelike° and wel.   *nobly, solemnly*
1330 Denemark shal be thin, evere-ilc° del°—   *every / part*
Have thou nouth ther-offe° douthe,°   *thereof / doubt*
Nouth the worth° of one nouthe!°   *amount / nut*
Ther-offe, withinne the firste yer,°   *year*

---

6. May Jesus Christ, who made the moon, turn your visions into happiness! (At least two lines
   appear to be missing after this, to judge from the rhyme and the sense.)
7. I know (it) as well as if I had (already) seen it!
8. Cf. ll. 31 ff.

Shalt thou ben King of evere-il del.

1335 But do nou als I wile rathe:°   *advise*
Nimen wit to Denemark bathe—
And do thou nouth on frest this fare;
Lith and selthe felawes are—[9]
For shal Ich nevere blithe be

1340 Til I with eyen° Denemark se;   *eyes*
For Ich woth that al the lond
Shalt thou haven in thin hond.
Prey° Grimes sones, alle thre,   *Pray, Ask*
That he° wenden° forth with the;   *they / go*

1345 I wot° he wilen the nouth werne.°   *know / refuse*
With the wende° shulen he yerne,°   *go / eagerly*
For he loven the hertelike°—   *heartily, from the heart*
Thou maght til he aren quike,
Hwore-so he o worde aren.[1]

1350 There ship thou do° hem swithe° yaren°—   *have / quickly / make ready*
And loke° that thou dwelle° nouth;   *see / delay*
Dwelling haveth ofte scathe wrouth!"[2]

Hwan Havelok herde that° she radde,°   *that (which) / advised*
Sone° it was day, sone he him cladde,°   *Forthwith / clad, dressed*

1355 And sone to the kirke° yede°   *church / went*
Or° he dide ani other dede,   *Before*
And bifor the rode° bigan falle,°   *rood, cross / to fall*
Croiz° and Crist bigan to kalle,°   *Cross / call upon*
And seyde, "Loverd,° that al weldes,°   *Lord / wields, controls*

1360 Wind and water, wodes° and feldes,°   *woods / fields*
For the holi milce° of you   *mercy*
Have merci of me, Loverd, nou!
And wreke° me yet on mi fo   *avenge*
That Ich saw biforn min eyne slo°   *slay*

1365 Mine sistres, with a knif,
And sithen wolde me° mi lyf   *(of) me*
Have reft;° for in the se   *reft, deprived*
Bad he Grim have° drenched° me.   *(to) have / drowned*
He haldes mi lond with mikel° unrith,°   *great / injustice*

1370 With michel wrong, with mikel plith°—   *injury*
For I ne misdede° him nevere nouth—   *wronged*
And haved me to sorwe° brouth.°   *sorrow, grief / brought*
He haveth me do mi mete to thigge[3]
And ofte in sorwe and pine° ligge.°   *pain, affliction / lie*

1375 Loverd, have merci of me,

9. Let us two betake ourselves to Denmark—and do not put off this journey; haste and success go together (*lit.* are fellows).
1. You could (so ask) for as long as they are alive, wherever in the world they are.
2. Delaying has often brought about harm.
3. He has made me beg for my food.

And late° wel passe° the se,   *let (me) / cross*
That Ich have ther-offe douthe and kare,[4]
Withuten stormes over-fare,°   *pass over*
That I ne drenched be ther-ine,
1380 Ne forfaren° for no sinne;   *dispatched, lost*
And bringge me wel to the lond
That Godard haldes° in his hond,   *holds*
That is mi rith,° everi del—   *rightful (legal) claim*
Jesu Crist, thou wost° it wel!"   *know*

1385   Thanne° he havede his bede° seyd,   *Then (when) / prayer*
His offrende° on the auter° leyd;   *offering / altar*
His leve at Jesu Crist he tok
And at His suete° moder° ok,°   *sweet / mother / also*
And at the croiz that he biforn lay;
1390 Sithen° yede sore grotinde° awey.   *Then / weeping*

       Hwan he com hom he° wore° yare,°   *they / were / ready*
Grimes sones, for-to fare
Into the se, fishes to gete
That Havelok mithe wel of ete;
1395 But Avelok thouthe al another:[5]
First he kalde the heldeste° brother,   *eldest*
Roberd the Rede, bi his naven,°   *name*
Wiliam Wenduth, and Huwe Raven—
Grimes sones, alle thre—
1400 And seyde, "Lithes° nou alle to me!   *Listen*
Loverdinges,° Ich wile you shaue°   *Sirs / show, relate*
A thing° of° me that ye wel knawe.   *matter / concerning*
Mi fader was King of Denshe° lond;   *(the) Danish*
Denemark was al in his hond
1405 The day that he was quik and ded.[6]
But thanne havede he wicke° red,°   *bad, disastrous / advice*
That he me and Denemark al
And mine sistres bitawte a thral—
A develes lime hus bitawte,
1410 And al his lond and al hise authe;[7]
For I saw that fule° fend°   *foul / fiend*
Mine sistres slo° with hise hend:°   *slay / hand*
First he shar° a-two° here° throtes,   *cut / in two / their*
And sithen hem al to grotes,°   *pieces*
1415 And sithen bad in the se
Grim, youre fader, drenchen me.[8]

4. About which I have fear and worry.
5. I.e., thought differently.
6. I.e., until the day he died. (Cf. l. 257.)
7. Such that he handed me and all Denmark and my sisters over to a villain—he handed us over to a limb (i.e., an imp) of Satan, and all his land and all his possessions.
8. And then bade Grim, your father, drown me in the sea.

Deplike° dede he him swere   *Deeply, Profoundly*
On bok° that he sholde me bere   *book, Bible*
Unto the se an drenchen ine,
1420 And wolde taken on him the sinne—[9]
But Grim was wis° and swithe° hende;°   *wise / very / gracious*
Wolde he nouth his soule shende.°   *destroy*
Levere° was him° to be forsworen°   *Preferable / (to) him / perjured*
Than drenchen me and ben forlorn;°   *forfeit (of soul), damned*
1425 But sone bigan he for-to fle°   *flee*
Fro Denemark, for-to berwen° me—   *save*
For yif° Ich havede ther ben funden,°   *if / found*
Havede° ben slayn, or harde bunden,°   *(He would) have / bound, tied up*
And heye ben henged° on a tre—   *hanged*
1430 Havede go for him gold ne fe.[1]
Forthi° fro Denemark hider° he fledde,   *Accordingly / hither*
And me ful fayre and ful wel fedde,°   *nurtured*
So that, unto this day,
Have Ich ben fed and fostred ay.°   *always*
1435 But nou Ich am up to that helde
Cumen that Ich may wepne welde,[2]
And I may grete dintes° yeve,°   *dints, blows / give*
Shal I nevere hwil° Ich lyve   *while*
Ben glad til that Ich Denemark se!
1440 I preie you that ye wende with me—
And Ich may mak you riche men;
Ilk° of you shal have castles ten   *Each*
And the lond that thor-til° longes,°   *thereto / belongs*
Borwes, tunes,° wodes, and wonges."°   *towns / fields*

[* * *][3]
1625 "With swilk° als Ich byen° shal.   *such / buy*
Ther-of biseche° you° nou leve°—   *(I) ask / (of) you / permission*
Wile° Ich speke with non other reve°   *Will / official*
But with you, that justise° are—   *justice, judge*
That I mithe° seken° mi ware°   *may / seek / wares*
1630 In gode borwes up and doun,
And faren° Ich wile, fro tun to tun."   *travel*

9. Cf. l. 536.
1. Gold nor property would have helped him.
2. But now (that) I have come to that age where I may wield weapons.
3. A page has been cut out of the manuscript at this point; four text columns of 45 lines each are lost (plus one more line, which, to judge from the rhyme of l. 1625, had been mistakenly omitted from the now-missing text). The plot of the missing text must have gone as follows. The three sons of Grim agree to accompany Havelok and Goldeborw to Denmark; they set sail. Once there, Havelok, Robert, and William, disguised as merchants, meet the Danish noble Ubbe (a former friend and ally of Havelok's father, King Birkabeyn) and request permission from him to sell their wares. The text resumes in the midst of Havelok's entreaty to Ubbe.

A gold ring drow° he forth anon   *drew, pulled*
(An hundred pund° was worth the ston)   *pounds*
And yaf it Ubbe for-to spede.[4]
1635 (He was ful wis that first yaf mede,[5]
And so was Havelok ful wis here;
He solde his gold ring ful dere°—   *dearly, expensively*
Was nevere non so dere sold
Fro° chapmen,° neyther yung ne old: *From, By / merchants*
1640 That sholen ye forthward° ful wel leren°   *forthwith / learn*
Yif that ye wile the storie heren.)

Hwan Ubbe havede the gold ring,
Havede he yovenet for no thing,[6]
Nouth° for the borw, evere-il° del.°   *Not / every / part*
1645 Havelok biheld he swithe wel,[7]
Hw° he was wel of bones maked,   *How*
Brod° in the sholdres, ful wel schaped,   *Broad*
Thicke in the brest, of bodi long;
He semede° wel to ben wel strong.   *seemed*
1650 "Deus!" hwat° Ubbe, "qui° ne were he knith?°   *said / why / (a) knight*
I woth° that he is swithe with;°   *know / doughty, courageous*
Betere semede him to bere[8]
Helm on heved,° sheld° and spere,   *head / shield*
Thanne to beye° and selle ware—   *buy*
1655 Allas, that he shal ther-with fare!
Goddot, wile he trowe me,
Chaffare shal he late be!"[9]
Netheles,° he seyde sone,   *Nevertheless*
"Havelok, have thi bone,°   *boon, request*
1660 And I ful wel rede° the   *advise*
That thou come and ete with me
Today, thou and thi fayre wif
That thou lovest al-so° thi lif—   *as*
And have thou of° hire° no drede;°   *for / her / dread, fear*
1665 Shal hire no man shame bede.°   *proffer*
Bi the fey that I owe to the,
Ther-of shal I meself borw be."[1]

---

4. I.e., and gave it to Ubbe to help matters along. (A diplomatic way, perhaps, of describing a bribe; for want of further details about Ubbe which may have been related on the missing leaf, and in light of the narrator's praise for Havelok's wise generosity in the next seven lines, it would seem that Ubbe is meant to be contrasted with Havelok as a less immediately ethical figure. He shares this unsettling ambivalence with Grim and, to a lesser extent, Godard: see the discussion of such figures in the Sources and Backgrounds headnote, pp. 317–18.)
5. He was very wise who first (ever) gave rewards.
6. He would not have given it (up) for anything.
7. I.e., he beheld Havelok throroughly.
8. It would seem better for him to bear.
9. God knows, if he will trust me, he will let trade be!
1. By the (good) faith that I owe to you, I myself will be guarantor to that.

Havelok herde that° he bad;°   *that (which)/bade, asked*
And, thow,° was he ful sore drad°   *though/afraid*
1670 With him to ete, for° hise wif—   *for (the sake of)*
For him wore levere that his lif
Him wore reft than she in blame
Felle or lauthe ani shame.[2]
Hwanne he havede his° wille yat,°   *(Ubbe's)/granted*
1675 The stede° that he° onne sat   *steed, war-horse/(Ubbe)*
Smot° Ubbe with spures° faste   *Struck/spurs*
And forth° awey—but, at the laste,°   *proceeded/last (moment)*
Or° he fro him ferde,°   *Before/went*
Seyde he, that° his folk herde,   *(so) that*
1680 "Loke° that ye comen bathe,°   *See/both*
For Ich it wile° and Ich it rathe."°   *will, desire/advise*

Havelok ne durste, thei° he were adrad,   *though*
Nouth with-sitten° that Ubbe bad;   *resist*
His wif he dide with him lede.°   *lead, take*
1685 Unto the heye° curt° he yede;°   *high/court/went*
Roberd hire ledde (that was red°—   *redheaded*
That havede° tholed° for hire the ded°   *would have/suffered/death*
Or ani° havede hire misseyd°   *anyone/spoken ill of*
Or hand with ivele onne leyd).[3]
1690 Willam Wendut was that other
That hire ledde, Roberdes brother,
That was with at alle nedes°—   *(times of) need*
Wel is him that god man fedes.[4]
Than he weren comen to the halle
1695 Biforen Ubbe and hise men alle,
Ubbe stirte° hem° ageyn,°   *started/them/toward*
And mani a knith and mani a sweyn,°   *swain, youth*
Hem for-to se° and for-to shawe.°   *see/scrutinize*
Tho° stod Havelok als° a lowe°   *Then/like/hill*
1700 Aboven that° ther-inne wore,   *(all those) who*
Rith al bi the heved more[5]
Thanne ani that ther-inne stod;
Tho was Ubbe blithe of mod°   *mood*
That° he saw him so fayr and hende—   *(When) that*
1705 Fro him ne mithe his herte wende,
Ne fro him, ne fro his wif;
He lovede hem sone so his lif.[6]

---

2. For it was preferable to him that his own life were taken from him than that she fell into disrepute or incurred any shame.
3. Cf. l. 50.
4. It goes well for him who nurtures a good man. (A proverbial reference to the kind of loyalty patently nurtured in Grim's family.)
5. Fully by more than a head.
6. His heart could not turn away from him—not from him, not from his wife; at once he loved

Weren° non in Denemark that him thouthe°   *(There) were / thought*
That he so mikel° love mouthe.°   *much / could*
1710 (More he lovede Havelok one°   *alone*
Than al Denemark, bi° mine wone°—   *by, in / opinion*
Loke nou hw God helpen kan
O° mani wise° wif and man!)   *In / ways*

    Hwan it was comen time to ete,
1715 Hise wif dede Ubbe sone in fete,°   *fetch*
And til° hire seyde al on° gamen,°   *to / in / game, jest*
"Dame, thou and Havelok shulen° ete samen,°   *shall / together*
And Goldeboru shal ete wit° me   *with*
That° is so° fayr so flour° on tre—   *Who / as / flower*
1720 In al Denemark nis° wimman°   *is not / (a) woman*
So fayr so sche, bi Seint Johan!"
Thanne he were set° and bord° leyd,   *seated / (the) table*
And the beneysun° was seyd,   *grace*
Biforn hem com° the beste mete°   *came / food*
1725 That king or cayser° wolde ete: *emperor*
Kranes, swannes, veneysun,°   *venison*
Lax,° lampreys, and god sturgun,   *Salmon*
Pyment to drinke and god claré,[7]
Win° hwit° and red, ful god plenté—   *Wine / white*
1730 Was ther-inne no page so lite
That evere wolde ale bite![8]
(Of the mete for-to telle,
Ne of the win, bidde° I nout dwelle;°   *wish / to dwell upon, to tarry*
That is the storie for-to lenge°—   *prolong*
1735 It wolde anuye° this fayre genge!)°   *annoy / group*
But hwan he haveden the kilthing° deyled,°   *drink / dealt, distributed*
And fele sithes haveden wosseyled,[9]
And with gode drinkes seten° longe,   *sat*
And it was time for-to gonge,°   *go*
1740 Il° man to ther° he cam fro,   *Each / there (where)*
Thouthe Ubbe, "Yf I late hem go
Thus—one foure, withuten mo—
So mote Ich brouke finger or to,
For this wimman bes mikel wo;
1745 For hire shal men hire loverd slo."[1]
He tok sone knithes ten,

---

them as much as his own life. (Yet another demonstration of the naturally commanding presence of Goldeborw and Havelok—and it is a presence which, in the case of Havelok, exists beyond his extraordinary physical prowess; cf. ll. 945–58 and 1211–36.)

7. Two varieties of spiced wine; the latter was also honeyed.
8. There was no page boy so small that he had to taste (mere) ale!
9. Cf. l. 1246.
1. If I let them go thus—four on their own, without any others—as I hope to use my finger or toe (i.e., as I hope to live), there will be much trouble because of this woman; men will slay her lord for her (i.e., in order to abduct her).

And wel° sixti other men   *well, fully*
Wit gode bowes and with gleives,°   *halberds*
And sende him unto the greyves°—   *greive's (house)*
1750 The beste man of al the toun,
That was named Bernard Brun—
And bad him, als he lovede his lif,
Havelok wel yemen° and his wif,   *to protect*
And wel do wayten° al the nith°   *watch / night*
1755 Til the other° day, that it were lith.°   *next / light*
Bernard was trewe and swithe with;°   *courageous*
In al the borw° ne was no knith   *borough*
That betere couthe° on stede riden,   *could*
Helm on heved, ne swerd° bi side.   *sword*
1760 Havelok he gladlike° understod°   *gladly / received*
With mike° love and herte° god,   *much / heart, affection*
And dide greythe° a super° riche   *prepare / supper*
(Al-so he was no-with chiche)[2]
To his bihove° everil° del,°   *need / every / portion*
1765 That° he mithe° supe° swithe wel.   *(So) that / could / sup*

    Al-so he° seten and sholde soupe,°   *they / sup*
So comes a ladde in a joupe,°   *loose tunic*
And with him sixti other stronge,
With swerdes drawen and knives longe,
1770 Ilkan in hande[3] a ful god gleive,
And seyde, "Undo,° Bernard the greyve!   *open up*
Undo swithe° and lat us in,   *quickly, right away*
Or thu art ded, bi Seint Austin!"°   *Augustine*
Bernard stirt up, that was ful big,
1775 And caste a brinie° upon his rig,°   *coat of mail / back*
And grop° an ax that was ful god;   *grasped, seized*
Lep° to the dore so° he wore wod,°   *Leaped / as if / mad*
And seyde, "Hwat° are ye, that are ther-oute,   *who*
That thus biginnen for-to stroute?°   *agitate, contend*
1780 Goth henne° swithe, fule° theves!   *hence / foul*
For, bi the Loverd° that man on leves,°   *lord (God) / believes*
Shol Ich casten the dore open;
Summe of you shal Ich drepen,°   *slay*
And the othre shal Ich kesten°   *cast, throw*
1785 In feteres° and ful faste festen!"°   *fetters, shackles / fasten*
"Hwat have ye seid?" quoth° a ladde,   *said*
"Wenestu° that we ben adradde?°   *Do you think / scared*
We shole at° this dore gonge°   *(in) at / go*
Maugré thin, carl, or outh longe!"[4]

2. As he was in no way mean.
3. I.e., each one handling.
4. Despite you, churl, before long!

1790 He gripen° sone a bulder-ston,°	*seized / boulder*
And let it fleye ful god won[5]	
Agen° the dore, that° it to-rof.°	*Against / (so) that / shattered*
Avelok it saw, and thider° drof,°	*thither / rushed*
And the barre° sone ut-drow°	*(door) bar / drew out*
1795 That was unride° and gret ynow,°	*immense / enough, in plenty*
And caste the dore open wide	
And seide, "Her shal I now abide;	
Comes swithe unto me—	
Datheyt hwo you henne fle!"[6]	
1800 "No!" quodh on, "that shaltou coupe!"[7]	
And bigan til° him to loupe,°	*to / run*
In his hond his swerd ut-drawe;	
Havelok he wende thore have slawe—[8]	
And with him comen other two	
1805 That him wolde of live have do.[9]	
Havelok lifte up the dore-tre,°	*door bar*
And at a dint° he slow° hem° thre;	*stroke / slew / them*
Was non of hem that hise hernes	
Ne lay ther ute ageyn the sternes![1]	
1810 The ferthe° that he sithen° mette,	*fourth / then*
Wit the barre so he him grette°	*assailed*
Bifor° the heved that the rith° eye	*In front of / right*
Ut° of the hole° made he fleye,	*Out / socket*
And sithe clapte° him on the crune°	*battered / crown, head*
1815 So that he stan-ded° fel thor dune.	*stone-dead*
The fifte° that he overtok	*fifth*
Gaf he a ful sor dint ok,°	*also*
Bitwen the sholdres ther° he stod,	*there (where)*
That he speu° his herte-blod.	*spewed out*
1820 The sixte wende° for-to fle,	*intended*
And he clapte him with the tre	
Rith in the fule° necke so	*foul, filthy*
That he smot hise necke on° to.°	*in / two*
Thanne the sixe weren doun feld,°	*felled, laid low*
1825 The sevenhte brayd° ut° his swerd,	*hastened / out*
And wolde Havelok riht° in the eye;	*slash*
And Havelok let the barre fleye	
And smot him sone ageyn the brest,	
That havede ne nevere schrifte of prest—[2]	
1830 For he was ded on° lesse hwile°	*in / time*

5. With abundant force.
6. Cursed be whoever flees hence from you!
7. "No!" said one, "you will pay for that!"
8. He intended there to have slain Havelok.
9. I.e., who would have taken his life.
1. There was not one of them whose brains did not there lie exposed to the stars!
2. So that he never received absolution from a priest.

Than men mouthe renne a mile![3]
Alle the othere weren ful kene;°   *keen, bold*
A red thei taken hem bitwene[4]
That he° sholde him bihalve°   *they / surround*
1835   And brisen° so that wit° no salve°   *beat / with / salve, remedy*
Ne sholde him helen° leche° non.   *heal / doctor*
They drowen ut swerdes ful god won,
And shoten° on him so° don° on bere°   *rushed / as / do / bear*
Dogges that wolden him to-tere,°   *tear apart*
1840   Thanne men doth the bere beyte.[5]
The laddes were kaske° and teyte°   *bold / eager*
And umbiyeden° him ilkon;°   *surrounded / each one*
Sum smot° with tre, and sum wit ston,   *smote, struck*
Summe putten° with gleyve in bac and side,   *thrust*
1845   And yeven° wundes° longe and wide   *gave / wounds*
In twenti stedes,° and wel mo,°   *places / more*
Fro the croune til the to.°   *toe*
Hwan he saw that, he was wod°—   *mad, enraged*
And was it ferlik° hw he stod,°   *a wonder / stood*
1850   For the blod ran of° his sides   *from*
So water that fro the welle° glides.   *spring*
But thanne bigan he for-to mowe°   *mow, cut down*
With the barre, and let hem shewe[6]
Hw he cowthe sore smite;
1855   For was ther non, long° ne lite,°   *tall / little, short*
That he mouthe° overtake   *could*
That he ne garte° his croune krake,°   *caused / to crack, to break*
So that, on° a litel stund,°   *in / time*
Felde he twenti to the grund.

1860   Tho° bigan gret dine° to rise,   *Then / din*
For the laddes on ilke wise°   *way*
Him asayleden wit grete dintes.
Fro fer° he stonden° him with flintes,°   *far / stoned / flints*
And gleyves schoten him fro ferne;°   *afar*
1865   For drepen him he wolden yerne—
But dursten he newhen° him no more   *approach*
Thanne he bor° or leun° wore!°   *boar / lion / were*

Huwe Raven that dine herde,
And thowthe° wel that men misferde°   *thought / did amiss*

---

3. Than that in which men could run a mile!
4. I.e., between them they set upon a plan.
5. When men bait the bear. (Bear-baiting was a popular medieval betting sport in which a chained bear was set upon by dogs; the object was to have one's favored dog be the first to compel the bear to submit. Other kinds of animals were also baited in similar ways; see ll. 2330–31, 2438–40.)
6. And let them find out.

1870 With his loverd, for his wif;
And grop an ore° and a long knif, *oar*
And thider drof al-so° an hert,° *like / hart*
And cham° ther on a litel stert,° *came / time*
And saw how the laddes wode° *mad, enraged*
1875 Havelok his loverd umbistode° *surrounded*
And beten on him so doth the smith
With the hamer on the stith.° *anvil*

"Allas!" hwat° Hwe, "that I was boren,° *said / born*
That evere et° Ich° bred of koren°— *eat / I / corn, grain*
1880 That Ich here this sorwe se!
Roberd! Willam! hware° are ye? *where*
Gripeth ether° unker° a god tre,° *each / of you two / beam*
And late we nouth° thise doges fle° *not / flee*
Til ure° loverd° wreke° be. *our / lord / avenged*
1885 Cometh swithe,° and folwes° me— *quickly / follow*
Ich have in honde a ful god ore—
Datheit wo ne smite sore!"[7]
"Ya!° leve,° ya!" quod Roberd sone, *Yes / beloved (brother)*
"We haven ful god lith° of the mone!"° *light / moon*
1890 Roberd grop a staf, strong and gret,
That mouthe ful wel bere a net;[8]
And Willam Wendut grop a tre,
Mikel grettere than his the;° *thigh*
And Bernard held his ax ful faste—
1895 I seye,° was he nouth the laste!— *say*
And lopen° forth so he weren wode *leaped*
To the laddes ther he° stode, *they*
And yaf° hem wundes swithe° grete. *gave / very*
Ther mithe° men wel se° boyes° bete,° *could / see / rascals / beaten*
1900 And ribbes in here° sides breke°— *their / broken*
And Havelok on hem wel wreke.° *avenged*
He° broken armes, he broken knes, *They*
He broken shankes,° he broken thes;° *shins / thighs*
He dide° the blod there renne° dune *caused / to run*
1905 To the fet,° rith° fro the crune— *feet / right*
For was ther spared heved° non; *head*
He leyden° on hevedes ful god won, *laid, set upon*
And made croune breke and crake
Of the broune and of the blake.[9]
1910 He maden here backes al-so° bloute° *as / soft, tender*
Als here wombes,° and made hem rowte° *bellies / roar*

7. Cursed be he who does not hit hard!
8. That an ox would do well to bear.
9. Cf. l. 1008.

Als he weren kradel-barnes,°   *infants in cradle*
So dos the child that moder° tharnes.°   *mother/is without, wants*

    Datheit wo recke, for he it servede!
1915 Hwat dide he thore? Weren he werewed![1]
So longe haveden he but° and bet,°   *thrust/beaten*
With neves under hernes set,[2]
That of tho° sixti men and on°   *those/one*
Ne wente ther° awey lives° non.   *(from) there/alive*

1920   On the morwen,° hwan it was day,   *morning*
Ilc on other wirwed° lay   *mangled*
Als it were dogges that weren henged;[3]
And summe leye° in dikes° slenget;°   *lay/ditches/slung*
And summe in gripes° bi the her°   *gutters/hair*
1925 Drawen° ware,° and laten° ther.   *Dragged/were/left*
Sket° cam tiding intil° Ubbe   *Quickly/unto*
That Havelok havede, with a clubbe,
Of hise slawen sixti and on
Sergaunz, the beste that mithen gon.[4]
1930 "Deus!"° quoth Ubbe, "hwat may this be?   *God*
Betere his° I nime° miself, and se   *(it) is/betake, go*
Hwat this baret oweth on wold[5]
Thanne I sende yunge or old,[6]
For yif° I sende° him unto,   *if/send (others)*
1935 I wene° men sholde° him shame° do.   *believe/would/violence*
And that ne wolde Ich for no thing;
I love him wel, bi Hevene King—
Me wore levere I wore lame[7]
Thanne men dide him ani shame,
1940 Or tok,° or onne handes leyde   *took, abducted*
Unornelike,° or same° seyde."   *disgracefully/insult*
He lep up on a stede lith,°   *lightly*
And with him mani a noble knith,
And ferde° forth unto the tun,°   *went/town*
1945 And dide calle Bernard Brun
Ut of his hus° wan° he ther cam;   *house/when*
And Bernard sone ageyn him nam,[8]
Al to-tused° and al to-torn,°   *tussled/torn up, ragged*
Ner° al-so naked so he was born,   *Nearly*
1950 And al to-brised° bac° and the.°   *bruised/back/thigh*

1. Cursed be he who feels pity, for they deserved it! What were they doing there? They were mangled!
2. With fists laid under brains (i.e., with uppercut blows to the head).
3. Like dogs that had been hanged.
4. I.e., slain sixty-one of his best men-at-arms.
5. What this fighting means.
6. I.e., than if I send anyone else.
7. I would sooner be lame.
8. And Bernard quickly went before him.

Quoth Ubbe, "Bernard, hwat is the?[9]
Hwo haves° the° thus ille° maked,   has / (to) thee / injury
Thus to-riven,° and al mad° naked?"   torn / made

   "Loverd,° merci!"° quot° he sone,   Lord / (have) mercy / said
1955 "Tonicht,° al-so ros° the mone,   Tonight / rose
Comen her mo than sixti theves
With lokene copes and wide sleves,[1]
Me for-to robben and to pine,°   inflict pain upon
And for-to drepe° me and mine.   slay
1960 Mi dore he broken up ful sket,
And wolde me binden, hond and fet.
Wan the godemen° that sawe—   worthy men
Havelok and he° that bi the wowe°   they / wall
Leye°—he stirten° up sone onon,°   Lay / started / anon
1965 And summe grop tre, and sum grop ston,
And drive° hem ut, thei° he weren crus,°   drove / though / fierce
So° dogges ut of milne-hous.°   Like / mill
Havelok grop the dore-tre°   door bar
And at a dint° he slow° hem° thre.   blow / slew / (of) them
1970 He is the beste man at nede°   (time of) need
That everemar° shal ride stede!   evermore
Als helpe God, bi mine wone,[2]
A thousend of men his° he worth one°—   is / alone
Yif he ne were, Ich were nou° ded;   now
1975 So have Ich don mi soule red!°—   help
But it is of° him mikel° sinne;°   concerning / great / pity
He maden him swilke woundes thrinne
That of the altherleste wounde
Were a stede brouht to grunde:[3]
1980 He haves a wunde in the side[4]
With° a gleyve,° ful unride;°   From / halberd / immense
And he haves on° thoru° his arum°   one / through / arm
(Ther-of is ful mikel harum);°   harm, pity
And he haves on thoru his the,
1985 The unrideste that men may se—
And other wundes haves he stronge,
Mo° than twenti, swithe longe.   More
But sithen° he havede lauth° the sor°   after / sustained / pain
Of the wundes, was nevere bor°   boar
1990 That so fauth° so° he fauth thanne!   fought / as

9. Cf. l. 453.
1. With fastened cloaks and wide sleeves (i.e., dressed to fight—for protection, perhaps to conceal
weapons).
2. So help (me) God, in my opinion.
3. They gave him three such wounds that the least one would have brought down a horse.
4. Cf. *The Sege off Melayne*, l. 702, n. Such a wound inevitably invites comparison with Christ,
but, in that context, a perhaps more immediately relevant recollection of Athelwold's model
kingship is in order; cf. ll. 217, n., and 228, n.

Was non that havede the hern-panne°   *brainpan, skull*
So hard that he ne dede al to-cruhsse,°   *crush*
And al to-shivere,° and al to-frusshe.°   *shatter / fracture*
He folwede° hem so hund° dos° hare!   *followed / hound / does*
1995 Datheyt on he wolde spare,[5]
That° he ne made hem everilkon°   *(So) that / everyone*
Ligge° stille so doth° the ston—   *Lie / does*
And ther nis he nouth to frie,
For other sholde he make hem lye
2000 Ded, or thei him havede slawen,
Or al to-hewen or al to-drawen.[6]

Loverd, havi no more plith
Of that Ich was thus grethed tonith.[7]
Thus wolde the theves me have reft;°   *robbed*
2005 But, God thank, he havenet° sure° keft.°   *have it / bitterly / paid for*
But it is of° him° mikel scathe;°   *about / (Havelok) / pity*
I woth° that he bes° ded ful rathe.”°   *believe / will be / quickly*

Quoth Ubbe, “Bernard, seyst thou soth?”°   *(the) truth*
“Ya, sire! That I ne leye oth;[8]
2010 Yif I, loverd, a word leye,
Tomorwen do me hengen° heye.”°   *hang / high*
The burgeys° that ther-bi stode thore   *burgesses*
Grundlike° and grete othes swore,   *Solemn*
Litle and mikle, yunge and holde,°   *old*
2015 That was soth that Bernard tolde—
Soth was that he° wolden° him bynde   *they (the thieves) / wished*
And trusse° al that he mithen fynde   *pack up*
Of hise in arke° or in kiste,°   *ark, coffer / chest*
That° he mouthe in seckes° thriste:°   *(So) that / sacks / thrust (it)*
2020 “Loverd, he haveden° al awey born   *they / would have*
His thing,° and himself al to-torn,   *things*
But als God self barw him wel
That he ne tinte no catel.[9]
Hwo mithe so mani stonde ageyn,
2025 Bi nither-tale, knith or swein?[1]
He weren bi tale° sixti and ten—   *count, number*
Starke° laddes, stalworthi° men   *Powerful / stalwart, strong*
(And on,° the mayster° of hem alle,   *one / master*
That was the name Giffin Galle).
2030 Hwo mouthe ageyn so mani stonde

5. Cursed be it that he would spare one of them.
6. And he is not to blame there, for either he had to lay them out dead or they would have slain him, or completely cut him to pieces or completely torn him apart.
7. Lord, I have no further harm from that with which I was thus (mis)treated tonight.
8. Yes, sir! I do not give the lie to an oath on that.
9. Except that God Himself protected him well, so that he lost no property.
1. Who could stand against so many in the middle of the night, (what) knight or young man?

But als this man of ferne londe
Haveth hem slawen with a tre?[2]
Mikel joie have he!°   *(may) he*
God yeve° him mikel god° to welde,°   *give / property / manage*
Bothe in tun and ek° in felde°—   *also / field, country*
Wel is set he etes mete!"[3]
Quoth Ubbe, "Doth° him swithe° fete,°   *have / quickly / fetched*
That° I mouthe° his woundes se,   *(So) that / can*
Yf that he mouthen holed° be;   *healed*
For yf he mouthe covere° yet   *recover*
And gangen° wel upon hise fet,°   *go about, walk / feet*
Miself shal dubbe him to knith[4]
Forthi° that he is so with.°   *Because / courageous*
And yif he livede, tho° foule theves,   *those*
That weren of Kaym kin and Eves,[5]
He sholden hange bi the necke—
Of here ded datheit wo recke,
Hwan he yeden thus on nithes[6]
To binde° bothe burgmen° and knithes;   *bind, tie up / townsmen*
For bynderes love Ich neveremo—[7]
Of hem ne yeve Ich nouht a slo!"°   *sloeberry*

Havelok was bifore Ubbe browth,°   *brought*
That° havede for him ful mikel thouth°   *Who / thought, concern*
And mikel sorwe° in his herte°   *sorrow / heart*
For hise wundes° that were so smerte.°   *wounds / painful*

But hwan his wundes weren shewed,°   *examined*
And a leche° havede knawed°   *doctor / made known*
That he hem mouthe ful wel hele°—   *heal*
Wel make him gange and ful wel mele,°   *speak*
And wel a palefrey° bistride°   *riding horse / sit astride*
And wel upon a stede° ride—   *steed, war-horse*

---

2. Who could stand against so many except as this man from a far-off land (who) has slain them with a wooden beam?

3. I.e., it is advantageous that he eats food! (The line may, however, be a corrupt recollection of the expression at l. 907.)

4. I myself shall dub him a knight. (Such an honor is conferred by touching lightly, or "dubbing," the shoulder of the recipient; knighthood can be conferred only by someone who is already a knight.)

5. Who were of Cain's kin, and Eve's. (It was commonly held that a race of murderers, thieves, monsters, and other ne'er-do-wells was descended from Cain, condemned to a life of brute vagabondage. That Eve alone is identified with the first murderer no doubt reflects the belief that she was more to blame for the Fall than Adam.)

6. Cursed be he who cares about their death when they so went about in the night.

7. I will nevermore be tolerant of "binders" (i.e., thieves who tie up their victims; Ubbe—using a word recorded nowhere else in English—seems inordinately outraged by this particular form of crime, perhaps because it involves the deprivation of freedom for those who are *de facto* "freemen" according to feudal law. In this sense, Godard and Godrich, the archcriminals of the tale, are also "binders," the extremity of their crime assured by their theft of rights and not just property. That Ubbe admits to having been formerly tolerant of "binders" implies a checkered past; cf. l. 1634, n.)

Tho° let Ubbe al his care°　　　　　　　　　　*Then/worry, distress*
And al his sorwe over-fare,　　　　　　　　　　*pass over, pass away*
And seyde, "Cum now forth with me,
2065　And Goldeboru thi wif° with the,　　　　　　　　　　　　　*wife*
And thine serjaunz,° alle thre;　　　　　　　　　　*men-at-arms*
For nou° wile° I youre warant° be.　　　　　*now/will/protector*
Wile I non of here frend
That thu slowe with thin hend
2070　Mouthe wayte the to slo
Al-so thou gange to and fro.⁸
I shal lene° the a bowr°　　　　　　　*lend/bower, chamber*
That is up in the heye tour°　　　　　　　　　　*tower*
Til thou mowe° ful wel go°　　　　　*can/go about, walk*
2075　And wel ben hol° of al thi wo.°　　　*whole, healed/injuries*
It° ne shal nothing ben bitwene　　　　　　　　　*There*
Thi bour and min,° al-so° I wene,°　　　*mine/so/believe*
But a fayr firrene° wowe;°　　　　　*(of) firewood/wall*
Speke° I loude or spek I lowe,　　　　　　　　　*Speak*
2080　Thou shalt ful wel heren° me,　　　　　　　　　　*hear*
And than° thu° wilt,° thou shalt me se.　　*then (when)/thou/wish*
A° rof° shal hile° us bothe o° nith,　　　*One/roof/cover/at*
That° none of mine, clerk ne knith,　　　　　　*(So) that*
Ne sholen thi wif no shame° bede°—　　　*violence/proffer*
2085　No more than min, so God me rede."°　　　　　　*help*

He dide unto the borw° bringe　　　　　　　　　*bower*
Sone anon, al with joyinge,°　　　　　　　　　*rejoicing*
His wif and his serganz thre—
The beste men that mouthe be.
2090　The firste nith he lay ther-inne,
Hise wif and his serganz thrinne,
Aboute the middel of the nith,
Wok° Ubbe and saw a mikel lith°　　　　　　　　*Awoke/light*
In the bour thar° Havelok lay,　　　　　　　　*there (where)*
2095　Al-so brith° so° it were day.　　　　　　　　*bright/as*

"Deus!"° quoth Ubbe, "hwat may this be?　　　　　*God*
Betere is° I go miself and se,　　　　　　　　*(it) is*
Hwether he° sitten nou and wesseylen,°　　*they/wassail, drink toasts*
Or of ani shotshipe° to-deyle°　　　*foolishness/take part in*
2100　This tid nithes, al-so foles—
Than birthe men casten hem in poles,
Or in a grip, or in the fen;
Nou ne sitten none but wicke men,
Glotuns, revres, or wicke theves,

---

8. I will see to it that none of the friends of those you slew with your hand can lie in wait to slay you as you go to and fro.

2105 Bi Crist that alle folk onne leves!"[9]

He stod and totede° in at a bord°   *peeked / (partition) board*
Her° he spak anilepi° word,   *Ere, Before / a single*
And saw hem slepen° faste ilkon°   *sleep / each one*
And lye stille so the ston,
2110 And saw° al that mikel lith   *saw (that)*
Fro Havelok cam that was so brith;
Of his mouth it com il° del°—   *each / part*
That° was he war° ful swithe° wel.   *(Of) that / aware / very*
"Deus!" quoth he, "hwat may this mene?"
2115 He calde bothe arwe men and kene,[1]
Knithes and serganz swithe sleie°—   *clever, discerning*
Mo than an hundred, withuten leye—
And bad hem alle comen and se
Hwat that selcuth° mithe° be.   *wonder / could*

2120 Als the knithes were comen alle
Ther° Havelok lay, ut° of the halle,   *(To) there (where) / out*
So stod° ut of his mouth a glem,°   *rose / gleam, ray*
Rith al swilk so the sunne-bem,[2]
That al-so° lith° was° thare, bi hevene,   *just as / bright / was (it)*
2125 So° ther brenden° serges° sevene   *As if / burned / candles*
And an hundred serges ok°—   *also, more*
That durste hi° sweren° on a bok.°   *they / swear / book, Bible*
He slepen faste, alle five,
So he weren brouth of live,[3]
2130 And Havelok lay on his lift° side,   *left*
In his armes his brithe° bride;   *splendid, fair*
Bi° the pappes° he leyen naked.   *As far as, Down to / breasts*
So faire two weren nevere maked
In a bed to lyen samen;°   *together*
2135 The knithes thouth of hem god gamen,
Hem for-to shewe and loken to.[4]
Rith° al-so he stoden alle so,   *Just*
And his bac° was toward hem went,°   *back / turned*
So weren he war of a croiz° ful gent°   *cross / excellent, fine*
2140 On his rith° shuldre—swithe brith,   *right*
Brithter than gold ageyn° the lith—   *against, exposed to*
So that he wiste, heye and lowe,[5]
That it was kunrik° that he sawe.   *of royal origin*

9. (At) this time of night, like fools—when it behooves men to throw themselves into pools or into a gutter, or in the mud; now none but wicked men sit (awake)—villains, robbers, or wicked thieves, (I swear) by Christ in whom all folk believe! (Ubbe himself sits awake; cf. l. 1634, n.)
1. Both timid men and bold (i.e., all kinds).
2. Altogether just like a sunbeam.
3. I.e., as if they were dead.
4. The knights thought them a delight to observe and watch.
5. I.e., in every way, without doubt.

It sparkede° and ful brith shon   *sparkled*
2145 So doth the gode charbucle-ston,
That men mouthe se by the lith
A peni chesen, so was it brith![6]
Thanne bihelden° he him faste,°   *beheld, scrutinized/closely*
So that he knewen, at the laste,
2150 That he was Birkabeynes sone,
That° was here° King, that was hem wone°   *Who/their/wont*
Wel to yeme° and wel were°   *look after/protect, defend*
Ageynes uten-laddes° here°—   *foreign men's/army*
"For it° was nevere yet a brother   *there*
2155 In al Denemark so lich° another,   *like*
So° this man, that is so fayr,   *As (is)*
Als° Birkabeyn: he is hise eyr!"°   *Like/heir*

He fellen sone at hise fet.°   *feet*
Was non of hem that he ne gret°—   *wept*
2160 Of joie he weren alle so fawen°   *elated*
So he him haveden of erthe drawen.[7]
Hise fet he kisten° an hundred sythes,°   *kissed/times*
The tos,° the nayles, and the lithes,°   *toes/tips of the toes*
So that he bigan to wakne°   *awaken*
2165 And wit hem ful sore to blakne—[8]
For he wende° he wolden him slo,°   *believed/slay*
Or elles binde him and do wo!°   *woe, harm*

Quoth Ubbe, "Loverd,° ne dred° the nowth;°   *Lord/fear/not at all*
Me thinkes that I se thi thouth.°   *thought*
2170 Dere sone, wel is me[9]
That I the with eyn° se!   *eyes*
Manred, loverd, bede I the;[1]
Thi man° auht° I ful wel to be,   *vassal/ought*
For thu art comen° of Birkabeyn   *descended*
2175 That havede° mani knith and sweyn.°   *ruled/swain, youth*
And so shalt thou, loverd, have;
Thou° thu° be yet a ful yung knave,°   *Though/thou/boy*
Thou shalt be King of al Denemark—
Was ther-inne nevere non so stark.°   *powerful*
2180 Tomorwen shaltu° manrede° take   *shalt thou/homage*
Of the brune and of the blake,[2]

6. As does the good carbuncle stone, such that men can see (well enough) by the light
   (thereof) to distinguish a penny (against an obscuring background), it was so bright! (The
   carbuncle, any one of a number of real or legendary rubious gemstones, was believed to shine
   in the dark.)
7. As if they had resurrected him from the grave.
8. And with (the sight of) them to turn exceedingly pale.
9. Dear boy, I am pleased.
1. Cf. l. 484, where Havelok was compelled to utter virtually the same words to his oppressor,
   Godard.
2. Cf. l. 1008.

Of alle that aren° in this tun,°   *are/town*
Bothe of erl and of barun—
And of dreng, and of thayn,³
2185 And of knith, and of sweyn—
And so shaltu ben mad knith,
Wit blisse,° for thou art so with!"°   *pleasure/courageous*

Tho was Havelok swithe blithe,
And thankede God ful fele° sithe.°   *many/times*
2190 On the morwen,° wan it was lith,   *morning*
And gon was thisternesse° of the nith,   *darkness*
Ubbe dide° upon a stede   *caused, had*
A ladde lepe,° and thider° bede°   *(to) leap/thither/call*
Erles, barouns, drenges, theynes,
2195 Klerkes,° knithes, burgeys, sweynes,   *Clerics*
That he sholden comen anon
Biforen him sone, everilkon,°   *everyone*
Al-so° he loveden° here° lives,   *As/loved/their*
And here children, and here wives.

2200 Hise bode° ne durste he° non at-sitte,°   *bidding/(of) them/resist*
That he ne neme for-to wite
Sone hwat wolde the justise;⁴
And bigan° anon to rise,   *(the justiciar) began*
And seyde sone, "Lithes° me,   *listen*
2205 Alle samen, theu° and fre.°   *serf/freeman*
A thing Ich wile you here shauwe°   *declare*
That° ye alle ful wel knawe;   *That (which)*
Ye witen wel that al this lond
Was in Birkabeynes hond
2210 The day that he was quic and ded,⁵
And how that he, bi youre red,°   *counsel*
Bitauhte° hise children thre   *Handed over*
Godard to yeme,° and al his fe.°   *look after/property*
Havelok his sone he him tauhte,°   *handed over*
2215 And hise two douhtres, and al his auhte.°   *possessions*
Alle herden° ye him swere,   *heard*
On bok and on messe-gere,⁶
That he shulde yeme hem wel,
Withuten° lac,° withuten tel.°   *Without/fault/reproach*

2220 He let his oth al over-go°—   *go by, be deserted*
Evere wurthe him yvel and wo!⁷

---

3. Cf. ll. 1327 ff.
4. That they did not betake themselves to find out forthwith what the justiciar (Ubbe) wished to do. (Ubbe's potential for meting out severe punishment is implied; cf. l. 1634, n.)
5. Cf. l. 1405.
6. On the missal and on the effects of the Mass.
7. May harm and misfortune befall him for ever!

For the maydnes here lif
Refte he bothen with a knif,[8]
And him° shulde ok° have slawen—   *(Havelok) / also*
2225 The knif was at his herte drawen.
But God him wolde wel have save;°   *safe*
He havede reunesse° of the knave,   *pity*
So that he with his hend°   *hand*
Ne drop° him nouth°—that sori° fend!°   *slew / not / vile / fiend*
2230 But sone dide he a fishere°   *fisherman*
Swithe grete othes° swere,   *oaths*
That he sholde drenchen° him   *drown*
In the se that was ful brim.°   *savage, turbulent*

    Hwan° Grim saw that he was so fayr,   *When*
2235 And wiste° he was the rith° eir,   *knew / rightful*
Fro Denemark ful sone he fledde
Intil° Englond, and ther him fedde°   *To / fed, nurtured*
Mani winter, that° til° this day   *(so) that / up to*
Haves he ben fed and fostred ay°—   *always*
2240 Lokes hware he stondes her![9]
In al this werd° ne haves he per,°   *world / peer, equal*
Non so fayr, ne non so long,°   *tall*
Ne non so mikel,° ne non so strong.   *great, large*
In this middelerd[1] nis no knith   *earth*
2245 Half so strong ne half so with.
Bes° of him ful glad and blithe,   *Be*
And cometh alle hider° swithe   *hither*
Manrede° youre loverd for-to make,   *Homage*
Bothe brune and the blake.
2250 I shal miself do first the gamen,°   *ritual*
And ye sithen° alle samen."   *then, thereafter*

    O° knes ful fayre he him sette—   *On*
Mouthe° nothing him ther-fro° lette°—   *could / from that / hinder*
And bicam° is° man° rith thare;   *became / his / vassal*
2255 That alle sawen that there ware.

    After him stirt° up laddes ten   *started*
And bicomen hise men,
And sithen everilk a baroun
That evere weren in al that toun—
2260 And sithen drenges, and sithen thaynes,
And sithen knithes, and sithen sweynes—
So that, or° that day was gon,   *before*
In al the tun ne was nouth on°   *one*

---

8. For he took the life of both of the maidens, with a knife.
9. I.e., behold, he stands before you!
1. Middle-earth (i.e., the place between heaven and hell, this world).

That it° ne was his man bicomen;   *he*
2265 Manrede of alle havede he nomen.°   *taken, received*

Hwan he havede of hem alle
Manrede taken in the halle,
Grundlike° dide° he hem swere°   *Solemnly / had / swear*
That he sholden him god feyth bere
2270 Ageynes alle that woren on live.
Ther-yen ne wolde never on strive
That he ne maden sone that oth,[2]
Riche and poure, lef and loth.[3]
Hwan that was maked, sone he sende
2275 (Ubbe) writes fer and hende[4]
After alle° that castel yemede,°   *all (those) / governed*
Burwes, tunes, sibbe an fremde,[5]
That thider sholden comen swithe°   *quickly*
Til him, and heren° tithandes° blithe   *hear / tidings*
2280 That he hem alle shulde telle.
Of hem ne wolde nevere on° dwelle°   *one / delay*
That he ne come sone plattinde;°   *spurring*
Hwo hors ne havede com gangande,°   *walking*
So that withinne a fourtenith°   *fortnight*
2285 In al Denemark ne was no knith,
Ne conestable, ne shireve,[6]
That com° of Adam and of Eve   *descended*
That he ne com biforn sire Ubbe—
He dredden him so thef doth clubbe.[7]

2290 Hwan he haveden alle the King gret°   *greeted*
And he weren alle dun° set,°   *down / sat*
Tho° seyde Ubbe, "Lokes° here   *Then / See*
Ure loverd° swithe° dere,   *lord / very*
That shal ben King of al the lond
2295 And have us alle under hond;
For he is Birkabeynes sone,
The King that was umbe stounde wone
Us for-to yeme and wel were[8]
Wit sharp swerd and longe spere.
2300 Lokes nou hw° he is fayr—   *how*

2. That they should support him in good faith against all who were alive. Against that would no one ever contend such that they did not quickly take that oath.
3. Cf. l. 261.
4. Forthwith he (Ubbe) sent out writs far and near at hand.
5. Boroughs, towns, kindred and unrelated (i.e., everyone).
6. Nor constable (a castle's chief military officer), nor sheriff.
7. They feared him as a thief does a club. (Cf. ll. 279 and 2568–69 where comparable similes are used to describe Godrich's rule; it is perhaps safest to take the similes only as measures of power and authority rather than of morality, but the observation is consistent with others which allude to Ubbe's darker side; cf. l. 1634, n.)
8. The king who was for a time wont to protect us and defend (us) well.

Sikerlike° he is hise eyr!°   *Certainly / heir*
Falles° alle to hise fet;   *Fall*
Bicomes hise men ful sket."°   *quickly*
He weren for Ubbe swithe adrad,°   *afraid*
2305   And dide sone al that he bad°—   *bade*
And yet deden he sumdel° more: *somewhat, rather*
O bok° ful grundlike he° swore   *book, Bible / they*
That he sholde with him halde,°   *hold, be loyal*
Bothe ageynes stille and bolde[9]
2310   That evere wolde his bodi dere.°   *harm, injure*
That dide hem o boke swere.

Hwan he havede manrede and oth
Taken of lef and of loth,[1]
Ubbe dubbede[2] him° to knith   *(Havelok)*
2315   With a swerd ful swithe brith;
And the folk of al the lond
Bitauhte him al in his hond,°   *hand*
The cunnriche,° everil° del,°   *kingdom / every / part*
And made him King heylike and wel.[3]
2320   Hwan he was King, ther mouthe men se
The moste joie that mouhte° be—   *could*
Buttinge° with sharpe speres,   *Thrusting*
Skirming° with talevaces° that men beres,   *Fencing / shields*
Wrastling with laddes, putting of ston,
2325   Harping and piping ful god won,[4]
Leyk of mine, of hasard ok,[5]
Romanz-reding, on the bok;[6]
Ther mouthe men here the gestes° singe,°   *heroic poems / sung*
The gleumen° on the tabour° dinge;°   *minstrels / small drum / beat*
2330   Ther mouhte men se the boles° beyte,°   *bulls / baited (cf. l. 1840, n.)*
And the bores,° with hundes° teyte;°   *boars / hounds / eager*
Tho mouthe men se everil° gleu;°   *every kind of / amusement*
Ther mouthe men se hw grim° greu°—   *excitement / grew*
Was nevere yete joie more
2335   In al this werd° than tho was thore.°   *world / there*
(Ther was so mike yeft of clothes[7]
That, thou I swore you grete othes,
I ne wore nouth ther-offe° trod°—   *thereof / believed*
That may I ful wel swere, bi God!)

---

9. I.e., against anyone.
1. Cf. l. 261.
2. Cf. l. 2042, n.
3. Cf. l. 1329.
4. In great abundance.
5. (The) game of *mine*, of *hasard* also. (Games played with dice.)
6. The recitation of romances, from manuscript.
7. Giving of clothes. (Probably a reference—self-advertising?—to a conventional method of rewarding minstrels.)

2340	There was swithe gode metes,°	*foods*
	And of wyn° that men fer° fetes°	*wine/(from) afar/fetch*
	Rith al-so mik and gret plenté	
	So it were water of the se.[8]	
	The feste° fourti dawes° sat—	*festivity/days*
2345	So riche was nevere non so° that.	*like*
	The King made Roberd there knith,	
	That was ful strong and ful with,°	*courageous*
	And Willam Wendut hec,° his brother,	*also*
	And Huwe Raven, that was that other,	
2350	And made hem barouns, alle thre,	
	And yaf hem lond and other fe°—	*property*
	So mikel that ilker twenti knihtes	
	Havede of genge, dayes and nithes.[9]	
	Hwan that feste was al don,	
2355	A thousand knihtes ful wel o bon	
	With-held the King with him to lede,[1]	
	That° ilkan havede ful god stede,°	*(Such) that/steed, war-horse*
	Helm and sheld° and brinie° brith,°	*shield/coat of mail/bright*
	And al the wepne° that fel° to knith;	*weapons/were befitting*
2360	With hem five thusand gode	
	Sergaunz, that weren to fyht wode,°	*madly eager*
	With-held he, al of his genge.°	*company*
	Wile I na more the storie lenge—[2]	
	Yet, hwan he havede of al the lond	
2365	The casteles alle in his hond,	
	And conestables don° ther-inne,	*placed, appointed*
	He swor he ne sholde nevere blinne°	*cease, give up*
	Til that he were of Godard wreken,°	*avenged*
	That° Ich have of ofte speken.°	*Whom/spoken*
2370	Half hundred knithes dede he calle,	
	And hise fif thusand sergaunz alle,	
	And dide° sweren on the bok°	*had (them)/book, Bible*
	Sone, and on the auter° ok,	*altar*
	That he° ne sholde nevere blinne,	*they*
2375	Ne for love, ne for sinne,°	*pity*
	Til that he haveden Godard funde°	*found*
	And brouth° biforn him, faste bunde.°	*brought/bound, tied up*
	Thanne° he haveden swor this oth,	*Then (when)*
	Ne leten° he nouth, for lef ne loth,	*hesitated*
2380	That° he ne foren° swithe rathe°	*(So) that/went/quickly*
	Ther° he° was, unto the pathe	*There (where)/(Godard)*

8. Just as much and in (such) great plenty as if it were (the) water of the sea.
9. So much that each had twenty knights in his retinue, day and night.
1. A thousand knights in very good condition the king kept back to take with him.
2. I will not draw the story out any more.

Ther he yet on hunting for°   went
With mikel genge and swithe stor.°   great
Robert, that was of al the ferd°   army
2385 Mayster, was girt° wit a swerd   girded, equipped
And sat upon a ful god stede
That under him rith° wolde wede;°   thoroughly / run madly
He was the firste that with Godard
Spak, and seyde, "Hede,° cavenard!°   Take heed / rogue
2390 Wat dos thu here at this pathe?
Cum to the King swithe and rathe!
That° sendes he the word, and bedes   (Of) that
That thu thenke° hwat thu him° dedes°   think, recall / to him / did
Hwan thu reftes° with a knif   took, stole
2395 Hise° sistres here° lif,   (Of) his / their
An sithen bede thu in the se°   sea
Drenchen° him—that herde° he!   to drown / heard
He is to° the swithe grim!°   towards / wrathful, vengeful
Cum nu° swithe unto him   now
2400 That King is of this kuneriche—
Thu fule° man, thu wicke° swike!°—   foul / wicked / traitor
And he shal yelde° the thi mede,°   yield, give / reward
Bi Crist that wolde on rode° blede!"°   rood, cross / bleed

Hwan Godard herde that he ther thrette,°   threatened
2405 With the neve° he Robert sette   fist
Biforn the teth° a dint ful strong;   teeth
And Robert kipt° ut° a knif long,   snatched / out
And smot° him thoru the rith° arum°— smote, stabbed / right / arm
Ther-of was ful litel harum!³

2410 Hwan his folk that sau° and herde,   saw
Hwou° Robert with here loverd° ferde,° How / lord / fared, behaved
He haveden him wel-ner browt of live,
Ne weren his two brethren, and othre five,
Slowen of here laddes ten,
2415 Of Godardes altherbeste men.⁴
Hwan the othre° sawen that, he fledden,   others
And Godard swithe loude gredde,°   cried
"Mine knithes, hwat do ye?
Sule° ye thus-gate° fro me fle?   Shall, Will / in this way
2420 Ich have you fed and yet shal fede—
Helpe me nu in this nede,°   (time of) need
And late° ye nouth° mi bodi spille,°   let / not / destroy
Ne Havelok don of me hise wille!
Yif° ye it do, ye do you shame   If

3. That was a matter for little pity! (Cf. Havelok's wounding in the arm, ll. 1982–83.)
4. I.e., they would very nearly have killed him if it were not for his two brothers, and five others,
who slew ten of their men, (ten) of Godard's best men.

2425	And bringeth youself in mikel blame!"°	*disrepute*
	Hwan he° that herden, he wenten° ageyn,	*they / turned*
	And slowen a knit and a sweyn°	*swain, youth*
	Of the Kinges oune° men,	*own*
	And wounededn abuten° ten.	*about*
2430	The Kinges men, hwan he that sawe,	
	Scuten° on hem, heye and lowe,	*Rushed*
	And everilk° fot° of hem slowe,	*every / foot (i.e., man)*
	But Godard one (that he flowe	
	So the thef men dos henge,	
2435	Or hund men shole in dike slenge).⁵	
	He bunden him ful swithe faste	
	Hwil the bondes wolden laste,⁶	
	That° he rorede als a bole°	*(So) that / bull*
	That wore parred° in an hole	*impounded*
2440	With dogges for-to bite and beite.°	*bait*
	Were the bondes nouth to leite;⁷	
	He bounden him so fele° sore	*inordinately*
	That he gan crien° Godes ore,°	*to cry (for) / mercy*
	That he sholde of° his hend plette°—	*off / strike*
2445	Wolden he nouht ther-fore lette°	*cease*
	That° he ne bounden hond and fet—	*(Such) that*
	Datheit that on that ther-fore let!—⁸	
	But dunten° him so man doth bere,°	*beat / bear*
	And keste him on a scabbed° mere;°	*scabby / mare*
2450	Hise nese went unto the crice.⁹	
	So ledden° he, that ful° swike,	*led / foul*
	Til he was biforn Havelok brouth,	
	That° he havede ful wo wrowht,°	*For whom / wrought*
	Bothe with hungre and with cold	
2455	Or° he were twelve winter old,	*Before*
	And with mani hevi° swink,°	*(a) heavy / travail*
	With poure mete and feble drink,	
	And with swithe wikke° clothes—	*disgraceful*
	For° al hise manie grete othes.	*Despite*
2460	Nu beyes° he his holde° blame;°	*buys, pays for / old / sin*
	Old sinne makes newe shame.	
	Wan he was so shamelike	
	Brouth biforn the King—the fule swike!—	
	The King dede° Ubbe swithe calle	*caused, had*
2465	Hise erles and hise barouns alle,	

5. Except for Godard alone (whom they [later] flayed, just as men have a thief hang, or will sling a [dead] dog into a ditch).
6. Cf. the description of Havelok's tight bonds, ll. 537–41.
7. The bonds were not to be sought after. (I.e., the existence of bonds could not be concealed.)
8. Cursed be the one who ceases thereof (to keep the bonds tight)!
9. His knees toward the crack. (Godard is placed, much to his disgrace, facing the horse's hindquarters).

Dreng and thein, burgeis and knith,[1]
And bad he sholden demen° him rith;°   *judge / accordingly*
For he kneu° the swikedam,°   *knew / treachery*
Everil del°—God was him° gram!° *part / (with) him / wrathful*
2470 He setten hem dun° bi the wawe,° *down / wayside*
Riche and povere, heye° and lowe,   *high(born)*
The helde° men and ek° the grom,° *old / also / boys*
And made ther the rithe dom,°   *doom, judgment*
And seyden unto the King anon,
2475 That stille sat so the ston,
"We deme° that he be al quic° flawen,° *judge / alive / flayed*
And sithen° to the galwes drawen° *then / dragged*
At this foule mere° tayl,°   *mare's / tail*
Thoru° is° fet a ful strong nayl,° *(Driven) through / his / nail*
2480 And thore ben henged wit° two feteres;° *with, by / fetters, chains*
And thare be writen thise leteres:
'This is the swike that wende wel
The King have reft the lond, il del,
And hise sistres, with a knif,
2485 Bothe refte here lif.'[2]
This writ shal henge bi him thare.
The dom is demd; seye we na more."

 Hwan the dom was demd and give,
And he was wit the prestes° shrive,° *priests / shriven, confessed*
2490 And it ne mouhte ben non other,[3]
Ne for fader ne for brother,
But that he sholde tharne° lif,   *lose*
Sket° cam a ladde with a knif *Quickly, Forthwith*
And bigan rith at the to°   *toe*
2495 For-to ritte° and for-to flo;°   *cut / flay*
And he bigan for-to rore
So it were grim or gore,[4]
That° men mithe° thethen° a mile *(So) that / could / thence*
Here him rore—that fule file!° *defiled thing, dregs*
2500 The ladde ne let nowith forthi,[5]
They° he criede, "Merci! Merci!"   *Though*
That he ne flow everil del,
With knif mad of grunden° stel.   *ground*
Thei garte° bringe the mere sone, *caused, had*
2505 Skabbed and ful ivele o bone,[6]
And bunden him rith at hire° tayl   *her*

---

1. Cf. ll. 1327 ff.
2. This is the traitor who fully intended to have taken the land of the king, every part, and (who) with a knife took the lives of both his sisters.
3. I.e., and there was nothing more to do.
4. As if it were out of excitement or rage.
5. The lad held back in no way because of that.
6. Scabby and in very poor condition.

With a rop° of an old seyl,°   *rope/sail*
And drowen him unto the galwes
(Nouth bi the gate,° but over the falwes)°   *road/plowed fields*
2510 And henge thore bi the hals°—   *neck*
Datheit° hwo recke;° he was fals!°   *Cursed be he/cares/untrue*

Thanne° he was ded, that Sathanas,°   *Then (when)/Satan*
Sket was seysed° al that his was   *seized*
In° the Kinges hand, il° del,   *Into/each*
2515 Lond and lith,° and other catel;°   *people, vassals/property*
And the King ful sone it yaf
Ubbe in the hond wit a fayr staf,[7]
And seyde, "Her Ich sayse° the,   *place in seisin, possess*
In° al the lond, in al the fe."°   *Of/property*
2520 Tho° swor Havelok he sholde make,   *Then*
Al for Grim, of monekes blake
A priorie to serven inne ay
Jesu Crist til Domesday,[8]
For the god° he havede him° don   *good (deeds)/(Havelok)*
2525 Hwil he was povere° and ivel o bon.   *poor*
(And ther-of held he wel his oth,
For he it made, God it woth,°   *knows*
In the tun° ther° Grim was graven,°   *town/there (where)/buried*
That of Grim yet haves the naven°—   *name (i.e., Grimsby)*
2530 Of Grim bidde° Ich na more spelle.)°   *wish/to speak*
But wan Godrich herde telle,
Of Cornwayle that was Erl—[9]
That fule traytour, that mixed° cherl!—   *feculent, filthy*
That Havelok was° King of Denemark,   *(who) was*
2535 And ferde° with him, strong and stark,°   *(an) army/powerful*
Comen° Engelond withinne,   *Came*
Engelond al for-to winne,
And that she° that was so fayr,   *(Goldeboru)*
That was of Engelond rith° eir,°   *rightful/heir*
2540 Was comen up at Grimesbi,
He was ful sorful° and sori,   *sorrowful*
And seyde, "Hwat shal me to rathe?
Goddoth, I shal do slon hem bathe!
I shal don hengen hem ful heye,
2545 So mote Ich brouke mi rith eie,
But yif he of mi lond fle.
Hwat! wenden he to desherite me?"[1]

---

7. By way of a handsome staff (a symbol of dominion over the property).
8. A priory of black (Benedictine) monks in which to serve Christ until Doomsday.
9. But when Godrich, who was the Earl of Cornwall, heard tell.
1. What plan of action should I follow? God knows, I will have them both slain! I will have them hanged very high, as I hope to enjoy my right eye (i.e., as I hope to live), unless they flee from my land. What! do they intend to disinherit me? (The last line resonates with irony; Godrich himself had, of course, done precisely that which now stirs his outrage.)

He dide sone ferd ut-bede,°   *call out, summon*
That al that evere mouhte° o° stede°   *could / on / steed, war-horse*
2550 Ride, or helm on heved° bere,   *head*
Brini° on bac,° and sheld° and spere,   *Coat of mail / back / shield*
Or ani other wepne° bere—   *weapon*
Hand-ax, sythe,° gisarm,° or spere,   *scythe / halberd*
Or aunlaz° and god long knif—   *dagger*
2555 That, als° he lovede leme° or lif,   *as / limb*
That they sholden comen him to—
"With ful god wepne ye° bere° so   *(that) you / bear, carry*
To Lincolne" (ther he lay)
"Of Marz the sevententhe day"—[2]
2560 So that he couthe° hem god° thank;   *could / well*
And yif° that ani were so rank°   *if / disdainful*
That he thanne ne come anon,
He swor, bi Crist and Seint Johan,
That he sholde maken him thral,°   *thrall, slave*
2565 And al his ofspring forthwithal.

The° Englishe that herde that,   *(Of) the*
Was non that evere his bode sat,[3]
For he° him dredde swithe sore°—   *they / sorely, bitterly*
So runci spore—[4] and mikle° more.   *much*
2570 At the day he come sone
That he hem sette,° ful wel o bone,   *set, appointed*
To Lincolne, with gode stedes
And al the wepne that knith ledes.°   *wields*
Hwan he wore come, sket was the Erl yare°   *eager*
2575 Ageynes Denshe° men to fare,°   *Danish / advance*
And seyde, "Lythes° nu,° alle samen!°   *listen / now / together*
Have Ich gadred° you for no gamen,°   *gathered / game, sport*
But Ich wile seyen° you for-wi:°   *tell / why*
Lokes° hware° here at Grimesbi   *See / where*
2580 Hise uten-laddes° here° comen,   *foreign men's / army*
And haves nu the priorie numen.°   *taken, seized*
Al that evere mithen he finde,
He brenne° kirkes,° and prestes binde;°   *burns / churches / binds*
He strangleth monkes and nunnes bathe.[5]
2585 Wat wile ye, frend, her-offe rathe?°   *advise*
Yif he regne° thus-gate° longe,   *reign / in this way*
He° moun° us alle over-gange°—   *They / may / overcome*
He moun us alle quic° henge,° or slo,°   *alive / hang / slay*

2. The seventeenth day of March. (Such a specific date invites historical inquiry and no doubt
   was included to give the impression of historical verisimilitude; Professor Smithers notes the
   existence of a writ of Edward I issued on that date in 1295, inquiring into the availability for
   military service of men in Huntingdonshire.)
3. There was no one who ever resisted his (Godrich's) bidding.
4. As (does) the horse the spur.
5. Godrich thus misleads his retainers, and again transgresses a solemn feudal bond.

	Or thral maken and do ful wo,	
2590	Or elles reve° us ure° lives,	take from / our
	And ure children, and ure wives.	
	But dos° nu als Ich wile you lere,°	do / instruct
	Als° ye wile be with me dere:°	As / dear, loyal
	Nimes° nu swithe forth and rathe,°	Betake (yourselves), Go / forthwith
2595	And helpes me and yuself bathe,	
	And slos° upo° the dogges swithe!	strike lethally / upon
	For shal I neveremore be blithe,	
	Ne hoseled ben, ne of prest shriven,[6]	
	Til that he ben of° londe driven.	(out) of
2600	Nime we swithe and do° hem fle,	cause, make
	And folwes° alle faste° me—	follow / closely
	For Ich am he, of al the ferd,	
	That first shal slo with drawen° swerd;	drawn
	Datheyt hwo ne stonde° faste	stands
2605	Bi me hwil° hise armes laste!"	while
	"Ye! lef,° ye!" quoth° the Erl Gunter;	beloved (lord) / said
	"Ya!" quoth the Erl of Cestre,° Reyner;	Chester
	And so dide alle that ther stode,	
	And stirte° forth so° he were wode.°	started / as if / mad
2610	Tho mouthe° men se the brinies brihte°	could / bright, shining
	On backes keste° and lace° rithe,	cast / laced
	The helmes heye on heved sette.	
	To armes al° so swithe plette°	all / hurried
	That thei wore on° a litel stunde°	in / time, while
2615	Grethet, als men mithe telle a pund,[7]	
	And lopen° on stedes sone anon;	leaped
	And toward Grimesbi, ful god won[8]	
	He foren,° softe,° bi the sti,°	advanced / stealthily / road
	Til he come ney° at° Grimesbi.	nigh, near / beside
2620	Havelok (that° havede spired° wel	who / found out
	Of here° fare°—everil del!)	their / advance
	With al his ferd cam hem ageyn.°	against
	Forbar° he nother° knith ne sweyn;	Spared / neither
	The firste knith that he ther mette	
2625	With the swerd so he him grette,[9]	
	That his heved of° he plette°—	off / struck
	Wolde he nouth° for sinne° lette.°	not / pity / hold back
	Roberd saw that dint so hende;°	adroit, skillful
	Wolde he nevere thethen° wende°	from there / go
2630	Til that he havede another slawen	

6. Cf. l. 212.
7. I.e., readied, in the time it takes for men to count out (the 240 pennies in) a pound.
8. In great numbers.
9. He attacked him so with his sword. (This is the first explicit reference to Havelok's use of a sword, a weapon appropriate to his newly acknowledged status.)

With the swerd he held ut-drawen.°   *drawn-out, unsheathed*
Willam Wendut his swerd ut-drow,
And the thredde° so sore he slow   *third*
That he made upon the feld°   *(battle)field*
2635 His lift° arm fleye with the sheld.   *left*

    Huwe Raven ne forgat nouth
The swerd he havede thider° brouth;°   *thither / brought*
He kipte° it up, and smot ful sore   *snatched*
An erl that he saw priken° thore°   *spur, ride / there*
2640 Ful noblelike° upon a stede   *nobly*
That with him wolde al quic° wede.°   *vigorously / run madly*
He smot him on the heved so
That he the heved clef° a-two,   *cleaved*
And that° bi the shudre-blade   *(such) that*
2645 The sharpe swerd let he wade°   *pass*
Thorw° the brest unto the herte;   *through*
The dint bigan ful sore to smerte°   *smart, inflict pain*
That the erl fel dun° anon,   *down*
Al-so° ded so° ani ston.°   *As / as / stone*
2650 Quoth Ubbe, "Nu dwelle° Ich to° longe!"   *tarry / too*
And leth° his stede sone gonge°   *let / go*
To Godrich, with a god spere
That° he saw another° bere,   *Whom / another (spear)*
And smoth° Godrich, and Godrich him,   *smote, struck*
2655 Hetelike,° with herte grim,   *furiously*
So that he° bothe felle dune   *they*
To the erthe, first the croune.[1]
Thanne he woren fallen dun bothen,
Grundlike° here swerdes ut-drowen   *Gravely*
2660 That weren swithe sharp and gode,
And fouhten so thei woren wode
That° the swot° ran fro the crune°   *(So) that / sweat / crown, head*
[. . .]
Ther mouthe men se two knicthes bete
2665 Ayther° on other dintes grete,°   *Either / great*
So that with the altherlest° dint   *least*
Were al to-shivered a flint.[2]
So was bitwenen hem a fiht,
Fro the morwen° ner° to the niht,   *morning / near*
2670 So that thei nouth ne blunne°   *ceased*
Til that to sette bigan the sunne.
Tho yaf Godrich thorw the side
Ubbe a wunde ful unride,[3]

---

1. Head-first.
2. A flint would have been shattered.
3. Then Godrich gave Ubbe an immense wound through the side.

So that thorw that ilke° wounde — *same*
2675 Havede° ben brouth to the grunde — *(He) would have*
And his heved al of-slawen,° — *struck off*
Yif God ne were and Huwe Raven,[4]
That drow him fro Godrich awey
And barw° him so that ilke day. — *protected*
2680 But er he were fro Godrich drawen,
Ther were a thousind knihtes slawen° — *slain*
Bi bothe halve, and mo ynowe,[5]
Ther the ferdes togidere slowe;° — *clashed lethally*
Ther was swilk dreping° of the folk — *slaughter*
2685 That on the feld was nevere a polk
That it ne stod of blod so ful
That the strem ran intil the hul.[6]
Tho° tarst° bigan Godrich to go — *Then / first*
Upon the Danshe° and faste to slo— — *Danish*
2690 And forthrith, al-so leun fares
That nevere kines best ne spares,
Thanne his gon;[7] for he garte° alle — *made, caused*
The Denshe men biforn him falle.
He felde° browne, he felde blake,[8] — *felled, laid low*
2695 That° he mouthe overtake; — *(All) that*
Was nevere non that mouhte° thave° — *could / endure*
Hise dintes, noyther knith ne knave,
That he ne felden° so dos the gres° — *fell / grass*
Biforn the sythe° that ful sharp es.° — *scythe / is*
2700 Hwan Havelok saw his folk so brittene° — *cut up*
And his ferd so swithe littene,° — *diminished*
He cam drivende° upon a stede, — *driving, hastening*
And bigan til him to grede,° — *cry*
And seyde, "Godrich, wat is the[9]
2705 That thou fare thus with me
And mine gode knihtes slos?
Sikerlike° thou mis-gos!° — *Surely / do wrong*
Thou wost° ful wel, yif° thu wilt wite,° — *know / if / acknowledge (it)*
That Athelwold the dide site° — *set*
2710 On knes° and sweren on messe-bok,° — *knees / missal*
On caliz° and on pateyn° hok,° — *chalice / paten / also*
That thou hise douhter sholdest yelde,° — *yield, hand over*
Than she were wimman° of elde,° — *woman / age*

4. I.e., if it were not for God and Huwe Raven.
5. On both sides, and plenty more.
6. Such that on the battlefield there was never a puddle that did not remain so full of blood that the stream ran into the hollow. (I.e., the blood not only pooled, but had to form running streams.)
7. And unswervingly forward, just as the lion makes its way, who spares no kind of beast, then is gone.
8. Cf. l. 1008.
9. Cf. l. 453.

Engelond, everil del°—   *part*
2715 Godrich the Erl, thou wost it wel!
Do nu° wel, with-uten fiht,°   *now / fight, strife*
Yeld hire the lond, for that is rith;
Wile Ich forgive the° the° lathe,°   *thee / the / enmity*
Al° mi dede,° and al mi wrathe,   *All (of) / (intended) death*
2720 For I se thu art so with°   *courageous*
And of thi bodi so° god knith."   *such (a)*
"That ne wile Ich neveremo!"°   *never*
Quoth Erl Godrich, "for Ich shal slo
The, and hire° for-henge° heye!   *her / hang*
2725 I shal thrist° ut° thi rith eye,   *thrust, put / out*
That thou lokes with on me,
But° thu swithe hethen° fle!"   *Unless / from here*
He grop° the swerd ut sone anon,   *grasped, seized*
And hew° on Havelok ful god won,   *hewed, struck*
2730 So that he clef his sheld on two.
Hwan Havelok saw that shame do
His bodi, ther biforn his ferd,[1]
He drow ut sone his gode swerd,
And smot him so upon the crune
2735 That Godrich fel to the erthe a-dune.
But Godrich stirt up swithe sket°—   *quickly*
Lay he nowth° longe at hise fet—   *not*
And smot him on the sholdre so
That he dide thare undo
2740 Of his brinie° ringes mo   *coat of mail*
Than that Ich kan tellen fro,°   *about*
And woundede him rith in the flesh,
That tendre was and swithe nesh,°   *soft*
So that the blod ran til his to.°   *toe*
2745 Tho was Havelok swithe wo°   *distressed*
That he° havede of him drawen   *(Godrich)*
Blod and so sore him slawen.°   *struck*
Hertelike° til him he wente   *Heartily, Boldly*
And Godrich ther fulike° shente,   *shamefully*
2750 For his swerd he hof° up heye,   *heaved, raised*
And the hand he dide of-fleye
That he smot him with so sore—[2]
Hw mithe° he don him shame more?   *could*

Hwan he havede him so shamed,
2755 His hand of-plat,° and yvele° lamed,° *struck off / badly / made lame*
He tok him sone bi the necke

---

1. When Havelok saw that humiliation done to his person, there in front of his army.
2. And he caused the hand to fly off with which he (Godrich) had (previously) struck him so painfully.

Als a traytour—datheyt wo recke!—[3]
And dide him binde and fetere° wel   *fetter, chain*
With gode feteres al of stel,°   *steel*
2760 And to the Quen he sende him,
That birde wel to him ben grim,[4]
And bad she sholde don° him gete,°   *have/guarded*
And that non° ne sholde him bete°   *no one/beat*
Ne shame do, for he was knith,
2765 Til knithes haveden demd him rith.[5]
Than° the Englishe men that sawe—   *Then (when)*
That thei wisten,° heye° and lawe,°   *knew/high(born)/low*
That Goldeboru, that was so fayr,
Was of Engeland rith° eyr,°   *rightful/heir*
2770 And that the King hire havede wedded,
And haveden ben samen bedded—[6]
He comen alle to crie° merci,°   *cry, beg/mercy*
Unto the King, at° one cri,°   *with/voice*
And beden him sone manrede and oth
2775 That he ne sholden, for lef ne loth,
Neveremore ageyn him go[7]
Ne ride, for wel° ne for wo.°   *good/bad*

   The King ne wolde nouth° forsake°   *not/neglect*
That he ne shulde of hem take
2780 Manrede that he beden, and ok°   *also*
Hold-othes° sweren on the bok;°   *Oaths of loyalty/book, Bible*
But or° bad° he that thider were brouth   *beforehand/bade*
The Quen for hem; swilk was his thouth
For-to° se° and for-to shawe°   *to/see/determine*
2785 Yif that he° hire wolde knawe°—   *they/acknowledge*
Thoruth hem witen wolde he
Yif that she aucte Quen to be.[8]

   Sixe erles weren sone yare°   *ready*
After hire for-to fare;
2790 He nomen° onon, and comen sone,   *betook (themselves), went*
And brouthen hire that under mone,°   *moon*
In al the werd,° ne havede per°   *world/peer, equal*
Of hendeleik,° fer° ne ner.   *graciousness/(from) afar*
Hwan she was come thider, alle
2795 The Englishe men bigunne to falle

---

3. Cursed be he who cares (about that)!
4. Who had good cause to be vengeful toward him.
5. Until knights had properly judged him. (According to feudal law, Godrich must be judged by a group of his peers.)
6. And had been bedded together. (I.e., the marriage had been consummated.)
7. I.e., and quickly proffered him homage and oaths (to the effect) that they would not, for anyone, ever again march against him.
8. By means of them he would know if she ought to be (their) queen.

O° knes, and greten° swithe sore,   *On / wept*
And seyden, "Levedi, Kristes ore[9]
And youres! We haven misdo° mikel,   *done wrong, transgressed*
That we ayen° you have be fikel°—   *towards / disloyal*
2800 For Englond auhte° for-to ben   *ought*
Youres, and we youre men.
Is° non of us, yung ne old,   *(There) is*
That we ne wot° that Athelwold   *know*
Was King of this kunerike°   *kingdom*
2805 And ye his eyr, and that the swike°   *traitor*
Haves it halden° with mikel wronge—   *held, kept*
God leve° him sone to honge!"°   *allow / hang*

Quot Havelok, "Hwan° that ye it wite,   *since*
Nu wile° Ich that ye doun site,°   *wish / sit*
2810 And, after Godrich haves wrouht,[1]
That° haves in sorwe himself brouth,   *Who*
Lokes° that ye demen° him rith—   *See / judge*
For dom ne spareth clerk ne knith;[2]
And sithen° shal Ich understonde°   *then / receive*
2815 Of you, after lawe of londe,
Manrede and holde-othes bothe—
Yif ye it wilen and ek rothe."°   *advise, sanction*
Anon ther dune he hem sette,
For non the dom ne durste lette,°   *hinder*
2820 And demden° him to binden° faste   *judged / be bound*
Upon an asse swithe unwraste°   *wretched*
(Andelong,° nouht overthwert°—   *Endlong / crosswise*
His nose went unto the stert)[3]
And so to Lincolne lede,°   *be led*
2825 Shamelike, in wicke° wede;°   *disgraceful / clothes*
And, hwan he cam unto the borw,°   *borough, town*
Shamelike ben° led ther-thoru   *to be*
Bi-southe° the borw unto a grene°   *To the south of / green*
(That thare is yet, als I wene)[4]
2830 And there be bunden° til a stake,   *bound*
Abouten him ful gret fir make,
And al to dust be brend° rith there.   *burned*
And yet demden he° ther more,   *they*
Other swikes° for-to warne:°   *traitors / deter*
2835 That hise children sulde° tharne°   *should / be deprived of*
Everemore that eritage°   *inheritance*

9. Lady, (we beg) Christ's mercy.
1. And, according to what Godrich has brought about.
2. I.e., for no one is spared of a (proper) judgment.
3. Toward the tail. (Cf. l. 2450; this and other details mirror those of Godard's trial and execution, and thus the dissolution of the villains is handled with the same kind of symmetry as is their rise to power: cf. l. 347, n.)
4. Cf. l. 875, n.

That his was, for° hise utrage.°   *because of/outrage, crime*

   Hwan the dom was demd and seyd,
Sket was the swike on the asse leyd,
2840 And led til° that ilke° grene   *to/same*
And brend til asken,° al bidene.°   *ashes/at once*
Tho° was Goldeboru ful blithe;   *Then*
She thanked God fele° sythe°   *many/times*
That the fule° swike was brend   *foul*
2845 That wende wel hire bodi have shend,[5]
And seyde, "Nu is time to take
Manrede of brune and of blake[6]
That Ich se ride and go,°   *go about, walk*
Nu° Ich am wreke° of mi fo."   *Now (that)/avenged*

2850   Havelok anon manrede tok
Of alle Englishe, on the bok,°   *book, Bible*
And dide° hem grete° othes swere   *had/great*
That he sholden him god° feyth bere,   *good*
Ageyn° alle that woren lives°   *Against/alive*
2855 And that sholde ben born of wives.

   Thanne he havede sikernesse
Taken of more and of lesse,[7]
Al at hise wille, so dide he calle
The Erl of Cestre, and hise men alle,
2860 That was yung knith wituten° wif,   *without*
And seyde, "Sire Erl, bi mi lif,
And° thou wile mi conseyl° tro,°   *If/counsel/trust*
Ful wel shal Ich with° the do,   *for*
For Ich shal yeve° the to° wive°   *give/as/wife*
2865 The fairest thing that is o-live,
That is Gunnild of Grimesby—
Grimes douther, bi Seint Davy,°   *David*
That me forth broute and wel fedde,[8]
And ut of Denemark with me fledde,
2870 Me for-to burwe° fro mi ded.°   *save/death*
Sikerlike, thoru° his red,°   *through, by/advice*
Have Ich lived into this day—
Blissed worthe his soule ay![9]
I rede that thu hire take,
2875 And spuse and curteyse make,[1]
For she is fayr, and she is fre,°   *magnanimous*

---

5. Who fully intended to have disgraced her person.
6. Cf. l. 1008.
7. I.e., when he had received assurance (of fealty) from everyone.
8. Who (i.e., Grim) brought me up and nurtured me.
9. May his soul be blessed forever!
1. And marry (her) and make her accustomed to courtly life.

And al-so° hende° so° she may be.	*as / gracious / as*
Thertekene, she is wel with me;²	
That shal Ich ful wel shewe the,	
2880 For Ich give the a give°	*given, assurance*
That, everemore hwil Ich live,	
For hire shaltu be with me dere—³	
That wile Ich that this folc° al here."°	*folk, people / hear*
The Erl ne wolde nouth ageyn	
2885 The King be, for knith ne sweyn,⁴	
Ne of° the spusing° seyen° nay,	*to / marriage / say*
But spusede° that ilke day.	*(would) get married*
That spusinge was god time maked,	
For it ne were nevere, clad ne naked	
2890 In a thede, samened two	
That cam togidere, livede so,	
So they dide al here live;⁵	
He geten° samen° sones five,	*begat / together*
That were the beste men at nede°	*(time of) need*
2895 That mouthe° riden on ani stede.	*could*
Hwan Gunnild was to Cestre brouth,	
Havelok the gode ne forgat nouth	
Bertram, that was the Erles kok,°	*cook*
That he ne dide callen ok,	
2900 And seyde, "Frend, so God me rede,°	*help*
Nu shaltu° have riche mede°	*shalt thou / reward*
For wissing° and thi gode dede°	*guidance / deed*
That tu° me dides in ful gret nede;	*thou*
For thanne I yede° in mi cuvel,°	*went about / cloak*
2905 And Ich ne havede bred ne sowel,°	*anything eaten with bread*
Ne I ne havede no catel,°	*property*
Thou feddes and claddes° me ful wel.	*clothed*
Have nu forthi° of Cornwayle°	*accordingly / Cornwall*
The erldom, il° del,° withuten fayle,°	*each / part / doubt*
2910 And al the lond that Godrich held,	
Bothe in towne and ek in feld;°	*field, country*
And ther-to wile Ich that thu spuse—	
And fayre bring hire until huse—⁶	
Grimes douther, Levive the hende,	
2915 For thider shal she with the wende.	
Hire semes° curteys° for-to be,	*befits / courtly, noble*
For she is fayr so flour on tre:	
The heu° is swilk° in hire ler°	*color / such / face, cheek*

2. In addition to that, she is in favor with me.
3. You shall be dear to me on her account.
4. For knight nor youth (i.e., for no one).
5. I.e., that marriage made for a time of happiness, for there were never two united, of any people in a nation, who came together, who so lived as they did all their lives.
6. I.e., and house her in fitting style.

	So° the rose in roser°	*As/rose bush*
2920	Hwan it is fayr sprad° ut newe°	*spread/newly*
	Ageyn the sunne brith° and lewe."°	*bright/warm*
	And girde° him sone with the swerd	*(he) girded*
	Of the erldom, biforn° his ferd,°	*before/army*
	And with his hond he made him knith,	
2925	And yaf° him armes,° for that was rith,	*gave/battle arms*
	And dide° him there sone wedde	*had*
	Hire (that was° ful swete in bedde).	*was (later)*

	After that he spused wore,	
	Wolde the Erl nouth dwelle° thore,	*tarry*
2930	But sone nam° until his lond,	*betook (himself), went*
	And seysed° it al in his hond,	*seized, took possession of*
	And livede ther-inne, he and his wif,	
	An hundred winter in god lif,	
	And gaten mani children samen,	
2935	And liveden ay° in blisse and gamen.°	*always/delight*
	Hwan the maydens were spused bothe,	
	Havelok anon bigan ful rathe°	*quickly*
	His Denshe men to feste° wel	*secure, endow*
	Wit riche landes and catel,	
2940	So that he weren alle riche—	
	For he was large° and nouth chiche.°	*generous/mean*

	Ther-after sone, with his here,°	*army*
	For° he to Lundone, for-to bere	*Went*
	Corune,° so that it sawe	*Crown*
2945	Henglische and Denshe, heye and lowe,[7]	
	Hwou° he it bar with mikel° pride,	*How/great*
	For his barnage° that was unride.°	*baronage/numerous*

	The feste° of his coruning°	*festivity/crowning*
	Laste° with gret joying	*Lasted*
2950	Fourti dawes and sumdel mo.[8]	
	Tho bigunnen° the Denshe to go	*began*
	Unto the King to aske leve;°	*leave (to go home)*
	And he ne wolde hem nouth° greve,°	*not/grieve, distress*
	For he saw that he woren yare°	*ready*
2955	Into Denmark for-to fare,	
	But gaf hem leve sone anon,	
	And bitauhte° hem Seint Johan,	*commended*
	And bad° Ubbe, his justise,°	*bade, asked/justiciar*
	That he sholde on ilke° wise°	*every/way*
2960	Denmark yeme° and gete° so	*protect/watch over*

---

7. English and Danish, high(born) and low. (By marrying Goldeboru, the rightful heir to the English throne, Havelok assumes the crown of England as well as that of Denmark.)

8. Forty days and somewhat more. (Cf. l. 2344.)

That° no pleynte° come him to.   *(So) that / complaint*

    Hwan he° wore parted alle samen,°   *they / completely*
Havelok bi-lefte° wit joie and gamen   *remained*
In Engelond, and was ther-inne
2965 Sixti winter King with winne,°   *happiness*
And Goldeboru Quen, that° I wene°   *(such) that / know*
So mikel love was hem bitwene
That al the werd° spak° of hem two.   *world / spoke*
He lovede hire, and she him so,
2970 That neyther other mithe° be   *could*
Fro° other, ne no joie se,°   *(Away) from / see, witness*
But yf he were togidere bothe.
Nevere yete° ne weren he wrothe,°   *yet / angered*
For here love was ay newe;
2975 Nevere yete wordes ne grewe
Bitwene hem hwar-of° ne lathe°   *(out) of which / enmity*
Mithe rise, ne no wrathe.

    He geten children hem bitwene
Sones and douthres rith fivetene,
2980 Hwar-of the sones were kinges alle—
So wolde God it sholde bifalle°—   *befall, come to pass*
And the douhtres alle quenes;
Him stondes wel that god child strenes.[9]
Nu have ye herd the gest° al thoru°   *record of (heroic) deeds / through*
2985 Of Havelok and of Goldeborw—
Hw° he weren born, and hw fedde,°   *How / nurtured*
And hwou° he woren with wronge ledde°   *how / treated*
In here youthe, with trecherie,
With tresoun, and with felounye;[1]
2990 And hwou the swikes° haveden tith°   *traitors / intended*
Reven hem that was here rith;[2]
And hwou he weren wreken° wel,   *avenged*
Have Ich seyd° you everil del—   *said, told*
And forthi Ich wolde biseken° you   *beseech*
2995 That haven herd the rim° nu,   *rhyme, poem*
That ilke of you, with gode wille,
Seye a Pater Noster stille[3]
For him that haveth the rym maked—
And ther-fore fele° nihtes° waked°—   *many / nights / remained awake*
3000 That Jesu Crist his soule bringe
Biforn his Fader at his endinge.

    Amen.

9. He is well set who begets a good child. (Cf. l. 1693.)
1. Cf. l. 444.
2. To rob them of that which was their rightful claim.
3. A quiet Pater Noster (i.e., the Lord's Prayer).

Ywain and Gawain†

Almyghti° God that made mankyn,°	*Almighty/mankind*
He schilde his servandes out of syn,[1]	
And mayntene° tham with might and mayne°	*maintain, uphold/strength*
That° herkens° *Ywayne and Gawayne*.[2]	*Who/listen to*
5 Thai° war° knightes of the Tabyl Rownde;	*They/were*
Tharfore° listens a lytel° stownde.°	*Therefore/little, brief/while*
Arthure, the Kyng of Yngland,°	*England*
That wan° al° Wales with his hand,	*won, conquered/all*
And al Scotland, als sayes the buke,[3]	
10 And mani mo,° if men wil luke°—	*more/look, inquire*
Of al knightes he bare the pryse;[4]	
In werld° was none so war° ne wise.	*(the) world/prudent*
Trew° he was in alkyn° thing,	*True/every*
Als it byfel° to swilk° a kyng.	*befell, was proper/such*
15 He made a feste,° the soth° to say,	*feast/truth*
Opon the Witsononday,[5]	
At Kerdyf° that es° in Wales;	*Cardiff/is*
And efter° mete,° thare° in the hales°	*after/dinner/there/pavilions*
Ful grete° and gay was the assemblé	*great*
20 Of lordes and ladies of that cuntré,°	*country*
And als° of knyghtes war and wyse	*also*
And damisels° of mykel° pryse.°	*damsels, maidens/great/esteem*
Ilkane° with other made grete gamin°	*Each one/game, amusement*

† Text of London, British Library MS Cotton Galba E. ix, ff. 4ʳ–25ʳ, printed with permission of the British Library. The manuscript dates from the first quarter of the fifteenth century; the poem's date of composition is held to have been sometime in the second quarter of the fourteenth century. The poem is written in nominally four-stress couplets. Paragraphing follows that of the MS, except in the following instances: (1) where the rubricator's eye has obviously skipped down a line (at ll. 105, 1337, 1727); and (2) where the sense is clearly interrupted (at ll. 525, 1177, 1489, 3027, 3811—in each case the paragraph break has been relocated to the nearest sensible verse, usually within two lines; a paragraph sign at l. 555 has been ignored because of the syntactical impracticality of assigning a near alternative).

  The poem is a translation of *Yvain* by Chrétien de Troyes; selections from a modern translation of *Yvain* are provided in the Sources and Backgrounds section, and a brief overview of Chrétien, his work, and his place in the history of Arthurian literature are given in the headnote to the selections. All subsequent references (in notes) to Chrétien to *Yvain*; line references to *Yvain* concur with T. B. Reid's augmented edition of W. Foerster's critical text (for details of which see the Selected Bibliography).

1. (May) He protect his servants from sin.
2. The title, a variation from either of those given to the source (see p. 329, n. 2), no doubt reflects Gawain's role in the climactic action of the poem (where he unwittingly crosses swords with Ywain, ll. 3509–74); the English title may also reflect the greater contemporary popularity of Gawain, nephew to King Arthur, in many other Middle English Arthurian romances—on Gawain's literary popularity, see the headnote to *The Awntyrs off Arthur* in the Sources and Backgrounds section, p. 365.
3. I.e., as the source text says. (Such an appeal to the authority of an earlier version of the story is common in the romances; it is often not possible to determine whether the assertion is strictly true or a rhetorical flourish—but, in this case, cf. Chrétien's introduction as reprinted in the Criticism section, p. 411.)
4. Of all knights he was the most highly esteemed.
5. Whitsunday, otherwise known as Pentecost; about the date, see the notes to *Sir Launfal*, ll. 50 and 133.

And grete solace° als° thai war samin.°   *pleasure/as, when/together*
25 Fast° thai carped,° and curtaysly,°   *Vigorously/spoke/courteously*
Of dedes° of armes and of veneri°—   *deeds/venery, hunting*
And of gude° knightes that lyfed° then,   *good/lived*
And how men might tham kyndeli° ken°   *naturally/know, recognize*
By doghtines° of thaire gude dede,°   *doughtiness/deeds*
30 On ilka syde, wharesum thai yede,[6]
For thai war stif° in ilka stowre,°   *unyielding/fight*
And tharfore gat° thai grete honowre.°   *got, acquired/honor, renown*
(Thai tald of more trewth tham bitwene
Than now omang men here es sene;
35 For trowth, and luf, es al bylaft—
Men uses now another craft.
With worde men makes it trew and stabil,
Bot in thaire faith es noght bot fabil;
With the mowth men makes it hale,
40 Bot trew trowth es nane in the tale.[7]
Tharfore hereof now wil I blyn;°   *cease, leave off*
Of the Kyng Arthure I wil bygin,°   *begin*
And of his curtayse° cumpany—   *courteous*
Thare was the flowre° of chevallry;°   *flower, paragon/knighthood, chivalry*
45 Swilk lose thai wan with speres horde,
Over al the werld went the worde.)[8]

After mete went the Kyng
Into chamber to slepeing,°   *sleep*
And also went with him the Quene.
50 That byheld° thai al bydene,°   *beheld, noticed/at once*
For thai saw tham never so
On high° dayes to chamber go.   *special, feast*
Bot sone, when thai war went to slepe   *soon, quickly*
Knyghtes sat the dor° to kepe;°   *door/guard*
55 Sir Dedyne and Sir Segramore,[9]
Sir Gawayn and Sir Kay sat thore,°   *there*
And also sat thare Sir Ywaine
And Colgrevance[1] of mekyl mayn.
This knight that hight° Colgrevance   *was called*
60 Tald° his felows of a chance°   *Told, Related/event, adventure*
And of a stowre he had in bene°—   *been*

6. In every place, wheresoever they went.
7. They valued more truth among themselves than is now seen among men; for truth, and love, are wholly abandoned—men practice another trade now. With words men make something seem true and secure, but in their pledge is nothing but falsehood; with their mouth they make a thing seem sound, but there is no real truth in the tale they tell.
8. Such renown did they win with point of spear, (that) the word spread all over the world.
9. "Dedine" translates Chrétien's "Dodiniaus"; possibly he is Dodinel, a knight of the Round Table who later figures in Malory's *Morte Darthur*, in which he is slain by Lancelot. Sagremor, another knight of the Round Table, is commonly known as the son of the King of Hungary and features in many Arthurian romances.
1. Calogrenant in *Yvain*; the knight figures very little in other romances.

And al his tale herd° the Quene. *heard*
The chamber dore sho° has unshet,° *she / opened*
And down omang° tham scho° hir° set; *among / she / herself*
Sodainli° sho sat downright,° *Suddenly / straight down*
Or° ani of tham of hir had sight. *Before*
Bot Colgrevance rase° up in° hy°— *rose / on / high*
And thareof° had Syr Kay envy,° *thereof / enmity*
For he was of his tong a skalde,[2]
And for-to boste° was he ful balde.° *boast, intimidate / daring*
"Ow° Colgrevance," said Sir Kay, *You*
"Ful light of lepes has thou bene ay![3]
Thou wenes° now that the sal fall° *hope / shall / befall, qualify*
For-to be hendest° of us all! *most gracious*
And the Quene sal understand
That here es none so unkunand;° *unknowing (as we), ignorant (as we)*
Al° if thou rase° and we sat styll, *Even / rose*
We ne dyd it for none yll,[4]
Ne for no manere° of fayntise°— *manner, kind / recalcitrance*
Ne for us° denyd° noght for-to rise, *we / deigned*
That we ne had resen° had we hyr° sene."° *risen / her / seen*
"Sir Kay, I wote° wele," sayd the Quene, *know (that)*
"And it war° gude thou° left swilk° sawes° *were / (if) thou / such / utterances*
And noght° despise so thi° felawes."° *(would) not / thy / fellows*
"Madame," he said, "by Goddes° dome,° *God's / doom, judgment*
We ne wist° nothing of thi come° *knew / coming*
And if we did° noght curtaysly, *acted*
Takes to no velany.[5]
Bot pray ye now this gentil man
To tel the tale that he bygan."
Colgrevance said to Sir Kay,
"Bi grete God that aw° this day, *controls*
Na mare manes° me thi flyt° *menaces, bothers / quarreling*
Than it war a flies byt.° *bite*
Ful oft° wele better men than I *often*
Has thou desspised° desspytusely.° *despised, resented / without pity*
It es ful semeli, als me think,
A brok omang men for-to stynk.[6]
So it fars° by° the, Syr Kay; *goes / with*
Of weked° wordes has thou bene ay,° *wicked / always*
And, sen thi wordes er wikked and fell

2. I.e., he had a reproachful tongue. (Kay, Arthur's foster brother, is traditionally depicted in Arthurian literature as discourteous.)
3. Very sparing of animated movements (*lit.* leaps) have you been before (this)!
4. I.e., we did it (failed to rise) for no evil purpose.
5. I.e., take it as no deliberately offensive act.
6. It is wholly appropriate, as far as I am concerned, for a badger to stink among men (i.e., it would be wrong to expect Kay to do anything other than act according to his disagreeable nature).

This time, tharto na more I tell.
Bot of the thing that I bygan—"[7]
   And sone° Sir Kay him answerd than   *immediately*
105 And said, ful tite,° unto the Quene,   *quickly*
"Madame, if ye had noght here bene,
We sold° have herd a selly° case;   *should/marvelous*
Now let° ye us of oure solace.°   *allow/pleasure, recreation*
Tharfore, madame, we wald° yow° pray°   *would/(of) you/pray, ask*
110 That ye cumand° him to say   *command*
And tel forth, als he had tyght."°   *intended*
Than answerd that hende° knight,   *gracious*
"Mi lady es so avyse°   *considerate*
That scho wil noght cumand me
115 To tel that° towches° me to ill°— *that (which)/touches, moves/distress*
Scho es noght of so weked will."
   Sir Kai said than ful smertli,°   *sharply*
"Madame, al hale° this cumpani   *whole, as one*
Praies yow hertly° now omell°   *heartily/all together*
120 That he his tale forth might tell.
If ye wil noght for oure praying,
For faith ye aw° unto the Kyng   *owe*
Cumandes him his tale to tell,
That we mai here how it byfell."
125   Than said the Quene, "Sir Colgrevance,
I prai the tak to no grevance[8]
This kene° karping° of Syr Kay;   *sharp, bitter/carping, diatribe*
Of weked wordes has he bene ay,
So that none may him chastise.
130 Tharfore I prai the, on° al° wise,°   *in/all, every/manner, way*
That thou let° noght for his sawes   *stop*
At° tel to me and thi felawes°   *To/fellows*
Al thi tale, how it bytid°—   *happened*
For my luf I the pray and byd."°   *bid*
135 "Sertes, madame, that es me lath,°   *loathsome (to do)*
Bot for° I wil noght mak yow wrath°   *so/wroth, enraged*
Yowre cumandment I sal fulfill—
If ye wil listen me untill,°   *unto, to*
With hertes and eres° understandes—   *ears*
140 And I sal tel yow swilk tithandes°   *tidings, news*
That ye herd never none slike°   *such (like)*
Reherced° in no kynges ryke.°   *Rehearsed/realm*
Bot word fares als dose the wind,
Bot if men it in hert bynd;[9]

---

7. And, since your words are wicked and vicious now, I will no longer speak thereof. But of the thing (i.e., the tale) that I began—[at this point Kay again interrupts].
8. I ask you not to take offense.
9. But speech goes the way of the wind, unless men secure it in their heart.

145 And, wordes, wo so trewly tase,
By the eres into the hert it gase,
And in the hert thare es the horde
And knawing of ilk mans worde.[1]

Herkens, hende, unto my spell;
150 Trofels° sal I yow nane° tell,   *Trifles / none*
Ne lesinges° for-to ger° yow lagh,°   *lies / make / laugh*
Bot I sal say right als I sagh.°   *saw*
Now als this time sex yere[2]
I rade° allane,° als ye sal here,   *rode / alone*
155 Obout for-to seke° aventurs,°   *seek / adventures*
Wele armid° in gude armurs.°   *armed / armor*
    In a frith° I fand° a strete°   *forest / found / path, way*
Ful thik° and hard,° I yow bihete,°   *dense / difficult / assure*
With thornes, breres,° and moni a quyn.°   *briars / whin, gorse (shrub)*
160 Nerehand° al day I rade thareyn,°   *Nearly / therein*
And thurgh° I past with mekyl° payn.° *through / great / pain, difficulty*
Than come I sone° into a playn,°   *quickly / plain*
Whare I gan se a bretise° brade;°   *fortification / broad*
And thederward° ful fast I rade.   *thither*
165 I saw the walles and the dyke,°   *ditch, moat*
And hertly wele it gan me lyke.[3]
    And on the drawbrig° saw I stand   *drawbridge*
A knight with fawkon on his hand.[4]
This ilk° knight, that be ye balde,[5]   *same*
170 Was lord and keper of that halde.°   *(strong)hold*
I hailsed° him kindly als I kowth;°   *hailed, greeted / knew how, could*
He answerd me mildeli° with mowth.   *mildly*
Mi sterap° toke that hende knight   *stirrup*
And kindly cumanded me to lyght;°   *alight*
175 His cumandment I did onane,°   *anon, forthwith*
And into hall sone war we tane.°   *taken*
He thanked God, that gude man
(Sevyn° sithes° or° ever he blan°) *Seven / times / before / ceased*
And° the way that me theder broght,   *And (he thanked)*
180 And als the aventurs that I soght.
    Thus went we in—God do him mede°—   *reward*
And in his hand he led my stede.°   *steed, war-horse*
When we war in that fayre palays°   *palace*
(It was ful worthly° wroght° always°), *nobly / wrought, made / in every way*
185 I saw no man of moder° born.   *mother*

1. And speech, for whoever comprehends it truly, goes past the ears and into the heart; and in the heart is the treasuring and understanding of every man's speech.
2. This time six years ago.
3. I.e., and (the sight of) it pleased me heartily.
4. On the significance of the falcon, see *Sir Launfal*, l. 961, n.
5. Of that you can be sure.

Bot a burde hang us biforn
(Was nowther of yren ne of tre,
Ne I ne wist whareof it might be)[6]
And by that bord hang a mall.°   *large mallet, hammer*
190 The knyght smate° on thar-with-all°   *smote, struck/therewithal*
Thrise,° and by then might men se   *Thrice*
Bifore him come a faire menyé,°   *company, retinue*
Curtayse men in worde and dede;°   *deed*
To stabil° sone thai led mi stede.   *stable*
195 A damisel° come unto me,   *damsel, maiden*
The semeliest° that ever I se°—   *most graceful/had seen*
Lufsumer° lifed° never in land.   *More lovely/lived*
Hendly° scho toke me by the hand,   *Graciously*
And sone that gentyl creature
200 Al unlaced myne° armure.   *my*
Into a chamber sho me led,
And with a mantil° scho me cled;°   *cloak/clad, dressed*
It was of purpure[7] faire and fine
And the pane° of riche ermyne.[8]   *lining*
205 Al the folk war went° us fra,°   *gone/from*
And thare was none than° bot we twa.°   *then/two*
Scho served me hendely te° hend;°   *to/hand*
Hir maners might no man amend.°   *improve*
Of tong sho was trew and renable°   *reasonable, lucid*
210 And of° hir semblant° soft and stabile.°   *by/appearance/dependable*
(Ful fain° I wald, if that I might,   *gladly*
Have woned° with that swete wight.)°   *dwelt, lived/person*
   And, when we sold° go to sopere,°   *should/supper*
That lady with a lufsom° chere°   *lovely/countenance*
215 Led me down into the hall.
Thare war we served wele at all;
It nedes noght to tel the mese,°   *portions (of food)*
For wonder° wele war we at esse.°   *wondrously/ease*
Byfor me sat the lady bright°   *splendid, fair*
220 Curtaisly my mete to dyght;°   *prepare, serve*
Us wanted° nowther° baken° ne roste.°   *lacked/neither/pie/roast*
And efter° soper sayd myne oste°   *after/host*
That he cowth noght tel° the day   *tell of, recall*
That ani knight are° with him lay,°   *before/stayed*
225 Or that ani aventures soght.

6. A ("sounding") board hung before us, but it was (made) neither of iron nor wood, nor did I know of what it might be (made). (In Chrétien, l. 216, the exotic gonglike object is said to be made of copper.)
7. Purple cloth. (Purple has traditionally been the color of high rank for millennia; the word itself derives from the Greek name given to the Mediterranean shellfish which originally provided the valuable purple dye. The actual color could range from true purple to a deep red.)
8. The white fur of the ermine (a kind of weasel), evenly punctuated by the black tip of the creature's tail, is a distinctive feature of royal robes.

Tharfore he prayed me, if I moght,°   *might, could*
On al wise, when I come ogayne,°   *again*
That I sold cum to him sertayne.°   *certainly, without question*
I said, 'Sir, gladly, yf I may'—
230 It had bene shame° have° said him° nay. *shameful/(to) have/(to) him*
  That night had I ful gude rest,
And mi stede esed° of the best.   *eased, accommodated*
Alsone° als it was dayes lyght,   *As soon*
Forth to fare sone was I dyght.
235 Mi leve° of mine ost toke I thare   *leave*
And went mi way withowten mare,°   *more (ado)*
Aventures for-to layt° in land.   *seek*
A faire forest sone I fand;
Me thoght mi hap thare fel ful hard,[9]
240 For thare was mani a wilde lebard,°   *leopard*
Lions, beres,° bath° bul° and bare,° *bears/both/bull/boar*
That rewfully° gan rope° and rare.° *ruefully/cry out/roar*
Oway° I drogh° me, and with that   *Away/withdrew*
I saw sone whare a man sat
245 On a lawnd,° the fowlest° wight° *clearing/foulest/creature*
That ever yit° man saw in syght.   *yet*
He was a lathly° creature,   *loathly*
For fowl he was out of mesure;°   *measure, proportion*
A wonder mace in hand he hade—
250 And sone mi way to him I made—
His hevyd,° me thoght, was als grete°   *head/great, large*
Als of a rowncy° or a nete.°   *large horse/ox*
  Unto his belt hang° his hare,°   *hung/hair*
And efter that byheld I mare.
255 To his forhede° byheld I than;   *forehead*
Was bradder than twa large span.[1]
He had eres° als° ane olyfant°   *ears/like/elephant*
And was wele more than geant.°   *a giant*
His face was ful brade° and flat;   *broad*
260 His nese° was cutted° als a cat;   *nose/forked*
His browes war like litel buskes,°   *bushes*
And his tethe like bare-tuskes.°   *boar-tusks*
A ful grete bulge opon his bak°   *back*
Thare was noght made withowten lac.[2]
265 His chin was fast° until° his brest.   *fastened/unto*
On his mace he gan him rest.
  Also it was a wonder wede,° *wondrous/piece of clothing*

---

9. I thought my luck there was hard to come by.
1. (It) was broader than two large spans. (A span is typically about nine inches, in principle the distance between tip of little finger and tip of thumb when the fingers are stretched farthest apart.)
2. Was there formed with no lack (of excess).

That the cherle° yn yede;°   churl / went
Nowther of wol° ne of line°   wool / linen
270 Was the wede that he went yn.
When he me sagh, he stode° upright.   stood
I frayned° him if he wolde fight—   asked
For tharto was I in gude will—³
Bot als° a beste° than stode he still.   like / beast
275 I hopid that he no wittes kowth,
No reson for-to speke with mowth.⁴
  To him I spak ful hardily°   boldly
And said, 'What ertow,° belamy?'°   art thou / good friend, fair friend
He said ogain,° 'I am a man!'   in return
280 I said, 'Swilk° saw I never nane.'°   such (like) / none
'What ertow?' alsone° said he.   at once
I said, 'Swilk als° thou here may se.'   as
I said, 'What dose° thou here allane?'°   do / alone
He said, 'I kepe thir bestes ilkane.'⁵
285 I said, 'That es mervaile,° think me;   a marvel
For I herd never of man bot the,
In wildernes ne in forestes,
That kepeing had of wilde bestes
Bot thai war bunden fast in halde.'⁶
290 He sayd, 'Of thire° es none so balde°   these (beasts) / daring
Nowther by day ne bi night
Anes° to pas° out of mi sight.'   Once / pass
I sayd, 'How so? Tel° me thi scill.'°   explain / skill, talent
'Parfay,'° he said, 'gladly I will.'   By my faith, Indeed
295 He said, 'In al this faire foreste
Es thare none so wilde beste
That remu° dar,° bot stil stand   stir, depart / dares
When I am to him cumand.°   coming
And ay,° when that I wil him fang°   in return / grasp
300 With mi fingers that er strang,°   strong
I ger° him cri° on swilk° manere   make / cry / such
That al the bestes, when thai him here,
Obout me than cum thai all,
And to mi fete fast thai fall
305 On thaire manere merci° to cry.   mercy
Bot understand now redyli,°   truly
Olyve° es thare lifand no ma°   Alive / more, other
Bot I that durst omang° tham ga,   among
That he ne sold° sone° be al to-rent.°   should / quickly / torn apart

3. For I was willing to do that.
4. I trusted that he was incapable of much intelligence and did not know how to talk.
5. I look after each one of these beasts.
6. For I never heard of a man except you who kept wild animals in (a) wilderness or forest unless
    they were securely confined.

310 Bot thai er at my comandment;°   *bidding*
    To me thai cum when I tham call,
    And I am maister° of tham all.'   *master*
    Than he asked onone right,
    What man° I was. I said, 'A knyght   *(kind of) man*
315 That soght aventurs in that land,
    My body to asai° and fande;°   *try/test*
    And I the pray of thi kownsayle,°   *counsel, advice*
    Thou teche° me to sum mervayle.'°   *direct/marvel, wonder*
        He sayd, 'I can no wonders tell,
320 Bot here-bisyde° es a well;   *nearby*
    Wend° theder° and do als I say—   *Go/thither*
    Thou passes noght al quite oway!⁷
    Folow forth this ilk° strete,   *same*
    And sone sum mervayles sal° thou mete.°   *shall/meet*
325 The well es under the fairest tre,°   *tree*
    That ever was in this cuntré;°   *country*
    By that well hinges° a bacyne°   *hangs/basin*
    That es of gold gude and fyne,
    With a cheyne,° trewly to tell,   *chain*
330 That wil reche° into the well.⁸   *reach*
        Thare es a chapel nere° tharby,°   *near/thereby*
    That nobil es and ful lufely.
    By the well standes a stane;°   *stone*
    Tak the bacyn sone° onane°   *quickly/anon, forthwith*
335 And cast on water with thi hand,
    And sone thou sal se new tithand;°   *tidings, news*
    A storme sal rise and a tempest
    Al obout, by° est° and west.   *from/east*
    Thou sal here° mani thonor° blast   *hear/thunder*
340 Al obout the blawand° fast;   *blowing*
    And thare sal cum slik slete° and rayne°   *sleet/rain*
    That unnese sal thou stand ogayne;⁹
    Of lightnes° sal thou se a lowe.°   *light/flash*
    Unnethes thou sal thi selven knowe—¹
345 And, if thou pas withowten grevance,°   *grievance, distress*
    Than has thou the fairest° chance°   *best/luck*
    That ever yit° had any knyght   *yet*
    That theder come to kyth° his myght.'   *make known*
        Than toke I leve and went my way
350 And rade unto° the midday.   *until*
    By than I come whare I sold be;
    I saw the chapel and the tre.

---

7. You will not come away unhindered!
8. On the significance of the well and its magical trappings, see l. 412, n.
9. That you will stand against it with difficulty.
1. With difficulty you shall find out about yourself.

Thare I fand° the fayrest thorne[2]   *found*
That ever groued° sen° God was born.   *grew / since*
355   So thik° it was with leves° grene,   *thick, overgrown / leaves*
Might no rayn cum° tharbytwene;   *come*
And that grenes° lastes ay,°   *greenness / always*
For no winter dere° yt may.   *harm, injure*
I fand the bacyn als he° talde,   *(the giant)*
360   And the wel with water kalde.°   *cold*
An amerawd° was the stane—   *emerald*
Richer saw I never nane—
On fowre rubyes on heght standand;[3]
Thaire light lasted° over al the land.   *continued on, extended*
365   And when I saw that semely syght,
It made me bath joyful and lyght.°   *lighthearted, cheerful*
I toke the bacyn sone onane
And helt° water opon the stane;   *poured*
The weder° wex° than wonder blak,°   *weather / grew / black, dark*
370   And the thoner fast gan crak.°   *crack*
Thare come slike stormes of hayl and rayn,
Unnethes° I might stand thare ogayn;   *With difficulty*
The store° windes blew ful lowd°—   *fierce, violent / loud*
So kene come never are of clowd.[4]
375   I was drevyn° with snaw° and slete;   *driven, pelted / snow*
Unnethes I might stand on my fete.
In my face the levening° smate;°   *lightning / struck*
I wend° have brent,° so was it hate.°   *expected to / burned / hot*
That weder made me so will of rede,[5]
380   I hopid° sone to have my dede°—   *expected / death*
And sertes, if it lang° had last,°   *long / lasted*
I hope I had never thethin past—[6]
Bot thorgh His° might that tholed° wownd,°   *(Christ's) / suffered / wound*
The storme sesed° within a stownde.°   *ceased / moment*
385   Than wex the weder fayre ogayne,
And thareof was I wonder fayne°   *well pleased*
(For best comforth of al thing
Es solace efter myslikeing).[7]
Than saw I sone a mery° syght: *merry, cheerful*

2. A thorn tree, probably hawthorn. Chrétien here describes a pine tree; the thorn may have been substituted by the translator because of its traditional associations with the supernatural, as a favorite haunt of fairies, and, in the form of cut branches, as a suitable defense against evil spirits. A context of supernatural sacrifice and redemption may well also be invoked; the thorn, especially in its connection with the spring, recalls the crown of thorns and the blood shed at the Crucifixion. Cf. the lyric "At a springe-well under a thorn," lyric no. 192 in Luria and Hoffman, eds., *Middle English Lyrics* (a Norton Critical Edition, New York, 1974), p. 181.
3. Standing aloft on four rubies.
4. Such sharp (winds) never came from the clouds before.
5. That weather left me at such a loss what to do.
6. I believe that I would never have passed out of that place.
7. The best of all consolations is pleasure after displeasure.

390 Of al the fowles that er in flyght[8]
    Lighted° so thik opon that tre   *Alighted*
    That bogh° ne lefe° none might I se.   *bough / leaf*
    So merily than gon thai sing
    That al the wode° bigan to ring.   *woods*
395 Ful mery was the melody
    Of thaire sang and of thaire cry;
    Thare herd never man none swilk,°   *such*
    Bot° if ani had herd that ilk.°   *Unless / same*
    And when that mery dyn° was done,   *din, noise*
400 Another noyse than herd I sone,
    Als it war of horsmen°   *horsemen, mounted men*
    Mo than owther° nyen° or ten.   *either / nine*

    Sone than saw I cum a knyght.
    In riche armurs° was he dight;   *armour*
405 And sone, when I gan on him loke,
    Mi shelde and spere° to me I toke.   *spear, lance*
    That knight to me hied° ful fast,   *moved*
    And kene wordes out gan he cast.
    He bad° that I sold tel him tite°   *bade, ordered / immediately*
410 Whi° I did him swilk despite,°   *why / contempt, harm*
    With weders° wakend° him of rest   *storms / waking*
    And done° him wrang° in his forest.[9]   *(had) done / wrong*
    'Tharfore', he said, 'thou sal aby.'°   *pay*
    And with that come he egerly°   *intently*
415 And said I had ogayn° resowne°   *against, without / reason, explanation*
    Done him grete° destrucciowne°   *great / destruction*
    And might it never more amend;°   *repair, put right*
    Tharfore he bad I sold me° fend.°   *myself / defend*
    And sone I smate° him on the shelde;°   *smote, struck / shield*
420 Mi schaft° brac° out in the felde,°   *lance / broke / (battle)field*
    And than he bare me sone bi strenkith
    Out of my sadel my speres lenkith.[1]

    I wate° that he was largely°   *know / in large measure*
    By the shuldres° mare° than I;   *shoulders / more, larger*
425 And, bi the ded° that I sal thole,°   *death / suffer*

8. All of the kinds of birds that fly.
9. At this point it should be clear that the magical well has no clearly plausible functions except the literary; one cannot really ask why the knight who guards the well does not remove the basin and stone, thus preventing his further exploitation. The principal literary functions of the episode are twofold. First, it provides a pretext for the remarkable encounter between the knight who guards the well and his challenger. More important, it links chivalric combat with public responsibility; whereas Colgrevance engages in combat for the sake of personal adventure, the knight of the well does so to protect his demesne.
    The motif of the magical well or spring may have Celtic precedents which appear only (perhaps deliberately) in half-remembered form in Chrétien, from whom the Middle English translator has produced this version; for a brief overview of Celtic influences on Chrétien and Arthurian literature generally, see the Sources and Backgrounds headnote, p. 329.
1. And then, through sheer force of strength, he quickly bore me out of my saddle (a distance about equal to) the length of my lance.

Mi stede by° his was bot a fole.°   beside, in comparison to / foal
For mate² I lay down on the grownde,
So was I stonayd° in that stownde.°   stunned / time
A worde to me wald° he noght say,   would
430   Bot toke my stede and went his way.
        Ful sarily° than thare I sat;   sorrily, wretchedly
For wa° I wist° noght what was what.   woe, anguish / knew
With my stede he went in hy°   haste
The same way that he come by;
435   And I durst folow him no ferr°   further
For dout me solde bite werr—³
And also yit,° by Goddes° dome,°   yet / God's / doom, judgment
I ne wist whare he bycome.°   went

        Than I thoght how I had hight°   promised
440   Unto myne° ost,° the hende knyght,   my / host
And also til his lady bryght,
To com ogayn if that I myght.
Mine armurs left I thare ilkane,°   every piece
For els° myght I noght have gane;°   otherwise / gone, made way
445   Unto myne in° I come by day.   lodging
The hende knight and the fayre may°   maid
Of my come° war° thai ful glade,   coming, arrival / were
And nobil semblant° thai me° made;   display / (for) me
In al thinges thai have tham born⁴
450   Als° thai did the night biforn.°   As / before
        Sone thai wist° whare I had bene,   knew
And said that thai had never sene
Knyght that ever theder° come°   there / came
Take the way ogayn home.
455   On this wise that tyme I wroght;⁵
I fand° the folies° that I soght.'"°   found / follies / sought

        "Now sekerly,"° said Sir Ywayne,   surely
"Thou ert my cosyn jermayne;°   germane, related by blood
Trew luf° suld be us bytwene,   love
460   Als sold° bytwyx brether° bene.   should / brothers
Thou ert a fole° at° thou ne had are°   fool / that / before
Tald me of this ferly° fare,°   wondrous / business
For, sertes,° I sold onone ryght   certainly
Have venged° the of that ilk knyght—   avenged
465   So sal I yit, if that I may."
And than als smertly° sayd Syr Kay   sharply

2. Out of dejected exhaustion.
3. For fear that I might suffer worse.
4. In all things they conducted themselves.
5. In this way I spent that time.

(He karpet to tham wordes grete),[6]
"It es sene now es efter mete!
Mare boste es in a pot of wyne
470 Than in a karcas of Saynt Martyne.[7]
    Arme the smertly,° Syr Ywayne;   *quickly*
And, sone that thou war cumen ogayne,
Luke thou fil wele thi panele[8]
And in thi sadel set the wele;
475 And, when thou wendes,° I the pray   *go*
Thi baner° wele that thou desplay;   *(heraldic) banner*
And, rede° I, or thou wende,   *advise*
Thou tak thi leve at° ilka° frende;   *from / every*
And, if it so bytide this nyght
480 That the in slepe dreche ani wight,
Or any dremis mak the rad,
Turn ogayn—and say I bad."[9]

    The Quene answerd with milde mode°   *disposition*
And said, "Sir Kay, ertow° wode?°   *art thou / mad*
485 What the devyl es the withyn,
At° thi tong may never blyn°   *That / cease, leave off*
Thi felows so fowly to shende?°   *reproach*
Sertes, Sir Kay, thou ert unhende!°   *ungracious*
By Him° that for us sufferd pine,°   *(Christ) / torment*
490 Syr, and thi tong war myne,
I sold bical it tyte of treson—[1]
And so might thou do, by° gude° reson;   *for / good*
Thi tong dose the grete dishonowre,
And tharefore es it thi traytowre."°   *traitor*
495   And than alsone° Syr Ywayne   *at once*
Ful hendly answerd ogayne°   *in return*
(Al° if men sayd hym° velany,°   *Even / (of) him / offensive things*
He karped° ay° ful curtaysly),   *spoke / always*
"Madame," he said unto the Quene,
500 "Thare sold na stryf° be us bytwene.   *strife, quarrel*
Unkowth° men wele may he shende   *Unknown, Strange*
That to his felows es so unhende;
And als, madame, men says sertayne

---

6. I.e., he spoke haughtily to them.
7. It is obvious enough that it is (now) after dinner! (Cf. ll. 18 ff.) There is more bravery to be
   had from a pot of wine than from a whole carcass of the kind hung up to air on St. Martin's
   Day. (I.e., a little wine makes for more courage than a lot of food. St. Martin's Day, November
   11, is traditionally associated with butchery of livestock before the onset of winter.)
8. And, so that you are quickly returned, see that you stuff your saddle pad well (for comfort on
   a long ride).
9. I.e., and if it so happens tonight that any creature troubles you in your sleep, or that any
   dreams make you frightened, turn back—and admit that I told you to do so.
1. I.e., if the tongue (which said that) were mine, I would immediately accuse it of treason.

That wo so flites or turnes ogayne,
505 He bygins al the mellé;°   *fight, quarrel*
So wil I noght it far by me.²
Lates° him say halely° his thoght;   *Let / wholly, entirely*
His wordes greves° me right noght."   *offend*

  Als thai war in this spekeing°   *conversation*
510 Out of the chamber come the Kyng.
The barons that war thare, sertayn,
Smertly rase° thai him ogayne.°   *rose / before*
He bad tham sit down al bydene,°   *at once*
And down he set him by the Quene.
515 The Quene talde him fayre and wele,
Als sho kowth,° everilka° dele°   *could / every / part*
Ful apertly,° al the chance°   *openly, plainly / adventure*
Als it bifel Syr Colgrevance.
When sho had talde him how it ferd,°   *went*
520 And the King hyr tale had herd,
He sware° by his owyn° crowne   *swore / own*
And his fader sowl Uterpendragowne,³
That he sold se that ilk° syght   *same*
By that day thethin a fowretenight—
525 On Saint Johns evyn, the Baptist⁴
(That best barn° was under° Crist).   *man / in the service of*
"Swith,"° he sayd, "wendes° with me,   *Forthwith / go*
Who so wil that wonder se."
  The Kynges word might noght be hid;°   *hidden*
530 Over al the cowrt° sone was it kyd,°   *court / made known*
And thare was none so litel° page°   *little, insignificant / (as a) page*
That he ne was fayn° of that vayage.°   *well-pleased / journey*
And knyghtes and swiers° war ful fayne—   *squires*
Mysliked° none bot Syr Ywayne;   *Disliked (it)*
535 To himself he made grete mane,°   *moan, complaint*
For he wald have went allane.°   *alone*
In hert he had grete myslykyng
For the wending° of the Kyng   *expedition*
Al for° he hopid,° withowten fayle,   *because / expected*
540 That Sir Kay sold ask° the batayle,   *ask (for), request*
Or els Sir Gawayn, knyght vailant—
And owther wald the King grant;⁵

---

2. Whoever argues or answers back, it is he who starts the fight; I will not let that happen with me.
3. And the soul of his father, Uther Pendragon. (Uther is traditionally identified as the father of Arthur; *Pendragon* probably derives from an ultimately Celtic title meaning "head leader.")
4. A fortnight thence from that day, on the eve of the feast of St. John the Baptist (i.e., Midsummer Night's Eve, June 23, a time traditionally held to be ripe for visitations from the world of faerie; recall just such activities in Shakespeare's *A Midsummer Night's Dream*).
5. And the King would grant either (the battle).

Who so it wald first crave,°   *request*
Of tham two, sone might it have.
545   The Kynges wil wald he noght bide,°   *abide, stand for*
Worth of him what may bityde;[6]
Bi him allane he thoght° to wend   *intended*
And tak° the grace that God wald° send.   *take, accept / would*
He thoght to be wele on hys way
550   Or° it war passed the thryd° day,   *Before / third*
And to asay° if he myght mete   *find out*
With that ilk narow strete°   *path, way*
With thornes and with breres° set   *briars*
That mens way might lightli° let°—   *easily / hinder*
555   And also for-to fynd the halde°   *(strong)hold, castle*
That Sir Colgrevance of talde,°   *told*
The knyght and the mayden meke.
The forest fast° than wald he seke   *dense*
And als the karl of Kaymes kyn[7]
560   And the wilde bestes with him,
The tre with briddes thareopon,
The chapel, the bacyn, and the stone.
His thoght wald he tel to no frende,
Until he wyst how it wald ende.[8]
565   Than went Ywaine to his yn;°   *lodging*
His men he fand redy thareyn.°   *therein*
Unto a swier gan he say,
"Go swith° and sadel my palfray,°   *at once / riding horse*
And so thou do my strang stede,
570   And tak with the my best wede°—   *armor*
At yone° yate° I wil out ryde;   *yonder / gate*
Withowten° town I sal the bide—   *Outside*
And hy° the smertly unto me;   *hasten*
For I most make a jorné°—   *journey*
575   Ogain, sal thou bring my palfray—
And forbede° the oght° to say.   *(I) forbid / anything*
If thou wil any more me° se,   *men*
Lat none wit° of my preveté;°   *know / secret*
And if ani man the oght° frayn,°   *anything / asks*
580   Luke now lely that thou layn."[9]
"Sir," he said, "with ful gude will,
Als° ye byd,° I sal fulfyll.   *As / bid*
At yowre awyn° wil may ye ride;   *own*
For me ye sal noght be ascryed."[1]

6. Regardless of what may become of him.
7. And also the man of Cain's kin. (On Cain's legacy, see *Havelok*, l. 2046, n.)
8. I.e., he would not reveal his intentions even to a friend until he knew how everything would turn out.
9. See that loyally you conceal (what you know).
1. You shall not be exposed because of me.

585   Forth than went Sir Ywayne;
         He thinkes,° or he cum ogayne,   *intends*
         To wreke his cosyn at his myght.[2]
         The squier has his hernays° dyght°—   *equipment / prepared*
         He did right als his mayster red;°   *directed*
590   His stede, his armurs, he him led.
         When Ywayn was withowten town,
         Of his palfray lighted he down
         And dight him right wele in his wede
         And lepe up on his gude stede.
595   Furth° he rade onone right,   *Forth*
         Until it neghed° nere the nyght.   *approached*
         He passed many high mowntayne
         In wildernes and mony a playne,°   *plain, field*
         Til he come to that lethir° sty°   *nasty / path*
600   That him byhoved° pass by—   *(it) behooved*
         Than was he seker° for-to se   *certain*
         The wel and the fayre tre.
             The c[ast]el[3] saw he at the last,
         And theder hyed° he ful fast.   *went*
605   More curtaysi and more honowre
         Fand° he with tham in that toure,°   *Found / tower, castle*
         And mare conforth,° by monyfalde,°   *comfort / many times*
         Than Colgrevance had him of talde.
         That night was he herberd° thare;   *harbored, sheltered*
610   So wele was he never are.[4]

             At morn he went forth by the strete,
         And with the cherel° sone° gan he mete   *churl (the giant) / soon*
         That sold° tel to him the way.   *should*
         (He sayned° him,° the soth to say,   *signed, crossed / himself*
615   Twenty sith° or° ever he blan,°   *times / before / stopped*
         Swilk mervayle° had he of that man,   *marvel, wonder*
         For he had wonder that nature
         Myght mak so fowl a creature.)
         Than to the well he rade gude pase,[5]
620   And doun he lighted in that place—
         And sone the bacyn has he tane°   *taken*
         And kest° water opon the stane,   *cast*
         And sone thare wex,° withowten fayle,   *grew, ensued*
         Wind and thonor,° and rayn and haile.   *thunder*

---

2. To avenge his cousin with all his might.
3. The manuscript here reads "chapel," probably the result of scribal overfamiliarity with the
   word recently (but so far exclusively) mentioned in connection with the magical spring.
4. He was never so well (lodged) before.
5. With good speed.

625	When it was sesed,° than saw he	*ceased*
	The fowles light opon the tre;	
	Thai sang ful fayre opon that thorn°—	*thorn tree*
	Right als thai had done byforn.	
	And sone he saw cumand° a knight	*coming*
630	Als fast so° the fowl in flyght	*as*
	With rude° sembland° and sterne chere,°	*severe/appearance/countenance*
	And hastily he neghed nere.	
	To speke of lufe° na° time was thare,	*love/no*
	For aither° hated uther° ful sare.°	*either/other/sorely, bitterly*
635	Togeder smertly gan thai drive;	
	Thaire sheldes sone bigan to ryve,°	*split*
	Thaire shaftes° cheverd° to thaire hand—	*lances/shivered, splintered*
	Bot thai war bath ful wele syttand.⁶	
	Out thai drogh° thaire swerdes kene°	*drew/sharp*
640	And delt° strakes° tham bytwene.	*dealt/strokes, blows*
	Al to peces thai hewed thaire sheldes—	
	The culpons° flegh° out in the feldes;°	*cuttings, splinters/flew/(battle)field*
	On helmes strake thay so with yre	
	At ilka strake outbrast the fyre.⁷	
645	Aither of tham gude buffettes° bede,°	*buffets, blows/gave*
	And nowther wald styr° of° the stede.°	*stir, move off/from/place*
	Ful kenely° thai kyd° thaire myght	*boldly/made known*
	And feyned° tham noght for-to fight—	*feigned, pretended*
	Thaire hauberkes that men myght ken;	
650	The blode out of thaire bodyes ren.⁸	
	Aither on other laid° so fast;	*laid on, struck*
	The batayl° might noght lang last.	*battle*
	Hauberkes er° broken and helmes reven°—	*are/riven, smashed*
	Stif° strakes war° thare gyfen.°	*Hard/were/given*
655	Thai faght on hors stifly° always;	*unyieldingly*
	The batel was wele more to prays.⁹	
	Bot at the last Syr Ywayne	
	On his felow kyd his mayne;°	*strength, power*
	So egerly° he smate° him than,	*fiercely/smote, struck*
660	He° clefe° the helme and	
	the hern-pan.°	*(That) he/cleaved/brainpan, skull*
	The knyght wist° he was nere° ded;	*knew/nearly*
	To fle° than was his best rede,°	*flee/plan*
	And fast he fled with al hys mayne—	
	And fast folowd Syr Ywayne.	
665	Bot he ne might him overtake	

6. I.e., but they both remained firmly set in their saddles.
7. They struck on (each other's) helms with such fury that fire (sparks) burst out at every stroke.
8. Their chain-mail coats might show men that; the blood ran out of their bodies. (Because of a belief that this couplet is corrupt, the chief editions add *At* to the beginning of l. 649, thus rendering a sense similar to that of ll. 3543–44.)
9. I.e., (because of that) the battle was that much more worthy of praise.

(Tharfore grete° murning° gan he make);   *great / mourning*
He folowd him ful stowtlyk°   *stoutly, determinedly*
And wald have tane him ded or quik.°   *alive*
He folowd him to the ceté—
670   Na man lyfand° met he;   *living*
When thai come to the kastel° yate,°   *castle / gate*
In he folowd fast thareate.°   *thereat*
At aither entré[1] was, iwys,°   *truly*
Straytly° wroght a portculis°   *Narrowly / portcullis, sliding grille*
675   Shod° wele with yren° and stele°—   *Tipped / iron / steel*
And also grunden° wonder wele.   *ground (sharp)*
    Under that than was a swyke°   *trap*
That made Syr Ywain to myslike.°   *be displeased*
His hors° fote° toched° thareon;   *horse's / foot / touched*
680   Than fel the portculis onone
Bytwyx him and his hinder° arsown°—   *rear / saddlebow*
Thorgh sadel and stede it smate al down;
His spores° of his heles° it schare°—   *spurs / heels / sheared*
Than had Ywaine murnyng° mare.   *grief, displeasure*
685   Bot so° he wend° have° passed quite,°   *as / expected / (to) have / free*
Than fel the tother bifore als tyte.[2]
(A faire grace yit fel him swa—
Al if it smate his hors in twa
And his spors of aither hele—
690   That himself passed so wele!)[3]
    Bytwene tha yates now es he tane;°   *held*
Tharfore he mase° ful mykel° mane,°   *makes / great / complaint*
And mikel murnyng gan he ma,°   *make*
For the knyght was went him fra.
695   Als he was stoken° in that stall,°   *shut / place*
He herd° byhind him in a wall   *heard*
A dore° opend faire and wele,   *door*
And thareout° come a damysel—   *thereout*
Efter° hir° the dore sho stak.°   *After, Behind / her / shut*
700   Ful hinde° wordes to him sho° spak.   *gracious / she*
    "Syr," sho said, "by Saint Myghell,°   *Michael*
Here thou has a febil° ostell!°   *feeble, inadequate / hostel, lodging*
Thou mon° be ded—es noght at laine—[4]   *will have to, must*
For my lord that thou has slayne;°   *slain*
705   Seker° it es that thou him slogh.   *Certain*

---

1. At either entrance. (Ywain is about to enter the castle barbican, a kind of fortification within the castle wall which houses the outer and inner gates and contains various chambers affording strategic vantage points over the portal way.)
2. Then the other (portcullis) immediately fell ahead.
3. Good fortune had still come his way—even if it (the gate) had cut his horse in two and cut his spurs from either heel—given that he had passed through (the event) in such (relatively) good condition!
4. (It) is not to be hidden.

My lady makes sorow ynogh°   *enough, in plenty*
And al his menyé° everilkane°—   *retinue / each one*
Here has thou famen° many ane.°   *foes / a one*
To be thi bane° er° thai ful balde;°   *destruction / are / determined*
710 Thou brekes° noght out of this halde°—   *(will) break / confinement*
And, for thai wate thai may noght fayl,
Thai wil the sla in playn batayl.[5]
       He sayd, "Thai ne sal,° so God me rede,[6]   *shall*
For al thaire might,° do me to dede,   *strength*
715 Ne no handes opon me lay.
Sho said, "Na, sertes, if that I may;
Al if thou be here straytly stad,
Me think thou ert noght ful adrad.[7]
And sir," sho said, "on al wise[8]
720 I aw° the honore° and servyse:°   *owe / honor, respect / service*
I was in message at the King[9]
Bifore this time, whils° I was ying;°   *whilst / young*
I was noght than savesé°   *so wise, so prudent*
Als a damysel aght° to be;   *ought*
725 Fro the tyme that I was lyght°   *alighted (from my horse)*
In cowrt was none so hend° knyght   *gracious*
That unto me than walde° take hede°   *would / heed, notice*
Bot thou allane°—God do the mede.[1]   *alone*
Grete honore thou did to me,
730 And that sal I now quite° the.   *repay*
       I wate (if thou be seldom sene)
Thou ert the Kyng son Uriene,[2]
And thi name es Sir Ywayne.
Of me may thou be sertayne;[3]
735 If thou wil my kownsail° leve,°   *counsel, advice / believe, trust*
Thou sal find na man the to greve;°   *harm*
I sal lene° the here mi ring,   *lend*
Bot yelde° it me at myne askyng—   *yield, return*
When thou ert broght° of al thi payn,°   *brought (out) / pain, distress*
740 Yelde it than to me ogayne.
Als° the bark hilles° the tre,   *As / covers, protects*

---

5. And, because they know that they cannot fail, they will kill you in open battle. (I.e., they
   will venture to kill you because they believe that you are trapped and helpless. The maiden
   thus implies the relative inadequacy of the dead knight's retainers; it is an implication she
   confirms later, ll. 952 ff., and which the retainers themselves verify, ll. 1187–1250).
6. I.e., so help me God.
7. Certainly not, if I can help it; although you are here severely beset, it seems to me that you
   are not completely afraid.
8. In every (other) way.
9. I was on an errand to the King.
1. God reward you.
2. I.e., I know (even if I have seen you but rarely since) you are the son of King Urien. (As well
   as his traditional role in Arthurian literature as Ywain's father, Urien is also identified with
   the rule of various Scottish and northern English territories.)
3. I.e., you can trust in me.

Right so sal my ring do the;
When thou in hand has the stane,[4]
Dere° sal thai do the nane°—   Harm / none
745 For the stane es of swilk° myght,°   such / power
Of the sal men have na syght."[5]
   Wit° ye wele that Sir Ywayne   Know
Of thir° wordes was ful fayne.°   these / pleased
In at the dore sho him led
750 And did° him sit opon hir bed;   made
A quylt° ful nobil lay thareon—   quilt
Richer saw he never none.
Sho said if he wald° any thing   wanted
He sold° be served at his liking.°   should / pleasure
755 He said that ete° wald he fayn.°   eat / gladly
Sho went and come ful sone° ogain;   soon, quickly
A capon[6] rosted° broght sho sone,°   roasted / soon, promptly
A clene klath° and brede° tharone,   cloth / bread / thereon
And a pot with riche wine
760 And a pece° to fil° it yne.   cup / pour
He ete and drank with ful gude° chere,   good
For tharof had he grete mystere.°   need
   When he had eten and dronken° wele,   drank
Grete noyse° he herd in the kastele.   noise
765 Thai soght overall° him to have slayn;   everywhere
To venge thaire lorde war° thai ful bayn°   were / eager
Or° that the cors° in erth was layd.   Before / corpse
The damysel sone to him sayd,
"Now seke thai the fast for-to sla;°   slay
770 Bot whosoever com or ga,
Be thou never the more adred,°   afraid
Ne styr° thou noght out of this stede.°   stir, move / place
In this° here seke° thai wyll,   this (place) / seek
Bot on this bed luke° thou be styll;°   see that / still, motionless
775 Of tham al mak thou na force.[7]
Bot when that thai sal bere° the cors   bear, carry
Unto the kyrk° for-to bery,°   church / bury
Than sal thou here° a sary° cry;   hear / sorrowful
So sal thai mak a doleful dyn.°   din, noise
780 Than wil thay seke the eft° herein;   again
Bot loke thou be of hert lyght,[8]

4. I.e., when you turn the stone of the ring toward the palm of your hand.
5. Men will not be able to see you. (Magic talismans such as this ring—and especially the stone it contains—are common in the romances, as they are in folk and fairy tales; cf. *Sir Launfal*, ll. 319–24, *The Sege off Melayne*, ll. 837, and Gaimar's Haveloc episode, printed in the Sources and Backgrounds section, p. 327, ¶ 681.)
6. A rooster castrated to improve the flavor of its meat—an expensive delicacy.
7. I.e., pay no attention to them.
8. I.e., be lighthearted, cheerful.

For of the sal thai have no syght.
Here sal thou be mawgré thaire berd,[9]
And tharfore be thou noght aferd;
785 Thi famen° sal be als° the blynd;   *enemies/like*
Both byfor the and byhind,
On ilka° side sal thou be soght.°   *every/sought*
Now most I ga;° bot drede the noght,   *go*
For I sal do that the es lefe,
790 If al it turn me to mischefe."[1]
         When sho come unto the yate,°   *gate*
Ful many men fand° sho tharate°   *found/thereat*
Wele armed, and wald° ful fayn   *(who) would*
Have taken and slane Sir Ywaine.
795 Half his stede thare fand thai
That within the yates lay;
Bot the knight thare fand thai noght—
Than was thare mekil° sorow unsoght.°   *great/unwanted*
Dore ne window was thare nane
800 Whare he myght oway gane.[2]
Thai said he sold thare be laft—[3]
Or els he cowth° of wechecraft,°   *knew the ways/witchcraft*
Or he cowth of nygromancy,°   *black magic*
Or he had wenges° for-to fly.   *wings*
805 Hastily than went thai all
And soght him in the maydens hall,
In chambers high (es noght at hide)[4]
And in solers° on ilka side.   *upper ("sun") rooms*
Sir Ywaine saw ful wele al that,
810 And still opon the bed he sat;
Thare was nane that anes° mynt°   *once/directed blows*
Unto the bed at° smyte° a dynt.°   *to/smite, strike/dint, blow*
All obout thai smate° so fast,   *smote, struck*
That mani of thaire wapins° brast;°   *weapons/broke*
815 Mekyl sorow thai made ilkane,
For thai ne myght wreke° thaire lord° bane.°   *avenge/lord's/destruction*
         Thai went oway with dreri° chere;°   *dreary, sad/countenance*
And sone thare-efter come the bere.°   *bier*
A lady folowd white so° mylk—   *as*
820 In al that land was none swilk.°   *such*
Sho wrang hir fingers—outbrast the blode.[5]

9. Here shall you be, in despite of all they can do.
1. For I shall do that which is agreeable to you, even if it gets me into trouble.
2. Where he might have got away. (The door through which the rescuing maid had passed
   earlier, ll. 697, 749, is either now considered by the knights to be unopenable from their side
   or is invisible to them—a feat quite possibly within the maid's capabilities, to judge from the
   magical ring she has given Ywain.)
3. I.e., they said that he should still be left lying there.
4. It (the fact) cannot be hidden.
5. She clenched her fingers—(so that) blood sprang forth (from her hands).

For mekyl wa° sho was nere wode;°   *woe, anguish / mad*
Hir fayre° hare° scho al to-drogh,°   *fair / hair / pulled out*
And ful oft° fel sho down in swogh.°   *often / swoon*
825   Sho wepe° with a ful dreri voice.   *wept*
The hali° water and the croyce°   *holy / cross*
Was born bifore the procession;
Thare folowd mani a moder° son.   *mother's*
Bifore the cors rade a knyght
830   On his stede that was ful wight,°   *strong*
In his armurs wele arayd,[6]
With spere and target gudely grayd.[7]
    Than Sir Ywayn herd the cry
And the dole of that fayre lady;
835   For more sorow myght nane° have   *no one*
Than sho had when he° went to grave.   *(the dead knight)*
Prestes° and monkes on thaire wyse[8]   *Priests*
Ful solempnly° did the servyse.°   *solemnly / service*
Als° Lunet[9] thare stode in the thrang,°   *As, While / throng, crowd*
840   Until Sir Ywaine thoght hir lang;[1]
Out of the thrang the wai° sho tase,°   *way / takes*
Unto Sir Ywaine fast sho gase.°   *goes*
Sho said, "Sir, how ertow stad?[2]
I hope° ful wele thou has bene rad."°   *expect / afraid*
845   "Sertes," he said, "thou sais° wele° thare;   *say / truly*
So abayst° was I never are."°   *abashed, dismayed / before*
    He said, "Leman,° I pray the,   *dear friend*
If it any wise may be
That I might luke a litel throw
850   Out at sum hole or sum window—[3]
For wonder fayn," he sayd, "wald I
Have a sight of the lady."
The maiden than ful sone unshet°   *opened*
In a place a prevé° weket.°   *secret / wicket gate*
855   Thare° of the lady he had a syght: *(From) there*
Lowd sho cried to God almyght,°   *almighty*
"Of his sins do hym pardowne,°   *pardon*
For sertanly in no regyowne°   *region*

6. The horse and armor may be that of the dead knight. This and the previous line are an addition by the English translator, perhaps reflecting a custom in Britain where important funerary processions included an effigy of the deceased or had a living person sporting such things as the armor or weapons of the deceased.
7. Well equipped with shield and lance.
8. In their way.
9. Though named for the first time here, Lunet is the maiden who has been helping Ywain. (See the extract from *Yvain* in the Sources and Backgrounds section, p. 337, in which Chrétien provides an etymology for the name.)
1. I.e., she grew concerned for Ywain.
2. I.e., how are you doing?
3. If it is at all possible that I might look for a brief time out of any small hole or window.

Was never knight of his bewté,°   *excellence*
860 Ne efter° him sal never nane be;   *after*
In al the werld° fro end to ende   *world*
Es none so curtayse° ne so hende.°   *courteous / gracious*
God grant the° grace thou mai won°   *thee / dwell*
In hevyn° with His owyn° Son;   *heaven / own*
865 For so large° lifes° none in° lede°   *generous / lives / among / people*
Ne none so doghty° of gude dede.'"°   *doughty, courageous / deeds*
When sho had thus made hir spell,°   *speech*
In swownyng° ful oft sithes° sho fell.   *swooning / times*

Now lat° we the lady be,   *let*
870 And of Sir Ywaine speke we.
Luf,° that es so mekil° of mayne,°   *Love / great / power*
Sare° had wownded° Sir Ywayne,   *Sorely / wounded*
That, whare-so° he sal ride or ga,   *wheresoever*
His hert sho has that es his fa.
875 His hert he has set al bydene
Whare himself dar noght be sene.[4]
Bot thus in langing° bides he   *longing*
And hopes that it sal better be.
Al° that war° at the enterement°   *All (those) / were / interment, burial*
880 Toke thaire leve at the lady gent,°   *gracious, noble*
And hame° now er thai halely° gane,   *home / wholly*
And the lady left allane°   *alone*
Dweland° with hir chamberere°   *Dwelling / lady-in-waiting*
And other mo that war hir dere.[5]
885 Than bigan hir noyes° al new;   *sorrows*
For sorow failed hir hide and hew.[6]
Unto his° sawl° was sho ful hulde;°   *(the dead knight's) / soul / devoted*
Opon a sawter al of gulde[7]
To say the Salmes° fast sho bigan   *Psalms*
890 And toke no tent° unto no man.   *notice*
Than had Sir Ywain mekyl drede,°   *dread, fear*
For he hoped° noght to spede;°   *expected / succeed*
He said, "I am mekil° to blame   *greatly*
That I luf tham that wald° me shame—   *would*
895 Bot yit I wite hir al with wogh,
Sen that I hir lord slogh.[8]
I can noght se, by nakyn° gyn,°   *no kind of / device, design*
How that I hir luf sold° wyn.°   *should / win*
That lady es ful gent and small,

---

4. His heart she possesses who is his enemy. He has altogether set his heart where he himself dare not be seen.
5. And others besides who were dear to her.
6. I.e., for sorrow she was drained of color.
7. Upon a psalter illuminated (or perhaps bound) in gold.
8. But I blame her wrongfully, since it was I who slew her lord.

900	Hir yghen° clere als es cristall;	*eyes*
	Sertes thare es no man olive°	*alive*
	That kowth° hir bewtese° wele descrive.”°	*could / beauty / describe*
	Thus was Syr Ywayne sted that sesowne;	
	He wroght ful mekyl ogayns resowne⁹	
905	To set his luf in swilk° a stede,°	*such / place*
	Whare thai hated him to the dede.°	*death*
	He sayd he sold have hir to° wive,°	*as / wife*
	Or els he sold lose his lyve.°	*life*
	Thus als he in stody° sat	*state of abstraction, perplexity*
910	The mayden come to him with that.¹	
	Sho sayd, “How hasto° farn° this day,	*hast thou / fared, done*
	Sen° that I went fro the oway?”	*Since*
	Sone° sho saw him pale and wan.°	*Immediately / wan, sickly*
	Sho wist° wele what him ayled° than;	*knew / ailed*
915	Sho said, “I wote° thi hert° es set,	*know (that) / heart*
	And sertes I ne sal noght it let,°	*hinder*
	Bot I sal help the fra° presowne°	*from, out of / prison*
	And bring the to thi warisowne.”°	*reward*
	He said, “Sertes, damysele,	
920	Out of this place wil I noght stele;°	*steal, sneak*
	Bot I wil wende° by dayes lyght,	*go*
	That° men may of me have sight	*(So) that*
	Opinly° on ilka° syde.	*Openly / every*
	Worth of me what so bityde,²	
925	Manly° wil I hethin° wende.”	*Courageously / from here*
	Than answerd the mayden hende,	
	“Sir, thow sal wend with honowre,	
	For thou sal have ful gude socowre;°	*succor, assistance*
	Bot, sir, thou sal be here sertayne°	*secure, safe*
930	A while unto° I cum ogayne.”	*until*
	Sho [wist] al trewly his entent,³	
	And tharfore es sho wightly° went	*quickly, directly*
	Unto the lady faire and bright°—	*splendid, beautiful*
	For unto hir right wele sho myght	
935	Say whatsom° hyr willes° es;	*whatsoever / desire*
	For sho was al° hir maystres,°	*altogether / confidante*
	Her keper,° and hir cownsaylere.°	*keeper, attendant / counselor*
	To hir sho said, als ye sal here,	
	Bytwix° tham twa° in gude cownsayl,	*Between / to*
940	“Madame,” sho sayd, “I have mervayl°	*marvel, wonder*

---

9. Thus was Ywain situated at that time; he worked very much against reason.
1. I.e., the maiden came to him then.
2. I.e., regardless of what becomes of me.
3. She knew his intentions fully. (The line as it exists in the manuscript lacks a verb. The chief editions supply *kend* (“knew, perceived”), but this particular form is attested nowhere in the text; *wist*, however, occurs more than two dozen times.)

That ye sorow thus ever on-ane.[4]
For Goddes luf, lat° be yowre mane°——   *let / moan, complaint*
Ye sold think over° alkyn° thyng   *above / all*
Of the Kinges Arthurgh cumyng.[5]
945   Menes° yow noght of the message   *Remember*
Of the Damysel Savage,
That in hir lettre° to yow send?[6]   *letter*
Allas, who sal yow° now defend   *(for) you*
Yowre land and al that es thareyn,°   *therein*
950   Sen° ye wil never of wepeing° blyn?°   *Since / weeping, mourning / cease*
A! Madame, takes tent to me![7]
Ye ne have na knyght in this cuntré
That durst right now his body bede[8]
For-to do a doghty dede,
955   Ne for-to bide° the mekil° boste°   *await / great / menace*
Of King Arthurgh and of his oste;°   *host, army*
And if he° find none hym ogayn,°   *(Arthur) / to oppose*
Yowre landes er° lorn°——this es sertayn!"   *are / lost*

The lady understode ful wele
960   How sho hyr cownsaild ilka° dele.°   *(in) every / part*
Sho bad° hyr go hir way smertly,°   *bade, ordered / quickly*
And that sho war° na more hardy°   *were, should be / daring (enough)*
Swilk wordes to hyr at° speke——   *to*
For wa° hir hert wold al to-breke.°   *woe, anguish / break asunder*
965   Sho bad, "Go wightly hethin° oway!"   *from here*
Than the maiden thus gan say,
"Madame, it es oft° wemens° will   *often / women's*
Tham for-to blame that sais tham scill."[9]
Sho went oway, als sho noght roght——[1]
970   And than the lady hyr bythoght°   *thought again, reflected*
That the maiden said no wrang;°   *wrong*
And so sho sat in stody lang.°   *long*
   In stody thus allane sho sat;
The mayden come ogayn° with that.   *again*
975   "Madame," she said, "ye er a barn!°   *child*
Thus may ye sone° yowre self for-farn."°   *soon, quickly / destroy*
Sho sayd, "Chastise° thi hert, madame;   *Control, Restrain*

---

4. That you mourn constantly in this way.
5. Of King Arthur's coming (cf. ll. 519–25).
6. Apart from being the author of the letter in question (evidently bearing news of Arthur's intended visit to the magical spring), the Damsel Savage ("Lady of the Wilds") remains an obscure figure; Chrétien's reference to her in *Yvain*, ll. 1619–21, is equally desultory. What is gained by such a precipitate reference, however, is a sense of the strange and exotic—a sense which may encourage one to be alive to the prospect of unforeseen and momentous incident (cf. the description of the hanging board at ll. 186–88).
7. Oh! Madam, take heed of me!
8. I.e., come forward (*lit.* offer his body).
9. For them to blame the one that speaks reason to them.
1. As if she thought nothing of it.

To swilk a lady it es grete° shame   *great*
Thus to wepe and make slike° cry—   *such*
980   Think opon thi grete gentri.°   *nobility*
Trowes thou the flowre of chevalry
Sold al with thi lord dy
And with him be put in molde?
God forbede that it so solde—
985   Als gude als he, and better, bene!"[2]
"Thou lyes!"° sho sayd, "by Hevyn° Quene!   *lie/Heaven*
    Lat° se if thou me tel kan,   *Let*
Whare es any so doghty man
Als he was that wedded me."
990   "Yis—and ye kun me na mawgré,[3]
And that ye mak° me sekernes°   *give/assurance*
That ye sal luf° me never the les."°   *love/less*
Sho said, "Thou may be ful sertayn
That for na thing that thou mai sayn°   *say*
995   Wil I me wreth° on° nane° manere."°   *become angry/in/no/manner*
"Madame," sho said, "than sal ye here.°   *hear*
I sal yow tel a preveté,°   *secret*
And na ma° sal it wit° bot we.   *more (people)/know*
    Yf twa° knyghtes be in the felde°   *two/(battle)field*
1000   On twa stedes with spere and shelde,
And the tane° the tother° may sla,°   *one/other/slay*
Whether° es the better of tha?"°   *which/those (two)*
Sho said, "He that has° the bataile."   *has (taken, won)*
"Ya," said the mayden, "sawnfayle°—   *without fail, certainly*
1005   The knyght that lifes° es mare° of maine°   *lives/greater/strength*
Than yowre lord that was slayne.
Yowre lord fled out of the place,
And the tother gan hym chace°   *chase*
Heder° into his awyn° halde;°   *Hither/own/(strong)hold*
1010   Thare° may ye wit,° he was ful balde."°   *(By) that/know/daring*
    The lady said, "this es grete scorne,°   *scorn, insult*
That thou nevyns° him me biforne;°   *mention/before, in front of*
Thou sais nowther° soth° ne right—   *neither/truth*
Swith,° out of myne eghen° syght!'   *Quick/eyes'*
1015   The mayden said, "So mot I the,
Thus ne hight ye noght me—
That ye sold so me myssay!"[4]
With that sho turned hir oway,°   *away*
And hastily sho went ogayn

---

2. Do you believe that the flower (i.e., the supreme achievement) of all knighthood must die with
   your lord and be put into the earth with him? God forbid that it should be so—there are
   (knights) as good as he, and better!
3. Yes—if you can (then) bear me no ill will.
4. As I hope to thrive, this is not what you promised me—that you would speak ill of me!

1020 Unto the chameber, to Sir Ywayne.
      The lady thoght than al the nyght,
  How that sho had na knyght
  For-to seke hir land thorghout[5]
  To kepe° Arthurgh and hys rowt.°   *receive, withstand / company*
1025 Than bigan hir for-to shame°   *grow ashamed*
  And hirself fast for-to blame.
  Unto hirself fast gan sho flyte°   *quarrel*
  And said, "With wrang now I hir wite;[6]
  Now hopes° sho I wil never mare   *expects, believes*
1030 Luf hir als I have done are.°   *before*
  I wil hir luf with main and mode;[7]
  For that° sho said was for my gode."°   *that (which) / good*
      On the morn the mayden rase,°   *rose*
  And unto chamber sone sho gase.°   *goes*
1035   Thare sho fyndes the faire lady
  Hingand° hir hevyd° ful drerily°   *Hanging / head / drearily*
  In the place whare sho hir left;
  And ilka° dele° sho talde hir eft,°   *every / part / again*
  Als sho had said to hir bifore.
1040 Than said the lady, "Me rewes° sore,° *rue, regret / sorely, bitterly*
  That I missayd° the yisterday;   *spoke ill of*
  I wil amend,° if that I may.   *make amends*
  Of that knyght now wald I here,°   *hear*
  What he war and whethen he were.[8]
1045 I wate° that I have sayd omys;°   *know / amiss*
  Now wil I do als thou me wys°—   *direct*
  Tel me baldely,° or° thou blin,°   *plainly / before / cease*
  If he be cumen of gentil kyn."[9]
  "Madame," sho said, "I dar° warand,°   *dare / warrant*
1050 A genteler° lord es none lifand.°   *more noble / living*
  The hendest° man ye sal him fynde   *most gracious*
  That ever come of Adams kynde."[1]
    "How hat° he? Sai° me for sertayne." *(is) called / Tell*
  "Madame," sho said, "Sir Ywayne.
1055 So gentil knight have ye noght sene—
  He es the Kings son Uryene."[2]
  Sho held hir° paid° of that tithyng,° *herself / satisfied / tiding, news*
  For that his fader° was a kyng: *father*
  "Do° me have him here in my sight   *Cause to*
1060 Bitwene this° and the thrid° night—   *this (night) / third*

5. I.e., even if she would seek (one) throughout her lands.
6. I blame her unjustly.
7. I.e., with strength and conviction.
8. Who he was and whence he came.
9. If he is descended from nobility.
1. I.e., who was ever born of man.
2. See l. 732, n.

	And are,° if that it are myght be.	*earlier*
	Me langes° sare° him for-to se—	*long* / *sorely*
	Bring him, if thou mai,° this night."	*may*
	"Madame," sho sayd, "that I ne might,	
1065	For his wonyng es hethin oway,³	
	More than the jorné° of a day—	*journey*
	Bot I have a wele-rinand° page,	*well-running, swift*
	Wil stirt thider right in a stage⁴	
	And bring him by to-morn° at nyght."	*tomorrow*
1070	The lady saide, "Loke° yf he myght	*See*
	To-morn by evyn° be here ogayn."	*evening*
	Sho said, "Madame, with al his mayn!"	
	"Bid him hy° on alkyn° wyse;°	*hasten* / *every* / *way*
	He sal be quit° wele his° servyse—	*paid* / *(for) his*
1075	Avancement° sal be hys bone°	*Advancement, Preferment* / *boon, reward*
	If he wil do this erand sone."	
	"Madame," sho said, "I dar yow hight°	*promise*
	To have him here or the thrid nyght.	
	Towhils° efter° yowre kownsayl° send	*Meanwhile* / *after, for* / *council*
1080	And ask tham wha sal yow° defend	*(for) you*
	Yowre well, yowre land, kastel and towre,	
	Ogayns the nobil King Arthure—	
	For thare es nane of tham ilkane⁵	
	That dar the batel undertane.°	*undertake*
1085	Than sal ye say, 'Nedes bus me take⁶	
	A lorde to do that° ye forsake—'	*that (which)*
	Nedes bus yow have sum nobil knyght,	
	That wil and may defend yowre right;	
	And sais also, to suffer ded,	
1090	Ye wil noght do out of thaire rede.⁷	
	Of that worde sal thai be blyth°	*blithe, pleased*
	And thank yow ful many sithe."°	*times*
	The lady said, "By God of myght,	
	I sal areson° tham this night.	*question*
1095	Me think thou dwelles ful° lang here;	*fully, too*
	Send forth swith° thi messangere."	*at once*
	Than was the lady blith and glad.	
	Sho did al als° hir mayden bad:	*as*
	Efter hir cownsail° sho sent onane°	*council* / *anon, forthwith*
1100	And bad thai sold° cum sone° ilkane.	*should* / *soon*
	The maiden redies° hyr° ful rath;°	*readies* / *herself* / *quickly*
	Bilive° sho gert° Syr Ywaine bath°	*Quickly* / *had* / *bathe*

3. Because his dwelling is (some distance) away from here.
4. Who will rush there without stopping.
5. I.e., for there is not one of them.
6. It is necessary for me to take.
7. I.e., on your life, you will not go against their advice.

And cled° him sethin° in gude scarlet°　　　*clad, cloathed / then / scarlet cloth*
　　　Forord° wele and with gold fret,°　　　　*Furred / wire fretting, purl*
1105　A girdel° ful riche for the nanes°　　　　　*belt / occasion*
　　　Of perry° and of preciows° stanes.°　　　　*jewels / precious / stones*
　　　Sho talde him al how he sold do,
　　　When that he come the lady to.
　　　　　And thus when he was al redy,
1110　Sho went and talde to hyr lady
　　　That cumen° was hir messagere.　　　　　　*come, returned*
　　　Sho° said smertly, "Do lat° me here°—　　　*(The lady) / let / hear*
　　　Cumes he sone, als have thou wyn?"[8]
　　　"Medame," sho said, "I sal noght blin,°　　　*cease*
1115　Or° that he be byfor yow here."　　　　　　*Until*
　　　Than said the lady with light° chere,°　　　*joyful / disposition*
　　　"Go, bring him heder,° prevely,°　　　　　　*hither / secretly*
　　　That° none wit° bot thou and I."　　　　　　*(So) that / know*
　　　　　Than the maiden went ogayn
1120　Hastily to Sir Ywayn.
　　　"Sir," sho sayd, "als have I wyn,[9]
　　　My lady wate° thou ert hereyn.°　　　　　　*knows / herein*
　　　To cum bifore hir luke° thou be balde,°　　　*see that / bold*
　　　And tak gode tent° what I have talde."　　　*heed (to)*
1125　By the hand sho toke the knyght
　　　And led him unto chamber right,
　　　Byfor hir lady—es noght at layne—[1]
　　　And of that come° was sho ful fayne.°　　　*coming, arrival / pleased*
　　　Bot yit Sir Ywayne had grete drede,°　　　*dread, fear*
1130　When he unto chamber yede.°　　　　　　　*went*
　　　　　The chamber flore° and als the bed　　　*floor*
　　　With klothes° of gold was al overspred.　　*cloths*
　　　Hir° thoght he was withowten lac;°　　　　*She (the lady) / lack, flaw*
　　　Bot no word to him sho spak—
1135　And, for dred, oway he drogh.°　　　　　　*drew*
　　　Than the mayden stode and logh;°　　　　　*laughed*
　　　Sho sayd, "Mawgré have that knyght
　　　That haves of swilk a lady syght
　　　And can noght shew to hir his nede.[2]
1140　Cum furth,° sir; the thar° noght drede　　　*forth / need*
　　　That mi lady wil the smyte!°　　　　　　　*smite, strike*
　　　Sho loves[3] the wele, withouten lite.[4]

8. I.e., so may you have joy.
9. So may I have joy.
1. (It) is not to be hidden.
2. May that knight receive ill will who has sight of such a lady and cannot declare to her his concerns.
3. From the context it is clear that "loves" cannot have the full modern sense of the word; the sense rather is that of "commends" or "values." Throughout this scene (to l. 1188) it is important to distinguish the lady's motives from those of Ywain; she is engaging him in a practical contract without any additional desire to requite his love.
4. Without fail.

Pray to hir of hir mercy
(And for thi sake right so sal I)
1145 That sho forgif the in this stede
Of Salados the Rouse ded[5]
That was hir lord, that thou has slayne."
On knese° him set than Syr Ywaine: (his) knees
"Madame, I yelde° me yow untill°   yield / unto
1150 Ever to be at yowre wyll
Yf that I might;° I ne wald noght fle."°   may / flee
Sho said, "Nay, whi sold so be?°   (it) be
To ded yf I gert do the now,
To me it war ful litel prow.[6]
1155 Bot for° I find the so bowsum°   because / willing, yielding
That thou wald thus to me cum,
And for thou dose the in my grace,[7]
I forgif° the thi trispase.°   forgive / trespass, offense
Syt down," sho said, "and lat me here,
1160 Why thou ert thus debonere."°   debonair, gracious
"Madame," he said, "anis° with a luke°   once / look, glance
Al my hert with the thou toke;
Sen° I first of the had syght,   Since
Have I the lufed with al my might.
1165 To mo than the, mi lady hende,
Sal never more my luf wende;[8]
For thi luf ever I am redy
Lely° for-to lif° or dy."   Loyally / live
Sho said, "Dar° thou wele undertake   Dare
1170 In my land pese° for-to make   peace
And for-to maintene al mi rightes
Ogayns King Arthure and his knyghtes?"
He said, "That dar I undertane—
Ogaynes ilka° lyfand° man."   each / living
1175 Sho said, "Sir, than er° we at ane."°   are / one
Swilk kownsail byfore had sho tane:[9]
Hir barons hir ful rathly° red°   quickly / (had) advised
To tak a lord hir for-to wed.
Than hastily sho went to hall;
1180 Thare abade° hir barons all   waited

---

5. Of the death of Salados the Rouse. (The name of the knight approximates "Esclados le Ros,"
   Esclados "the Red," the name given him in Chrétien's *Ywain*. It is not clear whether the name
   was chosen by Chrétien for any particular reason; the mentioning of the name is, however,
   as evocatively precipitate as that of the Damsel Savage at l. 946.)
6. If I were to have you put to death now, it would be of little advantage to me.
7. I.e., and because you put yourself at my mercy.
8. I.e., my love shall never go beyond you, my gracious lady.
9. I.e., she had taken the following advice beforehand. (The implication is, as is explicit in
   Chrétien, ll. 2038–39, that the lady has already met with her barons once. This and the
   previous line are transposed in the manuscript, thus making the sense difficult; the current
   order reproduces that of Chrétien.)

For-to hald° thaire parlement°	hold / discussion
And mari° hir by thaire asent.°	marry / assent
Sho sayd, "Sirs, with an° acorde,°	one / accord
Sen° me bus° nedely° have a lord	Since / must / necessarily
1185 My landes for-to lede° and yeme,°	lead, oversee / guard, protect
Sais° me sone howe ye wil deme."°	Tell / deem, judge
"Madame," thai said, "how so ye will,[1]	
Al we sal assent thartyll."°	thereto
Than the lady went ogayne	
1190 Unto chameber to Sir Ywaine.	
"Sir," sho said, "so God me save,	
Other° lorde wil I nane have;	Another
If I the left, I did noght right,	
A king son and a noble knyght.[2]	
1195 Now has the maiden done° hir thoght,°	fulfilled / intention
Sir Ywayne out of anger° broght.	trouble, misfortune
The lady led him unto hall;	
Ogains° him rase° the barons all,	Before / rose
And al thai said ful sekerly,°	certainly
1200 "This knight sal wed the lady."	
And ilkane° said thamself bitwene	each one
So° faire a man had thai noght sene—	(That) so
"For his bewté in hal and bowre	
Him semes to be an emperowre;[3]	
1205 We wald° that thai war trowth-plight°	would (have it) / betrothed
And weded sone°—this ilk° nyght."	soon, quickly / same
The lady set hir on the dese°	dais, raised platform
And cumand° al to hald° thaire pese,°	commanded / hold / peace
And bad hir Steward[4] sumwhat° say	something
1210 Or° men went fra cowrt oway.	Before
The Steward said, "Sirs, understandes,	
Were° es waxen° in thir° landes;	War / grown / these
The King Arthure es redy dight°	prepared
To be here byn° this fowretenyght.°	within / fortnight
1215 He and his menyé ha thoght[5]	
To win this land if thai moght.°	might, may
Thai wate° ful wele that he es ded	know
That was lord here in this stede°—	place
None es so wight° wapins° to welde°	strong / weapons / wield
1220 Ne that so boldly mai us belde.°	protect

1. Howsoever you wish (it).
2. I.e., if I rejected you, (who are) a king's son and a noble knight, I will have done wrong.
3. I.e., because of his excellence in courtly circumstances (lit., in hall and chamber), it would be fitting for him to be an emperor.
4. A steward is the head administrative official of an estate, typically responsible for managing the property and its finances. This particular Steward figures later in the poem as the persecutor of Lunet (see ll. 2163–64, 2555–2621).
5. He and his company intend.

And wemen may maintene° no stowre;°   *maintain, sustain / battle*
Thai most° nedes° have   *must / necessarily*
 a governowre.°   *governor, male master*
Tharfor mi lady most nede
Be weded hastily for drede;°   *dread, fear*
1225 And to na lord wil sho tak tent,[6]
Bot if it be by yowre assent."
  Than the lordes al on raw[7]
Held tham wele payd° of this saw;°   *pleased / speech*
Al assented hyr untill°   *unto*
1230 To tak a lord at hyr owyn wyll.
Than said the lady onone right,
"How hald ye yow paid of this knight?
He profers hym on al wyse[8]
To myne honore and my servyse;
1235 And sertes, sirs, the soth° to say   *truth*
(I saw him never or° this day,   *before*
Bot talde° unto me has it bene),   *told*
He es the Kyng son Uriene.[9]
He es cumen of hegh° parage°   *high / rank, birth*
1240 And wonder doghty of vasselage.°   *prowess*
War° and wise and ful curtayse,   *Wary, careful*
He yernes° me to° wife alwayse° *yearns for / as / in every way*
(And, nere-the-lese, I wate he might
Have wele better—and so war right)."[1]
1245 With a° voice halely° thai sayd, *one / wholly, together*
"Madame, ful wele we hald us payd.
Bot hastes° fast, al that ye may,[2]   *hasten*
That° ye war wedded this ilk day."   *(So) that*
And grete prayer° gan thai make   *pleas, entreaties*
1250 On al wise that sho suld hym take.
Sone unto the kirk° thai went   *church*
And war wedded in thaire° present.° *their (the barons') / presence*
Thare wedded Ywaine in plevyne°   *pledge*
The riche lady Alundyne,
1255 The Dukes doghter of Landuit—[3]
Els° had hyr lande bene destruyt.° *(Or) else / destroyed*
Thus thai made the maryage

---

6. I.e., will she pay attention.
7. Together (*lit.*, in a row).
8. In every way.
9. See l. 732.
1. I.e., and nevertheless, I know that he could have better (than I)—and rightfully so.
2. As much as you can.
3. Alundyne, the daughter of the Duke of Landuit. (The name Alundyne probably results from
the misreading of *a Laudine* ("to Laudine") at l. 2151 of the translator's source copy of Chrétien.
Chrétien names the lady nowhere else in his poem, and the name Laudine is not recorded
elsewhere in Arthurian literature. The name of Landuit is derived from some form of *Laudunet*
in Chrétien; it is possible that the name refers to the region of Lothian in Scotland.)

Omang al the riche barnage;°   *baronage*
Thai made ful mekyl° mirth that day,   *great*
1260 Ful grete festes° on gude aray.[4]   *feasts*
      Grete mirthes made thai in that stede.
And al forgetyn° es now the ded°   *forgotten / death*
Of him° that was thaire lord fre;°   *(Salados) / gracious*
Thai say that this es worth swilk thre,[5]
1265 And that thai lufed him mekil° more   *much*
Than him that lord was thare° byfore.   *there*
The bridal° sat,° for soth to tell,   *wedding feast / lasted*
Til Kyng Arthure come° to the well   *came*
With al his knyghtes everilkane°—   *each one*
1270 Byhind leved° thare noght ane.   *was left, remained*
      Than sayd Sir Kay, "Now whare es he
That made slike bost° here for-to be   *boast*
For-to venge° his cosyn germayne?[6]   *avenge*
I wist° his wordes war al in vayne;°   *knew / vain*
1275 He made grete boste bifor the Quene,
And here now dar he noght be sene.
His prowd wordes er now al purst,°   *withdrawn*
For, in fayth, ful ill he durst
Anes luke opon that knyght
1280 That he made bost with to fyght."[7]
      Than sayd Gawayn, hastily,
"Syr, for Goddes luf, mercy!°   *(have) mercy*
For I dar hete° the for sertayne   *promise*
That we sal here° of Sir Ywayne   *hear*
1285 This ilk day, that° be thou balde,°   *(of) that / confident*
Bot he be ded or done in halde—[8]
And never in no cumpany
Herd I him speke the° velany."°   *(of) thee / insulting things*
Than sayd Sir Kay, "Lo!° At thi will   *Look, Behold*
1290 Fra this time forth I sal be still."°   *silent*

      The King kest° water on the stane;   *cast*
The storme rase ful sone° onane°   *soon, quickly / anon, forthwith*
With wikked weders,° kene° and calde,°   *storms / sharp / cold*
Als° it was byforehand talde.   *As*
1295 The King and his men ilkane
Wend° tharwith to have bene slane,°   *Expected / slain*
So blew it store° with slete and rayn—   *fiercely, violently*
And hastily than Syr Ywayne

---

4. I.e., in fitting splendor.
5. I.e., they say that this new knight is worth three of the old.
6. See l. 458.
7. For, in truth, with great displeasure would he dare (even) once look upon that knight with whom he boasted he would fight.
8. Unless he is dead or imprisoned.

Dight° him graythly° in his gere,°   *Dressed/readily/equipment*
1300 With nobil shelde° and strong spere.°   *shield/spear, lance*
    When he was dight in seker° wede,°   *sure, reliable/armor*
Than he umstrade° a nobil stede;   *bestrode, mounted*
Him thoght that he was als lyght°   *light, unrestrained*
Als a fowl es to the flyght.
1305 Unto the well fast wendes° he;   *goes*
And sone, when thai myght him se,
Syr Kay—for he wald noght fayle°—   *fail (to do so)*
Smertly° askes° the batayl.   *Promptly/requests*
And alsone° than said the Kyng,   *immediately*
1310 "Sir Kay, I grante the thine askyng."°   *asking, request*
    Than Sir Ywayn neghed° tham nere°   *nighed, approached/near*
Thaire cowntenance° to se and here;°   *countenance/hear*
Sir Kay than on his stede gan spring—
"Bere° the wele now," sayd the Kyng.   *Bear, Conduct*
1315 Ful glad and blith° was Syr Ywayne   *blithe, pleased*
When Sir Kay come him ogayn.°   *against, toward*
Bot Kay wist noght wha° it was—   *who*
He findes his fere° now or° he pas;°   *match/before/leaves*
Syr Ywaine thinkes now to be wroken°   *avenged*
1320 On the grete° wordes that Kay has spoken.   *great, big*

    Thai rade togeder with speres kene°—   *sharp*
Thare was no reverence tham bitwene.
Sir Ywayn gan Sir Kay bere
Out of his sadel lenkith° of his spere;   *(the) length*
1325 His helm unto the erth smate°—   *smote, struck*
A fote° depe° tharein yt bate.°   *foot/deep/bit, dug in*
He° wald do him na more despite,°   *(Ywain)/humiliation*
Bot down he lighted als tyte;⁹
Syr Kay° stede he toke in hy°   *Kay's/haste*
1330 And presand° the King ful curtaysly.   *presented (it) to*
Wonder glad than war thai all
That Kay so fowl a shame gan fall;°   *fall (into)*
And ilkone° sayd til° other then,   *each one/to*
"This es he that scornes al men"—
1335 Of his wa war thai wele paid!¹
    Syr Ywain than to the Kyng said,
"Sir Kyng, I gif to the this stede,
For he may help the in thi nede;
And to me war it grete trispas°   *trespass, offense*
1340 For-to withhald that° yowres was."   *that (which)*
"What man ertow?"° quod° the Kyng,   *art thou/said*
"Of the have I na knawyng,

9. But he dismounted immediately.
1. They were very pleased with his misery!

Bot if thou unarmed were,
Or els thi name that I might here."[2]
1345 "Lord," he sayd, "I am Ywayne!"
Than was the King ferly° fayne.°   wondrously / pleased
    A sari° man than was Sir Kay,   sorry
That said that he° was stollen° oway;   (Ywain) / stolen, fled
Al descumfite° he lay on grownde—   overcome
1350 To him that was a sary stownde!°   time
The King and his men war ful glad,
That thai so Syr Ywayne had;
And ful glad was Sir Gawayne
Of the welefare° of Sir Ywayne—   success
1355 For nane was to him half so dere
Of al that in the court were.
The King Sir Ywayn sone bisoght°   asked
To tel him al how he had wroght;°   done
And sone Sir Ywaine gan him tell
1360 Of al his fare° how it byfell—   experience
With the knight° how that he sped,°   (Salados) / succeeded
And how he had the lady wed,
And how the mayden hym helped wele°—   well
Thus tald he to him ilka° dele.°   every / part

1365 "Sir Kyng," he sayd, "I yow byseke°   beseech, ask
And al yowre menyé° milde and meke,   company
That ye wald grante to me that grace
At° wend° with me to my purchace,°   To / go / acquired property
And se my kastel and my towre;
1370 Than myght ye do me grete honowre."
The Kyng granted him ful right°   privilege
To dwel with him a fowretenyght;°   fortnight
Sir Ywayne thanked him oft° sith.°   often, many / times
The knyghtes war° al glad and blyth   were
1375 With Sir Ywaine for-to wend—
And sone a squier has he send;°   sent
Unto the kastel the way he nome°   took
And warned the lady of thaire come,°   coming
And that his lord come° with the Kyng.   was coming
1380 And when the lady herd this thing,
It es no lifand man with mowth
That half hir cumforth tel kowth.[3]
    Hastily that lady hende°   gracious
Cumand° al hir men to wende   Commanded
1385 And dight tham in thaire best aray°   clothing

2. I.e., I have no way of knowing who you are, unless you remove your armor, or unless I might
    hear your name.
3. I.e., there is no man alive who could describe half her delight.

To kepe° the King that ilk° day.   *receive / same*
Thai keped him in riche wede°   *clothing*
Rydeand° on many a nobil stede;   *Riding*
Thai hailsed° him ful curtaysly   *hailed, greeted*
1390 And also al his cumpany—
Thai said he was worthy to dowt°   *fear, respect*
That so fele° folk led obowt.   *many*
Thare was grete joy, I yow bihete,°   *assure*
With clothes° spred in ilka strete°   *(rich) cloths / path*
1395 And damysels danceand° ful wele   *dancing*
With trompes,° pipes, and with fristele.°   *trumpets / flute*
The castel and the ceté° rang   *city*
With mynstralsi and nobil sang°—   *song*
Thai ordand° tham ilkane in-fere°   *made ready / together*
1400 To kepe° the King on° faire manere.   *accommodate / in*
      The lady went withowten° towne   *outside*
And with hir many bald° barowne°   *bold / baron*
Cled° in purpure and ermyne⁴   *Clad*
With girdels° al of gold ful fyne.   *belts*
1405 The lady made ful meri chere;
Sho was al dight with drewries dere.⁵
Abowt hir was ful mekyl° thrang;°   *great / throng, crowd*
The puple cried and sayd omang,°   *among (themselves)*
"Welkum ertou,° Kyng Arthoure.   *art thou*
1410 Of al this werld thou beres the flowre,⁶
Lord, Kyng of all kynges—
And blissed be he that the brynges."°   *brings (here)*
      When the lady the Kyng saw,
Unto him fast gan sho draw
1415 To hald his sterap° whils he lyght.°   *stirrup / alighted*
Bot sone° when he of hir had syght,   *immediately*
With mekyl myrth thai samen° met.   *together*
With hende° wordes sho him gret°—   *gracious / greeted*
"A thowsand sithes welkum," sho says,
1420 "And so es Sir Gawayne the curtayse."
      The King said, "Lady white so° flowre,   *as*
God gif the joy and mekil° honowre,   *great*
For thou ert fayre with body gent.°   *delicate*
With that he hir in armes hent,°   *took*
1425 And ful fair gan hir falde°—   *embrace*
Thare was many to bihalde.⁷
It° es no man with tong° may tell   *There / tongue*

4. See the notes to 11. 203–04.
5. The lady put on a merry display; she was endowed with expensive gifts of affection.
6. I.e., you are the best.
7. There were many people to behold that. (The Middle English text at this point omits a passage
   in Chrétien describing the relationship which develops between Gawain and Lunet; for the
   passage in Chrétien, see the Sources and Backgrounds section, p. 337.)

The mirth that was tham omell;°   *among*
Of maidens was thare so gude wane[8]
1430 That ilka° knight myght tak° ane.°   *each / accompany / one*
Ful mekil joy Syr Ywayn made
That he the King til° his hows° hade;°   *at / house / had*
The lady omang tham al samen
Made ful mekyl joy and gamen.°   *game, amusement*
1435 In the kastel thus thai dwell;
Ful mekyl myrth wase tham omell.
The King was thare with his knyghtes
Aght° dayes and aght nyghtes,   *Eight*
And Ywayn tham ful mery made
1440 With alkyn° gamyn tham for glade°—   *every kind of / to gladden*
He prayed the Kyng to thank the may°   *maid (lunet)*
That hym° had helpid in his jornay.   *(Ywain)*
And ilk day had thai solace° sere°   *(the) delight / various*
Of huntyng and als of revere°—   *hawking beside a river*
1445 For thare was a ful fayre cuntré,°   *country*
With wodes and parkes grete plenté°   *plenty*
And castels wroght with lyme° and stane,°   *mortar / stone*
That Ywayne with° his wife had tane.°   *through / acquired*

Now wil the King no langer lende,°   *delay*
1450 Bot til° his cuntré wil he wende.°   *to / go*
Aywhils° thai war thare, for sertayne,   *All the while*
Syr Gawayn did al his° mayne°   *(in) his / power*
To pray Sir Ywaine on al manere
For-to wende with tham in-fere.°   *together*
1455 He said, "Sir, if thou ly° at hame,°   *lie, stay / home*
Wonderly men wil the blame.
That knyght es nothing to set by[9]
That leves° al his chevalry   *leaves*
And ligges° bekeand° in his bed   *lies / warming (himself)*
1460 When he haves° a lady wed.   *has*
For when that he has grete endose,°   *backing, support*
Than war tyme to win his lose;°   *honor*
For when a knyght es chevalrouse,
His lady es the more jelows°—   *jealous*
1465 Also sho lufes him wele the bet.°   *better*
Tharfore, sir, thou sal noght let°   *cease*
To haunt armes in ilk cuntré;[1]
Than wil men wele more prayse the.
Thou hase inogh to thi despens;[2]
1470 Now may thow wele hante° turnamentes.   *attend to*

8. There was such abundance.
9. That knight is not to be valued.
1. To attend to deeds of arms in every country.
2. I.e., you now have enough resources at your disposal.

Thou and I sal wende in-fere,
And I will be at thi banere.[3]
    I dar° noght say, so God me glad,°   *dare/gladden*
If I so fayre a leman° had,   *mistress*
1475   That I ne most leve al chevalry[4]
At hame ydel° with hir to ly°—   *idly/lie, stay*
Bot yit a fole that litel kan
May wele cownsail another man."[5]
So lang Sir Gawayn prayed so,
1480   Syr Ywayne grantes° him for-to go   *agrees with*
Unto the lady and tak his leve
(Loth° him was hir for-to greve).°   *Loath, Unwilling/grieve, offend*
Til° hyr onane° the way he nome°   *to/anon, forthwith/took*
(Bot sho ne wist noght whi he come);
1485   In his arms he gan hir mete,°   *embrace*
And thus he said, "My leman swete,
My life, my hele,° and al my hert,   *salvation*
My joy, my comfort,° and my quert,°   *comfort/health*
A thing prai I the unto[6]
1490   For thine honore and myne also."
    The lady said, "Sir, verrayment,°   *truly*
I wil do al yowre cumandment."°   *commandment*
"Dame, he said, "I wil the pray
That I might the King cumvay°   *accompany*
1495   And also with my feres° founde,°   *companions/set out*
Armes for-to haunte a stownde—[7]
For in bourding° men wald me blame   *joking*
If I sold° now dwel° at hame."   *should/dwell, stay*
    The lady was loth him to greve.
1500   "Sir," sho said, "I gif yow leve
Until a terme° that I sal sayn°—   *final date/declare*
Bot° that ye cum than° ogayn.   *Provided/then, at that time*
Al this yere hale° I yow grante   *whole, entire*
Dedes° of armes for-to hante°—   *Deeds/attend to*
1505   Bot, syr, als° ye luf me dere,   *as*
On al wise that ye be here
This day twelmoth, how som it be,[8]
For the luf ye aw° to me.   *owe*
And if ye com noght by that day,
1510   My luf sal ye lose for ay.°   *ever*

---

3. And I will go under your banner (i.e., I will go by your side).
4. I.e., that I must abandon all knightly deeds.
5. I.e., and yet a fool who cannot advise himself will still try to advise another man.
6. I ask one thing of you.
7. To attend to deeds of arms for a time.
8. In every way (i.e., without exception) see that you are here a year (*lit.* a twelvemonth) today, regardless of what happens.

Avise yow wele now or ye gone—[9]
This day es the evyn of Saint Jon—[1]
That° warn I yow now or ye wende;   (Of) that
Luke° ye cum by the twelmoth ende."   See that
1515   "Dame," he sayd, "I sal noght let°   fail
To hald the day[2] that thou has set—
And if I might be at my wyll,
Ful oft are sold I cum the till—[3]
Bot, madame, this understandes,
1520   A man that passes° divers° landes   passes (through) / diverse
May sum tyme cum° in° grete destres,°   enter / into / distress
In preson° or els in sekenes;°   prison / sickness
Tharfore I pray yow, or I ga,
That ye wil out-tak thir twa."[4]
1525   The lady sayd, "This grant I wele,
Als ye ask, everilka° dele.°   every / part
And I sal lene° to yow my ring,   lend
That es to me a ful dere thing;
In nane anger° sal ye be—   trouble, misfortune
1530   Whils° ye it have and thinkes on me.   Whilst
   I sal tel to yow onane
The vertu° that es in the stane: magic power
It° es na preson° yow sal halde,°   There / prison / hold
Al° if yowre fase° be manyfalde;°   Even / foes / manifold
1535   With sekenes sal ye noght be tane,°   taken
Ne of yowre blode° ye sal lese° nane;   blood / lose
In batel tane sal ye noght be—
Whils ye it have and thinkes on me.
And aywhils° ye er trew of love,   all the while
1540   Over al sal ye be obove.[5]
I wald never for nakyn wight
Lene it are, unto na knyght—[6]
For grete luf I it yow take.°   give
Yemes° it wele now, for my sake."   Care for

9. Take you good heed before you go.
1. Cf. l. 525.
2. To keep the appointment.
3. And if I had it my way, I would return to you often before then.
4. That you will except those two (conditions).
5. You will be above everything (i.e., you will be triumphant).
6. I would never before lend it to any kind of man, unto no knight. (If Salados the Rouse had received this favor, he would, presumably, not have been defeated by Ywain. Two implications may be drawn from the lady's admission: that her past marriage, despite her extravagant grief at its end, was largely contractual—much after the fashion of the marriage with Ywain; and that her sense of attachment to Ywain is now growing beyond the contractual. Cf. the next line, which seems to signal a turning point in her feelings; cf. also l. 1624. It would perhaps be unwise, however, too much to psychologize Alandyne's gesture retrospectively; the ring—mentioned again only when it is taken back, ll. 1628–32—serves principally to focus our attention on the issue of what genuine truth and loyalty involve. Note, indeed, how the appeal to loyalty is stressed in the account of the ring, through repetition at ll. 1530 and 1538.)

1545	Sir Ywayne said, "Dame, gramercy."°	*many thanks*
	Than he gert ordain in hy[7]	
	Armurs and al other gere—	
	Stalworth° stedes, both sheld and spere,°	*Stalwart, Strong / spear, lance*
	And also squyere, knave,° and swayne.°	*knave, male servant / swain, youth*
1550	(Ful glad and blith was Sir Gawayne!)	
	No lenger wald Syr Ywayne byde;	
	On his stede sone° gan he stride,°	*soon / bestride, mount*
	And thus he has his leve tane—	
	For him murned° many ane.°	*mourned / a one*
1555	The lady toke leve of the Kyng	
	And of his menyé,° ald° and ying.°	*company / old / young*
	Hir lord Sir Ywayne sho bisekes,°	*beseeches, asks*
	With teris° trikland° on hir chekes,	*tears / trickling*
	On al wise that he noght let°	*fail*
1560	To halde° the day that he had set.	*hold (to), keep*
	The knightes thus thaire ways er went	
	To justing° and to turnament.	*jousting*
	Ful dughtily° did Sir Ywayne,	*doughtily*
	And also did Sir Gawayne.	
1565	Thai war ful doghty both in-fere°—	*together*
	Thai wan° the prise° both fer° and nere.	*won / prize / far*
	The Kyng that time at Cester° lay;	*Chester*
	The knightes went tham° for-to play.°	*themselves / amuse*
	Ful really° thai rade° obout	*royally / rode*
1570	Al that twelmoth, out and out,[8]	
	To justing and to turnament.	
	Thai wan grete wirships° als thai went;	*honors*
	Sir Ywaine oft had al the lose°—	*honor*
	Of him the word ful wide gose.°	*goes*
1575	Of thaire dedes was grete renown	
	To and fra° in towre° and towne.	*fro / castle*
	On this wise° in this life° thai last°—	*way / way of life / continued*
	Unto° Saint Johns day was past.	*Until*
	Than hastily thai hied° home,	*hurried*
1580	And sone unto the Kyng thai come;	
	And thare thai held grete mangeri,°	*feasting*
	The Kyng with al his cumpany.	
	Sir Ywaine umbithoght° him than—	*reminded*
	He had forgeten his leman!°	*mistress*
1585	"Broken I have hir cumandment!	
	Sertes," he said, "now be I shent!°	*ruined*
	The terme es past that sho me set—	
	How ever sal this bale° be bet?"°	*harm / mended*

7. Then he had made ready in haste.
8. I.e., through and through, entirely.

Unnethes° he might him hald fra wepe;°   *With difficulty / weeping*
1590 And right in this than toke he kepe:[9]
Into court come a damysele
On a palfray° ambland° wele.   *riding horse / ambling*
  And egerly° down gan sho lyght°   *eagerly, intently / alight*
Withouten help of knave or knyght;
1595 And sone sho lete hyr mantel° fall   *cloak*
And hasted hir fast into hall.
"Syr Kyng," sho sayd, "God mot the se,[1]
My lady gretes the wele by me,
And also Sir gude Gawayne,
1600 And al thi knyghtes—bot° Sir Ywayne;   *except*
He es ateyned° for° trayture,°   *attainted, convicted / as / traitor*
A fals and lither° losenjoure.°   *contemptible / flatterer*
  He has bytrayed my lady,
Bot sho es war with his gilry.[2]
1605 Sho hopid° noght, the soth to say,   *trusted*
That he wald so have stollen° oway;   *stolen, sneaked*
He made to hir ful mekyl° boste°   *great / boast*
And said of al he lufed hir moste.
Al was treson and trechery—
1610 And that° he sal ful dere° haby.°   *(for) that / dearly / pay*
It es ful mekyl° ogains° the right   *greatly / against*
To cal so fals a man a knight.
My lady wend° he had hir hert°   *believed / heart*
Ay° for-to kepe and hald in quert,°   *Always / wholeness*
1615 Bot now with grefe° he has hir gret°   *grief / greeted*
And broken the term that sho him set—
That was the evyn of Saynt John;
Now es that tyme for ever gone.
  So lang gaf sho him respite,
1620 And thus he haves hir led with lite.[3]
Sertainly, so fals a fode°   *progeny, child*
Was never cumen of kynges blode,
That so sone forgat his wyfe
That lofed him better than hyr life."
1625 Til° Ywayne sais sho thus: "Thou es   *To*
Traytur untrew° and trowthles°   *disloyal / deceitful*
And also an unkind° cumlyng°—   *ungrateful / newcomer, parvenu*
Deliver me my lady° ring!"   *lady's*
Sho stirt° to him with sterne loke,°   *rushed / look, expression*
1630 The ring fro his finger sho toke;
And alsone° als sho had the ring,   *as soon*

---

9. And right at that moment he took notice (of something).
1. I.e., may God protect you.
2. But she is apprised of his deception.
3. She gave him free time away for so long, and in this way has he misled her.

Hir leve toke sho of the King
And stirted up on hir palfray.
Withowten more° sho went hir way;   *more (ado)*
1635 With hir was nowther° knave ne grome,°   *neither / groom, manservant*
Ne no man wist where sho bycome.[4]

 Sir Ywayn, when he this gan here,°   *hear*
Murned and made simpil chere;[5]
In sorow than so was he stad,°   *placed*
1640 That nere for murning wex he mad.[6]
It° was no mirth that him myght mend;   *There*
At worth to noght ful wele he wend—
For wa he es ful wil of wane—[7]
"Allas, I am myne owin° bane.°   *own / destruction*
1645 Allas," he sayd, "that I was born;
Have I my leman thus forlorn,°   *deserted*
And al es for° myne owen foly°—   *because of / folly*
Allas, this dole° wil mak me dy!"   *grief*
An evyl° toke him als he stode;°   *illness / stood*
1650 For wa° he wex° al wilde and wode.°   *woe, anguish / grew / mad*
Unto the wod° the way he nome;°   *woods / took*
No man wist whore he bycome.
Obout he welk° in the forest—   *walked*
Als it wore a wilde beste.[8]
1655 His men on ilka° syde has soght,°   *each / sought, searched*
Fer° and nere, and findes him noght.   *Far*
 On a day, als Ywayne ran
In the wod, he met a man;
Arowes brade° and bow had he,   *broad-tipped*
1660 And when Sir Ywaine gan him se,
To him he stirt with bir° ful grim—   *attack*
His bow and arwes reft° he him.°   *seized / (from) him*
Ilka day than at the leste°   *least*
Shot he him a wilde beste.°   *beast*
1665 Fless he wan him ful gude wane—[9]
And of his arows lost he nane.
Thare he lifed a grete sesowne°   *(length of) time*
With rotes° and raw venysowne;°   *roots / venison*
He drank of the warm blode,
1670 And that did him mekil° gode.   *much*
 Als° he went in that boskage,°   *As / woodland*
He fand° a litil ermytage.°   *found, came upon / hermitage*

4. Nor did any man know what became of her.
5. Mourned and behaved miserably.
6. That for mourning he nearly went mad.
7. He expected to come to nothing—because of his anguish he is at a loss what to do.
8. Like a wild beast.
9. He gained for himself a good supply of meat.

The ermyte° saw and sone° was war°   *hermit / soon, quickly / aware*
A° naked man a bow bare.°   *(That) a / bore*
1675 He hoped° he was wode° that tide°—   *believed / mad / time*
Tharfore no lenger durst he bide;°   *abide, linger*
He sperd° his yate° and in he ran   *fastened, locked / gate*
For-fered° of that wode man.   *Afraid*
And for° him thoght it charité,   *because*
1680 Out at his window set he
Brede° and water for the wode man—   *Bread*
And tharto ful sone he° ran.   *(Ywain)*
Swilk° als he° had, swilk he him gaf—°   *such / (the hermit) / gave*
Barly-brede, with al the chaf.[1]
1685 Tharof ete he ful gude wane—[2]
And are° swilk° ete° he never nane.   *before / (of) such / had eaten*
   Of the water he drank tharwith,
Than ran he forth into the frith.°   *woods*
For if a man be never so wode
1690 He wil kum whare man dose him gode—[3]
And, sertanly, so did Ywayne;
Everilka° day he come ogayne,   *Every*
And with him broght he redy° boun°   *readily / prepared*
Ilka day new venisowne.
1695 He laid it at the ermite° yate   *hermit's*
And ete and drank and went his gate.°   *way*
   Ever alsone als he was gane,
The ermyt toke the flesh onane°—   *anon, forthwith*
He flogh° it and seth° it fayre and wele;   *flayed / boiled*
1700 Than had Ywayne at ilka mele°   *meal*
Brede and sothen° venysowne.   *boiled*
Than went the ermyte to the towne
And salde° the skinnes° that he° broght,   *sold / hides / (Ywain)*
And better brede tharwith he boght;°   *bought*
1705 Than fand Sir Ywayne in that stede
Venyson and better brede.
This life led he ful fele° yere,°   *many (a) / year*
And sethen° he wroght° als ye sal here.   *since then / fared*

   Als Ywaine sleped under a tre,
1710 By him come thare rideand° thre:°   *riding / three*
A lady, twa boure-wemen° alswa.°   *ladies in waiting / also*
Than spak ane° of the maidens twa,°   *one / two*
"A naked man me think I se—
Wit° I wil what it may be."   *Find out*
1715 Sho lighted doun and to him yede,°   *went*

---

1. Barley bread, with all the chaff (i.e., very coarse bread, of poor quality).
2. He ate a great amount thereof.
3. Even if a man has never been so insane (as he has now come to be), he will return to wherever a person does him some good.

And unto him sho toke gude hede;
Hir thoght wele sho had him sene[4]
In many stedes° whare sho had bene.   places
Sho was astonyd° in that stownde,°   astonished / moment
1720   For in hys face sho saw a wonde,°   wound
Bot it was heled° and hale° of hew;°   healed / hale, healthy / color
Tharby,° hir thoght, that sho him knew.   Thereby
Sho sayd, "By God that me has made,
Swilk a wound Sir Ywayne hade—
1725   Sertaynly, this ilk° es he!   same
      Allas," sho sayd, "how may this be?
Allas, that him° es thus bityd,°   (to) him / come to pass
So nobil a knyght als he was kyd.°   known
It es grete sorow that he sold° be   should
1730   So ugly now opon to se."°   look
So tenderly for him sho gret,°   wept
That hir teres° al hir chekes wet.   tears
"Madame," sho said, "for sertayn
Here have we funden° Sir Ywayne,   found
1735   The best knyght that on grund mai ga.[5]
Allas, him es bytid so wa;[6]
In sum sorow was he stad,°   placed
And tharfore es he waxen mad—
Sorow wil meng° a mans blode°   mix, corrupt / blood
1740   And make him for-to wax wode.
      Madame, and° he war° now in quert,°   if / were / good health
And al hale of will and hert,
Ogayns yowre fa° he wald yow° were°   foe / you / defend
That° has yow done so mekyl° dere.°   Who / great / harm
1745   And he ware hale, so God me mend,°   preserve
Yowre sorow war sone broght to end."
The lady said, "And° this ilk be he—   If
And° than° he wil noght hethin° fle°— If / then / from here / flee
Thorgh Goddes help than hope I yit
1750   We sal him win ynto his wyt.[7]
Swith° at hame° I wald° we were,   At once / home / wish
For thare I have an unement° dere°—   ointment / valuable
Morgan the Wise gaf it to me[8]
And said als I sal tel to the:
1755   He sayd, 'This unement es so gode,°   good

4. And she took a good close look at him; she thought that she had certainly seen him (before).
5. I.e., the best knight on earth.
6. Alas (that) such woe has befallen him.
7. Through God's help I hope that we shall then yet restore him to his senses.
8. This figure is better known in Arthurian tales as Morgan le Fay (or le Fée, "the fairy"), and, though here referred to as a man (two lines below), is traditionally a woman—the half sister of Arthur, and, in some stories, the mother of Ywain. Morgan is traditionally associated with great magic power (learned from Merlin), including the power to heal.

	That if a man be brayn-wode°	*mad*
	And he war anes° anoynt° with yt,	*once / anointed*
	Smertly° sold he have his wit.' "	*Quickly*
	Fro hame thai wer bot half a myle;°	*mile*
1760	Theder° come thai in a whyle.°	*Thither / (brief) time*
	The lady sone the boyst° has soght,°	*(ointment) box / sought*
	And the unement has sho broght.	
	"Have," sho said, "this unement here.	
	Unto me it es ful dere—	
1765	And smertly that thou wend ogayne—[9]	
	Bot luke thou spend° it noght in vaine;°	*expend / vain*
	And fra° the knight anoynted be,	*from (the time that)*
	That° thou leves,° bring it to me."	*That (which) / leave over*
	Hastily that maiden meke	
1770	Tok hose and shose° and serk° and breke.°	*shoes / shirt / breeches*
	A riche robe als gan sho ta°	*take*
	And a saint° of silk alswa,	*belt*
	And also a gude palfray;	
	And smertly come sho whare he lay.	
1775	On slepe fast yit sho him fande.[1]	
	Hir hors° until° a tre sho band,°	*horses / to / tied*
	And hastily to him sho yede—	
	And that was a ful hardy° dede.	*courageous*
	Sho enoynt hys heved° wele	*head*
1780	And his body ilka° dele.°	*every / part*
	Sho despended° al the unement,	*dispensed*
	Over° hir ladies cumandment;	*Against*
	For hir lady wald sho noght let°—	*stop*
	Hir thoght that it was ful wele set.[2]	
1785	Al his atyre° sho left hym by	*attire, clothing*
	At his rising to be redy,	
	That° he might him cleth° and dyght°	*(So) that / clothe / make ready*
	Or° he sold of hyr have syght.	*Before*
	Than he wakend of his slepe	
1790	(The maiden to him toke gude kepe),[3]	
	He luked up ful sarily°	*sorrily, miserably*
	And said, "Lady Saynt Mary,	
	What hard grace to me es maked[4]	
	That I am here now thus naked?	
1795	Allas, wher any have here bene?[5]	
	I trow sum has my sorow sene!"	

---

9. And see that you come back (with it) quickly.
1. She found him still fast asleep.
2. It seemed to her that it was (all) very well spent.
3. The maiden kept close watch over him (from a distance; see 11. 1806–10).
4. I.e., what kind of misfortune has befallen me.
5. Alas, is it possible that any (other people) have been here?

Lang he sat so in a thoght
How that gere was theder broght.[6]
    Than had he noght so mekyl myght[7]
1800   On his fete° to stand upright;   *feet*
     Him failed might° of fote° and hand,   *strength/foot*
     That° he myght nowther° ga° ne stand— *(So) that/neither/go, move*
     Bot yit his clathes on he wan.[8]
     Tharfore ful wery° was he than;   *weary*
1805   Than had he mister° for-to mete°   *need/meet*
     Sum man that myght his bales° bete.°   *sufferings/relieve*
     Than lepe° the maiden on hir palfray   *leaped*
     And nere° byside him made hir way.   *near*
     Sho lete° als° sho him noght had sene *let (it seem)/as (if)*
1810   Ne° wetyn° that he thare had bene.   *Nor/knew*
     Sone, when he of hir had syght,
     He cried unto hyr on hight;°   *high*
     Than wald sho no ferrer° ride,   *further*
     Bot fast sho luked on ilka syde
1815   And waited° obout fer and nere—   *looked*
     He cried and sayd, "I am here!"
     Than sone° sho rade him till°   *soon, quickly/to*
     And sayd, "Sir, what es thi will?"
     "Lady, thi help war me ful lefe,[9]
1820   For I am here in grete meschefe°—   *trouble*
     I ne wate° never by what chance   *know*
     That I have al this grevance.°   *hardship*
     Par charité[1] I walde the pray
     For-to lene° me that palfray   *lend*
1825   That in thi hand es redy° bowne,° *readily/prepared (saddled)*
     And wis° me sone unto some towne.   *direct*
     I wate noght how I had this wa,°   *woe, misfortune*
     Ne how that I sal hethin° ga."   *from here*
     Sho answerd him with wordes hende,°   *gracious*
1830   "Syr, if thou wil with me wende,°   *go*
     Ful gladly wil I ese° the   *ease, accommodate*
     Until that thou amended° be."   *recovered*
     Sho helped him up on his hors ryg,°   *back*
     And sone thai come until a bryg;°   *bridge*
1835   Into the water the boist° sho cast,   *(ointment) box*
     And sethin° hame sho hied° fast.   *then/hurried*
     When thai come to the castel yate°   *gate*
     Thai lighted and went in tharate.°   *thereat*

---

6. I.e., for a long time he thus sat in a state of perplexity about how that clothing came to be there.
7. At that time he had not enough strength.
8. I.e., but he still managed to get his clothes on.
9. Your help would be most welcome to me.
1. For the sake of (Christian) charity.

The maiden to the chameber went;
1840 The lady asked° the unement.   *asked (for)*
"Madame," sho said, "the boyst es lorn°—   *lost*
And so was I nerehand,° tharforn."°   *nearly / therefore*
"How so," sho said, "for Goddes tre?"[2]
"Madame," sho said, "I sal tel the
1845 Al the soth° how that it was: *truth*
Als° I over the brig sold° pas,°   *As / should / pass*
Evyn° inmyddes,° the soth to say,   *Right / in the middle*
Thare stombild° my palfray.   *stumbled*
    On the brig he fell al flat,
1850 And the boyst right with that
Fel fra me in the water down—[3]
And had I noght bene titter° boun°   *more quickly / ready*
To tak my palfray bi the mane,
The water sone had bene my bane."°   *destruction*
1855 The lady said, "Now am I shent°   *ruined*
That I have lorn my gude unement;
It was to me, so God me glade,°   *gladden*
The best tresure that ever I hade.
To me it es ful mekil° skath°—   *great / matter for regret*
1860 Bot better es lose° it than yow bath.°   *(to) lose / both*
Wend, sho said, unto the knight
And luke thou ese him at thi myght."[4]
"Lady," sho said, "els war me lathe."[5]
Than sho gert° him washe and bathe   *had*
1865 And gaf him mete and drink of main,°   *strength*
Til he had geten° his might ogayn.   *got, gained*
Thai ordand° armurs ful wele dight,°   *made ready / appointed*
And so thai did stedes° ful wight.°   *steeds, war-horses / strong*

    So it fell sone on a day,
1870 Whils he in the castel lay,
The ryche Eryl,° Syr Alers,   *Earl*
With knightes, serjantes,° and swiers,°   *men-at-arms / squires*
And with swith grete vetale,°   *victuals, provisions*
Come that kastel to asayle.°   *assail*
1875 Sir Ywain than his armurs tase°   *takes (up)*
With other socure° that he hase.°   *succor, reinforcements / has*
The Erel he kepes in the felde,[6]
And sone he hit ane° on the shelde°   *one (knight) / shield*
That° the knyght and als the stede   *(So) that*
1880 Stark° ded° to the erth thai yede.°   *Utterly / dead / went, fell*

2. I.e., for the sake of Christ's Cross.
3. Fell from me down into the water.
4. And see that you comfort him as best you can.
5. I would hate to do otherwise.
6. He constrains (the forces of) the Earl in the battlefield.

Sone another, the thrid,° the ferth,° *third / fourth*
Feld° he doun ded on the erth. *Felled*
  He stird° him so omang tham than, *bestirred*
At ilka° dint° he slogh° a man. *each / dint, blow / slew*
1885 Sum he losed of hys men,
Bot the Eril lost swilk ten;[7]
Al thai fled fast fra that syde° *part (of the field)*
Whare thai saw Sir Ywayn ride.
He herted° so his cumpany, *heartened, encouraged*
1890 The moste° coward was ful hardy° *greatest / courageous*
To fel° al that thai fand° in felde. *fell / found*
The lady lay° ever and bihelde; *stayed*
Sho sais, "Yon es a nobil knyght,
Ful eger° and of ful grete myght— *eager, fierce*
1895 He es wele worthy for-to prayse° *praise*
That es so doghty and curtayse."
  The mayden said, "Withowten let,° *fail*
Yowre oynement mai ye think wele set.° *spent*
Sese,° madame, how he prikes,° *See / rides forth*
1900 And sese also, how fele° he stikes°— *many (men) / sticks, stabs*
Lo° how he fars° omang his fase!° *Look, Behold / fares / foes*
Al that he hittes° sone° he slase.° *hits, strikes / quickly / slays*
War thare swilk other twa als he,[8]
Than hope° I sone thaire° fase sold fle; *expect / their*
1905 Sertes, than sold we se ful tyte° *immediately*
The Eril sold be descumfite.° *overcome*
Madame, God gif his wil were
To wed yow and be loverd here."[9]
  The Erils folk went fast to ded;° *death*
1910 To fle than was his best rede.° *plan*
The Eril sone bigan to fle,
And than might men bourd° se— *amusement*
How Sir Ywayne and his feres° *companions*
Folowd tham on fel° maners.° *many / ways*
1915 And fast thai slogh the Erils men;
Olive° thai left noght over° ten. *Alive / more than*
The Eril fled ful fast for drede,° *dread, fear*
And than Sir Ywaine strake° his stede *struck*
And overtoke him in that tide° *time*
1920 At a kastel thar-bysyde.° *nearby*
Sir Ywayne sone withset° the yate, *obstructed*

7. He lost some of his own men, but the Earl lost ten times as many.
8. If there were two more such as he.
9. May God make it so that he (Ywain) would marry you and be lord here. (This is, of course, not the first time that a lady-in-waiting has in this way recommended Ywain to her mistress —and it will not be the last: cf. l. 1962, n.)

That° the Eril myght noght in° tharate.°   *(So) that / (get) in / thereat*
    The Eril saw al might noght gain;[1]
He yalde° him sone to Sir Ywayn,   *yielded*
1925 And sone he has his trowth° plyght°   *truth, loyalty / pledged*
To wend° with him that ilk° night   *go / same*
Unto the lady of grete renowne
And profer him to hir presowne,
And to do him in hir grace,
1930 And also to mend his trispase.[2]
    The Eril than unarmed his hevid,[3]
And none armure on him he levid.°   *left*
Helm, shelde, and als his brand°   *sword*
That he bare naked° in his hand—   *unsheathed*
1935 Al he gaf to Sir Ywayne,
And hame with him he went ogaine.[4]
In the kastel made thai joy ilkane°   *each one*
When thai wist° the Eril was tane;°   *knew / taken*
And when thai saw tham cumand° nere,°   *coming / near*
1940 Ogayns° him went thai al in-fere.°   *Toward / together*
And when the lady gan tham mete,
Sir Ywaine gudely gan hir grete.
He said, "Madame, have thi presoun°   *prisoner*
And hald him here in thi baundoun"°—   *dominion*
1945 Bot he gert hir grante him grace
To mak amendes yn that space.
    On a buke the Erl sware
For-to restore bath les and mare,[5]
And big° ogayn bath toure and toune   *build*
1950 That by him war casten° doune,°   *cast, knocked / down*
And evermare to be hir frende.
Umage° made he to that hende;°   *Homage / gracious (lady)*
To this forward he borows fand,[6]
The best lordes of al that land.
1955 Sir Ywaine wald no lenger° lend,°   *longer / delay*
Bot redies° him fast for-to wend.   *readies*
At the lady his leve he takes;
Grete murnyng° tharfore sho makes.   *mourning*
Sho said, "Sir, if it be yowre will,
1960 I pray yow for-to dwel here still;

1. I.e., the Earl saw that he had nothing to lose.
2. And offer himself as her prisoner, and to put himself at her mercy, and also to make amends for his offense.
3. I.e., removed his helm.
4. And he was escorted back home (to the lady's castle) by Ywain.
5. I.e., the Earl swore on the Bible to restore everything.
6. For this agreement he found guarantors.

And I wil yelde° into yowre handes   *yield*
Myne awyn° body and al my landes."[7]   *own*
Hereof fast° sho hym bysoght,   *insistently*
Bot al hir speche avayles° noght.   *avails*
1965 He said, "I wil° no thing to° mede°   *desire / as / reward*
Bot myne armurs and my stede."
Sho said, "Bath stedes and other thing
Es yowres at yowre owyn likyng—[8]
And° if ye walde here with us dwell,   *But*
1970 Mekyl° mirth war° us omell."°   *Great / would be / among*
It was na bote° to bid him bide;°   *help / abide, stay*
He toke his stede and on gan stride.
The lady and hyr maydens gent
Wepid° sare when that he went.   *Wept*

1975   Now rides Ywayn, als° ye sal here,   *as*
With hevy° herte and dreri° chere°   *heavy / dreary, sad / countenance*
Thurgh a forest by a sty.°   *path*
And thare he herd a hydose° cry;   *hideous*
The gaynest° way ful sone° he tase° *quickest / immediately / takes*
1980 Til he come whare the noys° was.   *noise*
Than was he war° of a dragoun   *aware*
Had° asayled a wilde lyown;°   *(That) had / lion*
With his tayl he drogh him fast[9]
And fire ever on him he cast.
1985 The lyoun had over° litel myght   *(left) over, remaining*
Ogaynes° the dragon for-to fyght.   *Against*
Than Sir Ywayn made him bown°   *ready*
For-to sucore° the lyown;   *succor, assist*
His shelde bifore his face he fest°   *made fast, held securely*
1990 For the fyre that the dragon kest.°   *cast*
He strake° the dragon in at the chavyl,°   *struck / jowl, cheek*
That° it° come out at the navyl.°   *(So) that / (the stroke) / navel*
Sunder° strake he the throte-boll,°   *Asunder, Apart / adam's apple*
That° fra the body went the choll;°   *(So) that / jowl*
1995 By the lioun tail the hevid hang yit—
For tharby had he tane his bit.[1]
The tail Sir Ywayne strake in twa;°   *two*
The dragon hevid than fel tharfra.°   *from there*
He thoght, "If the lyoun me asayle,

---

7. This is the first of several new occasions in which Yvain is perceived as worthy of joining, and even governing, an important household—a role to which, of course, he had in the past been dramatically unequal; see also ll. 2486–2502, 2646–54, and 3286–91. At such points in the text it is important each time to gauge Ywain's *own* perception of his worthiness. One should also look for other events which might be emblematic of Ywain's participation in a kind of expurgatory retracing of steps; see for instance, l. 2030 and n.
8. Steeds and other things both are yours at your pleasure.
9. The dragon dragged the lion firmly by its (the lion's) tail.
1. From the lion's tail the head still hung—for it was there that he (the dragon) had taken hold.

2000	Redy° sal he have batayle."	Readily
	Bot the lyoun wald noght fyght—	
	Grete fawnyng° made he to the knyght.	fawning
	Down on the grund° he set him oft,	ground
	His fortherfete° he held oloft°	front feet / aloft
2005	And thanked the knyght als° he kowth,°	as (best) / could, knew how
	Al if² he myght noght speke with mowth.	
	So wele the lyon of him lete,³	
	Ful law° he lay and likked° his fete.	low / licked
	When Syr Ywayne that sight gan se,	
2010	Of the beste him thoght peté,°	pity
	And on his wai forth gan he ride;	
	The lyown folowd by hys syde.	
	In the forest al that day	
	The lyoun mekely° foloud° ay,°	meekly / followed / always
2015	And never for wele ne for wa	
	Wald he part Sir Ywayn fra.⁴	
	Thus in the forest als° thai ware°	as / were
	The lyoun hungerd° swith° sare.°	grew hungry / forthwith / sorely
	Of a beste° savore° he hade;	animal / a taste for
2020	Until° hys lord sembland° he made	Unto / a sign
	That he wald° go to get his pray	desired (to)
	(His kind it wald, the soth to say).⁵	
	For his lorde sold him noght greve,⁶	
	He wald noght go withowten leve.	
2025	Fra his lord the way he laght°	took
	The mountance of ane arow-draght;⁷	
	Sone he met a barayn° da,°	barren, without fawn / doe
	And ful sone he gan hir sla;°	slay
	Hir throte in twa ful sone he bate°	bit
2030	And drank the blode whils it was hate.⁸	
	That da he kest than in° his nek°	on, over / neck, withers
	Als it war a mele-sek;°	meal sack, sack of grain

2. Even though.
3. So much did the lion revere him.
4. And, for good or bad, he would never part from Sir Ywain. (The lion's extraordinary behavior, no doubt modeled more on that of people and dogs than that of true lions, can invite symbolic readings of the kind which suggest, for instance, that Ywain is now possessed of a leonine psychology of strength and determination; or that, in slaying the dragon, he no longer fights against threats to his, or his friends' pride, but instead, like the Christian hero St. George, fights against moral evil. One cannot be certain, however, that the Middle English translator, let alone Chrétien, intended the work in the first instance to be "decoded" systematically. What can more securely be said is that the advent of the lion provides Ywain with his first *selfless* assistance of another being and that the lion's unsolicited devotion presents him with his first practical example of abject loyalty; see also l. 2030, n.)
5. To tell the truth, his nature (i.e., instinct) demanded it.
6. So that his lord should not be distressed.
7. The distance of an arrow's flight.
8. Whilst it was hot. (Cf. l. 1669; there are also echoes of Ywain's wild state in the subsequent account of the lion's generous hunt, to l. 2050. The implication is of a process incomplete; though his sanity is restored, Ywain still attends to the life of an outcast.)

Unto his lorde than he it bare.
And Sir Ywayn parsayved° thare   *perceived*
2035 That it was so nere° the nyght   *near, close to*
That no ferrer° ride he might.   *further*
     A loge° of bowes° sone he made,   *lodge, shelter/boughs*
And flynt and fire-yren bath he hade,[9]
And fire ful sone thare he slogh°   *struck up (from the flint)*
2040 Of dry mos° and many a bogh.°   *moss/bough*
The lion had the da undone;°   *dismembered*
Sir Ywayne made a spit ful sone
And rosted sum to° thaire sopere.°   *for/supper*
The lyon lay als ye sal here:
2045 Unto na mete he him drogh°   *drew, went*
Until his maister had eten ynogh.°   *enough*
Him failed° thare bath salt and brede,°   *lacked/bread*
And so him did whyte° wine and rede;°   *white/red*
Bot of swilk° thing als thai had,   *such*
2050 He and his lyon made tham glad.
The lyon hungerd for the nanes;[1]
Ful fast he ete raw fless° and banes.°   *flesh/bones*
     Sir Ywayn in that ilk° telde°   *same/shelter*
Laid his hevid opon his shelde;
2055 Al nyght the lyon obout° yede°   *about/went*
To kepe° his mayster° and his stede.   *watch over/master*
Thus the lyon and the knyght
Lended° thare a fouretenyght.°   *Remained/fortnight*

     On a day, so it byfell,°   *befell, happened*
2060 Syr Ywayne come unto the well.
He saw the chapel and the thorne°   *thorn tree*
And said "Allas" that he was born—
And, when he loked on the stane,°   *stone*
He fel in swowing sone onane.[2]
2065 Als° he fel his swerde outshoke;°   *As/shook loose*
The pomel° into the erth toke,°   *pommel/took, settled*
The poynt toke until° his throte°—   *onto/throat*
Wel nere he made a sari note;[3]
Thorgh his armurs sone it smate,°   *pierced*
2070 A litel intil° hys hals° it bate.°   *into/neck/bit*
     And, wen the lyon saw his blude,°   *blood*
He brayded° als he had bene wode.°   *started about/mad*
Than kest he up so lathly rerde,[4]
Ful mani folk myght he have ferde.°   *terrified*

9. And he had both a flintstone and a fire iron (on which to strike the flint to make sparks.)
1. I.e., the lion then grew hungry indeed.
2. He immediately fell in a swoon.
3. I.e., very nearly did he do a nasty job (on himself).
4. Then he let forth such a horrible roar.

2075	He wend wele, so God me rede,[5]	
	That his mayster had bene ded;	*master*
	It was ful grete peté to here	
	What sorow he made on° his manere.°	*in / manner, way*
	He stirt° ful hertly,° I yow hete,°	*started / earnestly / promise*
2080	And toke the swerde bytwix° his fete;	*between*
	Up he set it by a stane,	
	And thare he wald himself have slane—	
	And so he had sone, for sertayne,	
	Bot right in° that° rase° Syr Ywayne;	*at / that (instant) / rose*
2085	And alsone° als he° saw hym stand,	*as soon / (the lion)*
	For fayn° he liked° fote and hand.	*joy / licked*
	Sir Ywayn said oft sithes° "Allas—"	*times*
	"Of alkins° men hard° es my grace.°	*all / (most) severe / fortune*
	Mi leman set me sertayn° day,	*(a) certain*
2090	And I it brak—so wayloway!°[6]	
	Allas, for dole° how may I dwell°	*grief / live, survive*
	To se this chapel and this well,	
	Hir° faire thorn, hir riche stane?	*Her*
	My gude° dayes er now al gane,°	*good / gone*
2095	My joy es done now al bidene,[7]	
	I am noght worthi to be sene.°	*seen*
	I saw this wild beste was ful bayn°	*eager*
	For my luf himself have° slayne;	*(to) have*
	Than sold° I, sertes,° by more right	*should / certainly*
2100	Sla my self for swilk a wyght°	*person*
	That I have for my foly lorn.°	*lost*
	Allas the while° that I was born!"	*time*
	Als° Sir Ywayn made his mane°	*As, While / moan, complaint*
	In the chapel ay° was ane°	*all the time / someone*
2105	And herd his murnyng,° haly° all,	*mourning / wholly*
	Thorgh° a crevice of the wall;	*Through*
	And sone° it said with simepel° chere,°	*soon / miserable / disposition*
	"What ertou° that murnes° here?"	*art thou / mourns*
	"A man," he sayd, "sum tyme I was—[8]	
2110	What ertow? Tel me or° I pas."°	*before / pass, go*
	"I am," it sayd, "the sariest° wight	*sorriest*
	That ever lifed° by day or nyght."	*lived*
	"Nay," he said, "by Saynt Martyne,	
	Thare es na sorow mete° to myne,°	*equal / mine*
2115	Ne no wight so wil of wane.[9]	
	I was a man; now am I nane.	

5. He fully believed, so help me God.
6. And I broke it—so woe is me!
7. My joy is now altogether over.
8. Cf. l. 279; the echo has similar resonances to those remarked in the note to l. 2030.
9. Nor any person so much at a loss what to do.

Whilom° I was a nobil knyght   *Once, Formerly*
And a man of mekyl° myght;°   *great / power*
I had knyghtes of my menyé[1]
2120   And of reches° grete plenté.°   *riches / plenty*
I had a ful fayre seignory°—   *domain*
And al I lost for my foly.
Mi maste° sorow als° sal thou here: *greatest / also*
I lost a lady that was me° dere.”°   *(to) me / dear*
2125   The tother sayd, “Allas, allas,
Myne es a wele sarier° case: *sorrier, sadder*
To-morn I mun bere my jewyse,
Als my famen wil devise.”[2]
“Allas,” he said, “what es the skill?”°   *reason*
2130   “That sal thou here, sir, if thou will.
I was a mayden mekil° of pride   *great*
With a lady here-nere-biside.°   *nearby*
Men me bikalles° of tresown°   *accuse / treason*
And has me put here in presown.
2135   I have no man to defend me;[3]
Tharfore to-morn brent° mun° I be.”   *burned / must*
He sayd, “What if thou get a knyght
That for the with thi fase° wil fight?”   *foes*
“Syr,” sho sayd, “als mot I ga,[4]
2140   In this land er bot knyghtes twa°   *two*
That me wald help to cover° of° care:°   *recover, save / from / trouble*
The tane° es went,° I wate° noght whare;   *one / gone / know*
The tother° es dweland° with the King   *other / dwelling*
And wate noght of my myslykyng.°   *unhappiness, distress*
2145   The tane of tham hat° Syr Gawayn   *is called*
And the tother hat Syr Ywayn—
For hym sal° I be done° to dede°   *shall / put / death*
To-morn, right in this same stede°—   *place*
He es the Kinges son Uriene.”[5]
2150   “Parfay,”° he said, “I have hym sene—   *By my faith, Indeed*
I am he! And for my gilt°   *guilt, fault*
Sal thou never more be spilt.°   *destroyed*
Thou ert Lunet, if I can rede,[6]
That helpyd me yn mekyl drede.°   *dread, fear*
2155   I had° bene ded had thou noght bene.°   *would have / existed*

1. I.e., I had a company of knights.
2. Tomorrow I must endure my judgment, according to what my enemies devise.
3. Trial of women through combat of elected champions was a bona fide judicial practice in
Chrétien's France, and remained so well into the fourteenth century. If a woman was charged
with a crime, or made a charge, and if litigation reached an impasse, she was liable to forfeit
her life, depending on the outcome of an appointed duel; the outcome was held to demonstrate
the will of God in the matter (cf. ll. 2589–90).
4. As I hope to live.
5. See l. 732.
6. I.e., if I am not mistaken.

Tharfore tel me us bytwene,
How bical° thai the of treson   *accuse*
Thus for-to sla,° and for what reson?"   *slay (you)*
 "Sir, thai say that my lady
2160 Lufed me moste specially
And wroght° al efter° my rede;°   *did/according to/advice*
Tharefore thai hate me to the ded.°   *death*
The Steward[7] says that done have I
Grete tresone unto my lady.
2165 His twa brether° sayd it als,   *brothers*
And I wist° that thai said° fals;° *know/spoke/falsely*
And sone I answerd, als° a sot°—   *like/fool*
For fole bolt es sone shot—[8]
I said that I sold find a knyght
2170 That sold me mayntene° in my right *maintain, support*
And feght° with tham, al thre.   *fight*
Thus the batayl wajed° we.   *wagered, pledged*
Than thai granted me als tyte
Fourty dayes unto respite.[9]
2175 And at the Kynges court I was;
I fand na cumfort° ne na solase° *comfort/solace, joy*
Nowther of knyght, knave,°   *knave, male servant*
  ne swayn."°   *swain, youth*
Than said he, "Whare was Syr Gawayn?
He has bene ever trew and lele;°   *loyal*
2180 He fayled never no damysele."
 Scho said, "In court was he noght sene,
For a knyght led oway the Quene;[1]
The King tharfore es swith° grym.° *forthwith/grim, solemn*
Syr Gawayn folowd efter him—
2185 He coms noght hame,° for sertayne,   *home*
Until he bryng the Quene ogayne.
Now has thou herd, so God me rede,
Why I sal be done to ded."
He said, "Als I am trew knyght,
2190 I sal be redy for-to fyght
To-morn with tham, al thre,
Leman,° for the luf° of the.   *Dear friend/love*
 At my might I sal noght fayl—
Bot, how so besé of the batayle,

---

7. On the post of steward, see l. 1209, n.
8. For a fool's (crossbow) bolt is soon shot (without discretion). (The sense of the proverb is similar to that of the more familiar "fools rush in where angels fear to tread.")
9. Then they granted me immediately a respite (a grace period) of forty days.
1. Because some knight had abducted the Queen. (The event is mentioned in the same perfunctory fashion in Chrétien—and such sudden references are characteristic of this text; cf. the notes to ll. 945–47 and 1146. The reference may echo an episode fully told in *Lancelot*, which romance some scholars suspect Chrétien was writing at the same time as *Yvain*.)

2195	If ani man my name the frayne,	
	On al manere luke thou yt layne;[2]	
	Unto na man my name thou say."	
	"Syr," sho sayd, "for soth, nay.	
	I prai to grete God alweldand°	*almighty*
2200	That thai have noght the hegher° hand.	*higher, upper*
	Sen° that ye wil my murnyng mend,°	*Since, Seeing that / remedy*
	I tak° the grace° that God wil send."	*accept / fortune*
	Syr Ywayn sayd, "I sal the hyght°	*promise*
	To mend thi murnyng at my myght.	
2205	Thorgh grace of God in trenyté°	*trinity*
	I sal be wreke° of tham, al thre."	*avenged*
	Than rade he forth into frith°—	*woods*
	And hys lyoun went hym with.	
	Had he redyn° bot a stownde,°	*ridden / brief time*
2210	A ful fayre castell he fownde;	
	And Syr Ywaine, the soth to say,	
	Unto the castel toke the way.	
	When he come at the castel yate,°	*gate*
	Foure porters he fand tharate.°	*thereat*
2215	The drawbryg° sone lete thai doun—	*drawbridge*
	Bot al thai fled for° the lyown;	*because of*
	Thai said, "Syr, withowten dowt,	
	That beste byhoves the leve tharout."[3]	
	He said, "Sirs, so have I wyn,[4]	
2220	Mi lyoun and I sal noght twyn;°	*separate*
	I luf him als wele, I yow hete,°	*assure*
	Als my self, at ane mete.[5]	
	Owther° sal we samyn° lende,°	*Either / together / remain*
	Or els wil we hethin° wende."°	*from here / go*
2225	Bot right with that the lord he met,	
	And ful gladly he° him gret°	*(the lord) / greeted*
	With knyghtes and swiers grete plenté,°	*plenty*
	And faire ladies and maydens fre;°	*gracious*
	Ful mekyl joy of him thai made—	
2230	Bot sorow in thaire hertes thai hade.	
	Unto a chameber was he led	
	And unarmed and sethin° cled°	*then / clothed*
	In clothes that war gay° and dere.°	*fine / dear, expensive*
	Bot ofttymes° changed thaire chere;°	*often / countenance*
2235	Sum tyme he saw thei weped° all,	*wept*
	Als thai wald to water fall.[6]	

---

2. With all my strength I shall not fail—but, however interested (he may be) in the battle, if any man asks of you my name, in every way see that you conceal it.
3. It behooves you to leave that beast outside.
4. As I may thrive.
5. In the same measure.
6. (So much so that it seemed) as if they would turn to water.

Thai made slike° murnyng and slik mane°   *such / moan*
That gretter° saw he never nane.   *more unhappy (people)*
   Thai feynyd° tham oft for hys sake   *feigned, pretended*
2240 Fayre semblant° for-to make.   *appearance, show*
Ful grete wonder Sir Ywayn hade,
For thai swilk° joy and sorow made;   *such*
"Sir," he said, "if yowre wil ware,
I wald wyt why ye make slike kare."[7]
2245 "This joy," he said, "that we mak now
Sir, es al for° we have yow;   *because*
And, sir, also we mak this sorow
For dedys° that sal be done tomorow.   *deeds*
   A geant° wons° here-nere-bysyde°   *giant / dwells / nearby*
2250 That es a devil of mekil° pryde;   *great*
His name hat° Harpyns of Mowntain.   *is called*
For° him we lyf in mekil payn;°   *Because of / pain, sorrow*
My landes haves° he robbed and reft°—   *has / reft, plundered*
Noght bot this kastel es me° left.   *(to) me*
2255 And, by God that in hevyn wons,
Syr, I had sex° knyghtis to° sons—   *six / as*
I saw my self the twa slogh he;[8]
To-morn the foure als° slane mun° be.   *also / must*
   He has al in hys presowne—
2260 And, sir, for nane other enchesowne°   *reason*
Bot for I warned° hym to wyve°   *forbade / wed*
My doghter, fayrest fode° olyve.°   *progeny, child / alive*
Tharfore es he wonder° wrath,°   *wondrously / wroth, enraged*
And depely° has he sworn hys ath°   *devoutly / oath*
2265 With maystry° that he sal hir wyn—   *mastery, the upper hand*
And that the laddes° of his kychyn°   *lads / kitchen*
And also that his werst° fote-knave°   *worst, lowliest / footman*
His wil of that woman sal have,
Bot° I to-morn might find a knight   *Unless*
2270 That durst with hym selven° fyght.   *self*
And I have none to him at° ga;   *to*
What wonder es if me be wa?"[9]
   Syr Ywayn lystend° hym° ful wele,   *listened / (to) him*
And when he had talde° ilka° dele,°   *told / every / part*
2275 "Syr," he sayd, "me think mervayl[1]
That ye soght° never no kounsayl°   *sought / counsel*
At the Kynges hous here-bysyde—
For, sertes, in al this world° so wyde   *world*
Es no man of so mekil myght,

---

7. I.e., if you would permit my asking, I would know why you are so distressed.
8. I saw for myself the two he slew.
9. Is it any wonder that I am desperate?
1. I think it a marvel.

2280　Geant, champioun, ne knight,
　　　That he ne has knyghtes of his menyé°   company
　　　That ful glad and blyth° wald be   blithe, pleased
　　　For-to mete with swilk a man
　　　That thai myght kyth thaire myghtes on."[2]
2285　　　He said, "Syr, so God me mend,°   preserve
　　　Unto the Kynges kourt I send°   sent
　　　To seke° my mayster° Syr Gawayn—   seek, find / master
　　　For he wald socore° me ful fain;°   succor, help / gladly
　　　He wald noght leve° for luf° ne drede°   hesitate / love / dread, fear
2290　Had he wist° now of my nede°—   known / need
　　　For his sister es my wyfe,
　　　And he lufes hyr als° his lyfe.   as
　　　Bot a knyght this other day,
　　　Thai talde, has led the Quene oway;[3]
2295　For-to seke hyr went Sir Gawayn,
　　　And yit ne come he noght ogayn."
　　　　Than Syr Ywayne sighed sare°   sorely, sadly
　　　And said unto the knyght right thare,
　　　"Syr," he sayd, "for Gawayn sake
2300　This batayl wil I undertake
　　　For-to fyght with the geant—
　　　And that opon swilk a covenant:[4]
　　　Yif he cum at swilk a time
　　　So that we may fight by prime;[5]
2305　No langer° may I tent° tharto,   longer / attend, wait
　　　For other thing I have to do.
　　　I have a dede that most be done
　　　To-morn, nedes° byfor the none."°   necessarily / noon
　　　　The knyght sare sighand° sayd him till,° sighing / to
2310　"Sir, God yelde the thi gode wyll."[6]
　　　And al that ware° thare in the hall,   were
　　　On knese° byfor hym gan thai fall.   knees
　　　Forth thare come a byrd° ful bryght,°   maiden / splendid, fair
　　　The fairest man might se in sight;
2315　Hir moder come with hir in-fere,°   together
　　　And both thai morned and made yll chere.[7]
　　　The knight said, "Lo!° verrayment°   Look, Behold / truly
　　　God has us gude socure sent—
　　　This knight that, of his grace, wil grant

2. With whom they might test their strength.
3. See l. 2182, n.
4. I.e., but (I will undertake) that according to the following conditions.
5. Prime was the first of the eight canonical hours making up the Divine Office, the sequence of prayer said every day and night by priests and other religious. Typically, Prime would begin at about six o'clock in the morning and end at nine; Ywain here uses the term less precisely to signify sometime in the later morning.
6. I.e., may God grant you success with your good intentions.
7. Mourned and behaved unhappily.

2320	For-to fyght with the geant."	
	On knese thai fel doun to his fete	
	And thanked him with wordes swete.°	*sweet, agreeable*
	"A!° God forbede," said Sir Ywain,	*Oh*
	"That the sister of Sir Gawayn	
2325	Or any other of his blode° born	*blood*
	Sold° on this wise° knel me byforn!"	*Should / way*
	He toke tham up tyte° both in-fere	*immediately*
	And prayd tham to amend thaire chere°—	*mood, disposition*
	"And praies° fast to God alswa°	*pray / also*
2330	That I may venge yow on yowre fa,°	*foe*
	And that he cum swilk° tyme of day	*such*
	That I by° tyme may wend° my way	*in / go*
	For-to do another dede—	
	For, sertes, theder most I nede.[8]	
2335	Sertes, I wald noght tham byswike	
	For-to win this Kinges rike."[9]	
	His thoght was on that damysel	
	That he left in the chapel.	
	Thai said, "He es of grete renowne,	
2340	For with hym dwels the lyoun!"	
	Ful wele confort° war thai all	*comforted, encouraged*
	Bath in boure and als in hall;[1]	
	Ful glad war thai of thaire gest.°	*guest*
	And when tyme was at go to rest,	
2345	The lady broght him to his bed;	
	And for the lyoun sho was adred°—	*afraid*
	Na man durst negh° his chamber nere	*approach*
	Fro° thai war broght thareyn in-fere.°	*From (the time that) / together*
	Sone° at morn, when it was day,	*Soon, Quickly*
2350	The lady and the fayre° may°	*fair / maid*
	Til Ywayn° chamber went thai sone,	*Ywain's*
	And the dore thai have undone.°	*opened*
	Sir Ywayn to the kyrk° yede°	*church / went*
	Or° he did any other dede;	*Before*
2355	He herd the servise of the day	
	And sethin° to the knyght gan say,	*then*
	"Sir," he said, "now most I wend;	
	Lenger° here dar° I noght lende°—	*Longer / dare / remain*
	Til other place byhoves° me fare."	*(it) behooves*
2360	Than had the knyght ful mekel° care;°	*great / distress*
	He said, "Syr, dwells° a litel thraw;°	*stay / while*
	For luf of Gawayn that ye knaw,°	*know*

8. For, certainly, I must necessarily go thither.
9. Certainly, I would not betray them for all this realm.
1. I.e., throughout the castle.

Socore us now or° ye wende.   *before*
I sal yow gif, withowten ende,[2]
2365 Half my land, with toun and toure,
And° ye wil help us in this stoure."°   *If / fight*
     Sir Ywayn said, "Nai, God forbede°   *forbid*
That I sold° tak any mede."°   *should / reward*
Than was grete dole,° so God me glade,°   *grief / gladden*
2370 To se the sorow that thai made.
Of tham Sir Ywayn had grete peté;°   *pity*
Him thoght his hert myght breke in thre,
For in grete drede ay° gan he dwell°   *constantly / remain*
For the mayden in the chapell—
2375 For, sertes, if sho war° done° to ded,°   *were / put / death*
Of° him war than none other rede°   *For / plan*
Bot oither° he sold hymselven sla°   *either (that) / slay*
Or wode° ogain to the wod° ga.°   *mad / woods / go*
     Ryght with that thare come a grome°   *groom, manservant*
2380 And said tham° that geant come—   *(to) them*
"Yowre sons bringes he him byforn,[3]
Wel nere naked als thai war born.
With wreched ragges war thai kled°   *clad*
And fast bunden;° thus er thai led."   *bound, tied up*
2385 The geant was bath large and lang°   *long, tall*
And bare a levore° of yren° ful strang;   *bar / iron*
Tharwith he bet° tham bitterly;   *beat*
Grete rewth° it was to here tham cry—   *pity*
Thai had nothing tham for-to hyde.
2390 A dwergh° yode° on the tother syde.   *dwarf / went*
     He bare a scowrge° with cordes ten;   *scourge, whip*
Tharwith he bet tha gentil men
Ever on-ane, als he war wode;[4]
Efter ilka band brast out the blode.[5]
2395 And when thai at the walles° were,   *(castle) walls*
He° cried loud that men myght here—   *(The giant)*
"If thou wil have thi sons in hele,°   *good condition*
Deliver me that damysele—
I sal hir gif to warisowne[6]
2400 Ane° of the foulest quisteroun°   *(To) one / scullions*
That ever yit ete° any brede!°   *ate / bread*
He sal have hir maydenhede°—   *virginity*
Thar sal none other lig° hir by   *lie*
Bot naked herlotes and lowsy!"[7]

2. I.e., forever.
3. He brings your sons ahead of him.
4. Constantly, as if he were mad.
5. After every lash the blood burst out.
6. I shall give her as a prize.
7. But naked and louse-ridden scoundrels!

2405 When the lord thir° wordes herd,	*these*
Als he war wode for wa he ferd.°	*behaved*
Sir Ywayn than, that was curtays,	
Unto the knyght ful sone he sais,	
"This geant es ful fers° and fell°	*fierce / vicious*
2410 And of his wordes ful kruell;°	*cruel*
I sal deliver hir of° his aw°	*from / power*
Or els be ded within a thraw.°	*short time*
For, sertes,° it war a misaventure°	*certainly / disaster*
That so gentil a creature	
2415 Sold ever so foul hap° byfall	*chance*
To be defouled° with a thrall."°	*defiled / servant*
Sone was he armed, Sir Ywayn;	
Tharfore the ladies war ful fayn.°	*pleased*
Thai helpid to lace him in his wede,°	*clothes, armor*
2420 And sone he lepe° up on his stede.	*leaped*
Thai prai to God that grace him grant	
For-to sla that foul geant.	
The drawbrigges° war laten doun,°	*drawbridges / down*
And forth he rides with his lioun;	
2425 Ful mani sari° murnand° man	*(a) sorry / mourning*
Left he in the kastel than,	
That on thaire knese to God of might	
Praied ful hertly° for the knyght.	*heartily*

Syr Ywayn rade° into the playne,°	*rode / plain, field*
2430 And the geant come hym ogayne°—	*against, toward*
His levore was ful grete and lang	
And himself ful mekyl° and strang.	*great*
He said, "What devil made the so balde°	*bold*
For-to cum heder° out of thi halde?°	*hither / (strong)hold*
2435 Whosever the heder send	
Lufed° the litel, so God me mend;°	*Loved / preserve*
Of the he wald be wroken° fayn!"°	*avenged / gladly*
"Do forth thi best," said Sir Ywayn.	
Al the armure he° was yn	*(the giant)*
2440 Was noght bot of a bul-skyn:[8]	
Sir Ywayn was to° him ful prest;°	*against / quick, ready*
He strake° to him inmiddes° the brest;	*struck / in the middle of*
The spere° was both stif and gode;	*spear, lance*
Whare it toke bit, outbrast the blode—	
2445 So fast Sir Ywayn on yt soght,	
The bul-scyn availed noght.[9]	
The geant stombild° with the dynt,°	*stumbled / dint, blow*

8. I.e., consisted of nothing more than a bull's hide.
9. I.e., the blood burst forth (from) where it took hold—so firmly did Sir Ywain bear down on it that the bull's hide was of no use.

And unto Sir Ywayn he mynt,°   *directed blows*
And on the shelde he hit ful fast;
2450 It was mervayl that it° myght last—   *(the shield)*
The levore bended° tharwithall!   *bent*
(With grete force he lete it fall;
The geant was so strong and wight°   *bold*
That never for no dint of knyght
2455 Ne for batayl that he sold° make,   *should*
Wald he none other wapyn° take.)   *weapon*
Sir Ywain left his spere of hand[1]
And strake obout him with his brand°—   *sword*
And the geant, mekil° of mayn,°   *great / strength*
2460 Strake ful fast to him ogayn,°   *again*
Til at the last, within a throw,
He rest him on his sadelbow.[2]
And that parcayved° his lioun,   *perceived*
That his hevid° so hanged doun;   *head*
2465 He hopid° that hys lord was hyrt,°   *believed / hurt*
And to the geant sone° he styrt.°   *quickly / started, rushed*
The scyn and fless° bath° rafe° he down   *flesh / both / tore*
Fro his hals° to hys cropoun;°   *neck / rump*
His ribbes° myght men se onane,°   *ribs / anon, forthwith*
2470 For al was bare unto bane!°   *bone*
At the lyown oft he mynt,
Bot ever he lepis° fro his dynt   *leaps*
So that no strake on him lyght.°   *alighted, settled*
By than was Ywain cumen° to myght—   *come, returned*
2475 Than wil he wreke° him° if he may.   *avenge / himself*
The geant gaf he ful gude pay:°   *settlement, repayment*
He smate° oway al his left cheke;°   *struck / cheek*
His sholder als of° gan he kleke,°   *off / clutch, draw*
That both his levore and his hand
2480 Fel doun law° open° the land.   *low / upon*
Sethin° with a stoke° to him he stert   *Then / stab, thrust*
And smate the geant unto the hert.
Than was nane other tale to tell,
Bot fast unto the erth he fell—
2485 Als it had bene a hevy tre.[3]
Than myght men in the kastel se
Ful mekil mirth on ilka side.
The yates° kest° thai opyn wyde;   *gates / cast*
The lord unto Syr Ywaine ran—
2490 Him foloud° many a joyful man.   *followed*
Also the lady ran ful fast—

1. I.e., let go of his spear.
2. Within a short time, he (Ywain) collapsed onto his saddlebow.
3. I.e., like a heavy tree.

And hir doghter was noght the last.
I may noght tel the joy thai had;
And the foure brether° war ful glad,   *brothers*
2495   For thai war out of bales° broght.   *sufferings*
The lord wist it helpid noght
At° pray Sir Ywayn for-to dwell,   *To*
For tales that he byfore gan tell;
Bot hertly with his myght and mayn°   *strength*
2500   He praied him for-to cum ogayn
And dwel with him a litel stage,°   *time*
When he had done hys vassage.°   *deed of prowess*
    He said, "Sir, that may I noght do;
Bileves° wele, for me bus° go."   *Believe / (it) behooves*
2505   Tham was ful wo he wald noght dwell,
Bot fain thai war that it so fell.[4]
The neghest° way than gan he wele,°   *nearest, shortest / choose*
Until he come to the chapele.
Thare he fand a mekil fire;
2510   And the mayden with lely° lire°   *lily-white / cheek*
In hyr smok° was bunden° fast,   *smock / bound*
Into the fire for-to be kast.°   *cast*
Unto himself he sayd in hy,°   *haste*
And prayed to God almyghty,
2515   That He sold° for His mekil myght   *should*
Save fro shame that swete wight°—   *person*
"Yf thai be many and mekil of pryse,°   *esteem*
I sal let° for no kouwardise;°   *cease / cowardice*
For with me es bath God and right,
2520   And thai sal help me for-to fight—
And my lyon sal help me:
Than er° we foure ogayns tham thre."   *are*

    Sir Ywayn rides and cries then,
"Habides,° I bid yow, fals° men.   *Abide, Wait / false*
2525   It semes° wele that ye er wode,°   *seems / mad*
That wil spill this sakles° blode;°   *innocent / blood*
Ye sal noght so,° yf that I may."°   *(do) so / can (help it)*
His lyown made hym redy way.[5]
Naked he saw the mayden stand,
2530   Bihind° hir bunden aither° hand.   *Behind / either*
Than sighed Ywain wonder oft;
Unnethes° might he syt° oloft°—   *With difficulty / sit / upright*
Thare was no sembland tham bitwene
That ever owther had other sene.[6]

---

4. I.e., but they were pleased with how everything else had gone.
5. I.e., his lion cleared the way for him (through the crowd).
6. They made no sign between them that suggested that they had ever seen each other before.

2535	Al obout hyr myght men se	
	Ful mykel° sorow and grete peté°	*great / pity*
	Of other ladies that thare were,	
	Wepeand° with ful sory° chere.°	*Weeping / sad / countenance*
	"Lord," thai sayd, "what es oure gylt?°	*guilt, offense*
2540	Oure joy, oure confort,° sal be spilt!°	*comfort / destroyed*
	Who sal now oure erandes° say?°	*tasks / dictate*
	Allas, who sal now for us pray?"	
	Whils thai thus karped° was Lunet	*spoke*
	On knese° byfore the prest° set,	*knees / priest*
2545	Of hir syns° hir for-to schrive.°	*sins / confess*
	And unto hir he° went bylive;°	*(Ywain) / quickly*
	Hir hand he toke, and up sho rase.	
	"Leman,"° he sayd, "whore° er° thi fase?"°	*Dear friend / where / are / foes*
	"Sir, lo° tham yonder in yone stede,°	*behold / place*
2550	Bideand° until I be ded.	*Waiting*
	Thai have demed me with wrang.[7]	
	Wel nere° had ye dwelt° over° lang—	*nearly / waited / too*
	I pray to God he do yow mede°	*reward*
	That ye wald help me in this nede."°	*need*
2555	Thir° wordes herd than the Steward.	*These*
	He hies° him unto hir ful hard—	*hurries*
	He said, "Thou lies, fals woman!	
	For thi treson ertow° tane.°	*art thou / taken, held*
	Sho has bitraied° hir lady—	*betrayed*
2560	And, sir, so wil sho the in hy—	
	And tharfore, syr, by Goddes dome,°	*doom, judgment*
	I rede° thou wend° right als° thou com;°	*advise / go / as / came*
	Thou takes a ful febil° rede°	*feeble / piece of advice*
	If thou for hir will suffer ded!"°	*death*
2565	Unto the Steward than said he,	
	"Who so es ferd,° I rede he fle.	*afraid*
	And, sertes,° I have bene this day	*certainly*
	Whare I had ful large pay—[8]	
	And yit," he sayd, "I sal noght fail."	
2570	To tham he waged° the batayl.	*wagered, pledged*
	"Do° oway° thi lioun," said the Steward,	*Send, Put / away*
	"For that es noght oure forward;°	*agreement*
	Allane° sal thou fight with us thre."	*Alone*
	And unto him thus answerd he,	
2575	"Of my lioun no help I crave°—	*desire*
	I ne have none other fote-knave;°	*footman*
	If he wil do yow any dere,°	*harm*
	I rede wele that ye yow° were."°	*yourself / protect*

7. They have accused me wrongly.
8. And, certainly, today I have (already) been where I have had ample satisfaction. (I.e., Ywain asserts that his motive in taking up the lady's defense is not vainglorious.)

The Steward said, "On alkins° wise°   *every/way*
2580 Thi lyoun, sir, thou most chastise°   *control, restrain*
That° he do here no harm this day—   *(So) that*
Or els wend forth on thi way,
For hir° warand° mai thou noght be   *her/defender*
Bot° thou allane fight with us thre.   *Unless*
2585 Al thir men wote,° and so wote I,   *know*
That sho bitrayed hir lady.
Als traytures sal sho have hyre;°   *reward*
Sho be° brent° here in this fire."   *(shall) be/burned*
Sir Ywayn sad, "Nai! God forbede."
2590 He wist wele how the soth yede—[9]
"I trow to wreke hir with the best."[1]
He bad his lyoun go to rest;
And he laid him sone° onane°   *soon/anon, forthwith*
Doun byfore tham everilkane.°   *each one*
2595 Bitwene his legges he layd his tail
And so biheld° to the batayl.   *looked*
    Al thre thai ride to Sir Ywayn,
And smertly° rides he tham ogayn.°   *quickly/against*
In that time nothing tint° he,   *wasted*
2600 For his an strake was worth thaires thre.[2]
He strake the Steward on the shelde,
That° he fel doun flat in the felde;   *(So) that*
Bot up he rase° yit at the last   *rose*
And to Sir Ywayn strake ful fast.
2605 Tharat the lyoun greved° sare;°   *grieved/sorely, bitterly*
No lenger wald he than lig° thare—   *lie*
To help his mayster he went onane.
And the ladies everilkane
That war thare for-to se that sight
2610 Praied ful fast ay° for the knight.   *constantly*

    The lyoun hasted° him ful hard,   *hastened*
And sone he come to the Steward.
A ful fel° mynt° to him he made;   *vicious/lunge, thrust*
He bigan at the shulder-blade,
2615 And with his pawm° al rafe° he downe   *paw/tore*
Bath hauberk° and his actoune°   *coat of mail/quilted underjacket*
And al the fless,° doun til his kne,°   *flesh/knee*
So that men myght his guttes se.
To ground he fell so al to-rent°—   *torn apart*
2620 Was thare no man that him ment.°   *mourned*
Thus the lioun gan hym sla;°   *slay*

9. I.e., Ywain knew what the truth of the matter was.
1. I.e., I intend to avenge her to the best of my ability.
2. For one stroke of his was (i.e., had to be) worth three of theirs.

Than war° thai bot twa° and twa.   *were/two*
(And, sertanly, thare Sir Ywayn
Als with wordes did his main[3]
2625 For-to chastis hys lyowne;
Bot he ne wald na more lig doun—
The liown thoght, how so he sayd,[4]
That with his help he was wele payd!)°   *pleased*
Thai smate the lyoun on ilka° syde   *every*
2630 And gaf him many woundes wide.
    When that he saw hys lyoun blede,
He ferd for wa als he wald wede,[5]
And fast he strake than in that stoure°—   *fight*
Might thare none his dintes° doure.°   *dints, blows/endure*
2635 So grevosly° than he bygan   *grievously*
That doun he bare bath° hors and man;   *both*
Thai yald° tham sone to Sir Ywayn   *yield*
(And tharof war the folk ful fayne)°   *pleased*
And sone quit° to tham thaire hire°—   *(he) paid/reward*
2640 For both he kest° tham in the fire,   *cast*
And said, "Wha juges men with wrang,
The same jugement sal thai fang."°   *receive*
Thus he helpid the maiden ying°—   *young*
And sethin° he made the saghtelyng°   *then/settlement, reconciliation*
2645 Bitwene hyr° and the riche lady.°   *(Lunet)/(Alundyne)*
Than al the folk ful hastily
Proferd tham to his servise[6]
To wirship° him ever on al wise.   *serve worthily*
    Nane of tham al wist bot Lunet
2650 That thai with thaire lord war met.
The lady° prayed him als the hend[7]   *(Alundyne)*
That he hame° with tham wald wende°   *home/go*
For-to sojorn° thare a stownd,°   *stay/time*
Til he wer warist° of his wound.   *healed*
2655 By his sare set he noght a stra—
Bot for his lioun was him wa.[8]
"Madame," he said, "sertes, nay,
I mai noght dwel, the soth° to say."   *truth*
Sho said, "Sir, sen° thou wyl wend,   *since*
2660 Sai° us thi name, so God the mend."°   *Tell/preserve*
    "Madame," he said, "bi Saint Symoun,°   *Simon*
I hat° the Knight with the Lyoun."   *am called*
Sho said, "We saw yow never or° now,   *before*

3. I.e., did everything in his power verbally.
4. I.e., regardless of what he (Ywain) said.
5. He feared he would grow mad for anguish.
6. I.e., offered to serve him.
7. In the most gracious manner.
8. He did not give a straw for his own wounds—but he was very unhappy for his lion.

Ne never herd we speke of yow."
2665 "Tharby," he sayd, "ye understand°   *can tell*
I am noght knawen° wide° in land."°   *known / widely / (the) land*
Sho said, "I prai the for-to dwell,
If that thou may, here us omell."°   *among*
(If sho had wist wele wha it was,
2670 She wald wele lever° have laten him pas—   *rather*
And tharfore wald he noght be knawen,°   *known*
Both for hir ese° and for his awyn.)°   *ease, peace of mind / own*
He said, "No lenger dwel I ne may;
Beleves wele and haves goday.⁹
2675   I prai to Crist, Hevyn Kyng,
Lady, len° yow gude lifing,°   *(that He) grant / living*
And len grace that al yowre anoy°   *annoyance, trouble*
May turn yow° unto mykel° joy."   *(for) you / great*
Sho said, "God grant that it so be."
2680 Unto himself than thus said he:
"Thou ert the lok,° and kay° also,   *lock / key*
Of al my wele° and al my wo."°   *joy / sorrow*

Now wendes he forth and morning° mase;°   *mourning / makes*
And nane of tham wist what° he was,   *who*
2685 Bot Lunet, that he bad sold layn—¹
And so sho did with al hir mayne.
Sho cunvayd° him forth on his way;   *accompanied*
He said, "Gude leman, I the pray
That thou tel to no moder° son   *mother's*
2690 Who has bene thi champion;
And als I pray the, swete wight,
Late and arly° thou do thi might   *early*
With speche° unto my lady fre°   *speech / noble*
For-to make hir frende° with me.   *(a) friend*
2695 Sen ye er now togeder glade,²
Help thou that we war frendes made."
"Sertes, sir," sho sayd, "ful fayn;°   *gladly*
Thare-obout wil I be bayn°—   *eager*
And that° ye have done me this day,   *(for) that (which)*
2700 God do yow mede, als He wele may."
Of Lunet thus his leve he tase,°   *takes*
Bot in hert grete sorow he hase;
His lioun feled° so mekill° wa°   *felt / much / woe, distress*
That he ne myght no ferrer° ga.   *further*
2705 Sir Ywayn puld° gres° in the felde   *pulled / grass*
And made a kouche° opon his shelde;°   *couch, litter / shield*

9. Stay well and have good day (i.e., farewell).
1. Who he said should conceal the matter.
2. Since you are now happy (i.e., reconciled) together.

Thareon his lyoun laid he thare,
And forth he rides, and sighes sare.
On his shelde so he him led;
2710   Than° was he ful evyl° sted.°   *At that time/badly/situated*
     Forth he rides, by frith° and fell,°   *wood/fell, ridge*
Til he come to a fayre castell.
Thare he cald° and swith° sone   *called/quickly*
The porter has the yates° undone.°   *gates/opened*
2715   And to him made he ful gude chere;[3]
He said, "Sir, ye er welcum here."
Syr Ywain said, "God do the mede,
For tharof° have I mekil nede."   *thereof*
Yn he rade right at the yate.
2720   Faire folk kepid° hym tharate;°   *attended to/thereat*
Thai toke his shelde and his lyoun,
And ful softly thai laid it doun;
Sum to stabil led his stede,
And sum also unlaced his wede.°   *clothing, armor*
2725   Thai talde° the lord than of that knyght,   *told*
And sone he and his lady bryght,°   *splendid, fair*
And thaire sons and doghters all,
Come ful faire him for-to kall.°   *call (upon)*
Thai war ful fayn he thore° was sted—   *there*
2730 To chaumber sone thai have him led;
His bed was ordand° richely   *appointed, made ready*
And his lioun thai laid him by.
Him was no mister for-to crave—[4]
Redy° he had what he wald have.   *Readily, At once*
2735 Twa° maydens with him thai laft°   *Two/left*
That wele war lered° of lechecraft.°   *learned/medicine*
The lordes doghters both thai wore°   *were*
That war left to kepe hym thore;
Thai heled° hym everilka° wound,   *healed/every*
2740 And hys lyoun sone made thai sownd.°   *sound, healthy*
I can noght tel how lang he lay;
When he was helyd° he went his way.   *healed*

    Bot whils he sojorned° in that place,   *stayed*
In that land byfel this case.°   *case, event*
2745 A litil° thethin° in a stede   *little (way)/from there*
A grete lord of the land was ded.
Lifand° he had none other ayre°   *Living/heir*
Bot two doghters that war ful fayre;
Als sone° als he was laid in molde,°   *soon/earth*
2750 The elder sister sayd sho wolde

3. And he behaved most pleasantly toward him.
4. For him there was no need to want (anything).

Wend° to court sone als sho myght	Go
For-to get hir som doghty° knyght	doughty, courageous
For-to win hir° al the land	(for) her
And hald it halely° in hir hand.	wholly
2755 The yonger sister saw sho ne myght	
Have that fell until hir right,[5]	
Bot° if that it war by batail;	Unless
To court sho wil° at° ask cownsayl.°	will (go) / to / counsel, advice
The elder sister sone was yare;°	ready
2760 Unto the court fast gan sho fare.	
To Sir Gawayn sho made hir mane,°	moan, complaint
And he has granted° hyr° onane—	granted (his aid) / (to) her
"Bot yt bus be so prevely,[6]	
That° nane wit° bot thou and I.	(So) that / know
2765 If thou of me makes any yelp,°	boast
Lorn° has thou al my help."	Lost
Than efter, on the tother° day,	other, next
Unto kourt come the tother may,°	maiden
And to Sir Gawayn sone sho went	
2770 And talde unto him hir entent.°	intent
Of his help sho him bysoght—	
"Sertes,"° he sayd, "that may I noght."°	Certainly / not (do)
Than sho wepe° and wrang hir handes—	wept
And right with that come new tithandes,°	tidings, news
2775 How a knyght with a lyoun	
Had slane° a geant° ful feloun.°	slain / giant / cruel
The same knight thare talde this tale	
That° Syr Ywayn broght fra° bale°	Who / from / suffering
That had wedded Gawayn° sister dere.°	Gawain's / dear
2780 Sho and hir sons war thare in-fere°—	together
Thai broght the dwergh,° that be ye balde,[7]	dwarf
And to Sir Gawayn have thai talde	
How the Knyght with the Lyowne	
Delivred tham out of presowne,°	prison
2785 And how he, for Syr Gawayn° sake,	Gawain's
Gan that batayl undertake,	
And als how nobilly that he wroght.°	fared
Sir Gawayn said, "I knaw him noght."	
The yonger mayden than alsone°	immediately
2790 Of the King askes this bone:°	boon, request
To have respite of fourti° dais,°	forty / days
Als it fel to landes lays—[8]	

---

5. The younger sister saw that she might not have that which should fall to her according to her rightful claim.
6. But it is necessary that it be done so secretly.
7. Of that you can be certain.
8. According to the laws of the land.

Sho wist thare was no man of main°   *strength*
That wald fyght with Sir Gawayn;
2795   Sho thoght to seke, by frith° and fell,°   *wood/fell, ridge*
The knyght that sho herd tham° of tell.   *them*
Respite was granted of this thing;
The mayden toke leve at the King
And sethen° at al the baronage,   *then*
2800   And forth sho went on hir vayage.°   *journey*
Day ne nyght wald sho noght spare;
Thurgh° al the land fast gan sho fare,   *Through*
Thurgh castel and thurgh ilka° toun,   *each*
To seke° the Knight with the Lyown—   *seek*
2805   He helpes al, in word and dede,
That unto° him has any nede.°   *of/need*
   Sho soght hym thurgh al that land,
Bot of hym herd sho na tythand;°   *tiding, news*
Na man kouth° tel hir whare he was.   *could*
2810   Ful grete sorow in hert sho has;
So mikel° murning° gan sho make   *great/mourning*
That a grete sekenes° gan sho take.   *sickness*
Bot in° hir way right wele sho sped;   *on*
At that kastell was sho sted°   *stopped, situated*
2815   Whare Sir Ywayn are° had bene   *previously*
Helid of his sekenes clene.⁹
Thare sho was ful wele knawen°   *known*
And als° welcum als til° hyr awyn;°   *as/to/own (people)*
With alkyn gamyn thai gan hir glade,¹
2820   And mikel joy of hir thai made.
   Unto the lord sho tald hyr case—
And helping hastily sho hase.²
Stil in lecheing° thare sho lay;   *medical treatment*
A maiden for hir toke the way
2825   For-to seke° yf that sho myght   *seek, find out*
In any land here° of that knyght.   *hear*
And that same kastel come sho by
Whare Ywayn wedded the lavedy,°   *lady (Alundyne)*
And fast sho spird° in ylk° sesown°   *asked/every/moment*
2830   Efter° the Knight with the Lioun.   *After*
Thai tald hir how he went tham fra,
And also how thai saw him sla°   *slay*

---

9. Healed completely of his sickness. (Between this point and l. 2879 the poem presents a much-reduced version of the story as told in Chrétien, resulting in a rather confusing identification of various castles. Evidently the castle mentioned here is that in which Ywain was cured of his madness—although it has since gained a lord, l. 2821. The castle mentioned at l. 2879 must consequently be that in which Ywain and his lion were healed of their wounds.)
1. They gladdened her with every kind of amusement.
2. And forthwith she has (been given) help.

Thre nobil knyghtes, for the nanes,[3]
That faght° with him al at anes.°   *fought / once*
2835 Sho said, "Par charité,[4] I yow pray,
If that ye wate,° wil ye me say   *know*
Whederward° that he es went?"   *Which way*
Thai said, for soth, thai toke na tent°—   *notice*
"Ne here es nane that the can tell[5]
2840 Bot° if it be a damysell   *Unless*
For whas° sake he heder° come,   *whose / hither*
And for hir the batayl he nome.°   *took up*
We trow° wele that sho can the wis°— *trust / inform*
Yonder in yone kyrk° sho ys—   *church*
2845 Tharfore we rede° to hyr thou ga."   *advise*
And hastily than did sho swa;°   *so*
Aither° other ful gudeli° gret,° *Either / kindly / greeted*
And sone sho frayned° at Lunet   *asked*
If sho kouth ani sertain° sayne.° *certain thing / say, relate*
2850 And hendly° answerd sho ogayne,° *graciously / in reply*
"I sal sadel my palfray°   *riding horse*
And wend° with the forth on thi way   *go*
And wis the als wele als I can."
Ful oft sithes° thanked sho hir than.   *times*
2855 Lunet was ful smertly° yare,° *quickly / ready*
And with the mayden forth gan sho fare.
Als thai went, al sho hyr talde—
How sho was taken and done in halde,[6]
How wikkedly that sho was wreghed,° *accused*
2860 And how that trayturs on hir leghed,° *placed charges*
And how that sho sold° have bene brent° *should / burned*
Had noght God hir socore° sent   *succor, help*
Of that Knight with the Lyoun—
"He lesed° me out of presoun."   *released*
2865 Sho broght hir sone° into a playn° *soon / plain, field*
Whare sho parted° fra Sir Ywayn; *(had) parted*
Sho said, "Na mare can I tel the,
Bot here parted he fra me.
How that he went wate° I no mare—   *know*
2870 Bot wounded was he wonder° sare.° *wondrously / sore*
  God that for us sufferd wounde,
Len° us to se him hale° and sownde. *Grant / hale, healthy*
No lenger with the may I dwell—
Bot cumly Crist that heried hell[7]

3. Three knights of high rank, indeed.
4. For the sake of (Christian) charity.
5. Nor is there anyone here who can tell you.
6. And imprisoned.
7. But (may) noble Christ who despoiled hell. (The story of the Harrowing of Hell, dependent largely on the apocryphal Gospel of Nicodemus, achieved wide popularity in the Middle Ages;

2875	Len the grace that thou may spede°	*succeed*
	Of thine erand als thou has nede."	
	Lunet hastily hies° hir home,	*hastens*
	And the mayden sone to the kastel come	
	Whare he° was helid° byforehand.[8]	*(Ywain) / healed*
2880	The lord sone at the yate° sho fand°	*gate / found*
	With knyghtes and ladies grete cumpani;°	*company*
	Sho haylsed° tham al ful hendely,	*hailed, greeted*
	And ful fayre praied sho to tham then,	
	If thai couth, thai° sold hyr ken°	*(that) they / inform*
2885	Whare sho myght fynd, in toure or toun,	
	A kumly° knyght with a lyoun.	*noble*
	Than said the lord, "By swete Jhesus,	
	Right now parted he fra us!	
	Lo° here the steppes° of his stede;	*Look, Behold / hoofprints*
2890	Evyn° unto him thai wil the lede."°	*Even, Right / lead*
	Than toke sho leve and went hir way;	
	With sporrs° sho sparid° noght hir palfray.	*spurs / spared*
	Fast sho hyed with al hyr myght	
	Until sho of him had a syght,	
2895	And of hys lyoun that by him ran.	
	Wonder° joyful was sho than,	*Wondrously*
	And with hir force° sho hasted so fast	*(utmost) effort*
	That sho overtoke him at the last.	
	Sho hailsed him with hert ful fayn,°	*glad*
2900	And he hir hailsed fayre ogayn.°	*in reply*
	Sho said, "Sir, wide have I yow soght—	
	And for my self ne es it noght,	
	Bot for a damysel of pryse°	*high esteem*
	That halden° es both war° and wise.	*held, considered / prudent*
2905	Men dose° to hir ful grete outrage;	*do*
	Thai wald hir° reve° hyr heritage.	*(from) her / seize*
	And in this land now lifes none	
	That sho traystes hyr opone[9]	
	Bot anly° opon God—and the,	*only*
2910	For thou ert of so grete bounté.°	*goodness*
	Thorgh° help of the sho hopes wele	*Through*
	To win° hyr right, everilka° dele.°	*gain / every / part*
	Scho sais no knyght that lifes now	
	Mai help hir half so wele als thou;	
2915	Gret word sal gang° of thi vassage°	*go (about) / deed of prowess*
	If that thou win hir heritage.	

---

according to the story, Christ descended to hell upon His Crucifixion and reclaimed many souls, including the necessarily unredeemed pre-Christian souls of Adam, Eve, and Moses.)

8. On the identity of this castle, see l. 2816, n.

9. In whom she places her trust.

For thoght sho toke slike sekenes sare,[1]
So that sho might travail° no mare;   *labor*
I have yow soght on sydes° sere°—   *parts / diverse*
2920   Tharfore yowre answer wald I here,
Whether ye wil with me wend,°   *go*
Or els wh[ether][2] yow likes° to lend.”°   *prefer / stay, tarry*
He said, “That knyght that idil° lies   *idle*
Oft sithes winnes ful litel pries.°   *esteem*
2925   Forthi° mi rede° sal sone be tane:°   *Therefore / (own) advice / taken*
Gladly with the wil I gane,
Wheder° so thou wil me lede,   *Wherever*
And hertly° help the in thi nede.   *heartily*
Sen° thou haves° me so wide soght,   *Since / have*
2930   Sertes,° fail the sal° I noght.”   *Certainly / shall*

Thus thaire wai° forth gan thai hald°   *way / take*
Until° a kastel that was cald°   *Unto / called*
The Castel of the Hevy Sorow;
Thare wald he bide° until the morow.   *abide*
2935   Thare to habide° him thoght it best—   *abide*
For the son° drogh° fast to rest—   *sun / drew*
Bot al the men that thai with met
Grete wonder sone on tham thai set[3]
And said, “Thou wreche!° Unsely° man!   *wretch / Unfortunate*
2940   Whi wil thou here thi herber° tane?°   *shelter / have taken*
Thou passes noght without despite.”[4]
Sir Ywain answerd tham als tyte°   *immediately*
And said, “For soth, ye er unhende°   *ungracious*
An unkouth° man so for-to shende;°   *unknown, strange / reproach*
2945   Ye sold noght say hym velany,°   *insulting things*
Bot° if ye wist° encheson° why.”   *Unless / know / (the) reason*
Thai answerd than, and said ful sone,
“Thou sal wit or° to-morn at none.”°   *before / noon*
Syr Ywaine said, “For al yowre saw°   *talk*
2950   Unto yon castel wil I draw.”
He and his lyoun and the may°   *maid*
Unto the castel toke the way.
When the porter of tham had sight,
Sone he said unto the knight,
2955   “Cumes° forth,” he said, “ye al togeder—   *Come*

1. For anxiety she contracted such a grievous sickness.
2. The manuscript reading here, “whare” (“where”), makes little sense of the maiden's question (and Ywain's answer) and probably represents scribal misapprehension after the copying of “els”; “Whether ye . . . /Or els wh[ether] yow . . .” translates, in sense, word order, and repetition, the maiden's words “Se vos . . . /Ou se vos . . .” in Chrétien (ll. 5093–94).
3. I.e., they regarded them with great amazement.
4. You will not come away without injury.

Ful ille hail er ye cumen heder!"[5]
Thus war° thai welkumd at the yate,   were
And yit° thai went al in tharate°—   yet / thereat
Unto the porter no word thai said.
2960   A hal° thai fand ful gudeli° graid,°   hall / well / prepared
And als Sir Ywaine made entré,°   entry
Fast bisyde him than saw he
A proper place and faire, iwis,°   indeed
Enclosed obout with a palis.°   palisade, defensive fence
2965   He loked in bitwix° the trese,°   between / wood (posts)
And many maidens thare he sese°   sees
Wirkand° silk and gold wire.   Working, Weaving
Bot thai war al in pover° atire;   poor
Thaire clothes war reven on evil arai.[6]
2970   Ful tenderly al weped° thai;   wept
Thaire face war lene° and als unclene,   lean, gaunt
And blak smokkes had thai on bidene.[7]
Thai had mischefs° ful manifalde,°   troubles / manifold
Of hunger, of threst,° and of calde°—   thirst / cold
2975   And ever on-ane thai weped all,
Als thai wald to water fall.[8]
When Ywaine al this understode,
Ogayn unto the yates he yode;°   went
Bot thai war sperred° ferli° fast   fastened, locked / amazingly
2980   With lokkes that ful wele wald° last.   would
The porter kepid tham with his main[9]
And said, "Sir, thou most wend ogain;°   back
I wate° thou wald° out at the yate,   know / would (go)
Bot thou mai noght, by na gate.°   way
2985   Thi herber° es tane° til tomorow—   lodging / taken
And tharfore° getes° thou mekill° sorow;   for that / get / great
Omang thi fase° here sted° ertow."°   foes / situated / art thou
He° said, "So have I bene or° now   (Ywain) / before
And past° ful wele; so sal I here—   passed, prevailed
2990   Bot, leve frend, wiltou me lere[1]
Of thise maidens, what° thai are   who
That wirkes° al this riche ware?"°   work / material
He said, "If thou wil wit trewly,
Forthermare° thou most° aspy."°   Elsewhere / must / espy, look
2995   "Tharfore," he° said, "I sal noght lett."°   (Ywain) / cease
He soght and fand° a dern° weket;°   found / secret / wicket gate
He opind it and in he yede—

5. Most disastrously have you come here!
6. Torn into a wretched state.
7. And black (i.e., dirty) smocks they had on, one and all.
8. And constantly they wept, as if they would turn to water.
9. I.e., the porter resolutely kept them back.
1. But, dear friend, will you inform me.

"Maidens," he said, "God mot yow spede,[2]
And, als° He sufferd woundes sare,°   as / sore
3000 He send yow covering° of° yowre care°   recovery / from / distress
So that ye might mak merier chere."[3]
"Sir," thai said, "God gif so were."[4]
"Yowre sorow," he said, "unto me say,°   relate
And I sal mend it, yf I may."
3005 Ane of tham answerd ogayne°   in reply
And said, "The soth° we sal noght layne;°   truth / hide
We sal yow tel or ye ga ferr°   further
Why we er here and what we err.°   are
        Sir, ye sal understand
3010 That we er al of Maydenland.
Oure kyng, opon his jolité°   sport, amusement
Passed thurgh many cuntré,
Aventures to spir° and spy   ask about
For-to asay° his owen body;   test
3015 His herber° here anes° gan he ta.°   lodging / once / take
That was biginyng of oure wa,
For heryn° er twa° champions—   herein / two
Men sais thai er the devil-sons
Geten of a woman with a ram;[5]
3020 Ful many° man have thai done gram°—   many (a) / grief, harm
What knight so herbers here a nyght,
With both at ones bihoves him fight.
So bus the do, by bel and boke—[6]
Allas, that thou thine yns° here toke!   lodgings
3025   Oure king was wight himself to welde[7]
And of fourtene yeres of elde°   age
When he was tane with tham to fyght.
Bot unto tham had he no myght,
And when he saw him bud be ded[8]
3030 Than he kouth° no better rede°   knew / plan
Bot did him haly in thaire grace,[9]
And made tham sureté° in that place   (a) surety, (a) pledge
For-to yeld° tham° ilka° yere,   yield / (to) them / each
So that he sold° be hale° and fere,°   should / unharmed / sound

2. May God help you.
3. I.e., so that you may be of a merrier disposition.
4. God grant that it were so.
5. Begotten of the union of a woman and a ram.
6. It behooves him to fight with both at once. So it behooves you to do, by bell and by book
   (i.e., with due solemnity; this conventional phrase, like the current "bell, book, and candle,"
   alludes to certain prescribed effects used either in the Mass or the rite of excommunication;
   cf. *Havelok*, ll. 388–91, *The Awntyrs off Arthur*, l. 30, and *The Sege off Melayne*, ll. 691–
   97).
7. I.e., our king was responsible for his actions.
8. I.e., and when he saw that he would have to die.
9. But put himself wholly at their mercy.

3035 Threty° maidens to° trowage°—	*Thirty / as / tribute*
And al sold be of hegh° parage°	*high / rank, birth*
And the fairest of his land—	
Herto held he up his hand.[1]	
This ilk rent byhoves° hym gyf°	*(it) behooves / (to) give*
3040 Als lang als the fendes° lyf,°	*fiends / live*
Or til thai be in batayl tane,°	*taken, defeated*
Or els unto° thai be al slane.°	*until / slain*
Than sal we pas° al hethin° quite°	*pass / from here / free*
That° here suffers al this despite°—	*Who / abuse*
3045 Bot herof es noght for speke;[2]	
Es none in werld that us mai wreke.°	*avenge*
We wirk° here silver, silk, and golde;	*work*
Es° none richer on this molde,°	*(There) is / earth*
And never the better er we kled,°	*clad, clothed*
3050 And in grete hunger er we sted.°	*situated, placed*
For al that we wirk in this stede,	
We have noght half oure fil of brede;°	*bread*
For the best that sewes° here any styk°	*sews / stitch*
Takes bot foure penys° in a wik°—	*pennies / week*
3055 And that es litel, wha som tase hede,[3]	
Any of us to kleth° and fede.	*clothe*
Ilkone of us, withouten lesyng,°	*lie*
Might win ilk wike° fourty shilling;[4]	*week*
And yit, bot° if we travail° mare,°	*unless / work / more*
3060 Oft thai bete us wonder sare.°	*sorely*
It helpes noght to tel this tale,	
For thare bese never bote of oure bale;[5]	
Oure maste° sorow, sen° we bigan,	*greatest / since*
That es that we se mani a man—	
3065 Doghty dukes, yrels,° and barouns—	*earls*
Oft sithes° slane with° thir° champiowns.	*times / by / these*
With tham to-morn bihoves the fight."°	*(to) fight*
Sir Ywayn said, "God, maste of myght,	
Sal strenkith° me in ilka dede	*strengthen*
3070 Ogains tha devils and al thaire drede;°	*horror*
That Lord deliver yow of yowre fase."[6]	
Thus takes he leve and forth he gase.°	*goes*
He passed forth into the hall.	
Thare fand he no man him to call;°	*greet*
3075 No bewtese° wald thai to him bede,°	*kindness / offer*
Bot hastily thai toke his stede	

1. I.e., he swore an oath to that.
2. I.e., but it is no use to speak of this.
3. To whoever takes notice (of the fact).
4. A shilling is equal to twelve pennies.
5. For there will never be a remedy for our suffering.
6. I.e., may that Lord (through me) deliver you of your foes.

And also the maydens palfray
(War° served wele with corn and hay;   *(The horses) were*
For wele thai° hoped that Sir Ywayn   *(the captors)*
3080 Sold never have had his stede ogayn).
Thurgh the hal Sir Ywain gase°   *goes*
Intil° ane orcherd playn pase—[7]   *Into*
His maiden with him ledes he.
He fand a knyght under a tre°—   *tree*
3085 Opon a cloth of gold he lay—[8]
Byfor him sat a ful fayre may.
A lady sat with tham in-fere.°   *together*
The mayden red° at° thai myght here   *read / so that*
A real° romance in that place   *royal, courtly*
3090 (Bot I ne wote of wham° it was).° *whom / was (about)*
Sho was bot fiftene yeres alde—°   *old*
The knyght was lord of al that halde,° *(strong)hold*
And that mayden was his ayre;°   *heir*
Sho was both gracious, gode, and fare.
3095 Sone,° when thai saw Sir Ywaine, *Soon, Quickly*
Smertly rase° thai hym ogayne,°   *rose / before*
And by the hand the lord him tase,°   *takes*
And unto him grete myrth he mase.°   *makes*
He said, "Sir, by swete Jhesus,
3100 Thou ert ful welcum until° us."   *unto*
  The mayden was bowsom° and bayne° *willing / eager*
For-to unarme° Syr Ywayne;   *unarm*
Serk° and breke° bath° sho hym broght *Shirt / breeches / both*
That ful craftily war wroght
3105 Of riche cloth soft als the sylk,
And tharto white als any mylk.
Sho broght hym ful riche wedes° to were,° *clothes / wear*
Hose and shose and alkins gere.[9]
Sho payned° hir° with al hir myght *pained, troubled / herself*
3110 To serve him and his mayden bright.
Sone thai went unto sopere;°   *supper*
Ful really° served thai were   *royally*
With metes and drinkes of the best—
And sethin° war thai broght to rest.   *then*
3115 In his chaumher by hym lay
His owin lyoun, and his may.
At morn, when it was dayes lyght,
Up thai rase and sone tham dyght.°   *prepared*
Sir Ywayn and hys damysele
3120 Went ful sone til° a chapele,   *to*

7. In all haste.
8. Presumably the knight lies on gold cloth wrought by the captive maidens.
9. Shoes and all kinds of (other) apparel.

And thare thai herd a mes° in haste   *mass*
That was sayd of° the Haly° Gaste.°   *for/Holy/Ghost, Spirit*
Efter mes ordand° he has   *made ready*
Forth on his way fast for-to pas;°   *pass*
3125 At the lord hys leve he tase,
And grete thanking to him he mase.°   *makes*
The lord said, "Tak it to na greve,
To gang hethin yit getes thou na leve;
Herein es ane unsely law
3130 That has bene used of ald daw
And bus be done for frend or fa.[1]
I sal do° com byfor the twa   *have*
Grete serjantes° of mekil° myght;   *men-at-arms/great*
And, whether it be wrang° or right,   *wrong*
3135 Thou most tak the shelde and spere°   *spear, lance*
Ogaynes° tham the for-to were.°   *Against/defend*
If thou overcum tham in this stoure,°   *fight*
Than sal thou have al this honoure,
And my doghter in mariage
3140 And also al myne heritage."
    Than said Sir Ywayn, "Als mot I the,
Thi doghter sal thou have for me;[2]
For a king or ane emparoure°   *emperor*
May hir wed with grete honoure."
3145 The lord said, "Here sal cum na knyght,
That he ne sal with twa champions fight;
So sal thou do on° al° wise,°   *in/every/way*
For it es knawen custum assise."[3]
Sir Ywaine said, "Sen I sal° so,°   *must/(do) so*
3150 Than es° the best that I may do   *(it) is*
To put me baldly° in thaire hend°   *boldly/hands*
And tak the grace that God wil send."
    The champions sone war forth broght.
Sir Ywain sais, "By Him me boght,[4]
3155 Ye seme° wele° the devils sons,   *seem/truly*
For I saw never swilk° champions."   *such*
Aither° broght unto the place   *Either*
A mikel° rownd° talvace°   *great/round/shield*
And a klub ful grete and lang,
3160 Thik fret° with mani a thwang;°   *bound/thong, strip of hide*
On bodies armyd wele thai ware,
Bot thare hedes° bath° war bare.   *heads/both*

1. Take no offense (at what I say), (but to intend) to go from here does not mean that you can leave; in this place there is an unfortunate rule that has been applied since the old days and must be observed by friend and foe alike.
2. As I hope to thrive, you shall keep your daughter for my sake.
3. For it is recognized (as an) established custom.
4. (I swear) by Him who redeemed my soul (i.e., by Christ).

The lioun bremly° on tham blist;°   *fiercely / glared*
When he tham saw, ful wele he wist
3165 That thai sold° with his mayster° fight.   *should / master*
He thoght to help him at his myght;[5]
With his tayl the erth he dang°—   *beat*
For-to fyght him thoght ful lang.[6]
Of him a° party° had thai drede;   *in / part*
3170 Thai said, "Syr knight, thou most nede
Do° thi lioun out of this place—   *Send*
For to us makes he grete manace°—   *menace, threat*
Or yelde° the til us als° creant."°   *yield / as / surrendered*
He said, "That war noght mine avenant."[7]
3175   Thai said, "Than do thi beste° oway,   *beast*
And als sone sal we samyn° play."   *together*
He said, "Sirs, if ye be agast,°   *aghast, terrified*
Takes the beste and bindes° him fast."   *bind, secure*
Thai said, "He sal be bun° or slane,°   *bound / slain*
3180 For help of him sal thou have nane;
Thi self allane° sal with us fight,   *alone*
For that es custume° and the right."   *customary*
Than said Sir Ywain to tham sone,
"Whare wil ye that the best be done?"
3185 "In a chamber he sal be loken°   *locked*
With gude lokkes ful stifly° stoken."°   *firmly / bolted*
Sir Ywain led than his lioun
Intil a chamber to presoun;°   *imprisonment*
Than war° bath tha devils ful balde°   *were / bold*
3190 When the lioun was in halde.°   *confinement*
  Sir Ywayn toke his nobil wede°   *armor*
And dight° him yn° (for he had nede),°   *dressed / (there)in / need*
And on his nobil stede he strade°   *bestrode*
And baldely to tham bath he rade.°   *rode*
3195   His mayden was ful sare adred°   *afraid*
That he was so straitly sted,[8]
And unto God fast gan sho pray
For-to wyn him wele oway.[9]
Than strake thai on him wonder sare
3200 With thaire clubbes that ful strang ware;
Opon his shelde so fast thai feld°   *fell, laid on*
That never a pece° with other held.°   *piece / held together*
Wonder it es that any man
Might bere° the strakes that he toke than;   *bear, endure*

---

5. With all his might.
6. I.e., he grew very impatient to fight.
7. That would not be honorable to me.
8. Because he was so severely constrained.
9. I.e., to bring him out of that situation with success.

3205	Mister° haved° he of socoure,°	*Great need / had / succor, help*
	For he come never° in swilk a stoure—	*never (before)*
	Bot manly evyr,° with al his mayn,°	*ever, always / strength*
	And graithly° hit he tham ogayn.	*readily*
	And, als it telles in the boke,[1]	
3210	He gaf the dubbil° of that° he toke.°	*double / that (which) / received*
	Ful grete sorow the lioun has	
	In the chameber whare he was;	
	And ever he thoght opon that dede—	
	How he was helpid in his nede—[2]	
3215	And he might now do na socowre	
	To him that helpid him in that stoure;	
	Might he out of the chamber breke,°	*break*
	Sone he walde his maister wreke.°	*avenge*
	He herd thaire strakes that war ful sterin,°	*strong, violent*
3220	And yern he waytes in ilka heryn;	
	And al was made ful fast to hald.[3]	
	At the last he come to the thriswald;°	*threshold*
	The erth° thare kest° he up ful sone°—	*earth / cast / soon*
	Als fast als foure men sold° have done,	*should*
3225	If thai had broght bath bill° and spade,	*pickax*
	A mekil° hole ful sone he made.	*great*
	Yn al this was Sir Ywayn	
	Ful straitly parred with mekil payn—	
	And drede he had, als him wele aght,[4]	
3230	For nowther° of tham na woundes laght.°	*neither / took, received*
	Kepe° tham cowth° thai wonder° wele	*Defend / could / (so) wondrously*
	That dintes derid° tham never a dele;[5]	*harmed*
	It° was na wapen° that man might welde°	*There / weapon / wield*
	Might° get a shever° out of thaire shelde.	*(Which) might / splinter*
3235	Tharof cowth Ywayn no rede;[6]	
	Sare he douted° to be ded.	*expected*
	And also his damysel	
	Ful mekil murnyng° made omell,°	*mourning / at once*
	And wele sho wend° he sold be slane—	*believed*
3240	And, sertes, than war hir socore gane.[7]	
	Bot fast° he stighteld° in that stowre°—	*resolutely / strove / fight*
	And hastily him° come socowre.	*(to) him*
	Now es the lioun outbroken—	
	His maister sal ful sone be wroken!°	*avenged*

1. Cf. l. 9 and n.
2. I.e., he constantly recalled the time that Ywain had helped him.
3. And longingly he inspects each corner; but every possible way out was fully secured for (his) confinement.
4. All this time was Sir Ywain severely constrained with great pain—and he had great fear, as he well ought to have.
5. Not in the least.
6. Because of this Ywain knew not what to do.
7. And certainly then her salvation would be lost.

3245	He rynnes fast with ful fell° rese—°	*savage/rush*
	Than helpid it noght to prai for pese!°	*peace, truce*
	He stirt unto that a glotowne,[8]	
	And to the erth he brayd° him downe.	*pulled*
	Than was thare nane obout that place	
3250	That thai ne war fayn° of that faire chace°	*pleased/chase, hunt*
	(The maiden had grete joy in hert);	
	Thai said, "He sal never rise in quert!"°	*one piece*
	His felow fraisted° with al his mayn	*attempted*
	To raise him smertly up ogayn—	
3255	And right so als he stowped° doun,	*stooped*
	Sir Ywain with his brand° was boun°	*sword/ready*
	And strake his nek-bane° right insonder.°	*neck vertebra/asunder*
	Thareof the folk had mekil wonder;	
	His hevid° trindeld° on the sand.	*head/trundled, rolled*
3260	Thus had Ywain the hegher° hand.	*higher, upper*
	When he had feld that fowl° feloun,°	*foul/felon, fiend*
	Of his stede he lighted° down.	*alighted*
	His lioun on that other lay;	
	Now wil he° help him, if he may.	*(Ywain)*
3265	The lioun saw his maister cum,	
	And—to hys part he wald have som—	
	The right sholder oway he rase;[9]	
	Both arm and klob° with him he tase°—	*club/takes*
	And so his maister gan he wreke.	
3270	And, als he° might, yit gan he speke	*(the wounded fiend)*
	And said, "Sir knight, for thi gentry,[1]	
	I prai the have of me mercy—	
	And, by scill, sal he mercy have	
	Wat man so mekely wil it crave;[2]	
3275	And tharfore grantes mercy to me."	
	Sir Ywain said, "I grant it the,	
	If that thou wil thi selven° say	*self*
	That thou ert overcumen° this day."	*overcome, vanquished*
	He said, "I grant, withowten fail,	
3280	I am overcumen in this batail	
	For pure ataynt,° and recreant."°	*exhaustion/defeated*
	Sir Ywayn said, "Now I the grant	
	For-to do the na mare dere,°	*harm*
	And fro my liown I sal the were.°	*protect*
3285	I grant the pese at° my powere."	*in*
	Than come the folk ful faire in-fere,°	*together*

8. He started unto the one fiend (*lit.*, glutton—a sinful creature).
9. The lion saw his master come, and—he wished to have his share—he tore away the right shoulder (of the fiend).
1. For the sake of your nobility.
2. And, according to reason, that man must have mercy who humbly asks for it.

The lord and the lady als;°   *also*
Thai toke him faire obout the hals°—   *neck*
Thai saide, "Sir, now saltou° be   *shalt thou*
3290 Lord and syre° in this cuntré,   *sire, master*
And wed oure doghter, for sertayn."
Sir Ywain answerd than ogayn—
    He said, "Sen ye gif me hir now,
I gif hir evyn° ogayn to yow;   *even, yet*
3295 Of me forever I grant hir quite.°   *free*
Bot, sir, takes it til° no despite;°   *to, as / insult*
For, sertes, whif may I none wed—
Until my nedes be better sped.³
Bot this thing, sir, I ask of the:
3300 That al thir° prisons° may pas fre—   *these / prisoners*
God has granted me this chance;
I have made° thaire delyverance."   *made (possible)*
The lord answerd than ful tyte°   *immediately*
And said, "I grant the tham al quite.
3305 My doghter als, I rede° thou take;   *advise*
Sho es noght worthi to forsake."
Unto the knyght Sir Ywain sais,
"Sir, I sal noght hir mysprays°—   *dispraise, disparage*
For sho es so curtays and hende°   *gracious*
3310 That fra hethin° to the werldes° ende   *here / world's*
Es no king ne emparoure,
Ne no man of so grete honowre,
That he ne might wed that bird bright—⁴
And so wald I, if that I myght.
3315   I wald hir wed with ful gude chere,⁵
Bot, lo,° I have a mayden here;   *look, behold*
To folow hir now most I nede,⁶
Wheder° so sho wil me lede.   *Wherever*
Tharfore at this time haves goday."⁷
3320 He said, "Thou passes noght so oway!
Sen thou wil noght do als I tell,
In my prison sal thou dwell."
He said, "If° I lay thare al my live,°   *(Even) if / life*
I sal hir never wed to wive;
3325 For with this maiden most I wend°   *go*
Until we cum whare sho wil lend."°   *stay*
The lord saw it was na bote°   *help, use*

---

3. For, certainly, I may wed no wife—until my difficulties are better dispatched. (Ywain thus makes a significant ironic reference to his own condition; he sees himself as a kind of suitor to his own marriage.)
4. That he would not wed that splendid maiden.
5. I.e., I would happily marry her.
6. I must now follow her.
7. Have good day (i.e., farewell).

Obout that mater° more to mote;°   *matter/argue*
He gaf him leve oway to fare—
3330 Bot he had lever° he had bene thare.   *rather*

Sir Ywayn takes than forth in-fere
Al the prisons that thare were;
Bifore hym sone° thai come ilkane,°   *soon, quickly/each one*
Nerehand° naked, and wobigane.°   *Nearly/woebegone, afflicted*
3335 Stil he hoved° at the yate°   *waited/gate*
Til thai war went al forth thareate;°   *thereat*
Twa-and-twa ay went thai samyn[8]
And made omang tham mikel° gamyn.°   *great/game, amusement*
If God had cumen fra hevyn° on hight°   *heaven/high*
3340 And on this mold° omang tham light,   *earth*
Thai had° noght made mare° joy, sertain,   *(would have) had/more*
Than thai made to Syr Ywayne.
Folk of the toun° com him biforn°   *town/before*
And blissed° the time that he was born.   *blessed*
3345 Of his prowes° war thai wele payd°—   *prowess/rewarded*
"In this werld es none slike,"° thai said.   *such*
Thai cunvayd° him out of the toun   *accompanied*
With ful faire processiowne.
The maidens than thaire leve has tane—
3350 Ful mekil° myrth thai made ilkane;   *great*
At thaire departing prayed thai thus:
"Oure Lord God, mighty Jhesus,
He° help yow, sir, to have yowre will   *(May) He*
And shilde yow ever fra alkyns ill."[9]
3355 "Maidens," he said, "God mot yow se[1]
And bring yow wele whare ye wald° be."   *would*
    Thus thaire way forth er° thai went.°   *are/gone*
(Na more unto tham wil we tent.)[2]
Sir Ywayn and his faire may°   *maid*
3360 Al the sevenight° traveld thai.   *week*
The maiden knew the way ful wele
Hame until that ilk° castele   *same*
Whare sho left the seke° may;   *sick*
And theder hastily come thai.
3365 When thai come to the castel yate,
Sho led Sir Ywain yn thareate.
The mayden was yit° seke lyand,°   *yet, still/lying*
Bot when thai talde hir this tithand,°   *tiding, news*
That cumen was hir messagere°   *messenger*
3370 And the knyght with hyr in-fere,

8. All the time they went together, two by two.
9. And shield you from every kind of evil.
1. May God watch over you.
2. I.e., we will follow their story no further.

Swilk° joy thareof sho had in hert   *Such*
Hir thoght that sho was al in quert.³
Sho said, "I wate° my sister will   *know*
Gif me now that falles me till."⁴
3375   In hir hert sho was ful light;
Ful hendly° hailsed° sho the knight.   *graciously/hailed, commended*
    "A!° Sir," sho said, "God do the mede°   *Oh/reward*
That thou wald cum in swilk° a nede."°   *such/(case of) need*
And al that in that kastel were
3380   Welkumd him with meri° chere—   *merry*
I can noght say, so God me glade,
Half the myrth that thai him° made.   *(for) him*
That night he had ful nobil rest
With alkins° esment° of the best.   *every kind of/ease, comfort*
3385   Als sone als the day was sent,°   *dawned*
Thai ordaind° tham,° and forth thai went.   *prepared/themselves*
Until that town fast gan thai ride
Whare the Kyng sojorned that tide.°   *time*
And thare the elder sister lay,
3390   Redy for-to kepe hyr day°—   *(appointed) day*
Sho traisted° wele on Sir Gawayn,   *trusted*
That no knyght sold° cum him ogayn;°   *should/against*
Sho hopid° thare was no knyght lifand°   *believed/living*
In batail that might with him stand.⁵
3395   Al a sevenight dayes bidene⁶
Wald noght Sir Gawayn be sene,°   *seen*
Bot in ane other toun he lay—
For he wald cum at the day
Als aventerous⁷ into the place,
3400   So that no man sold se his face;
The armes° he bare war noght his awyn,°   *arms and coat-of-arms/own*
For he wald noght in court be knawyn.°   *known, recognized*
Syr Ywayn and his damysell
In the town toke thaire hostell;
3405   And thare he held him° prevely°   *himself/secretly*
So that none sold him ascry.°   *expose*
(Had thai dwelt° langer° by a day,   *tarried/longer*
Than had sho lorn° hir land for ay.)°   *lost/ever*
Sir Ywain rested thare that nyght,
3410   And on the morn he gan hym dyght.°   *prepare*
On slepe left thai his lyowne
And wan° tham wightly° out of toun;   *passed/boldly*

---

3. She felt that she was fully recovered.
4. I.e., that which is rightfully mine.
5. I.e., that might withstand him.
6. I.e., for an entire week.
7. As if seeking adventure (i.e., armed, presumably with his visor down).

It was hir wil, and als° hys awyn,   *also*
At° cum to court als° knyght unknawyn.°   *To/as/unknown*
3415   Sone, obout the prime⁸ of day,
Sir Gawayn fra thethin° thare he lay°   *thence/stayed*
Hies° him fast into the felde,   *Hastens*
Wele armyd with spere° and shelde;   *spear, lance*
No man knew him, les ne more,⁹
3420   Bot sho that he sold fight fore.
The elder sister to court come,
Unto the King at° ask hir dome;°   *to/judgment*
Sho said, "I am cumen with my knyght
Al redy to defend my right.°   *rightful (legal) claim*
3425   This day was us set sesowne,°   *(as) the due time*
And I am here al redy bowne;°   *prepared*
And sen this es the last day,
Gifes° dome and lates us wend° oure way.   *Give/go*
My sister has al sydes° soght,   *parts, places*
3430   Bot, wele I wate,° here cums sho noght;   *know*
For, sertainly, sho findes nane
That dar the batail undertane°   *undertake*
This day for hir for-to fyght,
For-to reve° fra me my right.   *take (by force)*
3435   Now have I wele wonnen° my land,   *won, seized*
Withowten dint of knightes hand;
What so my sister ever has mynt,
Al hir part now tel I tynt—¹
Al es myne to sell and gyf;°   *give*
3440   Als a wreche° ay° sal sho lyf.°   *wretch/forever/live*
Tharfore, Sir King, sen° it es swa,°   *since/so*
Gifes yowre dome and lat us ga."

The King said, "Maiden, think noght lang."²
Wele he wist° sho had the wrang°—   *knew/wrong*
3445   "Damysel, it es the assyse,
Whils sityng, es of the justise;
The dome nedes thou most habide—³
For, par° aventure,° it may bityde   *by/chance*
Thi sister sal cum al bi° tyme,   *in*
3450   For it es litil passed° prime."   *past*
When the King had tald° this scill,°   *told, declared/reason*
Thai saw cum rideand° over a hyll   *riding*
The yonger sister and hir knyght;
The way to town thai toke ful right.

8. On *prime*, see l. 2304, n.
9. Less nor more (i.e., in no way).
1. Whatever my sister may have intended, all her share I now declare as forfeit.
2. I.e., do not be impatient.
3. Damsel, it is the court, while sitting, that is the judge; you must wait for the decision.

3455 (On Ywains bed his liown lay,
     And thai had stollen fra him oway.)
     The elder maiden made il chere⁴
     When thai to court cumen were.
     The King withdrogh° his jugement,   *withheld, held back*
3460 For wele he trowed° in his entent°   *trusted / conviction*
     That the yonger sister had the right,
     And that sho sold cum with sum knyght—
     Himself knew hyr wele inogh.°   *enough*
     When he hir saw, ful fast he logh;°   *laughed*
3465 Him liked it wele in his hert
     That he saw hir so in quert.°   *good health, good form*
          Into the court sho toke the way,
     And to the King thus gan sho say,
     "God that governs alkin° thing,   *every*
3470 The save and se,° Syr Arthure the Kyng,   *watch over*
     And al the knyghtes that langes° to the,   *belong*
     And also al thi mery menyé.°   *company*
     Unto yowre court, sir, have I broght
     An unkouth° knyght that ye knaw° noght;   *unknown / know*
3475 He sais that sothyly° for my sake   *truly*
     This batayl wil he undertake—
     And he haves yit in other land
     Ful felle dedes under hand;⁵
     Bot al he leves°—God do him mede°—   *leaves, puts off / reward*
3480 For-to help me in my nede."
          Hir elder sister stode hyr by,
     And tyl° hyr sayd sho hastily,   *to*
     "For Hys luf that lens° us life,   *grants*
     Gif me my right° withouten strife   *rightful (legal) claim*
3485 And lat no men tharfore be slayn."
     The elder sister sayd ogayn,
     "Thi right es noght,° for al es myne—   *nothing*
     And I wil have yt mawgré thine.⁶
     Tharfore, if thou preche° al day,   *preach, protest*
3490 Here° sal thou nothing bere° oway."   *(From) here / bear, take*
     The yonger mayden to hir says,
     "Sister, thou ert ful curtays,°   *courteous, gracious*
     And gret dole es it for-to se
     Slike° two knightes als thai be   *(That) such*
3495 For us sal put° thamself to spill.°   *venture / die*
     Tharefore now, if it be thi will,
     Of thi gude° wil to me thou gif   *goods, property*
     Sumthing that I may on lif?"°   *live*

4. Put on a show of displeasure.
5. I.e., and elsewhere he has important deeds yet to do.
6. I.e., in spite of you.

The elder said, "So mot I the,[7]
3500 Who so es ferd,° I rede° thai fle.°   *afraid / advise / flee*
Thou getes right noght, withowten fail,
Bot if thou win yt thurgh° batail."°   *through / battle*
The yonger said, "Sen thou wil° swa,   *will (have it)*
To the grace of God here I me ta;°   *take, commend*
3505 And Lord als He es, maste° of myght,   *most*
He° send His socore° to that knyght   *(May) He / succor, help*
That thus in dede° of charité   *deed*
This day antres° hys lif for me."   *ventures*
    The twa° knightes come bifor the King—   *two*
3510 And thare was sone° ful grete gedering,°   *soon / gathering (of a crowd)*
For ilka° man that walk might   *every*
Hasted sone to se that syght.
Of tham this was a selly° case,   *wondrous*
That nowther° wist what° other wase;   *neither / who*
3515 Ful grete luf was bitwix° tham twa,   *between*
And now er aither° other° fa°—   *either / other's / foe*
Ne the King kowth° tham noght knaw,   *could*
For thai wald noght thaire faces shew.°   *show*
If owther of tham had other sene
3520 Grete luf had bene° tham bitwene;   *been (expressed)*
Now was this a grete selly°   *wonder*
That trew luf and so° grete envy°   *such / enmity*
Als bitwix tham twa was than
Might bath° at anes° be in a man!   *both / once*
3525 The knightes, for thase maidens love,°   *devotion*
Aither til other kast a glove,[8]
And, wele armed with spere and shelde,
Thai riden both forth to the felde.
    Thai stroke° thaire stedes that war° kene°—   *whipped / were / keen, eager*
3530 Litel luf was tham bitwene;
Ful grevosly bigan that gamyn.°   *game*
With stalworth° speres strake thai samen°—   *stalwart, strong / together*
And thai had anes togeder spoken,
Had thare bene no speres broken—[9]
3535 Bot in that time bitid° it swa°   *befell / so*
That aither of tham wald other sla.°   *slay*
Thai drow° swerdes and swang obout;   *drew*
To dele° dyntes° had thai no dout.°   *deal / dints, blows / hesitation*
Thaire sheldes war shiferd° and helms rifen°—   *shattered / riven, smashed*
3540 Ful stalworth strakes° war thare gifen;°   *strokes / given*

---

7. As I hope to thrive.
8. I.e., either threw down the gauntlet to the other. (A chivalric custom which is the literal antecedent of the modern expression; the throwing down of the gauntlet—the gauntlet being seen as a symbol of its owner's martial authority—constitutes a challenge to combat.)
9. But if they had just once spoken together, no spears would have been broken (in battle).

Bath on bak and brestes thare
War bath wounded wonder sare.
In many stedes° might men ken°   *places / perceive*
The blode out of thaire bodies ren.°   *running*
3545   On helmes thai gaf slike° strakes kene   *such*
That the riche stanes° al bidene,°   *stones / together*
And other gere that was ful gude,
Was overcoverd al in blode.
Thaire helmes war evel° brusten° bath;   *badly / buckled*
3550 And thai also war wonder wrath.°   *wroth, enraged*
Thaire hauberkes° als war al to-torn,°   *coats of mail / torn up*
Both bihind and als byforn;°   *before, in front*
Thaire sheldes lay sheverd° on the ground.   *shattered*
Thai rested than a litil stound°   *time, while*
3555 For-to tak thaire ande° tham till—   *breath*
And that was with thaire bother° will,   *mutual*
Bot ful lang rested thai noght
Til aither of tham on other soght.°   *charged*
A stronge stowre° was tham bitwene—   *fight*
3560 Harder had men never sene.
    The King and other° that thare ware   *other (people)*
Said that thai saw never are°   *before*
So nobil knightes in no place
So lang fight bot by Goddes grace.
3565 Barons, knightes, squiers, and knaves
Said, "It° es no man that haves°   *there / has*
So mekil° tresore° ne nobillay,°   *much / treasure / high regard*
That might tham quite° thaire dede this day."   *requite, reward*
Thir° wordes herd the knyghtes twa;°   *These / two*
3570 It made tham for-to be more thra.°   *stubborn*

    Knightes went obout gude wane
To mak the two sisters at ane;[1]
Bot the elder was so unkinde,°   *unnatural (i.e., unsisterly)*
In hir thai might no mercy finde;
3575 And the right that the yonger hase,
Puttes sho in the Kinges grace.[2]
The King himself, and als the Quene
And other knightes al bidene,°   *together*
And al that saw that dede° that day,   *deed*
3580 Held° al with the yonger may.   *Kept, Sided*
And to the King al thai bisoght,°   *beseeched, implored*
Whether the elder wald° or noght,   *would*
That he sold° evin° the landes dele,°   *should / evenly / divide*
And gif the yonger damysele

1. A good many knights went about trying to bring the two sisters to one accord.
2. And the younger sister entrusts (the question of) her rightful claim to the King's discretion.

3585 The half (or els sum porciowne°   *portion*
     That sho mai have to° warisowne),°   *in / compensation*
     And part the two knightes intwyn°—   *apart*
     "For, sertis," thai said, "it war grete syn,°   *sin*
     That owther of tham sold other sla—
3590 For in the werld° es noght swilk° twa;   *world / such*
     When other knightes," said thai, "sold sese,°   *cease*
     Thamself° wald noght asent to pese."°   *(They) themselves / peace*
     Al that ever saw that batayl
     Of thaire might had grete mervayl;
3595 Thai saw never under the hevyn
     Twa knightes that war copled° so evyn.°   *matched / evenly*
     Of al the folk was none so wise
     That wist whether° sold have the prise;   *which (of the two)*
     For thai saw never so stalworth stoure.
3600 Ful dere boght thai that honowre;[3]
     Grete wonder had Sir Gawayn
     What° he was that faght him ogain°—   *Who / against*
     And Sir Ywain had grete ferly°   *wonder*
     Wha° stode ogayns him so stifly.°   *(About) whom / unyieldingly*
3605 On° this wise° lasted that fight   *In / way*
     Fra midmorn unto mirk° night;   *dark*
     And by that tyme, I trow, thai twa
     War ful weri° and sare alswa.°   *weary / also*
     Thai had bled so mekil blode,
3610 It was grete ferly that thai stode.
     So sare thai bet on bak and brest
     Until the sun was gone to rest—
     For nowther° of tham wald other spare.   *neither*
     For mirk might° thai than na mare;°   *might (do) / more*
3615 Tharfore to rest thai both tham yelde°—   *yielded, consented*
     Bot or thai past out of the felde,
     Bitwix tham two might men se
     Both mekil joy and grete peté.°   *pity*
       By speche might no man Gawain knaw,
3620 So was he hase° and spak° ful law,°   *hoarse / spoke / low*
     And mekil was he out of maght[4]
     For the strakes that he had laght;°   *taken, received*
     And Sir Ywain was ful wery—
     Bot thus he spekes and sais in hy:°   *haste*
3625 He said, "Syr, sen us failes light,[5]
     I hope it be no lifand° wight°   *living / person*
     That wil us blame if that we twin°—   *part*
     For of al stedes° I have bene yn,   *places*

---

3. Very dearly did they pay for that honor.
4. I.e., and he was greatly weakened.
5. I.e., since the light fails us.

With no man yit never I met
3630 That so wele kowth° his strakes set.°   *could / direct*
So nobil strakes has thou gifen
That my sheld es al to-reven."°   *ripped apart*
     Sir Gawayn said, "Sir, sertanly,
Thou ert noght so weri als I—
3635 For if we langer fightand° were,   *(in) fighting*
I trow° I might do the no dere.°   *trust, believe / harm*
Thou ert nothing in my det°   *debt*
Of strakes that I on the set!"
Sir Ywain said, "In Cristes name,
3640 Sai me what thou hat° at hame."°   *are called / home*
He said, "Sen thou my name wil here
And covaites° to wit° what it were—   *covet, desire / know*
My name in this land mani wote—°   *know*
I hat Gawayn, the King son Lote."[6]
3645 Than was Sir Ywayn sore agast;°   *aghast, horrified*
His swerde fra him he kast°—   *cast*
He ferd right als he wald wede—[7]
And sone° he stirt° down of his stede.   *soon, quickly / started*
He said, "Here es a fowl mischance,°   *misadventure*
3650 For defaut° of conisance.°   *fault / identification*
A! Sir," he said, "had I the sene,[8]
Than had here no batel bene;
I had me yolden to the als tite,
Als worthi war for descumfite."[9]
3655   "What man ertou?"° said Sir Gawain.   *art thou*
"Syr," he sayd, "I hat Ywayne,
That lufes the more, by se and sand,[1]
Than any man that es lifand,°   *living*
For mani dedes that thou me° did   *(for) me*
3660 And curtaysi ye have me kyd.°   *shown*
Tharfore, sir, now in this stoure
I sal do the this honowre:
I grant that thou has me overcumen
And by strenkyth° in batayl nomen."°   *strength, force / taken, subdued*
3665   Sir Gawayn answerd als curtays,
"Thou sal noght do, sir, als thou sais!
This honowre sal noght be myne—
Bot, sertes,° it aw° wele at° be thine;   *certainly / ought / to*

---

6. I am called Gawain, the son of King Lot. (As well as being the father of Gawain, Lot is also usually known, [as in this poem—see l. 3691] as brother-in-law to Arthur; he is also traditionally known as the King of Lothian—whence his name—and sometimes the King of Norway, sometimes of Orkney.)
7. He behaved as if he would go mad.
8. I.e., had I seen your face.
9. I would have yielded to you immediately, as worthy of defeat.
1. By sea and sand (i.e., for all the world).

I gif it the here withowten hone° — *delay*
3670 And grantes° that I am undone."° — *concede/defeated*
Sone thai light,° so sais the boke,[2] — *alighted*
And aither other in armes toke
And kissed so ful fele° sithe.° — *many/(a) time*
Than war thai both glad and blithe;
3675 In armes so thai stode togeder,
Unto° the King com ridand° theder°— — *Until/riding/thither*
And fast he covait for-to here° — *hear*
Of thir knightes what° thai were — *who*
And whi thai made so mekil° gamyn° — *much/amusement*
3680 Sen° thai had so foghten° samyn.° — *Since/fought/together*

Ful hendli° than asked the King — *graciously*
Wha° had so sone made saghteling° — *Who/settlement, reconciliation*
Bitwix tham that had bene so wrath
And aither° haved° done other scath.° — *either/had/harm*
3685 He said, "I wend° ye wald ful fain,° — *believe/happily*
Aither of yow, have other slayn—
And now ye er so° frendes dere!"° — *such/dear*
"Sir King," said Gawain, "ye sal here:
For unknawing and hard grace—[3]
3690 Thus have we foghten in this place.
I am Gawayn, yowre awin° nevow,° — *own/nephew*
And Sir Ywayn faght with me now.
When we war nere° weri,° iwys,° — *nearly/exhausted/indeed*
Mi name he frayned,° and I his; — *asked*
3695 When we war knawin,° sone gan we sese.° — *known, identified/cease*
Bot, sertes, sir, this es no lese;° — *lie*
Had we foghten forth° a stownde,° — *further, longer/time*
I wote wele I had gone to grounde
By his prowes and his mayne°— — *strength*
3700 I wate,° for soth, I had bene slayne." — *know*
Thir° wordes menged° al the mode° — *These/disturbed/mood*
Of Sir Ywain als he stode;
"Sir," he said, "so mot I go,[4]
Ye knaw yowre self it es noght so—
3705 Sir King," he said, "withowten fail,
I am overcumen in this batayl."
"Nai, sertes," said Gawain, "bot am I."
Thus nowther wald have the maistri;° — *mastery, upper hand*
Bifore the King gan aither grant
3710 That himself was recreant.° — *defeated*
Than the King, and hys menye,

2. Cf. l. 9 and n.
3. Because of ignorance and bad luck.
4. As I hope to live.

Had bath° joy and grete peté—   *both*
He was ful fayn thai frendes were
And that thai ware so funden° in-fere.°   *found / together*
3715   The Kyng said, "Now es wele sene°   *seen*
That mekil luf was yow bitwene."
He said, "Sir Ywain, welkum home!"
(For it was lang sen° he thare come).   *since*
He said, "I rede° ye both assent   *advise*
3720 To do° yow in my jujement,   *place*
And I sal mak so gude° ane ende°   *good / conclusion*
That ye sal both be halden hende."[5]
Thai both assented sone thartill°   *thereto*
To do tham in the Kynges will—
3725 If the maydens° wald do so.   *(i.e., the two sisters)*
Than the King bad knyghtes two
Wend° efter the maydens bath,   *(To) go*
And so thai did ful swith° rath.°   *quickly / forthwith*
Bifore the Kyng when thai war broght,
3730 He told unto tham als him thoght.
    "Lystens me now, maydens hende,
Yowre grete debate es broght til ende;
So fer forth now es it dreven[6]
That the dome° most nedes° be gifen,   *judgment / necessarily*
3735 And I sal deme° yow als° I can."   *judge (for) / as (best)*
The elder sister answerd than,
"Sen ye er King that us sold° were,°   *should / protect*
I pray yow do to me na dere."°   *harm*
He said, "I wil let for na saw
3740 For-to do the landes law:[7]
Thi yong sister sal have hir right,°   *rightful (legal) claim*
For I se wele that thi knyght
Es overcumen in this were."°   *war, battle*
(Thus said he anely° hir to fere,°   *only / frighten*
3745 And for° he wist° hir wil ful wele—   *because / knew*
That sho wald part with never a dele.)°   *part, fraction*
"Sir," sho said, "sen thus es gane,[8]
Now most I—whether I wil° or nane—   *wish (it)*
Al yowre cumandment fulfill;
3750 And tharfore dose° right° als ye will."   *do / just*
    The King said, "Thus sal it fall:°   *befall, happen*
Al yowre landes depart° I sall.   *partition*
Thi wil es wrang°—that have I knawin;°   *wrong / known*
Now sal thou have noght bot thin awin,°   *own (share)*

---

5. That you will both be held to be gracious (in this matter).
6. To such an extreme have these affairs been taken.
7. I will cease for no (such) saying to uphold the law of the land.
8. Since it (the decision) has gone thus.

3755 That es the half of al bydene."°   *together*
Than answerd sho ful tite° in tene°   *immediately / anger*
And said, "Me think ful grete outrage
To gif hir half myne heritage!"
    The King said, "For yowre bother esse
3760 In hir land I sal hir sese;
And sho sal hald hir land of the,
And to the tharfore mak fewté.[9]
Sho sal the luf als hir lady—
And thou sal kith° thi curtaysi,   *make known*
3765 Luf hir efter thine avenant—[1]
And sho sal be to the tenant."
This land was first, I understand,
That ever was parted in Ingland;[2]
Than said the King, withowten fail,
3770 "For the luf of that batayl,[3]
Al sisters that sold efter bene°   *be, exist*
Sold part the landes tham bitwene."

    Than said the King to Sir Gawain,
And als° he prayed Sir Ywain,   *also*
3775 For-to unlace thaire riche wede°   *clothes, armor*
(And tharto had thai bath grete nede).
Als° thai thusgate° stod and spak,   *As / in this way*
The lyown out of the chamber brak.°   *broke*
Als thai thaire armurs sold unlace,
3780 Come he rinand° to that place;   *running*
Bot he had, or° he come thare,   *before*
Soght his mayster whideware,°   *far and wide*
And ful mekil joy he made
When he his mayster funden hade.
3785 On ilka° side than might men se   *every*
The folk fast to toun gan fle—
So war° thai ferd for the liowne   *were*
Whan thai saw him theder° bown.°   *(for) there / bound, set out*
Syr Ywain bad tham cum ogayn°   *back*
3790 And said, "Lordinges,° for sertayn,   *Sirs*
Fra this beste I sal yow were
So that he sal do yow no dere.°   *harm*

9. To ease your annoyance, I shall place her in legal possession of her land as a feudal holding; and she shall hold her land from you, and therefore make fealty (take an oath of obedience) to you (as her feudal overlord). (On feudal bonds, see *Havelok*, l. 444, n.)
1. (And) love her as befits your honor.
2. This aside is not found in Chrétien, and would seem to reflect the English poet's admiration of matters pertaining to "trowthe," in this instance manifest in the contracting and keeping of agreements (cf. the headnote in the Sources and Backgrounds section, p. 333). The reference is to the practice known as partitioning; feudal custom sanctioned the inheritance of estates in their entirety by the eldest son, but in cases where only female heirs survived the property was, in principle, divided ("parted") evenly.
3. I.e., in fond memory of that battle (between Ywain and Gawain).

And, sirs, ye sal wele trow° mi sawes—°   *trust in / words*
We er frendes and gude felaws;
3795 He es mine and I am his.
For na tresore I wald him mys."°   *go without*
  When thai saw this was sertain,
Than spak thai al of Sir Ywaine:
"This es the Knight with the Liown,
3800 That es halden° of so grete renown!   *held to be, considered*
This ilk° knight the geant° slogh;°   *same / giant / slew*
Of dedis° he es doghty inogh!"°   *deeds (of arms) / enough*
Than said Sir Gawayn sone° in hi,°   *soon / haste*
"Me es bitid grete velani.[4]
3805 I cri° the° mercy, Sir Ywayne,   *beg, implore / (of) thee*
That I have trispast° the ogayn— *trespassed, offended against*
Thou helped mi syster in hir nede!
Evil have I quit° the now thi mede.°   *repaid / reward*
  Thou anterd° thi life for luf of me,   *ventured*
3810 And, als mi sister tald of the,
Thou said that we ful fele° dawes°   *many / days*
Had bene frendes and gude felawes,
Bot wha° it was ne wist I noght.   *who*
Sethen have I had ful mekil thoght—[5]
3815 And yit, for al that I do can,
I cowth never here of na man
That me cowth tell, in toure ne town,
Of the Knight with the Liown."
  When thai had unlaced thaire wede
3820 Al the folk toke ful gode hede°   *heed, notice*
How that beste,° his bales° to bete,° *beast / sufferings / relieve*
Likked his maister both hend° and fete.°   *hand / feet*
Al the men grete mervail hade
Of the mirth the lyown made.
3825 When the knightes war broght to rest,
The King gert° cum sone of the best   *had, caused*
Surgiens that ever war° sene°   *were / seen*
For-to hele° tham both bidene.°   *heal / together*
  Sone so° thai war hale° and sownd,   *as / hale, healthy*
3830 Sir Ywayn hies° him fast to found.°   *hastens / set out*
Luf was so in his hert fest,°   *fastened*
Night ne day haved he no rest;
Bot° he get grace of his lady,   *Unless*
He most go wode° or for luf dy.°   *mad / die*
3835 Ful preveli° forth gan he wende°   *secretly / go*
Out of the court, fra ilka° frende.°   *each / friend*
He rides right unto the well,

4. Great shame has befallen me.
5. I.e., I have since had great concern (about that).

And thare he thinkes for-to dwell.
His gode lyon went with him ay°—   *constantly*
3840 He wald noght part fro him oway.°   *away*
    He kest water opon the stane;
The storm rase ful sone onane,°   *anon, forthwith*
The thoner grisely gan outbrest—[6]
Him thoght als[7] al the grete forest,
3845 And al that was obout the well,
Sold have sonken° into hell.   *sunk*
The lady was in mekyl° dout,°   *great/fear*
For al the kastel walles obout
Quoke° so fast that men might think   *Quaked, Shook*
3850 That al into the erth sold° synk.   *should*
Thai trembled fast, both boure° and hall,   *bower, chamber*
Als° thai unto the grund° sold fall;   *As (if)/ground*
Was never in this mydlerde[8]
In no kastell folk so ferde.°   *afraid*
3855   Bot wha it was wele wist Lunet.
Sho said, "Now er we hard byset;°   *beset*
Madame, I ne wate what us° es best,°   *(for) us/best (to do)*
For here now may we have no rest.
Ful wele I wate ye have no knight
3860 That dar° wende to yowre wel and fight   *dare*
With him that cumes yow to asaile°—   *assail, attack*
And, if he have here no batayle,
Ne findes none yow to defend,
Yowre lose bese lorn withouten end."[9]
3865 The lady said sho wald° be° dede;   *wished/(to) be*
"Dere Lunet, what es thi rede?°   *advice*
Wirk° I wil by thi kounsail,°   *Work, Act/counsel*
For I ne wate noght what mai avail."°   *succeed*
"Madame," sho said, "I wald ful fayn°   *gladly*
3870 Kownsail yow, if it might gayn,°   *be of use*
Bot in this case it war mystere°   *needful*
To have a wiser kownsaylere."
And by desait° than gan sho say,   *deceit*
"Madame, par° chance this ilk day   *by*
3875 Sum of yowre knightes mai cum hame°   *home*
And yow defend of° al this shame."   *from*
    "A!"° sho said, "Lunet, lat be!   *Oh*
Speke na more of my menyé°—   *company, retinue*
For wele I wate,° so God me mend,°   *know/preserve*
3880 I have na knight me mai defend;

6. The thunder burst forth terribly.
7. It seemed to him as if.
8. In this world (on "middle-earth," see *Havelok*, l. 2244, n.).
9. Your honor is lost forever.

Tharfore my kownsail bus the be,
And I wil wirk al efter the—[1]
And tharfore help at° al thi myght."　　　　　　　　　　　　*with*
"Madame," sho said, "had we that knyght
3885　That es so curtais and avenant,°　　　　　　　*admirable, honorable*
And has slane the grete geant,
And als° that the thre° knightes slogh,°　　　　*also / three / slew*
Of him ye myght be trist° inogh.°　　　　　　*trusting, sure / enough*
Bot forthermar,° madame, I wate,　　　　　　　　　*furthermore*
3890　He and his lady er at debate°　　　　　　　　　　　　*odds*
And has bene so ful many day;
And, als° I herd hym selvyn° say,　　　　　　　　　*as / self*
He wald bileve° with no lady　　　　　　　　　　　　　*stay*
Bot on this kownand° utterly:°　　*covenant, condition / alone*
3895　That thai wald mak sertayn ath°　　　　　　　　　　　*oath*
To do thaire might and kunyng bath,[2]
Trewly, both by day and naght,°　　　　　　　　　　　*night*
To mak him and hys lady saght."°　　　　*settled, reconciled*
The lady answerd sone° hir tyll,°　　　　*soon, quickly / to*
3900　"That wil I do with ful gode will;
Unto the here mi trowth° I plight°　　*truth / plight, pledge*
That I sal tharto do mi might."[3]
Sho said, "Madame—be ye noght wrath—
I most nedes° have of yow an ath,　　　　　　　　*necessarily*
3905　So that I mai be sertayn."
The lady said, "That will° I fayn."　　　　　　　　*will (do)*
　　Lunet than riche relikes° toke,°　　*(holy) relics / took out*
The chalis,° and the mes-boke;°　　　　　*chalice / missal*
On knese° the lady down hir set　　　　　　　　　　*knees*
3910　(Wit ye wele, than liked Lunet!)[4]
Hir hand opon the boke sho laid,
And Lunet al-thus° to hir said,　　　　　　　　*accordingly*
"Madame," sho said, "thou salt swere here
That thou sal do thi powere,
3915　Both dai and night, opon al wise,[5]
Withouten alkyns° fayntise°　　　　*any / recalcitrance*
To saghtel° the Knyght with the Liown　　　　　*reconcile*
And his lady of grete renowne,
So that no faut be funden in the."[6]
3920　Sho said, "I grant it sal so be."
　　Than was Lunet wele paid° of this;　　　　　　*satisfied*
The boke sho gert° hir lady kys.°　　　　*had, made / kiss*

---

1. I.e., and therefore it behooves you to be my counsel, and I will follow you in everything.
2. I.e., to do, to the best of their power and ability.
3. I.e., do all in my power.
4. I.e., you can be sure that Lunet was pleased then!
5. In every way.
6. So that you are not found to be in default (of your oath).

Sone a palfray° sho bistrade,°	riding horse / bestrode
And on hir way fast forth sho rade;°	rode
3925 The next° way ful sone sho nome,°	nearest, shortest / took
Until sho to the well come.	
Sir Ywain sat under the thorn,°	thorn tree
And his lyoun lay him byforn.°	in front of
Sho knew him wele by his lioun,	
3930 And hastily sho lighted° downe;	alighted
And als sone als he Lunet sagh,°	saw
In his hert than list° him lagh.°	it pleased / (to) laugh
Mekil° mirth was° when thai met;	Great / (there) was
Aither° other ful faire has gret.°	Either, Each / greeted
3935 Sho said, "I love° grete God in trone°	praise / throne
That I have yow fun° so sone—	found
And tithandes° tel I yow biforn:	tidings, news
Other° sal my lady be manesworn°	Either / forsworn, perjured
On relikes and bi bokes bradc,°	broad, great
3940 Or els ye twa er frendes made!"	
Sir Ywain than was wonder° glad	wondrously
For the tithandes that he had.	
He thanked hir ful fele sith°	times
That sho wald him slike gudenes° kith°—	goodness / show
3945 And sho him thanked mekill° mare,°	much / more
For the dedes that war done are;°	before, in the past
So ather was in other det	
That both thaire travail was wele set.[7]	
He sais, "Talde° thou hir oght° my name?"	told / anything of
3950 Sho said, "Nay—than war I to blame—[8]	
Thi name sho sal noght wit° for° me,	know / because of
Til ye have kyssed, and saghteld be."	
Than rade thai forth toward the town,	
And with tham ran the gude lyoun.	
3955 When thai come to the castel yate,°	gate
Al went thai in thareat;°	thereat
Thai spak na word to na man born	
Of al the folk thai fand° byforn.°	found / before (them)
Als sone so the lady herd° sayn°	heard / reported
3960 Hir damisel was cumen ogayn,	
And als the liown and the knight,	
Than in hert sho was ful lyght—	
Scho covait ever of al thing[9]	
Of him to have knawlageing.°	acquaintance
3965 Sir Ywain sone on knese him set	

7. Each was so indebted to the other that the efforts of both were well spent.
8. No—for then I would be blameworthy.
9. I.e., she desired above all.

When he with the lady met.
  Lunet said to the lady sone,
"Take up the knight, madame, have done!
And, als covenand° bituix° us was,   *pledged / between*
3970 Makes his pese fast, or he pas."[1]
Than did the ladi him up rise;
"Sir," sho said, "opon al wise,
I wil me° pain° in al thing   *myself / take pains*
For-to mak thi saghtelyng
3975 Bitwix the and thi lady bryght."°   *splendid, fair*
"Medame," said Lunet, "that es right—
For nane bot ye has that powere.
Al the soth° now sal ye here: *truth*
Madame," sho said, "es noght at layn—[2]
3980 This es my lord, Sir Ywaine!
Swilk luf God° bitwix yow send,   *(may) God*
That may last to yowre lives end."
  Than went the lady fer° obak,°   *far / aback, backward*
And lang sho stode° or° that sho spak.   *stood / before*
3985 Sho said, "How es this, damysele?
I wend thou sold be to me lele,
That makes me, whether I wil or noght,
Luf tham that me wa has wroght—
So that me bus be forsworn
3990 Or luf tham that wald I war lorn.[3]
Bot, whether it torn° to wele° or ill,   *turns, comes / good*
That° I have said, I sal fulfill."   *That (which)*
Wit° ye wele, than Sir Ywaine   *Know*
Of tha° wordes was ful fayne;°   *those / pleased*
3995 "Madame," he said, "I have miswroght,°   *done wrong*
And that I have ful dere boght.[4]
  Grete foly° I did, the soth to say,   *folly, foolishness*
When that I past° my terme° day—   *passed / final*
And, sertes, wha so had so bityd,[5]
4000 Thai sold have done right° als I dyd—   *just*
Bot I sal never, thorgh° Goddes grace,   *through*
At mi might[6] do more trispase;
And what man so wil mercy crave,
By Goddes law, he sal it have."[7]

---

1. Make peace with him quickly, before he leaves.
2. (It) is not to be hidden.
3. I believe that you should be loyal to me, (you) who make me, whether I wish to or not, love them who have brought me misery—so that it behooves me either to perjure myself or love them that I would sooner be rid of.
4. And for that I have paid very dearly.
5. I.e., for anyone who experienced such a thing.
6. With all my strength.
7. And that man who begs for mercy shall have it, according to the law of God. (Ywain makes a similar appeal, both in content and in proverbial form, to that made by the vanquished fiend at ll. 3273–74.)

4005 Than sho asented° saghteling to mak;°   *assented, agreed / make*
     And sone in arms he gan hir tak
     And kissed hir ful oft sith—
     Was he never are° so blith.°   *before / blithe, happy*

        Now has Sir Ywain ending made
4010 Of al the sorows that he hade.
     Ful lely° lufed he ever hys whyfe   *loyally*
     And sho him als° hyr owin° life;   *as (much as) / own*
     That lasted to thaire lives ende.
     And trew Lunet, the maiden hende,
4015 Was honord ever with° ald° and ying°   *by / old / young*
     And lifed at hir owin likyng;[8]
     Of° alkins° thing sho has maystri,°   *Over / every / mastery*
     Next° the lord and the lady—   *Next to, After*
     Al honord hir in toure and toun.[9]
4020 Thus the Knyght with the Liown
     Es turned° now to Syr Ywayn,   *returned, changed back*
     And has his lordship al ogayn;
     And so Sir Ywain and his wive
     In joy and blis thai led thaire live—
4025 So did Lunet and the liown—
     Until that ded° haves dreven° tham down.   *death / driven, thrown*
     Of tham na mare have I herd tell,
     Nowther in rumance ne in spell.[1]
     Bot Jhesu Criste, for His grete grace,
4030 In hevyn blis grante us a place
     To bide in, if His wills be.
     Amen, amen, par charité.[2]

        Ywain and Gawain thus makes endyng.
     God grant us al Hys dere° blyssing.° Amen.   *dear / blessing*

8. And lived according to her own desire.
9. I.e., all people honored her everywhere.
1. Neither in a French story nor in spoken story.
2. For the sake of (Christian) charity.

Sir Orfeo†

[We redeth oft and findeth y-write—[1]
And this clerkes° wele° it wite°—   *clerks, scholars / well / know*
Layes that ben in harping
Ben y-founde of ferli thing:[2]
5   Sum bethe° of wer,° and sum of wo,°   *are / war / woe, misfortune*
And sum of joie and mirthe also,
And sum of trecherie and of gile,°   *guile, deceit*
Of old aventours that fel while,[3]
And sum of bourdes° and ribaudy°—   *jests, jokes / ribaldry, vulgarity*
10   And mani ther beth of fairy.°   *faerie, enchantment*
Of al things that men seth°   *see*
Mest° o° love, forsothe, thai beth.   *Mostly / of*
    In Breteyne, bi hold time,[4]
This° layes were wrought (so seith this rime)]   *These*
15   [Of aventures that fallen by dayes—[5]
Wherof Brytouns° made her° layes;]   *Bretons / their*
[When kinges might our° y-here°   *anywhere / (wish to) hear*

---

† Text of Edinburgh, National Library of Scotland MS Advocates' 19.2.1 (the "Auchinleck Manuscript"), ff. 299ʳ (the stub of an otherwise missing leaf)–303ʳ, printed with the permission of the Trustees of the National Library of Scotland. The manuscript dates from the fourth decade of the fourteenth century; the poem's date of composition is held to be around the beginning of the fourteenth century. Where the text is missing at f. 299, readings are supplied, as is the usual practice with editions of this poem, from two other sources, as follows: (1) ll. 1–14 are taken from the prologue to *Lai Le Freine,* also found in the Auchinleck MS (f. 216ʳ; two other surviving texts of *Sir Orfeo,* preserved in London, British Library MS Harley 3810 and Oxford, Bodleian Library MS Ashmole 61, have prologues very similar to that of *Le Freine* and suggest that the lost Auchinleck prologue was very nearly identical in dialect and orthography with that of *Le Freine*); (2) ll. 15–16, 25–38, and the latter parts of ll. 23 and 24 are from MS Harley 3810. Paragraphing is that of the Auchinleck MS. The poem is written in four-stress couplets.
    Sir Orfeo is related to the classical legend of Orpheus and Euridice, referred to periodically in the notes which follow; for a discussion of the relationship, see the headnote in the Sources and Backgrounds section, p. 345.
1. (As) we read often and find written.
2. I.e., lays that have been sung to the accompaniment of the harp are found to be wondrous things.
3. (And some of) adventures that once happened of old.
4. In Brittany, in olden times. (The poem identifies itself as a Breton lay, about which see the headnote in the Sources and Backgrounds section, p. 345. Cf. the first five lines of the Prologue to Chaucer's *Franklin's Tale,* which also identifies itself as a Breton lay.)
5. Concerning fortuitous events that happened once upon a time.

Of ani mervailes that ther were,
Thai token an harp in gle and game[6]
20 And maked° a lay and yaf° it name.   *made / gave*
Now, of this aventours that weren y-falle[7]
I can tel sum, ac° nought° alle—   *but / not*
Ac herkneth, lordinges°] [that ben trewe,°]   *lords, sirs / truthful, loyal*
[Ichil° you telle] [*Syr Orphewe.*   *I will*
25 Orpheo most of ony° thing   *any*
Lovede the gle of harpyng;
Syker° was every gode° harpure   *Sure, Certain / good*
Of° hym to have° moche° honour.   *From / receive / much, great*
Hymself° loved for-to harpe   *(He) himself*
30 And layde theron his wittes scharpe;
He lerned so, ther nothing was
A better harper in no plas.[8]
In the world was never man born
That,° onus° Orpheo sat byforn°   *Who / once (he) / before*
35 And he myght of his harpyng her,
He schulde° thinke that he wer   *should, would*
In one of the joys of Paradys,[9]
Suche joy and melody in his harpyng is.°]   *(there) is*
   Orfeo was a kinge,
40 In Inglond° an heighe° lording,   *England / high, elevated*
A stalworth° man and hardi bo;°   *stalwart, strong / both*
Large° and curteys° he was also.   *Generous / courteous, noble*
His fader was comen of King Pluto
And his moder of King Juno,[1]
45 That sum time were as godes° y-hold°   *gods / held to be, considered*
For aventours that thai dede° and told.   *did*
This King sojournd° in Traciens,[2]   *resided*
That was a cité of noble defens°   *fortification*
(For Winchester was cleped° tho°   *called, named / then*
50 Traciens, withouten no.)°   *denial, doubt*

6. They (the harpers) took up a harp in (the interests of) minstrelsy and amusement.
7. That had happened.
8. And thereto devoted his keen intelligence; he studied so, such that there was nowhere a better harpist.
9. I.e., participating in the kind of heavenly joy usually manifest by the music of angels.
1. His father was descended from King Pluto and his mother from King Juno. (Classical names are recalled here, but evidently without knowledge of their associated traditions. The stated geneaology is otherwise unheard of; for the conventional geneaology of Orpheus, see n. 2 to the Boethian version as represented in the Sources and Backgrounds section, p. 349. Juno is properly the *wife* of the god Jupiter, and Pluto (also known as Hades) is the god of the underworld, against whose dominion Orpheus contends in his attempt to reclaim his wife.)
2. A recollection of Thrace, the Greek city which, according to the classical legend, was home to Orpheus; cf. the Sources and Backgrounds selection, p. 349. Because of the admission at l. 40 that Orfeo was a king of England, Thrace is below (ll. 49–50) identified with Winchester, which city was once the capital of the Saxon kingdom of Wessex and which rivaled London in wealth and importance into the later Middle Ages. *Traciens* is an Old French adjectival form, possibly borrowed under constraint of rhyme from a French antecedent of the poem in which appeared a phrase like *li reis Traciens* (the Thracian king).

The King hadde a Quen° of priis°   *Queen/excellence, esteem*
That was y-cleped Dame° Heurodis—[3]   *Lady*
The fairest levedi,° for the nones,[4]   *lady*
That might gon on bodi and bones,[5]
55 Ful of love and of godenisse—
Ac no man may telle° hir° fairnise.   *(fully) relate/her*

Bifel° so in the comessing° of May—   *(It) happened/commencement*
When miri° and hot is the day,   *merry*
And oway° beth winter schours,°   *away, gone/showers*
60 And everi feld is ful of flours,
And blosme° breme° on everi bough   *blossom/bright*
Overal° wexeth° miri anough°— *Everywhere/grows/(more than) enough*
  This ich° Quen, Dame Heurodis,   *same*
Tok° to° maidens of priis,   *Took/two*
65 And went in an undrentide[6]
To play bi an orchard-side,
To se the floures sprede° and spring,   *spread, grow*
And to here the foules° sing.   *fowl*
Thai sett hem° doun al thre   *themselves*
70 Under a fair ympe-tre,[7]
And wel° sone° this fair Quene   *very/soon*
Fel on slepe° opon the grene.°   *sleep/green, lawn*
The maidens durst hir nought awake,
Bot lete hir ligge° and rest take.   *lie*
75 So sche slepe° til after none°   *slept/noon*
That° under-tide° was al° y-done. *(So) that/midday/all, wholly*
Ac, as sone as sche gan awake,
Sche crid and lothli bere gan make;
Sche froted hir honden and hir fet,
80 And crached hir visage[8]—it bled wete;°   *wet*
Hir riche° robe hye° al to-ritt,° *rich, splendid/she/tore apart*
And was reveyd° out of hir witt.°   *driven/mind*
The tvo° maidens hir biside°   *two/beside*
No durst with hir no leng° abide,°   *longer/remain*
85 Bot ourn° to the palays° ful right°   *ran/palace/directly*
And told bothe squier and knight

3. The name recalls Euridice, Orpheus's wife in the classical legend.
4. I.e., believe me.
5. I.e., who could exist as flesh and bone.
6. One midday. (Possibly late morning. (traditionally such was considered to be a favorite time for visitations from faerie and for other supernatural manifestations; cf. ll. 76, 133, 181, 282, and 402; cf. also *Sir Launfal*, l. 220, and *The Awntyrs off Arthure*, l. 72.)
7. Under a beautiful orchard tree with grafted branches. (Sitting under trees on or before noon is in a number of romances tantamount to inviting a supernatural visitation; cf. *Sir Launfal*, ll. 220 ff. and n., and *The Awntyrs off Arthure*, ll. 70 ff; the motif may be influenced by Psalm 91 [Vulgate Psalm 90] 5–6: "Thou shalt not be afraid for . . . the destruction that wasteth at noonday." The precise significance of a grafted tree here is unclear, though notionally such a tree represents a coincidence of the natural with the unnatural.)
8. She cried and did make a loathsome noise; she rubbed her hands and her feet, and scratched her face.

That her Quen a-wede wold,[9]
And bad° hem go and hir at-hold.°   *bade, commanded / restrain*
Knightes urn° and levedis also,   *ran*
90 Damisels° sexti° and mo,°   *Maidens / sixty / more*
In° the orchard to the Quene hye° come   *Into / they*
And her up in her° armes nome,°   *their / took*
And brought hir to bed atte last,
And held hir there fine° fast°—   *very / firmly*
95 Ac ever sche held in o cri
And wold up and owy.[1]
When Orfeo herd that tiding°   *news*
Never him nas wers for nothing.[2]
He come° with knightes tene°   *came / ten*
100 To chaumber,° right bifor the Quene,   *(bed)chamber*
And biheld,° and seyd° with grete pité,°   *beheld, looked on / said / pity*
"O lef liif! what is te[3]
That° ever yete° hast ben so stille°   *Who / yet / calm*
And now gredest° wonder schille?°   *weep, cry out / shrilly*
105 Thi bodi, that was so white y-core,[4]
With thine nailes is al to-tore.
Allas! thi rode° that was so red°   *complexion (of cheek) / i.e., flush*
Is al wan,° as° thou were ded;   *pale / as if*
And also thine fingres smale°   *small, slender*
110 Beth al blodi and al pale.
Allas! thi lovesom° eyghen° to°   *lovely / eyes / two*
Loketh° so° man doth on his fo!°   *Gaze / as / foe, enemy*
A,° dame! Ich° biseche° merci;   *Ah, Oh / I / beseech, beg*
Lete° ben° al this reweful° cri   *Let / be / pitiful*
115 And tel me what the is,[5] and hou,
And what thing may the° help now!"   *thee*
Tho° lay sche stille atte last,   *Then*
And gan° to wepe° swithe° fast,   *began / weep / very*
And seyd thus the King to:
120 "Allas, mi lord, Sir Orfeo,
Sethen° we first togider° were   *Since / together*
Ones wroth never we nere,[6]
Bot ever Ich have y-loved the
As mi liif, and so thou me;
125 Ac now we mot delen a-to—[7]
Do thi best, for I mot go!"

9. I.e., and told everyone that their Queen would go mad.
1. But constantly she persisted in the same outcry and wished to get up and make away.
2. He had never before been so badly troubled by anything.
3. Oh dear life! what is the matter with you.
4. That was of such a choice white (complexion).
5. See l. 102, n.
6. We were never once angry (with one another).
7. But now we must separate.

"Allas!" quath° he, "forlorn° Icham!°   *said/lost/I am*
Whider° wiltow° go, and to wham?°   *Whither/will you/whom*
Whider thou gost° Ichil° with the—   *go/I will (go)*
130 And whider I go thou schalt with me."
"Nay, nay! Sir, that nought nis!⁸
Ichil the telle al hou it is:
As Ich lay this under-tide
And slepe under our orchard-side,
135 Ther come to me to° fair knightes—   *two*
Wele y-armed al to rightes—⁹
And bad° me comen an° heighing°   *(they) bade/in/haste*
And speke with her° lord, 'the kinge';   *their*
And Ich answerd at° wordes bold,   *with*
140 I no durst nought, no I nold.¹
Thai priked ogain as thai might drive;
Tho com her king also blive²
With an hundred knightes and mo,
And damisels an hundred also,
145 Al on snowe-white stedes;°   *steeds, war-horses*
As white as milke were her wedes.°   *clothes*
I no seighe° never yete bifore   *saw*
So° fair creatours° y-core.°   *Such/creatures/(of) choice*
The king hadde a croun on hed;
150 It nas° of silver, no of gold red,³   *was not*
Ac it was of a precious ston—
As bright as the sonne it schon.
And, as son° as he to me cam,°   *soon/came*
Wold Ich nold Ich, he me nam,⁴
155 And made me with him ride
Opon a palfray,° bi his side,   *riding horse*
And brought me to his palays,
Wele atird° in ich° ways,°   *adorned/each, every/way*
And schewed me castels and tours,
160 Rivers, forestes, frith° with flours,   *woods*
And his riche stedes ichon;°   *each one*
And sethen me brought ogain hom°   *home*
Into our owhen° orchard,   *own*
And said to me thus afterward:
165 'Loke,° dame, tomorwe thatow° be   *See/that thou*
Right here under this ympe-tre;
And than° thou schalt with ous° go   *then/us*
And live with ous evermo;°   *evermore*

8. That is not how it is! (Orfeo's words do at length, however, turn out to be completely true.)
9. I.e., properly armed.
1. I durst not, nor would I.
2. They spurred back as fast as they could go; then came their king as quickly.
3. Nor of red gold. (On "red gold" see *Havelok*, l. 47, n.)
4. Whether I wished it or not, he seized me.

And yif thou makest ous y-let,[5]
170 Whar° thou be, thou worst° y-fet°   *Wherever / will be / fetched*
And to-tore thine limes° al   *limbs*
That nothing help the no schal—[6]
And thei° thou best° so to-torn,   *(even) though / be*
Yete thou worst with ous y-born!' "°   *born away*

175   When King Orfeo herd° this cas,°   *heard (about) / situation*
"O, we!"° quath he, "allas—allas!—   *alas*
Lever me were to lete mi liif[7]
Than thus to lese° the Quen, mi wiif."   *lose*
He asked conseyl° at° ich man;   *counsel, advice / from*
180 Ac no man him help no can.
A-morwe° the under-tide is come,   *The next day*
And Orfeo hath his armes° y-nome,   *arms, weapons*
And wele ten hundred knightes with him,
Ich y-armed, stout° and grim;°   *strong / formidable*
185 And with the Quen wenten he°   *they*
Right unto that ympe-tre.
Thai made scheltrom° in° ich a side,   *a shield-wall / on*
And sayd thai wold° there abide   *would*
And dye ther, everichon,°   *everyone*
190 Er° the Quen schuld° fram hem° gon—   *Before / should / them*
Ac yete amiddes hem ful right
The Quen was oway y-tvight,°   *snatched*
With° fairi° forth y-nome;   *By / faerie, enchantment*
Men wist° never wher sche was bicome.   *knew*
195 Tho was ther criing, wepe° and wo!°   *weeping / woe, sorrow*
The King into his chaumber is go,
And oft swoned° opon the ston°   *swooned / stone (floor)*
And made swiche° diol° and swiche mon°   *such / grief / moan*
That neighe his liif was y-spent—
200 Ther was non amendement.[8]
He cleped° togider his barouns,   *called*
Erls, lordes of renouns,°   *renown*
And when thai al y-comen were,
"Lordinges,"° he said, "bifor you here   *Lords, Sirs*
205 Ich ordainy min Heighe° Steward[9]   *High*
To wite° mi kingdom afterward.°   *watch over / hereafter*
In mi stede° ben he schal   *stead*
To kepe° mi londes° overal—   *protect / lands*
For now° Ichave° mi Quen y-lore,   *now (that) / I have*
210 The fairest levedi that ever was bore,

5. And if you cause us hindrance.
6. Such that nothing will help you.
7. It would be preferable to me to forfeit my own life.
8. Such that his life was nearly expended—there was no remedy (for it).
9. On the occupation of steward, see *Ywain and Gawain*, l. 1209, n.

Never eft° I nil no woman se.   *again*
Into wildernes Ichil te°   *go*
And live ther evermore
With wilde bestes, in holtes hore;[1]
215 And when ye understond° that I be spent°   *establish/i.e., dead*
Make you than° a parlement,   *then*
And chese° you a newe king—   *choose*
Now doth° your best with al mi thinge."[2]   *do*

     Lo,° was ther wepeing in the halle   *Look, Behold*
220 And grete cri among hem alle!
Unnethe° might old or yong   *With difficulty*
For wepeing speke a word with tong.
Thai kneled a-doun al y-fere°   *together*
And praid° him, yif his wille were,°   *beseeched/(it) were*
225 That he no schuld nought° fram hem go—   *not*
"Do way!"[3] quath he, "It schal be so!"
Al his kingdom he forsoke;
Bot a sclavin on him he toke.[4]
He no hadde kirtel° no hode,°   *tunic/hood*
230 Schert, no no nother gode—[5]
Bot his harp he tok algate,°   *anyway, nevertheless*
And dede° him barfot° out atte gate;   *betook, went/barefoot*
No man most° with him go.   *might*
O, way!° What ther was wepe and wo   *alas*
235 When he that hadde ben king with croun
Went so poverlich[6] out of toun!
Thurth° wode and over heth°   *Through/heath*
Into the wildernes he geth.°   *goes*
Nothing he fint that him is ays,[7]
240 Bot ever he liveth in gret malais.°   *discomfort*
He that hadde y-werd the fowe and griis,
And on bed the purper biis—[8]
Now on hard hethe he lith,°   *lies*

---

1. In gray woods. (On the possible senses of the expression, see *Sir Launfal*, l. 171, n.)
2. Cf. l. 126. (So begins a sequence of echoes of earlier details and/or phrases; the effect is to redouble the sense of absolute disparity between that which is lost and that which remains.)
3. Do away (with all that)!
4. He took only a pilgrim's mantle about him. (The choice of raiment suggests an intention to go on some kind of pilgrimage, but it is soon made clear that Orfeo seeks no kind of spiritual enlightenment or consolation of the kind traditionally sought by pilgrims.)
5. Shirt, nor any other possession.
6. I.e., in such a state of poverty.
7. He finds nothing to his ease. (The description of Orfeo's hardship employs repeated contrasts with his past well-being; the method is also employed above, ll. 105–8, in Orfeo's reflections on his wife's distress. The poem thus draws special attention to the conditions of possession and completion as defined by their opposites.)
8. He who had worn the variegated and gray fur, and who had covering his bed the fine purple linen. (Some trappings of royalty; the fur appears to have been variegated with alternating strips in gray and white—cf. *Sir Launfal*, l. 237; on purple cloth, see *Ywain and Gawain*, l. 203, n.)

With leves and gresse° he him writh.°   *grass / covers*
245 He that hadde had castels and tours,
River, forest, frith with flours,
Now, thei° it comenci° to snewe° and frese, *though / commenced / snow*
This king mot make his bed in mese.°   *moss*
He that had y-had knightes of priis°   *excellence, esteem*
250 Bifor him kneland,° and levedis,°   *kneeling / ladies*
Now seth° he nothing that him liketh;°   *sees / pleases*
Bot° wilde wormes° bi him striketh.°   *Only / snakes / slide*
He that had y-had plenté
Of mete and drink, of ich deynté,°   *delicacy*
255 Now may he al day digge and wrote°   *root about*
Er° he finde his fille of rote.°   *Before / roots*
In somer° he liveth bi° wild frut°   *summer / on / fruit*
And berien bot gode lite;[9]
In winter may he nothing finde
260 Bot rote, grases, and the rinde.°   *bark*
Al his bodi was oway duine°   *dwindled, wasted*
For missays,° and al to-chine.°   *poverty / scarred*
Lord! who may telle the sore
This king sufferd ten yere and more?
265 His here° of his berd,° blac and rowe° *hair / beard / rough*
To his girdel-stede° was growe.   *waist*
His harp, whereon° was al his gle,° *upon which / merriment, minstrelsy*
He hidde in an holwe tre;
And when the weder° was clere and bright, *weather*
270 He toke his harp to him wel right
And harped at his owhen° wille.   *own*
Into alle the wode the soun° gan schille,° *sound / resound*
That° alle the wilde bestes° that ther beth *(Such) that / beasts*
For joie abouten him thai teth,°   *come*
275 And alle the foules that ther were
Come and sete on ich° a brere° *each, every / briar, twig*
To here his harping a-fine,°   *to the end*
So miche° melody was therin°—   *much / therein*
And, when he his harping lete° wold,° *leave off / would*
280 No best bi him abide nold.[1]
He might se him bisides°   *nearby*
Oft, in hot under-tides,
The King o Fairy with his rout,°   *company*
Com to hunt him al about[2]
285 With dim° cri and bloweing,° *faint / blowing (of horns)*
And houndes also with him berking;
Ac no best thai no nome,°   *took*

9. And berries of little worth.
1. No beast would stay with him. (Note again the emphasis on dispossession; cf. l. 239, n.)
2. Come to hunt (in the wilderness) all around him.

No never he nist whider thai bicome.[3]
And other while he might him se
290 As a gret ost° bi° him te,°   *army/with/went*
Wele atourned,° ten hundred knightes,   *equipped*
Ich y-armed to his rightes,[4]
Of cuntenaunce° stout and fers,°   *appearance/fierce*
With mani desplaid° baners,   *unfurled, displayed*
295 And ich his swerd y-drawe° hold°—   *drawn/(he saw) to hold*
Ac never he nist whider thai wold.
And other while he seighe° other thing: *saw*
Knightes and levedis com dlaunceing°   *dancing*
In queynt° atire, gisely,°   *elegant/skillfully*
300 Queynt pas[5] and softly;
Tabours° and trunpes° yede° hem bi,   *Tabors, Small drums/trumpets/went*
And al maner° menstraci.°   *manner (of)/minstrelsy*

And on a day[6] he seighe him biside
Sexti° levedis on hors ride   *Sixty*
305 Gentil and jolif° as brid° on ris°—   *cheerful/bird/twig*
Nought° o° man amonges hem ther nis—   *Not/one*
And ich a faucoun on hond bere,
And riden on haukin bi o rivere.[7]
Of game thai founde wel° gode° haunt:°   *very/good/plenty*
310 Maulardes,° hayroun,° and cormeraunt.   *Mallards/heron*
The foules of the water ariseth;
The faucouns hem wele deviseth:°   *discerned*
Ich faucoun his pray slough.°   *slew*
That seighe Orfeo, and lough:°   *(he) laughed*
315 "Parfay!"° quath° he, "ther is fair game!   *By my faith, Indeed/said*
Thider Ichil, bi Godes name—[8]
Ich was y-won° swiche° werk° to se!" *(once) accustomed/such/activity*
He aros, and thider gan te.
To a levedi he was y-come—
320 Biheld,° and hath wele undernome,°   *(He has) looked/understood*
And seth bi al thing[9] that it is
His owhen Quen—Dam° Heurodis!   *Lady*
Yern° he biheld hir—and sche him eke;°   *Eagerly/also*

---

3. Nor did he ever know what became of them (Presumably the fairies catch nothing because
  they seek a rare kind of prey, namely people like Heurodis who have been made vulnerable
  by special circumstances—see ll. 65–70 and notes thereto; and cf. ll. 387–404 below.)
4. Each one appropriately armed.
5. (With) elegant steps.
6. At almost exactly the midpoint of the poem, reference to a particular day signals the introduction
  of new and different conditions into what for ten years has been an experience of routine and
  indistinct event; cf. l. 239, n.
7. And each bore a falcon in hand and rode in hawking beside a river. (Such hunts—and,
  indeed, the hunts, tourneying, and lyrical pageantry described above—are pastimes of nobility;
  cf. *Sir Launfal*, l. 961 and n.)
8. Thither will I go, (I swear) by God's name.
9. I.e., and sees in every way.

Ac neither° to other a word no speke.°   *neither/spoke*
325 For messais that sche on him seighe,[1]
The° had ben so riche and so heighe,   *(He) who*
The teres fel out of her eighe;°   *eye*
The other levedis this y-seighe
And maked hir oway to ride—
330 Sche most with him no lenger abide.[2]
"Allas!" quath he, "now me is wo;°   *sorrowful*
Whi nil° deth now me slo?°   *will not/slay*
Allas, wroche°, that I no might   *wretch (that I am)*
Dye now after this sight—
335 Allas! To° long last° mi liif   *too/lasts*
When I no dar° nought with mi wiif—   *dare*
No° hye° to me—o° word speke.   *Nor/she/one*
Allas, whi nil min hert breke?°—   *break*
Parfay!" quath he, "tide wat bitide,[3]
340 Whider-so° this° levedis ride,   *Wheresoever/these*
The selve° way Ichil° streche;°   *selfsame/I will/go*
Of liif no deth me no reche."[4]
His sclavain he dede on also spac[5]
And henge° his harp opon his bac,   *hung*
345 And had wel gode wil to gon;
He no spard noither stub no ston.[6]
In at a roche° the levedis rideth—   *(cleft in a) rock, cliff*
And he after, and nought abideth.
When he was in the roche y-go,
350 Wele thre° mile other° mo,°   *three/or/more*
He com into a fair cuntray
As bright so° sonne on somers day,   *as*
Smothe° and plain° and al grene;   *Smooth, Flat/level*
Hille no dale nas ther non y-sene.
355 Amidde the lond° a castel he sighe,   *land*
Riche° and real° and wonder° heighe: *Splendid/royal/wondrously*
Al the utmast° wal   *outermost*
Was clere° and schine° as cristal;   *(as) clear/bright*
An hundred tours° ther were about,   *towers*
360 Degiselich, and bataild stout;[7]
The butras° com out of the diche,°   *buttress(es)/moat*
Of rede gold y-arched riche—[8]

---

1. Because of the discomfort she saw he was in.
2. I.e., she was forbidden to stay with him any longer. (Cf. l. 280 and n.)
3. "By (my) faith!" said he, "come what may."
4. I care neither for life nor death.
5. He donned his cloak at once.
6. He avoided neither stump nor stone (i.e., he took the straightest route).
7. Beguiling and sturdily furnished with battlements.
8. (Made) of red gold splendidly enarched. (Evidently these are "flying" buttresses, graceful demi-arches ranged around the outside of a building and designed to transfer roof and vaulting loads

The vousour° was avowed° al   *vaulting / colored*
Of ich maner divers aumal;⁹
365 Within ther wer wide° wones,°   *vast / dwellings*
Al of precious stones—
The werst piler on to biholde¹
Was al of burnist° gold.   *burnished*
Al that lond was ever light;
370 For when it schuld be therk° and night   *dark*
The riche stones light° gonne°   *light up / did*
As bright as doth at none the sonne.²
No man may telle, no thenche° in thought,   *think of, imagine*
The riche werk that ther was wrought:
375 Bi al thing him° think° that it is   *(to) him / (it) seems*
The proude court of Paradis.³
In this castel the levedis alight;
He wold° in° after, yif° he might.   *intended / to go in / if*
        Orfeo knokketh atte gate;
380 The porter was redi therate,°   *thereat*
And asked what he wold have y-do.°   *done*
"Parfay," quath he, "Icham a minstrel—lo!—⁴
To solas° thi lord with mi gle,°   *entertain / merriment, minstrelsy*
Yif his swete wille be."⁵
385 The porter undede° the gate anon°   *opened / forthwith*
And lete him into the castel gon.

     Than he gan bihold about al
And seighe° liggeand° within the wal   *saw / lying, situated*
Of° folk that were thider y-brought,   *(Numbers) of*
390 And thought dede, and nare nought:⁶
Sum° stode° withouten hade,°   *Some / stood / head*
And sum non armes nade,°   *had (not)*
And sum thurth° the bodi hadde wounde,   *through*
And sum lay wode y-bounde,⁷

---

away from the walls and down to the ground. Such buttresses permitted more spacious interiors, allowed higher walls with larger windows, yet still permitted light to reach the windows.)

9. With every kind (i.e., color) of enamel. (Prominent structures, especially churches, were during the Middle Ages brightly painted both inside and out in a variety of colors.)

1. The meanest pillar to behold.

2. As bright as the sun at noon. (The implication is that time in this place is—like those abducted into it [see ll. 391–404 below]—arrested in a perpetual noon.)

3. Though this preternatural kingdom is hardly Paradise (see ll. 387–404, below), the description may nevertheless be influenced by the fantastical account given in Revelation 21.

4. I am a minstrel—behold! (Orfeo evidently displays his harp.)

5. If it were his dear will (that I do so).

6. And seemed to be dead, but were not. (At l. 400, the appalling harvest of the fairies is in fact shown to consist of the dead as well. Those who are not dead appear to have been taken for various reasons: some were seized on the point of death, mortally traumatized; others had gone mad; and others, like Heurodis, had exposed themselves to the fairies by sleeping at the wrong time, possibly also in the wrong place. All are held suspended in the circumstances of their abduction; the moment of abduction thus continues to exist in an abstracted, timeless form.)

7. Bound in madness.

395	And sum armed on hors sete,°	*sat*
	And sum a-strangled° as thai ete;°	*choked / ate*
	And sum were in water a-dreynt,°	*drowned*
	And sum with fire al for-schreynt;°	*shriveled*
	Wives ther lay on child-bedde,	
400	Sum ded and sum a-wedde;°	*gone mad*
	And wonder° fele° ther lay bisides	*(a) wondrous / many*
	Right as thai slepe her under-tides—[8]	
	Eche° was thus in this warld° y-nome,°	*Each / world / taken*
	With fairi thider y-come.[9]	
405	Ther he seighe his owhen° wiif,	*own*
	Dame Heurodis, his lef° liif,	*dear*
	Slepe under an ympe-tre—[1]	
	Bi her clothes he knewe that it was he.°	*she*
	And when he hadde bihold this° mervails alle	*these*
410	He went into the kinges halle.	
	Than seighe he ther a semly° sight,	*fair*
	A tabernacle° blisseful and bright:	*canopied structure*
	Therin° her° maister° king sete,°	*Therein / their / lord / sat*
	And her quen, fair and swete—	
415	Her crounes, her clothes, schine so bright	
	That unnethe° bihold he hem° might.	*with difficulty / them*
	When he hadde biholden al that thing	
	He kneled a-doun bifor the king:	
	"O Lord," he seyd,° "yif it thi wille were,	*said*
420	Mi menstraci thou schust y-here."[2]	
	The king answered: "What man artow°	*art thou*
	That art hider° y-comen now?	*hither*
	Ich,° no non° that is with me,	*I / none, no one*
	No sent never after the.°	*thee*
425	Sethen that Ich here regni° gan°	*reign / began*
	I no fond° never so° folehardi° man	*found / such (a) / foolhardy*
	That hider to ous durst wende,°	*come*
	Bot that Ichim wald of-sende."[3]	
	"Lord," quath° he, "trowe° ful wel,	*said / trust*
430	I nam° bot° a pover° menstrel—	*am not / but / poor*
	And, sir, it is the maner° of ous°	*custom / us*
	To seche° mani a lordes° hous;	*seek out / lord's*
	Thei° we nought welcom no be,	*Though*
	Yete° we mot° proferi forth our gle!"	*Yet / must*
435	Bifor the king he sat a-doun	
	And tok° his harp so miri° of soun,°	*took / merry / sound*

8. Just as they slept through their midday. (Cf. l. 65.)
9. Cf. l. 193.
1. Cf. l. 70.
2. You should hear my minstrelsy.
3. Unless I would send for him.

And trempreth his harp, as he wele can;[4]
And blisseful notes he ther gan,
That° al that in the palays were   *(Such) that*
440 Com to him for-to here,
And liggeth° a-doun to° his fete,   *lie/at*
Hem thenketh his melody so swete.[5]
The king herkneth° and sitt° ful stille;   *hearkens/sits*
To here his gle he hath gode wille.[6]
445 Gode bourde° he hadde of his gle;   *enjoyment*
The riche quen also hadde he.[7]
When he hadde stint° his harping   *ceased*
Than seyd to him the king,
"Menstrel, me liketh wel thi gle;
450 Now aske of me what it be—[8]
Largelich° Ichil° the pay—   *Generously/I will*
Now speke, and tow might asay."[9]
"Sir," he seyd, "Ich biseche° the   *beseech, beg*
Thatow° woldest yive° me   *That thou/give*
455 That ich levedi, bright on ble,[1]
That slepeth under the ympe-tre."
"Nay!" quath the king, "that nought nere![2]
A sori couple of you it were—[3]
For thou art lene,° rowe° and blac,°   *lean, thin/rough/black, dirty*
460 And sche is lovesum, withouten lac;°   *blemish*
A lothlich thing it were, forthi,[4]
To sen° hir in thi compayni."   *see*
   "O sir!" he seyd, "gentil° king,   *noble*
Yete were it a wele fouler thing
465 To here° a lesing° of° thi mouthe!   *hear/lie/from*
So, sir, as ye seyd nouthe°   *(just) now*
What Ich wold aski, have I schold—
And nedes thou most thi word hold."[5]
The king seyd, "Sethen° it is so,   *since*
470 Take hir bi the hond, and go—
Of hir Ichil thatow be blithe!"[6]
He kneled a-doun and thonked° him swithe.°   *thanked/quickly*

4. And tunes his harp, as he knows well how to do.
5. To them his melody seems so sweet.
6. I.e., he became favorably disposed to listen to Orfeo's music.
7. The splendid queen had such enjoyment as well.
8. Now ask anything of me.
9. Now speke (to me), and you may put it (my word) to the test.
1. That same lady, fair of complexion.
2. That could never be!
3. You would make a wretched match.
4. It would be a loathsome thing, therefore.
5. That of which I would ask, I should have—you must necessarily keep your word. (Orfeo appeals to the traditional understanding that a king above all others must keep his word; he also appeals to a central chivalric principle—cf. *Ywain and Gawain*, ll. 7–40.)
6. I would that you be glad of her!

His wiif he tok bi the hond
And dede° him swithe out of that lond,   *betook*
475 And went him out of that thede°—   *country, nation*
Right° as he come, the wey° he yede.°   *Just / way / went*
So° long he hath the way y-nome,°   *(For) so / taken*
To Winchester he is y-come,
That was his owhen cité;
480 Ac° no man knewe that it was he.   *But*
No forther° than the tounes° ende°   *further / town's / edge*
For knoweleche [he] no durst wende;[7]
Bot with a begger y-bilt ful narwe,[8]
Ther he tok his herbarwe°   *lodging*
485 (To° him° and to his owhen wiif)   *For / himself*
As a minstrel of pover liif,°   *living*
And asked tidinges° of that lond,   *tidings, news*
And who the kingdom held in hond.°   *hand*
The pover begger in his cote°   *cottage*
490 Told him everich a grot—[9]
Hou her° Quen was stole° owy°   *their / stolen / away*
Ten yer° gon° with fairy,   *years / ago*
And hou her King en exile[1] yede
(Bot no man nist° in wiche thede)   *knew (not)*
495 And hou the Steward the lond gan° hold—   *did*
And other mani thinges him told.

A-morwe, ogain none-tide,[2]
He maked his wiif ther abide.
The beggers clothes he borwed° anon   *borrowed*
500 And heng° his harp his rigge° opon,°   *hung / back / upon*
And went him into that cité
That° men might him bihold and se.°   *(So) that / see*
Erls and barouns bold,
Burjays° and levedis him gun° bihold: *Burgesses, Citizens / did*
505 "Lo,"° thai seyd, "swiche° a man!   *Behold / such*
Hou long the here° hongeth° him opan°—   *hair / hangs / upon*
Lo, hou his berd° hongeth to his kne!°   *beard / knee*
He is y-clongen° also° a tre."   *shrivelled / like*
And, as he yede in the strete,
510 With his Steward he gan mete,°   *meet*
And loude he sett on him a crie:[3]
"Sir Steward!" he seyd, "merci!°   *(have) mercy*
Icham° an harpour of° hethenisse°—   *I am / from / foreign lands*

7. In case of recognition he durst not go.
8. Housed very meanly.
9. Every single piece (of news).
1. Into exile. (An Old French phrase, perhaps used as a matter of course by the Middle English poet, but perhaps also suggesting a direct borrowing from a French source text.)
2. The next day, toward noon.
3. Loudly he called to him.

Help me now in this destresse!"°   *distress*
515 The Steward seyd, "Com with me—come!
Of that Ichave thou schalt have some;[4]
Everich° gode° harpour is welcom me to   *Every/good*
For mi lordes love, Sir Orfeo."[5]
    In the castel the Steward sat atte mete,°   *(his) meal*
520 And mani lording° was bi him sete.   *(a) lord*
Ther were trompours° and tabourers,°   *trumpeters/drummers*
Harpours fele° and crouders:°   *many/fiddlers*
Miche° melody thai maked° alle—   *Much/made*
And Orfeo sat stille in the halle
525 And herkneth;° when thai ben° al stille°   *listened/were/silent*
He toke his harp and tempred° schille.°   *tuned/resonantly*
The blissefulest notes he harped there
That ever ani man y-herd with ere;°   *ear*
Ich° man liked wele his gle.°   *Each/minstrelsy*
530 The Steward biheld, and gan° y-se,°   *did/see*
And knewe the harp als blive—[6]
"Menstrel!" he seyd, "so mot thou thrive,[7]
Where hadestow° this harp, and hou?°   *did you come by/how*
I pray that thou me telle now."
535   "Lord," quath he, "in uncouthe° thede;   *(an) unknown*
Thurth° a wildernes as I yede,°   *Through/went*
Ther I founde in a dale
With lyouns a man to-torn smale,[8]
And wolves him frete° with teth so scharp;   *had gnawed*
540 Bi him I fond° this ich° harp—   *found/very*
Wele ten yere it is y-go."[9]
"O!" quath the Steward, "now me is wo—°   *sorrowful*
That was mi lord, Sir Orfeo!
Allas! wreche,° what schal I do   *wretch (that I am)*
545 That° have swiche° a lord y-lore?°   *Who/such/lost*
A, way!° that Ich was y-bore,°   *alas/born*
That him was so hard grace y-yarked
And so vile deth y-marked!"[1]
A-doun he fel a-swon° to grounde: *in a swoon*
550 His barouns him tok up in that stounde°   *time*
And telleth him hou it gweth:
"It nis no bot of mannes deth."[2]
    King Orfeo knewe wele bi than

4. You will have something of what I have.
5. For (the sake of my) love for my lord, Sir Orfeo.
6. And recognized the harp immediately.
7. As you hope to thrive.
8. A man torn to small pieces by lions.
9. It was fully ten years ago.
1. (Alas) that such misfortune was appointed for him and such a vile death designed.
2. And tell him how things go: "There is no remedy for a man's death."

His Steward was a trewe° man   *true, loyal*
555 And loved him as he aught° to do,   *ought*
And stont° up, and seyt° thus: "Lo,   *stood / said*
Steward, herkne° now this thing: *hearken unto, attend to*
Yif° Ich were Orfeo the King,   *If*
And hadde y-suffred ful yore°   *long*
560 In wildernisse miche° sore°—   *much / sorrow, distress*
And hadde y-won° mi Quen owy°   *taken / away*
Out of the lond of fairy—
And hadde y-brought the levedi hende,°   *gracious, noble*
Right here to the tounes ende,
565 And with a begger her° in° y-nome°—   *here / lodging / taken*
And were miself hider° y-come   *hither*
Poverlich° to the,° thus stille,°   *In poverty / thee / quietly*
For-to asay° thi gode wille—   *test*
And Ich founde the thus trewe—
570 Thou no schust it never rewe!³
Sikerlich,° for love or ay,⁴   *Certainly*
Thou schust° be King aftcr mi day—   *would*
And yif thou of mi deth hadest ben blithe°   *pleased*
Thou schust have voided, also swithe."⁵
575 Tho° al tho° that therin° sete,°   *Then / those / therein / sat*
That it was King Orfeo underyete°—   *understood*
And the Steward him wele knewe:
Over and over the bord° he threwe,   *table*
And fel a-doun to° his fet°—   *at / feet*
580 So dede° everich° lord that ther sete,   *did / every*
And al thai seyd at o criing,⁶
"Ye beth our lord, sir, and our King!"
Glad thai were of his live.°   *life*
To chaumber thai ladde him als bilive⁷
585 And bathed him, and schaved his berd,
And tired him as a king apert—⁸
And sethen,° with gret° processioun,   *then / great*
Thai brought the Quen into the toun,
With al maner menstraci.⁹
590 Lord! ther was grete melody!
For joie thai wepe° with her° eighe°   *wept / their / eyes*
That hem so sounde y-comen seighe.¹
Now King Orfeo newe° coround° is—   *newly / crowned*

3. You would never regret it!
4. For love or fear (i.e., in any case).
5. You would have been banished, at once.
6. And all of them said with one voice.
7. They led him immediately.
8. And clothed him manifestly as a king.
9. Cf. l. 302.
1. Who saw them returned so safe.

And his Quen, Dame Heurodis—
595 And lived long afterward
(And sethen was King the Steward).[2]
Harpours in Bretaine[3] after than°   *then*
Herd hou this mervaile° bigan,   *marvel, wonder*
And made her-of a lay of gode likeing,[4]
600 And nempned° it after the King: *named*
That lay *Orfeo* is y-hote—°   *called*
Gode is the lay, swete is the note!
Thus com Sir Orfeo out of his care;°   *trouble*
God° graunt ous° alle wele to fare. Amen.   *(may) God / us*

Explicit.°   *(Here) ends (the text)*

Sir Launfal†

Be° doughty Artours° dawes,°   *By, In / Arthur's / days*
That° held Engelond yn° good lawes,   *Who / in*
   Ther fell° a wondyr° cas;°   *happened / wondrous, marvelous / event*
Of a ley that was y-sette
5 That hyght *Launval* (and hatte yette);[1]
   Now herkeneth° how hyt° was.   *listen to / it*
Doughty Artour somwhyle°   *at one time*
Sojournede° yn Kardevyle,[2]   *Resided*
   Wyth joye and greet° solas,°   *great / delight*
10 And knyghtes that wer profitable°   *able to do good*
Wyth Artour, of the Rounde Table;
   Never noon better ther nas:[3]

Sere Persevall and Syr Gawayn;
Syr Gyheryes and Syr Agrafrayn;
15   And Launcelet du Lake;
Syr Kay and Syr Ewayn[4]

---

2. And afterward the Steward was King.
3. Cf. ll. 13–24.
4. And composed of this a celebrated lay.
† Text of London, British Library MS Cotton Caligula A. II, ff. 35ᵛ-42ᵛ, printed with the permission of the British Library. The manuscript dates from the first half of the fifteenth century; the poem's date of composition is held to be around the end of the fourteenth century. The poem is written in twelve-line tail-rhyme stanzas, rhyming (nominally) *aabccbddbeeb*; the couplets nominally have four stresses and the tail lines three.
1. About that a lay was composed, which was called *Launval* (and is so called still). (See pp. 351 ff.)
2. *Kardevyle* is held by the chief editions of this poem to be Carlisle, one of the traditional residences of the King in the north of England; it seems more likely, however, that in this instance the name actually represents Cardiff in Wales—also one of Arthur's traditional residences (cf. *Ywain and Gawain*, l. 17), and a place certainly much closer to Cærleon-upon-Usk, which Launfal visits with some frequency (at ll. 88, 371, 490).
3. There were never better (knights).
4. Sir Perceval and Sir Gawain; Sir Gaheris and Sir Agravain; and Lancelot du Lac; Sir Kay and Sir Yvain. (Perceval is the titular hero of the first Grail romance, written by Chrétien de Troyes; for a brief account, see the headnote to *Ywain and Gawain* in the Sources and

(That well couthe° fyghte° yn playn,° — *could / fight / (battle)field*
　Bateles for-to take);° — *undertake*
Kyng Ban-Booght and Kyng Bos[5]
20　(Of ham° ther was a greet los°— — *them / praise, reputation*
　Men sawe tho° nowher her° make);° — *then / their / match, equal*
Syr Galafré[6]—and Syr Launfale,
Wherof° a noble tale — *Of whom*
　Among us schall awake!

25 Wyth Artour ther was a bacheler° — *young man*
(And hadde° y-be° well many a yer°); — *had / been / year*
　Launfal, forsoth,° he hyght. — *truly*
He gaf° gyftys° largelyche°— — *gave / gifts / generously*
Gold and sylver° and clothes ryche°— — *silver / rich, valuable*
30　To squyer° and to knyght. — *squire*
For hys largesse° and hys bounté° — *largess / generosity*
The Kynges° stuward[7] made was he — *King's*
　Ten° yer, I you plyght:° — *(For) ten / promise*
Of alle the knyghtes of the Table Rounde
35 So large° ther nas° noon y-founde,° — *generous / was not / found, known*
　Be dayes ne° be nyght. — *nor*

So hyt° befyll,° yn the tenthe yer — *it / befell, happened*
Marlyn° was Artours counsalere; — *Merlin*
He radde° hym for-to wende° — *advised / go*
40 To Kyng Ryon of Irlond ryght,[8]
And fette° hym ther a lady bryght,° — *fetch / splendid, fair*
　Gwennere,° hys doughtyr° hende.° — *Guenevere / daughter / gracious*
So he dede,° and hom her brought. — *did*
But Syr Launfal lykede her noght°— — *not*
45　Ne other knyghtes that wer hende—
For the lady bar los° of swych° word — *reputation / such*
That sche° hadde lemmannys° under° her lord, — *she / lovers / besides*
　So fele° ther nas noon° ende. — *many / no*

Backgrounds section, p. 332. Gawain is traditionally the most courteous of Arthur's knights; about his popularity in certain Middle English romances, see the headnote to *The Awntyrs off Arthur*, in the Sources and Backgrounds section, p. 365. Gaheris and Agravain are brothers to Gawain. Lancelot is best known as Arthur's champion but also the lover of his wife and Queen, Guenevere. About Kay, see *Ywain and Gawain*, l. 70, n; Yvain is the titular hero of another romance by Chrétien de Troyes, of which *Ywain and Gawain* is a translation.)

5. Probably the brothers Ban (King of Benwick) and Bors (King of Gaul), both allies of Arthur in his early struggles against rebellious lords.

6. This name is usually given to heathen warriors—such as the giant bridge warden in the *chanson de geste* of *Fierabras*—but it is not otherwise recorded in Arthurian literature.

7. On the office of steward, see *Ywain and Gawain*, l. 1209, n.

8. Directly to King Ryon of Ireland. (Otherwise known in Arthurian literature variously as King Rience of North Wales, Denmark, or Ireland, he is traditionally an enemy of Arthur. The poet appears to have confused him with Leodegrance, traditional father of Guenevere and King of Cameliard, with whom Rience was at war; Arthur first met Guenevere, his Queen, when becoming an ally with her father against Rience.)

They wer y-wedded, as I you say,
50   Upon a Wytsonday,[9]
          Before princes of moch° pryde.   *much*
No man ne may telle yn tale
What folk ther was at that bredale,°   *bridal feast*
          Of countreys fer° and wyde;   *far*
55   No nother° man was yn halle y-sette°   *other/seated*
But° he wer prelat° other° baronette   *Unless/prelate/or*
          (In herte ys naght to hyde).[1]
Yf° they satte noght all ylyke,°   *(Even) if/alike, of equal rank*
Har° servyse° was good and ryche,   *Their/manner of serving*
60   Certeyn, yn ech a syde.[2]

And whan° the lordes hadde ete° yn the halle,   *when/eaten*
And the clothes° wer drawen° alle   *tablecloths/withdrawn*
          (As ye mowe her and lythe),[3]
The botelers° sentyn wyn°   *butlers/wine*
65   To alle the lordes that wer theryn,
          Wyth chere bothe glad and blythe.°   *happy*
The Quene yaf° yftes,° for the nones[4]—   *gave/gifts*
Gold and selver and precyous stonys—
          Her curtasye° to kythe.°   *courtesy/make known*
70   Everych° knyght sche gaf broche other ryng;   *Every*
But Syr Launfal sche yaf nothyng:
          That grevede° hym many a sythe.°   *grieved, offended/time*

And whan the bredale was at ende,
Launfal tok° hys leve° to wende   *took/leave*
75   At° Artour the Kyng,   *Of*
And seyde° a lettere was to hym come,   *said*
That deth hadde hys fadyr° y-nome;°   *father/taken*
          He most to hys beryynge.[5]
Tho seyde Kyng Artour, that was hende,
80   "Launfal, yf thou wylt fro me wende,
          Tak wyth the° greet° spendyng°   *thee/great/spending money*
And my suster-sones° two;   *nephews*
Bothe they schull° wyth the go,   *shall*
          At hom the for-to bryng."

85   Launfal tok leve, wythoute fable,
Wyth knyghtes of the Rounde Table,
          And went forth yn hys journé°   *journey*

9. Whitsunday, otherwise known as Pentecost. The choice of this date (mentioned in Marie de France's *Lanval*, l. 11, but not in *Sir Landevale*) is conventional (cf. *Ywain and Gawain*, l. 16); but in this instance the date is also thematically significant—see l. 133, n.
1. I.e., there is no reason to conceal anything.
2. Certainly, on every side.
3. As you can (now) hear and listen.
4. I.e., indeed.
5. He must go to his burial.

Tyl he com to Karlyoun,[6]
To the Meyrys° hous of the toune,   *Mayor's*
90   Hys servaunt[7] that hadde y-be.
The Meyr stod, as ye may here,
And sawe hym come ryde, up anblere,[8]
Wyth two knyghtes and other mayné.°   *company, retinue*
Agayns° hym he hath wey° y-nome,   *Toward / (his) way*
95 And seyde, "Syr, thou art wellcome.
How faryth° our Kyng, tel me?"   *fares*

Launfal answerede and seyde than,
"He faryth as well as any man—
And elles greet ruthe hyt wore;[9]
100 But, syr Meyr, wythout lesyng,°   *lying*
I am departyd fram the Kyng—
And that rewyth me sore.[1]
Nether thar no man, bencthe ne above,
For the Kyng Artours love,
105   Onowre me nevermore.[2]
But, syr Meyr, I pray the, par amour,[3]
May I take wyth the sojour?°   *residence*
Somtyme we knewe us, yore."[4]

The Meyr stod and bethoghte° hym there   *considered*
110 What myght be hys answere—
And to hym than gan° he sayn,°   *began / to say*
"Syr, .vii.° knyghtes han her har in y-nome—   *seven*
And ever I wayte whan they wyl come,
That arn of Lytyll Bretayne."[5]
115 Launfal turnede hymself and lowgh;°   *laughed*
Therof he hadde scorn inowgh,°   *enough, in plenty*
And seyde to hys knyghtes tweyne,°   *two*
"Now may ye se; swych ys service
Under a lord of lytyll pryse—
120   How he may therof be fayn!"[6]

6. Cærleon-upon-Usk in Wales, traditionally held in much Arthurian literature to be the site of Camelot.
7. I.e., Launfal's servant.
8. Upon an ambling horse.
9. Otherwise it would be a great pity.
1. Sorely causes me regret.
2. There is no man, neither high(born) nor low, who will, for the love of King Arthur, honor me ever again.
3. By way of friendship.
4. Once we knew each other, (in days of) yore.
5. Sir, seven knights have here their lodging taken, and ever I wait for when they will arrive, who are from Brittany.
6. Now may you see; such is the service given to a lord of little account—(now may you see) how he may thereof be glad! (An ironic indictment of the Mayor's undoubtedly false excuse; in this instance Launfal's mocking laughter is the only "gladness" to be had.)

Launfal awayward gan to ryde;
The Meyr bad he schuld abyde,
   And seyde yn thys manere,
"Syr, yn a chamber by my orchardsyde,
125 Ther may ye dwelle wyth joye and pryde—
   Yyf° hyt your wyll were."   *If*
Launfal anoonryghtes,°   *forthwith*
He and hys two knytes,
   Sojournede ther yn-fere.°   *together*
130 So savagelych° hys good° he besette°   *wildly / property, wealth / spent*
That he ward° yn greet dette,°   *came to be / debt*
   Ryght yn the ferst yere.[7]

So hyt befell at Pentecost[8]—
Swych° tyme as the Holy Gost   *Such*
135   Among mankend gan lyght°—   *descend, alight*
That Syr Huwe and Syr Jon
Tok her° leve for-to gon   *their*
   At° Syr Launfal the knyght;   *Of*
They seyd, "Syr, our robes beth° to-rent,°   *are / torn up, ragged*
140 And your tresour ys all y-spent,
   And we goth° evyll° y-dyght."°   *go / badly / dressed*
Thanne seyde Syr Launfal to the knyghtes fre,
"Tellyth° no man of my poverté,   *Tell*
   For the love of God almyght."°   *almighty*

145 The knyghtes answerede and seyde tho
That they nolde° hym wreye° nevermo,   *would not / betray*
   All thys world to wynne.[9]
Wyth that word they wente hym fro
To Glastyngbery,[1] bothe two,
150   Ther° Kyng Artour was inne.   *There (where)*
The Kyng sawe the knyghtes hende,
And agens° ham he gan wende°   *toward / go*
   (For they wer of hys kenne°);   *kin*
Noon other robes they ne hadde
155 Than they owt wyth ham ladde—[2]

---

7. I.e., within the first year.
8. Precisely one year has now passed since Launfal left Arthur's court: cf. l. 50. The reference here to the date has its ironies. Pentecost is the 50th day after Easter, the day on which Christ's Apostles "were all filled with the Holy Ghost" (Acts 2.4) and on which the numbers of those following in Christ's teachings were seen to increase: "all that believed were together, and had all things common; and sold their possessions and goods, and parted them to all men, as every man had need" (Acts 2.44–45).
9. I.e., (not) for all the world.
1. Glastonbury was held, according to some traditions, to be Arthur's final resting place; for this reason the place is sometimes also identified with the Isle of Avalon, a mysterious world rooted in Celtic mythology for which the wounded Arthur departs after the final battle of his reign. Glastonbury is not otherwise known, however, as one of Arthur's residences; that detail appears to be an invention of the *Launfal* poet.
2. I.e., than they had taken with them on the outgoing journey.

And tho° wer to-tore° and thynne.°   *those/torn up/thin, threadbare*

Than seyde Quene Gwenore, that° was fel,°   *who/wicked*
"How faryth the prowde knyght, Launfal?
May he hys armes welde?"°   *wield*
160   "Ye,° madame!" sayde the knytes than,   *Yes*
"He faryth as well as any man—
And ellys God hyt schelde!"[3]
Moche worchyp° and greet honour   *renown*
To Gonnore the Quene and Kyng Artour
165   Of Syr Launfal they telde,°   *told, reported*
And seyde, "He lovede us so
That he wold us evermo
At wyll have y-helde;[4]

But upon a rayny day hyt befel
170   An-huntynge wente Syr Launfel
To chasy° yn holtes hore.[5]   *chase, hunt*
In our old robes we yede that day,
And thus we beth y-went away
As we before hym wore."[6]
175   Glad was Artour the Kyng
That Launfal was yn good lykyng;°   *health*
The Quene hyt rew° well sore,   *regretted*
For sche wold° wyth all her myght   *would (have it)*
That he hadde be,° bothe day and nyght,   *been*
180   In paynys° mor° and more.   *pains/more*

Upon a day of the Trinité[7]
A feste of greet solempnité°   *ceremony*
In Carlyoun was holde.
Erles and barones of that countré,
185   Ladyes and borjaes° of that cité,   *burgesses*
Thyder° come, bothe yong and old.   *Thither*
But Launfal, for hys poverté,
Was not bede to that semblé:°   *assembly*
Lyte men of hym tolde.[8]
190   The Meyr to the feste was of-sent;
The Meyrys° doughter to Launfal went,   *Mayor's*
And axede° yf he wolde   *asked*

In halle dyne° wyth her that day.   *dine*
"Damesele," he sayde, "nay!

3. I.e., and God forbid otherwise!
4. That he would always willingly have maintained us.
5. In gray woods (*lit.* in hoary woods; a conventional phrase, sometimes alluding to a winter scene, but often, as possibly here, evoking the antiquity of the place.)
6. In our old robes we went that day, and thus we are come away from him as we were (dressed) in his presence.
7. Trinity Sunday, the first Sunday after Pentecost.
8. I.e., people reckoned him of little account.

195 To dyne have I no herte.°	*heart*
Thre° dayes ther ben agon,°	*Three / gone (by)*
Mete ne drynke eet° I noon;	*(have) eaten*
And all was for° povert.	*because of*
Today to cherche° I wolde have gon,	*church*
200 But me fawtede° hosyn and schon,	*lacked / hose, stockings / shoes*
Clenly° brech° and scherte°—	*Clean / breeches / shirt*
And for defawte° of clothynge	*default, lack*
Ne myghte I yn wyth the peple thrynge°—	*make my way*
No wonder though me smerte.[9]	

But o° thyng, damesele, I pray the: *one*
Sadel and brydel lene° thou me   *lend*
    A whyle for-to ryde—
That I myghte confortede be
By a launde under thys cyté,
210   Al yn thys underntyde."[1]
Launfal dyghte° hys courser°   *harnessed / charger*
Wythoute knave° other squyer.   *groom, servant*
    He rood wyth lytyll pryde;
Hys hors slod° and fel yn the fen,°   *slipped / mud*
215   Wherfore hym scornede many men[2]
    Abowte hym fer and wyde.

Poverly° the knyght to hors gan sprynge;   *Wretchedly*
For-to dryve away lokynge[3]
    He rood toward the west.[4]
220 The wether was hot the underntyde;[5]
He lyghte adoun,° and gan abyde   *down*
    Under a fayr forest;
And, for hete of the wedere,°   *weather*
Hys mantell° he feld° togydere,   *cloak / folded*
225   And sette hym doun to reste.
Thus sat the knyght yn symplyté,°   *simplicity, indigence*
In the schadwe,° under a tre,   *shadow*
    Ther° that hym lykede° best.   *There (in the place) / pleased*

As he sat yn sorow and sore,
230 He sawe come out of holtes hore

---

9. No wonder I am in pain.
1. So that I might be comforted by (visiting) a park not far from this city, during the morning time.
2. For which many men scorned him.
3. To distance himself from (mocking) scrutiny.
4. I.e., into the distance; but westward is also traditionally the direction of the mysterious, the occult and magical; cf. l. 281. (Cf. also *The Weddyng of Syr Gawen and Dame Ragnell*, l. 385.)
5. The weather was hot that morning. Cf. the descriptions of fairy visitations in (hot) mornings in *Sir Orfeo*, ll. 65–82, 133–63, 281–86, and 402–3. The motifs involved (including sitting under trees, as Launfal does, l. 227 below) are traditional; see *Sir Orfeo*, l. 70, n.

Gentyll maydenes two.
Har° kerteles° wer of inde-sandel,°   *Their / frocks / indigo silk*
Y-lased° smalle,° jolyf,° and well;   *Laced / tightly / prettily*
Ther myght noon° gayer go.   *no one*
235   Har manteles° wer of grene felwet,°   *cloaks / velvet*
Y-bordured° wyth gold, ryght well y-sette,°   *Edged / adorned*
      Y-pelured° wyth grys° and gro.°   *Fur-trimmed / gray / gray-white fur*
Har heddys° wer dyght° well wythalle;   *heads / adorned*
Everych° hadde oon a jolyf coronall°   *Each one / coronet*
240   Wyth syxty gemmys° and mo.°   *gems / more*

Har faces wer whyt° as snow on downe;°   *white / hill*
Har rode° was red, her eyn° wer browne   *complexion (of cheek) / eyes*
      (I sawe never non swyche).
That oon bar of gold a basyn,
245   That other a towayle, whyt and fyn,
      Of selk that was good and ryche;[6]
Har kercheves wer well schyre,°   *sheer, finely woven*
Arayd° wyth ryche gold wyre°—   *Embroidered / wire, thread*
      Launfal began to syche.°   *sigh*
250   They com to hym over the hoth;°   *heath*
He was curteys,° and agens hem goth,   *courteous*
And greette° hem myldelyche.°   *greeted / mildly, gently*

"Damesels," he seyde, "God yow se."[7]
"Syr knyght," they seyde, "well the be.[8]
255   Our lady, Dame Tryamour,[9]
Bad thou schuldest com speke wyth here—
Yyf hyt wer thy wylle, sere°—   *sir*
      Wythoute more sojour."°   *delay*
Launfal hem grauntede° curteyslyche,   *consented*
260   And wente wyth hem myldelyche
      (They wheryn° whyt as flour!)   *were*
And when they come in the forest, an hygh[1]
A pavyloun y-teld, he sygh,
      Wyth merthe and mochell honour.[2]

6. The basin and silk towel are presumably to allow Launfal to wash the mud (of ll. 214–17)
   from his hands, in anticipation of a meal (cf. ll. 337–42). Soiling and cleansing are important
   motifs in the poem, linked with Launfal's success or failure; see, for example, ll. 200–1, 526–
   27, 742–43, and 1027–32.
7. God watch over you.
8. (May) it be well with you.
9. The lady's name is most likely a fitting composite of the Old French forms *trier*, "to choose,"
   and *amor*, "love."
1. Aloft.
2. He saw a pavilion (which had evidently been) pitched with joy and great ceremony.

265 The pavyloun was wrouth,° forsothe ywys,°	*wrought / indeed*
All of werk of Sarsynys,[3]	
The pomelles° of crystall;	*finial spheres*
Upon the toppe an ern° ther stod	*eagle*
Of bournede° gold ryche and good,	*burnished*
270 Y-florysched° wyth ryche amall;°	*floridly decorated / enamel*
Hys eyn wer carbonkeles[4] bryght—	
As the mone° the° schon anyght,°	*moon / they / by night*
That spreteth° out ovyr all.	*spreads*
Alysaundre the conquerour,[5]	
275 Ne Kyng Artour yn hys most honour,[6]	
Ne hadde noon swych° juell.°	*such / jewel*

He fond° yn the pavyloun	*found*
The Kynges doughter of Olyroun,[7]	
Dame Tryamour that hyghte;°	*(was) called*
280 Her fadyr was Kyng of Fayrye,°	*(the land of) Faerie*
Of occient,° fer and nyghe,	*occident, the west*
A man of mochell° myghte.	*much, great*
In the pavyloun he fond a bed of prys°	*great value*
Y-heled° wyth purpur[8] bys°	*Covered / linen*
285 That semylé° was of syghte.	*seemly*
Therinne lay that lady gent°	*graceful, noble*
That after Syr Launfal hedde° y-sent;	*had*
That lefsom° lemede° bryght.	*lovely (lady) / shone*

For hete her clothes down sche dede[9]	
290 Almest° to her gerdylstede;°	*Almost / waist*
Than lay sche uncovert.	
Sche was as whyt as lylye° yn May,	*lily*
Or snow that sneweth yn wynterys day;	
He seygh never non so pert.°	*beautiful*
295 The rede rose, whan sche ys newe,	
Agens her rode nes naught of hewe,[1]	
I dar° well say, yn sert.°	*dare / certain*
Her here° schon as gold wyre;	*hair*

3. Saracens. (Typically Muslim Arabs; the word probably derives, by way of Greek, Latin, and then French, from an Arabic word for "easterner." On western medieval conceptions of Araby, see *The Sege off Melayne*, l. 28, n, and 829, n.)
4. Carbuncles; see *Havelok*, l. 2146, n.
5. Alexander the Great (356–323 B.C.), King of Macedonia and conqueror of Egypt, the Persian Empire, and Greece.
6. I.e., in his best regalia.
7. I.e., the daughter of the King of Olyroun (the island of Oléron off the Breton coast; this degree of geographical realism is not found in other versions of the *Lanval* story, where the mysterious Isle of Avalon, traditionally the place to which Arthur was taken after his final battle, is the popular choice; cf. *Sir Landevale*, l. 92).
8. On the color purple, see *Ywain and Gawain*, l. 203, n.
9. Because of the heat she undid her clothes.
1. The red rose, when it is newly blossomed, against her complexion (of cheek) has no color.

May no man rede here atyre,
300   Ne naught well thenke yn hert.[2]

Sche seyde, "Launfal, my lemman° swete,   *beloved*
Al my joye for the I lete.°   *have lost*
    Swetyng,° paramour.°   *Sweetheart / lover*
Ther nys no man yn Cristenté
305   That I love so moche as the—
    Kyng, neyther emperour."
Launfal beheld that swete wyghth°   *person*
(All hys love yn her was lyghth!)°   *set*
    And keste° that swete flour,   *kissed*
310   And sat adoun her bysyde,
And seyde, "Swetyng, whatso° betyde,°   *whatsoever / happens*
    I am to° thyn honour."°   *at / service*

She seyde, "Syr knyght, gentyl and hende,°   *gracious, decent*
I wot° thy stat,° ord° and ende.   *know / condition / beginning*
315   Be naught aschamed of me;[3]
Yf thou wylt truly to me take—
And alle wemen for me forsake—
    Ryche I wyll make the.
I wyll the yeve an alner°   *purse*
320   Y-mad of sylk and of gold cler,°   *bright*
    Wyth fayre ymages° thre;   *pictures*
As oft° thou puttest the hond° therinne,   *often / hand*
A mark[4] of gold thou schalt wynne,°   *obtain*
    In wat° place that thou be.   *whatever*

325   Also," sche seyde, "Syr Launfal,
I Yeve the Blaunchard, my stede lel,°   *loyal*
    And Gyfré,[5] my owen knave.°   *servant*
And of my armes oo° pensel,°   *one / pennon, banner*
Wyth thre ermyns[6] y-peynted° well,   *painted*
330   Also thou schalt have.
In werre° ne yn turnement   *war*
Ne schall the greve° no knyghtes dent,° *grieve, harm / dint, blow*
    So well I schall the save."°   *protect*
Than answerede the gantyl knyght,

2. No man may describe her clothing, nor well imagine (it) in (his) heart.
3. I.e., be not ashamed on my account.
4. A mark was a quantity of money equal to thirteen shillings and fourpence, or two-thirds of a pound, equivalent in value to eight ounces of gold. In the fourteenth and fifteenth centuries, a well-to-do gentleman's annual income would be measured only in tens of pounds.
5. The assistant's name (and perhaps something of his impish manner) may be modeled on that of Guivret li Petiz ("the Small"), the impromptu and vigorous ally of Erec in Chrétien de Troyes' romance *Erec and Enide*. Both Gyfré and Blaunchard appear to be as supernatural as their mistress; see ll. 484–86 and 580–94.
6. A reference perhaps to the correct term for a heraldic charge, which in this case would be seen as three black lozenges on a white background. It is equally likely, however, that the weasel-like animals themselves are depicted; cf. l. 321.

335 And seyde, "Gramarcy,° my swete wyght;   *Many thanks*
         No bettere kepte I have."[7]

     The damesell gan her up sette,°   *sit*
     And bad her maydenes her fette°   *fetch*
         To hyr° hondys° watyr clere;   *her / hands*
340 Hyt was y-do° wythout lette.°   *done / delay*
     The cloth was spred, the bord was sette;
         They wente to hare sopere.°   *supper*
     Mete and drynk they hadde afyn,°   *in plenty*
     Pyement, claré,[8] and Reynysch° wyn,   *Rhenish (Rhine wine)*
345   And elles greet wondyr hyt wer.[9]
     Whan they had sowped,° and the day was gon,   *supped*
     They wente to bedde (and that anoon°),   *immediately*
         Launfal and sche yn-fere.°   *together*

     For play lytyll they sclepte° that nyght,   *slept*
350 Tyll on morn hyt was daylyght;
         Sche badd hym aryse anoon.
     Hy° seyde to hym, "Syr gantyl knyght,   *She*
     And° thou wylt speke wyth me any-wyght,°   *If / any time*
         To a derne° stede° thou gon;°   *secret / place / (must) go*
355 Well privyly° I woll come to the   *secretly*
     (No man alyve ne schall me se)
         As stylle° as any ston."   *still, quiet*
     Tho was Launfal glad and blythe—
     He cowde° no man hys joye kythe°—   *could / make known*
360   And keste her well good won.[1]

     "But of o thyng, syr knyght, I warne the,
     That thou make no bost of me—
         For no kennes mede![2]
     And yf thou doost°—I warny° the before!°—   *do / warn / in advance*
365 All my love thou hast forlore"°—   *lost*
         And thus to hym sche seyde.
     Launfal tok hys leve to wende:°   *go*
     Gyfré kedde° that he was hende,°   *made known / attentive*
         And brought Launfal hys stede.
370 Launfal lepte ynto the arsoun°   *saddle*
     And rood hom to Karlyoun
         In hys pover° wede.°   *poor, wretched / clothes*

---

7. Given Launfal's poverty, the sense of the line is ironic: "I have have kept no better (arrangement)." "Kepte" may also carry the sense of "embraced," in which case "better" may
   implicitly refer to a lady.
8. See *Havelok*, l. 1728.
9. I.e., and it would have been a wonder if it had been otherwise.
1. And kissed her a good many times.
2. That you do not boast of me—for no kind of reward!

Tho was the knyght yn herte at wylle;°   *ease*
In hys chaunber° he hyld° hym stylle   *chamber / held, kept*
375   All that underntyde.
Than come ther, thorwgh° the cyté, ten   *through*
Well y-harneysyd° men   *equipped*
      Upon ten somers° ryde,°   *sumpters, packhorses / riding*
Some wyth sylver, some wyth gold—
380   All to Syr Launfal hyt schold.°   *should (go)*
      To presente hym, wyth pryde,
Wyth ryche clothes and armure bryght,
They axede aftyr Launfal the knyght,
      Whar he gan abyde.

385   The yong men wer clothed yn ynde;°   *indigo*
Gyfré, he rood all behynde
      Up Blaunchard whyt as flour.
Tho seyde a boy that yn the markct stod,
"How fer schall all thys good?
390   Tell us, par amour."³
Tho seyde Gyfré, "Hyt ys y-sent
To Syr Launfal, yn° present,   *as a*
      That hath leved° yn greet dolour."°   *lived / sorrow*
Than seyde the boy, "Nys he but a wrecche;
395   What thar any man of hym recche?⁴
      At the Meyrys hous he taketh sojour."°   *lodging*

At the Merys hous they gon alyghte,
And presented the noble knyghte
      Wyth swych° good as hym was sent.   *such*
400   And whan the Meyr seygh° that rychesse°   *saw / wealth*
And Syr Launfales noblenesse,°   *distinction, importance*
      He held hymself foule° y-schent.°   *foully, grossly / disgraced*
Tho seyde the Meyr, "Syr—par charyté—
In halle today, that thou wylt ete wyth me!⁵
405   Yesterday I hadde y-ment°   *intended*
At the feste we wold han° be yn same°   *have / together*
And y-hadde solas° and game°—   *delight / amusement*
      And erst thou were y-went!"⁶

"Syr Meyr, God foryelde the.⁷
410   Whyles° I was yn my poverté   *While*
      Thou bede° me never dyne;   *bade*

3. I.e., how far do these goods have to go? Tell us, by way of friendship.
4. He is nothing but a wretch; what does any man care of him?
5. Sir—for the sake of (Christian) charity—I would that today you eat in hall with me!
6. I.e., but before (I could invite you), you were gone!
7. I.e., (may) God reward you. (An otherwise conventional welcome here suffused with irony.)

Now I have more gold and fe°   *wealth, property*
That myne frendes han sent me
   Than thou and alle thyne."
415 The Meyr for schame away yede.
Launfal yn purpure° gan hym schrede,°   *(purple) cloth / clothe*
   Y-pelured wyth whyt ermyne.[8]
All that Launfal hadde borwyd° before,   *borrowed*
Gyfré, be tayle and be score,[9]
420   Yald° hyt well and fyne.   *Yielded, Repaid*

Launfal helde ryche festes;°   *feasts*
Fyfty fedde povere gestes[1]
   That yn myschef° wer;   *distress*
Fyfty boughte stronge stedes;
425 Fyfty yaf ryche wedes°   *clothes*
   To knyghtes and squyere;
Fyfty rewardede relygyons;°   *religious orders*
Fyfty delyverede° povere prysouns,°   *freed / prisoners*
   And made ham quyt° and schere;°   *free of debt / free of guilt*
430 Fyfty clothede gestours.°   *minstrels*
To many men he dede honours
   In countreys fer and nere.

Alle the lordes of Karlyoun
Lette crye a turnement[2] yn the toun,
435   For love of Syr Launfel
(And for Blaunchard, hys good stede,
To wyte° how hym wold spede°   *know, find out / fare, succeed*
   That was y-made so well!)
And whan the day was y-come
440 That the justes° were yn y-nome°   *jousts / scheduled*
   They ryde out also snell.[3]
Trompours° gon har bemes° blowe;   *Trumpeters / trumpets*
The lordes ryden out arowe°   *in a row*
   That were yn that castell.

445 Ther began the turnement,
And ech knyght leyd on other good dent,°   *dints, blows*

8. On ermine, see *Ywain and Gawain*, l. 204, n.
9. According to tally and count. (*Lit.* by notch and by score; a pleonastic reference to the medieval custom of keeping accounts by cutting horizontal notches in a stick, splitting the stick down its length, and giving one half to debtor, one to creditor. The irregular nature of the break would prevent forgeries.)
1. I.e., (he) fed fifty guests. (Each subsequent sentence beginning with "Fifty" should, it seems, be understood in the same manner. The repetition of "fifty" probably results from the misreading of "L" as a Roman numeral rather than as an abbreviation for the hero's name. One surviving MS of Marie's Old French *Lanval* so abbreviates the hero's name at this point in the story; cf. ll. 210 ff. of MS "S" as printed in the edition of Jean Rychner—for details of which, see the Selected Bibliography. Cf. *Sir Landevale*, ll. 173–77, for the more competent ME reading.)
2. I.e., announced a tournament.
3. They ride out as quickly as possible.

Wyth mases° and wyth swerdes bothe;   *maces*
Me° myghte y-se° some, therfore,   *One/see*
Stedes y-wonne, and some y-lore°—   *lost*
450   And knyghtes wonder wroghth!°   *wroth, enraged*
(Syth the Rounde Table was,
A bettere turnement ther nas,
I dar well say, forsothe—
Many a lord of Karlyoun
455   That day were y-bore adoun,
Certayn, wythouten othe!)°   *(need to swear an) oath*

Of Karlyoun the ryche Constable[4]
Rod to Launfal, wythout fable;
He nolde° no lengere° abyde.   *would not/longer*
460   He smot to Launfal, and he to hym;
Well sterne° strokes and well grym°   *stern, cruel/grim, dreadful*
Ther wer yn eche a syde.
Launfal was of hym yware;°   *aware, careful*
Out of hys sadell he hym bar
465   To grounde that ylke° tyde.°   *same/time*
And whan the Constable was bore adoun,
Gyfré lepte ynto the arsoun°—   *saddle*
And awey he gan to ryde!

The Erl of Chestere° thys-of segh;°   *Chester/saw*
470   For wrethe° yn herte he was wod° negh,°   *wrath/mad/nearly*
And rood to Syr Launfale
And smot hym yn the helm, on hegh,[5]
That° the crest adoun flegh°   *(So) that/flew*
(Thus seyd the Frenssch tale).[6]
475   Launfal was mochel° of myght;   *great*
Of hys stede he dede hym lyght,
And bar hym doun yn the dale.[7]
Than come ther Syr Launfal abowte[8]
Of Walssche° knyghtes a greet rowte°   *Welsh/throng, host*
480   (The numbre I not° how fale°);   *(do) not (know)/many*

Than myghte me se scheldes° ryve,°   *shields/riven, cleft*
Speres° to-breste° and to-dryve,°   *Spears, Lances/broken/dashed apart*
Behynde and ek° before.   *also*
Thorugh Launfal—and hys stedes[9]—dent,
485   Many a knyght, verement,°   *verily, truly*

4. The chief military officer of the castle.
5. From above.
6. On such references to source texts, see *Ywain and Gawain,* l. 9, n.
7. Off his steed did he alight, and bore him (the Earl) down to the ground.
8. I.e., then there came around Sir Launfal.
9. Once Launfal has dismounted, Blanchard strikes well-aimed blows of his own.

To ground was i-bore.
So the prys° of that turnay   *prize*
Was delyvered to Launfal that day
    (Wythout oth y-swore).°   *sworn (cf. l. 456)*
490 Launfal rod to Karlyoun,
To the Meyrys hous of the toun,
    And many a lord hym before.

And than the noble knyght Launfal
Held a feste, ryche and ryall,°   *royal*
495   That leste° fourtenyght.°   *lasted / (a) fortnight*
Erles and barouns fale°   *many*
Semely° wer sette yn sale°   *(In a) seemly (manner) / hall*
    And ryaly wer adyght;°   *dressed*
And every day, Dame Triamour,
500 Sche com to Syr Launfal bour,°   *bower, chamber*
    Aday° whan hyt was nyght.   *Regularly, Often*
Of all that ever wer ther tho,
Segh her non but they two,
    Gyfré and Launfal the knyght.

505 A knyght ther was yn Lumbardye;°   *Lombardy*
To Syr Launfal hadde he greet envye;°   *envy*
    Syr Valentyne he hyghte.
He herde speke of Syr Launfal,
That he couth justy well
510   And was a man of mochel myghte.
Syr Valentyne was wonder strong;
Fyftene feet he was longe![1]
    Hym thoghte he brente bryghte
But he myghte wyth Launfal pleye
515 In the feld, betwene ham tweye
    To justy other to fyghte.[2]

Syr Valentyne sat yn hys halle.
Hys massengere° he let y-calle,   *messenger*
    And seyde he moste wende°   *go*
520 To Syr Launfal, the noble knyght
That was y-holde° so mychel of myght.   *held (to be)*
    To Bretayne° he wolde hym sende: *Britain*
"And sey hym, for love of hys lemman
    (Yf sche be any gantyle° woman,   *wellborn, of the gentry*

---

1. He was fifteen feet tall! (Valentyne's height, his audacity, and his probably heathen provenance—see l. 561, n.—are all typical of giants in medieval literature; cf. *Ywain and Gawain*, ll. 244–312, 2385–2404, and 2430–40. Giants were also often held to be descendants of Cain; see *Ywain and Gawain*, l. 559, n.)
2. It seemed to him that he would burn intensely (with envy) unless he could have some sport with Launfal in the field, (unless they could) joust or fight with each other.

525   Courteys, fre, other hende)³
      That he come wyth me to juste—
      To kepe hys harneys° from the ruste—   *armor*
        And elles hys manhod° schende!"°   *manhood / disgrace*

      The messengere ys forth y-went
530   To do hys lordys commaundement;
      He hadde wynde at wylle.⁴
      Whan he was over the water y-come
      The way to Syr Launfal he hath y-nome,
        And grette hym wyth wordes stylle,°   *quiet*
535   And seyd, "Syr, my lord Syr Valentyne—
      A noble werrour, and queynte° of gynne°—   *cunning / tricks*
        Hath me sent the tylle,
      And prayth the (for thy lemmanes sake)
      Thou schuldest wyth hym justes take."
540   Tho° lough° Launfal full stylle,   *Then / laughed*

      And seyde, as he was gentyl knyght,
      Thylke° day a fourtenyght   *The same*
        He wold wyth hym play.
      He yaf the messenger for that tydyng°   *tiding, news*
545   A noble courser and a ryng,°   *ring*
        And a robe of ray.°   *striped cloth*
      Launfal tok leve at Triamour
      That was the bryght° berde° yn bour   *splendid, fair / lady*
        And keste that swete may.°   *maid*
550   Thanne seyde that swete wyght,°   *person*
      "Dreed the nothyng, syr gentyl knyght;
        Thou schalt hym sle° that day."   *slay*

      Launfal nolde nothyng wyth hym have
      But Blaunchard hys stede and Gyfré hys knave,
555   Of° all hys fayr mayné.°   *From / company*
      He schypede,° and hadde wynd well good,   *took ship*
      And wente over the salte flod°   *sea*
        Into Lumbardye.
      Whan he was over the water y-come
560   Ther° the justes schulde be nome,°   *(To) there (where) / scheduled*
        In the cyté of Atalye,⁵
      Syr Valentyn hadde a greet ost—°   *host, army*

3. Courteous, noble, or gracious. (There is possibly an element of mockery in this pat itemization of a gentlewoman's qualifications; Valentyne perhaps values the conventions of chivalry only as a pretense for combat. Triamour's encouragement of Launfal in taking up this challenge, ll. 551–52, would seem to confirm that view; Triamour does not see the pact of secrecy she has with Launfal as threatened. Note also the other motivation suggested at l. 527.)

4. I.e., he had favorable winds.

5. A fictional name, probably derived from the Old French *chanson de geste* of *Otinel*, where the city is identified as a Saracen possession in Lombardy.

And Syr Launfal abatede° her° bost,   *abated, lessened / their*
 Wyth lytll companye!

565 And whan Syr Launfal was y-dyght°   *readied*
Upon Blaunchard hys stede lyght,°   *agile*
 Wyth helm and spere and schelde,
All that sawe hym yn armes bryght
Seyde they sawe never swych a knyght,
570 That hym wyth eyen beheld.
Tho ryde togydere thes knyghtes two,
That har schaftes° to-broste° bo°   *lances / broke apart / both*
 And to-schyverede° yn the felde;   *shattered*
Another cours° togedere they rod,   *charge, encounter*
575 That Syr Launfal helm of glod[6]
 (In tale as hyt ys telde).°   *told*

Syr Valentyn logh, and hadde good game;
Hadde Launfal never so moche schame
 Beforhond, yn no fyght.
580 Gyfré kedde° he was good at nede   *made known*
And lepte upon hys maystrys stede—
 No man ne segh wyth syght[7]—
And er° than thay togedere mette   *before*
Hys lordes helm he on sette,
585 Fayre and well adyght!°   *adjusted*
Tho was Launfal glad and blythe,
And thonkede Gyfré many sythe°   *(a) time*
 For hys dede° so mochel of myght.   *deed*

Syr Valentyne smot Launfal soo°   *so*
590 That hys scheld° fel hym fro,   *shield*
 Anoonryght° yn that stounde°—   *Immediately / moment*
And Gyfré the scheld up hente,°   *took*
And broghte hyt hys lord to presente
Er hyt cam doune to grounde!
595 Tho was Launfal glad and blythe,
And rode ayen the thrydde° sythe,   *third*
 As a knyght of mochell mounde;°   *valor*
Syr Valentyne he smot so there
That hors and man bothe deed° were,   *mortally wounded*
600 Gronyng° wyth grysly wounde.   *Groaning*

Alle the lordes of Atalye
To Syr Launfal hadde greet envye°   *hostility*
 That Valentyne was y-slawe,
And swore that he schold dye
605 Er he wente out of Lumbardye—

6. So that Sir Launfal's helmet glided off.
7. I.e., Gyfré leaped on behind Launfal—but was invisible.

And be hongede° and to-drawe.°		*hanged/drawn, cut to pieces*
Syr Launfal brayde° out hys fachon,°		*drew/falchion, (broad)sword*
And as lyght as dew he leyde hem doune[8]		
In a lytyll drawe.°		*time*

610 And whan he hadde the lordes sclayn°   *slain*
    He wente ayen ynto Bretayn,
       Wyth solas and wyth plawe.°   *delight*

    The tydying com to Artour the Kyng
    Anoon, wythout lesyng,°   *lying*
615 Of Syr Launfales noblesse.[9]
    Anoon, a° let to hym sende   *he*
    That Launfall schuld to hym wende
       At Seynt Jonnys Masse,[1]
    For Kyng Artour wold a feste holde
620 Of erles and of barouns bolde,
       Of lordynges more° and lesse;°   *greater/lesser*
    Syr Launfal schud be stward° of halle   *steward*
    For-to agye° hys gestes alle,   *manage*
       For cowthe of largesse.[2]

625 Launfal toke leve at Triamour
    For-to wende to Kyng Artour,
       Hys feste for-to agye.
    Ther he fond merthe° and moch honour,   *merriment*
    Ladyes that wer well bryght yn bour,
630 Of knyghtes greet companye.
    Fourty dayes leste° the feste,   *lasted*
    Ryche, ryall, and honeste°—   *honorable*
       What help hyt for-to lye![3]
    And, at the fourty dayes ende,
635 The lordes toke har leve to wende,
       Everych yn hys partye.[4]

    And aftyr mete Syr Gaweyn,
    Syr Gyeryes and Agrafayn,
       And Syr Launfal also,
640 Wente to daunce upon the grene°   *green, lawn*
    Under the tour ther° lay the Quene   *there (where)*
       Wyth syxty ladyes and mo.

---

8. I.e., and as gently as dew settles on the ground he laid them out.
9. These tidings evidently come seven years after the Valentyne episode; see ll. 678 and 696.
1. I.e., he (Arthur) allowed (a message) to be sent to Launfal (saying) that he should come to him on (the day of) St. John's Mass (probably June 24, feast day of St. John the Baptist, also very close to the summer solstice, a time by tradition associated—ironically, given what is about to happen to Launfal, l. 730—with fairy visitations; cf. *Ywain and Gawain*, l. 525, n. The date is mentioned in Marie de France's *Lanval*, l. 220, but not in *Sir Landevale*.)
2. I.e., because of (his) understanding of generosity.
3. I.e., to lie would not make it (sound) any better.
4. I.e., each to his part (of the world).

To lede the daunce Launfal was set;°   *appointed*
For hys largesse he was lovede the bet,°   *more, better*
645   Sertayn, of alle tho.
The Quene lay° out and beheld hem alle: *leaned*
"I se," sche seyde, "daunce large° Launfalle;   *generous*
   To hym than wyll I go.

Of alle the knyghtes that I se there
650   He ys the fayreste bachelere;°   *young man*
   He ne hadde never no wyf.°   *wife*
Tyde° me good other ylle,°   *Betide/ill*
I wyll go and wyte° hys wylle—   *know*
   I love hym as my lyf!"
655   Sche tok wyth her a companye—
The fayrest that sche myghte aspye,
   Syxty ladyes and fyf—
And wente hem doun anoonryghtes,
Ham to pley⁵ among the knyghtes,
660   Well stylle,° wythouten stryf.°   *quietly/conflict*

The Quene yede to the formeste° ende,   *leading*
Betwene Launfal and Gauweyn the hende,°   *gracious*
   And after, her ladyes bryght.⁶
To daunce they wente, alle yn same.
665   To se hem play hyt was fayr game:
   A lady and a knyght.⁷
They hadde menstrales° of moch honours,   *minstrels*
Fydelers, sytolyrs,° and trompours   *citole (lyre) players/trumpeters*
   (And elles° hyt were unryght).°   *otherwise/improper*
670   Ther they playde, forsothe to say,
After mete,° the somerys day   *midday meal*
   All-what° hyt was neygh° nyght.   *Until/nearly*

And whanne the daunce began to slake°   *dwindle*
The Quene gan Launfal to counsell° take,   *confidence*
675   And seyde yn thys manere:
"Sertaynlyche, syr knyght,
I have the lovyd wyth all my myght
   More than thys seven yere!
But° that thou lovye me,   *Unless*
680   Sertes° I dye for love of the,   *Certainly*
   Launfal, my lemman dere!"
Thanne answerede the gentyll knyght,
"I nell° be traytour,⁸ day ne nyght,   *will not*

---

5. I.e., to amuse themselves.
6. I.e., and her splendid ladies (followed) after.
7. I.e., to see them play it was a charming diversion: (they went one by one) a lady and (then) a knight. (Cf. *Sir Landevale*, ll. 209–10.)
8. I.e., I will not be traitor (to the King).

Be° God that all may stere!"°   *By/guide*

685 Sche seyde, "Fy on the, thou coward!
     Anhonged° worth° thou—hye and hard.°   *Hanged/will be/painfully*
        That thou ever were y-bore°—   *born*
     That thou lyvest—hyt ys pyté!
     Thou lovyst no woman, ne no woman the;
690   Thow wer worthy forlore!"⁹
     The knyght was sore° aschamed tho;   *sorely, bitterly*
     To speke ne myghte he forgo°   *refrain*
        And seyde the Quene before;
     "I have loved a fayryr° woman   *fairer, more beautiful*
695 Than thou ever leydest° thyn ey° upon   *laid/eye*
        Thys seven yer and more;

     Hyr lothlokste° mayde, wythoute wene,°   *loathliest/doubt*
     Myghte bet° be a quene   *better*
        Than thou, yn all thy lyve!"°   *life*
700 Therfore the Quene was swythe° wroghth.°   *very/wroth, angry*
     Sche taketh hyr maydenes and forth hy° goth   *they*
        Into her tour, also blyve;¹
     And anon sche ley doun yn her bedde.
     For wrethe syk sche hyr bredde,²
705   And swore, so° moste sche thryve,°   *as/(hope to) prosper*
     Sche wold of Launfal be so awreke°   *avenged*
     That all the lond° schuld of hym speke,   *land*
        Wythinne the dayes fyfe.°   *five*

     Kyng Artour com fro huntynge,
710 Blythe and glad yn all thyng.
        To hys chamber than wente he.
     Anoon the Quene on hym gan crye:
     "But I be awreke, I schall dye—
        Myn herte wyll breke a-thre!°   *into three*
715 I spak to Launfal, yn my game,³
     And he besofte° me of schame,°   *besought, asked/shameful act*
        My lemman for-to be.
     And of a lemman hys yelp° he made,   *boast*
     That the lothlokest mayde that sche hadde
720   Myght be a quene above me!"

     Kyng Artour was well wroth,
     And be° God he swor hys oth°   *by/oath*
        That Launfal schuld be sclawe.°   *slain*
     He wente aftyr doghty knyghtes

9. You are fit to be destroyed.
1. As quickly as possible.
2. She made herself sick with rage.
3. I.e., in play.

725   To brynge Launfal anoonryghtes
     To be honged and to-drawe.
    The knyghtes softe° hym anoon,   *sought*
    But Launfal was to hys chaumber gon
     To han° hadde solas and plawe.°   *had / play*
730   He softe hys leef,° but sche was lore°—   *beloved / lost*
    As sche hadde warnede hym before—
     Tho was Launfal unfawe!°   *unhappy*

    He lokede yn hys alner°   *purse*
    That fond° hym spendyng, all plener,°   *provided / in full*
735   Whan that he hadde nede—
    And ther nas noon, forsoth to say.
    And Gyfré was y-ryde away
     Up° Blaunchard hys stede.   *Upon*
    All that he hadde before y-wonne,
740   Hyt malt° as snow agens the sunne   *melted*
     (In romaunce as we rede).
    Hys armur, that was whyt as flour,
    Hyt becom of blak colour—
     And thus than Launfal seyde:

745   "Alas!" he seyde, "my creature,
    How schall I from° the endure,   *(away) from*
     Swetyng Tryamour?
    All my joye I have forlore—
    And the; that me ys worst fore,[4]
750   Thou blysfull berde° yn bour."°   *lady / bower, chamber*
    He bet° hys body and hys hedde ek,°   *beat / also*
    And cursede the mouth that he wyth spek°   *spoke*
     Wyth care° and greet dolour.   *distress*
    And for sorow yn that stounde°   *moment*
755   Anoon he fell aswowe° to grounde.   *in a swoon*
     Wyth that come knyghtes four

    And bond° hym, and ladde° hym tho°   *bound / led / then*
    (Tho was the knyghte yn doble° wo!°) *double / woe, distress*
     Before Artour the Kyng.
760   Than seyde Kyng Artour,
    "Fyle° ataynte[5] traytour,   *Vile*
     Why madest thou swyche yelpyng?°   *boasting*
    That thy lemmannes lothlokest mayde
    Was fayrer than my wyf, thou seyde—
765   That was a fowll lesynge!°   *lie*
    And thou besoftest her, befor than,
    That sche schold be thy lemman—

---

4. I.e., I have lost all my joy—and (I have lost) you; I am the worst for that.
5. Attainted, convicted. (Arthur begins to prejudge the case.)

That was mysprowd° lykynge!"°   *arrogant / desire*

The knyght answerede, wyth egre° mode°   *fierce, angry / mood, disposition*
770 Before the Kyng ther° he stode,   *there (where)*
    The Quene on hym gan lye:[6]
"Sethe° that I ever was y-born,   *Since*
I besofte° her herebeforn°   *besought of / before now*
    Never of no folye.°   *folly, foolish act*
775 But sche seyde I nas no man,
Ne that me lovede no woman,
    Ne no womannes companye.
And I answerede her, and sayde
That mý lemmannes lothlekest mayde
780   To be a quene was better° worthye.   *more*

Sertes, lordynges, hyt ys so.
I am aredy° for-to do   *ready*
    All that the court wyll loke."°   *foresee, ordain*
To say the soth, wythout les,
785 All togedere how hyt was,
    .xii. knyghtes wer dryve to boke:[7]
All they seyde ham° betwene°   *themselves / among*
That knewe the maners° of the Quene   *habits*
    And the queste toke,[8]
790 The Quene bar° los° of swych° a word°   *bore / reputation / such / report*
That sche lovede lemmannes wythout° her lord.   *besides*
    Har never on hyt forsoke.[9]

Therfor they seyden alle
Hyt was long on the Quene, and not on Launfal;[1]
795   Therof they gonne hym skere:[2]
"And yf he myghte hys lemman brynge
That he made of swych yelpynge
    (Other° the maydenes were°   *Or / (that) were*
Bryghtere than the Quene of hewe),
800 Launfal schuld be holde° trewe°   *held / truthful*
    Of that, yn all manere;[3]
And yf he myghte not brynge hys lef,°   *beloved*
He schud be hongede, as° a thef,"°   *like / thief*
    They seyden all yn-fere.°   *together*

805 Alle yn-fere they made proferynge°   *proposal*

6. I.e. (that) the Queen had lied about him.
7. To discern the truth, without lie, (to discern) altogether how it (the truth) went, twelve knights
   were directed to (swear an oath on a) book (i.e. the Bible). (In other words, a provisional jury
   was sworn in.)
8. And undertook the inquiry (i.e., who bothered to find out).
9. I.e., not one of them denied it.
1. It was owing to (i.e., the fault of) the Queen and not Launfal.
2. And thus they were prepared to free him.
3. In every way.

That Launfal schuld hys lemman brynge:
  Hys heed he gan to laye.[4]
Than seyde the Quene, wythout lesynge,
"Yyf he bryngeth a fayrer thynge—
810   Put out my eeyn° gray!"   *eyes*
Whan that wajowr was take on honde[5]
Launfal therto two borwes° fonde,   *guarantors, sureties*
  Noble knyghtes twayn—
Syr Percevall and Syr Gawayn,
815 They wer hys borwes, soth to sayn,
Tyll a certayn day.

The certayn day (I yow plyght)
Was .xii. moneth and fourtenyght,
  That he schuld hys lemman brynge.[6]
820 Syr Launfal, that noble knyght—
Greet sorow and care yn hym was lyght°—   *set*
  Hys hondys he gan wrynge.
So greet sorowe hym was upan,
Gladlyche hys lyf he wold a forgon[7]
825   In care and in marnynge°.   *mourning*
Gladlyche he wold hys hed forgo;
Everych man therfore was wo
  That wyste° of that tydynde.°   *knew / news*

The certayn day was nyghyng.°   *coming near*
830 Hys borowes hym broght befor the Kyng;
  The Kyng recordede° tho,°   *recalled (the charges) / then*
And bad hym bryng hys lef yn syght.
Syr Launfal seyde that he ne myght;
  Therfore hym was well wo.
835 The Kyng commaundede the barouns alle
To yeve jugement on Launfal,
  And dampny hym to sclo.[8]
Than sayde the Erl of Cornewayle°   *Cornwall*
That was wyth ham at that counceyle,
840   "We wyllyth naght° do so!   *not*

Greet schame hyt wer us alle upon
For-to dampny that gantylman
  That hath be hende° and fre.°   *gracious / generous*
Therfor, lordynges°—doth be my reed![9]—   *sirs*

4. He pledged his head.
5. When that wager was taken up.
6. That certain day (I promise you) was twelve months and a fortnight (hence), when he should
   produce his beloved.
7. Would have relinquished.
8. And condemn him to be slain.
9. I.e., follow my advice!

845 Our Kyng we wyllyth° another wey lede:°   *will/lead, direct*
    Out of lond¹ Launfal schall fle."
And as they stod thus spekynge,
The barouns sawe come rydynge
    Ten maydenes, bryght of ble²—
850 Ham° thoghte they wer so bryght and schene°   *They/beautiful*
    That the lothlokest, wythout wene,°   *doubt*
        Har quene than° myghte° be!   *then/could*

Tho seyde Gawayn, that corteys° knyght,   *courteous*
"Launfal, brodyr,° drede the no-wyght!³   *brother, friend*
855   Her cometh thy lemman hende."
Launfal answerede and seyde, "Ywys,°   *To be sure*
Non of ham my lemman nys,
    Gawayn, my lefly° frende!"   *beloved*
To that castell they wente ryght;
860 At the gate they gonne alyght.
        Befor Kyng Artour gonne they wende,°   *go*
And bede hym make aredy hastyly
A fayr chamber for her lady
    That was come of kynges kende.°   *kin, kind*

865 "Ho° ys your lady?" Artour seyde.   *Who*
"Ye schull y-wyte,'"° seyde the mayde,   *know*
    "For sche cometh ryde."°   *riding*
The Kyng commaundede, for her sake,
The fayryst chaunber for-to take°   *choose*
870   In hys palys that tyde.
And anon to hys barouns he sente
For-to yeve jugemente
    Upon "that traytour full of pryde."
The barouns answerede anoonryght,
875 "Have we seyn the madenes bryght—
    Whe schull not longe abyde."⁴

A newe tale they gonne tho,
Some of wele—and some of wo,
    Har lord the Kyng to queme.⁵
880 Some dampnede° Launfal there,   *condemned*
And some made hym quyt and skere;⁶
    Har tales° wer well breme.°   *debates/fierce*
Tho saw they other° ten maydenes bryght   *another*

---

1. I.e., into exile.
2. Fair of face.
3. Fear nothing!
4. We have now seen the splendid maidens—we shall not take long (to reconsider).
5. I.e., they began a new debate then, some (speaking) for (Launfal's) good fortune—and some for bad, to placate their lord, the King.
6. Acquitted and free.

Fayryr than the other ten of syght,
885   As they gone hym deme.[7]
They ryd upon joly moyles° of Spayne,°   *mules/Spain*
Wyth sadell and brydell of Champayne;°   *Champagne (in France)*
     Har lorayns° lyght gonne leme.°   *harnesses/shine*

They wer y-clothed yn samyt° tyre;°   *samite/attire*
890   Ech man hadde greet desyre
     To se har clothynge.[8]
Tho seyde Gaweyn, that curtayse knyght,
"Launfal! her cometh thy swete wyght
     That may thy bote° brynge!"   *salvation*
895   Launfal answerede wyth drery° thoght,°   *dreary/melancholy*
And seyde, "Alas, I knowe hem noght,
     Ne non of all the of sprynge."[9]
Forth they wente to that palys°   *palace*
And lyghte° at the hye deys,°   *alighted, dismounted/dais*
900   Before Artour the Kynge,

And grette the Kyng and Quene ek;
And oo° mayde thys wordes spak   *one*
     To the Kyng Artour:
"Thyn halle agrayde,[1] and hele° the walles   *cover, conceal*
905   Wyth clothes° and wyth ryche palles,°   *cloths/hangings*
     Agens° my lady Tryamour."   *In anticipation of*
The Kyng answerede bedene,°   *immediately*
"Wellcome, ye maydenes schene,°   *splendid, fair*
     Be Our Lord the Savyour."
910   He commaundede Launcelot du Lake[2] to brynge hem yn-fere
In the chamber ther har felawes° were,   *fellows, companions*
     Whyth merthe and moche honour.

Anoon the Quene supposede° gyle°—   *suspected/guile, trickery*
That Launfal schulld, yn a whyle,
915   Be y-made quyt and skere
Thorough hys lemman that was commynge;
Anon sche seyde to Artour the Kyng,
     "Syre, curtays yf thou were,
Or yf thou lovedest thyn honour,
920   I schuld be awreke° of that traytour   *avenged*
     That doth me changy chere.[3]

7. As they were about to pass judgment on him.
8. I.e., to get a good look at their clothing.
9. Possibly "nor nothing of whence they sprang." (The line appears to be corrupt, though something of the original sense may be gleaned from *Sir Landevale*, ll. 398–400.)
1. (Let) your hall be prepared.
2. Scribal favoritism for Launcelot may be responsible for the insertion of his polysyllabic name into an already hypermetric line; cf. *Landevale*, l. 413.
3. Who puts me through such distress (*lit.* who makes me change my expression).

To Launfal thou schuldest not spare.°   *be sparing*
Thy barouns dryveth° the to bysmare°—   *bring / mockery, scorn*
   He ys hem° lef and dere!"   *to them*

925 And as the Quene spak to the Kyng,
The barouns seygh° come rydynge   *saw*
   A damesele alone
Upoon a whyt comely palfrey;°   *riding horse*
They saw never non so gay
930   Upon the grounde gone,
Gentyll, jolyf as bryd° on bowe,°   *bird / bough*
In all manere fayr inowe
   To wonye yn wordly wone.[4]
The lady was bryght as blosme° on brere,° *blossom / brier*
935 Wyth eyen gray, wyth lovelych chere.°   *face*
   Her leyre° lyght schoone.   *countenance*

As rose on rys° her rode° was red.   *branch, spray / complexion (of cheek)*
The her° schon upon her hed   *hair*
   As gold wyre° that schynyth bryght.   *wire, thread*
940 Sche hadde a crounne° upon her molde°   *crown / head*
Of ryche stones, and of golde;
   That lofsom° lemede° lyght.   *lovely (lady) / shone*
The lady was clad yn purpere palle,°   *cloth*
Wyth gentyll body and myddyll° small,° *waist / slender*
945   That semely was of syght.
Her mantyll was furryd° wyth whyt ermyn,[5] *fur-trimmed*
I-reversyd° jolyf and fyn;   *Lined*
   No rychere be ne myght.[6]

Her sadell was semyly set:
950 The sambus° wer grene feluet°   *saddlecloths / velvet*
   I-paynted wyth ymagerye;°   *pictures*
The bordure° was of belles   *border, fringe*
Of ryche gold, and nothyng elles
   That any man myghte aspye.°   *see*
955 In the arsouns,° before and behynde,   *saddlebows*
Were twey° stones° of Ynde,° *two / (precious) stones / India*
   Gay° for the maystrye.[7]   *Brilliant*
The paytrelle° of her palfraye   *breast strap*
Was worth an erldome° stoute° and gay, *earldom / stately*
960   The best yn Lumbardye.

---

4. In all ways exceedingly fair to live a worldly existence (i.e., she was too extraordinary to be merely human).
5. Cf. l. 417, n.
6. There could be nothing more opulent.
7. Surpassing all others.

A gerfawcon° sche bar on her hond;[8]   *gyrfalcon, large falcon*
A softe° pas° her palfray fond,°   *gentle / pace / provided, maintained*
   That° men her schuld beholde.   *(So) that*
Thorugh Kar[devyle]°[9] rood that lady;
965 Twey whyte grehoundys ronne° hyr by—   *ran*
   Har° colers° were of golde.   *Their / collars*
And whan Launfal sawe that lady,
To alle the folk he gon crye an hy,[1]
   Bothe to yonge and olde:
970 "Her," he seyde, "comyth my lemman swete!
Sche myghte me of my balys° bete°—   *sufferings / relieve, cure*
   Yef° that lady wolde."   *If*

Forth sche wente ynto the halle
Ther° was the Quene and the ladyes alle,   *There (where)*
975   And also Kyng Artour.
Her maydenes come ayens° her, ryght,   *beside*
To take her styrop,° whan sche lyght,°   *stirrup / alighted, dismounted*
   Of° the lady, Dame Tryamour.   *Off*
Sche dede° of her mantyll on the flet°—   *put / floor*
980 That men schuld her beholde the bet—
   Wythoute a more° sojour.°   *greater, further / delay*
Kyng Artour gan her fayre° grete—   *fairly, courteously*
And sche hym agayn,° wyth wordes swete   *in turn*
   That were of greet valour.

985 Up stod the Quene and ladyes stoute,°   *stately*
Her for-to beholde all aboute
   How evene° sche stod upryght—   *straight*
Than wer they wyth° her also° donne°   *(in comparison) with / as / dun, dark*
As ys the mone ayen° the sonne   *beside*
990   Aday° whan hyt ys lyght!   *By day*
Than seyde sche to Artour the Kyng,
"Syr, hydyr I com for swych° a thyng;   *such*
   To skere° Launfal the knyght,   *clear*
That° he never, yn no folye,   *(To confirm) that*
995 Besofte the Quene of no drurye,°   *affection*
   By dayes ne be nyght.

Therfor, syr Kyng, good kepe° thou nyme;°   *notice, heed / take*
He bad° naght her, but sche bad hym   *bade, asked*
   Here lemman for-to be!

---

8. To carry a falcon so is a sign of nobility, for which class falconry was a favorite sport. The greyhounds in Tryamour's procession (l. 965), as hunting dogs, also bear the same prestige. Cf. the appearance of such animals at the proud coronation of the Sultan Garcy in *The Sege off Melayne*, ll. 845 and 849.
9. A copying error has rendered the wrong place-name at this point in the manuscript, which reads *Karlyon*; the actual setting is confirmed at l. 1021.
1. On high, aloud.

1000 And he answerede her and seyde
     That hys lemmannes lothlokest mayde
        Was fayryr than was sche."
     Kyng Artour seyde, wythouten othe,°   *(need to swear an) oath*
     "Ech man may y-se that ys sothe,
1005   Bryghtere° that ye² be."   *More beautiful*
     Wyth that, Dame Tryamour to the Quene geth
     And blew on her swych° a breth°   *such / breath*
        That never eft° myght sche se.³   *again*

     The lady lep an hyr palfray
1010 And bad hem alle have good day—
        Sche nolde° no lengere abyde.   *would not*
     Wyth that com Gyfré allso prest,⁴
     Wyth Launfalys stede, out of the forest,
        And stod Launfal besyde.
1015 The knyght to horse began to sprynge
     Anoon, wythout any lettynge,°   *delay, hesitation*
        Wyth hys lemman away to ryde.
     The lady tok her maydenys achon°   *each one*
     And wente the way that sche hadde er° gon,   *before*
1020   Wyth solas and wyth pryde.

     The lady rod thorgh Cardevyle
     Fer ynto a jolyf ile,°   *island*
        Olyroun⁵ that hyghte.°   *was called*
     Every er,° upon a certayn day,   *year*
1025 Me° may here Launfales stede nay,°   *One / neigh*
        And hym se wyth syght.
     Ho° that wyll ther axsy° justus—°   *He / ask (for), demand / jousts*
     To kepe hys armes fro the rustus—⁶   *rust*
        In turnement other fyght,
1030 Thar he never forther gon.⁷
     Ther he may fynde justes anoon
        Wyth Syr Launfal the knyght.

     Thus Launfal, wythouten fable,
     That noble knyght of the Rounde Table,
1035   Was take° ynto Fayrye.°   *taken / (the land of) Faerie*
     Sethe° saw hym yn thys lond no man,   *Since*
     Ne no more of hym telle I ne can,
        Forsothe, wythoute lye.

2. This is only the second time in the poem (see also l. 140) that a character has clearly used
   the second person plural pronoun in the "polite" singular form; Arthur's great respect for
   Tryamour is manifest.
3. The Quene's rash oath of l. 810 is thus honored.
4. Thereupon Gyfré came immediately.
5. Cf. l. 278, n.
6. Cf. l. 527.
7. He thence need go no further.

Thomas Chestre made thys tale[8]
1040 Of the noble knyght Syr Launfale,
    Good of chyvalrye.
Jhesus, that ys Hevene Kyng,
Yeve us alle Hys blessyng,
    And Hys modyr° Marye.   *mother*

1045   Amen.

Explicit° Launfal   *(Here) ends*

---

8. Though attempts have been made to identify Thomas Chestre and to name him as author of other romances, nothing conclusive in either of these matters has been found. It is possible, moreover, that "made" could simply refer to the act of copying.

The Awntyrs off Arthure at the Terne Wathelyne†

In the tyme of Arthur an aunter° bytydde°	*fortuitous event / occurred*
By the Turne° Wathelan,[1] as the boke telles,[2]	*Tarn, Lake*
Whan° he to Carlele° was comen, [that]	*When / Carlisle*
conquerour kydde,°	*renowned*

† Text of Oxford, Bodleian Library MS Douce 324 (*D*), printed with permission of the Bodleian Library. Emended readings—to fill in lacunæ, or to improve sense, consistency of alliteration, iteration, or concatenation—are supplied from the three other surviving manuscripts of the poem: the "Ireland-Blackburne" MS (*Ir*, now in the Robert H. Taylor Collection, Princeton University Library); Lincoln Cathedral Library MS 91 (*T*, the "Thornton Manuscript"); Lambeth Palace Library MS 491 (*L*). Readings from *Ir* are adopted at ll. 3, 8, 43, 59, 70, 82, 83, 84, 96, 112, 113, 119, 120, 124, 138, 143, 162, 165 (2nd only), 170, 176, 178, 179, 211, 215, 230, 236, 237, 253, 269, 276, 280, 286, 314, 381, 382, 396, 410, 415, 419–20, 438, 460, 482, 488, 490, 511, 528, 539, 540, 542, 550, 559, 565, 576, 602, 603, 610, 613, 618, 644, 652, 655, 679, 680, 703, 708, 709, 711; readings from *T* are adopted at ll. 18, 55, 81, 131, 132, 165 (1st only), 212, 220, 228, 240, 257, 270, 271, 316, 318, 334, 339, 352, 353, 354, 360, 371, 375, 418, 435, 443, 625, 637, 641; readings from *L* are adopted at ll. 87, 94, 115, 141, 158, 169, 173, 209, 272, 365, 392, 492, 522, 523, 544, 594–98. All four manuscripts date from the fifteenth century, *L* from the second quarter, *T* from 1430–40, *Ir* from 1450–60, and *D* from 1460–80; the poem's date of composition is held to be within the first quarter of the fifteenth century.

    The poem's versification is among the most sophisticated to be found in a Middle English poem, comprising a thirteen-line alliterative stanza which is made up of nine four-stress long lines rhyming *ababababc* and a four-line "wheel" rhyming *dddc*; the lines of the wheel have between two and three main stresses. Nominally the long line assumes a medial pause, or caesura, and each of its four stresses falls on alliterating words (thus, l. 5: "To *h*unte at the *h*erdes ~ that longe *h*ad bene *h*ydde;" the pattern here can be represented in a shorthand form as *xx ~ xx*—note that alliteration can occur on initial vowels); often lines with the form *xx ~ ax* (with a third nonalliterating stress) or *xx ~ xa* appear. The ninth line of each stanza (the first line of the wheel) nominally iterates (repeats one or more words, or a part of a word) with the eighth line (that practice is much less regular in the second half of the poem, but in the stanzas beginning at ll. 300 and 495 iteration occurs between the seventh and ninth lines, and, as Helen Phillips has pointed out, virtual iteration anywhere between the sixth and twelfth line is otherwise common). Iteration also occurs between the last and first lines of each stanza—it is a form of stanza-linking known as concatenation—and the last two short lines of the poem round off this pattern by repeating the first line of the poem.

1. Tarn Wadling is located less than ten miles south of Carlisle (in the northern English county of Cumberland), in the middle of Inglewood Forest (cf. l. 709). The Tarn and the Forest are favorite sites of Arthurian adventure; cf. *The Weddyng of Sir Gawen and Dame Ragnell*, ll. 16, 152, 215, etc., and *The Marriage of Sir Gawaine* (in the Sources and Backgrounds section), ll. 32 and 51. The Tarn was drained in the nineteenth century, but the name of the place is unchanged. Carlisle, located at the northern extreme of Inglewood Forest, is one of the traditional residences of Arthur; cf. *The Weddynge of Syr Gawen and Dame Ragnell*, ll. 127, 132, etc., *The Marriage of Sir Gawain*, ll. 1 and 20, and (also in the Sources and Backgrounds section), *Sir Landevale*, l. 4.

2. As the (source) book relates. (On such references, see *Ywain and Gawain*, l. 9, n.)

With dukes and dussiperes[3] that with the dere° dwelles,   *dear (king)*
5 To hunte at the herdes that longe had ben° hydde.°   *been / hidden*
On a day thei hem° dight° to the   *themselves / betook*
    depe delles,°   *small valleys*
To fall° of the females in forest frydde,°   *fell, slay / enclosed, protected*
Fayre by the [fermesones,[4]] in frithes° and felles.°   *woods / fells, ridges*
    Thus to wode arn° thei went, the wlonkest°   *are / most splendid*
      in wedes,°   *dress*
10   Bothe the Kyng and the Quene
      And al the doughti° bydene;°   *doughty (knights) / together*
      Sir Gawayn, gayest° on grene,°   *most handsome / green, field*
      Dame Gaynour° he ledes.°   *guenevere / leads, escorts*

Thus Sir Gawayn the gay Gaynour he ledes
15 In a gleterand° gide° that glemed full gay   *glittering / gown*
With riche ribaynes reversset, ho-so right redes,[5]
Rayled° with rybees° of riall° aray;°   *Arrayed / rubies / royal / splendor*
Her hode° of a [hawe°] huwe, that here°   *hood / blue-gray / her*
    hede hedes,°   *hides*
Of pillour, of palwerk, of perré, to pay;[6]
20 Schurde° in a short cloke that the rayne shedes,[7]   *Shrouded*
Set over with saffres,° sothely° to say—   *sapphires / truly*
    With saffres and seladynes set by the sides;
    Here sadel sette of that ilke,[8]
    Saude° with sambutes° of silke;   *Strewn / saddlecloths*
25   On a mule as° the mylke,   *(white) as*
      Gaili she glides.

Al in gleterand golde gayly ho° glides   *she*
The° gates° with Sir Gawayn, bi the   *(Along) the / paths, ways*
    grene welle.°   *pool*
And that burne° on his blonke° with the   *man, knight / horse*
    Quene bides°   *stays*
30 That° borne was in Borgoyne,[9] by boke and by belle.[1]   *Who*
He ladde° that lady so longe by the lawe° sides;   *led / hill*
Under a lorre° they light,°   *laurel tree / dismount*
    loghe° by a felle.   *low, down*

3. Nobles (for the origin of the ME word, see *The Sege off Melayne*, l. 806, n.).
4. Beautiful in the close season (i.e., the time between September 14 and June 24, during which it was forbidden to hunt male deer; females, moreover, could only be hunted between November 11 and February 2, a period consistent with the winter landscape described ll. 41 ff.).
5. Trimmed with fine ribbons, according to whosoever thinks rightly.
6. Of fur, of rich clothwork, of jewelry, (wrought) pleasingly.
7. I.e., that sheds the rain.
8. With sapphires and celidonies arranged on the sides; her saddle (was) adorned with the same kind (of decoration). (Celidonies are legendary precious stones, reputed to come from the belly of a swallow.)
9. Gawain (not Guenevere) is traditionally held to have been born in Burgundy; the choice of place-name does, however, serve alliteration.
1. I.e., (I tell you) with due solemnity. (On the background to the ME expression, see *Ywain and Gawain*, l. 3023, n.)

And Arthur with his erles° ernestly rides	*earls*
To teche hem to her tristres, the trouthe for to telle—[2]	
35 To here° tristres he hem taught, ho the trouth trowes,[3]	*their*
Eche° lorde withouten lette°	*Each / delay*
To an oke he hem sette,°	*directed, appointed*
With bowe and with barselette,°	*retrieving dog*
Under the bowes.°	*boughs*

40 Under the bowes thei bode,° thes burnes so bolde,	*abided*
To byker at thes baraynes in bonkes so bare.[4]	
There might hatheles° in° high herdes beholde,	*noble men / on*
Herken° huntyng [with horne] in holtes so hare.[5]	*Hear*
Thei kest° of° here couples° in cliffes so colde,	*cast / off / leashes*
45 Conforte her kenettes° to kele°	*small hounds / cool, relieve*
hem of care;°	*anxiety*
Thei fel of° the femayles ful° thik-folde°—	*on / fully / in great numbers*
With fressh houndes and fele° thei folowen her fare.°	*fierce / track*
[. . .]	
With gret° questes° and quelles,°	*great / forays (by hounds) / slayings*
50 Both in frethes° and felles,	*woods*
All the dure° in the delles	*deer*
Thei durken° and dare.°	*lie hidden / cower*

Then durken the dere in the dymme skuwes°	*woods*
That° for drede° of the deth droupes°	*(Such) that / dread / trembles*
the do.°	*doe*
55 [And by the stremys so strange that swithely swoghes][6]	
Thai werray the wilde and worchen hem wo—[7]	
The huntes° thei halowe° in hurstes°	*hunters / halloo / woods*
and huwes,°	*cliffs*
And bluwe rachas ryally; thei ran to the ro—	
Thay gaf to no gamon [no grythe] that on grounde gruwes,[8]	
60 The grete greundes° in the greves,° so gladly thei go.	*greyhounds / groves*
So gladly thei gon in greves so grene;	
The King blowe rechas	
And folowed fast on the tras,°	*track*
With many sergeant of mas,[9]	
65 That solas° to sene.°	*amusement, sport / see*

With solas° thei semble, the pruddest°	*joy / most splendid*
in palle,°	*rich clothes*

2. To direct them to their hunting stations, (as I aim) to tell (you) the truth (of the matter).
3. I.e., (I say to) whoever believes the truth.
4. To attack the barren does (i.e., fair game) on bare hillsides.
5. In very gray woods. (On the possible senses of the expression, see *Sir Launfal*, l. 171, n.)
6. And by the very strong (flowing) streams that powerfully murmur.
7. They make war upon the wild (creatures) and do them harm.
8. And grandly blew the call (for the greyhounds) to reassemble; they (the hounds) ran (then) to the roe deer—they gave no quarter to any (kind of) game that exists in the land.
9. Official men-at-arms.

And suwen° to the soverayne within schaghes° *follow / thickets*
 schene°— *fair*
Al but Sir Gawayn, gayest of all,
Beleves° with Dame Gaynour in greves so grene; *(Who) stays*
70 [By a lauryel° ho° lay, undur a lefesale°] *laurel tree / she / shelter, lean-to*
Of box° and of berber° bigged° *boxwood / barberry / assembled*
 ful bene.° *well*
Fast byfore undre this ferly con fall;[1]
And this mekel° mervaile,° that I shal *great / marvel, wonder*
 of mene°— *tell*
 Now wol I of this mervaile mene if I mote:° *am able*
75 The day wex° als° dirke° *grew / as / dark*
  As hit° were mydnight myrke;° *it / murky*
  Thereof the King was irke° *irked, annoyed*
   And light° on his fote.° *dismounted / foot*

Thus to fote ar thei faren,° thes frekes° unfayn,° *gone / men / unhappy*
80 And fleen° fro the forest to the fewe° felles; *flee / striated, multicolored*
[Thay rane faste to the roches° for reddoure° *rocks / rigor, severity*
 of the raynne,]
For the sneterand snawe [that] snartly hem snelles.[2]
There come [a lau oute of a loghe—in lede] is not to layne,[3]
[In lykenes of Lucifere, lauyst° in *lowest, most abject*
 hellus°—] *regions of hell*
85 And glides to Sir Gawayn, the gates to gayne,° *obtain, seize*
Yauland° and yomerand° with many loude yelles. *Yowling / lamenting*
 Hit° yaules, hit yameres, with [wonges° ful] wete,° *It / cheeks / wet*
  And seid, with siking° sare,° *sighing / sore, bitter*
  "I ban° the body me° bare;° *curse / (that) me / bore, gave birth to*
90 Alas! now kindeles° my care— *is aroused*
   I gloppen° and I grete!"° *am distraught / weep*

Then gloppenet and grete Gaynour the gay,
And seid to Sir Gawen, "What is thi good rede?"° *advice*
"Hit [is] the clippes° of the son°—I herd a *eclipse / sun*
 clerk° say—" *scholar*
95 And thus he confortes the Quene for his knightede.[4]
"Sir Cadour, Sir Clegis, Sir [Costantyne,] Sir Cay:[5]

---

1. Just before midday did this marvel occur. (Sitting under trees on or before noon is in a number of romances tantamount to inviting a supernatural visitation; cf. *Sir Launfal*, ll. 220 ff. and n., and *Sir Orfeo*, l. 70, n.)
2. (And) because of the falling snow that bitterly hurries them on.
3. There came a flame out of a lake—(the truth of) it cannot be denied among people.
4. I.e., by virtue of his chivalric status.
5. A panicked Guenevere is speaking. Constantine is traditionally known as a relative of Arthur and his successor (cf. the opening lines of the selection from Gaimar in the Sources and Backgrounds section, p. 319); Cador, ruler of Cornwall, is Constantine's father; on Sir Kay, see *Ywain and Gawain*, l. 69, n.; Cligés (the titular hero of one of the Arthurian romances of Chrétien de Troyes), may appear here, as may the other three names, via recollection of their naming in the alliterative *Morte Arthure*—notably, in the case of Cador, Cligés, and

Thes knyghtes arn uncurtays,° by Crosse and by crede,[6]   *discourteous*
That thus oonly° have me laft° on my deth-day[7]   *alone / left*
With the grisselist° goost that ever herd I grede!"°   *most horrible / weep*
100   "Of the goost," quod° the gome,° "greve° you   *said / man / grieve*
        no mare,°   *more*
        For I shal speke with the sprete,°   *spirit*
        And of the wayes I shall wete
        What may the bales bete
        Of the bodi bare."[8]

105   Bare was the body and blak° to the bone,   *black*
        Al biclagged° in clay, uncomly° cladde;   *clodded / repulsively*
        Hit waried,° hit wayment,° as°   *cursed / wailed / in the manner of*
            a woman—
        But on hide° ne on huwe° no heling°   *skin / complexion, face / covering*
            hit hadde;
        Hit stemered, hit stonayde, hit stode as a stone;[9]
110   Hit marred,° hit memered,° hit mused for madde.[1]   *grieved / muttered*
        Agayn° the grisly goost Sir Gawayn is gone;   *Toward*
        He rayked° [to hit in] a res° (for [he] was never   *went / rush*
            [radde°]—   *afraid*
        [Rad] was he never, ho-so right redes).
        On the chef° of the [cholle°]   *top / jowl*
115   A pade° pikes° on [hir] polle,°   *toad / picks / head*
        With eighen° holked° ful holle°   *eyes / sunken / hollow*
            That gloed as the gledes.[2]

        Al glowed as a glede the goste there ho glides,
        Umbeclipped° [in] a cloude of clethyng°   *Encompassed / clothing*
            unclere,°   *obscure*
120   Serkeled° with serpentes [that sate°] to the sides—   *Encircled / clung*
        To tell the todes theron my tonge wer full tere.[3]
        The burne braides° oute the bronde° and the   *draws / sword*
            body bides;°   *awaits*
        Therefor the chevalrous knight changed no chere.[4]
        The houndes highen° to the [holtes] and her° hedes hides,   *hasten / their*
125   For the grisly goost made a grym bere.°   *noise*
        The grete° greundes wer agast of the grym bere;   *great*

Kay, as alliterative complements at ll. 1637–38, 1706–7, 1997 (on the alliterative *Morte Arthure*, see the headnote in the Sources and Backgrounds section, p. 367).

6. (I swear) by the Cross and by the (Christian) creed.
7. Gueneuere subscribes to a common belief that a demonic visitation presages death.
8. And I shall learn of the ways by which the torments of that uncovered corpse may be relieved.
9. It stammered, it was bewildered, it stood (still) as a stone.
1. It gazed madly.
2. That glowed like embers. (On the imagery of the toads—and serpents, as described below, l. 120—see the headnote in the Sources and Backgrounds section, p. 367; see also the selections from the *Gesta Romanorum* printed thereafter, pp. 375 ff.)
3. It would be very difficult for my tongue to enumerate the toads thereon.
4. To that purpose the chivalrous knight did not change his expression. (I.e., he showed no fear.)

	The birdes in the bowes°	*boughs*
	That on the goost glowes,°	*stare*
	Thei skryke° in the skowes°	*screech / thickets*
130	That° hatheles° may here.	*(Such) that / (other) noble knights*

Hathelese might here, [hendeste° in] halle,   *most gracious*
How chatered° the cholle, the [chaftis,°   *chattered, shuddered / jaws*
    and] the chynne.
Then conjured° the knight; on Crist con he calle—   *abjured, invoked*
"As Thou was crucifiged on croys° to clanse° us of syn—   *cross / cleanse*
135 That° thou sei me the sothe,° whether°   *(May Christ see) that / truth / if*
    thou shalle,
And whi thou walkest thes wayes, the wodes within."
"I was of figure and face fairest of alle,
Cristened and [crisumpte,] with kinges in my kynne—[5]

	I have kinges in my kyn knowen° for kene.°	*renowned / bravery*
140	God has me geven of His grace	
	To dre° my [penaunce°] in this place;	*endure / penance*
	I am comen in this cace°	*case, matter*
	To [carpe°] with your Quene.	*speak*

	Quene was I somwile°—brighter of browes°	*sometime / brows (i.e., face)*
145	Then° Berell or Brangwayn,[6] thes burdes° so	*Than / women*
	bolde°—	*great*

Of al gamen° or gle° that on grounde growes[7]   *amusement / mirth*
Gretter then Dame Gaynour—of garson and golde,[8]

	Of palaies,° of parkes, of pondes, of	*palisades, enclosures*
	plowes,°	*arable lands*
	Of townes, of toures,° of tresour untolde,	*towers*
150	Of castelles, of contreyes, of cragges,° of clowes;°	*crags / ravines*

Now am I caught oute of kide to cares so colde—[9]
    Into care am I caught and couched in clay.[1]

	Lo,° sir curtays knyght	*Look, Behold*
	How delfulle° deth has	*doleful, grievous*
	me dight!°—	*dressed, appointed*
155	Lete me onys° have a sight	*once*
	Of Gaynour the gay."	

After Gaynour the gay Sir Gawyn is gon
And to the body he her brought, [the] burde [so] bright.°   *splendid, fair*
"Welcom, Waynour,° iwis,° worthi   *Guenevere / indeed*

5. Christened and anointed with (baptismal) chrism, with kings in my family.
6. Nothing is known in surviving romances of a Berell (perhaps an original reference to the stone has been misread; cf l. 587), but Brangwen figures as Iseult's maidservant in versions of the Tristan legend, where she is often characterized as beautiful.
7. That exists in the land.
8. More commanding than Dame Guenevere—of treasure and gold.
9. Now am I taken from home into bitter sorrows.
1. Laid in clay. (A reference not just to the ghost's appearance—cf. l. 106—but to the fact of her having been buried.)

in won;°	*(your) domain*
160 Lo, how delful deth has thi dame° dight!	*mother*
I was radder° of rode° then rose in	*redder / complexion (of cheek)*
the ron,°	*bush*
My ler° as° the lelé° lonched° [so lyghte;]	*face / like / lily / sprouted*
Now am I a graceles° gost, and grisly I gron.°	*damned / groan*
With Lucyfer in a lake logh am I light—	
165 [Thus am I lyke to Lucefere; takis] tent [by me:][2]	
For° al thi fressh foroure,°	*Despite / fur (trimmed garments)*
Muse on my mirrour,[3]	
For, king and emperour,	
Thus [dight] shul° ye be.	*shall*

170 Thus [dethe] wil you dighte, thare you not doute;[4]	
Thereon hertly° take hede° while thou art here,[5]	*diligently, to heart / heed*
Whan thou art richest araied° and ridest in	*dressed*
thi route.°	*company, retinue*
Have pité on the poer° [whil] thou art of power—[6]	*poor*
Burnes and burdes that ben besy the aboute,	
175 When thi body is bamed and brought on a ber,	
[Thay will leve the ful lyghteli,] that now wil the loute;[7]	
For then the° helpes nothing but holy praier°—	*thee / prayer*
The praier of [the] poer may purchas the pes	
Of that thou yeves at [thi] yete[8]	
180 Whan thou art set in thi sete,°	*seat*
With al merthes° at mete,°	*mirths, amusements / dinner*
And dayntes° on des.°	*delicacies / dais, high table*

Withe riche dayntes on des thi diotes° arn° dight;	*meals / are*
And in danger and doel° in dongon° I dwelle,	*grief / dungeon, prison*
185 Naxté,° and nedefull,° naked on night.	*In want / needy*
Ther folo° me a ferde° of fendes° of helle;	*follow / army, host / fiends*
They hurle° me unhendely,° thei harme me	*throw down / violently*
in hight—[9]	

2. I am fallen low in a lake—in this way am I like Lucifer; pay attention to my example. (The lake is thus to be understood not just as the Tarn Wadling but as a representation of the abyss of hell. More specifically, given that the ghost later speaks of the possibility of relief from her condition, ll. 176 ff., she lingers in the purifying fires of purgatory. According to the common medieval belief, those who repented of their sins but who had not confessed them in life, or who in life had not completed prescribed penances, were consigned to this place for the cleansing of their souls; such cleansing could be facilitated by prayers of the living, especially by prayers offered in the form of masses.)
3. I.e., consider how I mirror myself.
4. I.e., have no doubt about that.
5. I.e., in this world.
6. I.e., while you are powerful.
7. Men and women who are (now) attentive toward you, when your corpse is embalmed and carried on a bier, will readily abandon you, (they) who would now bow before you.
8. The (grateful) prayer of the poor can purchase (heavenly) peace for you from that which you give (them, as alms) at your gate. (I.e., the giving of alms and the consequent thankful prayer uttered by the poor is the only currency with which the rich may purchase a place in heaven.)
9. Excessively.

In bras and in brymston I bren as a belle.[1]
Was never wrought in this world a wofuller°   *more sorrowful*
    wight°—   *creature*
190 Hit were ful tore any tonge[2] my turment to telle;
    Nowe wil I of my turment tel or° I go.   *before*
      Thenk hertly on this:
      Fonde° to mende° thi mys°—   *seek / remedy / offense, sin*
      Thou art warned, ywys°—   *indeed, certainly*
195   Be war be my wo!"[3]

"Wo is me for thi wo," quod Waynour, "ywis!
But one thing wold° I wite° if thi wil° ware:°   *would / know / will / (it) were*
If auther matens or mas might mende thi mys,
Or eny meble on molde; my merthe were the mare
200 If bedis of bisshopps might bring the to blisse,[4]
    Or coventes° in cloistre might kere°   *(if) convents, religious orders / recover*
      the of care.
If thou be my moder,° grete [mervelle°] hit is   *mother / marvel, wonder*
That al thi burly° body is brought to be so bare!"   *grand, stately*
    "I bare° the of my body, what bote is hit I layn?[5]   *bore*
205   I brak a solempne avowe,
    And no man wist hit but thowe;[6]
      By that token° thou trowe°   *sign / know*
      That sothely° I sayn."°   *truthfully / speak*

"Say sothely what may the° saven [of° thi sytis,°]   *thee / from / sorrows*
210 And I shal make sere° men to singe for thi sake;   *various, diverse*
But the baleful° bestes° that on thi body [bites]   *harmful, malicious / beasts*
[Alle blendis my blode—thi blee es] so blake!"[7]
"That is luf paramour, listes, and delites,
That has me light and laft logh in a lake;[8]
215 Al the welth° of the world [thus] awey°   *wealth, delight / away*
      witis°   *vanishes*

1. In a caldron (*lit.* in brass) and in brimstone, I burn as a great fire.
2. Cf. l. 121, n.
3. Take caution by (the example of) my suffering.
4. If either (the singing) of matins or mass might remedy your sin, or (the provision of) any worldly goods; I would be that much happier if the prayers of bishops might transport you to (heavenly) bliss.
5. What good is it to deny (that)?
6. I broke a solemn vow, and no man knew what it was except you. (Though the general nature of the transgression is outlined forthwith, ll. 213–15, the precise details of the broken vow are never revealed. In the analogous *Trental of St. Gregory*, [printed in the Sources and Backgrounds section, pp. 369 ff.] the mother has broken a marriage vow of chastity and murdered those children of hers born out of wedlock; but in the analogous *exempla* from the *Gesta Romanorum* [also in the Sources and Backgrounds section, pp. 375 ff.] she has commited a variety of sins.)
7. (The creatures) stir my blood (i.e., distress me)—your face is so black!
8. That is (the effect of) illicit love, (improper) desires, and delights, which have drawn me down and abandoned (me) low in a lake. (The ghost speaks figuratively; cf. ll. 164–65, n. The poem no doubt assumes knowledge of Guenevere's traditional identification as one of the harbingers of the dissolution of the Round Table through her adulterous relationship with Lancelot. The ghost's comments here, and possibly at l. 207, are thus especially pointed.)

With the wilde wormes that worche me wrake—[9]
  Wrake thei me worchen, Waynour, iwys.
    Were thritty trentales don[1]
    Bytwene under° and non,°   *(mid)morning / noon*
220   Mi soule [were°] socoured° [full] son°   *would be / aided / soon*
      And brought to the blys."°   *bliss (of heaven)*

"To blisse bring the the barne that bought the on rode,[2]
That° was crucifiged on croys° and crowned with thorne, *Who / cross*
As thou was cristened and crisomed° with   *anointed*
    candel and code,°   *chrism cloth*
225 Folowed in fontestone frely byforne.[3]
Mary the mighti, myldest° of mode,° *most merciful / disposition*
Of whom the blisful° barne in Bedlem° was borne, *blessed / Bethlehem*
Lene me grace that I may grete [thy saule] with gode[4]
And mynge° the with matens and masses on morne." *remember*
230 "To mende[5] [me] with masses grete myster° hit *necessity*
    were;°   *would be*
    For° Him that rest on the Rode,° *For (the sake of) / Rood, Cross*
    Gyf° fast° of thi goode° *Give / copiously / goods, property*
    To folke that failen the fode,[6]
    While thou art here."[7]

235 "Here, hertly my honde, thes hestes to holde,[8]
With a myllion of masses to make [thy] mynnyng!° *commemoration*
A [thing,"] quod Waynour, "iwis,° yit° weten° *indeed / yet, still / know*
    I wolde:
What wrathed° God most, at° thi weting?"° *angered / to / knowledge*
"Pride with the appurtenaunce,[9] as prophetez han° tolde *have*
240 Bifore the peple [appertly°] in her° preching; *openly, clearly / their*
Hit beres bowes bitter—therof be thou bolde—
That makes burnes so bly to breke His bidding.[1]
    But ho° His bidding brekes, bare° thei ben° *whoever / bereft / are*
    of blys;

9. That bring about my affliction.
1. If thirty trentals were performed. (A trental is a sequence of thirty requiem masses offered to
reduce the duration of a soul's passage through purgatory; the sequence may be performed
over weeks, days, or even one day. The specificity of the request points to the *Trental of St.
Gregory* as a source cf. l. 206, n.)
2. (May) the man who redeemed you on a cross bring you to (the) bliss (of heaven).
3. Baptized nobly in the (baptismal) font beforehand.
4. (Mary) grant me the favor to salute your (the ghost's) soul with good (deeds).
5. *Mende* in the first instance suggests "repair," "heal;" but the near concatenation with *menge*
invites the additionally valid reading of "be mindful," "remember."
6. Who fail of (i.e., lack) food. (The reference is to the ghost's spiritual hunger as well as that
of the living poor; cf. ll. 320–23 below.)
7. Cf. l. 171.
8. Here earnestly I raise my hand (in sign of my pledge) to honor these behests.
9. With all that appertains to it.
1. I.e., Pride (envisioned allegorically as a tree) bears branches (i.e., the "appertenances" of Pride)
that are cruel—of that you can be certain—which make men very happy to transgress God's
commandment.

But° thei be salved° of that sare°   *Unless / healed / sickness*
245   Er° they hethen° fare,°   *Before / from here (this world) / go*
They mon weten of care—[2]
Waynour, ywys!"

"Wysse° me," quod Waynour, "som wey,°   *Show / way, direction*
if thou wost;°   *know*
What bedis° might me best to the blisse bring?"   *prayers*
250   "Mekenesse and mercy—thes arn the moost;
And sithen° have pité on the poer—that pleses   *then, next*
Heven King;
Sithen charité is chef,° and then is chaste,°   *chief / chastity*
And thene almessedede° aure° al [other] thing: *almsgiving / over, above*
Thes arn the graceful giftes of the Holy Goste
255   That enspires iche sprete withoute speling.[3]
Of this spiritual thing spute° thou no mare.   *dispute, reason formally*
[Whills°] thou art Quene in thi quert,°   *Whilst / good health, comfort*
Hold thes wordes in° hert.°   *to / heart*
Thou shal leve° but a stert;°   *live / short time*
260   Hethen shal thou fare."

"How shal we fare," quod the freke, "that fonden to fight
And thus defoulen the folke on fele kinges londes,[4]
And riches° over reymes° withouten eny right,   *ride / realms*
Wynnen worshipp in werre thorgh wightnesse of hondes?"[5]
265   "Your King is to° covetous, I warne the, sir knight: *too*
May no man stry him with strength while his whele stondes;
Whane he is in his magesté, moost in his might,
He shal light ful lowe on the se-sondes,[6]
And this chivalrous [Kynge] chef shall [a] chaunce.[7]
270   [False Fortune°] in fight,   *(goddess) Fortune*
[That] wonderfull

2. They must know (nothing but) sorrow.
3. Of the Holy Spirit which breathes life into each soul without (possibility of) destruction. (I.e., which creates immortal souls; the reference to the gifts of the Holy Spirit is not necessarily to be confused with the catechistic heptad; see the headnote in the Sources and Backgrounds section, p. 366.)
4. "How shall we (i.e., Arthur's forces) prevail," said the knight, "who seek to fight and in so doing violate the people of many kings' lands?" (Gawain's analytical self-censure here is one of the more remarkable manifestations in the poem of his renowned courtesy; cf. ll. 458–68.)
5. (Who seek to) win honor in war through strength of hand (i.e., through physical force).
6. No man can destroy him while his wheel (of Fortune) stands still; (but) when he is at the height of his power he will fall low on the sea sands. (A prophecy of events leading to Arthur's final defeat at the hands of his son Mordred; according to the Middle English alliterative *Morte Arthure*, ll. 3598–3711, Arthur's first battle against some of Mordred's forces occurred at sea, off the coast of Southampton. Fortune was commonly envisaged as a goddess turning a wheel to which people were fixed, their welfare being determined by the position of the wheel—either rising into glory or falling to ruin. The brief account in the *Awntyrs* appears to be indebted to ll. 3218–3467 of the *Morte Arthure*, where Arthur tells his counselors of a dream he has had in which Fortune enthrones him high on her wheel but then throws him down; the counselors interpret this as a sign that Fortune has turned against Arthur at the height of his powers and that he must now repent for the excesses of his conquests.)
7. In this way will your chivalrous King achieve a misfortune.

    [whelewryghte,°] *wheelwright, one who turns a wheel*
Shall make lordes [lowe] to light;
Take° witnesse by Fraunce.° *Bear/(the example of) France*

Fraunce haf ye frely° with your fight wonnen;° *totally/won, conquered*
275 Freol⁸ and his folke fey° ar they leved;° *fated to die/abandoned*
Bretayne [and] Burgoyne [is both] to you bowen,
And al the dussiperes of Fraunce with your dyn deved;⁹
Gyan¹ may grete° the werre was bigonen— *regret*
There ar no lordes on lyve² in that londe leved.° *left*
280 Yet shal the riche [Romans] with° [you] be aurronen° *by/overrun*
And with the Rounde Table the rentes° be *revenues*
    reved°— *taken away*
    Thus shal a Tyber untrue tymber with tene!³
    Gete° the,° Sir Gawayn! *Guard/thee, yourself*
    Turne the to Tuskayn,⁴
285   For ye shul lese° Bretayn° *lose/Britain*
    With° a [knyghte] kene.° *Through/bold*

This knight shal be clanly° enclosed° with a crowne, *fully/encircled*
And at Carlele° shal that comly° be crowned *Carlisle/handsome (man)*
    as king;
A sege° shal he seche° with a cession° *throne/seek/sitting (of parliament)*
290 That myche° baret° and bale° to Bretayn shal bring. *much/strife/misery*
Hit shal in Tuskan be tolde of the treson,⁵
And ye shullen turne ayen° for° the *again, back/because of*
    tything.° *tiding*
Ther shal the Rounde Table lese the renoune;° *renown*
Beside Ramsey ful rad° at a riding° *quickly/(mounted) battle*
295   In Dorsetshire shal dy the doughtest of alle—⁶
    Gete the, Sir Gawayn!
    The boldest of Bretayne,

8. Frollo, a Roman tribune who governed Gaul (France) and was defeated by Arthur in the first of his continental wars.
9. Brittany and Burgundy are both submissive to you, and all the nobles of France (cf. l. 4, n.) stunned (*lit.* deafened) by your tumult (*lit.* din).
1. Guienne (another region in France conquered by Arthur).
2. I.e., alive.
3. (And) in this way shall a treacherous Tiber frame (Arthur's ventures) with suffering! (A cryptic reference to the fatal distractions of Arthur's second continental war, traditionally viewed as a war of mere territorial aggrandizement. The implication is that the campaign will draw Arthur on toward Rome in territory through which the River Tiber runs; at that time, with the Tiber marking the limit of his foray, he will hear word of the ultimately ruinous usurpation of his throne by Mordred—the "kynghte kene" of l. 286, below—and he will turn back. Only in the alliterative *Morte Arthure* does Arthur's Roman campaign extend so far south; he turns back at Viterbo.)
4. Turn back to Tuscany. (I.e., take a route back northward, away from Rome; cf. *The Sege off Melayne*, ll. 13–24.)
5. I.e., word of the treason (of Mordred) will be had in Tuscany.
6. The boldest of all. (I.e., Gawain. *Ramsey* may in fact be Romsey, very near the Dorsetshire border, roughly between Southampton and Winchester—an area where, according to the alliterative *Morte Arthure*, ll. 3716–3863, Gawain is killed by Mordred's forces after injudiciously advancing into low-lying ground and finally charging forth in a frenzied rage.)

In a slake° thou shal be slayne;   *hollow*
Sich ferlyes° shull falle.°   *wonders / happen*

300 Suche ferlies shull fal, withoute eny fable[7]
Uppone Cornewayle coost[8] with a knight kene:
Sir Arthur the honest, avenaunt° and able,   *gracious*
He shal be wounded iwys—wothely,° I wene°—   *dangerously / believe*
And al the rial° rowte° of the Rounde Table.   *royal / company*
305 Thei shullen dye on a day, the doughty bydene,°   *altogether*
Suppriset with a surget: he beris [of] sable
With a sauter engreled of silver full shene.[9]
He beris hit° of sable, sothely° to say;   *it / truly*
In riche Arthures halle
310   The barne° playes at° the balle   *boy (Mordred) / with*
That° outray° shall you alle,   *Who / outrage, destroy*
Delfully° that day.   *Sorrowfully*

Have gode day[1] Gaynour, and Gawayn the gode;
I have no lenger tome° tidings [to] telle.   *leisure, opportunity*
315 I mot° walke on my wey thorgh this wilde wode   *must*
[Unto] my wonying-stid,° in wo for to [welle.°]   *dwelling place / boil*
Fore Him that rightwisly° rose and rest on the   *righteously*
    Rode,°   *Rood, Cross*
Thenke° on the danger [and the dole] that I yn dwell;
Fede folk, for my sake, that failen the fode,[2]
320 And menge° me with matens and masses in melle.°   *remember / together*
Masses arn medecynes to us° that bale bides;   *we*
Us thenke a masse as swete
As eny spice that ever ye yete."°   *ate*
With a grisly grete°   *wail, cry*
325   The goste awey glides.

Withe a grisly grete the goost awey glides,
And goes with gronyng sore thorgh the greves° grene.   *groves*
The wyndes, the weders,° the welken°   *weathers, tempests / sky*
    unhides°—   *clear*
Then unclosed° the cloudes; the son° con°   *separated / sun / did*
    shene.°   *shine*
330 The King his bugle has blowen and on the bent°   *open field*

---

7. (I tell you) without falsehood.
8. Beside the coast of Cornwall. (According to the alliterative *Morte Arthure*, Arthur's final battle occurred at Camelford, about five miles inland from Tintagel, on the north coast of Cornwall. Geoffrey of Monmouth also places the final battle in this vicinity, beside the river Camel. About Geoffrey, see the headnote to *Ywain and Gawain* in the Sources and Backgrounds section, pp. 331–32.)
9. Surprised by an insurgent: he bears (a coat of arms) of sable (i.e., black) background with a saltire (the X-shaped cross of St. Andrew) with scalloped edges of brilliant silver. (Such are the arms of Mordred, according to the alliterative *Morte Arthure*, ll. 4180–84.)
1. I.e., farewell.
2. Cf. ll. 232–33.

bides;°   *waits*
His faire folke in the frith,° thei flokken° bydene,   *woods / flock*
And al the riall route° to the Quene rides: *company*
She sayes° hem° the selcouthes° that thei hadde   *tells / them / wonders*
 ther seen—
 The wise° [on swilke° wondirs] for-wondred°   *people / such / astonished*
  they were.
335 Prince, proudest° in palle,°   *most splendid / rich clothes*
  Dame Gaynour, and alle,
  Went to Rondoles Halle³
   To the suppere.

The King to souper is set [and] served in [sale,°]   *hall*
340 Under a siller° of silke dayntly° dight,°   *canopy / delightfully / appointed*
With al worshipp° and wele° inne-with°   *honour / well-being / within*
 the walle,
Briddes brauden and brad in bankers bright.⁴
There come in a soteler° with a symballe,°   *citole (lyre) player / cymbal*
A° lady, lufsom° of lote,° ledand° a knight; (And) *a / lovely / manner / leading*
345 Ho° raykes° up in a res° bifor the rialle,°   *She / went / rush*
And halsed Sir Arthur hendly, on hight.⁵
 Ho said to the soverayne, wlonkest° in wede,°   *most splendid / dress*
  "Mon,° makeles° of might,   *Man / matchless*
  Here commes an errant knight;
350 Do him reson and right,⁶
   For° thi manhede."°   *For (the sake of) / manliness, valor*

[The mane in his mantyll° syttis at his] mete°   *mantle, robe / dinner*
In pal pured [with pane], prodly pight,
[Trofelyte and traverste wyth trewloves in trete];⁷
355 The tasses° were of topas° that were   *clasps / topaz*
 thereto tight.°   *attached*
He gliffed° up with his eighen° that grey   *glanced / eyes*
 wer and grete,°   *great, large*
With his beveren° berde,° on that   *reddish-brown / beard*
 burde° bright—   *lady*
He was the soveraynest of al, sitting in sete,⁸

3. Names from the vicinity of Inglewood Forest suggest the existence of a real place on which
 "Rondoles" Hall ("Rondallsete," "Rondolesette," or "Randolfsett" Hall in the other manuscripts) is based; there are records of a manor house named Randalholme to the northeast of
 Carlisle, a Randasset to the west about fourteen miles, and a Randerside Hall about six miles
 south of the Tarn, at Hutton-in-the-Forest.
4. (With) birds embroidered and spread out in splendid tapestries.
5. And hailed Arthur graciously, out loud.
6. I.e., treat him with propriety and with justice.
7. In rich cloth trimmed with fur superbly adorned, minutely embellished, and overlaid with
 true lover's knots all in a row.
8. The most noble of all, sitting on throne. (With this description of Arthur and the preceding
 description of the glories of the dining hall, recall the ghost's earlier descriptions, and her
 attendant warnings—e.g., ll. 166–69, 178–82.)

That ever segge° had sen° with his eghe-sight;°   *man / seen / sight*
360   King, crowned in kithe,[9] [carpis°] hir tille:°   *(he) speaks / to*
       "Welcom, worthely° wight;°   *worthy / person*
       He shal have reson and right.
       Whethen° is the comli knight,   *Whence, From where*
       If hit be thi wille?"[1]

365   Ho was the worthiest wight that eny° [weld°] wolde: *any (man) / possess*
       Here gide° was glorious and gay, of a gresse-grene;°   *dress / grass-green*
       Here belle was of blunket with birdes ful bolde
       Brauded with brende golde, and bokeled ful bene.
       Here fax in fyne perré was fretted in folde,
370   Contrefelet and kelle coloured full clene,[2]
       With a crowne craftly° al of [clere°] golde.   *skillfully made / shining*
       Here kercheves were curiouse, with many proude pene;[3]
           Her perré was praysed with° prise° men of might.   *by / esteemed*
           Bright birdes° and bolde   *women*
375   Had [ynoghe°] to beholde   *enough, plenty*
           Of that frely° to folde°—   *gracious (woman) / embrace*
           And the hende° knight.   *noble*

       The knight in his colours° was armed ful   *(heraldic) colors*
           clene,°   *completely*
       With his comly° crest clere to beholde,   *handsome*
380   His brené° and his basnet° burneshed ful bene,   *coat of mail / light helmet*
       With a [bordur°] abought al of brende° golde;   *border, rim / shining*
       His mayles° were mylke-white, [enclawet°   *rings of mail / riveted*
           ful clene,°]   *properly*
       His horse trapped° of that ilke° (as true   *outfitted / same (kind of armor)*
           men me tolde);
       His shelde° on° his shulder of silver so shene,   *shield / (hung) on*
385   With bere-hedes° of blake, browed°   *(images of) bears' heads / with brows*
           ful bolde.
           His horse in fyne sandel° was trapped to the hele°—   *thin silk / heel*
           And in° his cheveron° biforne°   *(fixed) in / head armor / in front*
           Stode as° an unicorne,   *resembling*
           Als sharp as a thorne,
390   An anlas° of stele.°   *spike / steel*

       In stele he was stuffed,° that stourne° uppon   *fitted / bold (man)*
           stede,°   *steed*
       Al of sternes° of golde [strynkelyd on stray;[4]]   *stars*
       His gloves, his gamesons,° glowed as a glede°   *protective surcoats / ember*

---

9. Crowned in (his) homeland (i.e., rightfully crowned).
1. I.e., if you would (tell me).
2. Her cloak was of fine woolen cloth extravagantly decorated with birds embroidered in shining gold, and (it was) fastened very handsomely. Her hair was fretted with precious stones in the plaits, (and also decorated with a) headband and hair net very brightly colored.
3. Her headscarves were elaborate, (set with) many (an) extravagant pin.
4. Strewn astray (i.e., all over).

With graynes° of rybé,° that graithed ben gay,[5]	*grains, beads / ruby*
395 And his schene° schynbaudes° that sharp wer	*bright / leg armors*
to shrede;[6]	
His poleinus with [pelidoddes] were poudred to pay.[7]	
With a launce° on loft° that lovely con° lede,°	*lance / high / did / go before*
A freke° on a freson° him folowed, in fay°—	*man / Frisian horse / truth*
The freson[8] was afered° for drede°	*afraid / dread*
of that fare,°	*proceeding*
400 For he was selden° wonte° to se°	*seldom / accustomed / see*
The tablet fluré;[9]	
Siche° gamen° ne gle°	*Such / sport / merriment*
Sagh° he never are.°	*Saw / before*

Arthur asked on hight, herand hem alle,[1]	
405 "What woldes thou, wee,° if hit be thi wille?	*man*
Tel me what thou seches,° and whether thou	*seek*
shalle,°	*shall (still do so)*
And whi thou, sturne° on thi stede, stondes° so stille."	*stern / stand*
He wayved° up his viser fro° his ventalle;°	*lifted / from / neck armor*
With a knightly contenaunce° he carpes him tille:	*countenance, bearing*
410 "Whether thou [be] cayser° or king, her I the°	*emperor / thee*
be-calle°	*call upon*
Fore to finde me a freke to fight with my fille;[2]	
Fighting to fraist° I fonded° fro home."	*seek / set out*
Then seid the King uppon hight,	
"If thou be curteys knight,	
415 [Lighte,° and] lenge° al nyght—	*Alight / stay*
And tel me thi nome."°	*name*

"Mi name is Sir Galaron,[3] withouten eny gile,	
The grettest of Galwey,[4] of greves° and [gyllis,°]	*groves / gills, ravines*
[Of Carrake, of Cummake, of Conyngame, of Kile,	
420 Of Lonwik, of Lannax, of Laudoune Hillus—]	
Thou has wonen hem in werre° with a	*war*
wrange° wile°	*wrong / wile, deception*

5. That (so) finished are splendid.
6. I.e., that had sharp edges which would cut.
7. His knee armors were pleasingly dusted with peridots (a clear green stone; a kind of olivine also known as chrysolite).
8. All four manuscripts refer to the horse at this point, but they may all preserve a misreading for "freke"; either way, the reading is unlikely to be taken as comic, standing rather as a measure of the splendor of the court.
9. The table decorated with fleurs-de-lys (i.e., a royal setting; cf. *The Sege off Melayne*, l. 94).
1. I.e., with all of them hearing.
2. I.e., with whom to have my fill of fighting.
3. A Sir Galeron appears briefly in a number of ME romances, including the alliterative *Morte Arthure*; but he appears most notably in Sir Thomas Malory's *Morte Darthur*, where he figures as one of Mordred's supporters in his subversive attempt to capture Lancelot in Guenevere's chamber at Carlisle.
4. Galloway is the Scottish district adjacent to Cumberland. The names listed in the next two lines also represent southwestern Scottish districts and places: respectively, Carrick, Cunningham, Cummock, Kyle, Lanark, Lennox, and Loudun Hill.

And geven° hem to Sir Gawayn; that my hert grylles°—   *given / angers*
But he shal wring his hondes and warry the wyle
Er he weld hem, ywis, agayn myn unwylles!⁵
425   Bi° al the welth° of the worlde, he shal hem   *(I swear) by / wealth*
        never welde
            While I the hede may bere,⁶
            But if he wyn⁷ hem in were,
            With a shelde and a spere,°   *spear, lance*
            On a faire felde.°   *(battle)field*

430   I wol fight on a felde—thereto I make feith°—   *faith, commitment*
With eny freke° uppon folde° that frely° is borne.   *man / earth / nobly*
To lese° suche a lordshipp me wold thenke°   *lose / think (it)*
        laith,°   *loathsome*
And iche lede opon lyve wold lagh me to scorne."⁸
"We ar in the wode went to walke on oure waith,⁹
435   To hunte at the [herdis] with hounde and with horne.
We ar in oure gamen; we have no gome graithe—¹
But yet thou shalt be mached be mydday to-morne—²
            Forthi° I rede° the, [rathe° mon, thou rest the]   *Therefore / advise / hasty*
            al night."
            Gawayn, grathest of all,
440   Ledes him oute of the hall
            Into a pavilon of pall°   *rich cloth*
                That prodly° was pight.°   *proudly, splendidly / pitched*

Pight was [it] prodly with purpour³ and palle,
Birdes brauden° above in brend gold bright;   *embroidered*
445   In-with° was a chapell, a chambour,° a halle,   *Within / (bed)chamber*
A chymné with charcole to chaufe° the knight.   *warm*
His stede was stabled and led to the stalle;
Hay hertly° he had in haches° on hight.   *generously / hayracks*
Sithen thei braide up a borde and clothes thei calle,⁴
450   Sanapes° and salers,° semly° to sight,   *Napkins / salt cellars / elegant*
        Torches, and brochetes,° and stondardes°   *candlesticks / tall candlesticks*
            bitwene.
            Thus thei served that knight,
            And his worthely wight,°   *person, woman*
            With riche dayntes° dight°   *delicacies / prepared*
455   In silver° so shene—   *silver (dishes)*

---

5. But he will wring his hands (in anguish) and curse the time (that was done) before he possesses them, indeed, against my unwillingness!
6. As long as I can hold up my head (i.e., as long as I live).
7. Unless he win.
8. And each person alive would laugh to scorn me.
9. We have (just) been in the woods to pursue the hunt.
1. We are at (i.e., dressed for) sport; we have no man ready (i.e., armed for combat).
2. But still you will be matched (in combat) by midday tomorrow.
3. Purple cloth (about which, see *Ywain and Gawain*, l. 203, n.).
4. Then they set up a table and called for (table)cloths.

In silver so semely were served of the best,
With vernage° in veres° and cuppes ful clene.   *white wine / glasses*
And thus Sir Gawayn the good glades hour gest,[5]
With riche dayntees endored° in disshes bydene.°   *glazed / completely*
460 Whan the riall° renke° was [rayket°] to his rest   *regal / knight / gone*
The King to counsaile has called his knightes so kene:°   *bold*
"Loke° nowe, lordes, oure lose° be not lost;   *See that / renown*
Ho° shal encontre° with the knight, kestes°   *Who / encounter, fight / decide*
     you bitwene."
     Then seid Gawayn the goode, "shal hit not greve:[6]
465   Here my honde;[7] I you hight°   *promise*
     I woll fight with the knight
     In defence of my right°—   *rightful claim*
          Lorde, by your leve."°   *leave, permission*

"I leve wel," quod the King, "thi lates ar light—[8]
470 But I nolde° for no lordeshipp se° thi life lorne."°   *would not / see / lost*
"Let go!" quod Sir Gawayn, "God° stond with the right!   *(may) God*
If he skape° skathelese,° hit° were a foule   *escape / unharmed / it*
     skorne."°   *insult*
In the daying° of the day the doughti°   *dawning / doughty (men)*
     were dight°   *armed*
And herden° matens° and masse erly   *hear / matins*
     on morne.°   *(the) morn*
475 By that on Plumton land a palais was pight[9]
Were° never freke opon folde had foughten biforne;°   *Where / before*
     Thei setten listes bylyve on the logh lande.[1]
          Thre soppes demayn[2]
          Thei brought to Sir Gawayn,
480   For to confort his brayn—
               The King gared° commaunde.°   *did / command (it)*

The King commaunded [kindeli] the Erlis son of Kent,[3]
Curtaysly in this case take kepe° to° the knight.°   *care / of / (Galeron)*
With riche dayntees or° day° he dyned in his tente;   *before / day(break)*
485 After buskes° him in a brené° that burneshed   *(he) readies / coat of mail*

5. Gawain the good entertains their guest. (It is to be assumed from this that Galeron bears
   Gawain no personal ill will; even so, under the circumstances of the visitor's challenge,
   Gawain's courtesy is extraordinary—cf. l. 262, n.)
6. I.e., it (the decision) shall not be a matter of contention.
7. See l. 235, n.
8. "I well believe," said the King, "your bearing is eager."
9. By that time a palisade (enclosing a place of combat) was pitched on cleared land about
   Plumpton (i.e., in the environs of Plumpton Foot, Plumpton, and Plumpton Head, between
   twelve and sixteen miles south of Carlisle).
1. They marked out the lists (i.e., the combat area) quickly on the low-lying ground.
2. Three wine-soaked sops of the highest-quality bread.
3. I.e., the son of the Earl of Kent.

was bright.

Sithen° to Waynour° wisly° he went;	*Then / Guenevere / prudently*
He laft° in here° warde° his worthly wight.	*left / her / keeping*
After [the hathels] in high hour horses thei hent,[4]	
And at the listes on the lande lordely° don°	*nobly / down*
lighte°—	*alighted*

490   [All butte] thes two burnes, baldest of blode.[5]

The Kinges chaier° is set	*chair, throne*
[Above,] on a chacelet.°	*platform*
Many galiard° gret°	*(a) stalwart (man) / wept*
For Gawayn the gode.	

495
Gawayn and Galeron gurden° her° stedes;°	*girded, prepared / their / steeds*
Al in gleterand° golde, gay was here gere.°	*glittering / gear, equipment*
The lordes bylyve° hom° to list ledes°	*quickly / them (the horses) / lead*
With many serjant of mace,[6] as was the manere.°	*custom*
The burnes broched the blonkes that the side bledis.	

500
Ayther freke opon folde has fastned his spere;	
Shaftes in shide-wode thei shindre, in shedes,[7]	
So jolilé thes gentil justed on were.[8]	
Shaftes thei shindr in° sheldes so shene;°	*on / shining*
And sithen, with brondes° bright,	*swords*

505
Riche° mayles° thei right.°	*fine / rings of mail / slash*
There encontres the knight	
With Gawyn on grene.°	*green, field*

Gawyn was gaily° grathed in grene,	*splendidly*
With his griffons of golde engreled full gay,	

510
Trifeled with tranes and true-loves bitwene.[9]	
On a [startand°] stede [he] strikes on stray;[1]	*prancing*
That other° in his turnaying° he talkes	*other (knight) / tourneying*
in tene:°	*anger*
"Whi drawes thou the on dregh and makes siche deray?"[2]	
He swapped° him yn at the swyre° with a swerde	*slashed / neck*
kene;°	*sharp*

515
That greved Sir Gawayn to his deth day—[3]	
The dyntes° of that doughty were doutwis°	*blows / fearsome*
bydene°:	*completely*

---

4. Afterward (all of) the noble knights in haste took their horses.
5. These two men, boldest of blood (i.e., most valiant of character).
6. Accompanied by many official men-at-arms.
7. The knights spurred the horses such that their flanks bleed. Each earthly man has firmly anchored his lance (in its saddle rest); (the) shafts into wood splinters they shiver, in pieces.
8. So gallantly did these noblemen joust in battle.
9. With his (coat of arms of) golden griffins (a mythical beast with the head and wings of an eagle, the body of a lion) with a splendidly scalloped border, minutely embellished with traceries and true lover's knots in between.
1. He strikes with abandon (*lit.* astray, out of the marked bounds of the lists).
2. Why do you withdraw yourself at a distance and cause such disarray?
3. That wound bothered Sir Gawain until his dying day.

Fifté° mayles and mo°   *Fifty/more*
The swerde swapt° in two—   *slashed*
The canel-bone° also—   *collarbone*
520   And clef° his shelde shene.   *cleaved, split*

He clef thorgh° the cantell° that covered   *through/corner (of the shield)*
      the knight,
Thorgh [shuldre and] shelde a shaftmon°   *hand span (six inches)*
      and mare°—   *more*
And then [lothely that lord] lowe uppon hight—
And Gawayn greches therwith and gremed ful sare:[4]
525 "I shal rewarde° the° thi route,° if I con rede right!"[5]   *repay/thee/stroke*
He° folowed in on the freke with a   *(Galeron)*
      fressh fare:°   *course of action*
Thorgh blason° and brené that burneshed wer bright   *shield*
With a [bytand°] bronde thorgh him he bare—   *biting*
      The bronde was blody° that burneshed was bright.   *bloody*
530   Then gloppened° that gay°—   *grew distressed/splendid (knight)*
      Hit° was no ferly,° in fay;°   *It/wonder/faith*
      The sturne° strikes on stray   *stern (knight)*
      In stiropes stright.[6]

Streyte in his steroppes, stoutely he strikes,
535 And waynes° at Sir Wawayn als° he were   *rushes/as (if)*
      wode°—   *mad, insane*
Then his lemman° on lowde skriles° and   *beloved (lady)/screams*
      skrikes°   *shrieks*
When that burly° burne° blenket° on° blode.   *great/knight/glistened/in*
Lordes and ladies of that laike° likes,°   *sport/are pleased*
And thonked God [of His grace] for Gawayn the gode.
540 With a swap° of a swerde [squeturly°] him   *stroke/powerfully*
      swykes°—   *cheats*
He stroke of the stede hede streite there he stode;
      The faire fole fondred and fel, [bi the Rode!7]
            Gawayn gloppened in hert°—   *(his) heart*
      [He was swithely°] smert;°   *very/quick*
545   Oute of sterops he stert°   *started, leaped*
            Fro Grissell° the goode.   *(the name of the horse; lit. "Gray")*

"Grissell," quod Gawayn, "gon is, God wote!°   *knows*
He was the burlokest° blonke° that ever bote brede—[8]   *greatest/horse*
By Him that in Bedeleem° was borne ever to ben   *Bethlehem*

4. Loathsomely that lord laughed aloud—and Gawain begrudged that and grew bitterly angry.
5. I.e., if I am not mistaken.
6. In stirrups (pushed) straight. (I.e., his great upper-body exertions must be counterbalanced with extra foot pressure on the stirrups.)
7. He struck off the steed's head right there where he stood; the fair horse foundered and fell, (I swear) by the Cross!
8. That ever bit bread (i.e., that ever lived; the phrase is usually reserved for people).

our bote,°   *salvation*
550 I shalle [revenge] the today, if I con right rede!"
    "Go, fecche me° my freson,° fairest   *(Galeron) / Frisian horse*
        on fote;°   *foot*
    He may stonde the in stoure in as mekle stede—"[9]
    "No more for the faire fole then° for a rissh° rote!°   *than / rush / root*
    But for doel of the dombe best that thus shuld be dede,[1]
555   I mourne for no montur,° for I may gete   *mount, horse*
        mare."°   *more, others*
        Als° he stode by his stede   *As, While*
        That was so goode at nede,°   *(time of) need*
        Ner° Gawayn wax° wede,°   *Nearly / grew, became / mad, insane*
        So [wepputte° he full] sare.°   *wept / sorely, bitterly*

560 Thus wepus for wo° Wowayn the wight,°   *woe, sorrow / brave*
    And wenys° him to quyte° that° wonded is sare.   *intends / repay / who*
    That other drogh him on dreght[2] for drede of the knight,
    And boldely broched° his blonk on the bent° bare:° *spurred / field / open*
    "Thus may thou dryve forthe the day to the derk night—
565   The son [is] passed [the merke of] mydday and mare!"[3]
    Within the listes the lede° lordly don° light;°   *man / down / alighted*
    Touard the burne with his bronde he busked° him   *hastened*
        yare.°   *quickly*
        To bataile they bowe° with brondes so bright: *turn*
        Shene sheldes wer shred,°   *shredded*
570   Bright brenes° by-bled°—   *coats of mail / bloodied*
        Many doughti were adred,°   *afraid*
        So fersely° thei fight.   *fiercely*

    Thus thei feght on fote on that fair felde—
    As fressh as a lyon that fautes° the fille.°   *is in default of / fill (of food)*
575 Wilelé° thes wight men thair wepenes they   *With wiles, Cunningly*
        welde°—   *wield*
    [Wete ye wele, Sir Wauan him wontut no wille;][4]
    He brouched° hym yn with his bronde, under the   *stabbed*
        brode° shelde,   *broad*
    Thorgh the waast° of the body, and wonded him ille.°   *waist / badly*
    The swerd stent for no stuf, hit was so wel steled;[5]
580 That other° startis° on bak° and stondis   *other (knight) / leaps / aback*
        ston-stille.
        Though he were stonayed° that stonde° he strikes   *stunned / moment*
            ful sare;

---

9. I.e., he can serve you (Gawain) in battle just as well instead.
1. Except for sorrow that the dumb beast must die in this way.
2. See l. 513.
3. You (Gawain) can pass the day in that way right through to the dark night—(but) the sun is well past its noonday zenith. (I.e., cease your mourning and fight.)
4. You well know that Sir Gawain had no lack of determination.
5. The sword was so well tipped with steel that it stopped for no defensive padding.

He gurdes° to Sir Gawayn   *strikes out*
Thorgh ventaile° and   *neck armor*
   pesayn°—   *chain mail about the neck*
He wanted noght to be slayn
585   The brede of an hare!⁶

Hardely° then thes hathelese° on helmes   *Boldly / noble knights*
   they hewe.
Thei beten downe beriles and bourdures bright;⁷
Shildes on° shildres° that shene were   *(slung) on / shoulders*
   to shewe,°   *view*
Fretted were in fyne golde, thei failen in fight;
590 Stones of iral° they strenkel° and strewe; *? (some precious variety) / scatter*
Stithe° stapeles° of stele they strike don stright.° *Strong / fasteners / directly*
Burnes bannen° the tyme the bargan° was   *curse / encounter*
   brewe,°   *contrived*
The doughti with dyntes° so delfully° were dight.° *blows / grievously / beset*
  [The dyntis of tho doghty were doutous° bydene;° *terrible / altogether*
595   Bothe Sir Lote and Sir Lake⁸
   Miche° mornyng thei make.   *Much*
   Gaynor° gret° for   *Guenevere / wept*
     her° sake   *their (Gawain's and Galeron's)*
     With her° grey eyen.°]   *her / eyes*

Thus gretis Gaynour with bothe her gray yene,
600 For gref° of Sir Gawayn, grisly° was wound.   *grief / (who) horribly*
The knight of corage was cruel and kene,⁹
And with a stele bronde [he strikes in that stounde;]
Al the cost° of [the] knyght he carf° downe clene,   *side, flank / carved*
Thorgh the riche mailes that ronke° were and rounde.   *strong*
605 With suche a teneful touche he taght him in tene¹
He gurdes° Sir Galeron groveling° on gronde.°   *knocks / facedown / ground*
   Grisly on gronde he groned, on grene;°   *(the) green*
    Als° wounded as he was,   *(But) as*
    Sone° unredely° he ras°   *Soon / violently / rose*
610   And folowed fast on° his° [face]   *after / (Gawain's)*
    With a swerde kene.

Kenely that cruel kevered on hight,
And, with a [cast of the carhonde,] in cantil he strikes²
And waynes° at Sir Wawyn, that worthely wight°   *rushes / person*
615 (But him lymped the worse,° and that me wel likes!)   *worse (for that)*

6. He did not fail of (nearly) being slain within the breadth of a hair!
7. They beat down beryls (decorative gems) and splendid (decorative) edgings (cf. l. 381).
8. Lot is Gawain's father (see *Ywain and Gawain*, l. 3644, n.); Lac is the father of Erec (cf. l. 654, n.).
9. The knight (Gawain) through (his) courage was fierce and bold.
1. With such a grievous stroke (that) he directed at him in anger.
2. Boldly that fierce knight recovered in haste, and, with a swing of the left hand, into a corner of the shield he strikes.

He atteled with a slenk haf slayn him in slight;[3]
The swerd swapped° on his swange° and on the   *struck / flank*
    mayle slikes°—   *slides*
And Gawayn bi the coler° [clechis°] the knight.   *collar / clutches*
Then his lemman on loft skrilles and skrikes;[4]
620   Ho° gretes° on Gaynour with gronyng grylle:°   *She / weeps / bitter*
    "Lady, makeles° of might,°   *matchless / power*
    Haf° mercy on yondre knight   *Have*
    That is so delfull° dight,°   *grievously / beset*
    If hit° be thi wille."   *it*

625 [Than wilfully] Dame Waynour to the King went;
Ho caught of her coronall and kneled him tille:[5]
"As thou art roy° roial, richest of rent,°   *king / revenue*
And I thi wife, wedded at thi owne wille—
Thes burnes in the bataile so blede on the bent,
630 They arn° wery° iwis,° and wonded full ille;   *are / weary / indeed*
Thorgh her° shene sheldes her shuldres ar shent;°   *their / smashed*
The grones of Sir Gawayn dos° my hert grille,°   *do / embitter*
    The grones of Sir Gawayn greven me sare—
    Woldest thou, leve lorde,[6]
635   Make thes knightes accorde?°   *reconcile*
    Hit were° a grete° conforde°   *would be / great / comfort*
    For all that [here] ware."°   *were*

Then spak Sir Galeron to Gawayn the good:
"I wende never wee in this world had ben half so wight;[7]
640 Here I make° the releyse,° renke, by   *grant / release (from all obligation)*
    the Rode,
[And, byfore thiese ryalle, resynge] the my right—[8]
And sithen make the monraden with a mylde mode,
As man of medlert makeles of might."[9]
He [stalket°] touard the King [in stid°]   *walked cautiously / (the) place*
    ther he stode,
645 And bede° that burly his bronde° that burneshed   *offered / sword*
    was bright—
    "Of rentes and richesse° I make the releyse—"   *property*
    Downe kneled the knight
    And carped wordes on hight.[1]

---

3. He intended with a glancing blow to have slain him skilfully.
4. Then his (Galeron's) beloved lady screams and shrieks loudly.
5. She took off her coronet and kneeled before him.
6. If you would, dear lord.
7. I believe no man in this world has ever been half as valiant (as you).
8. And, in the presence of these royal people, I resign unto you my rightful claim.
9. And I will do homage to you with a peaceful disposition, as (you are) a man of middle-earth of matchless power. (On the act of homage and its feudal background, see *Havelok*, l. 444, n.; on "middle-earth," see *Havelok*, l. 2244, n.)
1. And spoke (those) words loudly.

The King stode upright
650   And commaunded pes.°   *peace, truce*

The King commaunded pes and cried on hight;
And Gawayn was goodly and [sesutt°] for his sake.   *ceased (fighting)*
Then lordes to listes° they lopen°   *the combat area/leap*
    ful light°—   *quickly*
Sir Ewayne fiz Urian and Arrak fiz Lake,[2]
655 Sir [Meliaduke] and [Marrake][3] that most wer of might—
Bothe° thes travayled° men they truly up take;   *Both (of)/fatigued*
Unneth° might tho° sturne stonde upright.   *With difficulty/those*
What for buffetes° and blode her blees° wex° blak;   *blows/faces/grew*
    Her blees were brosed° for beting of brondes.   *bruised*
660   Withouten more lettyng°   *delay*
     Dight° was here saghtlyng;°   *Arranged/settlement, reconciliation*
     Bifore the comly° King   *handsome*
       Thei held up her hondes.[4]

"Here I° gif° Sir Gawayn, with gerson°   *(Arthur)/give/treasure*
    and golde,
665 Al the Glamergan° londe with   *Glamorgan (district of Wales)*
    greves° so grene;   *groves*
The worship of Wales, at wil and at wolde,[5]
With Criffones castelles curnelled ful clene;[6]
Eke° Ulstur Halle, to hafe and to holde,   *Also*
Wayford and Waterforde" (in Wales I wene)°   *believe*
670 "Two baronrees° in Bretayne,° with burghes° *baronies/Brittany/towns*
    so bolde
That arn batailed aboughte and bigged ful bene.[7]
    I shal dight° the a duke, and dubbe the with honde—[8]   *appoint*
       With-thi° thou saghtil° with   *Provided that/settle, reconcile*
       the knight
       That is so hardi and wight,
675   And relese° him his right°   *release (unto)/rightful (legal) claim*
       And graunte him his londe."

"Here I gif Sir Galeron," quod° Gawayn,   *said*
    "withouten any gile,°   *guile, deceit*

2. Ywain, son of Urien (cf. *Ywain and Gawain*, l. 732) and Erec, son of Lac. (Cf. l. 595 above; Erec, like Ywain, is the titular hero of one of the romances of Chrétien de Troyes—about whom see the headnote in the Sources and Backgrounds section, p. 329.)
3. A Merrake and a Meneduke are together named twice in the alliterative *Morte Arthure*; both also appear in Sir Thomas Malory's *Morte Darthur*; and a Marroke and a Mewreke are also named in the couplet and tail-rhyme versions respectively of the ME romance *Sir Gawain and the Carl of Carlise*—but little is known of any of these figures beyond their names.
4. See l. 235, n.
5. I.e., the honor (of possession) of Wales, to do with as you wish. (The place-names listed in the next three lines, as places *in Wales*, have not been identified; in all likelihood they represent substitutions by scribes unfamiliar with the names of the original text.)
6. Castles fully crenellated (constructed with battlements).
7. That are furnished with battlements all round and very well built.
8. And dub you with (my) hand (cf. *Havelok*, l. 2042, n.).

Al the londes and the lithes⁹ fro Laner to Layre:
[Carrake] and [Cummake,] Conyngham and Kile—¹
680 [Als the chevalrous knyghte hase chalandchede°   challenged for
        als] air°—   heir
The Lother, the Lemmok, the Loynak, the Lile,²
With frethis° and forestes and fosses° so faire.   woods / moats
Under your lordeship to lenge° here a while,   remain
And to the Rounde Table to make repaire,°   resorting
685   I shall refeff³ him in felde, in forestes so fair."
            Bothe the King and the Quene,
            And al the doughti bydene,
            Thorgh the greves so grene
                To Carlele° thei cair.°   Carlisle / ride

690 The King to Carlele is comen with knightes so kene
And al the Rounde Table on rial aray.°   splendor
The wees° that weren wounded (so wothely,°   knights / dangerously
        I wene)
Surgenes sone saved, sothely° to say.   truly
Bothe confortes the knightes the King and the Quene;
695 Thei were dubbed dukes both on a day.
There he wedded his wife (wlonkest,° I wene)   most splendid (woman)
Withe giftes and garsons,° Sir Galeron the gay.   treasures
        Thus that hathel in high withholdes that hende;⁴
            Whan he was saved° sonde,°   healed / soundly
700   Thei made Sir Galeron that° stonde°   (in) that / time
            A knight of the Table Ronde
                To his lyves° ende.   life's

Waynour gared wisely write [into] the west,
To al the religious to rede and to singe;⁵
705 Prestes° with procession to pray were prest,°   Priests / pressed, enjoined
With a mylion of masses to make the mynnynge;⁶
Boke-lered° men—bisshops the best—   Book-learned
Thorghe al Bretayne° [bellus°] the burde°   Britain / bells / woman
        gared° rynge.   caused to
This ferely° bifelle° in [Ingulwud] Forest,   wonder / happened
710 Under a holte so hore at a huntyng—⁷
        Suche a huntyng in [a holt] is noght to be hide.⁸

---

9. All the lands and the properties. (The names at the end of this line are, again, not identifiable
    with certainty—possibly they designate Lanark and Ayre, in southwest Scotland.)
1. Cf. l. 418, n.
2. More unidentified places; but cf. the similar-sounding Scottish names of l. 420.
3. Re-enfeoff (i.e., reestablish with a feudal holding; cf. Havelok, l. 444, n.).
4. In this way that noble man (Arthur) detains that gracious knight.
5. Wisely, Guenevere had writs sent west (i.e., far and wide), to all the men in religious orders
    to read (prayers) and to sing (masses).
6. Guenevere's promise of ll. 235–36 is thus fulfilled.
7. Cf. l. 43.
8. I.e., the story of such an extraordinary hunt in a wood should not be hidden.

Thus to forest they fore,°   *fared, went*
Thes sterne knightes in store;°   *battle*
In the tyme of Arthore
715   This anter betide.[9]

The Weddyng of Syr Gawen and Dame Ragnell
for Helpyng of Kyng Arthoure†

Lythe° and lystenyth° the lif of a lord riche!   *Hearken / hear (about)*
The while that he lyvid was none hym liche,°   *like*
    Nether in bowre ne in halle.[1]
In the tyme of Arthoure thys adventure betyd;°   *happened*
5   And of the greatt adventure, that he hymself dyd,[2]
    That Kyng curteys° and royall.   *courteous*

Of alle kynges Arture beryth the flowyr,[3]
And of alle knyghtod he bare away the honour[4]
    Wheresoever he wentt.
10 In his contrey was nothyng butt chyvalry
And knyghtes were belovid by that doughty,°   *doughty (man)*
    For cowardes were evermore shent.°   *disgraced, ruined*

Nowe, wyll ye lyst[5] a whyle to my talkyng,
I shall you tell of Arthoure the Kyng,
15   Howe ones° hym befell—   *(it) once*
On huntyng he was in Ingleswod[6]
With alle his bold knyghtes good—
    Nowe herken to my spell!°   *story, tale*

The Kyng was sett att his trestyll-tree°   *blind, hide (for hunting)*
20 With his bowe to sle° the wylde veneré,°   *slay / game*
    And his lordes were sett hym besyde.
As the Kyng stode,° then was he ware°   *stood / aware*
Where a greatt hartt was and a fayre,[7]

---

9. Cf. l. 1.
† Text of Oxford, Bodleian Library MS Rawlinson C. 86, ff. 129ʳ–140ʳ, printed with permission
  of the Bodleian Library. The manuscript dates from the very late fifteenth century, possibly
  the early sixteenth century; the poem's date of composition is held to have been no earlier
  than the middle of the fifteenth century. The poem is written mainly in six-line tail-rhyme
  stanzas, rhyming (nominally) *aabccb*; the couplets nominally have four stresses and the tail
  lines three. The rhyme scheme often breaks down into couplets which are irregularly inter-
  spersed with what appear to be orphaned tail-lines; they are no doubt relics of the textual
  corruption which has otherwise rendered the blocks of couplets. At such points "stanza" breaks
  have been assigned according to sense and cadence, not always to rhyme.
1. Neither in chamber nor in hall (i.e., nowhere).
2. I.e., and, concerning the great adventure, he was involved in that himself.
3. Arthur bears the flower (i.e., he excels).
4. I.e., and he was the most honored of all knights.
5. If you will listen.
6. Inglewood Forest; see *The Awntyrs off Arthure*, l. 2, n. 1.
7. Where a great and handsome hart was.

And forth fast dyd he glyde.°   *go*

25 The hartt was in a braken° ferne,°   *thicket / (of) fern*
    And hard° the houndes, and stode full derne.°   *heard / still, secretly*
        Alle that sawe the Kyng:
    "Hold you styll, every man,
    And I woll° goo myself, yf I can—   *will*
30   With craft° of stalkyng."   *skill, guile*

    The Kyng in hys hand toke° a bowe   *took*
    And, wodmanly, he stowpyd lowe[8]
        To stalk unto that dere.
    When that he cam the dere full nere,
35 The dere lept forth into a brere°—   *brier (patch)*
        And ever the Kyng went nere° and nere.   *near(er)*

    So Kyng Arthure went a whyle
    After the dere (I trowe° half a myle),   *believe*
        And no man with hym went;
40 And att the last to the dere he lett flye°   *fly (an arrow)*
    And smote hym sore° and sewerly°—   *sorely / surely*
        Such grace God hym sent.

    Doun the dere tumblyd so deron°   *subdued*
    And fell into a greatt brake° of feron°—   *thicket / fern*
45   The Kyng folowyd full fast.
    Anon the Kyng, both ferce° and fell,°   *fierce / bold*
    Was with° the dere and dyd hym servell°—   *upon / dash out the brains*
        And after the grasse he taste.[9]

    As the Kyng was with the dere alone,
50 Streyght° ther cam to hym a quaynt° grome°   *Immediately / strange / man*
        Armyd well and sure,
    A knyght fulle strong and of greatt myght,
    And grymly° wordes to the Kyng he sayd:°   *grimly, gravely / spoke*
        "Well i-mett,° Kyng Arthour!   *met*

55 Thou hast me done wrong many a yere,
    And wofully° I shall quytte° the° here!   *grievously / requite, repay / thee*
        I hold thy lyfe-days nygh° done;   *nigh, nearly*
    Thou hast gevyn° my landes in certayn[1]   *given*
    With greatt wrong unto Syr Gawen°—   *Gawain*
60   Whate sayest thou, kyng alone?"

8. And, like a (skilled) woodsman, he stooped low.
9. And thereafter he tested the grease (i.e., to establish the quality of his kill, Arthur examines
   the thickness of the deer's fat).
1. I.e., certainly.

"Syr Knyght, whate is thy name, with honour?"[2]
"Syr Kyng," he sayd, "Gromer-Somer Jour,[3]
   I tell the nowe, with ryght."[4]
"A!° Syr Gromer-Somer, bethynk° the well,   *Ah, Oh / consider*
65 To sle me here, honour getyst thou no dell.°   *part*
   Bethynk the thou artt a knyght;

Yf thou sle me nowe in thys case,
Alle knyghtes woll refuse the in every place—
   That shame shall° never the froo.°   *shall (go) / from*
70 Lett be thy wyll° and folowe wytt;°   *desire / reason*
And that° is amys,° I shall amend itt,   *that (which) / amiss, wrong*
   And° thou wolt,° or° that I goo."   *If / will (allow it) / before*

"Nay!" sayd Syr Gromer-Somer, "by Hevyn° Kyng,   *Heaven*
So shalt thou nott skape,° withoute lesyng;°   *escape / lie, deception*
75 I have the nowe att avayll—
Yf I shold lett the thus goo with mokery,
Anoder tyme thou wolt me defye—
   Of that I shall nott fayll."[5]

"Now," sayd the Kyng, "so God me save,
80 Save my lyfe, and whate° thou wolt crave,   *whatever*
   I shall now graunt itt the—
Shame thou shalt have to sle me in veneré,°   *hunting*
Thou armyd and I clothyd butt in grene, perdé!"[6]

"Alle thys shall nott help the,° sekyrly,°   *thee (Arthur) / truly*
85 For I woll° nother° lond ne gold, truly;   *wish, desire / neither*
Butt° yf thou graunt me att a certayn day   *Unless*
   Suche as I shall sett,° and in thys same araye°—"   *appoint / array, attire*

"Yes!" sayd the Kyng, "lo!° here my hand!"[7]   *look, behold*
"Ye,° butt abyde, Kyng, and here° me a stound;°   *Yea, Yes / hear / while*
90 Fyrst, thou shalt swere° upon my sword broun°   *swear / bright*

2. I.e., with respect.
3. A knight named Gromore Somer Joure also appears in Malory's *Morte Darthur*, where—and like the challenging Sir Galeron of the *Awntyrs off Arthur* (which see, l. 417, n.)—he is one of the band of knights loyal to Mordred in the attempt to capture Lancelot in Guenevere's chamber. A Sir Gromer appears in the ME romance *The Turke and Gowin*; there, a strange dwarflike man (a "turke"), after a series of adventures with Gawain, asks to be beheaded by him, upon which he miraculously arises as the well-formed knight Gromer.
4. I.e., with just cause, truly.
5. I.e., I have you now in my power—if I were to let you go, merely having joked about, you would denounce me at another time—I shall not fail in that respect.
6. And I clothed but in the green cloths of the hunt, indeed! (Cf. Arthur's more commanding response in *The Awntyrs off Arthur*, ll. 434–38.)
7. I.e., I raise my hand (as a pledge of good faith in this matter). (By so interrupting Sir Gromer, Arthur, in his evident haste to get away, attempts to agree to nothing; cf. the more fulsome versions of such a pledge in *The Awntyrs off Arthur*, ll. 235–36 and 465–68.)

To shewe me att thy comyng whate wemen love best,
    in feld and town;[8]

And thou shalt mete° me here, withouten   *meet*
    send,°   *appointed company*
Evyn att this day .xij. monethes end;[9]
And thou shalt swere upon my swerd good
95 That of thy knyghtes shall none com with the, by° the   *(I swear) by*
    Rood,°   *Cross*
    Nowther° fremde° ne freynd—   *Neither / stranger*

And yf thou bryng nott answere withoute fayll,
Thyne hed thou shalt lose for thy travayll°—   *travail, effort*
    Thys shall nowe be thyne oth.°   *oath*
100 Whate sayst thou, Kyng? Lett se! Have done!"[1]

"Syr, I graunt° to thys; now lett me gone.°   *accede / go*
    Though itt be to me full loth,°   *loathsome*

I ensure° the, as I am true Kyng,   *assure*
To com agayn att thys .xij. monethes endyng
105 And bryng the thyne answere."
"Now go thy way, Kyng Arthure;
Thy lyfe is in my hand, I am full sure;
    Of thy sorrowe thow artt nott ware—[2]

Abyde! Kyng Arthure, a lytell whyle—
110 Loke° nott today thou me begyle,°   *See (that) / beguile, deceive*
    And kepe alle thyng in close;[3]
For and I wyst, by Mary mylde,
Thou woldyst betray me in the feld,
    Thy lyf fyrst sholdyst thou lose."[4]

115 "Nay," sayd Kyng Arthure, "that may nott be;
Untrewe knyght shalt thou never fynde me;
    To dye yett were me lever.[5]
Farwell, syr knyght, and evyll mett;[6]
I woll com, and I be on lyve[7] att the day sett—
120 Though° I shold scape never."   *(Even) though*

8. I.e., to reveal to me upon your return what women everywhere (*lit.* in field and town) desire most.
9. Just at this day, at the end of twelve months.
1. I.e., Let it be seen! Be done with it! (Such expressions of impatience are found throughout the poem, often undermining any sense of stately composure one might tend to attribute to Arthur, his followers, or his interlocutors.)
2. I.e., you do not fully realize the grief you are about to incur. (After this taunt, Gromer, evidently having forgotten to secure a promise of secrecy from Arthur, has to recall the King, who is already stealing away.)
3. I.e., and keep everything to yourself.
4. For if I knew, by gracious Mary, that you intended to betray me in the field (of battle), you would lose your life first (before you could do that).
5. I would sooner die.
6. Unfortunately met. (Cf. l. 54.)
7. If I am (still) alive.

The Kyng his bugle gan° blowe—   did
That hard° every knyght and itt gan knowe;°   heard / recogize
  Unto hym can° they rake.°   did / hasten
Ther they fond° the Kyng and the dere°   found / deer
125 With sembland sad and hevy chere,
  That had no lust to layk.[8]

"Go we home nowe to Carlyll;[9]
Thys huntyng lykys° me nott well,"   like, enjoy
  So sayd Kyng Arthure.
130 Alle the lordes knewe by his countenaunce
That the Kyng had mett with sume dysturbaunce.

Unto Carlyll then the Kyng cam,
Butt of his hevynesse° knewe no man;   sadness
  His hartt° was wonder° hevy.   heart / wondrously

135 In this hevynesse he dyd abyde
That° many of his knyghtes mervelyd°   (So) that / wondered
  that tyde,°   time
Tyll, att the last, Syr Gawen
To the Kyng he sayd than,
"Syr, me marvaylyth ryght sore,°   grievously
140 Whate thyng that thou sorrowyst fore."

Then answeryd the Kyng as-tyght,°   at once
"I shall the tell, gentyll Gawen knyght.
In the forest as I was this daye,
Ther I mett with a knyght in his araye,°   array, armor
145 And serteyn° wordes to me he gan sayn°   certain / say
And chargyd° me I shold hym nott bewrayne;°   ordered / betray
His councell° must I kepe therfore,   confidence, secret
Or els I am forswore."°   perjured

"Nay, drede° you nott, lord, by Mary flower!   dread, fear
150 I am nott that man that wold° you dyshonour,   would
  Nother by evyn ne by moron."[1]

"Forsoth,° I was on huntyng in Ingleswod—   Indeed
Thowe knowest well I slewe an hartt, by the Rode,°   Cross
  Alle mysylf° alon;   (by) myself
155 Ther mett I with a knyght armyd sure.°   surely, fully
His name, he told me, was Syr Gromer-Somer Joure;

---

8. With a sad appearance and a grave countenance, who had no desire for (further) sport.
9. Carlisle (about which, see *The Awntyrs off Arthure*, l. 2, n. 1).
1. By neither evening nor morning (i.e., at no time).

Therfor I make my mone.°   *complaint*

Ther that knyght fast° dyd me threte°   *soon, quickly / threaten*
And wold have slayn me with greatt heatt;°   *ferocity*
160   Butt I spak fayre° agayn°—   *skilfully, courteously / in reply*
Wepyns with me ther had I none;[2]
Alas, my worshypp° therfor is nowe gone."   *renown, honor*
"What thereof?"[3] sayd Gawen.

"Whatt nedys more? I shall nott lye—[4]
165   He wold have slayn me ther withoute mercy,
And that me° was full loth!   *(to) me*
He made me to swere that, att the .xij. monethes end,
That I shold mete hym ther in the
        same kynde°—   *manner, state (of dress)*
To that I plyght my trowith—[5]

170   And also I shold tell hym att the same day
Whate wemen desyren moste, in good faye;°   *faith*
        My lyf els° shold I lese.°   *else, otherwise / lose*
This oth I made unto that knyght,
And that I shold never tell itt to no wight°—   *creature, person*
175   Of thys I myght nott chese—[6]

And also I shold com in none oder° araye,°   *other / array, attire*
Butt evyn° as I was° the same daye;   *just / was (attired)*
And yf I faylyd of myne answere,
I wott° I shal be slayn ryght there—   *know*
180   Blame me nott though° I be a wofull° man!   *if / woeful, sorrowful*
Alle thys is my drede and fere."°   *fear*

"Ye syr, make° good chere!   *be of*
Lett make your hors redy
To ryde into straunge° contrey;   *strange, unfamiliar*
185   And ever wheras ye mete owther° man or woman, in faye,   *either*
Ask of theym whate thay therto saye.
And I shall also ryde anoder waye
And enquere° of every man and woman, and gett whatt I may   *inquire*

2. I had no weapons with me there. (That is not strictly true—like most assertions made in this poem—but Arthur presumably refers to his lack of chivalric weaponry: sword, lance, armor, and shield.)
3. I.e., how so? (But perhaps also with the cursory sense of "what of it?"—cf. Gawain's rather detached, even platitudinous, optimism at ll. 182, 212, and 219–224.)
4. What more needs to be said? I will not lie (concerning this matter). (The repetition in Arthur's subsequent answer suggests a certain irritated impatience.)
5. On that I gave my word (*lit.* pledged my truth).
6. I could make no choice in this (matter).

Of every man and womans answere—
190 And in a boke I shall theym wryte."[7]

"I graunt," sayd the Kyng as-tyte,°   *immediately*
"Ytt° is well advysed, Gawen the good,   *It*
Evyn° by the holy Rood."   *Even, Right*
Sone° were they both redy,   *Soon*
195 Gawen and the Kyng wytterly.°   *plainly, certainly*
The Kyng rode on° way and Gawen anoder   *one*
And ever enquyred of man, woman, and other,[8]
    Whate wemen desyred moste dere.°   *dearly*

Somme sayd they lovyd to be well arayd;
200 Somme sayd they lovyd to be fayre prayed;°   *besought, wooed*
Somme sayd they lovyd a lusty man
That in theyr armys can clypp° them, and kysse them than;   *embrace*
Somme sayd one,° somme sayd other;   *one (thing)*
And so had Gawen getyn° many an answer.   *got*
205 By that° Gawen had geten whate he maye   *that (time)*
And come° agayn° by a certeyn daye.   *came/in return, back*

Syr Gawen had goten answerys so many
That had made a boke greatt, wytterly;
    To the courte he cam agayn.
210 By that was the Kyng comyn with hys boke,
And eyther on others pamplett° dyd loke;   *pamphlet, book*
    "Thys may nott fayl!" sayd Gawen.

"By God," sayd the Kyng, "I drede me sore;[9]
I cast° me to seke° a lytell° more   *aim, intend/search/little*
215   In Yngleswod Forest—
I have butt a moneth° to° my day sett;   *month/until*
I may hapen on somme good tydynges to hytt—[1]
    Thys thynkyth me nowe best."

"Do as ye lyst,"° then Gawen sayd,   *please*
220 "Whate-so-ever ye do, I hold me payd°—   *satisfied*
    Hytt° is good to be spyrryng!°   *It/inquiring*
Doute° you nott, lord, ye shall well spede;°   *Doubt/succeed*
Sume of your sawes° shalle help att nede°—   *sayings/(time of) need*
    Els itt were yll lykyng!"[2]

7. Gawain's jollity presides over a subversion of knightly standards: the collection of more than one answer to allow Arthur to hedge his bets goes against any chivalric aspiration to ethical certainty; the compiling of the answers *in a book* is surely a job for clerks and a ridiculous prospect for a knight; Gawain's willingness to assist Arthur violates the promise of secrecy made to Gromer.
8. "Other" presumably indicates children. (Though this is in the first instance an inept rhyme found amid an obviously corrupt passage, it does suggest something of the desperate nature of the quest.)
9. I am sorely afraid.
1. I may happen to hit upon some good news.
2. Otherwise it would be displeasing!

225 Kyng Arthoure rode forth on the other° day	*next*
Into Yngleswod, as hys gate° laye—	*path, way*
And ther he mett with a lady;	
She was as ungoodly° a creature	*unpleasant, ugly*
As ever man sawe, withoute mesure.°	*measure, moderation*
230 Kyng Arthure mervaylyd securly:°	*certainly*
Her face was red, her nose snotyd° withall,°	*snotted / moreover*
Her mowith° wyde, her teth yalowe° over all,	*mouth / yellow*
With bleryd° eyen gretter° then a ball;	*bleared / greater*
Her mowith was nott to lak;³	
235 Her teth hyng° over her lyppes,	*hung*
Her chekys° syde° as wemens hyppes;°	*cheeks / prominent / hips, buttocks*
A lute° she bare upon her bak,	*lute-shaped hump*
Her nek long and therto greatt,⁴	
Her here° cloteryd° on an hepe.°	*hair / knotted / heap, pile*
240 In the sholders she was a yard brode;°	*broad*
Hangyng pappys to be an hors lode;⁵	
And lyke a barell she was made;	
And to reherse the fowlnesse of that lady,	
Ther is no tung may tell, securly—	
245 Of lothlynesse inowgh° she had.	*enough, in plenty*
She satt on a palfray was gay begon,⁶	
With gold besett and many a precious stone;	
Ther was an unsemely° syght,	*unseemly, inappropriate*
So fowll a creature withoute mesure,	
250 To ryde so gayly, I you ensure°—	*assure*
Ytt was no reason ne ryght.⁷	
She rode to Arthoure, and thus she sayd:	
"God spede, syr King! I am welle payd	
That I have with the° mett;	*thee*
255 Speke with me, I rede,° or° thou goo,	*advise / before*
For thy lyfe is in my hand, I warn the soo—⁸	
That shalt thou fynde, and I itt nott lett."⁹	
"Why, whatt wold° ye, lady, nowe with me?"	*would*
"Syr, I wold fayn° nowe speke with the,	*gladly*
260 And tell the tydynges good;	
For alle the answerys that thou canst yelpe,°	*boast*

3. I.e., not lacking (in size).
4. I.e., her neck was as long as it was thick.
5. I.e., (she had) hanging breasts massive enough to be a load for a horse.
6. She sat on a riding horse which was gayly bedecked. (Cf. the equestrian trappings of the magical—but also beautiful—Dame Tryamour, *Sir Launfal*, ll. 949–60.)
7. I.e., there was no reason or justification for it. (Thus ends the first of a number of allusions to the lady's mysterious embodiment of opposing qualities.)
8. Cf. l. 107.
9. You shall find that out, if I do not prevent it (i.e., your death).

None of theym° alle shall the helpe—   *them*
　　That shalt thou knowe,° by the Rood!   *find out*

Thou wenyst° I knowe nott thy councell;°   *believe / secret*
265　Butt I warn the, I knowe itt, every deall°—   *part*
　　Yf I help the nott, thou art butt dead.
Graunt° me, syr Kyng, butt one thyng,   *Grant, Promise*
And for thy lyfe I make warrauntyng°—   *guarantee*
　　Or elles° thou shalt lose thy hed.”   *else*

270　“Whate mean you, lady? Telle me tyghte,°   *quickly*
For of thy wordes I have great dispyte;°   *contempt*
　　To° you I have no nede.°   *Of / need*

What is your desyre, fayre lady?[1]
Lett me wete,° shortly,°   *know / briefly*
275　Whate is your meanyng,
And why my lyfe is in your hand;
Tell me, and I shall you warraunt
　　Alle your oun° askyng.”°   *own / request*

“Forsoth,”° sayd the lady, “I am no qued!°   *In truth / wretch*
280　Thou must graunt me a knyght to wed—
　　His name is Syr Gawen—
And suche covenaunt I woll make the:
Butt° thorowe° myne answere thy lyf   *Only / through / (shall) be*
　　savyd be°—
　　Elles lett my desyre be in vayne—

285　And yf myne answere save thy lyf,
Graunt me to be Gawens wyf.
　　Advise° the nowe, syr Kyng,   *Think carefully*
For itt must be so, or thou artt° butt dead;   *are*
Chose nowe, for thou mayste° sone lose thyne hed—   *may*
290　Tell me nowe, in hying.”°   *haste*

“Mary!” sayd the Kyng, “I maye nott graunt the
To make warraunt Syr Gawen to wed the;
　　Alle lyeth in hym alon—
Butt, and itt be so, I woll do my labour
295　In savyng of my lyfe to make itt secour;
　　To Gawen woll I make my mone.”[2]

“Welle!”° sayd she, “nowe go home agayn   *Good*
And fayre wordes speke to Syr Gawen,
　　For thy lyf I may save.

---

1. Given the three previous lines, “fayre lady” here is far more sarcastic than it is polite, and
   Arthur's response, though largely disconsolate, manages also to be condescending.
2. I cannot promise you to guarantee that Gawain will wed you; all depends upon him alone—
   but, though it is so, I will take pains in (the interests of) saving my life to secure it (i.e., what
   you ask); I will make my complaint to Gawain.

300 Though I be foull, yett am I gaye;°   *vigorous, amorous*
     Thourgh° me thy lyfe save he maye—   *Through*
        Or sewer thy deth to have."[3]

     "Alas!" he sayd, "nowe woo° is me   *woe, unhappy*
     That I shold cause Gawen to wed the
305   (For he wol be loth° to saye naye);   *loath*
     So foull a lady as ye ar° nowe one   *are*
     Sawe I never in my lyfe on ground gone,°   *go*
        I nott° whate° I do may."   *know not / what*

     "No force,° syr Kyng, though I be foull;   *matter*
310 Choyse for a make hath an owll.[4]
        Thou getest of me no more;[5]
     When thou comyst agayn to° thyne answere,   *to (give), with*
     Ryght in this place I shall mete the here—
        Or elles I wott thou artt lore."°   *lost*

315 "Now farewell," sayd the Kyng, "lady fowll."
     "Ye syr," she sayd, "ther is a byrd men call an owll—
        And yett a lady I am."[6]
     "Whate is your name? I pray you tell me."
     "Syr Kyng, I hight° Dame Ragnell,[7] truly,   *(am) called*
320   That never yett begylyd° man."   *beguiled, deceived*

     "Dame Ragnell, now have good daye."
     "Syr Kyng, God spede the on thy way!
        Ryght here I shall the mete."
     Thus they departyd fayre and well.
325 The Kyng full sone com to Carlyll,
     And hys hartt° hevy and greatt.°   *heart (was) / ponderous*

     The fyrst man he mett was Syr Gawen,
     That unto the Kyng thus gan° sayn,°   *did / say*
        "Syr, howe have ye sped?"°   *succeeded, got on*
330 "Forsoth," sayd the Kyng, "never so yll!°   *ill, badly*

3. Or surely obtain your death.
4. Choice of a mate has (even) an owl. (The owl was traditionally held to be one of the uglier
   and more disagreeable birds.)
5. I.e., I have nothing more to say.
6. Editors usually attribute the woman's cryptic response to corruption of the text at this point,
   but it is possible that she alludes, with characteristic playfulness, to the two senses available
   in Arthur's disdainful "fowll." She takes the word to mean "fowl" and thus transforms the
   insult into a reprise of the self-salutary proverb about the owl. This, combined with her assertion
   that she is after all "a lady" (and by implication really neither foul nor fowl), hints at her full
   transformative potential; cf. l. 251, n.
7. *Dame* is a respectful title; but *Ragnell* is recorded elsewhere in Middle English literature as
   the name of a devil—see, for instance, the alliterative poem *Patience*, l. 188, and the Chester
   mystery play of *Antichrist*, ll. 645–47. (Cf. l. 251, n.)

Alas, I am in poynt myself to spyll,
   For nedely I most be ded."[8]

"Nay!" sayd Gawen, "that may nott be!"
I had lever myself be dead, so mott I the—[9]
335   Thys is ill° tydand!"°   *bad / news*
"Gawen, I mett today with the fowlyst lady
   That ever I sawe, sertenly.

She sayd to me my lyfe she wold save—
Butt fyrst she wold the to° husbond have,   *as*
340   Wherfor I am wo-begon;°   *woebegone, mournful*
   Thus in my hartt I make my mone."

"Ys° this all?" then sayd Gawen,   *Is*
"I shall wed her, and wed her agayn!
   Thowgh she were a fend°—   *fiend, demon*
345   Thowgh she were as foulle as Belsabub—[1]
Her shall I wed, by° the Rood;°   *(I swear) by / Cross*
   Or elles were nott I your frende—

For ye ar my Kyng with honour
And have worshypt° me in many a stowre;°   *honored / battle*
350   Therfor shall I nott lett.°   *refrain, hold back*
To save your lyfe, lorde, itt were my parte°—   *duty*
   Or were I false and a greatt coward—
   And my worshypp° is the bett."°   *honor / better*

"Iwys,° Gawen, I mett her in Inglyswod;   *Indeed*
355   She told me her name, by the Rode,°   *Cross*
   That itt was Dame Ragnell.
She told me butt I had of her answere,
Elles alle my laboure is never the nere;[2]
   Thus she gan me tell—

360   And butt° yf her answere help me well,   *only*
Elles lett her have her desyre no dele;[3]
   This was her covenaunt—
And yf her answere help me, and none other,° *other (person's answer)*
Then wold she have you—here is alle togeder;
365   That made she warraunt."[4]

8. Alas, I am on the point of killing myself, for I must necessarily die. (Note how, before revealing the conditions of his difficulty, Arthur leads Gawain into an assertion of absolute devotion. Arthur has, moreover, anticipated Gawain's response; see l. 305.)
9. As I hope to thrive. (A less-than-apposite complement to the first part of the line.)
1. Beelzebub, "the prince of the devils" (Matthew 12. 24), another name for Satan.
2. She told me that unless I got the answer from her all my labors would be no nearer (a solution).
3. Or else let her have no part of her request.
4. I.e., this is what it amounts to; she made me guarantee it. (But cf. Arthur's refusal to do just that at ll. 291–93; the current ploy, unnecessary in the light of Gawain's previous answer, suggests a lingering sense of desperation—cf. Arthur's insecurity at ll. 213–15.)

"As for this," sayd Gawen, "shall I nott lett;[5]
I woll wed her att whate° tyme ye woll sett.°   *whatever / appoint*
   I pray you make no care,[6]
For and° she were the most fowlyst wyght°   *(even) if / creature*
370 That ever men myght se° with syght,   *see*
   For your love I woll nott spare."°   *hold back*

"Garamercy° Gawen!" then sayd Kyng Arthor,   *Many thanks*
"Of alle knyghtes thou berest the flowre[7]
   That ever yett I fond.°   *found*
375 My worshypp and my lyf thou savyst for ever;
Therfore my love shall nott frome the dyssevyr,°   *part*
   As° I am Kyng in lond."°   *While / (the) land*

Then within .v.° or .vj.° days   *five / six*
The Kyng must nedys° goo his ways   *necessarily*
380   To bere his answere;
The Kyng and Syr Gawen rode oute of toun,
No man withe them, butt they alone,
   Neder ferre ne nere.[8]

When the Kyng was within the forest:
385 "Sry Gawen, farewell, I must go west;[9]
   Thou shalt no furder° goo."   *further*
"My lord, God spede you on your jorney.
I wold° I shold nowe ryde your way,   *would (prefer)*
   For to departe I am ryght wo."

390 The Kyng had rydden butt a while—
Lytell more then the space of a myle—
   Or° he mett Dame Ragnell: *Before*
"A!° syr Kyng, ye arre nowe welcum here,   *Ah, Oh*
I wott° ye ryde to bere your answere;   *believe*
395   That woll avayll you no dele."[1]

"Nowe," sayd the Kyng, "sith° itt woll none   *since*
   other° be,   *other (way)*
Tell me your answere nowe, and my lyfe save me;°   *(for) me*
   Gawen shall you wed—
So he hath promysed me, my lyf to save—
400 And your desyre nowe shall ye have,
   Both in bowre° and in bed.   *(bed)chamber*

Therfor tell me nowe, alle in hast,°   *haste*
Whate woll help now, att last—

5. (*I* is lacking in the MS, and is inserted on the model of l. 350.)
6. I.e., do not worry.
7. See l. 7, n.
8. But they alone (rode out), (and) no man (was) with them, from neither far (off) nor nearby.
9. See *Sir Launfal*, l. 219, n.
1. That will help you in no way.

Have done!² I may nott tary!"°   tarry, delay
405 "Syr," quod° Dame Ragnell, "nowe shalt thou knowe   said
       Whate wemen desyren moste, of high and lowe;³
       From this I woll nott varaye:⁴

       Summe men sayn we desyre to be fayre;
       Also we desyre to have repayre°   resort, sexual relations
410   Of diverse straunge° men;   strange
       Also we love to have lust in bed
       And often we desyre to wed—
         Thus ye men nott ken.⁵

       Yett we desyre anoder° maner° thyng,   another / manner, kind (of)
415 To be holden° nott old, butt fresshe and yong;   considered
       With flatryng and glosyng and quaynt gyn,⁶
       So ye men may us° wemen ever wyn°   (from) us / obtain
         Of whate ye woll crave.

       Ye goo full nyse,⁷ I woll nott lye!
420 Butt there is one thyng is alle oure fantasye,⁸
         And that nowe shall ye knowe:
       We desyren of men, above alle maner thyng,
       To have the sovereynté,° withoute lesyng,°   sovereignty, rule / lie
         Of° alle, both hygh and lowe.   Over

425 For where we have sovereynté, alle is ourys;°   ours
       Though a knyght be never so ferys,°   fierce
         And ever the mastry° wynne   mastery, victory (in combat)
       Of the moste manlyest,° is° oure desyre   heroic / (it) is
       To have the sovereynté of suche a syre;°   sire, master
430   Suche is oure crafte° and gynne.°   skill, cunning / design, plan

       Therfore wend,° syr Kyng, on thy way,   go
       And tell that knyght as I the° saye,°   thee / tell
         That itt is as we desyren moste;
       He wol be wroth° and unsought°   angry / irreconciled
435 And curse her fast that itt the taught,
         For his laboure is lost.

       Go forth, syr Kyng, and hold promyse,
       For thy lyfe is sure° nowe in alle wyse;°   secure / respects
         That dare I wele undertake."°   affirm

2. See l. 100, n.
3. Among highborn and low (i.e., among all kinds).
4. I will not digress. (A promise immediately broken with a desultory answer of a length teasingly
   disproportionate to Arthur's requested "hast.")
5. I.e., and in this way you men perceive nothing.
6. With flattery and inducement and elegant contrivance.
7. You (men) go (about such business) very subtly.
8. I.e., the desire of all of us.

440	The Kyng rode forth a greatt shake,[9]	
	As fast as he myght gate,°	*go*
	Thorowe myre, more,° and fenne°	*moor/fen, marsh*
	Whereas° the place was sygnyd° and	*(To) where/assigned*
	sett° then.	*appointed*

	Evyn° there with Syr Gromer he mett,	*Right, Precisely*
445	And stern wordes to the Kyng he spak with that:[1]	
	"Com of syr Kyng! nowe lett se[2]	
	Of thyne answere, whate itt shal be—	
	For I am redy grathyd."°	*prepared (with arms)*

	The Kyng pullyd oute bokes twayne;°	*two*
450	"Syr, ther is myne answer, I dare sayn,	
	For somme woll help att nede."[3]	
	Syr Gromer lokyd° on theym everychon;°	*looked/every one*
	"Nay! nay! syr Kyng, thou artt butt a dead man—	
	Therfor nowe shalt thou blede!"°	*bleed*

455	"Abyde, Syr Gromer!" sayd Kyng Arthoure,	
	"I have one answere shall make ale sure."[4]	
	"Lett se!"[5] then sayd Syr Gromer,	
	"Or els, so God me help, as I the say,	
	Thy deth thou shalt have—with large° paye°	*great/pleasure*
460	I tell the nowe, ensure!"°	*assuredly*

	"Now," sayd the Kyng, "I se, as I gesse,°	*guess, suppose*
	In the is butt a lytell gentilnesse,°	*graciousness, kindness*
	By God that ay is helpand.[6]	
	Here is oure answere, and that is alle,	
465	That wemen desyren moste speciall	
	Both of fre and bond:[7]	

	I saye no more butt, above al thyng,	
	Wemen desyre sovereynté, for that is theyr lykyng°	*pleasure*
	And that is ther moste° desyre—	*greatest*

---

9. I.e., in a hurry.
1. I.e., he spoke thereupon.
2. I.e., Come on, Sir King! now let it be seen. (See. l. 100, n.)
3. I.e., for some (one) of them will do in (this) crisis. (The ridiculousness of Arthur's hedging of bets here is equaled only by the strategy's unquestioning acceptance by Gromer; cf. the more decisive response of the challenger in the analogous *Marriage of Sir Gawaine* [in the Sources and Backgrounds section], ll. 88–95. One advantage Arthur's strategy does afford, however, is that it would keep the King from honoring his promise to Dame Ragnell should an answer from one of the books work first; further, Arthur now has a chance to tease through delay, as he himself has been teased.)
4. I have one answer which will make everything secure.
5. See l. 100, n.
6. By God, who is ever helping.
7. Concerning that which women desire most especially of both freeman and servant (i.e., of all men).

470 To have the rewll° of the manlyest men,   *rule*
     And then ar they well° (thus they me dyd ken)°—   *happy / instruct*
       To rule the, Gromer syre!"[8]

     "And she that told the nowe, Syr Arthoure,
     I pray to God I maye se her bren° on a fyre!   *burn*
475   For that was my suster,° Dame Ragnell,   *sister*
     That old stott!° God geve° her shame!   *cow / give*
     Elles° had I made the° full tame—   *Else, Otherwise / thee*
       Nowe have I lost moche° travayll.°   *much / travail, effort*

     Go where thou wolt,° Kyng Arthoure,   *would*
480 For of° me thou maiste° be ever sure°—   *from / may / secure*
       Alas, that I ever se° this day!   *(live to) see*
     Nowe, welle I wott, myne enimé° thou wolt be;   *enemy*
     And att suche a pryck° shall I never°   *torment, coercion / never (again)*
       gett the—
     My song may be 'well-awaye!' "[9]

485 "No!" sayd the Kyng, "that make I warraunt;[1]
     Some harnys° I woll have to make me defendaunt°—   *armor / defensible*
       That make I God° avowe!°   *(to) God / vow*
     In suche a plyght° shallt thou never me fynde,   *plight*
     And yf thou do, lett me bete° and bynde,°   *(be) beaten / bound*
490   As is for° thy best prowe."°   *to / advantage*

     "Nowe have good day," sayd Syr Gromer;
     "Fare wele,"° sayd Syr Arthoure, "so mott I the,[2]   *well*
     I am glad I have so sped!"°   *succeeded*
     Kyng Arthoure turnyd° hys hors into the playn;°   *directed / plain, field*
495 And sone° he mett with Dame Ragnell agayn,   *soon*
       In the same place and stede:°   *stead, location*

     "Syr Kyng, I am glad ye have sped well—
     I told howe itt wold be, every dell;°   *part*
       Nowe hold that ye have hyght.[3]
500 Syn° I have savyd your lyf, and none other,°   *Since / other (person has)*
     Gawen must me wed, Syr Arthoure,
       That° is a full gentill° knyght."   *Who / noble, gracious*

     "No, lady, that° I you hyght I shall nott fayll—   *(of) that (which)*
     So ye wol be rulyd by my councell,[4]
505   Your will then shall ye have."
     "Nay! syr Kyng, nowe woll I nott soo;°   *(do) so*

8. I.e., in providing the answer to Arthur, a woman has obtained sovereignty over Gromer.
9. I.e., I have good cause to lament.
1. I can guarantee that.
2. See l. 334, n.
3. Now keep to that which you promised.
4. Provided that you will be governed by my advice. (Dame Ragnell anticipates the nature of Arthur's advice in her response.)

Openly° I wol be weddyd or° I parte the froo,°   *Publicly/before/from*
   Elles° shame woll ye have!   *(Or) else*

    Ryde before,° and I woll com after   *ahead*
510 Unto thy courte, syr King Arthoure;
   Of no man I woll shame—[5]
   Bethynk° you° howe I have savyd your lyf;   *Remind/yourself*
   Therfor with me nowe shall ye nott stryfe,°   *strive, contend*
    For and° ye do, ye be to blame!"   *if*

515 The Kyng of° her had greatt shame;   *(because) of*
   Butt forth she rood,° though he were grevyd°—   *rode/grieved, distressed*
   Tyll they cam to Karlyle forth they mevyd.°   *moved*
   Into the courte she rode hym by;°   *beside*
   For no man wold she spare, securly—
520   Itt likyd the Kyng full yll![6]

    Alle the contraye° had wonder greatt   *country*
   Fro whens° she com, that foule unswete;°   *whence/unlovely (person)*
    They sawe never of so fowll a thyng.
   Into the hall she went, in certen:[7]
525 "Arthoure, Kyng, lett fetche me Syr Gaweyn[8]
   Before° the knyghtes, alle in hying!°   *In front of/haste*

    That I may now be made sekyr,
   In welle and wo trowith-plyght us togeder[9]
   Before alle thy chyvalry.°   *knights*
530 This is your graunt—Lett see! Have done![1]
   Fett° forth Syr Gawen—my love—anon,°   *Fetch/forthwith*
    For lenger tarying kepe nott I!"[2]

    Then cam forthe Syr Gawen the knyght:
   "Syr, I am redy of° that° I you hyght,   *for/that (which)*
535   Alle forwardes° to fulfyll."   *promises*
   "God-have-mercy!" sayd Dame Ragnell then,
   "For thy sake I wold° I were a fayre woman,   *wish*
    For thou art of so° good wyll!"   *such*

    Ther Syr Gawen to her his trowth° plyght,°   *truth/pledged*
540 In well and in woo, as he was a true knyght—
   Then was Dame Ragnell fayn!°   *pleased*
    "Alas!" then sayd Dame Gaynour°—   *Guenevere*

---

5. I will be shamed by no man. (In asking Arthur to ride ahead, Dame Ragnell effectively makes him a servile escort.)
6. She would hold back for no man, truly—it (her behavior) displeased the King greatly!
7. Assuredly.
8. Have Sir Gawain fetched for me.
9. So that I may be made secure (in marriage), trothplight (i.e., betrothe) us together, for good and for bad (cf. "in sickness and in health"). (On the literal meaning of "trowyth-plyght," see l. 539.)
1. See l. 100, n.
2. For I do not care for further delay.

So sayd alle the ladyes in her bower°—   *chamber*
   And wept for Syr Gawen.

545 "Alas!" then sayd both Kyng and knyght,
   "That ever he shold wed such a wyght!°"   *creature*
     She was so fowll and horyble:
   She had two teth,° on every° syde,   *teeth / each*
   As borys tuskes—I woll nott hyde—
550   Of length a large handfull;³

   The one tusk went up, and the other doun;
   A° mouth full wyde and fowll° i-grown°   *(She had) a / foully / formed*
    With grey herys° many on;°   *hairs / (a) one*
   Her lyppes° laye lumpryd° on her chyn;   *lips / lumped, piled*
555 Nek, forsoth, on her was none i-seen—
    She was a lothly on!°   *one*

   She wold nott be weddyd in no maner
   Butt° there were made a krye° in alle the   *Unless / proclamation*
     shyre,°   *shire*
    Both in town and in borowe:°   *borough*
560 Alle the ladyes nowe of the lond
   She lett kry to com to hand
    To kepe that brydalle thorowe.⁴

   So itt befyll° after, on a daye,   *befell, came to pass*
   That maryed shold be that fowll maye°   *maid*
565   Unto Syr Gaweyn.
   The daye was comyn the daye shold be;⁵
   Therof the ladyes had greatt pitey—
    "Allas!" then gan° they sayn.°   *did / say*

   The Queen prayd Dame Ragnell sekerly°   *certainly, firmly*
570 To be maryed in the mornyng, erly°—   *early*
    "As pryvaly° as we may."   *secretly, privately*
   "Nay," she sayd, "by Hevyn° Kyng!   *Heaven*
   That woll I never,° for no thyng,   *never (do)*
    For ought° that ye can saye.   *anything*

575 I wol be weddyd alle openly,°   *publicly*
   For with the Kyng suche covenaunt made I,
    I putt you oute of doute.°   *fear, doubt*
   I woll nott to° church tylle high masse tyme,⁶   *(go) to*
   And in the open halle I woll dyne—

---

3. Like boars' tusks—I will not hide the fact—the length of a large hand. (Note in the next line
   how the teeth, before only compared to tusks, are now seen to be tusks.)
4. I.e., she had summoned to make the wedding festivities complete.
5. I.e., the appointed day had come.
6. I.e., at noon.

580   In myddys° of alle the rowte."°   *midst / company*

"I am greed,"° sayd Dame Gaynour,   *agreed*
"Butt me wold thynk more honour
And your worshypp moste—"[7]
"Ye, as for that, lady, God you save;
585   This daye my worshypp woll I have,
I tell you withoute boste."°   *boasting, arrogance*

She made her° redy to church to fare,°   *herself / fare, go*
And alle the states that there ware—
Syrs, withoute lesyng.[8]
590   She was arayd° in the richest maner   *arrayed, clothed*
(More fressher° than Dame Gaynour);   *finely dressed*

Her arayment was worthe .iij. .m^l. mark
Of good red nobles styff and stark,[9]
So rychely she was begon.°   *bedecked, adorned*
595   For all her rayment she bare the bell
Of fowlnesse that ever I hard tell—[1]
So fowll a sowe° saw never man!   *sow*

For to make a shortt conclusion,
When she was weddyd, they hyed° theym° home;   *hastened / themselves*
600   To mete° alle they went.   *dinner*
This fowll lady bygan the high dese;[2]
She was full foull and nott curteys,°   *courteous*
So sayd they alle verament.°   *truly*

When the servyce° cam her before,   *service of food*
605   She ete° as moche as .vj.° that ther wore;°   *ate / six (people) / were*
That° mervaylyd° many a man.   *(At) that / marveled*
Her nayles were long ynchys .iij^e.;[3]
Therwith, she breke° her mete° ungoodly°—   *broke / food / unpleasantly*
Therfore, she ete alone.

610   She ette .iij^e. capons[4] and also curlues° .iij^e.,   *curlews (shorebirds)*
And greatt bake° metes she ete up, perdé°—   *baked / to be sure*
Al men therof had mervayll.
Ther was no mete cam her before,

---

7. I.e., but I would think it more honorable and to your greatest esteem. . . . (Dame Ragnell interrupts before the Queen can utter something to the effect of "in the way I first suggested.")
8. And (so did) all the estates (of people) that were there—sirs, (I tell you this) without lie.
9. Her attire was worth three thousand marks in good red nobles (gold coins worth six shillings and eightpence), strong and rigid. (On the value of a mark, see *Sir Launfal*, l. 323, n.; on "red gold," see *Havelok*, l. 47, n.)
1. I.e., despite all her raiment she took the prize for foulness among any (such) that I ever heard speak of.
2. Began (i.e., was served first at, and presided over) the high dais (a raised table for honored guests).
3. Her nails were three inches long.
4. On capons, see *Ywain and Gawain*, l. 757, n.

Butt she ete itt up, lesse and more,[5]
615   That praty fowll[6] damesell.°   *damsel, maiden*

All men then that ever her sawe
Bad° the devill her bonys° gnawe,   *Bade, Prayed / bones*
   Both knyght and squyre.
So she ete tyll mete was done,
620   Tyll they drewe clothes and had wasshen,
   As is the gyse and maner.[7]

Meny men wold speke of diverse service;
I trowe ye may wete inowgh ther was,
   Both of tame and wylde—[8]
625   In Kyng Arthours courte ther was no wantt°   *lack*
That° myght be gotten with mannys° hand, *(Of) that (which) / man's*
   Noder° in forest ne in feld.°   *Neither / field*

Ther were mynstralles of diverse contrey°   *countries*

[* * *][9]

"A!° Syr Gawen, syn° I have you wed,   *Ah, Oh / since*
630   Shewe me your cortesy in bed—
   With ryght itt may nott be denyed!"[1]

Iwyse,° Syr Gawen," that lady sayd,   *Certainly*
"And I were fayre ye wold do anoder brayd—[2]
   Butt of wedlok ye take no hed.°   *heed*
635   Yett, for Arthours sake, kysse me att the leste°   *least*
   I pray you do this att my request—
   Lett se[3] howe ye can spede!"°   *get on, succeed*

Syr Gawen sayd, "I woll do more
Then° for to kysse, and God before!"°   *Than / in the sight of*
640   He turnyd hym° her untill°—   *himself / unto, toward*
He sawe her the fayrest creature
That ever he sawe, withoute mesure!°   *moderation*

5. I.e., all of it.
6. Pretty foul (i.e., very ugly, but possibly also "clever [and] ugly"; further, the oxymoronic sense of "fair [and] foul" also applies in the larger context of other allusions to Dame Ragnell's transformative potential—cf. l. 317, n.)
7. Until they took up (hand)cloths and had washed, as is the practice and custom.
8. Many men would (now) tell of diverse services of food; I trust you may know that there was plenty, both of domestic and wild (kinds).
9. A page has been lost from the manuscript at this point; at least 64 lines are lost. The missing text will have continued the description of the wedding celebrations and then noted the departure of the newlyweds to the bridal chamber. The text resumes with Dame Ragnell and Gawain in bed; she teases him (while he has his back turned to her) about one of the ways in which he has yet to demonstrate his exemplary courtesy.
1. It may not justly be denied! (A reference to the notion of the "conjugal debt," according to which each partner in a marriage has from the other a rightful claim to sexual relations; see 1 Corinthians 3.)
2. If I were beautiful you would take another course of action. (With a possible reference to additional senses of *brayd*, "sudden movement," "charge.")
3. See l. 100, n.

She sayd, "Whatt is your wyll?"

"A! Jhesu!"° he sayd, "whate are ye?"	*Jesus*
645 "Syr, I am your wyf, securly!°—	*truly*
Why ar ye so unkynde?"[4]	
"A! lady, I am to blame;	
I cry° you mercy, my fayre madame—	*beg (of)*
Itt was nott in my mynde;[5]	
650 A lady ye ar, fayre in my syght,	
And today ye were the foulyst wyght	
That ever I sawe with myne ie°—	*eye(s)*
Wele is me,[6] my lady, I have you thus!"	
And brasyd° her in his armys and gan her kysse	*(he) embraced*
655 And made greatt joye, sycurly.	
"Syr," she sayd, "thus° shall ye me have;	*in the following way*
Chese° of the one—so God me save,[7]	*Choose*
My beawty woll nott hold:°	*keep, last*
Wheder° ye woll have me fayre on nyghtes	*Whether*
660 And as foull on days, to alle men sightes;[8]	
Or els to have me fayre on days	
And on nyghtes on° the fowlyst wyse.°	*in / manner*
The one ye must nedes° have;	*necessarily*
Chese the one or the oder;°	*other*
665 Chese on, syr Knyght! Which you° is lever,°	*(to) you / preferable*
Your worshypp° for to save?"	*honor*
"Alas!" sayd Gawen, "the choyse is hard!	
To chese the best, itt is froward,°	*perverse, difficult*
Wheder° choyse that I chese!	*Whichever*
670 To have you fayre on nyghtes and no more,[9]	
That wold greve° my hartt ryght sore°	*grieve, vex / sorely, bitterly*
And my worshypp shold I lese;°	*lose*
And yf I desyre on days to have you fayre,	
Then on nyghtes I shold have a symple°	*modest*
repayre!°	*(conjugal) resort*
675 Now fayn° wold I chose the best;	*gladly*
I ne wott° in this world whatt I shall saye!	*know*
Butt do as ye lyst° nowe, my lady gaye;	*please*

4. Why are you (being) so cruel? (*Unkynde* also has the senses of "unnatural," "unfamilial," and "ungrateful"; Dame Ragnell continues to play on Gawain's failure to respond to the usual attractions of the bridal bed.)
5. I.e., it slipped my mind.
6. I.e., I am delighted.
7. I.e., as God is my savior.
8. And proportionately foul during the day, in the sight of all men.
9. I.e., and nothing else.

     The choyse I putt in your fyst°—   *hand*

     Evyn° as ye wolle,° I putt itt in your hand,   *Just/wish*
680   Lose° me when ye lyst, for I am bond—°   *Loose, Free/bound, enslaved*
       I putt the choyse in° you.   *to*
       Both body° and goodes, hartt, and every dele,°   *(my) body/part*
       Ys° alle your oun,° for to by° and sell—   *Is/own/buy*
       That make I God° avowe!"°   *(to) God/vow*

685   "Garamercy,° corteys° knyght," sayd the lady,   *Many thanks/courteous*
     "Of alle erthly° knyghtes blyssyd° mott° thou be,   *earthly/blessed/may*
       For now am I worshypped.[1]
     Thou shall have me fayre both day and nyght
     And ever whyle I lyve as fayre and bryght;[2]
690   Therfore be nott grevyd—

     For I was shapen° by nygramancy,°   *(mis)shaped/necromancy*
     With° my stepdame[3]—God have on her mercy!—   *By*
       And by enchauntement,
     And shold have bene oderwyse, understond,[4]
695   Evyn° tyll° the best° of Englond   *Right/until/best (knight)*
     Had wedyd me, verament;°   *truly, indeed*

     And also he shold geve me the sovereynté
     Of° alle his body and goodes, sycurly.   *Over*
       Thus° was I disformyd;°   *In this way/deformed*
700   And thou, syr Knyght, curteys Gawen,
     Has gevyn me the sovereynté, serteyn,°   *certainly, indeed*
       That woll nott wroth the, erly ne late.[5]

     Kysse me, syr Knyght, evyn now here!
     I pray the° be glad and make good chere,   *thee*
705   For well is me begon!"[6]
     Ther they made joye oute of mynde,
     (So was itt reason and cours of kynde)[7]
       They° two theymself alone.   *Those*

     She thankyd God and Mary mylde
710   She was recoverd of that she was defoylyd—[8]
       So dyd Syr Gawen;
     He made myrth° alle in her boure°   *mirth/bower, chamber*
     And thankyd of° alle° oure Savyoure,   *for/everything*

---

1. Cf. ll. 585–86.
2. And for as long as I live as beautiful and splendid (as I am now).
3. Stepmothers (and stepfathers—witness the case of Ganelon as reported in the *Sege off Melayne*, ll. 169 ff.) are traditionally depicted in medieval literature as jealous and treacherous figures.
4. I.e., and was otherwise intended to have remained so, you understand.
5. I.e., who will not anger you, at any time.
6. I.e., be glad and put on a pleasant countenance, for I am fortunate!
7. As was reasonable and in the natural course of things.
8. That she was recovered from that by which she had been defiled.

I telle you, in certeyn.

715 With joye and myrth they wakyd° tyll daye;   *remained awake*
And than wold° ryse that fayre maye—   *wished (to)*
   "Ye shall nott," Syr Gawen sayd,
"We woll lye and slepe tyll pryme⁹
And then lett the Kyng call us to dyne."
720   "I am greed,"° then sayd the mayd.   *agreed*

Thus itt passyd° forth tyll mid-daye.   *passed*
"Syrs," quod° the Kyng, "lett us go and asaye°   *said / try to find out*
   Yf Syr Gawen be on lyve—
I am full ferd° of° Syr Gawen   *afraid / for*
725 Nowe, lest the fende° have hym slayn;   *fiend*
   Nowe wold I fayn preve.°   *find out*

Go we nowe," sayd Arthoure the Kyng,
"We woll go se theyr uprysyng,¹
   Howe° well that he hath sped."°   *(To see) how / succeeded, got on*
730 They cam to the chambre, alle in certeyn:²
"Aryse!" sayd the Kyng to Syr Gawen,
   "Why slepyst thou so long in bed?"

"Mary," quod Gawen, "syr Kyng, sicurly,
I wold be glad and° ye wold lett me be,   *if*
735   For I am full well att eas°—   *ease*
Abyde, ye shall se the dore° undone;°   *door / opened*
I trowe that ye woll say I am well goon—³
   I am full loth° to ryse!"   *loath, ill-disposed*

Syr Gawen rose, and in his hand he toke°   *took*
740 His fayr lady, and to the dore he shoke°   *went*
   And opynyd° the dore full fayre:°   *opened / elegantly*
She stod in her smok° alle by that fyre°   *undergarment, slip / fire(place)*
Her her° was to her knees, as red as gold wyre°—   *hair / wire, thread*
   "Lo!° This is my repayre!⁴   *Look, Behold*

745 Lo!" sayd Gawen Arthoure untill,
"Syr, this is my wyfe, Dame Ragnell,
   That savyd onys° your lyfe—"   *once*
He told the Kyng and the Queen hem beforn°   *before, in front of*
Howe sodenly° from her shap° she dyd   *suddenly / shape*
   torne°—   *turn, change*

9. On *prime*, see *Ywain and Gawain*, l. 2304, n.
1. We will go to witness (the circumstances of) their waking.
2. Assuredly.
3. I.e., I trust you will agree that I am fortunate.
4. Cf. ll. 409 and 674 for the range of meaning available in *repayre*.

750   "My lord, nowe be° your leve°—"   *by, with/leave, permission*

And whate was the cause° she forshapen° was,   *reason (why)/transformed*
Syr Gawen told the Kyng both more and lesse.[5]
   "I thank God," sayd the Queen,
"I wenyd,° Syr Gawen, she wold the have   *believed*
   myscaryed;°   *brought to grief*
755 Therfore in my hartt I was sore° agrevyd°—   *sorely/distressed*
   Butt the contrary is here seen."

There was game, revell,° and playe   *revelry*
And every man to other gan° saye,   *did*
   "She is a fayre wyght!"°   *creature, person*
760 Than the Kyng them alle gan tell
How did held° hym att nede° Dame Ragnell—   *support/(a time of) need*
   "Or my deth had bene dyght!"[6]

Ther the Kyng told the Queen, by the Rood,°   *Cross*
How he was bestad° in Ingleswod   *beset, constrained*
765 With° Syr Gromer-Somer Joure   *By*
And whate othe° the knyght made hym swere—   *oath*
   "Or elles he had slayn me ryght there
   Withoute mercy or mesure.

This same lady, Dame Ragnell,
770 From my deth she dyd help me ryght well—
   Alle for the love of Gawen."
Then Gawen told the Kyng alle togeder[7]
Howe forshapen she was with her stepmoder
   Tyll° a knyght had holpen° her agayn.   *Until/helped*

775 Ther she told the Kyng fayre and well
Howe Gawen gave her the sovereynté, every dell,°   *part*
   And whate choyse she gave to hym—
"God thank hym of° his curtesye!   *for*
He savid me from chaunce° and vilony°   *misfortune/(an) ignoble condition*
780 That was full foull and grym.

Therfore, curteys knyght and hend° Gawen,   *gracious*
Shall I never wrath the, sertayn—[8]
   That promyse nowe here I make;
Whilles° that I lyve I shal be obaysaunt°—   *Whilst/obedient*
785 To God above I shalle itt warraunt°—   *guarantee, promise*
   And° never with you to debate."°   *And (promise)/quarrel*

"Garamercy, lady," then sayd Gawen,
"With you I hold° me full well content,   *consider*

---

5. I.e., everything.
6. Or my death would have been secured.
7. I.e., entirely.
8. Cf. l. 702.

And that I trust to fynde."[9]
790 He sayd, "My love shall she have;
     Therafter nede she never more crave,°   want
       For she hath bene to me so kynde."

The Queen sayd, and the ladyes alle,
"She is the fayrest nowe in this halle,
795   I swere by Seynt John!
My love, lady, ye shall have ever,°   forever
     For that[1] ye savid my lord Arthoure,
       As I am a gentilwoman."

Syr Gawen gatt° on her Gyngolyn,[2]   begot, fathered
800 That° was a good knyght of strength and kynn,°   Who / kin, family
       And of the Table Round.
Att every greatt fest° that lady shold° be;   feast / must
Of fayrnesse she bare away the bewtye[3]
     Wher° she yed° on the ground.   Wherever / went

805 Gawen lovyd that lady, Dame Ragnell—
In alle his lyfe he lovyd none so well,
       I tell you, withoute lesyng.°   lie
As a coward[4] he lay by her, both day and nyght—
Never wold he haunt justyng aryght;[5]
810   Ther-att mervayled° Arthoure the Kyng!   wondered

She prayd the Kyng, for° his gentilnes,   for (the sake of)
"To be good lord to Syr Gromer, iwysse,°   certainly
     Of that to you he hath offendyd."
"Yes, lady, that shall I nowe,° for your sake—   (do) now
815 For I wott° well he may nott amendes make—   know
       He dyd to me full unhend!"[6]

Nowe, for to make you° a short conclusyon,   (for) you
I cast° me for to make an end full sone°   purpose / soon
     Of this gentyll lady:

9. I.e., and I trust to find that it will always be so.
1. I.e., because.
2. Gawain's son is the hero of the ME romance *Libeaus Desconus* (from the French for "the fair unknown"), in which his name is eventually revealed as Gingelein (Guinglain in the French source). In Malory's *Morte Darthur* he figures—curiously enough, like Gromer Somer Joure—as one of Mordred's supporters in the attempt to capture Lancelot in Guenevere's chamber (cf. l. 62, n.).
3. In matters of elegance she took the prize for beauty. (Cf. ll. 595–96.)
4. I.e., timidly. (Though the more usual sense would seem to obtain in Arthur's eyes, to judge from the next two lines; Arthur's view, however, does him no real credit, seeming in light of his own lapses more a measure of relative immaturity than of chivalric authority. Concerning the condition of both Arthur and Gawain as implied in these lines, the opening assertions of ll. 7–12 seem pointedly ambiguous.)
5. He would no longer properly attend to jousting.
6. He behaved very disgracefully toward me! (Arthur's leniency is loudly begrudging; cf. his response to the analogous situation in *The Awntyrs off Arthure*, ll. 664–76.)

820 She lyvyd with Syr Gawen butt yerys .v.—[7]
That grevyd° Gawen alle his lyfe,[8]   *distressed*
    I telle you, securly;

In her lyfe she grevyd hym never;
Therfor was never woman° to hym lever°—   *(any) woman / more dear*
825   Thus leves my talkyng.[9]
She was the fayrest lady of ale Englond,
When she was on lyve, I understand—
    So sayd Arthoure the Kyng.

Thus endyth the adventure of Kyng Arthoure,
830 That° oft in his days was grevyd sore,   *Who*
    And of the weddyng of Gawen—
Gawen was weddyd oft in his days;
Butt so well he never lovyd woman, always,
    As I have hard° men sayn.   *heard*

835 This adventure befell in Ingleswod,
As good Kyng Arthoure on huntyng yod;[1]
    Thus have I hard men tell.
Nowe God, as thou were in Bethleme° born,   *Bethlehem*
Suffer never her° soules be° forlorne°   *their / (to) be / lost*
840   In the brynnyng° fyre of hell!   *burning*

And, Jhesu,° as thou were borne of a virgyn,   *Jesus*
Help hym oute of sorowe that this tale dyd devyne°—   *recount*
    And that° nowe in alle hast°—   *(do) that / haste*
For he is besett with gaylours many,[2]
845 That kepen hym full sewerly,°   *securely*
    With wyles° wrong° and wraste.°   *wiles / unjust / powerful*

Nowe God, as thou art veray° Kyng royall,   *very, true*
Help hym oute of daunger that made this tale,
    For therin° he hath bene long.   *therein*
850 And of° greatt pety° help thy servaunt—   *(out) of / pity*
For body and soull I yeld° into thyne hand—   *yield*
    For paynes he hath strong.

Here endyth *The Weddyng of*
Syr Gawen and Dame Ragnell
For helpyng of Kyng Arthoure.

7. Only five years. (The line would be pathetic were it not for the irreverent ambiguity which results from the promise made in the previous three lines. The effect is perhaps meant to be parodic of the way some romances finish by "finishing off" their principal characters: cf. *Ywain and Gawain*, l. 4026; *Havelok*, l. 2966; *Sir Orfeo*, ll. 593–96; *The Awntyrs off Arthure*, ll. 713–15.)
8. Cf. *The Awntyrs off Arthure*, l. 515.
9. Thus my talking leaves off. (Another promise broken immediately; cf. also ll. 829 ff.)
1. Went hunting. (Cf. ll. 4–16—and cf. *The Awntyrs off Arthure*, ll. 1–5 and 709–15.)
2. By many gaolers. (Again, a line of questionable pathos; see the headnote in the Sources and Backgrounds section, pp. 379–80.)

The Sege off Melayne†

Here Bygynnys the Sege off Melayne

All werthy° men that luffes° to here°   *worthy / love / hear*
Off chevallry that byfore us were[1]
    That doughty° weren of dede°—   *doughty, valiant / deed*
Off Charlles° of Fraunce, the heghe°   *Charles (Charlemagne) / exalted*
    Kynge of alle
5 That ofte° sythes° made hethyn° men for-to falle,   *often / times / heathen*
    That styffely° satte one° stede°—   *proudly / on / steed, war-horse*
This geste es sothe; wittnes the buke,
The ryghte lele trouthe, whoso will luke,
    In cronekill for-to rede.[2]

10 Alle Lumbardy,[3] thay made thaire mone,°   *complaint*
And saide thair gammunes° weren alle gone,   *joys, joyous times*
    Owttrayede with hethen thede:[4]

The Sowdane Arabas[5] the stronge
Werreyde appon Crystyndome with wronge,[6]
15 And ceties° brake° he downn,   *cities / broke*
Robbyde° the Romaynes° of theire rent;°   *Robbed / Romans / revenues*

---

† "The Siege of Milan"; text of London, British Library MS Additional 31,042 (the "London Thornton Manuscript"), ff. 64ᵛ–77ᵛ, printed with permission of the British Library. The manuscript is dated c. 1450; the poem's date of composition is held to be c. 1400. The poem is written in twelve-line tail-rhyme stanzas, rhyming (nominally) *aabccbddbeeb*; the couplets nominally have four stresses and the tail lines three; alliteration is common but not regular. The manuscript is now illegible in places; an approximation of the space occupied by illegible text is in the edition marked out by dots within square brackets; partially legible words are silently reconstructed where their original form is reasonably certain.

1. I.e., of knights who lived before us.
2. This account is true; whosoever will investigate, take witness by the (source) book, the wholly faithful truth, (available) to be read in a chronicle. (As an ostensibly historical record, a chronicle is a natural choice for appeals to authenticity—though in this case the appeal is likely to be an artifice, as no chronicle containing this story is known to exist; for similar references, cf. *The Awntyrs off Arthure*, l. 2, and *Ywain and Gawain*, l. 9, n.)
3. (The people of) Lombardy (the northern Italian region of which Milan is the largest city.)
4. Violated by the heathen nation.
5. The Sultan Arabas. (*Arabas* is generic; cf. *Arabaunt*, l. 230: both appear to inflect "Arab" as if it were a Latin verb in the imperfect tense, indicative mood—second person singular and third person plural, respectively.)
6. Wrongly made war upon Christendom.

The Popys° pousty° hase he schente,°   *Pope's/power/destroyed*
    And many a kynges with crownn.[7]
In Tuskayne townnes gon he wyn[8]
20 And stuffede° tham° wele with hethyn kyn,°   *filled/them/people*
    This lorde of grete° renownn;   *great*
And sythen° to Lumbardy he wanne°—   *then/went*
    Mighte° to lett° hym hade no man;   *Strength/stop*
      Thus wynnes he many a town.

25 The emagery that ther solde bee,
Bothe the Rode and the Marie free,[9]
    Brynnede° tham in a fire;   *(He) burned*
And than his mawmettes[1] he sett up there
In kirkes° and abbayes that there were—   *churches*
30 Helde° tham for° lordes and syre.°   *(He) regarded/as/master*
To Melayne° sythen he tuke° the waye   *Milan/took*
And wanne the cyté apon a daye—
    Gaffe his men golde till hyre.[2]
Many a martyre made he there
35 Off men and childire that there were,
    And ladyes swete of swyre.[3]

The lorde of Melayne, Sir Alantyne,
Sawe the Crystynde° putt to   *Christians (lit. Christened)*
    pyne;°   *pain, torment*
    Owte of the townn he flede
40 To a cyté that was thereby—
Alle nyghte he thoghte° therin to ly.°   *intended/lodge*
    He was full straytly stede—[4]
Thay myghte it wynn with spere° and schelde;   *spear, lance*
Appon the morne hym buse it yelde,
45 Or laye his lyfe in wede.[5]
Was never no knyghte putt to mare° care;°   *more/trouble, distress*
Full° hertly° to Criste than prayes he thare,   *Very/earnestly*

---

7. And many a crowned king's (power).
8. He did conquer towns in Tuscany (the region between Rome and Lombardy).
9. The (devotional) effigies that should be there, both of the Cross (i.e., a crucifix) and of gracious Mary.
1. His idols. (*Mawmettes* is derived from the Old French rendering of *Mohammed*. In reality, Islam, of course, spurns idols and representational images and does not worship the Prophet as a god; medieval Christian theologians and no doubt Europeans who traveled to the Middle East (pilgrims, missionaries, crusaders) could not but be aware of this, but such misrepresentations of which *mawmettes* is an example fulfilled a need to depict Islam as antithetical to all things Christian and thence found their way into the general currency of ignorance.)
2. Gave his men gold as payment. (Gold as material plunder is cited throughout the poem as a measure of material excess, often in contrast to the higher spiritual rewards available to a warrior; cf. ll. 403–8, 982–98, 1265–67.)
3. And ladies fair of throat (i.e., beautiful ladies).
4. He was very strictly constrained.
5. It would behoove him to yield up that town in the morning, or offer (them) his life as a pledge (of submission).

To knawe° the lyfe he ledde.   *know (of)*

The Sawdane° sent hym messangers free°   *Sultan / noble*
50　And bade hym torne° and hethyn bee—   *turn, convert*
    And he solde° have his awenn,°   *should, would / own (possessions)*
Melayne, that was the riche cité,
And alle the lanndis of Lumbardye—
    And to his lawe be knawenn:[6]
55　"And if he ne will noghte to oure lawe be swornne,
He sall° be hangede or° other° mornne   *shall, will / before / next*
    And with wylde horse be drawen,°   *dragged (to pieces)*
His wyffe and his childire three,
Byfore his eghne° that° he myghte see,   *eyes / (so) that*
60　 Be in sondre sawenn."[7]

He prayede° the Sowdane than of° grace,°   *begged / (out) of / goodwill*
That he wolde° byde° a littill space°—   *would / abide, wait / space of time*
    Whils one the morne at daye—[8]
And he sall do° hym for-to witt°   *cause, enable / know*
65　If that he wolde assent to itt,
    To leve° apon his laye.°   *believe / religion*
Bot° than heves° he up his handis to heven;   *But / heaves, raises*
To Jesu Criste, with mylde steven,°   *voice*
    Full hertly gane° he praye: *did*
70　"Lorde," he saide, "als° thou swelte° appon the   *as / died*
      Tree,°   *i.e., Cross*
Of° thy man thou hafe° peté,°   *For / have / pity*
    And Mary mylde, that maye.[9]

If I solde Crystyndome forsake
And to hethyn lawe me take,
75　 The perill mon° be myn;°   *must / mine*
Bot, Lorde, als thou lete me be borne,
Late° never my sawle° be forlorne,°   *Let / soul / lost, destroyed*
    Ne dampnede° to helle-pyne.°   *condemned / torments of hell*
Bot, Lorde, als thou swelte on the Rode°   *Rood, Cross*
80　And for mankynde schede° thi blode,°   *shed / blood*
    Some concelle° sende thou me—   *counsel, advice*
Whethire° that me° es° better to doo: *Which (of the two) / (for) me / is*
The hethyn lawe to torne too,
    Or my lyfe in lande to tyne."[1]

85　Than wente that knyghte unto bedde.
For sorowe hym thoghte his hert bledde,

6. I.e., and acknowledge his (the Sultan's) religion.
7. Be sawn apart.
8. Until daybreak on the morrow.
9. And (so also may) that maiden, mild Mary.
1. On earth to lose.

And appon Jesu than gan he calle;
And sone aftire that gane he falle one slepe,
Als man that was wery for-wepe—[2]
90 Than herde° by hym on a walle   *(he) heard*
Ane angelle that unto hym gane saye,
"Rysse° up, sir kynge, and wende° thy waye—   *Rise/go*
For faire the sall byfalle—[3]
To Charles that beris the flour-de-lyce;[4]
95 Of other kynges he berys the pryce[5]
And he sall wreke° thy wrethis° alle."   *avenge/tribulations*

The angelle bade hym ryse agayne—
"And hy° the° faste to Charlemayne,   *hasten/thee*
The crownnede Kynge of Fraunce;
100 And say° hym God byddis° that he sall° go   *tell/commands/must*
To helpe to venge° the of thy foo,   *avenge*
Bathe° with spere and launce."°   *Both/lance*
The kynge was full fayne° of that;   *glad*
His swerde° in his hande he gatt°   *sword/took*
105 And therto graythely° he grauntis.°   *readily/agrees*
He garte swythe sadyll hym a palfraye[6]
And even° to Fraunce he tuke the waye—   *right, straight*
Now herkenys of this chaunce![7]

The same nyghte byfore the daye,
110 Als Kyng Charls in his bedde laye
A swevn° than gan he mete:°   *dream/dream*
He thoghte ane angele lyghte° als leven°   *(as) bright/lightning*
Spake° to hym with mylde steven,   *Spoke*
That gudly° hym gane grete.°   *pleasantly/greet*
115 That angele bytaughte° hym a brande,°   *handed/sword*
Gaffe° hym the hiltis° in his hande   *Gave/hilt*
That even was hande-full mete,[8]
And saide, "Criste sende° the this swerde,   *sends*
Mase° the his werryoure° here in° erthe,   *Makes/warrior/on*
120 He dose the wele to weite.[9]

He biddes thou sall resceyve° it tyte°   *receive, accept/at once*
And that thou venge alle His dispyte,

2. As a man who was worn out by weeping.
3. For (henceforth) it will go well for you.
4. (Go) to Charles who bears the fleur-de-lys (a formalized iris flower having three petals, used in England and France as a heraldic emblem of royalty).
5. He is preeminent among (all) other kings.
6. He had a riding horse saddled for him quickly.
7. Now hear about (what came of) this occurrence!
8. That matched his grip perfectly. (The divine bestowal of a sword as a sanction for warfare against God's enemies has a biblical antecedent, and a Carolingian analogue in a late-medieval crusading sermon; see the headnote in the Sources and Backgrounds section, p. 390.)
9. He has you to understand this fully.

For thynge that ever may bee—[1]
And sla° alle there thou° sees me stryke, *slay/(that) thou (in this vision)*
125 And sythen thou birnne° up house and dyke°— *burn/ditch, rampart*
 For beste° He traystis° in thee." *(the) best/trusts*
The walles abowte Melayne townne,
Hym thoghte the angele dange° tham downn, *struck*
 That° closede in that cité— *(The walls) that*
130 Sythen alle the lanndis of Lumbardy,
Townnes, borows,° and bayli°— *boroughs/bailey, castle wall*
 This was selcouthe° to see! *wondrous*

When Charls wakenede of his dreme
He sawe a bryghtenes° of a beme° *radiance/beam (of light)*
135 Up unto hevenwarde glyde.
Bot when he rose, the swerde he fande° *found*
That the angelle gaffe hym in his hande,
 Appon his bedde syde.
He schewede° it thanne to his barouns alle; *showed*
140 And than saide his lordes bothe grete and smalle,° *lesser*
 "The sothe° is noghte° to hyde:° *truth/not/be hidden*
We wote° wele that Goddis will it es *know*
That thou sall conquere of hethennesse
 Countres lange and wyde."[2]

145 To mete° than wente that riche Kynge, *dinner*
Bot sone° come° there newe tydynge° *soon/came/tidings, news*
 Als he in sete° was sette; *seat, throne*
The lorde of Melayne he sawe come in
(That° was his cosyn nere° of kyn) *Who/near*
150 And hym full gudely grett.
The grete lordis alle hailsede° hee *hailed, greeted*
And prayede tham all sesse° of theire glee,° *cease/merriment*
 And sayse to Charls, withowtten° lett,° *without/delay*
"Jesu Criste hase comannde° thee *commanded*
155 To fare° to the felde° to feghte° for mee, *fare, go/(battle)field/fight*
 My landis agayne to gett."° *get, regain*

He tolde tham alle at the borde° and by° *(dinner) table/nearby*
That the Sarazenes[3] had wonn Lumbardy—
 Thay mornede° and made grete mone°— *mourned/complaint*
160 And how the angelle bade hym goo.
The Kynge tolde° his sweven alsoo: *told (of), related*

---

1. I.e., and that you avenge all defiant injury done to Him, at any cost.
2. That you will conquer great countries among the heathen lands. (The prediction is important in two respects. Firstly, it defines openly the need for Charlemagne to act *personally*—it is a responsibility which he will be persuaded not to countenance for some time to come; cf. Turpin's galvanizing complaint at ll. 745–50—and, secondly, it implies that we are dealing with a relatively early stage in Charlemagne's career; cf. ll. 178–80 and 1085–87. Perhaps his inexperience accounts for his impending impressionability and recalcitrance.)
3. Saracens. (On the background of the name, see *Sir Launfal*, l. 266, n.)

Thay accordede bothe in one.[4]
Thane sayde the Beshop° Turpyne,   *Bishop*
"Hafe done! Late semble the folke of thyne—[5]
165   Myn hede, I undirnome[6]
That Gode es grevede° at the Sarazenes   *angered, offended*
          boste;°   *arrogance*
We salle stroye° up alle theire hoste,°   *destroy/host, army*
Those worthely men in wone."[7]

Bot alle that herde hym Genyenn[8]
170   That was a lorde of grete renownn
And Rowlande modir hade wedde—[9]
Thare° wery° hym bothe God and Sayne° John!   *For that/curse/Saint*
The falseste° traytoure was he one   *most untrustworthy*
That ever with fode° was fedde: *food*
175   For landis° that Rowlande solde have° thare   *lands/(i.e., inherit)*
Dede fayne he wolde that he ware,
The resone ryghte who redde.[1]
His first tresone now bygynnes here[2]
That the lordis boghte° sythen° full° dere,°   *paid for/thereafter/very/dearly*
180   And to ladyse° grete barett° bredde:°   *ladies/sorrow/bred, caused*

"Sir," he sayde, "that ware° a synfull chaunce!°   *would be/risk*
Whatt solde worthe° of us in Fraunce   *become*
          And° thou in the felde were slayne?   *If*
Thyselfe, and we, at home will byde°—   *abide, wait*
185   And latte° Rowlande thedire° ryde,   *let/thither*
That° ever to bekyre° es bayne°   *Who/fight/ready*
With batelle and with brode banere;[3]
Of his wyrchipp° wolde° I here,°   *honorable deeds/would/hear*

4. I.e., they corresponded so as to give a (convincingly) unified account.
5. Be done with it! Have your people assemble (to form an army).
6. (By) my head (i.e., by my life), I perceive.
7. Those men worthy in (their) domain. (Although this is a conventional alliterative collo-
cation—cf. *The Awntyrs off Arthure*, l. 159—its use here is not necessarily indiscriminate;
admiration for the achievements of Saracens as worthy opponents, regardless of their perceived
religious status, is common; cf. ll. 228, 1064–66, 1118–34.)
8. I.e., but Ganelon heard all that.
9. And had wedded Roland's mother. (I.e., Ganalon is Roland's stepfather. Roland is traditionally
known as Charles's nephew, his sister's son; he is the most accomplished, and proudest, of
the French warriors.)
1. I.e., he would gladly see him dead, (according to) whoever related the right interpretation (of
the facts).
2. Another indication that the poem deals with the early stages of Charles's career (cf. l. 144,
n.). Some years hence, Ganelon's treacherous ways will bring about the deaths of Roland,
Oliver, and most of Charles's great lords; in league with Saracen lords of Spain, he will
orchestrate the ambush of the French heroes at Roncevaux in the Pyrenees. That is the essential
episode of the great French *Chanson de Roland*; it is also described (ostensibly by Turpin
himself and with different details) in the *Pseudo-Turpin Chronicle*. About both works and their
possible influences on this poem, see the headnote in the Sources and Backgrounds section,
pp. 388 ff.
3. With a battle formation and a large (heraldic) banner. (I.e., with everything ready to ride into
battle. The banner was used both for identification and as a rallying point during battle; cf.
ll. 923–24.)

Witt° ye wele,° full fayne!"   *Know/well*
190 For Rowlande this resone he wroghte;°   *wrought, contrived*
Evermore in his herte° he thoghte   *heart*
He° solde never come° agayne.   *(Roland)/come (back)*

The Kynge than sent a messangere
To grette lordes bothe ferre° and nere   *far*
195   And bade tham make tham yare°—   *ready*
Bot the peris° take° a concelle° newe   *peers, chief lords/took/plan of action*
That made alle Fraunce ful sore° to rewe,°   *sorely, bitterly/regret*
And byrdis of blyse full bare:[4]
Thay prayede the Kynge on° that tyde°   *at/time*
200 That he hymselfe at home walde° byde,   *should*
To kepe° that lande right thare—   *watch over, protect*
"And sendis° Rowlande to Lumbardy   *send*
With fourty thowsande chevalry°   *knights*
Of worthy men of were."°   *war*

205 Then° Rowlande thus his were° than   *Then (when)/army*
        made,°   *assembled*
Fares° forthe with baners brade.°   *(He) goes/broad, large*
The Kynge byleves° thare still,   *stays back, remains*
Within the cité of Paressche°   *Paris*
For-to kepe that townn of pryce,°   *renown*
210   Als° thay accordede° till°—   *As/agreed/unto*
And if the Sowdane wane the felde,[5]
Lyghtly° walde thay it noghte yelde°   *Easily/yield, surrender*
To° thay had foughtten thaire fill.   *Until*
Bot be-comen was the feftenede daye;[6]
215 Therfore° myghte mornne° bothe man and   *for that/mourn*
        maye,°   *maiden*
And ladyse lyke full ill.[7]

To Melayne even thay made tham bownn
And batelde tham thare byfore the townn,[8]
Those knyghttis that were kene;°   *bold*
220 And in to the Sowdane thay sent a knyghte
And bade hym come owte with tham to fyghte,
To witt withowtten wene.[9]
The Sowdane grauntis° wele thertill°—   *agrees/thereto*
That tornede oure gud men all to gryll,

4. And (which made) women wholly bereft of joy.
5. I.e., was victorious.
6. But the fifteenth day (after Alantyne's arrival) had come around (i.e., two weeks had now passed by).
7. And ladies be very displeased.
8. To Milan directly they appointed themselves, and drew up their lines of battle outside the town.
9. (I will have you) know that without doubt.

225 And many one mo to mene;[1]
     Than the Sarazens come owte of that cité,
     Forty thowsandes of chevalrye,
     The beste in erthe myghte bene.[2]

     The° forthirmaste° come a Sarazene wyghte,°   *(As) the/foremost/valiant*
230 Sir Arabaunt[3] of Perse° he highte,°   *Persia/was called*
     Of Gyon° was he kynge: *? Gijon*
     He saide ther was na° Cristyn knyghte,   *no*
     Ware he never so stronge ne wyghte,
     To dede he ne solde hym dynge;[4]
235 And one° Sir Artaymnere of Beme°   *on/? Beaune*
     (That was Sir Olyvers eme)[5]
     Byfore the stowre thay thrynge;[6]
     And even at the firste countire° righte,   *encounter, bout*
     The Sarazen slewe oure Cristyn knyghte:
240 It was dyscomforthynge.°   *discouraging*

     The lorde of Melayne to hym° rade,°   *(Arabaunt)/rode*
     Sir Alantyne, withowtten bade,°   *delay*
     The Crystyn knyghte to wreke;°   *avenge*
     Bot he° stroke oure Cristyn knyghte that°   *(Arabaunt)/(at) that*
          stownde°   *time*
245 That° dede he daschede° to the grounde,   *(Such) that/dashed, sped*
     Mighte no worde after° speke.   *thereafter*
     Sythen aftewarde he bare down
     Worthy lordes of grete renownn,
     Ay° to° his launce° gane breke°—   *All the time/until/lance/break*
250 And sythen areste° thaire nobill° stedis°   *seized/noble/steeds, war-horses*
     And to the hethyn hoste tham ledis°—   *leads*
     Loo, thusgates fares the freke![7]

     Bot by that was done, the grete gon mete;[8]
     Barouns undir blonkes° fete°   *horses/feet*
255 Braythely° ware borne doun.   *Violently*

---

1. That caused all our good men to come to grief, and (caused) many another to lament. (The narrator's reference to "our men" is the first of many such second-person identifications which appear to be designed to evoke from us a strong sense of partisanship with the Christian forces; see also ll. 239, 244, 259, 266–67, 271, 274–75, 283, 316, 322, 346–47, 352, 365, 386, 388, 429, 465, 492, 496, 502, 565, 950, 1084, 1125, 1194, 1199, 1246, 1256, 1260, 1267, 1274, 1289, 1295, 1300, 1331, 1484, 1495, 1518, 1527, 1533, 1547, 1593 [oure]; 1099, 1147, 1288 [us], and 1098 [we]. The density of such reference is unmatched in other Middle English romances; but cf. similar heavy usage in the late crusading poem *Capystranus*, in the Sources and Backgrounds section.)
2. The best knights that could be (found) on earth. (Cf. l. 168, n.)
3. See l. 13, n.
4. (That) he would not beat him to death.
5. Who was Sir Oliver's uncle. (Oliver is Roland's chief companion, usually judged to be second only to him in prowess. In this poem he is mentioned just once more, at l. 376).
6. Ahead of the melee they throng.
7. Behold, in this way the man carries on!
8. But by the time that was accomplished, the greater parts of the armies did meet.

Thay stekede° many a staleworthe° knyghte,   *stabbed / stalwart, strong*
The hethen folke in that fyghte;
    The moste° were of renownn.   *greater part (of those killed)*
Oure knyghtis one the gronde lyse°   *lie*
260 With wondes wyde, one wafull wyse:⁹
    Crakkede was many a crownn,°   *crown, head*
Riche hawberkes° were all to-rent,°   *coats of mail / torn apart*
And beryns thorowe thaire scheldis schent,¹
    That° many to bery° was bownn.°   *(Such) that / be buried / ready*

265 The Sarazens semblede° so sarely°   *attacked / violently*
That thay felde° faste of° oure chevalrye;   *felled, laid low / (those) of*
    Oure vawarde° down thay dynge.   *vanguard*
Righte at the firste frusche° thay felde   *charge*
Fyve thowsande knyghtis trewly telde°—   *counted*
270   This is no lesynge!°   *lie*
Oure knyghtis lyghtede° one the bent;°   *alighted, dismounted / field*
Thorowe thaire scheldis are they schent—
    Of sorowe than myghte thay synge!°   *sing*
Than oure medillwarde° gane tham mete°   *middle guard / meet*
275 Thare myghte no beryns° oure bales° bete°   *men / suffering / relieve*
    Bot° the helpe of Hevens Kynge.   *Except*

The medillwarde Sir Rowlande ledde;
That doghty° in felde was never drede°   *doughty (man) / afraid*
    To do what solde° a knyghte.   *should*
280 Fyfty lordis of gret empryce°   *renown, valor*
Of Fraunce that bare the floure-de-lyce²
    Hase loste bothe mayne° and myghte;   *strength*
Our medillwarde sone° hade thay slayne,   *soon, quickly*
And Rowlande was in handis tane,³
285   And other seven that were knyghtes
(But, als God gaffe° hym that chaunce,°   *gave / good fortune*
Thay wende° he hade bene Kynge of Fraunce,   *thought*
    That lyfede° in thase° fyghtis).   *(had) survived / those*

Bot of a knyghte me rewes° sore°   *feel sorrow / sorely, bitterly*
290 That in the felde laye wondede thore,°   *there*
    The Duke of Normandy.
He lukes° up in the felde;   *looks*
His umbrere° with his hande up helde,   *visor*
    On Rowlande gane he cry:
295 "Rowlande, if the° tyde° that chaunce   *(to) thee / happens*
That thou come evermore into Fraunce,

9. With great wounds, in a woeful state.
1. And men slain (by strokes which pierced) through their shields.
2. See l. 94, n.
3. Taken in hands (i.e., captured).

For the lufe° of mylde Marie   *love*
Comande° me till oure gentill° Kynge,   *Commend / noble*
And to the Qwene my lady yynge,°   *young*
300   And to all chevalrye.

And if thou come into Normandy,
Grete° wele my lady,   *Greet*
  And Sir Richerd, my sonne—
And dubbe[4] hym Duke in my stede,°   *stead, place*
305   And bydde° hym venge his fadir° dede,°   *tell / father's / death*
  Of myrthe if he will mone;[5]
Bid hym hawkes and houndes forgoo[6]
And to dedis° of armes hym° doo,°   *deeds / himself / give*
  Thase° craftes° for-to konn,°   *Those / skills / learn*
310   Appon the cursede Sarazens for-to werre—
Venge me with dynt° of spere!°   *dint, stroke / spear, lance*
  For my lyfe es° nere° done.   *is / nearly*

A,° Rowlande! byhaulde° nowe whatt I see!   *Ah, Oh / behold*
More joye ne myghte never bee,
315   In youthe ne yitt° in elde°—   *yet / old age*
Loo!° I see oure vawarde ledde to hevene   *Look, Behold*
With angells songe and merye° stevene,°   *merry, joyous / sound*
  Reghte° as thay faughte in the felde!   *(Looking) just*
I see moo° angells—loo!—with myn eghe,°   *more / eye*
320   Then° there are men within Cristyanté   *Than*
  That any wapyn° may welde!°   *weapon / wield, handle*
To heven thay lede oure nobill knyghtis
And comforthes tham with mayne and myghtis,[7]
  With mekill° blysse and belde.'"°   *much / encouragement*

325 Bot by Rowland gan a Sarazene stande
. That braydede° owte with a bryghte brande°   *rushed / sword*
  When he harde° hym say soo,   *heard*
And to the Duke a dynt he dryvede:°   *drove, directed*
At° the erthe he smate° righte of° his hede—   *To / cut / off*
330   Therfore was Rowlande woo°—   *grieved*
And Rowland styrte° than to a brande   *started, rushed*
And hastily hent° it owte of a Sarazene hande,   *snatched*
  And sone he gane hym sloo.°   *slay*
With that swerde he slewe sexty°—   *sixty*
335 The beste of the Sarazens chevalrye°—   *knights*
  Off hardy men, and moo.

4. See *Havelok*, l. 2042, n.
5. If he complains of (a loss of) joy.
6. Tell him to forgo (the pleasures of hunting with) hawks and hounds. (Cf. l. 33, n.)
7. I.e., with all their strength. (Richard's speech thus ends with a vision of that ultimate incentive for martyrs to holy war, an assured place in heaven; cf. ll. 908–10.)

Than Rowlande in handis is taken agayne
And putt unto full harde payne,[8]
  That° sorowe it was to see;   *(Such) that*
340 And foure nobill knyghtis than have thay slayne
Byfore that were in handis tane[9]
  With Sir Rowlande the free.°   *noble*
The Sowdane comandis of his men
And° hundrethe knyghtis to kepe° tham then,   *A / watch over, guard*
345   Rowland and other three.[1]
And to oure rerewarde° sythen thay rode;   *rearguard*
Oure barouns boldely tham abode°—   *awaited*
  Nowe helpe tham the Trynytee!

The Duke of Burgoyne,° Sir Belland,   *Burgundy*
350 The fadir of Sir Gy of Nevynlande,°   *? Neuville*
  The rerewarde than rewlis° hee: *rules, commands*
He comforthede° alle oure nobyll knyghtis—   *encouraged*
Said, "Lordis, halde your feldes and your ryghttis,[2]
  And no Sarazene yee flee—
355 And thofe° ye see thies° lordis be slayne   *though / these*
Ne hope ye noghte, for alle thaire payne,
  That we ne sall solance see;[3]
Bot° the werkynge° of oure wondis sare,   *Except for / aching, pain*
Of the paynes of helle fele° we no mare   *feel (will)*
360   Bot hy° to heven one heghe."°   *hasten / high*

Thay fruschede° in fersely° for Goddis sake;   *rushed, charged / fiercely*
Grete strokes gane thay gyffe and take,
  With wondis werkande° wyde.   *painful (and)*
Bot yitt the Sarazens with thayr speris
365 Full ferre on bakke oure batelle berys[4]
  And knyghtis felde undir fete.
Walde° never no Crystyn knyghte thethyn° flee   *Would / thence*
Thoghe that he wyste° ryghte there to dye,   *expected*
  I doo yowe wele to wytt,[5]
370 Bot alle in-fere° thay endide° righte thare: *together / died*
That sowede the Sarazenes sythen full sare,
  For lordis that levede the swete.[6]

---

8. And subjected to very cruel punishment.
9. I.e., who beforehand had been captured. (Roland's anger unnecessarily claims the lives of fellow Christians—and yet his vengeance is undoubtedly meant to be admired; this is the first of several audacious acts detailed throughout the poem which champion individual abandonment to pure zeal in the struggle against enemies of the faith; cf. ll. 542–71, 1364–1423.)
1. I.e., and three others.
2. Protect your lands and your rightful inheritances.
3. Do not believe, despite all their suffering, that we will not receive (heavenly) comfort.
4. Push our army very far in retreat.
5. I will have you know well.
6. That deed was later revisted upon the Saracens very bitterly, on account of the (Christian) lords who departed this life (*lit.* the [thing which is] dear).

Thus fourty thowsande hafe thay slayne,
Safe° foure that were in handis tane—   *Save, Except for*
375   Rowlande ande other three:
One was the gentill Erle° Sir Olyvere,   *Earl*
Another was Sir Gawtere
      (The Kyngis cosyns° nere);°   *relatives/near, close*
The thirde was Sir Gy of Burgoyne—
380   His fadir[7] in the felde laye there slone;°   *slain*
      The soryare° myghte he bee.   *more sorrowful*
They ledde thies lordes into Melayne;
With that the Sowdane turnes agayne,°   *back*
      Righte gladde of his menyee.[8]

Prymus passus: *the first Fytt*[9]

385   To the Sowdane° chambir many a man   *Sultan's*
Oure foure lordis ledd thay than
      To rekken of theire arraye.[1]
Thay ette° and dranke and made tham° glade—   *ate/themselves*
Bot littill myrthe oure lordis hadde.
390   The Sowdane gane tham saye,
"Welcome be thow, Kynge of Fraunce—
The bytide a cely chaunce;[2]
      Thi lyfe was savede this daye!
The false lawes° of Fraunce sall°   *religion/shall, will*
      downn;°   *be thrown down*
395   The rewme° sall leve° one Seynt Mahownn°   *realm/believe/Mohammed*
      That° alle the myghtyeste° maye!"°   *Who/mightiest (deeds)/can (do)*

And Rowlande answerde, full gentilly:°   *honorably*
"I ne rekke° whethir I lyfe or dye,   *care*
      By God that awe° this daye.   *controls*
400   Kynge of Fraunce ame I none,
Bot a cosyne ame I one
      To Charlles, by my faye.°   *faith*
He will gyffe me golde and fee,[3]
Castells ryche with towris° heghe,   *towers*
405   That lorde full wele he maye;
Bot Goddis forbode and the holy Trynytee[4]
That ever Fraunce hethen were for° mee   *because of*

---

7. Cf. ll. 349–50.
8. Very pleased with his army.
9. The latter three words effectively translate the first two; a *fit* is a section of a poem, used in a similar sense to the more familiar *canto*; *passus*, however, further conveys the sense of a step or stage in a process. The notice here marks the *end* of the first stage of the poem.
1. To consider how they should be dealt with.
2. A momentous piece of luck has come about for you.
3. Gold and possessions. (Cf. l. 33, n.)
4. But may God and the holy Trinity forbid.

And lese° oure Crysten laye!°   *(should) lose / religion*

For sothe, thou Sowdane, trowe thou moste[5]
410   One° the Fader and the Sone and the Holy Goste: *In*
      Thire° thre are alle in one   *These*
That borne was of Marye free,
Sythen for us dyede° one a tree°—   *died / i.e., cross*
      In other trowe we none."[6]
415   Thane loughe° the Sowdane withe   *laughed*
          eghne° full smale,°   *eyes / small, squinted*
And saide, "Ane hundrethe of youre goddis alle hale[7]
Have I garte° byrne° in a firre with bale°   *made / to burn / destruction*
      Sen° firste I wanne° this wone.°   *Since / conquered / domain*
I sawe at° none no more powstee°   *from / power*
420   Than att another° rotyn° tree,   *any other / rotten*
      One erthe so mote I gone![8]

Goo, feche° one of theire goddis in,   *fetch*
And if he in this fire will byrne,
Alle other sett att noghte."[9]
425   Than furthe° ther rane a Sarazene in that tyde   *forth*
To a kyrke° was° there byside;°   *church / (that) was / nearby*
      A faire rode° in he broghte,°   *rood, crucifix / brought*
Fourmede ewenn als He gane blede.[1]
Oure Cristen knyghtis bygane thaire Crede[2]
430   And Rowland God bysoughte,°   *beseeched*
And saide, "Thou that was borne of a may,°   *maiden, virgin*
Schewe thou, Lorde, thi meracle this day,
      That with thi blode us boghte."[3]

They keste° the rode into the fire   *cast, threw*
435   And layde brandis with mekill ire—[4]
      Fayne° wolde° thay garre° hym° birne! *Gladly / would / make / it, the effigy*
The Sowdane saide, "Now sall ye see
What myghte° es° in a rotyn tree   *power / is*
      That youre byleve° es in!   *belief, faith*
440   I darre° laye my lyfe full ryghte   *dare*
That of° hymselfe he hase no myghte   *for*

5. In truth, Sultan, you must believe.
6. I.e., we believe in none other.
7. Fully a hundred of your gods. (The Sultan projects a view, no doubt inflammatory to a
   medieval Christian reader, of crucifixes (and possibly other devotional images) as mere idols;
   cf. ll. 25–28 and nn.)
8. As I hope to thrive in this world.
9. Value all such others at nothing.
1. Fashioned even as Christ did bleed (i.e., depicting accurately Christ's wounds).
2. I.e., began to say the Creed (a concise declaration of articles of the Faith, echoes of which
   appear at ll. 410–13 above; see also the *Capystranus*, l. 2, n.).
3. Demonstrate this day, Lord, a miracle of yours, (you) who redeemed us with your blood.
4. And with great anger laid (upon it) burning brands.

Owte of this fire to wyn:°   *gain way, escape*
How solde he than helpe another man
That for hymselfe no gyn ne kan,
445   Nother crafte ne gyn?"[5]

Thay caste one it full many a folde:[6]
The rode laye still ay° as° it were colde;   *all the time/as (if)*
  No fire wolde in hym too.°   *take, ignite*
All° if the crosse were makede° of tree°   *Even/made/wood*
450   The fire yode° owtt that come° ther nee°—   *went/came/near*
  Than wexe° the Sowdan woo!   *grew, became*
"And yif° the devell,"° he sayde, "be hym within,   *if/devil*
He sall be brynt or° ever I blyne"°—   *before/cease*
  Of hert° he was full throo°—   *heart, mood/stubborn, quarrelsome*
455 "Thies cursede wreches° that are herein   *wretches*
Hase° wethede° thaire goddis that thai may not byrn—   *Have/wetted*
  I wote° wele° it es soo!"   *know/well*

Than bromstone° that wele walde birn,   *brimstone, sulfur*
And pykke° and terre° mengede° therin,°   *pitch/tar/mixed/therein*
460   Thay slange° in the fire full bolde;°   *slung/boldly, confidently*
Torches that were gude and grete
For-to helpe that mekill hete
  Thay caste in many a folde:
The fire wexe owte at the laste.[7]
465 Oure knyghtis made thaire prayere faste
  To Criste that Judas solde;[8]
The rode braste° and gaffe a "Crake!"   *split*
That thamm thoghte that alle the byggynge brake[9]
  That° was within that holde.°   *Who/(strong)hold*

470 A fire than fro° the crosse gane frusche,°   *from/discharge*
And in the Sarazene eghne it gaffe a dosche°—   *strike*
  Ane element als it were—[1]
That° thay stode still als° any stone;   *(So) that/as*
Hanndis° nore fete myghte thay stirre° none,   *Hands/stir, move*
475   Bot drery wexe in chere—
Thay wyste nother of gude ne ill![2]
Than Rowlande sais his felawes untill,°   *unto*
  "Sirs, hy° us alle hethyn° in-fere;°   *(let us) hurry/from here/together*
This meracle es° schewede° thorowe° Goddis grace,   *is/manifest/through*

---

5. Who knows no trick (of escape) for himself, (who knows) neither skill nor trick.
6. Manifold times.
7. The fire faded out eventually.
8. Cf. *Havelok*, ll. 319–20, n.
9. Such that they thought that the whole building was breaking up.
1. I.e., as if it were lightning. (All created things were believed to be made up of one or more of four essential elements, wind, fire, water, and earth; but *element* could also signify the sky and weather generally.)
2. But took on a dreary expression—they knew of neither good nor bad (i.e., they were senseless).

480   For alle the Sarazenes in this place
    May nother see nore here!"

Sayde Sir Gy of Burgoyne, "Yitt,° or I goo,   (And) yet
The Sowdane sall have a stroke or twoo
    That glade sall hym no glee!"[3]
485   He ferkes° owte with a fawchon°   lashes / falchion, (broad)sword
And hittis the Sowdane one the crownn
    Unto the girdyll welle nee.[4]
Thay tuke the grete lordes with ire
And brynte tham in that bale fire;
490   Those doughty garte they dye.
(Bot sythen° the Sarazenes crouned° Sir Garsy,[5]   then, thereafter / crowned
That ofte sythes° chaste° oure chevalry;°   times / harassed / knights
    A bolde Sarazene was he.)

Alle that was than in that place
495   Thay slewe clenly° thorow Goddis grace,   completely
    Oure worthy men and wyghte,°   valiant
And sythen owte at the yates° they yede:°   gates / went
Ilkone° of tham fande° a whitte stede,° Each one / found / steed, war-horse
    Sadilt and redy dighte.[6]
500   Thay stirtt° up on those stedis full steryn°— started, mounted / strong
Thay fande no man that tham wolde warne,°   challenge
    Oure ferse° men felle° in fighte—   fierce / cruel, formidable
And, als the cronekill yitt will saye,[7]
Even° to Fraunce thay tuke the waye;   Directly
505   To Paresche° thay ryde full righte.   Paris

Bot yitt thay wolde noghte come att° Paresche   to
To thay had offerde to Seyne Denys;[8]
    And wendis° to that abbaye,   (they) go
And leves° thaire stedis righte at the yate   (they) leave
510   And wightly in thay tuke the gate,°   way
    Thaire prayers for-to say;
And by° thay hade thayre prayers made   by (the time that)
Agayne° they come withowtten bade°   Back / delay
    Thaire horse than were away!°   gone
515   And alle the bellis that in that abbaye was
Range° allone,° thorowe Goddis grace,   Rang / on their own
    Whils° it was pryme of the day![9] While, For as long as

3. That will give him no joy!
4. (And slices him) very nearly to the waist.
5. See ll. 821 ff.
6. Saddled and made ready.
7. Cf. l. 9, n.
8. Until they had offered thanks at (the Abbey of) Saint Denis. (St. Denis is the patron saint of France; the abbey is located in the Parisian suburb of the same name.)
9. On *prime*, see *Ywain and Gawain*, l. 2304, n.

And thereby wiste° those lordis of pryce°   *knew/renown*
That the myghte of God and Seynt Denys
520   Had broghte tham thethyn° away;   *thence (from Milan)*
Thaire horse° that so there come° to handes   *horses/came*
Was° thorowe the prayere of Seynt Denys—   *Were (there)*
    Thus will the cronecle say.
Bischope Turpyne than come fro Paresche townn
525   To Seynt Denys with grete processiownn,°   *ceremony*
    For thiese lordes for-to pray
That was in Lumbardy at the were;°   *war*
And when he sawe Rowlande there,
    He saide, "Lordis, morne° we may."   *mourn, lament*

530   Thay mervelde° why the bellis so range;   *marveled*
And the clergy lefte theire sange,°   *singing (of the Mass)*
    Thoughte ferly of that fare—[1]
Thay hade mervelle whate it myghte mene.°   *mean, signify*
Als sone als the Byschoppe hade Rowlande sene,°   *seen*
535   To hym he went full yare°—   *quickly, readily*
Sayd, "A° Rowlande, how fares° Lumbardye,   *Ah, Oh/goes*
And all oure nobill chevallry
    That thou hade with the° thare?"   *thee*
"Certis,° sir Bischoppe, it is noghte to layne,°   *Certainly/be concealed*
540   The Sarazenes hase oure gude men slayne—
    Thou seese° of tham namare!"°   *will see/no more*

The Bischop keste his staffe° hym fro,   *crozier*
The myter° of his hede also—   *miter*
    "I sall° never were° the more,°   *shall, will/wear/again*
545   Ne other habite for-to bere,[2]
Bot buske me bremly to the were,
    And lerene one slyke a lore![3]
A! Mary mylde, whare° was thi myght°   *where/power*
That° thou lete thi men thus to dede°   *(Such) that/death*
    be dighte°   *consigned*
550   That wighte and worthy were?
Art thou noghte halden of myghtis moste,
Full conceyvede of the Holy Goste?[4]
    Me ferlys of thy fare.

Had thou noghte, Marye, yitt bene borne,
555   Ne had noghte oure gud men thus bene lorne—[5]

1. Thought that happening a marvel.
2. Nor (wish) to wear any other dress (of a religious order).
3. But equip myself resolutely for war, and learn about such a doctrine!
4. Are you not held to be in possession of the greatest powers, (which were) wholly conceived by the Holy Ghost? (Turpin's querulous stance may seem to amount to apostasy, but it is a traditional measure of zeal in texts which advocate the crusade; see the headnote in the Sources and Backgrounds section, pp. 388–89, and the *Capystranus*, ll. 465 ff.; see also l. 341, n., above.)
5. (Then) would our good men not have been lost in that way.

The wyte° is all in the! *blame*
Thay faughte holly° in° thy ryghte,° *wholly / in (sevice of) / just cause*
That thus with dole⁶ to dede es dyghte—
A! Marie, how may this bee?"
560 The Bischoppe was so woo° that° stownnd,° *aggrieved / (at) that / time*
He wolde noghte byde° appon the grownnd *wait*
 A sakerynge for-to see,⁷
Bot forthe he wente—his handis he wrange,° *wrang*
And flote with Marye ever amange⁸
565 For the losse of oure menyee.° *army*

Then come Kynge Charls appon pilgremage
Fro Paresche town, with his baronage;° *barons*
 To Seynt Denys he went.
Bot when the Bischoppe mett with the Kynge
570 He wolde noghte say "gud mornynge,"
 Ne ones his browes blenke.⁹
The Kynge hade mervelle what that myght be,° *be (about)*
Bot als sone als he Rowlande see,° *saw*
 Wyghtly° to hym he went: *Immediately*
575 Be° Rowlande had his tale tolde *By (the time that)*
The Kynge myghte noghte a tere° holde°— *tear / withhold*
 For bale hym thoght he brynt.¹

"Allas," he saide, "cosyn° fyne, *cousin, relative*
Whare are alle the nobill knyghtis of myne
580 That ever to fighte were fayne?"° *glad*
"Sir, bi God and by Sayne John,
The Sarazenes alle bot° us hase slone;° *except for / slain*
 It is no bote to layne—²
Bot° we were taken into holde;° *Only / custody*
585 Bot, als that Criste Hymselfe wolde,³
 That° we wan° owte agayne— *(From) that / got*
Thorowe the grace of God omnipotent,
In his chambir or° we went *before*
 The Sowdane have we slayne."

590 Genyonn saide, "Lorde, by my rede,° *reckoning*
All° if the Sowdane thus be dede, *Even*
 Thay will have another newe°— *anew*
A more schrewe° than was the tother°— *wicked (man) / other*
Garcy, that is his awenn° brothir, *own*

6. Who so grievously.
7. To preside over a consecration (of the Host).
8. And all the while contended with Mary.
9. Nor once blink his brows (i.e., acknowledge Charles's presence).
1. He felt as if he were burning for sorrow.
2. There is no use in concealing (the truth).
3. As Christ Himself wished it.

595	That more barett° will brewe.	*strife*
	These landes of hym I rede ye halde,[4]	
	Or he will kindill° cares° full calde°—	*kindle / troubles / cold, bitter*
	Yhe trowe this tale for trewe!—[5]	
	Or ells within thies monethes° three	*months*
600	Als qwhitte° of Fraunce sall yhe bee	*deprived*
	Als° yhe it never ne knewe."	*As if*
	"Now Cristis malyson,"° quod° the Bischoppe,	*curse / said*
	"myghte he have	
	That Charls firste this concell° gaffe°—	*counsel / gave*
	And noghte bot it be righte![6]	
605	To make homage to a Sarazene—	
	Jesu kepe us fro that pyne,°	*misery, harm*
	And Marie His modir° bryghte!°	*mother / splendid, fair*
	Bot at home, sir Kynge, thou sall keep nanne,°	*no one*
	Bot alle thy gud men with the tane°	*(will) take*
610	That worthy are and wighte	
	Appon yone cursede Sarazenes for-to were—	
	And venge the one tham with dynt of spere	
	That thus thi peris hase dyghte![7]	
	And alle the clergy undirtake° I:	*promise, pledge*
615	Off° alle Fraunce, full sekerly,°	*From / surely, certainly*
	Thay sall wende° to that were.	*go*
	Of the Pope I have pousté;[8]	
	Att my byddynge° sall thay bee,	*bidding, command*
	Bothe with schelde and spere."	
620	The Bischoppe sendis ferre and nere,[9]	
	To monke, chanoun,° preste,° and frere,°	*canon / priest / friar*
	And badd° tham graythe°	*commanded / prepare*
	thaire gere°	*gear, weaponry*
	And keste thaire care clene tham froo—[1]	
	"Come helpe to feghte° on Goddis° foo°	*fight, make war / God's / foe*
625	Alle that° a swerde may bere!"°	*(those) who / bear, carry*
	The clergy grauntes° alle° therto—	*agree / fully*
	Als doghety men of dede solde do—[2]	
	That worthy were and wyghte.	

4. I advise you to hold these lands from him (as a vassal). (On the feudal background to such an arrangement, including the requisite act of homage, mentioned at l. 605 below, see *Havelok*, l. 444, n.)
5. You can trust this prediction is true!
6. And it would be nothing but just (to be so cursed).
7. And avenge yourself with dint of spear on those who have so treated your nobles.
8. I have the authority of the Pope. (A bona fide crusade had to be sanctioned by the Pope, as would any substantial involvement by the clergy; cf. the *Capystranus*, ll. 229–336.)
9. Far and near (i.e., to everywhere).
1. And to discard their worries completely.
2. As valiant men of action must do.

Be-comen was wekes three;[3]
630 Thare semblede° a ful faire menyhe,°   *assembled / army*
   In baneres burneschid bryghte.[4]
A hundrethe° thowsande were redy bownn°   *hundred / prepared*
Of prestis that werede schaven crownn,[5]
   And fresche° men for-to fighte.   *fresh, eager*
635 Thay lightede appon a lawnde so clere
Undir the mownte Mowmartere;[6]
   It was a ful faire syghte.

With that the Bischoppe Turpyn come,
And also a Cardynall° of Rome   *Cardinal*
640 With a full grete powere;°   *force, army*
Thay semblede appon another syde
Baners bett° with mekill° pryde,   *embroidered / great*
   The clergy that was so clere.°   *pure, virtuous*
And appon thaire knees thay knelide down;
645 The Bischoppe gafe tham his benyson°   *blessing*
   Alle hollyly° in-fere.°   *wholly / together*
And thane sent he in to the Kynge,
And badde hym forthe his barouns brynge,
   And saide, "My prestis are here."

650 Bot yitt this false Genyonn
Conselde the Kynge, ay with treson,[7]
   That hymselfe solde duelle° ther still—   *stay*
"And lette the Bischoppe wende his waye,
Doo at yone Sarazenes that he maye—[8]
655   There sall he feghte his fill—
And byde° thiselfe in this citee: *stay*
Slayne in the felde° gife° that thou bee,   *(battle)field / if*
   Alle Fraunce may like it full ill."[9]
And with his concelle and his fare°   *carrying on*
660 Slyke° concell he gaffe tham thare: *Such*
   The Kynge grauntis thertill.°   *thereto*

And forthe to the Bischopp than sendis he,
And, for thynge that ever myghte bee,
   He solde hym never beswyke,[1]
665 Bot take his nobill chevalrye°   *knights*
And wende forthe into Lumbardy—
   "For I will kepe° my ryke."°   *watch over, guard / realm*

---

3. Three weeks had come around.
4. With splendid shining banners. (Cf. l. 187, n.)
5. I.e., of tonsured priests.
6. They dismounted on a clearing below Montmartre ("Hill of the martyrs," a suburb of Paris.)
7. Counseled the King, all the time with treasonous intent.
8. Do to those Saracens what he can.
9. I.e., will be very displeased.
1. He then sends forth to the Bishop, and (bids him that), at all costs, he must never betray him.

The Bischopp saide, "By Goddes Tree,°   *Cross*
Or° that Charls doo° so with mee,   *Before/does, deals*
670   Full ill it sall° hym lyke!   *shall, will*
I sall hym curse in myddis his face—[2]
What! sall he nowe, with sory grace,
    Become ane eretyke?"[3]

The Bischoppe leves his powere thare
675 And into the cité gane he fare,
    And the Cardenall with hym;
And when he come byfore the Kynge
There was none other haylsynge°   *greeting*
    Bot stowte° wordes and grym:°   *stout, strong/grim, solemn*
680 He saide, "Allas, sir Charllyone,°   *Charles*
That thou thus sone° becomes a crayon°—   *soon, quickly/craven, coward*
    Me thynke thi body full dym!*[4]
Alle the false councell that touches the crown,[5]
Here gyffe I tham Goddis malyson,
685   Bothe in lyfe and lyme°—   *limb*

And Cristis malyson myghte he have
That fyrste to the° that concell gaffe—   *thee*
    And here I curse the, thou Kynge!
Because thou lyffes in eresye°   *heresy*
690 Thou ne dare noghte fyghte one Goddes enemy!"[6]
    And a buke° forthe gane° he brynge;   *book, missal/did*
And, the sertayne° sothe° als I yow telle,   *certain/truth*
He dyde all that to cursynge felle—
    This was no manere of lesynge:[7]
695 "Nowe arte thou werre° than any Sarazene,   *worse*
Goddes awenn° wedirwyne°—   *own, personal/adversary*
    Of sorowe now may thou synge!

If Cristyndome loste bee,
The wyte° bese° casten° one° the—   *blame/will be/cast, laid/on*
700   Allas that thou was borne!
Criste for the sufferde mare° dere,°   *more/harm, injury*
Sore wondede with a spere,[8]
    And werede° a crown of thorne—   *wore*

---

2. To his face (*lit.* in the midst of his face).
3. Will he now, with misfortune (willed upon him), become a heretic? (I.e., will he be excommunicated from the Faith?)
4. I.e., I think you are very weak.
5. I.e., all those who give false counsel to the King.
6. Here Turpin points out the irony of Charles's excommunicate status: his refusal to fight in person for God is now theologically acceptable.
7. He performed all (the ceremony) that appertained to excommunication—in this there was no kind of lying (i.e. it was no bluff). (Cf. *Ywain and Gawain*, l. 3023, n.)
8. A reference to the great wound in Christ's side, inflicted at the Crucifixion: ". . . one of the soldiers with a spear pierced his side, and forthwith came thereout blood and water" (John 19.34).

And now thou dare noghte in the felde
705 For Hym luke undir thy schelde!⁹
   I tell° thi saule° forlorne.°   *judge/soul/to be damned*
Men will deme° aftir thi daye   *declare*
How falsely° thou forsuke° thi laye,°   *faithlessly/abandoned/religion*
   And calle° the 'Kynge of Skorne.' "°   *pronounce/Contempt*

710 Bot then Kyng Charls, withowtten wene,°   *doubt*
At° the Byschopp was so tene,°   *With/vexed, angry*
   A fawchone° hase he drawen;°   *falchion, (broad) sword/drawn out*
And the Bischopp styrte° than to a brande°— *started, rushed/sword*
Hent° it owt of a sqwyers° hande   *Snatched/squire's*
715   Both with myghte and mayne°—   *strength*
And braydes° owte the blade bare.°   *draws/unsheathed*
"By myghtfull° God," than he sware,°   *almighty/swore*
   "If I wiste to be slayne,
Charls, and thou touche mee,
720   Thou fares noghte forthir fete thre
   Or it be qwitt agayne!"¹

Than grete lordes yede° tham bytwene;   *moved, went*
The Kynge comande° his knyghtis kene°   *commanded/bold*
   The Bischopp for-to taa;°   *take, seize*
725 And the Bischopp said, "Sirris, I will yow no scathe,²
And,° bi my faythe, it es° grete° wathe° *But/is/(a) great/danger*
   Bot if ye late me gaa—³
For, certis,° I will noghte taken bee   *certainly*
With° nane° that I now here see,   *By/no one*
730   Bot if yee firste me slaa;°   *slay*
And whilk° of yow that touches me,   *whichever*
Withowtten harme passes° noghte hee."   *escapes*
   Than with his horse com° thay—   *came*

"Here," he said, "I avowe° to mylde Marie   *swear*
735 And to hir Sone, God almyghttye,
   I sall noghte leve the soo—
For we are halden with the righte,
Clerkes appon cursede men to fighte:⁴
   I calle the Goddes foo.
740 I sall gerre buske my batelle bownn⁵
And halde° the, Charls, within this townn—   *imprison*

9. For Him watch under (cover of) your shield! (I.e., be prepared to do battle for Christ.)
1. If I find I am mortally threatened, Charles, if you (so much as) touch me, you will not go (more than) three feet farther before your intention is repaid!
2. Sirs, I wish you no harm.
3. Unless you let me go.
4. I will not depart from you (with the situation unresolved) so—because we, (as) clerics (determined) to fight against accursed men, keep to that which is just.
5. I will have my forces made ready.

Withowt° thou sall noghte goo: *Outside (the town)*
Was never kynge that werede° a crown   *wore*
So foule rebuytede with relygyon!⁶
745   Thou sall sone witt° of woo.°   *know / anguish*

Goddes byddynge° hase thou broken—   *commandment*
Thurghe the traytour° speche° spoken,   *traitorous / speech, words*
   Alle Cristendom walde° thou schende!°   *would / destroy*
When Criste sent the a suerde untill⁷
750   Thou myghte wele wiete° it was His will   *know*
That thiselfe solde thedir° wende: *thither*
Therefore I sall stroye° the,   *destroy*
Bryne° and breke downn thi cité,   *Burn*
   If thou be never so tende.⁸
755   Then to yone° Sarazenes wende sall I,   *those*
Fighte with tham whils I may dry,⁹
   In Goddes servyce to ende."°   *end (my life), die*

The Bischopp and the Cardynere°   *Cardinal*
Appon thaire horses gatt° both in-fere;°   *got / together*
760   Owte of the townn thay rade°   *rode*
Also° faste als° thay myghte dryve°   *As / as / spur on, go*
To the grete batelle° belyfe°—   *army / at once*
   And buskede baners full brade.¹
They romede° towarde Paresche° town   *made their way / Paris*
765   And thoghte° to bete the cyté downe   *intended*
   With the powere that he hade.
(Slyke° clerkes° beris° my benysone,°   *Such / clerics / have / blessing*
For trewere° men of relygyonn   *more faithful*
   In° erthe were never none made.)   *On*

770   Charls over the walles bihelde°   *looked*
And sawe the hoste° come in° the felde°   *host, army / into / (battle)field*
   And drawe towardes the town.
Bot than said Duke Naymes unto the Kynge,
"Sir, yonder comes us° new tythynges°—   *to us / tidings, news*
775   With baners buskede alle bown!
I rede° ye praye° yone clergy sesse°   *advise / ask / to cease, to stop*
And aske° the Bischopp forgyfnesse   *ask of*
   And absolucioun;
And graunt hym graythely for-to goo²
780   For-to feghte° appon Goddis° foo°—   *fight, make war / God's / foe, enemy*

6. So shamefully reproached by religious orders.
7. Unto you a sword. (Recall ll. 109–68.)
8. No matter how enraged you are.
9. For as long as I can endure.
1. See l. 187, n.
2. And consent to him readily to go.

Or loste es thi renownn."

"In faithe," saide the Kynge, "I graunt:
The Bischopp es gude° and evynhaunt,°   *good, honest / proper, compelling*
   With baners bryghte of hewe."[3]
785 Before tham a furlange and mare,[4]
The Kynge undid° his hede° alle bare—   *uncovered / head*
   The Bischopp wele hym knewe°—   *recognized*
And appon his knees he knelid down
And tuke his absolucyoun:
790   Theire joye bygane to newe.°   *renew*

The Kynge says, "Haly° fader° free,°   *Holy / father / gracious, noble*
This gilte° I pray the forgyffe me   *guilt, sin*
   And I will wirke your will;[5]
And with your clergye tournes° agayne°—   *turn / back*
795 Riste and ryott yow by the water of Sayne[6]
   Ay-whills° I come yow till."°   *All the time until / to*
The Bischoppe grauntis hym in that tyde,
And pyghte° pavylyons with mekill° pryde,   *pitched / great*
   With wyne and welthes at will.[7]
800 The Kynge into the citee went,
And aftir his baronage° he sent   *barons*
   Alle forwardes° to fulfill.   *agreements*

And by the thre wekes comen were[8]
Charls had semblede° a faire powere;°   *assembled / force, army*
805   Hymselfe come all at hande—[9]
Erles, dukes, and the twelve duchepers,[1]
Bothe barouns and bachelers,°   *young knights*
   Knyghtis full hevenhande.°   *noble*
Thay offerde° alle at Seynt Denys,   *made offerings*
810 And grete lordes to armes chesse—
   And Charls tuke his brande.[2]
And thus remewes° that grete powere: *moves off*

---

3. With brightly colored banners. (Cf. l. 187, n. The implication of Charles's observation is that Turpin's cause must be right if he has been able to mount such a splendid opposition.)
4. In front of them (Turpin's forces), from a distance of more than a furlong (one eighth of a mile).
5. And I will do what you will.
6. Rest and enjoy yourselves by the Seine River.
7. With wine and good things (available) at will.
8. See l. 629.
9. I.e., all placed themselves under his control.
1. I.e., the twelve peers of France, Charles's chief knights. (*Duchepers* derives from Old French *douze pers*, "twelve peers," but in Middle English the compounded form often loses its contextual specificity, designating "nobles"—whence the pleonasm here; cf. *The Awntyrs off Arthure*, ll. 4 and 277. The membership of this group varies from text to text (and even within texts), but Roland and Oliver are invariably included. The analogy with the twelve Apostles is obvious but need not be insisted upon.)
2. And great lords took up arms—and Charles took his sword (presumably the sword given by the angel at l. 115, and a sign of the King's personal commitment to the war; cf. l. 144, n.).

The levenynge° of thair baners clere°   *shining / bright*
  Lyghtenes° all that lande.   *Lightens, Illuminates*

Passus: *a Fitt*[3]

815 Thus Charls with his chevalrye,
    Unto° he come at° Lumbardy,   *Untill / to*
      In no place wolde° he hone.°   *would / stay*
    And to the Sarazenes was it tolde
    That Charls make werre° appon tham wolde   *war*
820   To venge° that° are° was done.   *avenge / that (which) / previously*
    The grete lordes than togedir spake:°   *spoke*
    "It is better that we Sir Garcy take
      And crownn hym the Sowdane° sonne."°   *Sultan / soon, quickly*
    Than sent thay to many an hethyn° knyghte;   *heathen*
825 Thay badde° that alle solde° come   *bade, commanded / should*
      that myghte,
      By the heghten° day, at nonne.°   *eighth / noon*

    When thay were semblede, sekerly,°   *truly*
    Thay crownnede the Sowdane Sir Garcy,
      That solance was to seene.[4]
830 Sexty° knyghtis of dyverse lande,   *Sixty*
    Ilkon° sent hym sere° presande,°   *Each one / many / presents*
      To witt withowtten wene.[5]
    Thay dressede° on hym a dyademe°   *set / diadem, crown*
    And made hym emperour so hym seme,[6]
835   Those knyghtis that were kene;
    Syne° present hym with golde   *Then*
    And stones of vertu that was holde,[7]
      The beste in° erthe myghte° bene.°   *on / (that) could / be*

    The Kynge of Massedoyne° lande   *Macedonia*
840 Sent the Sowdane a presande,
      The meryeste° one molde:°   *merriest / earth*
    Sexty maydyns faire of face
    That cheffeste° of his kyngdome was,   *best*
    And faireste appon folde;°   *earth*
845 Sexty fawcouns° faire of flyghte;   *falcons*
    And sexti stedis° noble and wyghte,°   *steeds, war-horses / swift*

3. The end of the second stage of the poem; cf. l. 384b, n.
4. (Such) that it was (a) delightful (ceremony) to see. (The subsequent processional description is largely conventional in manner and content; cf. *Sir Launfal*, ll. 230–48, 421–32, 847–52, 883–91, 925–66. From the poem's militant Christian point of view, however, the orderly extravagance of the Saracen court is to be understood further as a reflection of heathen overindulgence in wordly materialism [cf. l. 33, n.]—though the length of the description also reflects a characteristic admiration held by western Christendom for exotic levantine artistry; cf. *Sir Launfal*, ll. 265–76.)
5. See l. 222, n.
6. As was befitting to him.
7. And stones of proven (*lit.* old) quality.

In everilke° journay° bolde;   *every/day's fighting, battle*
And appon ilke° a° stede a knyghte sittande°   *each/single/sitting*
With a fawcon appon his hande
850   And a cowpe° full of golde;   *cup*

Sexty grewhondes° unto° the gamen;°   *greyhounds/for/sport*
And sexti raches° rynnande° in samen,°   *hunting dogs/running/together*
    The beste in erthe myghte bee.
He come hymselfe with this presande
855   And broghte in his awenn hande,
    That was worthe thiese three,[8]
In visebill,° a full riche stone—   *? plain view*
A safre—the beste that myghte be one
    To seke alle Crystiantee.[9]
860   The Sowdane was full fayne° of this   *pleased*
And kyndely gan° his cosyn° kysse   *did/cousin, relative*
    With mekill solempnytee.°   *ceremony*

When he his powere semblede hade,
A ryalle° feste° the Sowdan made   *royal/feast, festivity*
865   Of worthy men in wede.°   *clothing, armor*
Of alle the damesels bryghte° and schene,°   *splendid/fair*
The Sowdane hade hymselfe, I wene,
    Thaire althere maydynhede:[1]
By tham ilkone he laye a nyghte,
870   And sythen° mariede° hir unto a knyghte;   *then/married*
    Thay leffed one haythen lede—[2]
So mekill luste° of lechery   *desire*
Was amange° that chevalry°   *among/company of knights*
    That thay myghte noghte° wele° spede.°   *not/well/succeed*

875   To Charls now will I torne° agayne   *turn*
That° passes over mountayne and playne;   *Who*
    At Melayne wolde he bee.
And when he come into that stede°   *place*
Where als° the Cristyn men byfore weren dede°   *as/killed*
880   Off Fraunce, so grete plentee,[3]
There, heghe appon an hill appon highte,[4]
Turpyn garte° an awtre° dyghte,°   *had/altar/prepared*
    That alle the folke myghte see;
And off° the Trynytee a messe° he says,   *of, for/mass*
885   And hertly° for the saules° he prayes,   *heartily, earnestly/souls (of the dead)*

---

8. (Something) which was worth three of (each of) those (other presents).
9. A sapphire—one of the best that could be found in all Christendom.
1. The Sultan took their virginity for himself, I believe, from all of them.
2. They believed in heathen ways.
3. I.e., in such great numbers.
4. I.e., there, raised aloft on a high hill.

And the bodyes that thare gan° dye.   *did*

The Bischopp sone° gane hym revesche;°   *soon, quickly / put on vestments*
In gude entent⁵ he says a messe,
In the name of God almyghte:
890 He blyssede° the awtere with his hande—   *blessed*
And a fayre oste of brede therappon he fande
That ever he sawe with syghte!⁶
His chalesse° was so full of wyne   *chalice*
There myghte no more hafe° gone therin!   *have*
895 It come fro° heven on highte.   *from*
He dide° his messe forthe° to the ende   *celebrated / on, through*
And thankede Gode that it° hym sende,°   *(the bread and wine) / sent*
And Marie His modir° bryghte.   *mother*

The Bischopp in his hert was fayne°   *pleased*
900 And thankede God with all his mayne,°   *power*
And Marie His modir free.°   *noble, gracious*
He tolde the hoste with lowde° steven°   *(a) loud / voice*
How brede and wyne was sent fro heven,
Fro God of moste poustee°—   *power, authority*
905 "And all that ever hase sene this syghte,
Yee are als clene° of syn, I plyghte,°   *cleansed / promise*
Als that day borne were yee;
And whoso° endys° in this felde°   *whosoever / dies / (battle)field*
In His byggynge° sall° he belde°   *dwelling (i.e., heaven) / shall, will / settle*
910 Ever more in blysse to bee."⁷

The Bischopp than keste° of his abytte,°   *cast / habit, vestments*
And aftir° armours he askede tytte°—   *for / immediately*
For egernesse° he loughe:°   *eagerness, zeal / laughed*
A kirtill° and a corsett° fyne;   *knee-length tunic / bodice*
915 Therover he keste an acton° syne,°   *padded (leather) underjacket / then*
And it to hym he droughe;°   *drew tight*
An hawbarke° with a gesserante;°   *coat of mail / coat of scale armor*
His gloves weren gude and avenaunte;°   *handsome*
And, als blythe° als birde one boughe,   *blithe, happy*
920 He tuke° his helme and sythen his brande   *took up*
Appon a stede; a spere in hande
Was grete and gud ynoghe—⁸

Sayse, "I praye yow, all my cleregy here,
Assembles undire my banere;
925 The vawarde° will I have:°   *vanguard / take*

5. With good will, faithfully.
6. And he found thereupon as fine a host of (consecrated) bread as he had ever seen!
7. On such promised rewards, see l. 323, n.
8. (With) a lance in hand (which) was exceedingly large and dependable.

Charls and his knyghtis kene,°   *bold*
Lete erles and barouns with hym bene,°   *be*
  Bothe sqwyers and knave.°   *boys, servants*
I beseke the freschely° for-to fyghte,   *vigorously*
930 That° the lewede° men may se° with syghte *(So) that/nonclerical, lay/see*
  And gud ensample° have.   *example*
Standis now baldly° for youre trouthe;° *boldly/righteousness, faith*
Appon yone Sarazenes haves no rewthe°—   *pity*
  For golde° in erthe, none save!"° *(all the) gold/spare*

935 Thus Charls ledeth° a faire menyhé°   *leads/army*
Bifore Melayne, that riche cité,
  Braydes up baners yare—[9]
And when the Sowdane hase tham sene,
He comandes his knyghtis kene
940   That thay solde make tham° yare.° *themselves/ready*
And or° he wolde passe owte of the townn, *before*
He made his offerande° to Mahownn° *offerings/Mohammed*
  (The wars, leve Gode, thay fare!)[1]
And sythen owt° of that citee   *(led) out*
945 Off° heythen men an hugge° menyhee *Of/huge*
  That semyde° als breme° als bare.° *seemed, appeared/fierce/boar(s)*

Sir Arabaunt, with ire° and hete,° *ire, anger/eagerness, dispatch*
A furlange bifore the batelle grete,[2]
  Come and askede° fighte—   *demanded*
950 And byfore oure folke had he slayne
Bothe the lorde of Melayne
  And many another knyght!
Than sayde the Bischopp, "So mot I spede,
He sall noghte ruysse hym of this dede
955   If I cane rede aryghte!"[3]
And or any knyght myght gete° his gere° *ready, present/gear, armor*
The Bischopp gart° hym with a spere *struck*
  Appon his tepet° lighte.° *neck armor/shining*

Turpyn strake° hym so sekerly°— *struck/surely*
960 Thurgh the breste bone all plenerly,
  A lange° yerde° and more— *long/yard*
That dede° he daschede° to the *mortally wounded/dashed, sped*
  grounde,
Grysely° gronannde° in that stownde,° *Horribly/groaning/moment*
  Woundede wonderly° sore.° *wondrously/grievously*
965 The Bischopp than lighte° full apertly,° *alighted, dismounted/boldly*
And off he hewes his hede° in hy° *head/haste*

9. (And) raises up banners ready. (Cf. l. 187, n.)
1. Dear God, may they fare the worse (for that)!
2. A furlong ahead of the main army.
3. As I hope to succeed, if I am not mistaken he will not boast of this deed!

That° are° was breme als bare.   *Who/previously*
His horse unto the Cristen oste° gan° spede;°   *host, army/did/speed off*
A sqwyere broghte agayne his stede,
970   And one° he leppe° righte thare.   *on/leaped*

The Bischopp° sqwyere in the place   *Bishop's*
Saw that the kynge° dede was   *(Arabaunt)*
      That had bene of grete powere;
His° helme and his hawberke holde,°   *(He saw) his/old, proven*
975   Frette overe with rede golde,
      With stones of vertue dere,⁴
His gowere pendande on the grounde—⁵
It was worthe a thowsande pownde—⁶
      Off° rubys° and safere;°   *(Made) of/rubies/sapphires*
980   He lowttede° down, up wolde itt ta:°   *bent/take*
The Bischopp bad° hym fro° it ga°—   *bade, commanded/from/go away*
      "Go fonnge the another fere!⁷

To wyn° the golde thou arte a fole°—   *take/fool*
Thou bygynnes sone for-to spoyle!—⁸
985   Loo!° yonder comes moo!°   *Look, Behold/more (Saracens)*
Thou settis more by⁹ a littill golde
That thou seese° lye appon the molde,°   *see/earth*
      Than to fighte one Goddes° foo°—   *God's/foe, enemy*
Loo! yonder comes Sarazenes in the felde!
990   Go kill tham down under thi schelde:
      Slyk° worchippes° were gude to do."   *Such/worthy deeds*
He° tuke the pendande in his hande;   *(The squire)*
The Bishopp bett° hym with his brande,°   *beat, slapped/sword*
      That° he keste° it hym fro.   *(Such) that/cast, threw*

995   With that come girdande° Sir Darnadowse,   *rushing*
A nobill knyghte and a chevallrouse,
      Prekande° one a stede.°   *Riding hard/steed, war-horse*
He was the chefe° of Famagose,°   *chief, lord/Famagusta*
A Sarazene that fayne° wolde wyn lose,°   *gladly/renown*
1000 And to the Cristen oste gan spede.
He bad sende owte Charlyon—¹
      "If he dare come to wynn pardonn°"—   *(divine) approval*
      A bofett° for-to bede:°   *blow/offer*
He wolde noghte fighte bot with a kynge—

4. Ornamented all over with red gold, (and) with stones of valuable quality. (On "red gold," see *Havelok*, l. 47 n.)
5. The pendant attached to the lower part of his mail shirt lay on the ground.
6. A thousand pounds. (On the relative value of such a sum, cf. *Sir Launfal*, l. 323, n.)
7. Go and get yourself another opponent! (Another speech against material gains begins; cf. ll. 294–312 and l. 13, n.)
8. You begin all too soon to take up looting!
9. I.e., you value more highly.
1. He commanded that Charles be sent out (to fight with him).

1005 He calde hymselfe, withowt lesynge,
      The chefe of hethyn thede!²

      Then Kyng Charls tuke his spere hym to;
      The Bischopp Turpyn and other mo°   *more*
      Prayede God solde° hym spede.°   *should/help*
1010 "A,° dere Lorde," said Rowlande in heghe,³   *Ah, Oh*
      "Late° me fare° to fighte for thee,   *Let/go*
      For Hym that one rode° gan blede."   *rood, cross*
      Than Charls sweris,° by Saynt Paule,   *swears*
      "Sen ilke a man feghtis for his saule,
1015 I sall for myn do mede.⁴
      Slayne in the felde gif° that I bee   *if*
      Kynge off Fraunce here make I the,°   *thee*
      With reghte the reme to lede."⁵

      Than withowtten any more habade°   *delay*
1020 Theis° two kynges togedir rade°   *These/rode*
      With ire and grete envy;°   *enmity, hostility*
      And at the firste course that thay ranne
      Thies kynges two, with° horse and manne,   *with (both)*
      At the grounde bothe gun° ly.°   *did/lie*
1025 Delyverly° up sone bothe thay stirtt°   *Quickly, Nimbly/started, leaped*
      And drewe thaire swerdis with noble hertt,⁶
      Withowtten noyse or cry;
      Thay dalt° so derfely° with thaire brandes,   *dealt (blows)/violently*
      Thay hewe theire scheldis to thaire handis
1030 In cantells hyngand by.⁷

      So darfely bothe thaire dynttis° thay driste,°   *dints, blows/struck*
      A littill while thay wolde tham riste—⁸
      The Sarazene prayede° hym styntt:°   *asked/(to) stop*
      "Nowe certis,° sir," he saide, "me rewes of thee,⁹ *certainly*
1035 A Cristynn man that thou solde bee—
      Thou arte so stronge of dyntt!
      Bot torne unto oure lawes and take tham to,¹
      And I sall gyffe° the rewmes° two—   *give/realms, kingdoms*
      And° elles° will thou harmes° hentt!"° *Or/otherwise/misfortunes/receive*
1040 Bot the Bischoppe Turpyn than cryes on heghte,

---

2. He called himself, (I tell you) without lie, the best (warrior) of the heathen nation!
3. On high, aloud.
4. Since every single man fights for (the salvation of) his soul, I will reward mine so. (This is the first time that Charles has declared a willingness to fight without any sign of being coerced.)
5. With a rightful claim to govern the realm.
6. I.e., with worthy courage.
7. (That) they hew their shields into fragments hanging from their hands.
8. (That) they wished to rest themselves for a little while.
9. I pity you.
1. I.e., but convert to and embrace our religion.

"A, Charles, thynk appon Marie brighte
   To whayme oure lufe es lentt!²

And if ever that thou hade any myghte,³
   Latt° it nowe be sene in syghte   *Let*
1045   What pousté° that thou hase: *power, authority*
   Latte never oure Kynge with dynt of brande
   Be slayne with° yone° Sarazene hande,   *by / that*
      Ne° ende,° Lady, in this place.   *Nor / die*
   A [. . . .] wote° we sall° be safe   *knows / will*
1050   [. . . . . .]y the l[. .] wolde we hafe°   *have*
      Of oure comly Kynge of face.⁴
   B[. . . .] makere bathe° of son° and see,°   *both / sun / sea*
   [. . . . . .]he dole° we dree° for thee,   *anguish / endure*
      And graunte us of thi grace!"

1055   [. . . . . .]° saide, "Sir Bischopp, nay,   *[Charles]*
   [. . . . . .]° forsake my lay"—   *[I will never]*
      And togedir gan thay goo.⁵
   So stiffely° aythere° at othere strake,°   *unyieldingly / either / struck*
   Appon his° helme Sir Charles brake°   *(the Saracen's) / broke*
1060   His nobill swerde in two;
   Bot than the Franche° folke, with nobill stevenn,° *French / voice*
   Thay cry up unto the Kynge of Hevenn,
      And for thaire lorde were wo.°   *distressed*
   The Sarazene was curtays° in that fighte   *courteous (cf. l. 168, n.)*
1065   And lawses° owt a knyfe full righte;°   *draws / properly*
      His swerde he keste hym fro.

   And Charles voydede° his broken brande;   *discarded*
   Owte he hent° a knyfe in hande,   *pulled*
   And samen° thay wente full tytte.°   *together / quickly*
1070   Thay daschede full darfely with thaire dynt—
   Mighte no steryn stele tham stynt,⁶
      So styffely bothe thay smyte.
   In sondre⁷ braste° thay many a mayle;°   *burst (apart) / ring of mail*
   Thaire hawberghes° thurgh° force° gan *coats of mail / by / force of blows*
      fayle—
1075   To see had lordis delitte!⁸

---

2. To whom our love is given! (Turpin's entreaty here reveals an understandable lack of confidence in Charles's newfound militancy.)
3. And if you ever had any power. (Turpin now addresses Mary—with characteristic aggression; cf. l. 552, n. Portions of his address are now illegible in the manuscript but the general sense is that Charles is irreplaceable and must be protected at all costs.)
4. I.e., of our handsome King.
5. I.e., and Charles and Darnadowse went at each other.
6. No strong steel (armor) could withstand them (the dints).
7. Asunder.
8. Lords took great delight in seeing that!

Bot a felle° stroke Sir Charls gafe hym one,   *fierce*
Evyn° at the breste° bone: *Right / breast*
   That strake his hert° gan blende.°   *heart / stop*

The Sarazene was dede° of that strake;   *killed*
1080 And Charls gan this fende° up take,°   *fiend / lift*
   And with his awenn° brande   *own*
He broches° hym so boldely   *stabbed*
That his hert blode,° sekerly,°   *blood / truly*
   Rane to oure Kynges hande.

1085 And thare he wane° the Sarazene swerde—   *won*
And, certis, that with one this erthe
   He conquered many a lande.[9]
The Cristen folke were never so fayne;
Bot by° the Kynge was horsede°   *by (the time that) / mounted on horse*
   agayne,
1090 The batells° were doande°—   *general battles / under way*

And hawberkes sone in schredis° were schorne,°   *shreds / shorn, cut*
And beryns° thorowe° the bodys borne,°   *men / through / pierced*
   And many a Sarazene slayne.
Knyghtis one the bent° bledis;°   *battlefield / bleed*
1095 Many lay stekede° undir stedis,   *stabbed*
   In gilten gere full gayne;[1]
Other with glafes were girde thurgh evyn.[2]
We may thanke Gode that is in heven
   That lent us myghte and mayne;°   *power*
1100 Thay sloughe° tham downn with swerdis bright;   *slew*
The Cristynnd° faughte in Goddis righte;°   *Christians / just cause*
   The Bischopp loughe for fayne.[3]

Bot als the cronakill yitt will telle,[4]
Ther come a Sarazene fers° and felle,   *fierce*
1105 And to the Bischoppe glade,°   *(he) went*
And stroke hym righte thorowe the thee,°   *thigh*
And agayne to the hethen oste° gane flee—   *host, army*
   And Turpyn after hym rade.
The Bischoppe folouede hym so ferre°   *far*
1110 That the Sarazene hade the werre°   *worst (of it)*
   For the maystrie that he made:[5]
He stroke hym so in the Sowdane° syghte,   *Sultan's*
He fande° never man° that after° myghte   *found / (a) man / afterward*

9. And, certainly, with it he conquered many a nation on this earth. (Cf. l. 144, n.)
1. In very fine gilt armor.
2. Others were run right through with halberds.
3. Laughed for joy. (Cf. l. 913.)
4. I.e., but as the chronicle yet survives to tell. (Cf. l. 9, n.)
5. For the advantage he had (earlier) taken.

Hele° the hurt° he hade!   *Heal/wound*

1115 Bot they helde in the Bischoppe in that rowtte°   *throng, company*
     That° he ne myghte noghte wyn° owte,   *(Such) that/escape*
         And th[. .]he[. . . . . .]
     The Kynge of Massedoyne land with a spere[6]
     The Bischop fro his horse gane bere,°   *bear, knock*
1120   And s[. . . . .]
     The Sarazenes sware° he solde° be dede,   *swore/must*
     And° the Kynge sayde "Naye!" in that stede°—   *But/place*
         "For no Sarazene liffande!"[7]
     And righte° als° thay solde oure Bischopp slo,°   *even/as/slay*
1125 Thay smote the Kynge of Massaydoyne fro
     Clenly of his reghte hande![8]

     Bot the kynges men of Massaydoyne weren wo°   *aggrieved*
     When thay saughe° thaire lorde was wondede soo,   *saw (that)*
     And trowed° he walde° be dede;   *believed/would*
1130 Thay braydede° owte swerdes full bryghte   *drew*
     Agaynes° the Sowdane folke to fighte   *Against*
         Full styffely in that stede;
     For that gane fyfetene° thowsandez dy°   *fifteen/die*
     Of the Sowdans chevalry°   *knights*
1135   Laye° bledande° than full rede.°   *(Who) lay/bleeding/red*
     And with that Turpyn gatt awaye
     To Charls oste—full fayne were thay;
         A horse thay to hym lede.°   *led*

     Bot when the Bischoppe was horsede agayne,
1140 Alle the cleregy weren full fayne
         And presede° into the place;   *pressed, thronged*
     So° depe wondes that day thay dalt°   *Such/dealt out*
     That many on wyde opyn walt
         That wikkidly wondede was.[9]
1145 Thay sloughe so many an heythen kynge
     That, at the laste, thay tuke° to flyinge°   *took/fleeing*
         Als God us gaffe the grace.
     Many a Sarazene garte° thay falle;°   *made/fall (dead)*
     And Turpyn with his clergy alle
1150   Folowede faste one the chase.

6. Cf. l. 839.
7. For no living Saracen! (On a point of honor, the King of Macedonia does not wish to slay
   the unhorsed Turpin; cf. l. 168, n.)
8. They struck off the King of Macedonia's hand completely! (Presumably he held up his hand
   in an effort to block a stroke leveled at Turpin. While implicitly valuing the King of Macedonia's
   chivalry, the episode also demonstrates the inconstancy of the heathen cause; cf. Turpin's
   observation below, l. 1169.)
9. That many spread wide open among those who were severely wounded.

And Charls on the tother syde
Sloughe tham downn with wondis wyde;
    The doughty° garte tham dy.   *valiant (men)*
The Sowdane hymselfe so harde was stedde°   *put, pressed*
1155 That with ten thowsande away he fledde,
    And faste to Melayne gatt° he.   *went*
The Cristen men chasede tham to the barres°   *gates*
And sloughe righte there fele folke and fresche,[1]
    All that there walde byde° and bee.   *abide, stay*
1160 Bot than Kynge Charls tuke the playne°   *field*
And semblede° all his folke agayne   *assembled*
    To luke how beste myghte the.[2]

Thay myghte noghte the cité wynn,°   *conquer*
The strenghe[3] of the Sarazenes that were within;
1165   The Bischoppe said, "I rede:°   *advise (as follows)*
Of oure knyghtes in the felde°   *(battle)field*
Es° many woundede under schelde,   *Are*
    And also some are dede—
And yone Sarazenes full of tresone° es;   *treachery*
1170 There I concelle bothe more and lesse
    We stirre noghte of this stede,
Ne or to-morne serche never a wounde,
Bot luke than who may be sownde:
    Lete Criste wirke"[4]—and forthe he yede.°   *went*

1175 Here-to acordes° everilkon;°   *agrees / everyone*
Lordes haf° thaire horses tone,°   *have / taken*
    And comen es the nyghte.
Fo[. . . .]f the Sarazenes there,
Th[. . . . .]ste no forthir° fare,°   *further / go*
1180   Bot bydis° in brenys° bryghte.   *wait / coats of mail*
Ch[. . . . . . .] als thay rade,
Al[. . . . .]e the bent° thay bade,°   *battlefield / waited*
    With standardes even up streghte.[5]
The Kynge prayede° the Bischoppe fre°   *asked / noble*
1185 His wonde that he wolde late hym see[6]
    That he hade tane° in that fighte;   *taken, received*

Bot the Bischoppe saide, "A vowe to God make I here:
There sall° no salve° my wonde come *shall, will / healing ointment*
    nere,°   *near*

1. Many and vigorous folk.
2. To see how they might best proceed.
3. (That is to say) the force (of numbers).
4. Concerning that, I advise everyone that we do not move from this place, nor tend to any wound before morning, only then looking to find out who is left unhurt: let Christ work (among them). (I.e., let Christ decide who lives and who dies.)
5. With standards (banners) held strictly upright.
6. If he would let him see (to) his wound.

	Ne no hose of my thee,[7]	
1190	Ne mete° ne drynke my hede° come in,	*food / head*
	The cité of Melayne or° we it wyn—	*before*
	Or ells° therfore to dye."	*else*
	He garte dele his vetells then[8]	
	Furthe° amanges oure wonded men—	*Forth*
1195	Bot no mete neghe° wolde hee.	*go near, approach*
	Bot als so sore wondede als he was,	*as*
	Knelande° he his prayers mase°	*Kneeling / makes, says*
	To Gode of most pousté.°	*power, authority*

	Oure folke hade done° so doughtily	*performed*
1200	That many of tham weren ful wery,°	*weary*
	So° hade thay foghten° than.	*So (much) / fought*
	Bot one the morne the Cristen stode,	
	A thowsande, over theire fete in theire blode	
	Of theire awenn wondes wanne;[9]	
1205	Othere refreschynge noghte many hade	
	Bot blody water of a slade	
	That thurghe the oste ran.[1]	
	The Sowdanne sent a messangere	
	To Kynge Charles, als ye may here,	
1210	And that sawe many a man.	

	The messangere bare a wande°	*branch*
	Of ane olefe° in his hande,	*olive tree*
	In takynnynge he come of pece;[2]	
	And lowde he cryede° appon Charls the Kynge,	*called*
1215	And saide, "He° myghte his handis	*(Charles)*
	wrynge°—	*wring (in anguish)*
	Appon lyfe if that he es!—[3]	
	For oure Sowdane hase by Mahownn° sworne	*Mohammed*
	That he salle mete° hym here to-morne°	*meet / tomorrow*
	With full prowde men in prese,°	*(thick of) battle*
1220	With fowrty thowsande of° helmes bryghte—	*with*
	Was never yitt° frekkere° men to fighte	*yet / bolder, more eager*
	Sene in hethynnesse!"°	*the heathen world*

| | And Charles ansuerde at that tide,° | *time* |
| | "In faythe, I sall tham here habyde°— | *await* |

7. Nor the leggings (taken) off my thigh.
8. He then had his victuals dealt (out).
9. I.e., a thousand Christians stood in blood which pooled over their feet (i.e., up to their ankles) from their own dark wounds.
1. Not many had refreshment other than from the bloody water of a ravine that ran amid the army. (The image of pooled battlefield blood is conventional—cf. *Havelok*, ll. 2684–87— but the drinking of that blood—notably mixed with water; cf. l. 702, n.—is extraordinary, at once sacrificial and sacramental, in the manner of the Eucharist.)
2. Signifying that he came in peace.
3. If he is (still) alive!

1225	Wode giffe that thay were!⁴
	If that he brynge alle the Sarazenes
	That es° alle heythynnesse within,	are, exist
	Hyne° will I noghte fare!"°	From here / go, move back
	The messangere agayne° than rade,	
1230	And they sett wache and still habade	
	Whills pryme was passede and mare.⁵	
	Bot or the nonnee neghede nee,	
	To tham than soughte a felle semblé°⁶	
	With baners,⁷ breme° als bare.°	fierce / boar(s)

1235	Bot than Sir Charles spekes full gudely°	well, properly
	To Rowlande, his nevewe° that stode hym by,	nephew
	And seid, "Sir, so God the spede,	
	This day wirke thou manfully⁸	
	With thi nobill chevalry,	
1240	And of the Sarazens hafe thou no drede.°	dread, fear
	Thou sall see that I sall noghte be sparede;°	kept safe
	Myselfe sall have the vawarde."°	vanguard
	"There Jesu Crist the spede."⁹	
	The trumpetes trynes° one° righte than;	play / on
1245	To joyne° so jolyly° thay bygane,	join (in combat) / gallantly
	Oure worthy men in wede.°	clothing, armor

	Thay ruysschede° samen° with swilke°	rushed / together / such
	a rake°	charge
	That many a Sarazene laye one° his bake—	on
	And one the lawnde° righte ther thay lay,	land, ground
1250	Full grisely° gronande° one the grete,°	horribly / groaning / grit, earth
	Stekyde° undir stedis fete,°	Stabbed / feet
	And liste nothynge of playe.¹	
	So darfely° than thay° dynge°	violently / (did) they / knock, beat
	tham downn,	
	Thay saide the myghte° of Saynt Mahownn°	power / Mohammed
1255	Was clenely all awaye;²	
	"A,° Mountjoye!"³ oure lordes gane crye,	Ah, Oh
	And Charles with his chevalrye	
	Full freschely° faughte that day.	vigorously

	They hewe of hethen hedis in hye;°	haste

---

4. (Even) if they were insane! (A retort to the messenger's boast of ll. 1221–22.)
5. And they set watch and did not move until prime was past, and longer. (Cf. l. 517, n.)
6. But before noon drew near, a fierce assembly of warriors came toward them.
7. See l. 187, n.
8. As God may grant you success, conduct yourself valiantly this day.
9. May Christ give you success there. (Roland is speaking.)
1. And had no desire for amusement.
2. Was completely gone.
3. A traditional battle cry of French warriors, from Old French *monjoie*, with a general sense of "exaltation, lofty delight."

1260 Oure Cristen men so sekirly°   *surely*
    Of tham hade littill drede,
Bot brittenesse° tham with brandis° bare,   *cut up/swords*
And Sarazenes thurghe° the schuldirs°   *through/shoulders*
    schare°   *sheared, cut*
    That to the girdill it yode.[4]
1265 Thay tuke none hede° of gudes° nore golde—   *heed/property, plunder*
Lay never so mekill appon the molde—[5]
    Oure worthy men in wede,
Bot beris abake the batells brade:[6]
    Fowrty thowsande in a slade
1270   Laye stekede under stede.

And so harde bystade° was the Sowdane,   *beset, endangered*
Hymselfe with ten thowsande than
    To Melayne tuke the gate;°   *way*
Oure Cristen knyghtis with thaire speres°   *spears, lances*
1275 The hyndirmaste° fro thaire blonkes° beres,   *hindmost/horses*
    And chacede° tham to the yate.°   *chased/gate*
The owte° barres° hew thay downn,   *outer/(wooden) gates*
And slewe hethynn kynges with crownn
    And thaire powere therate.[7]
1280 To sawtte° the cité sadly° thay bygann   *assault, attack/earnestly*
Off Cristyn men many a cruelle man:[8]
    The hethyn wex° all mate.°   *grew, became/dejected, frustrated*

With speris and with spryngaldes° faste,   *catapults*
With dartis° kenely° owte thay caste,   *arrows/fiercely*
1285   Bothe with myghte and mayne,°   *power*
With gownnes° and with grete° stones.   *guns/great*
Graythe° gounnes stoppede those gomes°   *Ready, Emplaced/men*
    With peletes,° us to payne;°   *cannonballs/pain, punish*
Oure Cristyn men that were of price
1290 Bendis up bowes of devyce,
    And bekirs tham agayne.[9]
Appon bothe the sydis so freschely thay fighte
That by° it drewe unto the nyghte   *by (the time)*
    Fele° folke of Fraunce were slayne.   *Many*

1295 There were of° oure clergy dede,   *(members) of*
And other lordes in that stede,°   *place*
    Or thay of sawte walde sesse;[1]

---

4. Such that a sword traveled (down through the body) as far as the waist.
5. Never had so much lain upon the ground. (Cf. l. 33, n.)
6. But push back the vast divisions (of Saracens).
7. I.e., crowned heathen kings and their attendant forces.
8. With many a fierce Christian man.
9. Our excellent Christian men load siege engines (*lit.* bend engineered bows) and launch at them in return.
1. Before they would cease in the assault.

By than thay sawe it was no bote to byde
And fro the cité warde thay ryde,[2]
1300 Oure prynces provede° in presse.   *proven, tested*
The Bischoppe es so woundede that tyde
With a spere thorowe-owte the syde[3]
    That one° his ribbis gan rese:°   *one of/stick out*
Thurgh the schelde and the browne bare,[4]
1305 A schaftemonde° of his flesche he   *hand span (six inches)*
        schare°—   *cut through*
    Lordynnges,° this es no lese.°   *Sirs/lie*

He pullede it owte, keste° it hym fro,   *cast, threw*
And weryde° the handis that it come fro   *cursed*
    And that it lete forthe glyde.
1310 The Sowdane over the wallis° byhelde,°   *(city) walls/looked*
And sawe the Cristen in the felde°   *(battle)field*
    Frowarde° the cité ride;   *Away from*
And appon Kynge Charls than cryes he:
"What, Charls, thynkes° now to flee?   *(do you) intend*
1315 I trowe° the most° habyde!°   *trust, believe/must/stay*
I sall the mete to-morne in felde
With fourty thowsand under schelde—
    Sall fonde to felle thi pryde!"[5]

Says Charls, "Thou false° hethyn hownde!°   *treacherous/hound*
1320 Thou ne dare noghte byde appon the grounde—
    Ther ever more worthe the woo—[6]
Bot aythire° of thies dayes ilyke°   *either, both/alike, in the same way*
Hase thou stollen awaye lyke a tyke:°   *mongrel*
    The develle° myghte with the° goo,   *devil/thee*
1325 That cité bot thou yelde to me
And fully trowe and Cristyn be,
    Appon one God and no moo.[7]
In felde yif° ever I see the mare,°   *if/more, again*
I sall"—by myghtfull° God he sware°—   *almighty/swore*
1330 "Hewe thi bakke in twoo!"

Then of oure Cristen men in the felde
Many semblede under schelde—
    And some ware° wondede sare;°   *were/sorely, grievously*
Thay that were bothe hale° and sownnde°   *whole/sound*

2. By then they saw there was no use in staying and they ride away from the city.
3. Right through the side.
4. Through the shield and the exposed brown leather (of his acton—cf. l. 915). (The manuscript reads *browe*, "eyebrow, forehead," but the reading *browne*, after the edition of Dr. Mills, better suits the sense.)
5. (I) will set out to crush your pride!
6. For that may misfortune befall you evermore.
7. Unless you yield that city to me, become Christian, and believe completely in one God and no others.

1335	Comforthed tham that were evyll° wounde,°	*badly / wounded*
	So als Criste wolde it were.[8]	
	The Kynge than of° his helme tase°	*off / takes*
	And to the Bischoppe swythe° he gase,°	*quickly / goes*
	And sayde, "Fadir,° for Goddes° are,°	*Father / God's / mercy*
1340	Thy woundes that thou walde late me see;[9]	
	If any surgeoun myghte helpe thee,	
	My comforthe ware the mare."°	*greater*

	"What! wenys° thou, Charls," he said, "that I	*expect*
	faynte° bee,	*fearful*
	For° a spere was in my thee,°	*because / thigh*
1345	A glace° thorowte my syde?	*glancing blow, graze*
	Criste for me sufferde mare;[1]	
	He askede no salve to His sare,	
	Ne no more sall I this tyde.[2]	
	I sall never ette ne drynke,	
1350	Ne with myn eghe° slepe a wynke,	*eye(s)*
	Whate bale als ever I byde,[3]	
	To° yone° cité yolden° bee,	*Until / that / surrendered*
	Or ells therfore in batelle dye—	
	The sothe is noghte to hyde."[4]	

1355	Als thay stode spekande° of this thynge,°	*speaking / matter*
	To Charls come a newe tydynge°	*tiding, piece of news*
	That blenkede° all his blee:°	*transfixed / facial expression*
	Thay saide that one Sir Tretigon,	
	That was the Sowdane syster son[5]	
1360	And the beste° of Barbarye°—	*best (knight) / Barbary*
	"Certys,° Charls, he comes at hande[6]	*Certainly*
	With men of armes a° sexty° thowsande,	*a (force of) / sixty*
	To strenghe° with yone cité."	*strengthen, reinforce*

[* * *][7]

1365	"Now sone when I hafe foughten my fill,
	I sall avise me gif that I will
	One thi message to wende."[8]

8. Just as Christ would have it. (Cf. such charitable confraternity as recommended at ll. 1193–94.)
9. Would that you might let me see to your wounds.
1. Cf. ll. 701–3 and l. 1207, n.
2. Here, and in the next line, Turpin continues to honor his vow of ll. 1187–92.
3. (Despite) whatever suffering I endure.
4. The truth cannot be hidden.
5. I.e., the Sultan's nephew.
6. I.e., he comes near.
7. At least one page (some 120 lines) has been lost from the manuscript at this point. The missing text will have recounted how, with the advent of Tretigon's Saracen force, Charles decides to select a messenger to ride to France and call upon Christian reinforcements. The text resumes with Sir Baldwin refusing to go.
8. Just as soon as I have had my fill of fighting, I will consider whether I will go on your mission.

"Now! Sir Bawdwyne, buske and make the bownn!"[9]
He saide, "Allas, thou Charelyoun,°   *Charles*
1370   That ever I tuke thi fee![1]
For yitt myselfe es saffe and sownnde,
My body hole,° withowttyn wounde,   *whole, unharmed*
         Als° thou thiselfe may see;   *As*
I walde° noghte, for all thi kyngdome,   *would (have it)*
1375   That ever that worde unto France come[2]
         I° solde° so feyntly° flee!   *(That) I/should, would/fearfully*
Gett the° a currour° whare thou may,   *thee/courier, messenger*
For, by God that awe° this day,   *controls*
         Thou sall have none of mee."

1380   "A, Sir Ingelere, for a knyghte thou art kyde!"[3]
"Whi, Sir Charls, what walde thou that I dide?"
         "I pray the, wende thi waye!"
"Bi Jesu Criste that sittis aboffe,°   *above*
Me thynke thou kydde me littill luffe[4]
1385   When thou that worde wolde saye!
Bot me sall never betyde that taynte;[5]
I hope° thou wenys° myn herte° be°   *believe/expect/heart/(to) be*
         feynte—
     I say the° schortly,° naye!   *(to) thee/in short, briefly*
That I sall never so fremdly flee,
1390   God lett me, yif it His wille bee,
         Never habyde that daye!"[6]

The Duke Berarde was wondede sare:
Thurgh the schelde into the body bare
         He was borne° with a brande.   *pierced*
1395   Of° this message thay gun° hym frayne,°   *Concerning/did/ask, beseech*
Bot he hade no worde to speke agayne,°   *in reply*
         Bot grymly stude° lukande.°   *stood/looking, staring*
Than Turpyn gan to Charls say,
"Here arte thou servede,° bi° my fay!°   *well served/(I swear) by/faith*
1400   Thou fayles of that thou fande.[7]
The Duke es woundede so wonder° sare,   *wondrously*
It ware grete° syn to greve° hym mare—   *great/grieve, trouble*

---

9. Make yourself ready (to go)!
1. (Alas) that I ever became your vassal! (Normally such a refusal as Baldwyn's would be seen as a serious violation of feudal vows—Charles's anger indicates as much; but here, as with other such manifestations of unorthodox behavior in the poem, it stands as a recommendation of commitment to the higher cause of the holy war; cf. l. 341, n. On the conditions of vasselage, see l. 596, n.)
2. I.e., that word ever reached France.
3. You are renowned as a knight! (Charles now tries to convince Engelier to go on the mission.)
4. I believe that you showed me little respect.
5. I.e., I will never be tainted so.
6. If it be His will, may God never let me see the day that I would so perversely flee!
7. You fail in that which you attempt.

Gude° sir, thou late° hym stande."   *Good / (must) let*

Thay prayede a banarett than of pryce,[8]
1405 One sir Barnarde of Parische,
  For° grete gyftis he wolde wende;   *(If) for*
And he saide, "Lordynges, by my faye,
I ame over symple to yow to saye,[9]
  Where ever ye will me sende;
1410 I aske ordir of knyghte° thertill°—   *knighthood / in respect of that*
Bot giffe your giftis where ye will;[1]
  Elles° ye be my frende."   *In another way*
Thay made hym knyghte with full gud chere;[2]
He tuke° leve° at° the twelve dugepere,[3]   *took / (his) leave / of, from*
1415   This curtayse° knyghte and hende:°   *courteous / gracious*

He saide than, "Have gud daye, Charls, in this stede,°   *place*
For thou sall never gyffe me brede,
  Ne in thy burdynge say,
If I be pore of golde and fee,
1420 That I fro this grete journee
  Fayntly fledde away!"[4]
He rydis even° to the yatis° of Melayne   *straight / gates*
And there with° Sarazenes was he slayne: *by*
  He dide full wele that day.[5]
1425 And Charls for hym in hert was woo,°   *grieved*
Bischoppe Turpyn, and othere moo;°   *more, in addition*
  For his dede° sore murnede° thay.   *death / mourned*

Thus have thay prayede everylkone,°   *everyone*
Bot there wolde goo never one
1430   (The symple thay bade none sende).[6]
The Bischoppe Turpyn cryede appon highte,°   *high*
"Sen° ye are so frekke° for-to fighte,   *Since / eager*
  God of His myghte yow mende![7]
Yitt° are we ten thowsande here   *Yet, Still*
1435 (That are yitt bothe hole and fere,°   *proud*
  That wele for kene are kende,[8]

8. They then asked a respected bannerer (a standard-bearer). (*Banarett* properly designates a knight of superior rank, but the word may represent a copying error made in anticipation of the knighthood about to be bestowed.)
9. I.e., I am of too low a rank to deliver a message for you.
1. I.e., give your gifts elsewhere.
2. I.e., gladly.
3. See l. 806, n.
4. For you will never need to provide for me (*lit.* give me bread), nor in moments of leisure say that, even though I was poor, I fled fearfully from this great day's fight!
5. A remarkable observation, given that Barnard rode in the opposite direction expected and essentially committed suicide; yet again, unmitigated martial zeal is recommended at the expense of all other considerations.
6. They commanded that no one of low rank be sent.
7. May God renew you with His strength!
8. Who are well known for ferocity.

And of° gude men that none° will flee) *(consisting) of / (from) no one*
To fourty thowsande—or° we dye   *before*
 In the felde to make thaire ende!"[9]

1440 Bot als° Turpyn lenys° hym on his brande, *as / leans*
Over an hill he saw comande°   *coming*
 Ful many a brade° banere: *broad, large*
The Duke of Bretayne,° Sir Lyonelle,   *Brittany*
That Charls was thare he herde telle,
1445 And hade mystere of powere.[1]
He broghte hym thirty thowsande fyne,° *fine (warriors)*
Vetaylls° gude and nobill engyne,° *Victuals, Provisions / siege engines*
 This bolde,° with full blythe chere.[2]   *bold (man)*
Than Turpyn gan to Charls say,
1450 "I see a felle° hoste,° bi my fay,   *formidable / host, army*
 That sone° will neghe° us nere.   *soon / approach*

Yone are the Sarazenes mekill° of mayne,° *great / strength*
The full powere owt of Spayne,
 That sone sall full ill spede—[3]
1455 For, by Hym that swelt° on tree,°   *died / i.e., cross*
This day no Sarazene sall I see
 Sall gerre me torne my stede!"[4]
And in his hande he caughte a launce—
"Have gud day, Charls, and grete wele Fraunce—"[5]
1460 And agayne° that hoste he yede;° *against, toward / went*
In fewter° sone he keste his spere *the saddle's lance-rest*
And thoghte° the boldeste down to bere° *intended / knock*
 That batelle walde hym bede.[6]

So blody was that Bischoppis wede,°   *clothing, armor*
1465 His conysaunce, ne yit his stede,
 The Bretons ne couthe noghte knawe;[7]
Bot als an harawde° hym byhelde,° *herald / beheld*
He lukede up into° his schelde   *at*
 And sayde to alle one rawe,[8]
1470 "If Bischoppe Turpyn appon lyve be,[9]
In faythe, lordynges, yone° es he   *yonder, there*
 That ye se hedirwarde° drawe!"   *hither*

---

9. I.e., to bring about their deaths!
1. Who had heard that Charles was there and was in need of forces.
2. I.e., gladly.
3. Who will soon get on very badly.
4. Who will make me turn my steed (in flight)!
5. I.e., and give my regards to France. (Turpin implies that, like Barnard, he will not return.)
6. Who would proffer him battle.
7. The Bretons could not make out his cognizance (coat of arms), or even that on his horse.
8. All (who there were marshaled) in a row.
9. Is alive.

Thay ferlyde° why he fewterde° his spere;   *marveled / set in (its) rest*
"A, Mountejoye!"[1] cryes one that° he myghte here°—   *(so) that / hear*
1475   He° was glade of that sawe!°   *(Turpin) / utterance*

The wardayne° rydis hym agayne   *warden*
And said, "Sir Bischoppe, for Goddis payne,[2]
   Who hase greved° the?"   *grieved, annoyed*
He tuke his spere owt of reste adowne
1480   And gaffe tham alle his benysoun,°   *blessing*
   The Bretonns, when he tham see.°   *saw*
The Bischoppe tolde tham of his care;°   *trouble*
Bot than the Bretonns hertis were sare°   *sorrowful*
   For the dole° oure oste gun dryee.°   *anguish / endure*
1485   A messangere went to telle the Kynge;
So fayne was Charles never of thynge
   With eghe that he gan see.[3]

And or° Turpyn myghte his tale halfe telle   *before*
He sawe come hovande° over a felle°   *appearing / fell, ridge*
1490   Many a brade banere,
Standardis grete, with stalworthe° men: *stalwart, strong*
Sexti thowsande wele myghte thay ken,°   *reckon, discern*
   In brenyes burnescht clere.[4]
Under the cante° of an hille   *side*
1495   Oure Bretonns beldis° and bydis° stille   *tarried / waited*
   When thay wiste° whate thay were;   *knew, realized*
The Bischoppe saide, "Bi Goddis myghte,
Thaym° sall rewe,° or it be nyghte,   *They / regret*
   The tyme that thay come here:

1500 Go we to yone company;
With° "Mountjoye!" baldly° tham   *With (cries of) / boldly*
    ascrye°—   *shout at, defy*
   Late ther be no lettynge![5]
An hawrawde° said, "To° fewe are we   *herald / Too*
To fighte with slyke° a grete menyé°—   *such / army*
1505   It is better wende° to the Kynge,   *to go*
A° sir, whare° thay° are sexti thowsande   *Ah, Oh / since / (the Saracens)*
    men!"
"And if thay were mo bi thowsandis ten,
   Bi° God that made all thynge,   *(I swear) by*
The more powere that thay be,
1510 The more honour wyn sall we—

---

1. See l. 1256, n.
2. I.e., for the sake of Christ's suffering (on the Cross).
3. I.e., Charles was never so pleased with anything he had seen.
4. In brightly burnished coats of mail.
5. Let there be no hesitation!

We dowte° noghte tham to dynge!"°   fear/strike down

The Bischoppe to the Kyng sent
And prayes hym to byde° appon the bent,°   stay/battlefield
  The cité for-to kepe°   watch over
1515 That° there no Sarazene solde come owte,   (So) that
To° thay had rekkenede° with that rowte°   Until/reckoned, dealt/company
  Thay sawe come overe the depe.[6]
Oure Bretonns kyndely comforthes° he—   encourages
Sayse, "Alle the Sarazenes ye yonder see,
1520   Thaire frendis° sore may wepe;°   friends, relatives/weep
We sall wirke° tham° wondis° full wyde—   work, create/(in) them/wounds
I hete° tham be° thaire lemans° syde   promise/by/lovers'
  Sowndely never sall thay slepe!"

For isschuynge owte of the cité,[7]
1525 Kynge Charles with his menyé
  Helde his batelle° still.°   army/in place
Oure Bretons bolde that fresche° come in   fresh, vigorous
Thoghte that thay wolde wirchipp° wyn,   honor, renown
  And gatt° the cante of the hill.   won
1530 The Sarazenes were so strange and stowte,
Thay late no lede that thay wolde lowte,[8]
  Thay were so wykkede of will;°   disposition, nature
Oure Bretonns dide so doughtyly°   valiantly
That lange° or° none,° sekerly,°   long/before noon/truly
1535   The Sarazenes lykede full ill![9]

Samen° than strake° that grete stowre°   Altogether/drove, clashed/battle
Als° it were aftire the none ane houre—   Until
  It was noghte mekille° mare°—   much/more, later
Bot many a Sarazene in that stownde°   time
1540 Lay grysely° gronande° on the grownde,   horribly/groaning
  Woundede wonderly sore.
Bot there° God will helpe ther es no lett;°   there (where)/hindrance
So° stronge strokes thay one tham sett   Such
  With burneschede bladis° bare   blades
1545 That fourty thowsande Sarazenes kene
With brandis lay brettenyde° one the grene,°   cut up/green, field
  So bolde oure Bretonns were.

And to the cité the tother° wolde have flede;   remaining warriors
And Rowlande thoghte he wolde tham stedde°—   stop
1550   Ten thowsande was with hym;
And when he with the Sarazenes mett,

6. (Who) they saw come from beyond the depths (of the city).
7. Against the issuing out (of Saracens) from the city.
8. That they acknowledged no other people to whom they would bow down.
9. I.e., became very displeased!

Full grym strokes he on tham sett
   With growndyn speris and grym.[1]
Charles, appon the tothere° syde,   *other*
1555 Sloughe° tham downn with woundis wyde—   *Slew*
   And made thaire dedis full dyme![2]
And thus thay chase tham here and thare,
  Als the howndes dose° the hare,   *do*
   And refte° tham lyfe and lyme.°   *took from / limb*

1560 Rowlande rydis to Letygon
(That was the Sowdane sister sone)[3]
   And stroke hym with a spere,
That° dede° he daschede° in the felde—   *(Such) that / dead / sped down*
Helme ne hawberke° he myghte none welde°   *coat of mail / wield, use*
1565 Ne never after none bere!°   *bear, carry*
Of sexti thowsande, sothely to say,
Passede° never one qwyke° away,   *Escaped / alive*
   Bot evyll° thay endide° there.   *wretchedly / died*
The Cristenyde knelide down in that place
1570 And thankede God that gaffe tham grace
   So worthily tham to were.[4]

The false° in the felde thus gun thay felle;°   *heathen / fell, lay low*
The Kynge callede Sir Lyonelle,
   And avauncede° hym full heghe:°   *advanced, promoted / highly*
1575 The Duke of Burgoyne bifore was dede;
He sessede hym in his stede,
   And gafe hym his doughter free.[5]
And to the Bischoppe than swythe° he gase°   *quickly / goes*
That wery° and sore woundede was,   *weary*
1580 And fastande° dayes three.   *(had been) fasting*
Be° that tyme he myghte note wele a worde out-wyn;[6]   *By*
The teris° rane over Charles chynn,   *tears*
   That° sorowe° it was to see—   *(Such) that / a sorrowful thing*

"And° thou dy, than dare I saye   *If*
1585 The floure° of presthode° es awaye°   *flower, paragon / priesthood / gone*
   That ever hade schaven crownn,[7]
For there ne is kynge ne cardynere°   *cardinal*

1. With cruel sharply ground lances.
2. I.e., and made their performance forgettable.
3. See l. 1359, n.
4. For them to fight so admirably.
5. The Duke of Burgundy had earlier died; Charles placed Lionel in legal possession of the Duke's feudal holding (cf. *Ywain and Gawain*, l. 3760, n.), and he gave him the Duke's noble daughter in marriage.
6. He could not properly get out a single word. (Turpin has strictly honored his vow; often in the romances such vows are merely rhetorical—cf. *Havelok*, l. 317. Turpin's self-mortification, however, though through combat obtaining the additional merit of sacrifice for others, is normative, concordant with penitential traditions: cf. *Havelok*, l. 217, n.)
7. Cf. l. 633.

In Cristyndome may° be thi pere,°   *(who) can / peer*
    Ne man of religiownn."[8]
1590 He will no man his wondes late° see,°   *let / see (to)*
    Ne mete ne drynke none neghe° hym ne,   *come near*
        For prayer ne for pardownn;°   *pardon*
    Oure oste for the Bischoppe mournes alle,
    And graythes° tham° to° Melayne walle   *ready / themselves / in sight of*
1595   With baners buskede bownn.[9]

    New vetailles° the Bretons broghte than   *victuals, provisions*
    That refresschede many of oure men,
        Of brede, brawne,° and wyne.   *meat*
    A nobill hurdas° ther was graythede   *rampart*
1600 And baners to the walles displayede;
        And bendis up thaire engyne. . . .[1]

---

8. Nor any man of religious orders.
9. With banners made ready. (Cf. l. 187, n.)
1. (For this line, cf. ll. 1289–91, n.) The pages containing the rest of the poem are missing from
the manuscript. Clearly the Christians are moving toward the final victory predicted early on
by the angel, at ll. 127–32. The Sultan Garcy will probably succeed in escaping, for he is
known as the principal Saracen leader in the popular *Otuel* story, in which Charlemagne is
engaged in further wars against the heathen in Lombardy (three different versions of *Otuel*
survive in Middle English). Turpin, of course, will survive (miraculously), for we know he
must live to witness the full flowering of Charles's career and the tragedy of Roncevaux; cf.
l. 178, n.
    The angel's prediction of the throwing down of the city walls suggests that the conclusion
may have been modeled on a chapter in the *Pseudo-Turpin Chronicle* (about which see the
headnote in the Sources and Backgrounds section, p. 389): failing to capture the city of
Pamplona in Spain after a six-month siege, Charles at last prays for assistance, at which point
the city walls are miraculously thrown down. (That episode is itself no doubt modeled on the
siege of Jericho; Joshua 6.)

SOURCES AND BACKGROUNDS

Havelok[1]

Though only one complete manuscript of the romance exists (there are also a few all-too-brief fragments),[2] a handful of other texts survives of sufficient variety to suggest that the Havelok *story* at least was quite popular. Most of these texts also provide glimpses of the kinds of sources from which *Havelok* was composed and in what ways *Havelok* might represent an original treatment of the story.

The most remarkable such "text" (for want of a better term in this instance) is that of the early-thirteenth-century town seal of Grimsby (the town in Lincolnshire which, as ll. 743–46 of *Havelok* relate, was named after its founder and the hero's guardian, Grim). The seal depicts three figures, each one named: the large figure of GRYEM (holding a sword and shield) stands in the center with the smaller figures of HABLOC (crowned, holding an ax and a ring) and GOLDEBVRGH (crowned, holding a scepter) standing to either side. With the exception of two other texts, only *Havelok* names Goldeboru as Havelok's wife and queen; even so, Grim does not engage in combat in *Havelok*, and no mention is made of Havelok's use of an ax. Such details could represent iconographic formulae (the ring could be a wedding ring, held out to Goldeboru), in which case the sculptor of the seal could have known the story from *Havelok* itself; but the meticulousness of the detail suggests otherwise, and it is safer to assume that there was another source, one which dealt more comprehensively with the legend of the founding of the town.

Another text in which Goldeboru is named is the Anglo-Norman (French) *Petit Brut*,[3] written in 1310 by Rauf de Bohun. In the space of 24 lines, Rauf summarizes the Havelok story, noting that his source was *L'Estoire de Grimesby* ("The History of Grimsby"). Other details, such as the naming of Godrich of Cornwall—a figure otherwise mentioned only in *Havelok*— and a measuring of England from Roxburgh and Dover (cf. *Havelok*, ll. 139, 265), suggest that *Havelok* was in fact Rauf's source. Nevertheless, like the anomalies of the Grimsby seal, the name he gives to his source just hints at the existence of a popular founding legend. Similar if not stronger hints emerge from Robert Mannyng's 1338 translation of Pierre Langtoft's

---

1. Editions and translations of the texts mentioned in this headnote, as well as references to related scholarship, are cited in the Selected Bibliography. On the date of the poem, see the leading footnote to the edition proper.
2. The "Cambridge fragments" of Cambridge University Library MS Add. 4407 (19): four fragmentary leaves, two of which have text corresponding (but not identical) to ll. 174–83, 341–64, and 537–50.
3. "Small *Brut*," an abbreviated history of the kings of Britain from the time of Brutus, the legendary Trojan founder of Britain.

Anglo-Norman *Chronicle* (c. 1300, a history of England). Responding to a reference in his source to Gunter (the equivalent of Birkabeyn in *Havelok*, so named in Gaimar and the *Lai d'Haveloc*—see below), Mannying complains that there are no authoritative written histories of Havelok; he only knows of that matter which unlettered men relate in English ("That thise lowed men upon Inglish tellis"). Presumably that is a reference to orally transmitted accounts, folktales perhaps, as opposed to poems the length of *Havelok*; indeed, Mannying (it is perhaps significant that he was from Bourne in Lincolnshire) then proceeds to describe three different stories: of the chapel which still stands in Lincoln in which Havelok married Goldeboru ("that saw [story] is yit [still] rife"); of the stone which Havelok once cast farther than anyone else and which yet lies at Lincoln castle; and of Grim, who founded Grimsby and whose story "men redes (read, relate) yit in ryme." As with the *Petit Brut*, there are overlaps with *Havelok*, but also divergences and obvious variations of emphasis which point to the existence alongside *Havelok* of local folkloric/legendary material which the author of *Havelok* may well have adapted (as noted below, the poet was certainly familiar with local details).[4]

Perhaps the best evidence about the background of *Havelok* is available in two French texts, both written in octosyllabic verse (so too is *Havelok*) and both of which predate *Havelok*. The earlier of the two covers ll. 41–816 of *L'Estoire des Engleis*,[5] written in Anglo-Norman c. 1135–40 by the chronicler Geffrei Gaimar; a prose translation is here printed. The second text is the anonymous Anglo-French *Lai d'Haveloc*,[6] a 1112-line adaptation of Gaimar's "Haveloc episode," written c. 1190–1220; many lines in the *Lai* are taken over verbatim from Gaimar. Neither text can conclusively be shown to be a direct source for *Havelok*; then again, it is not impossible that, armed with a formidable imagination, the *Havelok* poet relied upon little more than the story matter represented by these two texts. In either case, a comparison of the French material with the ME text gives an impression of the kinds of ideas and motifs which the *Havelok* poet could have adapted from preexisting material. The principal difference between the *Lai* and Gaimar concerns the way in which the chronology of events is handled at the beginning: after the opening 23 lines, which declare that this is a salutary tale about good and noble conduct (an introductory approach taken up and much elaborated in *Havelok* with the important idealizing account of Athelwold), the *Lai* relates the equivalent of Gaimar ll. 377–454 (the death of Gunter, Grim's flight to England with Haveloc, the settlement at

---

4. One manuscript of Mannyng, Lambeth Palace MS 131, replaces Mannyng's complaint with an 82-line summary (the "Lambeth interpolation") based upon the version of the Havelok story represented by Gaimar and the *Lai d'Haveloc*. Another brief account of the story, in the Anglo-Norman prose *Brut* (composed originally not long after 1272 and successively augmented to 1333), attests to the diverse background of *Havelok*; it is based on the story as represented in Gaimar, but two manuscripts of the earliest portion of the text name Goldeboru.

5. "The History of the English"; the history appears to have been written as a continuation of Gaimar's own translation, now lost, of Geoffrey of Monmouth's *Historia Regum Brittaniae* (about which see the Sources and Backgrounds headnote to *Ywain and Gawain*, pp. 331–32).

6. "Lay of Haveloc"; in an attempt perhaps to appear exotic the poem belies its dependence on Gaimar by purporting to be a "Breton Lay." The appellation has since erroneously been foisted upon *Havelok*. For a discussion of the authentic elements of the *lai* genre, see the Sources and Backgrounds headnote to *Sir Orfeo*, p. 345 ff.

Grimsby), 41–97 (the death of Edelsi, the placing of Argentile in Adelbriht's care), 105–66 (the life of Cuaran as Adelbriht's cook), and 167–76 (the forced marriage of Argentille to Cuaran), in that sequence. From there on, the action is fundamentally the same: with that in mind the following discussion will refer mainly to Gaimar (other notable differences in the *Lai* are recorded below and in the footnotes to Gaimar).

A cultivation of ironies and inherent contradictions of character motivates some of the *Havelok* poet's more conspicuous contributions to the received story. The result is a sophisticated (but not necessarily unfeeling) exposure of the morbid duplicities which attend an unnatural ambition—namely the desire of both Godrich and Godard to confound the divine right of a legitimate royal heir. At the outset, the *Havelok* poet takes ingenious advantage of the existence in the received story of the double usurpation: in contrast to Gaimar, *Havelok* frames the usurpers' exploits with an unmistakable symmetry (cf. 1. 347, n.), and the ultimate punishment meted out to the villains is treated in kind (see 1. 2823, n.). *Havelok* thus develops the impression of a type of insurgent evil which is repeatable and predictable, and which can in turn be met with a predictable corrective (in the form of a legitimate king loyally nurtured). Certain ironies in detail elaborate the impression: see, for example, ll. 1178, 2437, 2547, and notes thereto.

Telling contradictions as expressions of character are first evident in Godard's servant, later Havelok's guardian, Grim. In Gaimar he is straightforwardly presented as Haveloc's savior and guardian; but in *Havelok* he is first seen as a foolishly ambitious lacky capable of gratuitous cruelty (ll. 537 ff.). Only when he witnesses the supernatural manifestations of Havelok's innate royalty does he become an exemplary guardian (ll. 606 ff.). Even Godard (whose equivalent in Gaimar, Odulf, is plainly described as a usurper much hated by the Danes) is subject to a lapse in outright villainy when he just once takes pity on Havelok (ll. 496 ff.). It is a lapse which eventually costs him his life, but also one which suggests that he could have been a superior royal servant had Havelok been old enough to master him. That is also the implication in the case of the other villain, Godrich, when in the thick of the final battle Havelok offers to reprieve him (ll. 2704–21): in Gaimar the equivalent figure, Edelsi, quickly capitulates and then dies (we know not how) within a fortnight.

The most complex of all such characterizations is that of Ubbe. The status of his equivalent in Gaimar, Sigar Estalre, is clear: formerly the seneschal to Gunter, he is said later to have developed a reclusive hatred for Gunter's usurper Odulf, and it is he who rallies supporters of the true heir and is instrumental in restoring him to the throne. Ubbe also performs the latter function in *Havelok*, but his career leading up to his declaration of loyalty to Havelok seems checkered. A page is missing in the manuscript at a point which might have provided an introductory declaration of Ubbe's history and present loyalties, but as things stand we first meet him accepting a bribe from Havelok (see l. 1634, n.), and he seems to enjoy a measure of authority and prosperity under Godard (ll. 1685, 1724 ff.). While he later becomes the premier champion of loyalty to Havelok (ll. 2168 ff.), earlier he seems all too familiar with lawlessness and the ways of brigands (e.g., ll. 1659–

65, 1741–45, 2047–51, 2096–2105).[7] He also possesses a ruthlessness comparable to that of Havelok's enemies (e.g., ll. 2284–89 and 2200–2). And yet in the case of Havelok he is capable of pity (ll. 2052–55) and unstinting support (ll. 2180 ff.); like Grim, he makes good only under the influence of Havelok's nascent royalty. In any other condition it seems even the most able subjects are prone to an invidious corruption.

Gaimar and the *Lai* both conceive Havelok's exploits in a distant past, but *Havelok*, though still telling of "are-dawes" (l. 27), brings to the story a greater immediacy; to its early-fourteenth-century audience it may well have invited reflection upon the contemporary life of the realm. There are allusions to state history (from the not-too-distant past, if the evidence is judged collectively; see the notes to ll. 375, 1178, 2559); and also references to specific conjunctions of time and place (especially at Lincoln; ll. 264–65, 875, 2828–29). There is also the inordinate level of material detail for which the poem is renowned, references to the stuff of everyday life, best exemplified by the lists of food (e.g., ll. 750–59, 895–97, 1240–41, 1726–29), but also evident with such touches as the description of the gag thrust in Havelok's mouth as "unwraste" (l. 547), or the observation that Godard was bound with "a rop of an old seyl" (l. 2507). Traces of that kind of detail can be found in Gaimar (less so the *Lai*), especially in the lists of food; but in *Havelok* the detail is almost always invested with greater meaning: thus Godard's rope recalls with bitter irony the seafaring background to Havelok's salvation (cf. ll. 707–863); the filthiness of the gag intensifies the impression of outrage done the young king; and the lists of food support the poem's marked advocacy of devoted and generous nurture, particularly as it applies to the rightful heir (cf., for example, 908, 926, 1693, 2236–39, 2420—symbolically, the gag is inimical to all this).

Against Gaimar, *Havelok* is also replete with details of law and order, illegalities, jurisdiction, form and ceremony, all ultimately informing a

7. The ambiguity of Ubbe's character may have been assisted by some alterations to the received story, their existence evidenced by lingering inconsistencies. For example, the "ten . . . and . . . sixti" men he sends (ll. 1746–47) to help guard Havelok's band at the house of Bernard Brun never appear; but they do seem suspiciously like the one "ladde" and sixty others (ll. 1767–68) who attack Bernard's house, bent on plunder (significantly, a later report at ll. 1928–29 names them as Ubbe's men, and another report, at l. 2026, says they were seventy in number). In Gaimar, six of Sigar's own men attack Havelok and his retinue, but their aim is to rape Argentille; interestingly, that is the motive Ubbe (wrongly) predicts for any attack against Havelok (ll. 1659–65, 1741–45).

Dr. Mills has posited the influence in these discrepancies of an episode cognate with that in the French romance *Richars li Biaus* (written c. 1250–75), in which the hero and two companions, invited by a villain to stay at his house, are attacked in their private chamber, at dinner, by the villain's sixty-one cohorts; eventually all sixty-one are killed. Earlier one of the hero's companions had overheard the villains plotting to murder and then rob them, and thus Richard and his men were suitably prepared to mount their successful defense. It is possible that the *Havelok* poet supplemented a faulty recollection of the events in the story as represented by Gaimar and the *Lai* with a recollection of a similar episode like that in *Richars* (that *Richars* is in fact the source is suggested by the hero's cruciform birthmark, a detail found in no other version of the Havelok story except the Middle English poem).

That the story generally has been subject to some reconstruction is evident in a number of other inconsistencies. For example, Havelok knows his own identity from the beginning, and yet his wife only finds out who he is through supernatural revelations (ll. 1247 ff.); and Havelok tells Grim's sons of his own history even though everyone there already knows it (ll. 1401 ff.). Though unnecessary to the development of the action, both examples are analogous in place to similar events in the French texts.

view of what constitutes the righteous and just administration of the nation (e.g., ll. 27–28, 185–89, 210–32, 442–44, 1089–99, 2464–87, 2512–19); even the usurping kings of the French have been demoted to regents, with consequent stress laid on the formal impropriety of their claims. It is important to be vigilant for such details; it is all too easy to overlook them beside the wealth of material detail and to see the poem in turn as some kind of common folk's idyll set in opposition to the polite dynastic preoccupations of the French antecedents. *Havelok* lies somewhere between those extremes; the administrative detail suggests that the poem was composed by a representative of and must have held a special appeal for the official ranks it names so frequently—indeed (and the irony is pointed) they are the kinds of figures Godard enlists to secure his unlawful power:

> Justises dede he maken newe
> Al Engelond to faren thorw,
> Fro Dovere into Rokesborw.
> Schireves he sette, bedels and greyves,
> Grith-sergeans wit longe gleyves. . . .
>
> (263–67)

GEFFREI GAIMAR

From L'Estoire des Engleis†

⁴¹   * * *¹two kings once ruled in Britain when Constantine was chieftain; this Constantine was the nephew of Arthur who wielded the sword Excalibur. One of the kings had the name Adelbriht.² He was a powerful man; he was Danish. The other had the name of Edelsi;³ his were Lincoln and Lindsey—from the Humber to Rutland the country was in his command. The other was king of the country which is now called Norfolk. So well acquainted were these two kings that they were companions indeed, and between the two was such love that Edelsi gave his sister [in marriage] to Adelbriht, that powerful king who was of Danish lineage. The other king who had the name of Edelsi was a Briton. His

---

† Translated by Stephen H.A. Shepherd from the text represented in the edition of Alexander Bell, Anglo-Norman Text Society, Nos. 14, 15, 16 (Oxford, Basil Blackwell, 1960). Paragraphing and punctuation are the translator's; to aid clarity, proper names are sometimes substituted in square brackets for the original pronouns. All references to the *Lai d'Haveloc* are to the edition of A. Bell, *Le Lai d'Haveloc and Gaimar's Haveloc Episode* (Manchester, 1925).
1. The first part of the sentence is subject to different manuscript readings, having the senses of "if what Gildas said he found written in the chronicle is true" or "if what Gildas said in the chronicle he wrote is true." Gildas (c. 500–c. 570, also known as St. Gildas "the Wise") wrote *De Excidio Britanniae* ("Concerning the Ruin of Britain") in the 540s; it is the only surviving historical British work roughly contemporary with the time in which Arthur (if he ever existed) was supposed to have lived. Gildas may have written another work to which Gaimar is referring, but *De Excidio Britanniae* does not mention Havelok.
2. Athelwold in *Havelok.*
3. Godrich in *Havelok.*

sister had the name of Orwain; she was of great nobility and of good descent. By her lord she had a daughter which they called Argentille.[4]

65 The maiden grew and thrived (for she had been raised kindly enough) and it came to pass in very truth that her father did not have any other heir. In the kingdom of Denmark he had four rich earldoms, and in Britain he had conquered Colchester with the [surrounding] country: from Colchester to Holland[5] at a stretch extended his realm. For as long as he was so powerful, Edelsi was his good friend; but then Adelbriht was dead, in the city of Thetford. To Colchester was the King taken, where he was interred; and Orwain and Argentille—they were the Queen and his daughter—were gone to Lindsey, to [the Queen's] brother, King Edelsi. They delivered the kingdom that Adelbriht held unto Edelsi to guard, for the Queen was infirm—nor but eight days [longer] did she last after Adelbriht. When she had died, they buried the Queen; and Argentille was raised at Lincoln and at Lindsey. As the ancients record,[6] she did not have any near relative on her father's side, of the Danish.

96 Hear what this felon king did. For the inheritance which he coveted, he had his niece mismarried; he gave her to a knave who had the name of Cuaran. Because he wished to debase her he purposed to give her to him [in marriage].[7] This Cuaran was a scullion, but a very attractive youth; he had a handsome face and beautiful hands, a shapely body, graceful and smooth. His own countenance was always happy. He had good legs and good feet. But because he was courageous and fought willingly, there was no youth in the household who made him a challenge and who started an altercation with him that [Cuaran] did not throw the [youth's] legs aloft;[8] and when he was very angry he bound [the youth] with his belt, and, if [the youth] then had no protection, he would beat him well with a rod! And nevertheless he was of such noble disposition that if the youth promised him that he would not love him the less for having done that, immediately he would untie him. When they were reconciled, then was Cuaran pleased! And the King and the knights gave to him from their food; some gave him cakes, some portions of simnel cakes; others gave him pieces of roast meat and fowl which came to them from the kitchens. He had so much such bread and provision because he had two servants with him; and to servants of the household he often made large donations of simnels, of biscuits, and of pieces of roast meat and of cakes. For this he was very well liked and so praised and so esteemed that there was no freeman in the household

---

4. Goldeboru in *Havelok*.
5. I.e., from Colchester to the district of Holland in Lincolnshire.
6. Another possible translation is "as the old people tell."
7. The *Lai* adds that the dying Achebrit (= Adelbriht) entrusted Edelsi to marry Argentille to the "strongest" (*plus fort*; i.e., most powerful) man in the kingdom (l. 228); as in *Havelok*, ll. 1077–84, the usurper then takes advantage of the strictly literal meaning in justifying the heiress's marriage to the physically superior knave.
8. I.e., head over heels.

who, if Cuaran needed a donation, would not willingly give to him—
but he did not seek rewards. He would give whatever he had—it was
little to him—and when he had nothing to give, willingly he would
borrow, then give it and spend. That which he borrowed he repaid well.
Whatever he had, he gave all—but never asked anyone for anything.

151   He was thus in the household dishwasher to a scullion. There were
two servants whom he looked after—hear now why he did that. He
thought that they were his brothers—but his father was not theirs, nor
his mother, nor his lineage, nor was he of their kindred. Even though
he was of such lowliness he was come of noble birth—and if the King
had realized that, [Cuaran] would never have had his niece [in marriage]!
Of whom he was born, [the King] did not know. He made him his
clown; so as to take away the land of Adelbriht he made his niece, the
daughter of a king, lie with [Cuaran] in a poor bed.

168   Now is it necessary that God help! For here has great cruelty been
done out of covetousness for this kingdom—when, in order to possess
the kingdom alone, he subjected his niece to his ambition. He gave her
to his scullion who had the name of Cuaran. [Cuaran] did not know
what a woman was nor what he should do with her; as soon as he came
to bed, he lay facedown and went to sleep. Argentille was in great
perplexity about why he lay facedown so and marveled greatly that he
never turned toward her nor wished to approach her as a man should
do with his wife. The niece complained to the King; she often cursed
her uncle who had disinherited her so and given her to such a man—
until it came to pass one night that they first took their pleasure. After
that they went to sleep; they loved and enjoyed each other very much.

193   In her sleep the daughter of the King dreamed that she was with
Cuaran, between the sea and a wood where a savage bear dwelt. Toward
the sea she saw come pigs and boars ready to attack this great bear,
which was very fierce—which wanted to eat Cuaran. With the bear
were many foxes—who were imperiled throughout the day because the
boars attacked them, and destroyed and killed many of them. When
those foxes were destroyed, this bear—which made great noise—a single
fierce and hardy boar alone assailed his body. He gave him a single
blow, such that in two pieces he cut the body. When the bear sensed
that he was done to death, he threw up a cry and then fell to the ground.
And the foxes came running from all sides toward Cuaran, their tails
between their legs, their heads bowed like kittens,[9] and made a show as
if to seek mercy from Cuaran on whom they had made war. When he
had made them all lie down, toward the sea he wished to repair. The
great trees which were of the wood bowed toward him on all sides. The
sea rose and the flood came, so that he could not keep to the wood.
The wood fell; the sea came; Cuaran was in great distress. After that

9. I.e., with caution.

came two lions; they fell to their knees—but they had killed many of the beasts who in the wood were in their way. Cuaran, for the fear he had, had climbed onto one of the great trees; and the lions came forward, kneeling before that tree.

235   Throughout the wood there was such a great cry that the lady roused herself; and because she had had this dream, she embraced her lord tightly. She found him lying on his back; between her arms she clasped him. For fear she opened her eyes; she saw a flame which issued from the mouth of her husband,[1] who was still fast asleep. She marveled at the vision, at the mouth of her lord and at the flame which she saw.

248   Now listen to what she said. "Sir," said she, "you burn! Wake yourself, if you would! From your mouth a flame issues—I know not who put it there!" She embraced him and drew him toward her, so that he awoke, and said, "Why have you wakened me, beautiful beloved? Why are you frightened? So he entreated her, so he blandished her to recount to him and reveal all concerning the flame and the vision concerning her lord which she had seen. Cuaran responded to her concerning the vision which she had had of him. According to his understanding he explained the dream (whatever he said, all of it was wrong!): "Lady," said he, "this will be fitting both to your use and mine. This is my opinion about what that may be: the King will hold a feast tomorrow. Many of his barons will be there; stags and roe deer and venison and much other meat will be left over there in the kitchen; so much will we take in abundance—I will make the squires wealthy with good sides of meat and roast meats from the dishes of the barons! The squires are devoted to me both night and day: that is what the foxes that you dreamed of signify—this is they. And the dead bear, it was killed yesterday, taken wild, in a wood. Two bulls there are for the lions; and for the sea, take the boiling-caldrons where the water rises like the sea until cooling makes it stop—the meat of the bulls will be cooked therein. Lady, the vision is explained!"

289   Argentille, when she heard this [said]: "Tell me further, sir, how that fire can be explained which I saw burning in your mouth." "Lady," said he, "I know not what it should be, but in sleeping it deceived me so. While I sleep my mouth catches fire; I sense nothing of the flame. Truly, I have great shame for it, that it happens to me in my sleep!"[2] Said Argentille, "Beloved, listen: we exist here shamefully—it were better we became exiles among strangers and the banished than dwell here in such shame. Beloved, where is your family?" "Lady," said he,

---

1. The *Lai* mentions the flame as part of its introductory account of Havelok and adds that the flame was accompanied by a pleasant odor (ll. 71–76).
2. At this point in the *Lai* (ll. 491 ff.), Argentille, assisted by a chamberlain, the next day seeks out a hermit who will explain the dream: he says that the dream indicates that Cuaran is of royal birth, that he and she will be king and queen, and that they both must go to Cuaran's country of birth to realize their destiny.

"at Grimsby; from there I departed when I came here. If I do not find my relatives there, I know not where I was born." "Beloved," said she, "then let us go there to know if we will ever find any there—who love me or you better or give us better counsel." Said Cuaran, "My own beloved, if it be wisdom or if it be folly, I will do what you wish; there will I take you, if you so advise." They lay all night until clear day. In the morning they went to their lord; to the King they came to take his leave. When he heard that, he was pleased; all smiles, he granted it them. To all his men he made fun of it, and said, "If they are just a little hungry, by tomorrow or the third day they will direct themselves to return when they can fare no better."

327   Then they take themselves to Grimsby. There they find a good friend who was a fisherman; there he dwelt. The daughter of Grim he had [as his wife]. When he recognized the three young men—Cuaran and the two sons of Grim[3]—and he knew of the daughter of the King (who was his better according to the law), he was very thoughtful in his heart. He said to his wife, who was very wise: "Lady," said he, "what will we do? If you so advise, we will reveal to Haveloc,[4] the son of the King, our counsel and the secret—let us tell him quite openly of whom he was born and of what people." Said the lady, "If he knew it—I think that he would reveal it in such a situation, through his own recklessness— soon great harm would come to him. He is certainly not so wise that he would know how to conceal his aspirations. If he knew that he was born of a king, for a brief time would it stay secret—and yet let us now call him, let us now ask of whom he was born; and if his wife comes with him, I think we can tell him of whom he was born and of what land, how he went into exile because of war."

357   With that they called Haveloc, and Argentille came with him. And the worthy man and his wife began intently to speak with them: "Friend," they say, "of whom were you born? In what place is your family?" "Lady," said he, "here I left my family when I departed. You are my sister; I am your brother by both mother and father. Grim was my father, a fisherman;[5] my mother, his wife, had the name of Sebruc.[6] When they were dead, I departed from here, took my two brothers with me. Now we are grown, we have returned; but we do not recognize our

---

3. I.e., Cuaran travels with the two servants usually in his charge—the true identity of whom the fisherman recognizes. (In *Havelok* Grim has an additional son, and all three are given names: see *Havelok* ll. 1397–98.)

4. Cuaran's true identity is thus revealed. (At this point it is worth noting that the name *Cuaran* probably recalls that of a true historical figure, Anlaf Cwaran, a Viking ruler of York and Northumbria, on separate occasions, during the first half of the tenth century; the name *Haveloc* can be shown, consequently, to be a linguistic descendant, via Welsh, Irish, and Icelandic intermediary equivalents, of the name *Anlaf*. Unfortunately, too few details about Anlaf Cwaran survive to enable one securely to draw further links between his life and the events of the *Haveloc* story.)

5. The *Lai* makes Grim a baron as well as a fisherman (l. 57).

6. Dame Leve in *Havelok*.

relatives—except only you and your lord. I know well you are our sister!" Kelloc[7] replied, "All that is otherwise! Never did your father sell salt, nor was your mother a salter; Grim sold salt, was a fisherman. For my brothers I owe you great rewards—I will repay you for having raised them. Yesterday, down at the port, arrived a good ship, large and strong; bread and meat and wine and wheat—such have they in very great plenty. Over the sea they will pass. If you would like to go with them, I think that they will go to the country where your supporters and family are. If you would like to go with them, we can hire them for you; we will give you cloth to offer in exchange; also, you will partake of our money, and bread, and meat, and good clear wine to take at night and in the morning. You will have provision, as much as you wish. You will take with you your two servants.

397   "But conceal well your secret: you were son to a good king. He had Denmark for his inheritance, as had his father and his lineage. Your father had the name of Gunter,[8] who took [as wife] the daughter of King Gaifer—Alvive was her name ('She kept me well; for as long as she lived she raised me'—so said my mother). I was the daughter of Grim, one of [the Queen's] companions. But this came to pass in your land: King Arthur came to conquer it for his tribute, which they withheld; with a very large army he came to the country. To King Gunter he seemed a threat; beside the sea he proffered him battle. King Gunter was killed there, and many knights on both sides; the land yielded whatever pleased Arthur. But, because of the war, the Queen could not remain in the country; so she fled, with the rightful heir—who I believe is you—Lord Haveloc, the son of the King. My father had a very good boat and took the Queen secretly. Toward this country he took her— when it came to pass, as it pleased God, that pirates attacked us. All were thrown into the sea, our knights and our people, and the Queen likewise. No man was saved there but my father, nor any woman but my mother. My father was known to them—for that they spared the children, and me and you and my two brothers, by the entreaties of my father.

435   "When we had arrived in this country[9] we cut our great boat in two—for it was smashed and damaged throughout when the Queen was killed. We made a house of our boat; with a [second] boat were we well provided for, in which our father went fishing. We had fish to eat— turbot, salmon and mullet, whale, porpoise, and mackerel. In great plenty and in abundance we had bread and good fish—the fish we exchanged for the bread (for men brought us plenty). And, when we had some money, my father became a salter. While he lived, he and

---

7. Gunnild in *Havelok*.
8. Birkabeyn in *Havelok*.
9. The *Lai* adds at the equivalent point (l. 132) that the place of landing was thence named Grimsby, after Grim.

my mother nurtured you well—better than my brother. And I stayed and took a husband; he has kept me with great honor. He is a merchant; he knows how to cross the sea and he knows well how to buy and sell. He was in Denmark the other day and heard many plead that if any man found you, you should come and challenge [possession of] the country. We well advise you to return there; take with you your two servants to be with you so as to serve you. If all goes well for you, send for us; we will follow you, if you wish—if God restores to you your inheritance."

467   Said Haveloc and his wife, "We will give to you a very good reward—we will give you more than you desire—if God restores to us our inheritance. And we will take the servants with us. Know that we will cross for God!" The lady responded, "Truly, here shall you stay until you have a wind—and, if I can see to it before you cross, in better clothes you will be dressed." They remained then, waiting; they were clothed with great honor. They waited until a breeze came; and then they had entered into the boat—and master Algiers, the merchant, made the deal for them. He and Kelloc gave the clothes for Haveloc's retinue and he put away for them ample victuals (he would not have them fail for as long as a month; he put in the boat for them bread and wine and meat and fish in great abundance). And forthwith the boat was afloat; the steersman conducted himself well. There were two boats, in fact; they set their sails against the wind.

493   So far have they been rowed and guided that they are arrived in Denmark. In the region where they arrived, they went to a town; there they sought packhorses and carts and had their effects brought there. The merchants were all returned with their gear back to the two boats, and Haveloc and his wife went to the town to take lodgings. A powerful man dwelt there who had the name of Sigar Estalre;[1] he had been a seneschal to King Gunter and justiciar of his land. But now was it so that he kept his own peace and had developed a hatred for the [current] king—who then was a powerful king over the people of this country—on account of his lord whom he had had killed (through the power of Arthur the strong, who, by treason, he had empowered and who had won for him this country). Because he was a traitor and cruel, others had taken the counsel never to hold with him or take land from him, until they knew of the rightful heir, of the truth about his life or death. This King who then was in the country (he was brother to King Aschis who for Arthur suffered death there where Mordred did him great wrong)[2] had the name of Odulf the King;[3] much was he hated by his Danes.

---

1. Ubbe in *Havelok*.
2. A reference to Arthur's final battle against Mordred, at which, according to the great Arthurian chronicler Geoffrey of Monmouth, the Danish king Aschil(lus) was one of Arthur's allies.
3. Godard in *Havelok*.

527   As God and destiny would have it, God placed Haveloc in [Sigar's] care. Because of his wife (Lady Argentille, daughter of the King) who was so beautiful, six young men then assailed him. They took his beloved, they beat him, and injured his servants—in many places bruised their heads. As they went off with his beloved, Lord Haveloc was enraged. He took up a very sharp ax which he found hanging in the house. He caught them in the road as they took away Lady Argentille: he killed three, mortally wounded two, and cut off the hand of the sixth. He took up his wife and went to their lodging—[but] behold the [public] outcry of foul play! He took his servants and his wife and so fled into a church; he closed the doors for fear. Then they ascended into the tower. There he had such a defensible position that he would never be taken without great travail—indeed they defended themselves so well that they wounded all those who attacked. When master Sigar came riding there he saw how Lord Haveloc, who was very strong, went on throwing stones—[and] he had [already] killed the five brigands! Sigar saw this and reflected; he was reminded of King Gunter. As soon as he had recognized Haveloc, he no longer hated him for the sake of his [dead and injured] men; he resembled his [old] lord so much that when he saw him he had such pity that he could speak only with great pain. He had the assault fully stopped, promised peace and truce to him, and led them to his hall—Haveloc and his wife and his companions (the two servants mentioned before); and when they were safe, this powerful man asked who he was and what his name was and who his companions were. And concerning the lady he asked him whence she came and who gave her to him [in marriage].

575   "Sir," said he, "I know not who I am—I believe I was born in this country; a mariner who had the name of Grim took me away as a little boy. He made for Lindsey; when we were making way on the high sea, we were assailed by pirates by whom I was badly treated. My mother was there; she was slain. I was spared—I know not in what manner— and the good man escaped, who then raised me and loved me very much. He and his wife raised me, loved me very much, and cherished me. When they were dead, I left; I served a king where I went, and two young men were with me all the time I was with that king. For some time I was with him in my youth—and this lady was of his kindred; as it pleased him, he gave her to me and together we were married. Then I came to this country; I know none of my supporters, nor do I know if in fact I have a single relative here. But, according to the report of a merchant—he is living at Grimsby, a very good man who has the name of Algier—he and his wife advised me to come here, to search for my supporters and relatives in this land. But I cannot name one of them, and I do not know if I can find them." The worthy man said, "What is your name?" "Sir, I do not know," (so he responded to him), "but when I was at the great court they called me Cuaran—and, though I

was a servant, I now know well that I have the name of Haveloc; when I was at Grimsby the other day, Algier called me Haveloc. Now I am here, by which of these two names will you call me?"

619   Sigar stood and listened; he remembered the son of the King by this name of which he spoke—the son of Gunter had that name. Then he was reminded of another means of identification which he long ago learned from the [boy's] nurse, concerning the flame which issued from his mouth when he was sleeping. That night he had him very closely watched, there where he lay with his wife. Because [Haveloc] was greatly tired from the battle and from the anxiety which before he had had in the day, he went to sleep without taking leave of anyone. As soon as he slept, the flame issued from his mouth—and the servants who had observed that quickly related it to their master; and the worthy man rose out of bed. When he went there, he saw the flame. Then he knew well that what he had suspected about him was true—but that knowledge was then so precious to him that he would never tell [even] his wife, until the next day when he rose. Then he sent for his men; he called for his knights, for spearmen, and for foot soldiers. Many came from all parts. After he had assembled many of them, he then went to speak with Haveloc. He had him bathed and provided for; in new clothes he had him dressed. He had him come into the hall.

653   When he had entered into the hall, where he saw so many men assembled, he had great fear that this group would make a bad judgment for him—he thought they had assembled on account of the five men he had killed. He wanted to make for an ax which a young man held there; he wanted to seize it to defend himself. Sigar saw that and had him taken. As they held him, from all sides, Sigar said to him, "Do not be afraid, do not be defensive, my friend. Fully I assure you—I promise you—that now I love you more than I ever did yesterday when I sat you at my dinner." Then he seated him beside him and had the Horn of the King brought; this was the horn of King Gunter. Under the skies there had been no knight who could ever sound that horn— not hunter, not young man—such that no one ever heard the horn blown, unless the King or rightful heir did so. Truly, the rightful heir of Denmark could blow the horn well, but another man could never blow it; any other man tried for nought.

681   Sigar had guarded this horn; King Gunter had entrusted it to him. When he took it, he could not sound it; he had it presented to a knight, and said to him, all [the while] laughing, "He who sounds it, he who knows how to blow the horn, I will give him a good ring, which, if needs be, is worth a castle. He who has it on his finger, if he fall in the sea, will not drown; nor can fire damage him at all, nor can any weapon wound him—such as I tell you is the ring." Then the company, the knights and the men-at-arms, came to blow the horn. It would not sound at any time for anyone; for none of them would it ever sound.

698   Then they handed it to the young man—whom they called "the
prisoner"—who had the name of Haveloc. When he took it, he looked
at it and said that he had never blown a horn. To the lord he said, "I
will leave it be. Since no other man can blow the horn, I withdraw
from any claim to your ring; I do not wish to offend the company."
Responded Sigar, "Do it you will! Put it to your mouth." "Sir," said
he, "I do not refuse you that; now will it be tried by me." Then he took
up the horn, made the sign of the cross over it, and tried it at his mouth.
As soon as it touched his mouth the horn sounded so superbly that no
one had ever heard its equal; no man could blow a horn so well! Sigar
heard it, jumped to his feet, and embraced him in his arms. Then he
cried, "God be praised! Now have I found my rightful lord, now I have
him whom I have desired—for whom I will wage war. This is the rightful
heir and the person who must wear the crown of gold!"

725   He then summoned all his men who forthwith swore fealty to Haveloc;
[Sigar] himself kneeled and vowed to hold with him. Then he sent for
his barons with whom the King [(Odulf)] had had disputes; they then
became [Haveloc's] men and received him as their lord. When they had
done that, they assembled forces; in four days they had many hundreds,
and, on the fifth day, of knights they had fully thirty thousand. They
then challenged King Odulf; and on a level field they met. Many great
blows were wrought; King Odulf was then vanquished—indeed Havelok
conducted himself so that he alone slew more than twenty! Two princes
of the country[4] were there who had been his enemies, who had held
with Odulf; now they came to [seek] Haveloc's mercy. The common
people of the country came likewise to [seek] his mercy; and Haveloc
gave them pardons by the counsel of his barons. All of them pledged
fidelity to him; the knights of that realm and the worthy men and the
burgesses made him their lord and king. They made great festivity and
great rejoicing, as the true history tells us.

757   After that he summoned his entire fleet and all the forces of his realm;
and his great host crossed the sea. Then he challenged King Edelsi. To
him he declared that he defied him unless he handed over to him the
rightful inheritance of his beloved. And Edelsi replied to him that he
would fight against him. They fought in a field from morning until
evening. There were many men wounded and killed on both sides, until
black night separated them, until the next day dawned. But, by counsel
of the Queen, who disclosed a remedy to make good their misfortune
and the battle, he won his realm without [further] great harm. All night
he had stakes erected, taller and greater than large staffs; they stood the
dead men up and through the night set them thereupon. They so assembled two divisions of them, who truly appeared as if they were alive
and eager for battle—they [who] the day before had been killed! For

---

4. The Earl of Chester and Earl Gunter in *Havelok*.

men who regarded them from a distance, all their flesh crept; both from a distance and from up close hideous seemed the unconfessed dead. The next day they prepared themselves, very much determined to fight. And the enemy scouts went ahead to see the valiant "Lord Cuaran." When they saw the resources he had there, all their flesh crept; for, against one man that they had, they saw seven on the other side! Back they went to declare to the King that it was no use fighting, to give to the lady her rightful inheritance, and to make peace before things got worse. The King could not proceed otherwise. Thus was it necessary for him to concede—for so had the barons advised him.

803 He caused to be handed over to [Haveloc] all the kingdom from Holland to Colchester. There King Haveloc held his festivities, [and] received the homage of his barons from throughout his territories. King Edelsi lived little more than fifteen days after. He had no heir with rightful claims such as Haveloc and his wife; he had children, but they were dead. The barons fully granted that Haveloc and his beloved should have the land of King Edelsi. Once he had it so, he was King for twenty years and with the Danes obtained much by conquest.   [816]

* * *

Ywain and Gawain[1]

Chrétien de Troyes

Ywain and Gawain is an abbreviated fourteenth-century translation of the Old French *Yvain*,[2] written c. 1177 by Chrétien de Troyes. Chrétien produced five Arthurian romances; beside *Yvain* survive *Erec and Enide*, *Cligés*, *Lancelot*, and *Perceval* (he may have written others, and he tells us in *Cligés* that he had translated works attributed to the Roman poet Ovid, but none of these survive). He was in many ways the founder of a new mode of poetry, one which reflected the values of a new kind of courtly society (and we know that he worked for aristocratic patrons). As Erich Auerbach notes at the beginning of his essay on *Yvain* (included in this volume, pp. 411–27), less than a century separates Chrétien's poem from the heroic *Chanson de Roland*,[3] and yet the poems seem worlds apart. The *Chanson* conceives a

1. Editions and translations of the texts mentioned in this headnote, as well as references to related scholarship, are cited in the Selected Bibliography. For further remarks on the date of the poem and its manuscript, see the leading footnote to the edition proper.
2. Also known as *Li Chevalier au Lion* ("The Knight with the Lion").
3. About which, and the genre of *chanson de geste* of which it is the best example, see also the Sources and Backgrounds headnote to *The Sege off Melayne*, p. 388.

severe, even brutal (though historically plausible) warrior society in which tension between a warrior's need both to maintain personal pride and to sustain certain public (indeed feudal) loyalties to God and King is resolved only in a tragic, albeit glorious, self-destruction. Chrétien's poetry, on the other hand, conceives the unlikely (often supernaturally destined) adventures of a lone knight whose values are conditioned by a devotion to high courtesy, to the service of women (especially to women who are the objects of an unrequited, much-psychologized love), and to a personal spiritual growth. With the latter comes the admission of initial unworthiness; it is an admission which, like the other preoccupations described, is at best peripheral to the ethos of the *Chanson*. Additionally, Chrétien's Arthurian setting liberates the experience of the knight from the constraints of a historical plausibility like that evinced by the *Chanson*—for that is a poem which, however apocryphally, does look back to the deeds of a genuinely historical king who really did fight wars against various non-Christian peoples.

Arthurian Literature before Chrétien: Chronicle and Celtic Traditions

Novel though Chrétien's use of this setting may have been, the setting itself was adopted from what even at the time was an ancient and diverse body of Arthurian lore. If a real "King" Arthur ever existed, he may have been a sixth-century (post-Roman) warlord, a Briton (a member of the Celtic peoples from whom the Bretons, Cornish, Irish, Welsh and Scots are descended), who enjoyed some success in battles against invading forces of Angles and Saxons (whence the Anglo-Saxons descend). There are some records dating from the sixth and seventh centuries which identify a few British rulers and one Irish ruler named Arthur; it seems likely that legendary accounts of their namesake were already in wide circulation.[4] Arthur is first named in a historical source of about the year 800, the *Historia Brittonum* ("History of the Britons," usually attributed to the Welsh monk Nennius). But even at this relatively early date Arthur's record is invested with fantasy; Nennius appends to his history accounts of local marvels, one of which describes a stone bearing the paw print of Arthur's dog Cabal, the print having been set during Arthur's hunt for a boar named Troit. The supernatural conception of the boar seems to be confirmed in the twelfth-century Welsh *Culhwch and Olwen*, which describes the hunt by Arthur and his men for Twrch Trwyth, an evil king who had been transformed into a boar. That the later Welsh tale echoes the story in Nennius implies the probability that some form of the tale led a folkloric existence much earlier.

Scholars frequently invoke Celtic "influences," and "traditions" to account for the sources of the often seemingly unmotivated marvels which perhaps more than anything else sustain the evocative appeal of Arthurian literature. The terms can seem nebulous, but it is often difficult to be more precise in isolating sources; Celtic tradition has always favored the oral/ memorial transmission of tales, and so the vast majority of attested written Celtic material is preserved as folktales recorded in relatively modern times, and the earliest of all records appear only in late medieval Irish and Welsh

4. The name itself appears to be a Welsh form of the Roman name Artorius.

manuscripts. Many so-called sources may thus document only the end of a chain of manifold oral adaptations of numinous myths and legends dating from the virtually prehistoric heyday of the Celtic peoples. Archaeology can provide some evidence to verify the authenticity of such records—by, for example, discovering the ceremonial uses to which certain sites may have been put, or in distinguishing iconographic trends represented by various artifacts (boars, for instance, are ubiquitous, appearing not only in the surviving artwork but also as remains of the real thing, found in ceremonial interments, sometimes alongside human remains; the real beast is quite ferocious and would have been considered a worthy measure of prowess in the killing). Some investigative headway can also be made by cross-reference between surviving analogous tales and names. It is possible, for instance, to identify Twrch Trwyth with Torc-Triath (or Orc-Triath), the destructive King of the Boars of Irish legend, and by so doing to catch another glimpse of what once was a religion incorporating certain wilderness spirits.

In the same way Arthur's famous Grail quest—and, of more immediate interest, the magical spring and its guardian in *Yvain*—can be linked with ancient fertility myths in which the well-being of a realm is inextricably tied to its ruler's health or his ability to procure or sustain a life-giving source. Such figures as the fairy mistresses of the romances, the dwarves, giants, water fays, and other fabulous beings, the magical tokens and locations of mysterious power, the self-referential notes of admiration for lyric (whence poetic) power, all can be identified with a Celtic culture. To that culture such things must have had a figural role in that attempt to make sense of existence which is the essence of myth. The proposition of Celtic sources is all the more reliable when such elements are found in combination; but it is important to remember that even for texts of a demonstrably Celtic orientation, fabulous elements can have other ancient sources: the classical basis of *Sir Orfeo* is an obvious case in point;[5] Chrétien's sportive irony owes much to the influence of Ovid; and Yvain's Lion must owe something to the classical fable of Androcles and the Lion. It should go without saying, moreover, that the dominant Judeo-Christian tradition of the Western Middle Ages itself admits of supernatural agencies. An interesting twist on such circumstances, however, is that, given the evidence for the existence of a distinctively Celtic culture at least as far back as the fifth century B.C., it is not impossible that even classical sources could have Celtic antecedents.[6]

Arthur's legendary status as a member of a Celtic people no doubt played a part in the coming-of-age of Arthurian legend which began in Britain in the first half of the twelfth century. The works of Geoffrey of Monmouth[7] and Robert Wace[8] in particular enjoyed considerable popularity among the educated and aristocratic classes which were dominated by descendants of the Normans, who had conquered the native Anglo-Saxon peoples a century

5. See the Sources and Backgrounds headnote, pp. 345 ff.
6. Again, see the Sources and Backgrounds headnote to *Sir Orfeo*.
7. We know little about him, but it is evident that by 1129 he was a cleric who probably taught at pre-university Oxford; in 1151 he was consecrated bishop of the see of St. Asaph in Wales. He died c. 1154.
8. Wace was born c. 1110 on the island of Jersey, a Norman possession. Like Chrétien, he appears to have been a professional writer all his life and enjoyed aristocratic patronage. He probably died sometime soon after 1174.

before. Geoffrey's *Historia Regum Brittaniæ* ("History of the Kings of Britain," written c. 1137) elevates Arthur to the status of a world leader. It tells, among other things, of Arthur's successful conquest of Gaul, his aborted campaign against the Roman emperor Lucius, his subsequent devastating battle against his usurping son Mordred, and his final repair to the Island of Avalon. It also brings to prominence the remarkable figure of Merlin the Magician and lays stress on the verity of his prophecies concerning Arthur's reign. Twenty years later Wace introduced an Anglo-Norman (French) version of the *Historia*, the *Roman de Brut* (finished in 1155), the first text to mention the Round Table, and the first to "modernize" the Arthurian court—to see it as an exemplary institution moderated by a devotion to chivalry and courtesy. Such innovations as both writers introduced, however, remained subordinate to the historical and heroic attitude toward their matter; the chivalric romance did not, of course, rise to prominence until the second half of the century, with Chrétien in France.

Chrétien's work presupposes a knowledge of Geoffrey and Wace, and Wace was an especially important influence; but Chrétien's most inspiring sources appear in the main to have been Celtic, and must naturally have appealed more to his fondness for imaginative intricacies. In the case of *Yvain*, a thirteenth-century Welsh poem, *Owein* (also known as *Iarlles y Ffynnawn*, "The Lady of the Fountain") tells fundamentally the same story as that of *Yvain*, and yet the Welsh text appears not to be extensively indebted to Chrétien, thereby suggesting the existence of an older common source for both French and Welsh texts. Chrétien's immediate sources may have been in the form of Breton stories translated into French (they may have been like the lyrical Breton poems which Chrétien's influential contemporary Marie de France acknowledges as sources for her "Lais"—among them *Lanval*, the nominal source of *Sir Launfal*).[9] Most famous of Chrétien's putative Celtic influences is the Grail story, which he introduced to Arthurian legend in his *Perceval*.

Ywain and Gawain and *Yvain*

Ywain and Gawain is the only surviving Middle English translation of a romance by Chrétien; unlikely as this may seem, given Chrétien's obvious importance, one must bear in mind that romances were not as a matter of course being translated into English (much less independently composed) until the second half of the thirteenth century. During that time some areas of Arthurian literature developed according to certain trends. The Grail quest had, for instance, been Christianized. In Chrétien it was simply "a grail," Perceval's informed knowledge of which would restore the health of the maimed Fisher King and his realm; in later texts it becomes the cup used by Christ at the Last Supper, the "Holy Grail," the achievement of which promises the transcendence of essential Christian mysteries. Another trend developed where knights such as Lancelot, Perceval, and Tristan attracted their own following in romances dedicated to celebrating their exploits; Gawain, known for his courtesy (and flirtatiousness), enjoyed particular favor in romances written

9. See the Sources and Backgrounds headnote, p. 351.

in English, as attested by the survival of many different texts featuring him.[1]

In Britain, moreover, romancers were typically less interested in the kinds of elaborate psychologizing—especially in matters amorous— which often captivated their continental precursors; their work also seems more consistently to have retained the kind of heroic gravity germane to the earlier historical treatments of Arthur. Such distinctions exist even in *Ywain and Gawain*, despite the eminent authority of the source, their disposition evident from the outset. Where, for instance, Chrétien notes at the beginning of his poem that Calogrenant tells a story "not to his honor but to his shame," Colgrevance in the ME text tells, without notice of self-incrimination, simply "of a chance / And of a stowre he had in bene" (ll. 60–61; Chrétien's introduction is quoted at the beginning of Erich Auerbach's essay). And, earlier, where Chrétien laments the abandonment of love, the ME text laments more the abandonment of "trowth" (ll. 35–40). For the English poet, "trowth" encompasses a range of virtues, from loyalty and honesty, to, as the introductory passage stresses, the keeping of real truth ("trew trowth"), the maintenance of an unshifting interdependence of word and deed. It is an emphasis on such virtues which distinguishes the meaning of the ME translation throughout. Chrétien revels in ironic explorations of the fragile paradoxes generated by the finest love (usually in its relation to the severe knightly contests which afford its privileged courtly existence) and bears often ironic witness to the interior process toward true self-lessness of a chivalric lover; by contrast, the English poet concentrates on the import of keeping agreements—honoring oaths and scriptural edicts, obeying laws—and bears ingenuous witness to the exterior deeds which mark a process toward the selfless "trowth" of, instead, a lover of chivalry.

The selections from *Yvain* printed below will give an impression of such differences. They will also give some idea of how close the ME translation can be—although a disadvantage to the necessary economy of providing only selections is that subtle affinities do tend to be under-represented in the interest of illustrating differences. Nevertheless, the selections reveal that *Ywain and Gawain* should be credited, for instance, with abstracting something of the exigence of Chrétien's dialogues—an accomplishment evident in Kay's mocking tirades (e.g., ll. 71–124, 466–82, 1271–80; like the other examples cited below, these must be taken as an invitation to examine the whole of Chrétien's poem), in Lunet's sardonically pragmatic observations (e.g., ll. 927–30, 975–76, 990–92, 1136–47) and in her sometimes deliberately melodramatic entreaties (e.g., ll. 3855–98); note also the giant herdsman's surprised and skeptical intonations (ll. 279–348). To the translation's further credit are its sometimes imaginative, sometimes reverential, adaptations of Chrétien's figurative expressions (e.g., ll. 97–98, 143–48, 2681–82). It is ultimately the alliance of such Chrétienesque touches with a thematic plan decisively different from that of Chrétien which secures the poem's place among the better ME romances.

1. See the Sources and Backgrounds headnote to *The Awntyrs off Arthure*, p. 365.

CHRÉTIEN DE TROYES

From Yvain†

[1]
[*Yvain stricken by love*]
[*cf. Ywain and Gawain*, 11.869–908]

[Yvain] is perturbed to see them burying the corpse when he can get nothing as evidence that he overcame and slew him and which he would be able to display openly. If he has no conclusive evidence, then he is utterly shamed. Kay is so extremely malicious and spiteful, so full of mockery and abuse that he would never be left in peace by him: he would always go on insulting him and hurling taunts and mockery at him as he did the other day. Those taunts are still fresh and rankling in his heart. But new-found Love, with his sugar and honeycomb, has brought him fresh sweetness, having hunted through his lands and fastened on his prey. His heart is carried away by her who is his enemy, and he loves the person who most hates him.[1] The lady, without knowing it, has fully avenged her husband's death. For it she has taken a greater revenge than she would have found possible had not Love avenged her by attacking him so gently and, through his eyes, striking him to the heart.

1369   The effect of this thrust lasts longer than that of one from any lance or sword. A sword-blow is cured and heals very quickly once a doctor attends to it: Love's wound, though, grows worse the nearer it is to its doctor. My lord Yvain's wound is such that he will never recover from it, for Love has dedicated himself entirely to him. Love goes round examining the places he used to frequent and then abandons them, unwilling to have any lodging or host but this one; and he acts worthily in withdrawing from a poor place in order to devote himself entirely to Yvain. Not wishing any part of himself to remain elsewhere, he scours all the mean lodging-places. It is disgraceful that Love's way is at times to behave so badly as to take shelter in the basest place he finds just as readily as in the very best of all. But now he is well off: here he will be treated honourably and find it good to stay. Such is the proper behaviour

---

† The selections are taken from Chrétien de Troyes, *Arthurian Romances*, translated by D.D.R. Owen, reproduced from the Everyman's Library edition. © David Campbell Publishers Ltd. (In addition to these selections, Owen's translation of the introductory passages of *Yvain* is reprinted at the beginning of the essay by Erich Auerbach, *Criticism*, pp. 411 ff. —*Editor*.)

1. Chrétien's fondness of this kind of paradox is one example among many of an essentially intellectual attitude to the predicaments of his characters. In *Yvain* this raises the question of how seriously he treated the love theme and whether we are entitled to see in it the main interest of the romance. Nevertheless, in the following scenes he does his best to make Laudine's sudden remarriage psychologically plausible within the limits allowed by his source-story. His development of the role of Lunete is especially skilful: she has much of the character of the soubrettes of later theatrical tradition* * * *

for Love, who is such a noble being that it is amazing how he dares to incur the shame of falling as low as he does. He is like a man who spreads his balm in ashes and dust, hating honour and preferring blame, blending sugar with gall and mixing soot with honey. Now, however, Love has not acted like that, but has instead lodged in a noble place, for which he is beyond reproach.

1406   When the dead man had been buried, all the people went away. There remained behind no cleric, knight, servant or lady other than the one who makes no secret of her grief. She, however, stays there quite alone, often clutching at her throat, wringing her hands and slapping her palms, and reading her psalms from a psalter illuminated with gold lettering. My lord Yvain is still at the window gazing at her; and the longer he observes her, the more he loves and is attracted by her. He would have liked her to stop weeping and reading and wished he might have the opportunity of speaking to her. Love, who has caught him at the window, has filled him with this desire; but he despairs of having what he wishes, for he cannot suppose or believe that what he wants can come about.

1428   He says: "I may well think myself stupid to want what I shall never have. Having mortally wounded her husband, do I think I can be reconciled with her? That's no sensible idea, I swear, for at this moment she hates me more than any living thing, and justly so.—I was right to say 'at this moment', because a woman has more than a thousand fancies. Perhaps she will change again from her present frame of mind: or rather she will change it, with no 'perhaps', so I'm foolish to despair of it. God grant she change before long! I must be in her power for ever more, since Love wishes it. Anyone who doesn't make Love welcome when he seeks his company commits a crime and treason; and I declare to any who is prepared to hear that such a person deserves neither success nor happiness. But I'll not be a loser on that account, though instead I'll be loving my enemy; for I shouldn't hate her unless I want to betray Love. I should love whatever Love wishes. And should she call me her lover? Yes indeed, because I do love her. And I call her my enemy as she hates me, and rightly, since I slew the object of her love. Am I her enemy for that reason? Certainly not—rather her friend, for I was never set on loving anyone so much.

1462   "I am much grieved for her hair, which surpasses gold, so very brightly does it shine; and to see her tear and cut it racks and torments me with grief. And the tears that fall from her eyes can never be dried. All this is repugnant to me. Despite their being full of tears that flow on without ceasing, there never existed such lovely eyes. I'm grieved to see her weep, and nothing distresses me as much as the way she wounds her face, for it couldn't have deserved such treatment. Never have I seen one so shapely or so freshly complexioned. It has hurt me very deeply too to watch her clutching at her throat. Indeed she can't keep from doing herself the greatest harm in her power; yet no crystal or mirror is so bright or smooth. God! Why does she commit such great folly, and why does she not do herself less injury? Why does she wring her lovely hands and beat and tear her breast? For would it not be truly wonderful to look at her if she were happy, when she is now so lovely in her grief? Yes indeed, I can certainly vouch for that. Never before has Nature succeeded in achieving such an extreme of beauty, for here she has doubtless passed the bounds of all her previous work. How, then, could this have come about? Where might such great beauty have come from? God surely made her with His bare hand in order to astound Nature. Should she wish to make a copy of her, she might spend all her time without ever being able to achieve it. Not even God, I think, if He might want to attempt it, could ever manage to create another like her, however hard He might try."

1507   Thus my lord Yvain represents to himself the lady who is torturing herself with grief. And I do not believe it could ever happen again that any man who was imprisoned (as is my lord Yvain, and fearing for his head) would be so madly in love with someone to whom he will never himself make an approach nor, in all likelihood, have another do so for him. There at the window he stood until he saw the lady go away again and both the portcullises had been lowered. Anybody else would have been distressed at this, preferring escape to continued imprisonment: to him it makes no difference whether they are closed or opened. He would certainly not go away were they opened for him, even if the lady gave him leave and freely pardoned him the death of her husband so that he might depart in safety. For he is held back by Love and Shame, who confront him on either hand. If he goes away, it is to his shame, for no one would ever believe he had acquitted himself to such effect; and on the other hand, he has such longing at least to see the beautiful lady, even if she may afford him nothing else, that he is not worried by his imprisonment and would rather die than go away.

[2]
[Gawain and Lunete]
[cf. Ywain and Gawain, 11.1427–34]

2388   I shall say nothing of [Laudine's] warm welcome to the others; but I have never heard of any people so warmly greeted, so honoured or well served. I could tell you much of that joy, except that I should be wasting my words. But I would just like to make a brief mention of the friendship that was struck up in private between the moon and the sun. Do you know of whom I want to tell you? The man who was chief of the knights and honoured above them all should indeed be called the sun. I refer to my lord Gawain, for chivalry gains lustre from him just as in the morning the sun casts its rays and lights up all the places where it shines. And by the moon I mean she who is uniquely endowed with good sense and courtly ways. Yet I say this not only because of her good reputation, but because her name is Lunete.

2415   The damsel's name was Lunete, and she was a charming brunette, very sensible, shrewd and intelligent. She develops a friendship with my lord Gawain, who gains a high opinion of her and loves her well; so he calls her his sweetheart, since she had saved his companion and friend from death, and is generous with his offers of service.[2] And she tells him and describes how difficult it had been to persuade her mistress to take my lord Yvain as her husband, and how she kept him out of the hands of the people who were looking for him, when they could not see him despite his being in their midst. My lord Gawain laughed heartily at her story and said: "My young lady, I place at your disposal such a knight as I am when you need me and when you don't. Never exchange me for anyone else, unless you believe you'll be better off. I am yours, and you be my own damsel from now on!"—"I thank you, sir," says she. That is how these two formed their relationship.

[3]
[Yvain's failure]
[cf. Ywain and Gawain, ll.1567–1656]

2672   Meanwhile the year passes; and throughout it my lord Yvain did so well that my lord Gawain was at great pains to honour him, and so kept him back so long that the whole year had passed together with a good part of the next until mid-August came round, when the king held court at Chester. The previous evening they had returned from a tournament where my lord Yvain had been and had carried off all the honour. And the story as I know it says that the two companions were unwilling to lodge together in the town, but had their tents erected outside it and

2. Gawain here shows, perhaps for the first time in Chrétien (though see *Lancelot*, ll. 548 ff.), that flirtatious streak which was to be developed in the second part of the *Conte du Graal* and led in later literature to a deterioration in his reputation.

held court there, not once coming to the king's court, but the king coming to theirs; for the majority, and the best, of the knights were with them. King Arthur was sitting among them, when there occurred to Yvain a thought which took him more aback than any he had had since the moment he took leave of his lady; for he realised he had broken his pledge to her and that the time-limit had passed. He had great difficulty in holding back his tears, but shame forced him to do so. He remained deep in thought until he saw a damsel coming straight towards them at a very fast amble on a black palfrey with white feet. In front of the tent she dismounts, without anyone helping her down or going to take her horse.

2711   As soon as she spotted the king she let her mantle fall and, entering the tent uncloaked, went right up to him. She said that her lady sends greetings to the king and my lord Gawain and all the others except my lord Yvain, the disloyal traitor, liar and deceiver, who has abandoned and duped her. "She has quite seen through his lying talk, pretending as he did to be a true lover, though he is a false, treacherous thief. This thief has betrayed my lady, who suspected no wrong and had not the slightest idea he would steal her heart. Those who truly love don't steal hearts away, though they are called thieves by some who go about practising deceit in love without knowing anything at all about it. The lover takes his beloved's heart in a way that is not theft: rather he guards it from being stolen from her by thieves in the guise of honest men. These are hypocritical thieves and traitors, competing in the theft of hearts to which they are indifferent; but the lover, wherever he may go, treasures the heart and brings it back again.

2742   "Yvain, though, has dealt my lady a mortal blow, for she believed he would keep her heart for her and, before the year was out, return it to her. Yvain, you were indeed highly forgetful to fail to remember that you were to return to my lady within a year. She permitted you to be away until the festival of Saint John, and you held her in such scorn that after that you never thought of her again. In her room my lady has marked out every single day and all the seasons; for a person in love is ill at ease and never able to sleep soundly, but all night long counts up and reckons the days as they come and go. Do you know how lovers behave? They keep account of the time and season. Her complaint has not been premature or made without reason. And, without making a formal accusation, I maintain that the person who married you to my lady has betrayed us. Yvain, my lady has no further concern for you, but instructs you through me never to return to her and not to keep her ring any longer. She demands through me whom you see here present that you send it to her. Hand it over, for you're obliged to return it to her!"

2774   Yvain cannot reply to her, having lost his senses and power of speech. The damsel jumps forward and pulls the ring off his finger, then com-

mends to God the king and all the others except him, whom she leaves
in great distress. And his distress continually increases: everything he
hears afflicts him, and all he sees grieves him. He would have wished
to take flight, quite alone, in a land so wild that nobody would know
where to look for him, and where there was no man or woman or
anybody knowing anything more of him than if he were in the pit of
Hell. He hates nothing so much as himself and does not know to whom
to turn for comfort now he has caused his own death; but he would
rather go out of his wits than fail to take vengeance on himself now he
has robbed himself of his own joy. He leaves the company of the nobles,
fearing to go out of his mind in their midst; and they did not notice
this, but let him go off alone. They are well aware that he does not care
about their conversation or their doings.

2802   He went away until he was far from the tents and pavilions. Then
his head is assailed by so wild a delirium that he loses his senses,
whereupon he tears and rends his clothes and goes fleeing across fields
and ploughed land, leaving his men at a loss, wondering where he can
be. They go looking for him throughout the whole neighbourhood, in
the knights' lodgings, under hedges and in gardens, seeking him where
he is not to be found. He continued his rapid flight until, near a park,
he came across a serving-lad holding a bow and five barbed arrows, very
sharp and broad. He had enough sense to go up to this lad and take the
bow and arrows he was holding, without, however, remembering anything he had done. He lies in wait for the animals in the woods, kills
them, and then eats the game quite raw.

[4]
[Yvain and the lion happen upon the magic spring]
[cf. Ywain and Gawain, ll. 2059–2102]

3485   In the morning they set off again together; and the two of them, it
seems, led the same kind of existence as that night for the best part of
the week, until chance led them to the spring beneath the pinetree.
There my lord Yvain almost went out of his mind a second time once
he had come up to the spring and its slab and chapel.[3] A thousand times
he calls "Alas!", voicing his grief, then falls in a swoon, such is his
anguish. His sword slips from its scabbard, and its point passes through
the links of his hauberk and into his neck close to the cheek. There is
not a link that does not open, and the sword cuts the flesh of his neck
under the bright mail, making the blood run down.

3506   The lion thinks it sees its companion and master dead. Never have
you heard told or described greater grief over anything than it began to
display over this! It writhes about, scratches itself and cries and wants

---

3. This scene contains an amusing parody of the lovers' suicides in the story of Pyramus and
Thisbe, probably known to Chrétien in an Old French version* * * *

to kill itself with the sword which it supposes to have slain its good master. It pulls the sword from him with its teeth, props it up against a fallen log, and wedges it against a treetrunk behind so that it will not slip or give way when it strikes its breast against it. Its intention was about to be realised when the knight came out of his swoon; and the lion, which was rushing full tilt to its death like an enraged boar that dashes on without heeding where, held itself back.

3526   Thus my lord Yvain swoons beside the slab. When he comes to, he reproaches himself bitterly for having overstayed the year and so incurred his lady's hatred. He says: "Why should he not kill himself, this wretch who has deprived himself of joy? What am I doing in my misery not to take my own life? How can I stay here and see my lady's possessions? Why does my soul linger in my body? What is a soul doing in so miserable a breast? Had it left it, it would not be in such torment. Truly I should hate and blame and despise myself greatly, as indeed I do. Someone who loses joy and contentment through his own misdeed and fault should have a quite mortal hatred of himself. He should hate and kill himself. And why do I, while no one is watching me, spare myself from ending my own life? Have I not, then, seen this lion suffering such great grief on my account that it was quite determined to impale itself through the breast on my sword? Should I, then, fear death, having turned my joy to grief? Joy has abandoned me.—Joy? What joy? I shall speak no more of it, for no one could tell of it, and I have asked a quite futile question. The one that was vouchsafed me was the most joyful of all joys; but it lasted far too briefly for me. And anyone who loses that through his own fault has no right to enjoy good fortune."

[5]
["You hold the key"]
[cf. Ywain and Gawain, ll. 2637–2710]

4566   Now [Yvain] has rescued [Lunete] exactly as he wishes; and the lady was quite happy to forgive her for the grief she had caused her. Then the defeated men were burnt on the pyre that had been kindled for her burning, since it is right and just that someone who wrongly condemns another should die by the same death as he had demanded for him. Now Lunete is joyful and glad to be reconciled with her mistress, and they rejoiced more freely than anybody had ever done before. And one and all duly offered their services to their lord, but without recognising him. Even the lady, who possessed his heart without knowing it, begged him insistently to agree to stay and rest until he had cured his lion and himself.

4588   He then says: "My lady, it will not be today on this occasion that I shall stay—not until my mistress frees me from her displeasure and anger. Then all my hardships will be at an end."—"Indeed," she says,

"I'm sorry. I don't consider the lady who bears you ill-will to be very courtly. She should not close her door against a knight of your merit, unless he had wronged her very grievously."—"My lady," he says, "however much it hurts me, all that pleases her I find agreeable. But don't question me any further! For on no account would I tell the offence or the penalty to any but those who are well aware of them."—"Does anyone know, then, other than you two?"—"Yes indeed, my lady!"—"Please tell us, good sir, at least your name. Then you will be quite free to leave."—"Quite free, my lady? That I should not be. I owe more than I could repay. Nevertheless, I shouldn't hide from you the name I've adopted. You will never hear about the Knight with the Lion without hearing about me. I wish to be known by this name."—"In God's name, good sir, how can it be that we never saw you before or heard your name mentioned?"—"That shows, my lady, that I'm not very well known." Then the lady says once more: "If you didn't object, I would again beg you to stay."—"Truly, my lady, I wouldn't dare to until I knew for certain that I had my lady's goodwill."—"Then go, good sir, and God be with you; and may He be pleased to change your sorrow and unhappiness to joy!"—"My lady," says he, "may God hear your prayer!" Then, softly under his breath, he said: "You have the casket in which my joy is locked, and, though you don't know it, you hold the key."

4635   With that he leaves in deep distress; and there is nobody who recognises him except for Lunete alone, who accompanies him for some distance. Lunete is his only escort; and he begs her urgently never to reveal who her champion was. "I won't, my lord," she says. After this he made a further request, namely that she should remember him and put in a good word for him with her lady, if she had the opportunity. She tells him to say no more, for she will never be forgetful or dilatory or lazy on that score. He thanks her a hundred times for that, then goes off deep in thought and worried about his lion, which he has to carry, since it cannot follow him. He makes for it a litter of moss and bracken in his shield; and having made its bed for it, he lays it there as gently as he can and carries it along stretched out on the inside of his shield.

[6]
[*Yvain and Gawain*]
[*cf. Ywain and Gawain*, ll. 3513–34]

. . . the men intending to fight and who used to be the greatest of
friends did not recognise each other at all.[4] So do they not love one
another now? My reply to you is "yes and no", and I shall find arguments
to prove the one and the other. Certainly my lord Gawain loves Yvain
and declares him to be his companion, and Yvain reciprocates, wherever
he is. Even here, if he recognised him, he would make much of him;
and each would give his head for the other sooner than do him harm.
Is this not true and total love? Yes indeed.—Their hatred, then: is not
that also quite evident? Yes, because it is a certain fact that each would
doubtless be glad to have broken the other's head or to have inflicted
on him such disgrace that he would be the worse for it. Upon my word,
to have found love and mortal hatred in the one receptacle is an absolute
miracle!

6024   God! How can two so contrary things dwell together in one single
lodging? It seems to me they cannot be together in one house; for one
could not stay with the other in one place without there being discord
and quarrelling once each knew the other's presence. But in one dwelling
there are a number of apartments: a gallery and separate rooms. The
situation might well be like this: perhaps Love had shut himself away
in some hidden room, and Hate had gone to the gallery overlooking
the street, wanting to be in full view. Now Hate is quite ready for action,
for he spurs, pricks and gallops against Love as hard as he can; and Love
makes no move at all. Ah, Love, where have you hidden?[5] Come out,
and you will see what an ally your friends' enemies have brought and
set against you!—The enemies are those very same men who love each
other with a most sacred love; for love which is neither false nor a sham
is a most precious and holy thing.

6053   Here Love is totally blind, and Hate sees nothing either; for Love,
had he recognised them, should have forbidden them to lay hands on
each other or do anything that might distress him. Love, then, is blind,
thrown into confusion and duped because he sees, yet does not recognise,
those who rightly belong entirely to him. And Hate, though he cannot
say why one of them should detest the other, nevertheless intends to
engage them in a wrongful combat, with each having a mortal hatred
of the other. A man, you may be sure, is not loved by someone who

4. This rather precious debate takes up in allegorical terms the [recurrent theme of the relationship
between love and hate]. One has the impression here, as in *Erec*, that Chrétien is spinning
out his story in order to achieve a particular quota of lines* * * * The duel with Gawain
nevertheless provides an admirable climax to Yvain's adventures, partly because it shows his
prowess to be once more second to none, and partly since we see him standing against the
man who had lured him from Laudine's side.

5. By deploying Hate against Love, Yvain and Gawain, whose mutual affection makes them
Love's friends, are also his enemies.

would wish to have him put to shame and desires his death. What? Does Yvain, then, want to slay his friend my lord Gawain? Yes, and the wish is mutual. So would my lord Gawain wish to slay Yvain with his own hands or do even worse than I say? No, I swear and promise you. The one would not want to have shamed or harmed the other for all that God has made for man or for the sake of Rome's entire empire. Now I have told a grave lie; for it is very plain to see that each of them, with his lance at the ready in its rest, is intending to attack the other, wishing to do him harm and injury without holding back at all.

6088   Now tell me: when one has defeated the other, whom will the one who gets the worst of the blows have to blame? For, if they do come to attacking each other, I am very much afraid they will keep up the combat and fight until it ends in the victory of one of them. Will Yvain, if he gets the worst of it, be able to claim with justice that that man has caused him injury and shame who counts him among his friends and has never named him otherwise than as friend and companion? Or, if it should happen by chance that it is Yvain who does Gawain some injury or gets the better of him in any way, will the latter, then, have the right to complain? No, for he will not know whom to blame.

6106   As they do not recognise each other, they both take their distance; then, as they clash, their lances, which were massive and made of ash, shatter.

[7]
[*Conclusion*]
[*cf. Ywain and Gawain*, ll. 3959–4032]

. . . And the lady was full of joy as soon as she heard the news that the maiden was coming and that she was bringing the lion and the knight, whom she was very anxious to see, meet and get to know. My lord Yvain, still fully armed, fell at her feet; and Lunete, who was at his side, said to her: "My lady, raise him to his feet again and apply your efforts and strength and skill to obtaining the reconciliation and pardon that no one except yourself in the whole world can procure for him!" Then the lady has him rise and says: "I'll do all I can for him. I would very much like to be able to meet his wishes and desires."— "Indeed, my lady," says Lunete, "I should not say this if it weren't true: it's entirely in your power to do this, and far more so than I've told you. But now I shall tell you the truth of the matter, and you'll understand: you never had and never will have a friend as close as this one. God, whose will it is that between you and him there should be true and enduring peace and love, caused me to find him today so close at hand. There's nothing I need say to prove the fact other than this: my lady, forgive him for incurring your wrath, for he has no lady except you— this is your husband, my lord Yvain!"

6759 The lady starts at these words and says: "God save me, you've got me well and truly in a trap![6] You'll have me love in spite of myself that man who neither loves nor respects me. Now you've done a fine thing and have just performed a most pleasing service for me! I'd rather suffer gales and storms all my life! And were it not such a vile and base thing to break one's word, he would never, try as he might, make his peace or be reconciled with me! There would always have smouldered within me, just as fire smoulders in ashes, that experience I don't want to go back over or care to bring up again now that I have to be reconciled with him."

6777 My lord Yvain hears and understands that his cause is going well and that he will be peacefully reconciled with her. He says: "Lady, one should show compassion to a sinner. I've paid for my folly, and it was only right that I should pay for it. It was foolishness that made me stay away, and I acknowledge my guilt and my crime. I've acted with very great boldness in daring to come into your presence; but if you are willing to keep me now, I shall never again wrong you in any way."— "Indeed," she says, "I am very willing, since I should perjure myself if I didn't do all I could to make peace between you and me. If that's your wish, I grant it to you."—"My lady," he says, "five hundred thanks! For, as I call on the Holy Spirit for aid, God could give me no other happiness in this mortal life!"

6799 Now my lord Yvain has found his peace; and you may well believe that he was never so happy for anything, great though his distress had been. All has ended very well for him, for he is loved and cherished by his lady, and she by him. He remembers none of his troubles, as they are driven from his mind by the joy he finds in his dearly beloved mistress. And Lunete too is very content: her pleasure is complete now that she has made a lasting peace between my excellent lord Yvain and his beloved and matchless mistress.

6814 Thus CHRÉTIEN concludes his romance of the Knight with the Lion; for I never heard any more of it told, nor will you ever hear more of it related, unless someone chooses to make some lying addition.

6818

---

6. The *dénouement*, which seems to be Chrétien's own, is cleverly contrived though psychologically unsatisfying. Laudine is persuaded to take Yvain back by a stratagem, just as Arthur had tricked the elder sister into recognising the injustice of her action. The final reassurance that love was restored and endured is scarcely enough to persuade us that Chrétien has not been more interested all along in the formal conditions and etiquette of courtly love than in the psychology of a deep human relationship.

Sir Orfeo[1]

The poem represents an evocative and masterful transformation of the classical legend of Orpheus and Eurydice. Where Eurydice dies from the bite of a serpent and is consigned to the underworld by default, Heurodis is abducted by the "King o Fairy" (we never do learn from the poem just why the abduction occurred); where the harpist Orpheus descends immediately to the underworld in the attempt to reclaim his wife, Orfeo, a king as well as a harpist, renounces his kingdom and possessions—and then for ten years leads a wild existence without a purpose beyond that of determined abnegation; and where Orpheus loses his own life in the attempt to restore that of his wife, Orfeo regains not just his wife but his kingdom as well—and he and Heurodis live "long afterward."

Many such differences appear to have been brought about under the influences of Celtic tradition—though no specific source texts are known to have survived, and it is consequently difficult to develop a clear sense of just how or when the classical legend came so to be transformed.[2] The poem nevertheless openly proclaims a Celtic heritage by referring to its original form as a lay composed and sung by Breton minstrels (ll. 13–24, 597–602). Three Old French texts, *Floire et Blanceflor* (l. 855), *Le Lai de l' Espine* (l. 181), and the prose *Lancelot* (book iv), all refer to the singing of a *lai d'Orphey* and suggest the possibility that *Sir Orfeo* had a French source which in turn may well have translated a Breton original.[3] Because bona fide Breton lays were transmitted orally (they were sung to the accompaniment of a harp or perhaps recited between musical interludes), none have survived; but an approximation of their spirit and a sense of the genre as understood by later medieval writers may be available in the very accomplished *lais* of Marie de France. At least a dozen *lais* survive which can be linked with Marie; they were probably written in the third quarter of the twelfth century, perhaps in England. Marie claims in some of them that they were first composed by Bretons.

Marie's *lais* are short (the longest is 1,184 lines) and often, in their compactness, manifest a close interdependence of form and meaning. Indeed, it has been demonstrated in various ways that the *lais* lend themselves to interpretations of an almost geometric kind. John A. Frey has, for instance,

1. Editions and translations of the texts mentioned in this headnote, as well as references to related scholarship, are cited in the Selected Bibliography. On the date of the poem, see the leading footnote to the edition proper.
2. For a brief overview of what is meant by "Celtic tradition," see the Sources and Backgrounds headnote to *Ywain and Gawain*, pp. 330–32.
3. There is some evidence in the text to suggest that *Sir Orfeo* had a French source: see ll. 47, 493, and notes thereto.

noted that they display a fondness for doublings (of character, say—as in *Le Fresne*, which traces the opposing and yet ultimately unified experiences of twin sisters—or of action—as in *Guigemar*, where the titular hero is magically wounded by his own arrow, which has rebounded off a marvelous doe; the doe then tells him that his wound will only heal if he can find a lady of equal distress to his). As early as 1929, S. Foster Damon noted a pervasive sense of symmetry in Marie's *lais*, whereby the poems appeared to form thematically corresponding pairs or groups of four. And it is surely telling that the earliest and most complete surviving manuscript of Marie's *lais* (British Library MS Harley 978) evenly alternates the longer *lais* with the shorter; the shorter *lais* (those under 320 lines—all others are over 500 lines) are invariably unhappy and tell of love or well-being thwarted through such things as banishment, murder, permanent separation, vindictive execution, and death through pain of grief or shame. The longer *lais* generally see happy resolutions brought about by the recovery from the ordeal such disagreeable things (or their prospect) can bring. In the case of the longer *lais*, a good example is Marie's *Lanval* (a Middle English translation, *Sir Landevale*, is printed in this volume, beginning p. 352). Great emphasis is given to examining the hero's indigent suffering and its causes; and much the same level of emphasis is then given over to documenting the extent to which the hero prevails by regaining all that he lost. It is helpful to see Lanval's experience in contradistinction to that of the hero of Chrétien's *Yvain*;[4] Lanval's progress out of his ordeal is much less the spiritual discovery of self experienced by Yvain than it is a material *recovery* of self.

Sir Orfeo develops the same kinds of patterns as appear in *Lanval* and in the *lais* generally. Orfeo's traumatic loss and his triumphant recovery are documented with a sense of symmetry; not only must he recover his wife, but he must recover everything that was lost—and so the effective climax of the poem comes not with the liberation of Heurodis but with the recovery of the kingdom.[5] On a rhetorical level, too, the poem defines circumstances through paired oppositions (and surely much of the art of the poem resides in its harrowing evocations of temporality abused): see ll. 105–112, 239–56, 280, and the notes thereto.[6]

The kind of ending the poem adopts against that of the classical legend has precedent in analogous Celtic tales (though none of these tales could be said to be a direct source). The Irish *Tochmarc Etaine*,[7] for example, tells of how the king of Ireland, Eochaid Airem, loses his wife, Etain, to a fairy prince, Midir; after nine years, during which he has all the fairy mounds in Ireland dug up, the king eventually recovers his wife (the story also describes how the king stations armies in rings around his wife in a futile attempt to block her abduction). In his *De Nugis Curialium*,[8] Walter Map relates the story of a man who, having been widowed and having grieved

4. About which, see the Sources and Backgrounds headnote to *Ywain and Gawain*, pp. 329 ff.
5. Cf. also l. 303, n.
6. For a study of a possible English background to such rhetorical devices, see the article by Betty Hill cited in the Selected Bibliography; on certain aspects of the treatment of time in the poem, see the article by Felicity Riddy.
7. The *Wooing of Etain*; the manuscript dates from c. 1100, but the story is probably much older.
8. "Courtiers' Trifles," a collection of marvelous, notably Welsh, tales recorded by Walter in the last quarter of the twelfth century; the tale in question is found at section IV, chapter 8.

over his loss for many years, happens upon his wife one night amid a company of women (whose presence he associates with the agency of fairies); this takes place in an otherwise deserted valley. He seizes his wife and takes her back with him; they live happily and normally thereafter. As Dorena Allen has observed, such tales represent a widespread belief—and one recorded in parts of Ireland just in the last century—that those who appear to have died may not be dead at all but may instead have been seized by fairies into a separate otherworld.

A number of other elements in the poem can be related to Celtic traditions, but in some cases it may be safer to speak of the confluence of two or more streams of tradition. When the poem near its end exclaims, "Gode is the lay, swete is the note!" (l. 602), it reminds us that an essential theme—the transcendent power of the lyrical—has been *demonstrated* as well as depicted. In thus celebrating the power of its own medium the poem reflects a traditional Celtic reverence for the incanted word; that Orfeo is made a king further reflects a Celtic reverence for the powers of one who commands music. But the classical legend itself does of course celebrate Orpheus's musical powers; and Judeo-Christian tradition admits a similar reverence in the case of King David, a skillful harpist (according to 1 Samuel 16) traditionally held to be the author of the Psalms.[9] Again, Orfeo's self-exile—something approximated in some versions of the classical story only after Orpheus loses Eurydice the second time—may be associated with more than one tradition. There is the Celtic tradition of the "wild man of the woods," perhaps best exemplified by accounts of Merlin's periods of wilderness distraction in Geoffrey of Monmouth's *Vita Merlini* ("Life of Merlin," written c. 1150 and based on older Welsh tales); but it would not be impossible for a medieval writer further to associate Orfeo's self-exile with Christ's period of temptation in the wilderness (Matthew 4.1–11).[1] The poem's account of the fairy world (it is the earliest such account in English) is comparable with that of numerous Celtic tales: the fairies dwell not in a subterranean world like that in the classical story, but rather in an otherworld into which one passes but does not descend (cf. *Sir Launfal*, ll. 1021 ff.); the fairies engage in festive excursions and of course hunt for and abduct mortals from this world; they also have the power magically to manipulate time and space. But it is still worth noting besides all this that, in the case of the description of the fairy castle, whose lapidary and gilt brilliance is similar to that of fairy structures described in other Celtic tales, the text nevertheless intimates that the castle may also owe something of its design to the poet's knowledge of the Book of Revelation (see l. 376, n.). J. B. Friedman has further suggested that the otherworld in *Sir Orfeo* may also ultimately owe something to the description of the underworld in Book 6 of Virgil's *Aeneid*; there, apart from accommodating the shade of Orpheus, the place is, as in *Sir Orfeo* (ll. 387–

9. J. B. Friedman points out that from the sixth century on, Orpheus was sometimes conceived as a figure of King David and suggests that such a comparison may lie behind the representation of Orfeo as a king. For a further possible link with King David, see l. 70, n.
1. As some scholars (notably J. B. Friedman and Peter Dronke) have demonstrated, moreover, Orpheus, surrounded by animals, was commonly envisioned by early Christianity as a type of Christ in His role as the Good Shepherd. The analogy was sometimes extended further in the recognition that Orpheus manifested the power to retrieve the dead from infernal regions; consequently the unhappy ending of his story was sometimes suppressed.

408 *vs.* ll. 409–16, 439–46), divided into regions inhabited respectively by dejected or happy shades.

The classical legend of Orpheus and Eurydice was known to the Middle Ages mainly through the versions presented in Ovid's *Metamorphoses* (Book X, 1–85, and XI, 1–66), Virgil's *Georgics* (Book 4, 453–527), and the *Consolation of Philosophy* of Boethius (Book III, Metrum 12). The versions are substantially the same up to the point of Orpheus's second loss of Eurydice. Thereafter Boethius concludes with a moral, while Virgil and Ovid tell of how Orpheus mourned and wandered for a long time until he was met by Thracian women (in Ovid they are Maenads, frenzied female worshipers of the god Dionysus) who tore him apart and threw his severed head (as well as his lyre, according to Ovid) into the river Hebrus. Ovid adds, among other things, that Orpheus's shade now walks with that of Eurydice, but however they walk he may never look back on her.

A medieval rendering of Boethius's version is here printed; it is attributed to Alfred the Great (849–99), King of Wessex from 871. Alfred was a great patron of learning and oversaw the translation of several favorite Latin works of his age into English (i.e., the early form of English we now call Old English). Alfred's version (here represented by W. J. Sedgefield's modern English translation) has been selected because, as J. Burke Severs first observed, there are places where Alfred has expanded upon his source and which parallel certain details in *Sir Orfeo* (Alfred's additions are rendered in italics). The implication is that *Sir Orfeo* may bear the impress of a very old but particularly British Orpheus tradition—one perhaps which Alfred originated, or, more likely, one which influenced Alfred. Note in particular the following: (1) Alfred's version, like *Sir Orfeo*, begins with a summary of the harper's qualifications and the qualities of his wife, and describes the setting; (2) the special attention Alfred gives to Orpheus's ability to charm animals (beside trees and stones) is reflected in *Sir Orfeo*, ll. 273–77, which mentions only "bestes;" (3) the addition in Alfred of a passage describing Orpheus's willful solitude *before* he attempts to recover his wife presages, if briefly, the extraordinary period of self-exile found in *Sir Orfeo*.

BOETHIUS

From *King Alfred's Translation of* The Consolation of Philosophy†

BOOK III, METRUM 12

Blessed is the man that is able to see the clear wellspring of the Highest
Good, and cast off the darkness of his mind. We must tell thee yet
another from the fables of old. Once on a time it came to pass that a
harp-player lived *in the country called* Thracia, *which was in the kingdom
of the Crecas.*[1] *The harper was so good, it was quite unheard of. His
name was Orfeus, and he had a wife without her equal, named Eurudice.
Now men came to say of the harper* that he could play the harp so that
the forest swayed, and the rocks quivered for the sweet sound, *and wild
beasts would run up and stand still as if they were tame, so still that
men or hounds might come near them, and they fled not. The harper's
wife died, men say, and her soul was taken to hell. Then the harpman
became so sad that he could not live in the midst of other men, but was
off to the forest, and sate upon the hills both day and night,* weeping,
and playing on his harp so that the woods trembled and the rivers stood
still, and hart shunned not lion, nor hare hound, *nor did any beast feel
rage or fear towards any other for gladness of the music.* And when it
seemed to the harper that nothing in this world brought joy to him *he
thought he would seek out the gods of hell and essay to win them over
with his harp, and pray them to give him back his wife.*[2] *When he came
thither, the hound of hell, men say, came towards him, whose name was
Cerverus*[3] *and who had three heads; and he began to welcome him with
his tail, and play with him on account of his harp-playing.* There was
likewise there a most *dreadful* gateward *whose name was Caron;*[4] *he had
also* three heads, *and was very, very old. Then the harper fell to beseeching*

---

† From W.J. Sedgefield, trans., *King Alfred's Version of the Consolations of Boethius Done into
Modern English, with an Introduction* (Oxford, 1900), pp. 115–18. Reprinted with the permission of Oxford University Press.

    Boethius, probably a Christian, lived in Italy c. 480–c. 524 and was an adviser to Theodoric,
King of the Ostrogoths. *The Consolation of Philosophy* was written in prison while Boethius
awaited execution for certain political activities; the work as a whole advocates the attainment
of a vision of the divine through the pursuit of philosophy. The selection provided comprises
verses sung to Boethius by Lady Philosophy. Sedgefield's italics indicate readings unique to
Alfred. All notes are the editor's.

1. I.e., the Greeks.
2. Alfred omits a few lines in Boethius which note that Orpheus's mother was Calliope, one of
the nine Muses, goddesses who presided over different arts and sciences. Calliope was the
goddess of lyric inspiration and was held in the Middle Ages to be the chief Muse.
3. Cerberus, the three-headed dog who guards the entrance to the underworld.
4. Charon, the ferryman who transports the dead across the river Styx to join the underworld.
Normally he will admit only those who have received proper burial rites and who can pay
the fare of an obol (a small silver coin which will have been placed in the mouth of the
corpse).

him that he would shield him while he was in that place, and bring him back again unharmed. And he promised him to do so, being overjoyed at the rare music. Then he went on farther until he met the *fell goddesses that men of the people call Parcae,*[5] *saying that they know no respect for any man,* but punish each according to his deeds; *and they are said to rule each man's fate. And he began to implore their kindness;* and they fell to weeping with him. *Again he went on, and all the dwellers in hell ran to meet him, and fetched him to their king;*[6] *and all began to speak with him and join in his prayer.* And the ever-moving wheel, that Ixion *king of the Levitas*[7] *was bound to for his guilt,* stood still *for his harping, and King* Tantalus,[8] *that was in this world greedy beyond measure, and whom that same sin of greed followed there,* had rest, and the vulture, it is said, left off tearing the liver of *King Ticcius*[9], *whom he had thus been punishing. And all the dwellers in hell had rest from their tortures whilst he was harping before the king. Now when he had played a long, long time,* the king of hell's folk cried out, saying, 'Let us give the good man his wife, for he hath won her with his harping.' Then he bade him be sure never to look back once he was on his way thence; *if he looked back, he said, he should forfeit his wife.* But love may hardly, nay, cannot be denied! Alas and well-a-day! Orpheus led his wife along with him, until he came to the border of *light and* darkness, and his wife was close behind. *He had but stepped into the light* when he looked back towards his wife, and immediately she was lost to him.

These fables teach every man that *would flee from the darkness of hell and come to the light of the True Goodness that he should not look towards his old sins, so as again to commit them as fully as he once did. For whosoever with entire will turneth his mind back to the sins he hath left, and then doeth them and taketh full pleasure in them, and never after thinketh of forsaking them, that man shall lose all his former goodness, unless he repent.*[1]

---

5. *Parcae* is here used in error; it is the Latin name for the Fates, the three goddesses who respectively hold the distaff, spin out, and cut the thread of one's life. As the subsequent account indicates, the reference here is in fact to the three Furies, winged goddesses who brought vengeance upon those who had gone unpunished for their crimes.
6. I.e., Hades (also known as Pluto), king of the dead, god of the underworld.
7. As punishment for attempting to seduce the goddess Hera, Ixion is bound in the underworld to an eternally revolving wheel.
8. This figure gives his name to his punishment. For the crime of a greed directly offensive to the gods (different versions of the legend change the details of the crime), Tantalus is deprived of food and water, and yet tantalized with fruit suspended over his head and with water which rises to his neck; the food and water withdraw if he moves to consume them.
9. For assaulting the goddess Leto, the giant Tityus is tied down forever to have vultures devour his constantly regenerated liver.
1. Boethius's moral is briefer and more allusive, to the effect that all hard-won (moral) excellence is lost to one who gazes back on infernal things.

Sir Launfal[1]

Apart from employing a smattering of traditional Arthurian lore—such as the details of King Arthur's court and his marriage (ll. 13–42)—*Sir Launfal* is notable for being an inventive composite of motifs and events which could have been taken from any number of medieval tales. For instance, the tournament at Arthur's court (ll.433–504) and the "Valentyne" escapade (ll. 505–612)—both episodes unique to this version of the story—may in part have been suggested by similar episodes in the Middle English romances of *Libeaus Desconus* (thought also to have been written by the *Launfal* poet, ll. 769 ff.) and *Guy of Warwick* (ll.895 ff. and 1261 ff., known episodic sources for *Libeaus*). Occasional details suggest the further influence of other romances and *chansons de geste* (cf. ll. 327, 561, and notes thereto).

The poem's nominal source is the Old French *lai* of *Lanval*, written by the great poet Marie de France in the last third of the twelfth century (and probably sometime before 1189). A more immediate source, however, would have been a relatively faithful Middle English translation of *Lanval* very close to that represented by the poem *Sir Landevale*, here printed. The dependency of *Sir Launfal* on such a text is evident in the many lines repeated verbatim and other close verbal echoes; we also know, however, that *Launfal* occasionally reflects the peculiarities of yet other surviving English versions of the story, perhaps even a specific version of Marie's *Lanval*.[2] A comparison with *Landevale* nevertheless provides invaluable insights into the methodological and aesthetic proclivities of the *Launfal* poet—notably in the ways in which the extremes of Launfal's success and failure are amplified and their measure taken. At the same time it ought to be said that, for all its arabesques, *Launfal* is not necessarily a better poem than *Landevale*.[3]

The next most important influence on *Sir Launfal* is a version of the Old French *lai* of *Graelent*, a close (non-Arthurian) analogue to, and itself quite

---

1. Editions and translations of the texts mentioned in this headnote, as well as references to related scholarship, are cited in the Selected Bibliography. On the date of the poem, see the leading footnote to the edition proper. For an overview of the backgrounds of Arthurian literature, see the headnote to selections from Chrétien's *Yvain*, pp. 329 ff.

2. Cf., for instance, the notes to ll. 50, 422, and 618 of *Sir Launfal*. For further insights into the possible links between *Launfal* and other versions (namely *Sir Lambewell* from the Percy Folio MS—about the MS, see the leading Sources and Backgrounds footnote to *The Marriage of Sir Gawaine*, p. 380—and *Sir Lamwell*, surviving fragmentariliy in Cambridge University Library MS Kk.v.30 and in two printed fragments: 1) Malone 941 and 2) Douce Fragments e.40, in the Bodleian Library, Oxford), see the review by M. Mills cited in the Selected Bibliography.

3. A case could be made, however, for arguing that *Launfal* was written for comic ends and that this has been accomplished with tantalizing skill; see, for instance, the article by Carol Nappholz cited in the Selected Bibliography.

possibly a source for, Marie's *Lanval*. *Sir Launfal* appears to be indebted to *Graelent* for the following: (1) the episode of the Queen's selective generosity which in turn makes the knight destitute (*Launfal*, ll. 67–72; in *Graelent* the Queen of Brittany, whose amorous advances have been rejected by the knight, Graelent, advises the King to withhold his pay); (2) the assistance given to the ostracized knight by the landlord's daughter (*Launfal*, ll. 191–216); (3) the episode of the knight's waiting in his chamber and the subsequent arrival of a procession of gifts (*Launfal*, ll. 373–420); (4) the details of the knight's loss upon betraying the existence of his mistress (*Launfal*, ll. 733–44).

Sir Landevale†

	Sothly,° by° Arthurys day	*Truly / by, in*
	Was Bretayn yn grete° nobley,°	*great / nobility, high regard*
	For, yn hys tyme, a grete whyle°	*while*
	He sojourned° at Carlile;[1]	*resided*
5	He had with hym a meyné° there,	*company, retinue*
	As he had ellyswhere,	
	Of the Rounde Table the knyghtys all,	
	With myrth° and joye yn hys hall.	*mirth*
	Of eache lande yn the worlde wyde°	*wide*
10	There cam men on every syde—	
	Yonge knyghtys and squyers	
	And othir bolde bachelers°—	*young men*
	For-to se° that nobley	*see*
	That was with Arthur allwey;°	*always*
15	For ryche yeftys° and tresour	*gifts*
	He gayf° to eache man of honour.	*gave*
	With hym there was a bachiller	
	[(And hadde° y-be° well many a yer°),]	*had / been / year*
	A yong° knyght of muche myght;	*young*
20	Sir Landevale, forsoith,° he hight.°	*forsooth, truly / was called*
	Sir Landevale spent blythely°	*gladly*
	And yaf° yeftys largely;°	*gave / generously*
	So wildely his goode° he sett°	*property, wealth / spent*
	That he fell yn grete dette.°	*debt*
25	[Then he began to mak his moane:°][2]	*complaint*

† Text of Oxford, Bodleian Library MS Rawlinson C. 86, ff. 119ᵛ–128ᵛ, printed with permission of the Bodleian Library. The manuscript dates from the very late fifteenth century, possibly the early sixteenth century; the poem's date of composition (as a translation from French) is held to have been in the first half of the fourteenth century. The poem is written in nominally four-stress rhyming couplets. Unless otherwise stated, lines in square brackets are supplied from *Sir Launfal* where a lacuna is obvious and the rhyme suggests little deviation from the original; "[. . .]" indicates a line which is missing (to judge from the rhyme) and cannot be reconstructed.
1. Carlisle (about which, see *The Awntyrs off Arthure*, l. 2, n. 1.)
2. Line supplied from Cambridge University Library MS Kk.v.30 (*Sir Lamwell*).

"Who hath no good, goode can he none—[3]
And I am here in uncuth londe
And no gode have under honde.
Men will me hold for a wrech;
30 Where I become, I ne reche!"[4]
He lepe° upon a coursier,°   *leaped / charger*
Withoute grome° or squier,   *groom, servant*
And rode forth yn a mornynge
To dryve awey longyng.
35 Then he takyth° toward the west,   *takes, turns*
Betwene a water° and a forest.   *stream*
The sonne was hote° that underntyde;°   *hot / morning*
He lyght° adowne, and wold abyde,   *alighted, dismounted*
For he was hote yn the weddir.°   *weather*
40 Hys mantell° he toke and fold° togeder;°   *cloak / folded / together*
Than lay downe that knyght so free°   *magnanimous, gracious*
Undre the shadow of a tree.
"Alas!" he said, "no good I have.
How shall I doo? I can not crave![5]
45 All the knyghtys that ben° so feers,°   *are / fierce*
Of the Rounde Table they were my pyers;°   *peers*
Every man of me was glade,°   *glad*
And now they be for me full saide."°   *sad*
"Alas! Alas!" was his songe;
50 Sore° wepyng, his hondis° he wronge.°   *Sorely, Bitterly / hands / wrung*
Thus he lay yn sorow full sore.
Than he sawe, comynge oute of holtys° hore,°   *woods / gray, ancient*
Owte of the forest cam° maydyns two,   *came*
The fayrest on grounde that myght goo.°   *go*
55 Kyrtyls° they had of purpyl° sendell,°   *Frocks / purple / silk*
Small° i-lasid,° syttyng° welle;   *Tightly / laced / fitting*
Mantels of grene velvet,
Frengid° with gold were° wele i-sette.   *Fringed / wire*
They had on° atyre° therwithall°,   *over / attire, clothing / with that*
60 And eache of them a joly cornall,°   *coronet*
With facys° white as lely° floure,   *faces / lily*
With ruddy, rede°-as-rose coloure.°   *red / coloring, complexion (of cheek)*
Fayrer women never he see;
They semyd° angels of hevin° hie.°   *seemed / heaven / high*
65 That on° bare° a gold basyn,   *one / bore*
That othir a towail,° riche and fyn.   *towel*

---

3. I.e., he who has no wealth can do no good. (Landevale is the speaker.)
4. And I am here in an unfamiliar land and have no wealth to hand. Men will treat me as an
outcast; I do not know what will become of me! (The implication that Landevale is a foreigner
comes from Marie de France's *Lanval*, ll. 27–28, where it is noted that the knight, though
a king's son, held his heritage far away.)
5. I.e., I do not know where to ask for help.

To hymwarde com the maydyns gent.°   *gracious, noble*
The knyght anon agaynse° hem went;   *toward*
"Welcom" he said, "damsels fre."
70   "Sir knyght", they seid, "Wel thu be.[6]
My lady, that is as bright as floure,°   *flower*
The gretith, Landavale, paramour;°   *with love*
Ye must come and speke with her—
Yef° it be your will, sir."   *If*
75   "I graunt,"° he said, "blythely,"°   *grant, agree / with pleasure*
And went with them hendly.°   *graciously*
Anone he in that forest sy°   *saw*
A pavylion,° i-pight an hy[7]   *pavilion, tent*
With treysour i-wrought° on every syde,   *wrought*
80   Al of werke of the faryse.°   *fairies*
Eche° pomell° of that pavilion   *Each / finial sphere*
Was worth a citie,° or a towne;   *city*
Upon the cupe° an heron was—   *top*
A richer nowher ne was;
85   In his mouthe a carboncle,° bright   *carbuncle, rubious gem*
As the mone° that shone light.   *moon*
Kyng Alexander the conquerour,
Ne Salamon° yn hys honour,   *Solomon*
Ne Charlemayn° the riche kyng—   *Charlemagne*
90   They had never suche a thing.
He founde yn that pavilion
The Kyngys doughter of Amylion[8]
That ys an ile° of the fayré   *isle, island*
In occian,° full faire to see.   *occident, the west*
95   There was a bede° of mekyll° price,°   *bed / much, great / value*
Coverid with purpill byse;°   *linen*
Thereon lay that maydyn bright,
Almost nakyd, and upright.
Al her clothes byside her lay;
100   Syngly° was she wrappyd,° parfay,°   *Solely / wrapped, covered / indeed*
With a mauntell of hermyn,°   *ermine*
Coverid° was with alexanderyn.°   *(Which) covered / alexandrine purple*
The mantell for° hete down she dede°   *because of / (un)did*
Right to hir gyrdillstede.°   *waist*
105   She was white as lely° in May,   *lily*
Or snowe that fallith yn wynterday;
Blossom on brere,° ne no floure,   *brier*
Was not like° to her coloure—   *comparable*
The rede rose whan it is newe

6. (May) it be well with you.
7. Pitched high aloft.
8. I.e., the daughter of the King of Amylion. (The name is a corruption of Marie de France's Avalun, or Avalon—about which see *Sir Launfal*, l. 149, n.)

110	To her rud° is not° of hewe.°
	complexion (of cheek) / nothing / color
	Her hcire° shon as gold wire—
	hair
	Noman can tell° her atyre.
	describe
	"Landavale," she seid, "myn hert swete,[9]
	For thy love now I swete.°
	sweat, perspire
115	There is kyng ne emperour—
	And° I lovyd hym, paramor,
	If
	As moche as I do the—
	But he wold be full glad of me."
	Landevale beheld the maydyn bright;
120	Her love persyd° hys hert right.
	pierced
	He sette hym down by her syde:
	"Lady," quod° he, "whatso° betyde,°
	said / whatsoever / happens
	Evermore, lowde and stylle,
	I am redy at your wylle."[1]
125	"Sir knyght," she said, "curteyse and hend,°
	gracious
	I know thy state,° every ende.°
	condition / aspect
	Wilt thow truliche° the to me take,°
	truly / betake
	And all other for me forsake?
	And I will yeve° the grette honoure,
	give
130	Gold inough,° and grete tresour;
	enough, in plenty
	Hardely° spende largely!°
	Boldly / generously
	Yife yeftys blythely!°
	gladly
	Spend and spare not!—for my love.
	Thow shalt inough to thy behove."[2]
135	Tho° she said to his desyre;°
	Then, At that time / liking
	He clyppid° her abowte the swire°
	clasped, embraced / neck
	And kyssyd her many a sith.°
	time
	For her profer° he thankyd hir swyth.°
	offer / at once
	This lady was son° up sette,°
	soon / sitting
140	And bad hir maydyns mete° fette,°
	food / fetch
	And to thir° handys water clere,
	their
	And sothyn° went to soupere.°
	thence / supper
	Bothe they togedirs° sette;
	together
	The maydyns servyd theym of mete—
145	Of mete and dryng° they had plentie,
	drink
	Of all thing that was deynté.°
	choice, delicious
	After soper the day was gone;
	To bedde they went both anon.
	All that nyght they ley yn-fere°
	together
150	And did what° thir will were—
	whatever
	For pley they slepyd litill that nyght.
	Tho it began to dawe° light;
	dawn
	"Landavale," she said, "goo hens° now.
	hence

9. I.e., sweetheart.
1. I.e., in every way (lit. loud and quiet) I am prepared to do your will.
2. You shall have enough for your need.

Gold and sylver take with you,
155 Spend largely on every man—
I will fynd you inough than.
And when ye will,° gentil knyght,   *would*
Speke° with me, any night   *Speak*
To sum° derne° stede° ye goo,   *some/secret/place*
160 And thynke on me, soo and soo;[3]
Anon to you shall I tee.°   *come*
Ne make ye never bost° of me!   *boast*
And yff thou doyest,° beware beforn°—   *do/in advance*
For thow hast my love forlorn!"
165 The maydeyns bringe hys horse anon;
He toke hys leve, and went sone.°   *soon*
Of tresour he hath grete plentie,
And ridith forth ynto the cieté.°   *city*
He comyth hom to hys in,°   *inn, lodging*
170 And mery he makyth hym therin.
Hymsylf he clothyd full richely,
Hys squyer, hys yoman,° honestly.°   *yeoman/decently*
Landavale makyth° nobile festys;°   *arranges/feasts*
Landevale clothys the pore gestys;°   *guests*
175 Landevale byith° grette stedys;°   *buys/steeds*
Landevale yevyth riche wedys;°   *clothes*
Landevale rewaredith religionse,°   *religious orders*
And acquiteth the presons;°   *prisoners*
Landevale clothes gaylours;°   *gaolers, jailers*
180 Landevale doith° each man honours.   *does (to)*
Of his largesse eche man wote;°   *knows*
But how it comyth,° noman wote.   *comes*
And he will, dern or stelle,
Hys love ys redy at his wylle.[4]
185 Upon a tyme, Sir Gawyn
The curteys knyght, and Sir Ewayn,
And Sir Landavale with them also,
And othir knyghtys twente° or moo,°   *twenty/more*
Went to play° theym° on a grene°   *amuse/themselves/green, lawn*
190 Under the towre where was the Quene.
Thyse knyghtys with borde[5] playd tho;
Atte the last to daunsyng° they goo: *dancing*
Sir Landevale was to-fore° i-sette°—   *in front/placed*
For his largesse he was lovyd the bette.°   *best*
195 The Quene hersylf beheld this all;
"Yender,"° she said, "ys Landavall.   *Yonder, There*

3. I.e., in one way or another.
4. If he wills it, secretly or quietly, his beloved is immediately at hand.
5. I.e., at a board game (probably backgammon).

Of all the knyghtys that ben here
There is none so faire a bachyler;
And° he have noder° leman° ne wyf,°   *If/ neither/ lover/ wife*
200 I wold he lovyde me as° his lif.   *as (much as)*
Tide° me good or tyde me ille,   *Betide*
I wille assay° the knyghtys wille."   *assay, test*
She toke with her a company,
Of faire laydys thyrty;°   *thirty*
205 She goith adown anonrightys°   *immediately*
For-to daunce with the knyghtys.
The Quene yede to the first° ende   *leading*
(Betwene Landavale and Gawyn so hend)
And all her maydens forth aright,°   *properly*
210 One-be-one, betwyxt° eche knyght.   *between*
Whan the daunsynge was i-slakyd,°   *dwindled*
The Quen Landavale to° concell° hath takyd.°   *(In)to/ confidence/ taken*
"Shortely,"° she said, "thu gentil knyght,   *In short*
I the love with all my myght,
215 And as moche desire I the° yere°   *thee/ eagerly*
As the Kyng—and moche more!
Gode° hap° is to the tanne°   *Good/ luck/ brought*
To love more me⁶ than any woman."
"Madame," he said, "be° God, nay!   *by*
220 I wil be traitour never, parfay;
I have do the Kyng oth and feaulté—⁷
He shall not be traid° for° me!"   *betrayed/ because of*
"Fy!" said she, "thow fowle° coward!   *foul*
An harlot° ribawde,° I wote, thou harte!°   *scoundrel/ villainous/ art, are*
225 That thow livest, it is pitie;°   *(a) pity*
Thow lovyst no woman, ne no woman the!"
The knyght was agreved° thoo;°   *offended/ then*
He her ansurid° and said, "Noo!   *answered*
Madame," quod he, "thu seist thi will,⁸
230 Yet can I love dern° and stelle,°   *secretly/ quietly*
And am i-loved, and have a leman
As gentill and as faire as° any man.   *as (has)*
The semplest° maide with her, I wene,°   *simplest, plainest/ believe*
Over the may be a quene."
235 Tho was she ashamyd and wroth.
She clepid° her maydens bothe;   *called*
To bede° she goith alle drery;°   *bed/ dreary, miserable*
For doole° she wold dye, and was sory.°   *sadness/ sorrowful*
The Kyng cam from huntyng,

6. I.e., to love me more.
7. I.e., I have sworn an oath of fealty (a solemn feudal contract of loyalty) to the King.
8. I.e., say what you will.

240	Glade and blithe yn all thing,	
	And to the Quene can he tee.[9]	
	Anon she fel upon her knee;	
	Wonder° lowde° can she crie,	*Wondrously/loud*
	"A! helpe me, lorde, or I die!	
245	I spake to Landavale on a game,[1]	
	And he besought me of shame°	*shameful act*
	As a foule viced° tratour;	*depraved*
	He wold have done me dishonour—	
	And of a leman bost he maide:°	*made*
250	That werst° maide that she hade	*worst*
	Myght be a quene over me—	
	And all, lorde, in dispite of the!"	
	The Kyng wax° wondir wroth,	*grew*
	And forthwith swore hys othe	
255	That Landavale shulde bide° by the lawe—	*abide*
	Be bothe hangyd and drawe°—	*drawn, disemboweled*
	And commanded .iiii.° knyghtys	*four*
	To fetche "the traitour" anonrightys,	
	They° .iiii. fechyng° hym anon.	*Those/fetching*
260	But Landavale was to chamber gone;	
	Alas, he hath hys love forlorne!—	
	As she warnyd hym beforne.	
	Ofte he clepid° her, and sought,	*called (for)*
	And yet it gayneth hym nought.	
265	He wept and sobbet° with rufull° cry,	*sobbed/rueful, piteous*
	And on hys kneys° he askyth mercy;	*knees*
	[He bet° hys body and hys hedde ek,°]	*beat/also*
	And cursed hys mouth that of hir spake.	
	"O!" he said, "Gentill creature,	
270	How shall my wrechyd body endure,	
	That worldys° blysse° hath forlore	*earthly/delight*
	And her that I am under arest° for,	*arrest*
	With suche sorowe?—alas that stounde!"°	*moment*
	With that he fel dede° on the grounde,	*deathly, as if dead*
275	So long° that the knyghtys comyn;°	*until/came*
	And ther so they hym namyn,°	*took up*
	And as theff° hym ladde° soo	*(a) thief/led away*
	(Than was his sorow doble° woo!°)	*(a) double/woe, sorrow*
	He was brought before the Kyng.	
280	Thus he hym grete° at the begynnyng:	*greeted*
	"Thow atteynt° takyn° traytour,	*attainted, convicted/captured*
	Besoughtest thou my wiff° of dishonour?	*wife*
	That she was lothely thou dedist° upbrayde,°	*did/reproach*
	That of thy leman the lest° mayde°	*least/maid*

9. And he made his way to the Queen.
1. I.e., in jest, in play.

285 Was fayrer than ys my wyff—
Therefore shalt thu lose thy lyffe!"
Landavale ansuryd at hys borde[2]
And told hym the sothe,° every worde,   *truth*
That it was nothing so—
290 And he was redy for-to die tho°   *then*
That° all the countrey wold looke.°   *(If) that / foresee, ordain*
Twelve knyghtys were drevyn to a boke[3]
The soth to say, and no leese,°   *lies*
Alltogedir as° it was.   *how*
295 Thise .xii.° wist,° withouten wene,°   *twelve / knew / doubt*
All the maner° of the Quene: *habits*
The Kyng was good, all aboute,
And she was wyckyd, oute and oute—
For she was of suche comforte°   *constitution (that), temperament (that)*
300 She lovyd men ondir° her lorde.   *besides*
Therby° wist thei it was all   *Therefore*
Longe on her, and not on Landewalle.[4]
Herof they quytten° hym as treue° men,   *acquitted / true*
And sith° spake they farder° then,   *since, thereafter / further*
305 That yf he myght hys leman bryng,
Of whom he maide knolishyng°—   *acknowledgment*
And yef° her maydenyse° bryght and shyne   *if / maidens*
Wern faircr than the Quene
In maykyng,° semblaunt,° and hewe°— *proportion / appearance / complexion*
310 They wold quyte hym gode and true;
Yff he ne myght stonnd thertill,[5]
Thann° to be at the Kyngys will.   *Then*
This verdite° thei yef to-fore° the Kyng.   *verdict / before*
The day was sett her for-to bryng;
315 Borowys° he founde to com ayen,°   *Guarantors, Sureties / again*
Sir Gawyn and Sir Ewyn.
"Alas!" quod° he, "now shall I die;   *said*
My love shall I never see with ee!"°   *eye*
Ete ne drynke wold° he never,   *desired*
320 But wepyng° and sorowyng° evir   *weeping / grieving*
(Syres, sare° sorow hath he nom;°   *sore, painful / taken*
He wold hys endyng day wer com,
That he myght ought° of lif goo!)   *out*
Every man was for hym woo;
325 For larger° knyght than he   *more generous*
Was ther never yn that countrey.
The day i-sett° com on hyynge;°   *appointed / quickly*

2. I.e., in his place. (A trial setting is implied.)
3. See *Sir Launfal*, l. 786, n.
4. See *Sir Launfal*, l. 794, n.
5. (And) if he could not abide by that (proposal).

His borowys hym brought before the Kyng.
The Kyng lett recorte° tho   *be recounted*
330 The sewt° and the answer° also,   *suit, charge/verdict*
And bad hym bryng his [lef°]⁶ in syght;   *love*
Landevall sayd that he ne myght.
Tho were comaundyd the barons alle
To gyve judgement on Sir Landevall.
335 Then sayd the Erle of Cornwayll
That was att the councell,
"Lordyngys,° ye wott° the Kyng oure lord;   *Sirs/know*
His oun mowth beryth° record   *bears*
That yf we go by the lawe,
340 Landevale is worthy to be drawe.
Butt greatt vilany° were therupon   *dishonor*
To fordo° suche a man,   *destroy*
That is more large° and fre°   *generous/magnanimous*
Then° eny° of us that here be.   *Than/any*
345 Therfore, by oure read,°   *advice*
We woll the Kyng in suche a way lede°   *lead, direct*
That he shall comaund hym to goo
Oute of this land for evermo."°   *evermore*
While they stode thus spekyng,
350 They sawe in-fere° cum rydyng   *together*
Two maydyns, whyte as flower,
On whyte palfrays,° with honour.   *riding horses*
So fayre creaturys with yen°   *eyes*
(Ne better attyrd°) were never seen.   *dressed*
355 Alle the° judgyd theym so sheen   *they*
That over Dame Gaynour they myght be a queen.
Then sayd Gawen, that curteys knyght,
"Landevale, care the no-wyght!⁷
Here comyth thy leman, kynde i-core,⁸
360 For whom thow art anoied° sore."   *troubled*
Landevale lokyd and said, "Nay, i-wysse!°   *to be sure*
My leman of hem ther non is."
Thise maidens come so riding
Into the castell, befor the King.
365 They light adown, and grete hym so,
And besought hym of a chamber tho,
A place for their lady that was cummyng.
Than said Arthour, the nobill King,
"Who is your lady, and what to done?"⁹

---

6. The manuscript reads "borowis" (guarantors, sureties), which makes no sense, given that the presence of these figures is noted three lines above; the supplied reading is from *Sir Launfal,* l. 832.
7. I.e., let nothing worry you!
8. Of such choice nature.
9. Who is your lady, and what (is she) to do?

370 "Lord," quod° they, "ye may wetyn° sone."   *said / know*
    The King lete,° for her sake,   *allowed*
    The fairest chamber to be take;°   *chosen*
    Thise maidens gon to bowre° on hye.   *bower*
    Than said the King to his baronye,
375 "Have i-do,° and gyve jugement!"   *done*
    The barones saide, "Verament,°   *Truly*
    We have beholde these maidens bright—
    We will do anonright."[1]
    A new speche began they tho;
380 Summe said wele,[2] and summe said not so.
    Summe wolde hym to dethe deem—°   *sentence*
    The King their lorde for to queme;°   *please*
    Summe hym wolde make clere.°   *innocent*
    And while they spake thus in-fere,°   *together*
385 Other maidens ther commyn tho;
    Well more fairer than the other two—
    Riding upon moilés° of Spayne,°   *mules / Spain*
    Bothe sadellys and bridels of Almayn—°   *Germany*
    They were i-clothed in atire;
390 And eache a man had grete desire
    To beholde her gentrise,°   *good manners, breeding*
    They came in so faire assise.°   *setting*
    Than sade Gawyn the hend,
    "Landevale, broder, heder thou wende![3]
395 Here comyth thy love—thou maist wel se!
    That one herof, I wote,° ys she."   *know, am sure*
    Landevale,° with dropyng° thought:°   *L. (said thus) / depressed / countenance*
    "Nay, alas, I know them nought;
    I ne wote who they beith,°   *are*
400 Ne whens they com, ne whethir they lith."[4]
    These maidens reden° ynto the paleys,°   *ride / palace*
    Right afore the Kyngys deys,°   *dais*
    And gretith° hym and his Quene ek.°   *greet / also*
    That on° of them thise wordys spake: *one*
405 "Sir, riche Kyng Arthure,
    Lete dight° thyn hall with honour,   *adorn*
    Bothe rofe° and grounde and wallys   *ceiling*
    With clothys of gold and riche pallys;°   *hangings*
    Yet° it is lothely,° yef° thou so doo,   *Otherwise / loathly / unless*
410 My lady for-to light° therto."   *alight, dismount*
    The Kyng said, "So shall it be;
    My lady ys welcom, and soo be ye."

1. We have now seen the splendid maidens—we will act immediately (to reconsider).
2. Some spoke of (Landevale's) good fortune.
3. There you go!
4. I.e., nor whence they came, nor whither they go.

He bade Sir Gawyn bryng hem yn-fere

With honour ther° the othir° were.   *there (where)/others*

415   The Quen therfore trowid° of gyle,°   *imagined/guile, trickery*

That Landevale shuld he holpyn° in a while   *helped*

Of° his leman that ys comyng;   *By*

She cried, and said, "Lorde and Kyng,

And° thow lovyst thyn honour   *If*

420   I were° avenged on that tratour;   *would be*

To sle Landevale thu woldest not spare°—   *refrain*

Thy barons do thy besmare!"[5]

While she spake thus to the Kyng

They saw where cam ridyng

425   A lady, herself all alone—

On erthe fayrer was never none—

On a white palfrey comlye°   *attractive*

(There nesse° kyng that hath gold ne fee°   *is not/property*

That myght by° that palfrey   *buy*

430   Withoute sellyng of lond awey!)

This lady was bright as blossom on brere°—   *brier*

Her yeen° lofsum,° bright and clere—   *eyes/lovely*

Jentyll and jolyff° as birde° on bowgh,°   *merry/bird/bough*

In all thing faire ynowgh.°   *enough, in plenty*

435   As rose in May her rude° was rede,   *complexion (of cheek)*

Here here° shynyng on her hede   *hair*

As gold wyre° yn sonn° bright.   *wire, thread/sun*

In this worlde nas so faire a wight.°   *person*

A crown was upon her hede,

440   Al of precious stones and gold rede;[6]

Clothid she was yn purpyll pall,°   *cloth*

Her body gentill and medill° smale;°   *waist/narrow*

The pane° of hir mantell, inwarde,°   *side/inward, on the inside*

On hir harmes° she foldid owtewarde,   *arms*

445   Whiche wel becam that lady.

There white grehoundys went hyr by;

A sparowhauke she bare upon hir hand.

A softe° paas° her palfrey comaunde;°   *gentle/pace/established*

Throw the citie rode she

450   For° every man shuld hir see.   *So that*

Wiff and childe, yong and olde,

Al com hir to byholde;

There was man ne woman that myght

Be wery° of so faire a sight.   *weary, tired*

455   Also° son° as Landevale hir see,   *As/soon*

To all the lordys he cryed on he,[7]

---

5. I.e., your barons make a mockery of you!
6. Red gold (about which, see *Havelok*, l. 47, n.)
7. On high, aloud.

"Now comyth my love! Now comyth my swete!
Now comyth she° my bale° shall beete!°   *she (who)/suffering/relieve, cure*
Now I have her seyn with myn ee!
460 I ne reke° when that I dye."   *care*
The damsell com rydyng stoute°   *(in a) stately (manner)*
Alone yn the citie throwoute,
Throw the palys ynto the hall
Ther° was the Kyng and the Quene all.   *There (where)*
465 Her .iiii. maidens with gret honour
Agayne° her came oute of the bowre,°   *Toward/bower, chamber*
And held her steroppys° so;   *stirrups*
The lady dyd alight tho,
And they gently can hyr grete,
470 And she hym° with wordys swete.   *them*
The Quene and othir ladyes stoute
Behelde her all aboute;
They to° her were allso° donn°   *(compared, next) to/as/dun, dark*
As the monelyght° to the sonne!   *moonlight*
475 Than every man had grete deynté°   *pleasure*
Her to beholde, and preiseth hir beauté.
Than said the lady to the Kyng,
"Sir, I com for suche a thinge:
My trew leman, Sir Landevalle,
480 Is accusyd amonges you all
That he shuld with tratoury°   *treachery*
Beseche° the Quen of velony.°   *Beseech, Beg/shame, dishonor*
That ys fals, by Seynt Jame!°   *James*
He bad° her not, but she bad hym!   *bade*
485 And of that othir°—that he saide   *other (charge)*
That my lothliest maide
Was fairer than the Quene—
Loke anone yf yt so bene!"[8]
The Kyng beheld and sawe the southe,°   *truth*
490 Also erlys° and barons bothe;   *earls*
Every lorde said than
Landevale was a trew man.
When the jugement gyvyn was,
At the Kyng her leve she takys,
495 And lepe upon hir palfrey
And betoke° them to Gode and goode day.   *commended*
The Kyng full fare,° and all his,   *courteously*
Besechit hir, withoutyn mys,°   *wrong, fail*
Longer to make sojournyng;
500 She said, "Nay," and thankyd the Kyng.
Landevale saw hys love wold gone;°   *go*

8. Look now if it is so!

Upon hir horse he lepe anon,
And said, "Lady, my leman bright
I will with° the, my swete wight,   *(go) with*
505 Whedir° ye ride or goo—   *Whither*
Ne will I never parte you froo!"
"Landevale," she said withoutyn lette,°   *delay*
"Whan we first togedir mete,
With dern° love, withouten stryfe,°   *secret / strife*
510 I chargyd° you yn all your lyff   *charged, entreated*
That ye of me never speke shuld;
How dare ye now bie° so bolde   *be*
With me to ride withoute leve!°   *leave, permission*
Ye ought to thyng° ye shuld° me greve."° *think / would / grieve, offend*
515 "Lady," he said, "faire and goode,
For His love that shed His blode,
Foryef° me that trespace,°   *Forgive / offense*
And put me hole° yn your grace."   *wholly*
Than that lady to hym can speke,
520 And said to hym wyth wordys meke,° *meek, gentle*
"Landevale, lemman, I you forgyve
That trespace; while ye leve°   *live*
Welcom to me, gentill knyght—
We woll never twyn,° day ne nyght!" *separate, part*
525 So they rodyn° evynryght,°   *rode (off) / straight away*
The lady, the maydyns, and the knyght—
Loo!° howe love is lefe° to wyn° *Look, Behold / desirable / gain*
Of wemen that arn of gentyll° kyn!° *noble / kind, sort*
The same way have they nomyn°   *taken*
530 Ryght as before she was comyn;[9]
And thus was Landevale brought from Cardoyll° *Carlisle (cf. l.4)*
With his fere,° into a joly yle° *companion / isle, island*
That is clepyd° Amylyon[1]   *called*
That knowith every Brytan.[2]
535 Of hym syns° herd never man—   *since*
No further of Landevall tell I can;
Butt God, for His greatt mercy,
Bryng us to His blysse on highe.

Amen.

540 Explicit°   *(Here) ends (the text)*

---

9. I.e., just as she had taken earlier when she was coming.
1. see l. 92, n.
2. That is known by every Breton.

The Awntyrs off Arthure
at the Terne Wathelyne[1]

Four surviving MSS attest to the popularity of the *Awntyrs* in the fifteenth century at least;[2] and each MS presents variant readings of a kind which suggest antecedent currency in some form of oral transmission. The readings of each of the four versions are, nevertheless, substantially close most of the time, and the omission in all of the ninth line of the fourth stanza shows that they derive from a common original. That "original" was itself, however, a sophisticated composite of several favorite thematic and textual traditions—and the effectively bipartite structure of the poem is the most obvious sign of that composite provenance. The second episode (beginning at l. 339), with its account of a knightly duel fought to establish rightful claim over certain lands, is the more conventional for an Arthurian romance—the final duel between the titular heroes of *Ywain and Gawain* (ll. 3499 ff.) comes to mind. Indeed, because it is Gawain who agrees to take up Galeron's challenge, the episode aligns itself with a group of English romances in which the ideals of Arthurian courtesy (most often exemplified by Gawain) are examined, usually by being tested against often discourteous, often supernatural, challengers. Best-known and most accomplished of these is *Sir Gawain and the Green Knight*; *The Weddyng of Syr Gawen and Dame Ragnell* and *The Marriage of Sir Gawaine*, both edited in the present volume, are also representatives of the group.[3]

The first episode has the more complex background. The ghost of Guenevere's mother not only requests the singing of masses for the repose of her soul, but also utters monitory prophecies about the demise of Arthurian civilization, draws plangent attention to the implications of her own putre-faction, and gives advice to the highborn (in particular to Gawain and Guenevere) on how they must achieve salvation: the association of topics

---

1. For a brief overview of the background to Arthurian literature (and related Celtic traditions), see the Sources and Backgrounds headnote to *Ywain and Gawain*, pp. 329 ff. Editions and translations of the text mentioned in this headnote, as well as references to related scholarship, are cited in the Selected Bibliography.
2. The MSS are identified in the leading footnote to the edition proper.
3. The others are *The Avowynge of King Arthur, Sir Gawan, Sir Kaye, and Sir Bawdewyn of Bretan* (preserved uniquely in the "Blackburne Ireland" MS—one of the MSS in which the *Awntyrs* is found); *The Grene Knight*; *The Turke and Gowin*; *The Jeaste of Syr Gawayne*; *Golagrus and Gawain*; *Syre Gawene and the Carle of Carelyle*; and *King Arthur and King Cornwall*. The *Awntyrs* also belongs to a subgroup of these texts which are set in Inglewood Forest or which feature Tarn Wadling; about the group, see the Sources and Backgrounds headnote to *The Weddyng of Syr Gawen and Dame Ragnell*, pp. 378–79.

—often mercurial and seemingly unresolved—draws from several traditions and at least two specific texts.

In response to Guenevere's query about what kinds of prayers are best for her to say in the interests of obtaining heavenly bliss (l. 249), the ghost responds with a catalogue not of prayers, but of disposition and action: meekness, mercy, pity for the poor, charity, chastity, and almsgiving (ll. 250–53). With the exception perhaps of chastity, all of these values pertain to the right treatment of the disenfranchised, and they reinforce the ghost's earlier appeals to have pity upon the poor (ll. 173–82), to give to the poor (ll. 231–34), and to feed them (l. 319; and cf. ll. 321–23). The ghost concludes by calling these values "the graceful giftes of the Holy Goste" (l. 254). Her choice of words recalls the traditional catechistic heptad known as the Seven Gifts of the Holy Spirit; but the Seven Gifts are in fact Wisdom, Understanding, Counsel, Fortitude, Knowledge, Piety, and Fear of the Lord (so originally recorded in the Vulgate Isiah ll.2). In truth, as Dr. Hanna has observed, the values named by the ghost more closely reflect the Seven Corporal Acts of Mercy: feeding the hungry, giving drink to the thirsty, harboring the stranger, clothing the naked, comforting the sick, visiting the prisoner, and burying the dead (the list is based on Matthew 25.35); this is not to say, however, that the Seven Gifts are inconsistent with much of what the ghost advises. One might in turn be reminded of the Seven Deadly Sins; the ghost speaks of three of them explicitly: Pride at ll. 239–43, Covetousness at ll. 265–83, and Lust at ll. 213–14.[4] Middle English texts devoted to rehearsing such catechistic tallies as a means of lay instruction in elements of the Christian Faith are legion;[5] and yet none can be said to represent a direct source for the material as it appears in the Awntyrs. The *tradition* represented by such texts, nevertheless, is a source; and the ghost's pietistic catalogues are enough to provide an impression of the irreducible truth of her words, while also, in their incompleteness, perhaps reflecting the chronic distraction of her purgatorial torments (cf. ll. 109–10).

In a similar though somewhat more specific way, details of the ghost's condition and her requests are derived from a type of popular story in which a son is visited by the ghost of his mother, who suffers hellish or purgatorial torments for having committed adultery, and possibly other sins; the ghost then confirms certain theological truths and usually makes certain requests for the sake of her own salvation. Three Middle English examples of the type are printed here (though there are earlier Latin and continental versions). The first example, the *Trental of St. Gregory* (or *St. Gregory's Trental*), has long been recognized as a source, obviously because of the ghost's request for a trental (*Awntyrs*, ll.218–21, 230), but also because of corresponding incidental details—such as the darkness which attends the

---

4. It could be argued that the rest are treated by implication: Gluttony (ll. 178–82), Anger (see l. 295, n.), Sloth (as complacency, ll. 283, 296, 309–12), and perhaps Envy, in the prophecy of Mordred's usurpation (ll.285–312), coming as it does after an account of Arthur's foreign conquests (ll. 274–81).

5. And they are not just confined to heptads: there are, to cite some examples that were popular in their day, *The Sixtene Condiciouns of Charité*, *XII Degrees of Humility*, *Foure Errours*, *Four Tokens of Salvation*, *The Five Wits*, *Nine Virtues*, and so on. Few have been published in modern editions, but section XX of Volume 7 of *The Manual of the Writings in Middle English* (New Haven, 1986) provides a useful guide to the variety and content of such works—see pp. 2255–2378 and 2467–2582.

ghost, the man's challenging request for the ghost to identify itself, and the emotional, even homely, exchange thereafter between mother and child. The other two versions of the story type come from the *Gesta Romanorum* ("Deeds of the Romans"), a large collection of *exempla* (sg. *exemplum*, a kind of parable often used in sermons to illustrate a particular moral point). As D.N. Klausner has noted, besides illustrating the popularity and inter-textual variability of the story, each of these tales reflects (and suggests explanations for) details found in the *Awntyrs*. Both provide specific inter-pretations for the burning suffered by the ghost and for the raptorial toads and serpents. The first, moreover, shows how the story could be conceived as a warning about the prospect of unmitigated damnation rather than the hope of salvation;[6] the second perhaps shows the influence of the *Trental* in the son's misidentification of his transformed mother as the Blessed Virgin.

In all these texts, including the *Awntyrs*, the ghost's condition and her related warnings about what awaits sinners in death belong to the very widespread tradition of the *memento mori* ("remember that you must die"). The tradition is represented not just in texts, but in art—most dramatically on tombs having a sculpture of the naked and emaciated cadaver—where the dead are sometimes depicted as infested with vermin such as worms, serpents, mice, snails, spiders, or toads (and sometimes the sculpture is matched by a second which depicts the deceased as known in hale life). The cadaver is the inescapable end of all worldly ambition; the implication is just that framed by Guenevere's mother at ll. 165–69 and 259–60. A related tradition invoked by the ghost concerns the vicissitudes of Fortune's Wheel. The immediate source is identifiable in the Middle English allit-erative *Morte Arthure*, an accomplished heroic work devoted to tracing the rise and sudden fall of Arthur's achievement; see ll. 265–312 and notes thereto. The second part of the poem also shows the influence of *Morte Arthur*, albeit in less significant ways (cf. the notes to ll. 417 and 655).

Besides the *Morte Arthure*, two other alliterative poems, *Somer Soneday* and *De Tribus Regibus Mortuis* ("Concerning the Three Dead Kings"), show notable affinities with the first part of the *Awntyrs*. Both, like the *Awntyrs*, employ a thirteen-line alliterative stanza with end rhyme;[7] *Somer Soneday* employs concatenation, and *De Tribus Regibus Mortuis* employs iteration between the eighth and ninth lines of each stanza. Both poems open with scenes of a splendid aristocratic hunt[8] and then move quickly to familiar monitory episodes. In *Somer Soneday* the narrator walks far away from the hunt and, having grown weary, sits down under a tree. He then has a vision of Fortune ("so wonder a whelwryghth," l.63; cf. *Awntyrs*, l. 271) and her wheel. Four men are seen on the wheel: the first, rising upward, declares his ambition to succeed; the second, a crowned king at the height of his power, sits in glory at the top of the wheel; the third, moving downward, is an old king now divested of his possessions and his rule; the fourth, at the bottom of the wheel, lies dead, a "Duke" who has met his end with

---

6. Something of the desperation of this version is latent in the *Awntyrs*. Although presumably the ghost's torments are ended by Guenevere's delegated trentals, traditional Arthurian history of course dictates that her prophecies of Arthur's downfall cannot have been heeded.

7. For details about the versification of the *Awntyrs*, see the leading footnote to the edition proper.

8. Such hunt scenes are to an extent conventional, their use often ironic; see the Sources and Backgrounds headnote to *The Weddyng of Syr Gawen and Dame Ragnell*, pp. 378–79.

"drouping and dare" (suffering and grief)—and those words abruptly end the poem, so pointing the severity of the traditional theme. *De Tribus Regibus Mortuis* relates a version of the widespread story (often depicted in medieval illustrations) of "The Three Living and the Three Dead." Whilst hunting, three young kings are enveloped suddenly in a mist and then confronted by the cadaverous shades of their fathers. The first shade warns that the living kings should repent of cruelties done to those who do not do their bidding, and declares his regret that the sons are not disposed to "mynn us with a mas" (l. 104; cf. *Awntyrs*, ll. 229–30, 236, 320, and 706); the second punningly reminds the living kings, "Thagh ye be never so fayre, thus schul ye fare" (l. 110; cf. the argument of *Awntyrs*, ll. 137–69) and warns them against the further seeking of fleshly pleasures; the third commands them, "Makis your merour be me!" (l. 120; cf. *Awntyrs*, l. 167) and warns against the mistreatment of common folk. Central to both poems, as to the *Awntyrs*, is a concern for the uncompromisingly devout conduct of the powerful.

It is important to keep in mind that the *Awntyrs* as a whole is governed by traditions associated with the alliterative (verse) medium; the poem finds analogues in both form and content with a number of Middle English alliterative poems. The medium is in principle at least as ancient as the written language, manifest in such texts as the *Anglo-Saxon Chronicle*, *Beowulf*, and Ælfric's *Lives of the Saints*. Predominantly alliterative (as opposed to mainly rhyming) verse experienced an apparent hiatus from texts written between the beginning of the thirteenth century and the middle of the fourteenth; thereafter such verse is held to have enjoyed a "Revival" (just how and why this happened is not entirely clear) out of which some of the great works of medieval English literary art were conceived—among them *Morte Arthure*, *Sir Gawain and the Green Knight*, *Pearl*, *Piers Plowman*, the *Wars of Alexander*. At first sight the choice of such a medium—especially one to which is added the intricate stanza form adopted by the *Awntyrs*—may seem unduly restrictive; but there are advantages. The medium is rhythmically insistent, even relentless, capable of an impressive mimetic palpability in accounts of action and high emotion; it is also capable of an arresting gravity in moments of reflection and an apposite sense of rigor in depictions of form, ceremony, and manners. Another advantage lies in the way in which the essential facts and actions of nearly every line are thrown into relief as the alliterating words. Further, the demands of finding alliterative complements for any given line have given rise to a specialized synonymic vocabulary (witness the various forms of "going" in the *Awntyrs*—in the passive, there are *went*, *glode*, *brayd*, *fore* and *dight*). In better alliterative poems, as in the *Awntyrs*, the effect can be to invite a sensitivity to the ways in which an original meaning is subjected to modulations which are accretive rather than substitutive. For example, between lines 83 and 104 the ghost is identified as a *lau*, *goost*, *sprete*, and *bodi*; an impression is thus constructed of a creature at once of this world and ethereal, decomposing but aflame, spiritual (in the sense of a soul capable of reaching heaven) and yet ghostly (in the sense of a soul confined to the earth and infernal regions).

It has long been a commonplace to remark that the *Awntyrs* comprises two poems somewhat incongruously thrown together, each the work of a different author (with the final stanza belonging to the first part but having been displaced by the second). Certainly each part bears the impress of different source traditions, but recent scholarship has tended to find more to be said for the notion that the poem represents an eschatological unity wrought by one poet. In light of such a proposition, it can be useful to stand back from the poem and keep a few general observations in mind. Firstly, it can be argued that both parts in fact constitute "testing" stories of the kind remarked above; both tell of challenges thrown down to the Arthurian court which demand that the court serve the needy better—be they repentant souls in purgatory, the poor, or the dispossessed. It could be said that either part, as a tale of pride admonished and charity tested, is an analogue to the other. If, moreover, the first part, with its impressively variegated intercalation of texts and traditions, stands as a testimony to the recombinant genius of its author, then it is possible to see the addition of the second part as simply providing further such testimony. Finally, the alliteration and the formalized concatenation and iteration all draw together images and ideas, the potential links between which might otherwise have gone unnoticed or been thought unlikely;[9] the very fabric of the poem, then, is associative, and one should be invited by that circumstance constantly to seek affinities on the larger scale.

The Trental of St. Gregory†

The Pope Trental

I-writen° I fynde a good stori;	*Written*
The Pope hit° wrot,° Seint Gregori,[1]	
Of° his modur,° and of hire° lyf,°	*About / mother / her / life*
That alle men heolden an holi hosewyf,[2]	
5 So sad° of maner, so mylde° of mood,	*steadfast, sober / mild, gentle*
That alle men heolden hire° holi and good;	*her*
Deboner,° devout, so milde of stevene,°	*Humble / voice, speech*
That alle men gesset° hire worthi to° hevene.°	*supposed / of / heaven*
As holi i-holden as heo° was,	*she*

---

9. In instances of concatenation, note for example the transformation of sense or the transposition of action at ll. 91–92, 195–96, 611–12, 624–25. Some notable examples of alliteration which renders meaningfully unlikely complements are at ll. 150–52, 162 and 164, 183–84, 215, 530, 640–41.

† Text of Oxford, Bodleian Library MS Eng. Poet. A.1 (the "Vernon Manuscript"), ff. 231ʳ-232ᵛ. The manuscript is dated c. 1390; the poem's date of composition is held to have been sometime after 1350. The poem is written in nominally four-stess rhyming couplets; alliteration is common but not regular.

1. St. Gregory "the Great" (c. 540–604), Pope from 590. The essence of the story most likely predates Gregory and, as the two other texts in this Sources and Backgrounds section suggest, is but one of many varaiations on the motif of the cautionary visitation of a dead relative. The attribution of authorship to Gregory reflects the supposition that he originated the scheme of saying thirty masses for the help of departed souls; Gregory was also one of the most important early proponents of the doctrine of purgatory (about which see *The Awntyrs off Arthur*, l. 165, n.).

2. Who all men held to be a devout family woman.

10 The fend yit falled hire in a foul cas:[3]	
He truyled° hire with his tricherye°	*cheated / treachery*
And ladde° hire in to lecherye,	*led*
That lust with love hire so be-gylede[4]	
So foule° til heo was with childe.	*shamefully*
15 So priveliche notheles heo hire bar	
That therof nas no wiht i-war.[5]	
And, for° no wiht° schulde wite°	*so that / person / know*
hire cas,°	*situation*
Anon as hire child i-boren° was,	*born*
The nekke° heo nom,° the child heo woriede,°	*neck / seized / strangled*
20 And anon the child heo buriede.	
Thus was heo cumbred° in careful° cas,	*encumbered / (a) sorrowful*
Ne schewed never schrift therof, allas,	
For heo wolde holy i-holde be;[6]	
Heo tolde never prest° hire privité.°	*priest / secret*
25 Al folk fayn° was of hire fame,	*delighted*
So holy as heo was holden of name.°	*reputation*
Eft-sones hir fel the same cas	
Riht as bi-foren bi-tyd hire was![7]	
For° heo was comen° of prys° parage,°	*Because / descended / noble / rank*
30 Of riche kun,° of gentil° lynage°—	*kin / noble / lineage*
Hire° sone° was Seynt Gregori the Pope—	*(Because) her / son*
Men heolden hire holy with al heore° hope;°	*their / belief, trust*
Therfore heo schonede° hir schrift°	*shunned / confession*
to schowe°	*make known*
Leste° by schrift hire cas weor° knowe.°	*Lest / were / known, exposed*
35 So schome° maketh men schone heor schrift	*shame*
And leose the grace of Godus gift,[8]	
And sithen° to liven so sunfulli,°	*thereafter / sinfully*
And sorily dyen and sodeynli.[9]	
This wommones dedes ner° not aspyet,°	*were / spied out, detected*
40 And softly° sone° theraftur heo dyed;	*quietly, peacefully / soon*
Whon° heo was seyen° so softly dye,	*When / seen to*
Men hopede heo weore in hevene ful highe.	
Men heolden hir holy and so devoute	
That of hire deth men hedden° no doute,°	*had / fear*
45 But wenden° witerly° alle to wisse°	*expected / undoubtedly / know, discover*
That heo weore set in sovereyn° blisse.	*sovereign, highest*

---

3. I.e., the devil still disgraced her in one shameful situation.
4. Such that desire for (illicit) love so beguiled her.
5. So discreetly nonetheless did she conduct herself that nobody was aware of that.
6. Nor, alas, did she ever make known a confession to it, for she wished to be considered devout.
7. Again the same situation befell her just as had happened to her before! (I.e., she became pregnant again, and again killed the child.)
8. And lose the grace of God's gift (i.e., forfeit everlasting life).
9. I.e., and die wretchedly and unexpectedly.

Theraftur, withinne a luytel° tyme,   *little*
Upon a day, sone aftur prime,[1]
Hire sone° the Pope at masse stood—   *son*
50   And of his modur° trouwed° bote° good.   *mother / believed / (nothing) but*
Al sodeynliche,° amidde his messe,°   *suddenly / mass*
Ther drouh° touward him such a derknesse°   *drew / darkness*
That lakkede° al the dayes lyht;°   *failed / light*
And was° derk as° hit° weore midniht,°   *(it) was / as (if) / it / midnight*
55   And in that derknesse a myst among;[2]
Al stoneyd° he was—such stunch° ther stong!°   *astonished / stench / stank*
Therof so grislich° he was agast°   *horribly / frightened*
That al swounyng he was almast.[3]
Beosyde he loked undur his leor:[4]
60   Amidde the derknesse ther drough on ner°   *near(er)*
A wonder° grisli° creature—   *wondrously / horrific*
Riht aftur a fend ferde hire feture—[5]
So ragget, so rent,° so elyng,° so uvel,°   *torn / ailing, morbid / evil*
As hidous° to biholden as helle-devel;   *hideous*
65   Mouth and neose, eres and eghes°   *eyes*
Flaumed al ful of furi lighes.[6]

He asked hit heighlich,° "Thorwh° His miht°   *solemnly / Through / power*
That alle develes schal dreden° and diht,°   *dread, fear / contend with*
And eke° bi vertu° of His blood   *also / power*
70   That for monkynde dighed° on rod,°   *died / rood, cross*
Sey° me anon the sothe° soone: *Tell / truth*
What hastou° in this place to done?°   *have you / do*
What is thi° cause,° thou cursede wrecche,°   *thy / purpose / wretch*
Thus me at masse to derve° and drecche?"°   *harass / torment*

75   The gost onswerde with dreri° cher,°   *dreary, sad / countenance*
"I am thi moodur that the° beer,°   *thee / bore, gave birth to*
That for unschrivene dedes derne[7]
In bitter peynes° thus I berne."°   *pains, torments / burn*

Then onswerd the Pope, "Allas!
80   Allas, my modur, this wondur° cas!   *wondrous*
Allas, my modur, hou may this be
In such aray° I the to° seo?°   *condition / (come) to / see*
Men wenden witerli to wisse
Thou weore wel worthi to habbe° blisse,   *have, receive*

---

1. On *prime*, see *Ywain and Gawain*, l. 2304, n.
2. And (there was) a mist within that darkness.
3. He was almost completely (on the point of) fainting.
4. He looked downward and to the side over his cheek.
5. Her features took after those of a fiend.
6. Were aflame, all full of fiery lights.
7. Who for secret unconfessed deeds.

85	And that ful wel° with God thou were,	*fittingly, certainly*
	To preyen° for us that liven yit° here.	*pray / yet, still*
	Sei° me, modur, withouten feyne,°	*Tell / dissembling*
	Whi art thou put to al this peyne?"	
	Heo seide, "My sone, sothfastly°	*truly*
90	I schal the telle the cause why:	
	For I nas not such as I seemed,	
	But wikked, and worse then° men me demed.°	*than / judged*
	I sungede° wikkedliche in my lyve,	*sinned*
	Of° whuch I ne dorste° for schome me schrive."	*For / durst*
95	Heo tolde him trewely al° hire cas	*all (about)*
	From ende° to othur, riht° as hit was.	*(one) end / just*

	"Sei me, modur, for Marie flour,°	*flower*
	Yif° ought° may beo° thi socour,°	*If / anything / be / salvation*
	Wher° penaunce of° fasting mai ought alegge,°	*Whether / by / alleviate*
100	Beodes° or masses thi peynes abregge,°	*Prayers / reduce*
	Or eny° maner° othur thyng	*any / manner (of), kind (of)*
	That the mai helpe of° eny lissyng?"°	*with / relief from pain*

	"Mi deore° blessede sone," seide heo,	*dear*
	"Ful wel i-holpen° I mihte° beo;	*helped / might, may*
105	Holpen and saved I mihte beo wel	
	Hose° undurtoke a trewe trentel[8]	*(By) whosoever*
	Of ten cheef° festes° of al the yer°	*chief / feast days, festivals / year*
	To synge for me, in this maneer:	
	Threo° masses of° Cristes Nativité,[9]	*Three / celebrating*
110	And of the Ephiphan[1] othur° thre;	*others*
	Threo of the Purificaciun,[2]	
	And threo of the Annunciaciun;[3]	
	Threo of the Resurrexiun,[4]	
	And threo of the Ascenciun;[5]	
115	Of the Pentecost[6] othur thre,	
	And threo of the Holy Trinité;[7]	
	Threo of Maries Nativité,[8]	

8. A true trental. (Cf. *The Awntyrs off Arthure*, l. 218, n.)
9. The feast of the Nativity (i.e., Christmas), December 25.
1. The feast of the Epiphany (celebrating the manifestation of Christ, in the persons of the Magi, to the Gentiles—see Matthew 2.1–12), January 6.
2. The feast of the Purification (also known as Candlemas, celebrating the purification of the Virgin Mary in the Temple—see Luke 2.21–39), February 2.
3. The feast of the Annunciation (also known as Lady Day, celebrating the announcement to Mary by the archangel Gabriel of the Incarnation of Christ and His conception in her womb—see Luke 1.26–38), March 25.
4. The feast of the Resurrection (i.e., Easter), held on the first Sunday after the full moon which occurs on or after March 21.
5. The feast of the Ascension (Christ's repair to heaven), held on the sixth Thursday after Easter.
6. See *Sir Launfal*, l. 133, n.
7. The feast of the Holy Trinity (i.e., Trinity Sunday), the first Sunday after Pentecost.
8. The feast of the Nativity of the Blessed Virgin, September 8.

And of hire Concepcioun[9] other thre.
Theose weoren the cheef festes ten
120 That sovereynliche° socourde synful men;   *chiefly*
What godmon syngeth theos masses, saunfaile[1]
To synful soule° thei schullen° avayle°—   *souls / shall, will / be helpful*
With the yeer, with-outen treyne,[2]
Diliveren° a soule ful out of peyne.   *Deliver, Release*
125 Let sei theos masses bi youre hestes
With-inne the utaves of the festes—[3]
And he that schal theos masses do,
Let sei therwith the orisun therto,[4]
Treoweliche,° withouten were,°   *Faithfully / doubt*
130 Everi day thorwhout° the yere;   *throughout*
Heet° him sei hit° everi day,   *Bid, Command / it*
Othur he that doth the masses to say.[5]
  Hose° wol knowe this orisun clene,°   *(For) whosoever / completely*
Hit is on° Englisch thus much to mene:°   *in / say*
135 'God, ur° verrey° redempciun,   *our / true*
Ur sothfast° soules savaciun°   *true / salvation*
That chose al othur londes biforn
The Lond of Biheste in to beo born,[6]
And thi deth suffredest in that same,°   *same (land)*
140 Dilivere this soule from gult° and blame;°   *guilt / censure*
Tak hit out of the fendes bond°—   *bonds*
And that lond from the hethene hond—[7]
And people that leveth° not in the   *believe*
Thorwh thi vertu amendet° mote° be;   *corrected / may (they)*
145 And alle that trusteth in thi merci,
Lord, save hem sone° and sothfastli.' "   *soon*

  "A,° modur," he seide, "that wol I do!   *Ah, Oh*
For I am mon most i-holde therto;[8]
Thou weore my modur, I was thi sone.
150 To synge the masses I schal not schone;°   *shun, avoid*
God graunte me, modur, the stonde in stede[9]
Ayeynes° the° synnes that ever thou dude.°   *Against / (all) the / committed*

---

9. The feast of the Immaculate Conception of the Blessed Virgin (celebrating the conception of Mary as free from all stain of the original sin of Adam), December 8.
1. Without fail, whatever worthy man sings these masses.
2. (They will) with the passing of the year, (I tell you) without deceit.
3. Have these masses performed according to your bidding within the octaves of the feasts (i.e., within the eight-day periods which comprise the feast day and the week following).
4. Have said with it the appertaining prayer.
5. Or he who has the masses said (i.e., you Gregory yourself).
6. Who chose before all other lands to be born in the Promised Land (i.e., Palestine).
7. And (take also) that land from the hands of the heathens. (A reference to the fact that the Holy Land had for most of the time since the eleventh century been in Muslim hands.)
8. For I am the man most (closely) committed to that.
9. May God allow me, mother, to be of help to you.

I halse° the heighliche, modur deere,	*beseech*
This tyme twelf-moneth° to me apeere;	*(in) a twelvemonth*
155 Hol° thin astat to me thou schowe,°	*Wholly / show, reveal*
That° hou thou fare° I mouwe° wel knowe."	*(So) that / fare, get on / may*

"Mi sone," heo seide, "I wole, in fey—"°	*faith*
And with that word heo wente hir wey.	
So, day from day the yer con° passe:	*did*
160 The Pope forlette° never his masse	*neglected*
The° same° dayes that weoren asignet,°	*(On) the / very / assigned*
To helpen his modur that was so pynet,°	*pained, tormented*
And tok° the orisun algate° therto	*undertook / always*
Als° as his modur preiyede° him do.	*Just / besought*

165 That tyde° twelf-moneth at masse he stod,	*time*
Holyliche,° with devociun good:	*Religiously*
And in that same tyde apliht°	*promised*
He sayz a swithe selli siht,[1]	
A comeli° ladi, so dresset° and diht°	*noble / dressed / adorned*
170 That al the world of° hire schon briht—	*(because) of*
Comeli° corouned° as a qweene,	*Nobly / crowned*
Tweyn angeles ladden hire hem bitwene.[2]	
He was so ravischt° of° that siht,	*ravished, overcome / by*
Almost for joye he swounede riht.[3]	
175 He fel doun flat biforen hire feet;	
The teres of his eyen° he doun leet.°	*eyes / let*
He grette° hire with wel° mylde stevene°	*greeted / very / voice*
And seyde, "Ladi, Qween of Hevene,	
Moodur of Jhesu, mylde Marie,	
180 For my moodur merci I crie!"°	*cry, beg*

"Do wey!" heo seide, "I nam not heo,[4]	
Ne whom thou wenest° that I beo,	*(could) imagine*
Bote, sothlyche, as thou seost° me her,°	*see / here*
I am the mooder that the° beer!°	*thee / bore*
185 Biforen I ferde°—thou wustest° wel—	*went about / know*
Farynge° as° a fend of hel;°	*Behaving, Seeming / like / hell*
I am nou° such as thou sest her,	*now*
Thorwh help and vertu of thi preyer	
From derknesse i-dresset° to blisse cleer°—	*turned, advanced / bright*
190 The tyme beo blesset° that I the beer!	*blessed*
And for the kuyndenesse° of thi deede	*kindness*
Sovereyn joye schal beo thy meede.°	*reward*
And alle° that leteth theos masses thus do,°	*all (those) / be performed*

1. He sees a very wonderful sight.
2. Two angels escorted her between them.
3. Cf. l. 58; note how this and other parts of the subsequent description play antithetically on the former description of the ghost.
4. "Do away (with all that)!" she said, "I am not she."

Schul save hemslef and soules also;[5]
195 Therfore, sone,° this storie thou preche!°   son / preach
Mi dere sone, God° I the beteche."°   (to the care of) God / commend
    Whon heo hedde endet this wordes evene,[6]
Angeles token hire hom° to hevene—   home
The same hom to God us sende,
200 To wone° with Him withouten ende.   dwell
Amen.

Two Exempla *from the* Gesta Romanorum†

[I]
[A Mother Eternally Damned Appears to Her Son]

A woman there was some tyme that had a sone° by   son
here° housbonde that was sette° to the scole;° and   her / sent / school
when he was of age, he was made a preste,° and   priest
studied to lyve religeously. This wyfe had
conseyved afterward .ij.° sonys in avoutery;° and,   two / adultery
when the childryn were waxen,° she deyed.° Then   grown / died
the fyrste sone that she had by here housbond,
that was a preste, was full besy° for to pray° the   diligent / pray (for)
salvacion of his modyrs° soule, and songe° many   mother's / sang
masses for here, prayeng to God devoutely that
he myght wete° how his modre fared.° On a day as   know / fared, got on
he prayde, there aperid° to hym a fourme° of a   appeared / apparition
woman, fro° whose hede° he sawe a derke° flawme° from / head / dark / flame
rise up; and on here lippes and on here tonge° he   tongue
sawe an horreble tode° gnawe, and sesid° not; and   toad / (it) ceased
fro hire tetis° he sawe hange .ij. serpentes, sore°   breasts / sorely
soukynge° hem;° and the skyn° on here back was   sucking / them / skin
drawen downe to here hammes,[1] and trayled°   trailed
after here, all on fyre.° Then seide° the preste,   fire / said
"What arte thou, in the name of God?" She answerid, and
seide, "I am thy modyre; beholde and se° to what   see
paynes° I am putte everlastyngly for my synnes."° pains, torments / sins
Then he asked here for what synnes she suffred
thes° paynes. She seide, "I am tormentid with this   these
blew° fyre on my hede for my lecherouse   blue

---

5. I.e., will save themselves as well as the souls for whom they have had the masses sung.
6. As soon as she had concluded these words.
† Text of London, British Library MS Additional 9066, printed with the permission of the British Library; the first selection is edited from f. 66ᵛ, the second from ff. 76ʳ-76ᵛ. The manuscript is dated c. 1440; the original translation from the Latin may have been done only twenty years before that.
1. Peeled down to the backs of her knees.

anourement of myn heere and other array theron;[2]
in my lyppes and my tonge, for wicked and veyne°   *vain*
speches° and lecherouse kyssynges I suffere thes   *speaking, talk*
todes to frete;° on my tetis I have thes .ij.   *gnaw*
serpentes soukyng—so sore that me thinketh they
souke° oute my herte-blode°—for I gafe° souke and   *suck / lifeblood / gave*
noryshed my .ij. hore-coppis;° and my brennynge°   *bastards / burning*
skynne, drawene of° and folowyng me, is for my   *off*
large trayne° of clothe, that I was wonte to drawe   *train*
aftire me while I levyd° on erthe." "A! modre," he   *lived*
seide, "mowe° ye not be savyd?" "No," she saide,   *might*
and wente away from his sight.

[II]
[A Son Releases His Mother from Purgatory]

There was a man that dred° the paynes of   *dreaded, feared*
Purgatorie,[3] and prayde° oure Lorde that He wolde   *prayed, asked*
sende hym a sekenesse° in the stid° of Purgatorie;   *sickness / stead, place*
and God sente into hym the fallyng evyll,[4] and the
lipre,° and the fyre of helle.[5] And he suffred tho°   *leprosy / those*
.iij.° sekenesse .xv.° yere, and than come an   *three / fifteen / angel*
aungille°
to hym, and seide, "Thy sekenesse are take° from   *removed*
the,° and God hathe forgevyn the thy synne." And   *thee*
when he was hole,° he spake to the aungille, and   *cured*
seide, "I pray the that I may have the same
paynes agayne, for to delyver° my modre,° if that   *release / mother*
she be in payne."° The aungill seide, "If thou   *pain (of Purgatory)*
suffred thes peynes fro° the fyrste day of thy   *from*
byrthe unto thyn ende,° thou shuld not delyver   *end, death*
here° the peynne of oo° day that she sufferith. But   *her (from) / one*
make the° a preste,° and pray to God that He wil   *(of) yourself / priest*
shewe° to the the state of thy modre, and how she   *show*
may be holpyn."° He did so; and when he had   *helped*
songen his fyrste masse, he lefte° still, alone in the   *remained*
kyrke.° And his modre aperid to hym, and shewed   *church*
to hym a brennyng° hande, in the which she was   *burning*
wonte to bere rynges.[6] After this she shewed here
herte brennyng, and a tode gnawyng thereon for°   *because of*
pride that she had in here herte for here clothyng

---

2. For my wanton adornment of my hair and other such display.
3. On Purgatory, see *The Awntyrs off Arthur*, l. 165, n.
4. The falling sickness (i.e., epilepsy).
5. Fire of hell (i.e., an inflammatory disease of the skin, perhaps erysipelas, also known as St. Anthony's Fire.)
6. (The one) on which she was wont to wear rings.

and here arraye.° And anone° sho was   *appearance/anon, forthwith*
brente,° and turnyd° into askys,°   *burned/(she) turned/ashes*
and rose agayne—
and saide that sevynty tymes on the day she
suffred this payne. Than the sonne askid how this'
payne myght be released. She answerid, prayeng
hym that he wolde syng° for here all° a yere. He   *sing (masses)/all (of)*
grauntid° therto, and did° it; and anone she   *granted, agreed/began*
was out of his sight. And after the yeris° ende he   *year's*
sawe twoo [aungilles], and betwene hem° a fayre°   *them/fair, beautiful*
woman, the which he had wende° hadben Oure   *imagined, thought*
Ladie, Seynte° Marie; and she seide to hym, "I   *Holy, Saint*
am not Marie, but I am thy modere that, for° the   *because of*
and thy messes syngyng for me, I ame delyvered
from allpeynes, and go to the joyes of paradise.
And, forthou haste done thus, thou haste bothe
delyvered me and the from all woo;° and thy   *woe, anguish*
merite° is sette in hevyn redy agayne thou   *reward*
come[7]—and sone° shalte   *soon*
thou come therto."

---

7. Ready against your coming.

The Weddyng of Syr Gawen and Dame Ragnell for Helpyng of Kyng Arthoure[1]

As students of Chaucer's Wife of Bath's Tale (WBT) will remark, *The Weddyng of Syr Gawen and Dame Ragnell* (a recognized analogue to the WBT) employs the common European folk-tale motif of the "Loathly Lady" transformed. As is also the case with the WBT, the poem links the transformation of the hag with a worthy man's abdication to her of complete sovereignty over him. The linking of the two motifs appears to have Celtic origins and has been traced by G. H. Maynadier to an Irish tradition evidenced by tales such as the *Adventures of the Son of Eochaid Mugmedon*, where a would-be king takes up the challenge of a hag and kisses her, whereupon she is transformed into a beautiful woman personifying the Sovereignty of Ireland. Sigmund Eisner further argues for the intermediary influence of cognate Welsh, Breton, and French tales, by which the sovereignty at issue is transformed from the regnal to the domestic.

Like the WBT, the *Weddyng* sets these motifs in an Arthurian context.[2] More specifically, it sets them in the context of a distinctive corpus of Middle English texts in which Gawain usually has his renowned courtesy and martial prowess tested (this is usually done by supernatural or otherwise extraordinary challengers; and sometimes it is not Gawain but Arthur or other knights of the Round Table who are so tested).[3] Further, the *Weddyng* is a member of a subgroup of these texts which sets much of the action in the enchanted environs of Inglewood Forest.[4] Besides the *Weddyng*, that group consists of *The Avowynge of King Arthur, Sir Gawan, Sir Kaye, and Sir Bawdewyn of Bretan*; *The Awntyrs off Arthure at the Terne Wathelyne*; and, closer to the *Weddyng* than the others, *The Marriage of Sir Gawaine*, here printed. The

---

1. For a brief overview of the background to Arthurian literature (and related Celtic traditions), see the Sources and Backgrounds headnote to *Ywain and Gawain*, p. 329 ff. Editions and translations of the texts mentioned in this headnote, as well as references to related scholarship, are cited in the Selected Bibliography. On the date of the poem, see the leading footnote to the edition proper.
2. Two other early English treatments of this type of tale (both of which exclude an Arthurian context) are the ballad *King Henry* and the Tale of Florent in John Gower's *Confessio Amantis*; the latter is edited with glosses and explanatory notes in the Sources and Backgrounds section of V. A. Kolve and Glending Olsen, eds., *The Canterbury Tales: Nine Tales and the General Prologue* (a Norton Critical Edition, New York, 1989), pp. 359–69.
3. All of the texts of this group are named in the Sources and Backgrounds headnote to *The Awntyrs off Arthure*, p. 365, and n. 3.
4. On the region, see *The Awntyrs off Arthure*, l. 2, n. 1.

prelude to adventure in these tales is very often a hunt in the forest, which event develops the familiar irony of the hunter becoming the hunted.

Although the *Weddyng* participates in this group, it also stands in a derivative relationship to it (and to other Arthurian texts) inasmuch as the poem's impudent humor (not unlike some of the humor of the WBT) presupposes a secure familiarity with conventional and serious Arthurian values. Thus, while the *Weddyng*, just like other "testing" poems, questions the integrity of Arthurian excellence, it does so not as does, say, the *Awntyrs*, on the exalted level of personal honor, political justice, chivalric service of women, and charity, but at the antithetical and ridiculous level of such things as bumbling and furtive breaches of contract (e.g., ll. 173–90), opportunistic deal-making and manipulation (e.g., ll. 279–335), the dismissal of a woman on the basis of her appearance (e.g., ll. 252–84), and begrudging bravado (e.g., ll. 485–90, 814–16).

The *Marriage* too has elements of this kind of subversion—as in the way Arthur in effect volunteers Gawain for marriage to the hag without first consulting with him (*Marriage*, ll. 77–80, *Weddyng*, ll. 303–5), or in the way he has, like some sort of uncertain bureaucrat attempting to confound an inquiry, written down many proposed answers to the challenger's question (*Marriage*, l. 88, *Weddyng*, ll. 190–211). At the same time, however, it should be clear that any humor the *Marriage* possesses is not as various and, dare one say, sophisticated as it is in the *Weddyng*. One manifestation of the difference lies in the probability that, as P. J. C. Field has remarked, the *Weddyng* may glance at the Wife of Bath's Tale—notably at ll. 199–203 (though the rhyme scheme is disturbed, suggesting a later interpolation; cf. WBT 925–28), 409 ff. (cf. WBT 927–28, where the hag speaks in the first person plural), 416–19 (cf. WBT 929–34) and 622–24 (cf. WBT 1073–76). Perhaps, moreover, l. 631 recalls the Wife of Bath's triumphant reference, in her prologue (ll. 197–98), to the attractions of the "conjugal debt." And perhaps it is the influence of Chaucer generally which inspires a number of exquisitely inane one-liners (there are too many for all to be accidental: e.g., ll. 30, 163, 221, 472, 556, 609, 667, 738), and Dame Ragnell's impressively quick-witted rejoinders (e.g., ll. 309–17, 581–86, 644–46).

A further difference is noticeable between the *Marriage* and the *Weddyng* in the way that the humor of the *Weddyng* at times presupposes a familiarity not just with the values of related texts but also with elements of their very form; at such points the poem tends toward literary travesty (a mode related to parody, burlesque, and caricature—the term does not indicate that it is a *bad* poem). Most obvious perhaps in this respect is the way the poem concludes with two false endings, the first promising to "make an end full sone" of (the subject of) Dame Ragnell and then promptly killing her off (see ll. 817–28 and notes thereto), the second mimicking the repetition of introductory lines which concludes "testing" poems like *Sir Gawain and the Green Knight* (ll. 2525 vs. 1), the *Avowynge of King Arthur* (ll. 1148 vs. 1), and the *Awntyrs* (see the note to l. 836 of the *Weddyng*).[5] The third

---

5. It is also worth noting the presence in the *Weddyng* of what might just be construed as vestiges of concatenating stanza-linking of the kind found, for instance, in the *Awntyrs* and, to a lesser extent, in the *Avowynge of King Arthur*; cf. the *Weddyng*, ll. 36–37, 133–35, 493–97, 508–

and final conclusion also smacks of irreverent imitation. If we assume the poem to have been written late in the fifteenth century, the third conclusion probably constitutes an allusion to Sir Thomas Malory's *Morte Darthur* (completed 1470–71), notably to the end of Book IV, where Malory admits to writing his work as a "knyght presoner" and prays that "God sende hym good recover."[6] But where Malory's admission achieves considerable gravity amid his grand nostalgic evocation of (among other things) the ethical superiority of Arthurian civilization, the *Weddyng* poet's admission rounds off a near-anecdotal and amusingly knowing account of ethical deficiency and ineptitude—and it has been an account which could easily make the imprisonment of its ostensible "author" seem a laughable and not inappropriate fate.

The Marriage of Sir Gawaine†

Kinge Arthur lives in merry Carleile,[1]	
And seemely° is to see;	*seemly, comely*
And there he hath with him Queene Genever,°	*Guenevere*
That bride° soe bright° of blee°—	*lady / fair / face, complexion*

5 And there he hath with him Queene Genever,
    That bride soe bright in bower;
And all his barons about him stoode
    That were both stiffe° and stowre.°   *bold / strong*

The King kept° a royall Christmasse   *held*
10   Of mirth and great honor,°   *renown*
And when. . . ."

11-15, 664–69, 678–81, and 821–23. The *Marriage* also, however, has a number of lines repeated wholesale; this may suggest that some form of repetition was a deliberate part of the common original of both poems, but it is equally if not more likely that the *Marriage* has just adopted the "incremental repetition" characteristic of the ballad form. Another perhaps more secure indication of the *Weddyng* poet's imitative inclinations lies in the opening line, which is studiously alliterative.

6. As P. J. C. Field has observed, Malory makes further similar plaintive entreaties to God at the ends of Books VII, XXI, and possibly XIX. The *Weddyng* also suggests a familiarity with Malory elsewhere; see the notes to ll. 62 and 799.

† Text of London, British Library MS Additional 27879 (the "Percy Folio Manuscript"), pp. 46–52, printed with permission of the British Library. The manuscript dates from the middle of the seventeenth century but preserves in a somewhat modernized form many texts which, like the *Marriage*, have a demonstrably medieval origin. To determine the date of composition of the *Marriage* is difficult, but sometime in the fifteenth century seems likely. The poem employs the ballad measure, having four-line stanzas rhyming *abcb*; the first and third line of each stanza have four stresses; the second and fourth have three stresses.

    The text, like many others in the manuscript, is defective in several places where half-pages have been torn out. Thomas Percy (1729–1811, Bishop of Dromore from 1782) discovered the MS sometime after 1753, in the Shropshire home of his friend Humphrey Pitt; in a note on the flyleaf of the MS he says he first saw the MS "lying dirty on the floor under a Bureau in the Parlour, being used by the Maids to light the fires." Text lost to the kindling half-pages is indicated by "[* * *]." A few lines near the damaged edges of the paper have been concealed by repairs made since the manuscript came into the possession of the British Museum in 1868; readings for those lines are incorporated silently from the edition of F. J. Child (about which see the Selected Bibliography).

1. Carlisle (about which see *The Awntyrs off Arthure*, l. 2, n. 1.).

[* * *]²

"And bring me word what thing it is
    That a woman will most desire;
This shalbe° thy ransome, Arthur," he sayes,   *shall be*
15   "For I'le have noe other hier!"°   *hire, ransom*

King Arthur then held up his hand,³
    According thene as was the law.⁴
He tooke his leave of the Baron there,
    And homward can° he draw.°   *did/withdraw*

20 And when he came to merry Carlile,
    To his chamber he is gone;
And ther came to him his cozen° Sir Gawaine   *relative (i.e., nephew)*
    As he did make his mone°—   *complaint*

And there came to him his cozen Sir Gawaine,
25   That was a curteous knight—
"Why sigh you soe sore,° uncle Arthur?" he said,   *sorely, bitterly*
    "Or who hath done thee unright?"°   *wrong*

"O peace!° O peace, thou gentle Gawaine,   *quiet*
    That faire may thee befall—⁵
30 For if thou knew my sighing° soe deepe   *sorrow, grief*
    Thou wold° not mervaile° att all.   *would/wonder*

For when I came to Tearne Wadling
    A bold barron there I fand°   *found*
With a great club upon his backe,
35   Standing stiffe and strong.

And he asked me wether I wold fight
    Or from him I shold begone—
Or else I must him a ransome pay
    And soe depart him from.

40 To fight with him I saw noe cause;
    Methought° it was not meet,°   *It seemed to me/proper*
For he was stiffe and strong withall°—   *indeed*
    His strokes were° nothing sweete!   *i.e., would be*

Therefor, this is my ransome, Gawaine,
45   I ought to him to pay:

2. A missing half-page, in which the following events were probably related: later (most likely on New Year's day) King Arthur rode out to Tarn Wadling (about which see *The Awntyrs off Arthure*, l. 2, n.); there he was confronted by an obstreperous "Baron" (possibly a misreading of *barn*, "man") wielding a great club who challenged him either to fight or pay a ransom. Arthur elects to pay the ransom; the Baron then instructs him to return the following New Year's day . . .
3. See the *Weddyng*, l.88, n.
4. According to what then was the law.
5. Such that things may go well for you.

I must come againe,° as I am sworne,   *back, in return*
    Upon the New Yeers day;

And I must bring him word what thing it is. . . .

[* * *]⁶

Then King Arthur drest° him for to ryde,   *dressed, prepared*
50   In one soe rich array,⁷
Toward the foresaid Tearne Wadling,
    That° he might keepe his day.   *(So) that*

And as he rode over a more,°   *moor*
    Hee see° a lady where shee sate,   *saw*
55 Betwixt an oke and a greene hollen⁸—
She was cladd in red scarlett.⁹

Then there as shold have stood her mouth,
    Then there was sett her eye;
The other° was in her forhead fast,   *i.e., her mouth*
60   The way that she might see.¹

Her nose was crooked and turnd owtward;
    Her mouth stood foule° awry:°   *foully, badly/to one side*
A worse formed lady than shee was
    Never man saw with his eye!

65 To halch° upon him, King Arthur,   *greet*
    This lady was full faine;°   *pleased*
But King Arthur had forgott his lesson°   *instruction (in courtesy)*
    What° he shold say againe.°   *(Concerning) what/in reply*

"What knight art thou" the lady sayd,
70   "That will not speak to me?
Of° me be thou nothing dismayd,   *(Because) of*
    Tho I be ugly to see;

For I have halched you curteouslye,
    And you will not me againe—

---

6. Text is lost here to the second missing half-page. The next line would most likely repeat l. 13; from there the story would probably have related how Gawain suggested that Arthur collect answers to the question and write them down. This he did, and, as the appointed time grew near . . .
7. I.e., in a splendid set of gear.
8. Between an oak and a green holly. (Both plants have familiar symbolic associations, the oak with uncommon sturdiness, the holly with evergreen longevity; the lady is thus by association invested with an air of extraordinary potential. There are further associations of trees with fairies and other supernatural phenomena; cf. *Ywain and Gawain*, l. 353, n., and *Sir Orfeo*, l. 70, n.)
9. She was dressed in rich red cloth. ("Scarlet" indicates the quality of cloth, not necessarily the color; the wearing of such material in red is a sign of nobility or an aspiration thereto; cf. *Ywain and Gawain*, l. 203, n. The detail recalls the "hosen . . . of fyn scarlet reed" worn by Chaucer's Wife of Bath [General Prologue to the *Canterbury Tales*, l. 456]; the Wife of course later tells a tale analogous to the *Marriage*.)
1. I.e., in the place from which she would normally see.

75 Yett I may happen, Sir Knight," shee said,
        "To ease thee of thy paine!"°   *distress*

    "Give° thou ease me, lady," he said,   *If*
        "Or helpe me any° thing,   *(in) any*
    Thou shalt have gentle Gawaine, my cozen,
80   And marry him with a ring!"[2]

    "Why, if I help thee not, thou noble King Arthur,
        Of thy owne hearts desiringe,°   *desire*
    Of gentle Gawaine . . ."

    [* * *][3]

    And when he came to the Tearne Wadling,
85   The Baron there cold° he finde   *could, did*
    With a great weapon on his backe,
        Standing stiffe and stronge.

    And then he tooke King Arthurs letters° in his hands, *writings*
        And away he cold them fling;
90 And then he puld out a good browne° sword   *shining*
        And cryd° himselfe a king—   *proclaimed*

    And he sayd, "I have thee and thy land, Arthur,
        To doe° as it pleaseth me;   *do (with)*
    For this° is not thy ransome sure°—   *this (response) / secure*
95   Therfore yeeld thee to me!

    And then bespoke him noble Arthur,
        And bad° him hold his hand—   *bade, commanded*
    "And give me leave to speake my mind
        In defence of all my land."

100 He said, "As I came over a more,
        I see a lady where shee sate,
    Betweene an oke and a green hollen;
        Shee was clad in red scarlett.

    And she says a woman will have her will,
105   And this is all her cheef° desire: *chief, principal*
    Doe me right, as thou art a baron of sckill—[4]

2. Ballads typically move their stories on apace, and that tendency alone may account for the suddenness and apparent pitilessness of Arthur's promise; that the hag appears in the next stanza to continue to argue her case, however, suggests that the promise was uttered with the same kind of mocking contempt with which the King first greets Dame Ragnell in the *Weddyng* (cf. l. 273, n.). Contempt soon turns to desperate compliance, nevertheless, as it is revealed later that Arthur has indeed made a compact with the hag.

3. Text is lost here to the other side of the second missing half-page: the poem would probably have told how Arthur concedes to the hag to give her Gawain in marriage in return for her answer to the Baron's question. The hag then gives the answer (cf. ll. 104–5, below), and Arthur rides off.

4. Do right by me, as you are a reasonable baron.

This is thy ransome and all thy hyer!°   *hire, ransom*

He° sayes, "An early vengeance light° on her! *(The Baron)/alight, descend*
  She walkes on yonder more—
110 It was my sister that told thee this—
  And she is a misshappen hore!

But heer I'le make mine avow to God
  To doe her an evill turne—
For an° ever I may thate fowle theefe get,   *if*
115 In a fyer I will her burne!"

[* * *]⁵

The Second Part

Sir Lancelott and Sir Steven⁶ bold,
  They rode with them that day,
And the formost of the company
  There rode the steward Kay—⁷

120 Soe did Sir Banier and Sir Bore,⁸
  Sir Garrett⁹ with them soe gay;°   *handsome*
Soe did Sir Tristeram¹ that gentle knight—
  To the forrest, fresh and gay.

And when he° came to the greene forrest,   *(Arthur)*
125 Underneath a greene holly tree
Their sate that lady in red scarlet
  That unseemly was to see.

Sir Kay beheld this ladys face
  And looked uppon her swire;°   *neck (i.e., countenance)*
130 "Whosoever kisses this lady," he says,
  "Of° his kisse he stands in feare!"   *From*

Sir Kay beheld the lady againe,
  And looked upon her snout:
"Whosoever kisses this lady," he saies,

---

5. The third missing half-page: the text evidently related how Arthur returned to Carlisle and told his knights that a bride awaited one of them in the forest (it seems that Gawain is not approached directly). Several knights, including Gawain, then agree to ride out with him; some go with hounds and hawks to take advantage of the hunting afforded by the forest.
6. On Lancelot, see *Sir Launfal*, l. 16, n; a Sir Steven is not recorded in Arthurian romance, but the name may represent a misappropriation of Sevain, identified in the Old French Vulgate Cycle of Arthurian romance as the grandfather of Arthur's illegitimate son Borre—about whom see l. 120 below, n.
7. About Kay, see *Ywain and Gawain*, ll. 68–70.
8. Possibly Kings Ban and Bors; cf. *Sir Launfal*, l. 19, n. Other candidates, however, include Banin, Ban's godson, and Borre, who in Malory's *Morte Darthur* is the son of Lionors and Arthur.
9. Sir Gareth of Orkney, brother of Gawain.
1. Tristan (Tristram in Malory), nephew of Mark, King of Cornwall, and tragic lover of Iseult.

135   "Of his kisse he stands in doubt!"°   *danger*

"Peace! cozen Kay," then said Sir Gawaine,
      "Amend thee of thy life!²
For there is a knight amongst us all
      That must marry her to° his wife."   *as*

140   "What! wedd her to wiffe?" then said Sir Kay,
      "In the divells° name anon!   *devil's*
Gett me a wiffe where-ere I may,³
      For I had rather be slaine!"

Then some tooke up their hawkes in hast,°   *haste*
145   And some tooke° up their hounds,
And some sware° they wold not marry her   *swore*
      For citty° nor for towne.   *(the reward of a) city*

And then bespake him noble King Arthur,
      And sware there, "By this day,
150   For a litle foule sight and mislikng . . ."⁴

[* * *]⁵

Then shee said, "Choose thee, gentle° Gawaine,   *noble*
      Truth as I doe say,
Wether thou wilt have me in this liknesse
      In the night or else in the day.

155   And then bespake him gentle Gawaine
      With° one soe mild of moode—   *To*
Sayes, "Well I know what I wold say
      (God grant it may be good):°   *right*

To have thee fowle in the night
160   When I with thee shold° play—   *should, would*
Yet I had rather, if I might,
      Have thee fowle in the day."

"What! when lords goe with ther feires,"° shee said,   *companions*
      "Both to the ale and wine?
165   Alas, then I must hyde my selfe—

2. I.e., amend your ways.
3. I will get myself a wife from wherever else I can.
4. (Just) because of a little ugliness and revulsion. . . .
5. The other side of the third missing half-page would have concluded Arthur's patently unconvincing appeal. However unconvincing the appeal, it seems that in the missing text Gawain,
because of his exemplary courtesy and his desire to honor Arthur's promise, does agree to
marry the hag. All then return to Carlisle, where the wedding takes place and the newlyweds
take to the bridal chamber. There the hag is transformed into a beautiful woman . . .

I must not goe withinne!"°   *within (the hall)*

And then bespake him gentle Gawaine—
    Said, "Lady, that's but a skill;[6]
And, because thou art my owne lady,
170   Thou shalt have all thy will."[7]

Then she said, "Blesed be thou, gentle Gawain,
    This day that I thee see—[8]
For as thou see me att this time,
    From hencforth I wilbe!°   *will be*

175 My father was an old knight,
    And yett it chanced° soe   *happened*
That he marryed a younge lady
    That° brought me to this woe;   *Who*

Shee witched° me, being a faire young lady,   *bewitched, cast a spell over*
180 To the greene forrest to dwell;
And there I must walke in womans liknesse,
    Most like a feend of hell.[9]

She witched my brother to° a carlish° b . . .   *into/churlish*

[* * *][1]

"That looked soe foule, and that was wont
185 On the wild more to goe!"

"Come kisse her, brother Kay," then said Sir Gawaine,
    "And amend the of thy liffe;[2]
I sweare this is the same lady
    That I marryed to my wiffe!"

190 Sir Kay kissed that lady bright,°   *splendid, fair*
    Standing upon his feete;
He swore, as he was trew knight,
    The spice was never soe sweete!

"Well, cozen Gawaine," sayes Sir Kay,
195 "Thy chance° is fallen arright,°   *luck/the right way*
For thou hast gotten one of the fairest maids
    I ever saw with my sight."

6. I.e., that (which has been said) was just for the sake of argument.
7. Cf. l. 104.
8. On this day in which I behold you.
9. A fiend of hell. (Cf. the *Weddyng*, l. 725, and *The Awntyrs off Arthure*, ll. 83–84.)
1. The fourth missing half-page: in the missing text the transformed woman will have explained that Gawain has permanently released her from the curse by granting her all her will—in other words, by granting that which all women most desire. Gawain then escorts his wife into the presence of an amazed court . . .
2. Cf. l. 137.

"It is my fortune," said Sir Gawaine;
   "For my unckle Arthurs sake,
200 I am glad as grasse wold be of raine
   Great joy that I may take!"[3]

Sir Gawaine tooke the lady by the one arme,
   Sir Kay tooke her by the tother:
They led her straight to King Arthur,
205 As° they were brother and brother.   As (if)

King Arthur welcomed them there all—
   And soe did Lady Genever, his Queene,
With all the knights of the Round Table
   Most seemly to be seene.

210 King Arthur beheld that lady faire
   That was soe faire and bright;
He thanked Christ in Trinity
   For Sir Gawaine that gentle knight—

Soe did the knights; both more° and lesse°   *greater / lesser*
215 Rejoyced all that day
For the good chance that hapened was
   To Sir Gawaine and his lady gay.

---

3. I.e., that I may take great pleasure in this.

The Sege off Melayne[1]

The poem is in a number of ways a good example of what is commonly called a *chanson de geste*. Like the best and most famous representative of the genre, the Old French *Chanson de Roland* (written c. 1100), the *Sege off Melayne* assumes a conceivably historical setting and tells of surpassingly heroic deeds of arms rendered in the service of national and especially Christian dominion; it is a tale in which sworn loyalty to one's lord is of supreme importance, and in which proud treachery—as opposed to self-doubt, supernatural interference, conflict of personality, or sin—is the greatest evil; vengeance is the preferred corrective to that evil. The world of these poems is primarily homosocial; erotic love is an almost nonexistent concern. As with the *Chanson de Roland* and most other *chansons de geste*, the circumstance under which such values are examined in *Melayne* is war with the Saracen.[2]

Melayne is one of a group of thirteen Middle English texts commonly known as the "Charlemagne romances" (it is the second-largest group after the Arthurian romances); most are translations from Old French sources and deal with Charlemagne's legendary campaigns against the heathen, first in Lombardy and then in Spain (where eventually Charlemagne's most worthy lords are treacherously ambushed and slain—see the note to l. 178 of *Melayne*).[3] Besides *Melayne*, three other texts deal with the Lombardy campaign: all three present versions of the story of the Saracen warrior Otuel (*Otinel* in the French sources), who is converted to Christianity upon losing a duel with Roland; Otuel then fights with Charlemagne's forces in Lombardy against the Sultan Garcy, who is eventually defeated and brought to Paris to be baptized by Archbishop Turpin. Though *Melayne* is set in the same place, it is set at an earlier time, for in it we have the extended account of the coronation of Garcy after the death of the Sultan Arabas (ll. 827 ff.); there are also allusions to the relative newness of Charlemagne's regime (see l. 144, n.).

Melayne shows little further direct dependence on related Charlemagne

---

1. Editions and translations of the texts mentioned in this headnote, as well as references to related scholarship, are cited in the Selected Bibliography. On the date of the poem, see the leading footnote to the edition proper.
2. On "Saracens," see *Sir Launfal*, l. 266, n.
3. The other Charlemagne romances in verse are *The Sowdon of Babylon*; the "Ashmole" *Sir Ferumbras*; the "Fillingham" *Firumbras*; *Roland and Vernagu*; *Otuel and Roland*; *Otuel A Knight*; *Duke Roland and Sir Otuel of Spain*; the fragment of *The Song of Roland*; and *The Taill of Rauf Coilyear*. There are also three late prose translations: William Caxton's *Charles the Grete* and *The Foure Sonnes of Aymon*, and Lord Berners's *Boke of Duke Huon of Burdeux*. The true historical Charlemagne lived from 742 to 814; though he never besieged Milan he did wage a campaign against the Lombards, and annexed Lombardy in 773.

legends; no true source is known, and the indications are that the poem is in all likelihood apocryphal not only in its plot but to some extent also in its governing aesthetic. Turpin, for instance, has long been recognized as extraordinary (if not baffling), both in his unprecedented dominance and in the egregious things he does. His dominance may have something to do with the influence of what in the Middle Ages was an extremely popular text, the *Pseudo-Turpin Chronicle* (written c. 1140). The author claims (falsely, to modern eyes, given the probable date of composition) to be Turpin himself, who writes while recovering from wounds suffered at Roncevaux, and who purposes to record the untold details of Charlemagne's campaigns in Spain. The *Pseudo-Turpin* contains accounts of numerous miracles and is punctuated by several moralizing passages: Turpin's authority, his wounds, his moralizing, and the miracles are also components of his experience in *Melayne*.[4] But these details still do not account for such things as his reviling of the Blessed Virgin, his excommunication of Charlemagne (let alone his refusal to say "gud mornynge" to him, l. 570), and his dazed and near-suicidal zeal—all of which appear to constitute, within the terms of the poem, wholly admirable behavior.

All of that is, however, normative within the context of crusade propaganda and historical crusading practice. Thus, one will find in crusading chronicles reverent accounts of knights who gladly advanced against impossible odds toward certain death, and who sometimes encouraged others to do so as well. In the first official call to the crusade, made by Pope Urban II at Clermont in 1095, those who set out on the venture (which at the time was simply called a "pilgrimage") were promised remission of all sins and an assured place in heaven (cf. *Melayne*, ll. 905–10); the Pope further encouraged his listeners to take advantage of their traditionally warlike instincts and to remember the deeds of forebears like Charlemagne. He also spoke of the venture as a journey to Jerusalem undertaken with the willingness to sacrifice one's life for the greater good of fellow Christians. Later crusading texts (and the visual arts) draw direct parallels between this conception and Christ's redeeming Crucifixion in Jersualem. The crusader could be seen to be engaged in a kind of *imitatio Christi* ("imitation of Christ"); perhaps it is this notion which informs the depiction of Turpin's extraordinary ordeal (cf. ll. 1301–2 and 1343–48 and, in the case of the army generally, ll. 1205–7). Only the Pope had the authority to call a crusade, and his authority was considered, in principle, to be above that of national rulers in matters pertaining to the security of Christendom; and so throughout the history of crusades, from the first, which resulted in the capture of Jerusalem in 1099, through to the movement's practical demise in the sixteenth century, there are records of papal threats of excommunication to recalcitrant kings (cf. *Melayne*, ll. 617–97). Expressions of anger at the Godhead also attend the propaganda and the historical accounts; as D. H. Green observes, one finds in texts which advocate the crusade the implication of a kind of feudal contract held by crusaders in their special relationship with God. According to such a contract, crusaders assumed they had a right to expect certain rewards for their sworn loyalty, just as they would in the case of their

---

4. A useful guide to the basic contents of the *Pseudo-Turpin* is available in the third book of Caxton's *Charles the Grete*.

relationship with a feudal overlord[5]—and it was, of course, well within their rights to voice their dissatisfaction, as does Turpin, should they find their loyalty unreciprocated.

Melayne finds analogues in two crusade-oriented pieces which speak of Charlemagne. In broad outline *Melayne* is analogous to a popular legend known in its literary form as the *Descriptio*. According to the legend, Constantine, Emperor of Constantinople, having been asked for help by the Patriarch of Jerusalem, whose city has been besieged by Saracens, is visited by an angel who recommends that he seek the assistance of Charlemagne. Charlemagne duly comes to the rescue, and for his efforts is rewarded with the relics of the Passion, which he brings back to France. The legend—no doubt once a useful tool in the persuasion of would-be crusaders—is itself analogous to the circumstances which prompted the First Crusade, where Alexis, the Emperor of Constantinople, requested help from western Christendom against Muslim incursions; and *Melayne* is analogous to the legend represented by the *Descriptio*, inasmuch as Alantyne, the lord of Milan, is also overrun by Saracens and is provided with an angelic recommendation to seek the assistance of Charlemagne. Some versions of the *Pseudo-Turpin Chronicle* are prefaced with the *Descriptio*, and one of the English Charlemagne romances, *Roland and Vernagu* (RV), begins with a summary of the legend (RV is in fact a free-verse translation of the *Pseudo-Turpin*, adapted as a kind of preface to the story of Otuel). The other analogue in question concerns only the scene in which Charlemagne receives the sword from an angel and is commanded to avenge injuries done to Christendom (ll. 109–32). As S. J. Herrtage noted over a century ago in the introduction to his edition of *Melayne*, the episode recalls that in the second of the (apocryphal) Old Testament books of Maccabees (xv. 15, 16), where Judas Maccabeus (a favored hero among crusade propagandists) recounts a dream in which the spirit of Jeremiah gives him a golden sword with which to defeat the enemies of the people of Israel. Further, a closer and more elaborate version of the analogue has recently surfaced in an Old French crusading chronicle identified by D. A. Trotter. There, the same episode from the Maccabees is related, and then it is asserted that a similar vision happened to Charlemagne as he was about to go to the Holy Land at the request of the Emperor of Constantinople (this is obviously an allusion to the *Descriptio*); St. Denis (the patron saint of France) appeared to him and (as a sign of heavenly approval of the projected conflict) gave him a golden halbert.

There is another medieval English text which is very close to *Melayne* in its crusading aesthetic. It is the little-known "romance" of *Capystranus*, here printed. It celebrates, with considerable embellishment of the historical facts, the raising of the Turkish siege of Belgrade in 1456. In it are many of the same kinds of distinctive elements as are found in *Melayne*: (1) a situation analogous to the *Descriptio*—less so than that described in *Melayne*, perhaps, but prefaced nonetheless with a summary of the events of the *Descriptio* (ll. 46–8); (2) an angry complaint to the Godhead based on an almost contractual sense of mutual obligation (ll. 465 ff.); (3) declarations of belief in certain martyrdom (ll. 90–92, 291–97); and (4) special

5. On the background to such a relationship, see *Havelok*, l. 444, n.

emphasis given to Papal sanction for the venture (ll. 232 ff.). The poem could have been written any time after 1456, but survives only in fragments of three different printed editions published between about 1515 and 1530; in the early sixteenth century the Turks continued to pose a considerable threat to Europe, and the multiple editions of the *Capystranus* may well suggest an (albeit fanciful) English concern with that threat.

Perhaps *Melayne* represents the same kind of concern from an earlier period (and it is interesting to note in addition that both texts share a particular interest in championing clerical participation in holy war—*Melayne*, ll. 911–34; *Capystranus*, ll. 319, 331–36—as if to suggest that both poets had a particular audience in mind). But it is important to remember that all of the English Charlemagne romances display some form of crusading interest, and that *Melayne*, for all its eccentricities, is in this respect not so very different. What difference there is, is one of elaboration, where *Melayne* strives not only to present the traditional attractions of the *chanson de geste*, but also to recommend the superior resilience of the crusading state of mind.

Capystranus†

[I]

O Myghty Fader° in heven on hye,°

	O Myghty Fader° in heven on hye,°	*Father/high*
	One God and Persones thre[1]	
	That made bothe daye and nyght—[2]	
	And after, as it was thy wyll,	
5	Thyn owne Sone thou sent us tyll[3]	
	In a mayden to lyght;°	*alight, descend*
	Syth,° the Jewes that were wylde°	*Since then/violent*
	Hanged° Hym that was so mylde,	*I.e., crucified*
	And to dethe Hym dyght;°	*put, consigned*
10	Whan He was deed,° the sothe° to saye,°	*dead/truth/tell*
	To lyfe He rose on the thyrde daye	

---

† Text of London, British Library incunable C. 71. c. 26 (*Short Title Catalogue* no. 14649; most likely printed by Wynkyn de Worde c. 1515), here printed with permission of the British Library. The text has been collated with that of two other fragments from later prints: British Library C. 40. m. 9(18) (*STC* no. 14649.5, Wynkyn de Worde, c. 1527, preserving ll. 1–102), and Oxford, Bodleian Library, Douce frag. f. 5 (*STC* no. 14650, Wynkyn de Worde, c. 1530, preserving ll. 161–397). The title is derived from the quire signatures of the print.

The poem is written mainly in twelve-line tail-rhyme stanzas, rhyming (nominally) *aabccbdd-beeb* (nine- and six-line stanzas are also common); the couplets nominally have four stresses and the tail lines three. A number of obviously corrupt rhymes (e.g., *doute* for *lete* at l. 221, *lande* for *stede* at l.294, *anone* for *agayne* at l. 436—all such errors are silently emended in the edition) suggest that the poem was in existence for some time before printing; it could have been composed anytime after 1456, the date of the events related. This edition divides the text into sections according to the presence in the early prints of woodcuts and/or large capitals.

1. I.e., One God consisting of the three Persons of the Godhead (the Father, Son, and Holy Spirit).
2. The syntactic force of the opening two lines, which appear to begin a prayer, gives way by the fourth to a paraphrase of elements of the Athanasian and Apostles' Creeds; cf. *The Sege off Melayne*, l. 429, n. The opening prayer resumes at l. 34.
3. Sent to us.

Thoroughe° His owne myght;°   *Through/power*

Then to helle He wente anone,
And toke out soules; many one
15   Out of that holde He hente;[4]
Maugré° the fendes° that were bolde,   *Despite/fiends*
He toke the prysoners out of holde;
    With them to heven He wente;
On His Faders ryght hande He hym sette
20 That° all sholde knowe, withouten lette,°   *(Such) that/delay, hindrance*
    That He was omnypotente;

And after° wysdome He was sente   *for the sake of*
That° all sholde kepe His commaundemente,   *(So) that*
    And for to byleve in Hym verray°   *truly*
25 That is our Savyour,
That borne was of that blyssed° floure,°   *blessed/flower*
    That hyght° Mary, I saye,   *is called*
That shall us deme,° withouten mysse,°   *judge/fail*
Some to payne° and some to blysse,   *pain, punishment (in hell)*
30   At dredefull Domes-daye;°   *Doomsday*
Tho° that byleve on Hym aryght,°   *Those/properly, earnestly*
To blysse they gone° with aungelles° bryght,   *(will) go/angels*
    To blysse and joye for aye°—   *ever*

Now Jhesu, as thou bought° us dere,°   *redeemed/dearly*
35 Gyve them joye this gest wyll here,
    And herken on aryght.[5]
Some men loveth to here tell
Of doughty° knyghtes that were fell,°   *doughty, valiant/fierce*
    And some of ladyes bryght,°   *splendid*
40 And some [of] myracles that are tolde,°   *reported, related*
And some of venterous° knyghtes olde°   *adventurous, bold/(of) old*
    That for our Lorde dyde° fyght—   *did*
As Charles° dyde, that noble Kynge,   *Charlemagne*
That hethen° downe dyde brynge,   *heathen (warriors)*
45   Thrughe the helpe of God almyghty.

He wanne fro the hethen houndes
The spere and nayles of Crystes woundes,
    And also the crowne of thorne—[6]
And many a ryche relyke mo°   *more*

4. Many a one He seized out of that prison. (A reference to the Harrowing of Hell, about which see *Ywain and Gawain*, l. 2874, n.; the reference is of course appropriate to the main story of the poem.)
5. Give them joy (i.e., heavenly bliss) who will listen to this account, (who will) hearken earnestly.
6. On the popular legend which held that Charlemagne had brought back to France the relics of the Passion, see the Sources and Backgrounds headnote, p. 390.

50 Mawgré° of them he wanne° also,	*In spite / won, obtained*
And kylled them even° and morne.	*(by) evening*
The Turkes[7] and the paynyms° bolde	*pagans*
He felled doune many a folde;[8]	
Durst none stande hym beforne.°	*in opposition*
55 Charles gan° them so affraye°	*did / frighten*
That the catyves° myght curse the daye	*wretches*
And the tyme that they were borne!	

[II]

Now Machamyte,[9] that Turke untrue°	*unfaithful*
To our Lorde Cryst Jhesu,	
60 And to His lawe° also,	*religion*
Many Crysten° man slayne hath he	*Christian*
And wanne Constantyne,° that noble cyté,	*Constantinople*
With many townes mo.	
He brent° and slewe and lefte none on lyfe,[1]	*burned*
65 Neyther man, chylde, ne wyfe;	
To dethe he made them go.	
Yonge innocentes° that never dyde gylte°	*children / offense*
That false° Turke hath them spylte;°	*heathen / slain*
He played° the kynge Pharao.[2]	*acted like*
70 All the stretes of Constantyne	
Ranne blode reder than wyne	
That mervayle was to se;[3]	
There coude° no man his fote° downe sette,	*could / foot*
I gyve you knowlege withouten lette,	
75 But on a deed body.	
The Crysten men wente to wrake;°	*wrack, destruction*
The chirches and our ymages they brake,	
That were made of stone and tree.[4]	
The crucyfyxe of our Savyour,	
80 They kest° it downe with dyshonour,	*cast*
And also Our Lady.	

7. The poem thus modernizes its "historical" authority; the Turks as such were no threat to Christendom in the real Charlemagne's time.
8. I.e., he laid low manifold numbers of them.
9. Mehmed (Mohammed) II (1432–81), the Sultan of the Ottoman Turks from 1451 to 1481; he had succeeded in capturing Consantinople (Istanbul) in 1453, thus presenting Christendom with one of its greatest losses (the city has been Turkish ever since). During 1454–55 he moved northward, annexing Serbia; he began to station his troops around Belgrade at the beginning of June 1456 and had the bombardment of the city started on July 1.
1. None alive.
2. A reference to Pharaoh's charge that all newborn Hebrew sons were to be slain, Exodus 1.15–22.
3. Ran with blood redder than wine such that it was a marvel to see.
4. Cf. *The Sege off Melayne*, ll. 25 ff.

They slewe our preestes° at the Masse;   *priests*
 Goddes men had no grace.[5]
They kylled them downe in every stede;°   *place*
85 Bothe preestes and clerkes° they put to dede° *clerics / death*
 Within Goddes° holy place.   *God's*
The Turkes kene,° with shelde° and spere,° *cruel / shield / spear*
Our preestes before the hye aultere°   *altar*
 They ranne thrughe in a race.
90 Many gan dye for Crystes love;
Aungelles theyr soules bare above[6]
 To blysse and moche° solace.° *much / delight, consolation*

Thus the Turke—the wycked quede!°—   *wretch*
Crysten people he put to dede,
95 And lefte few upon lyve.
The hethen cryed with grete dyspyte[7]
On Mahounde and Macamyte,
 The Turkes° men full ryve;°   *Turkish / rife, abundant*
There was none that durst on Jhesu crye
100 But they were taken and slayne in hye,°   *haste*
 Anone, and that belyve![8]
The Turke° hymselfe a crye° dyde make— *(Mehmed) / proclamation*
 "There sholde no man a prysoner take—"
 God, lette them° never thryve!° *(the Turks) / thrive, succeed*

105 Then the dogges that byleved° on Mahounde *believed*
The Crysten people kylled to the grounde;
 No golde myght be theyr mede.°   *reward*
The Crysten saw that they sholde° dye,   *must*
And on theyr maystres° layde hande quycly *masters, conquerors*
110 And faught a wele good spede:[9]
Every prysoner then on lyve
Kylled of the Turkes foure or fyve;
 To helle theyr soules yede.°   *went*
Or our prysoners after were take;
115 Many a Turke they made blake:[1]

There was no helme, nor haubergyon,°   *coat of mail*
Plate, or male, nor good aucton,° *padded (leather) underjacket*
 Theyr dyntes myght refrayne.[2]

5. I.e., men of God were given no reprieve.
6. Angels bore their souls aloft. (A sign of martyrdom; cf. *The Sege off Melayne*, ll. 289–324.)
7. Called with great insult (to Christendom) on Mohammed. (On western medieval conceptions of Araby, see *The Sege off Melayne*, ll. 28, n., and 829, n.)
8. Forthwith, and quickly at that!
9. And fought with some considerable success.
1. Before our captured people were eventually subdued, they killed many a Turk (*lit.* made many a Turk pale [in death]).
2. That could check their blows.

Macamyte sawe his men so dye,
120 And loude on Mahounde he gan crye;
 In herte° he was not fayne.°   *heart, spirit / pleased*
Our Crysten neded no wepen° crave;°   *weapon / go without*
The stretes laye full, take who wolde have.
 To fyght with men of mayne.³
125 Anone, within a lytell throwe,°   *time*
Fyve .m. Turkes on a rowe⁴
 In the stretes lay slayne.

Whan Mychamyte that spyed,
Out on Mahounde he cryed,
130 And as a fende dyde yell.
Our Crysten stode° in full grete doubte°   *stood / fear*
As doughty men layde fast aboute
 Upon the houndes of helle;
Our Crysten men were then to° fewe,   *too*
135 For the Turkes came° ever newe,°   *came (on) / anew, renewed*
 In sothe° as I you tell.   *truth*
Our men hewed on hastely,°   *in haste*
And made Turkes loude to crye;
 The false° downe they fell.   *heathen*

140 Thus they countred with Sarasyns⁵ kene
Tyll .lxxx.m. were layde bedene⁶
 In a lytell thought.°   *space of time*
Mychamyte was never so wo°   *distressed*
To se° so fewe so many slo;°   *see (how) / slew*
145 His sorwe° was not shorte.°   *sorrow / little*
He cryed Mahounde as he wolde braste;⁷
Our Crysten on Jhesu cryed faste,
 That° all the worlde wrought.°   *Who / made*

Some scaped° away, with Goddes grace   *escaped*
150 On lyve, maugré the Turkes face;⁸
 But many than gan dye.
At the dystruccyon° of Cyvys⁹   *destruction*
Were not so many slayne, ywys,°   *indeed*
 As were on bothe partye.°   *parties, sides*
155 Alas, saufe Crysten wyll of heven,
Our Crysten were made uneven

3. For the taking of whoever would have them, in order to fight against powerful men.
4. Five thousand Turks altogether.
5. Saracens. (On the background of the name, see *Sir Launfal*, l. 266, n.)
6. Until eighty thousand were laid out (dead) altogether.
7. He called upon Mohammed as if he would burst (with rage).
8. Alive, despite the Turks.
9. Possibly the battle of Kosovo, October 17–20, 1448, where Christian forces led by János Hunyadi suffered a devastating defeat at the hands of the Turkish Sultan Murad II.

With a false company—[1]
For of the Turkes and Sarasyns kene,
An .c.° were, withouten wene,°   *hundred / doubt*
160   Agaynst one of our meny!°   *army*

[III]

The Emperour of Constantyne,
A doughty man at a° tyme,   *one*
The Turke hym toke,° that hethen hounde,   *took, captured*
And gave hym many a grysly° wounde—   *horrific*
165   I praye God gyve hym grame!°   *grief, pain*
He bounde hym tyll the blode out braste°   *burst*
And badde° hym forsake Jhesu in haste—   *bade, commanded*
"Or elles thou shalte have shame!°   *disgrace, injury*
Have done anone, and Hym defye—[2]
170   And also His moder Marye
That thou callest His dame."°   *lady, mother*

Valeryan[3] answered, and sayd, "Nay!
Thou shalte never se that daye
That I shall Hym forsake—
175   Turne° the,° Turke, and all thy men,   *Convert / thee, yourself*
Or elles in helle thou shalte brenne°   *burn*
Amonge the fendes blacke!
Leve° in Jhesu full of myght,   *Believe*
And that Mayden that he in lyght°   *alighted, descended*
180   For Crysten men sake."
Than the Turke wexed evyll apayed,
Commaunded his men at a brayed[4]
Anone to make hym naked.

He bad them bete° hym with scourges kene,°   *beat / cruel, sharp*
185   And, after, bore out his eyen°   *eyes*
With wymbles hote and reed;[5]
They plucked his here,° by and by;[6]   *hair*
And bothe his eeres° on hy   *ears*
They cut of° his heed;   *off of, from*
190   With pynsors° his tethe they brake,   *pincers*
Bad hym anone his God forsake,
Or sholde never ete breed.[7]

1. I.e., save for the (effect of the) Christian desire for heavenly reward, our Christians were
   outnumbered by a heathen army.
2. Be done with it forthwith and renounce Him.
3. I.e., Constantine XI (1404–53), Emperor of Byzantium from 1449 to 1453; he was killed in
   combat during the Turkish assault on Constantinople. (Cf. the more provocative version of
   his death as related below, ll. 181–95.)
4. Then the Turk grew displeased, (and) commanded his men at once.
5. With red-hot wimbles (tools for boring holes).
6. I.e., one hair after another.
7. Or he would never (again) eat bread (i.e., or he would be killed).

They sawe in no wyse° that it° wolde be;	*way, manner/(their desire)*
Anone, they made a sawe of tre°	*wood*
195 And sawed hym to deed.°	*death*

Tho° the Turkes, with moche payne,	*Then*
This° doughty men have they slayne—	*These*
For Crystes sake, I saye.	
And so they dyde with many mo;	
200 The Turkes myght curse the tyme also	
That they there came that daye:	
Of Crystes people was many a part° marte;°	*share/? martyred*
There was no Turke payed of his parte	
By the laste ende of the fraye—[8]	
205 They had° helle for theyr fyght;	*received*
The Crysten wente to heven bryght	
To bye° in blysse for aye.	*abide, dwell*

Thus is Constantyne the noble cyté wonne,	
Beten doune with many a gonne,°	*gun*
210 And Crysten people slayne.	
There the Turke with his meyné°	*army*
Keped° styll° that noble cyté;	*Guarded/immovably*
Durste no man hym with-sayne.°	*oppose*
Forty myle° rounde aboute	*miles*
215 Durst no man by hym route,°	*assemble forces*
Neyther on hyll ne playne.	
The Turke kepte the felde° many a day;	*(battle)field*
Crysten people in the countray	
Of hym were dredde,° I sayne.°	*afraid/say*

220 Where they myght ony° Crysten gete,°	*any/capture*
I tell you now, withouten lete,°	*delay, hindrance*
They lefte there lyfe to wedde:[9]	
All suffred dethe for Crystes sake	
That this Turke myght overtake;°	*meet*
225 But thus they for° hym fledde.	*because of*
Therof herde° a holy Frere,°	*heard/Friar*
The werkes of the fendes fere,[1]	
And to Rome hym spedde.	

Johan Capystranus the Frere hyght—[2]

---

8. No Turk was rewarded for his part at the ultimate end of the conflict.
9. They (the Christians) departed their life as a pledge (that the Turks would ultimately be defeated).
1. (About) the deeds of the fiend's companion.
2. The Friar was called Johan Capistranus. (This is St. Giovanni da Capistrano [1386–1456]; after studying law at Perugia, he pursued a political life in Naples, where he was imprisoned for his involvement in a local family war. While in prison he experienced a vision of St. Francis of Assisi which compelled him to join the priesthood. As a Franciscan friar [from 1416] he eventually became famous for his missionary expeditions, for his remarkable gifts as a preacher, and for his ability to work extraordinary healing miracles. After the conquest of Constantinople in 1453 [see l. 62, n.], his efforts were increasingly turned toward preaching

230   I dare say he was Goddes knyght;[3]
      An holy man was he.
  To the Pope anone he wanne,°   *went*
  Capystranus, that holy man,
      And kneled upon his kne—
235   He sayd, "Fader, for Crystes love of heven,[4]
  That° made this worlde and dayes seven,   *Who*
      Herken now to me.
  There is a Turke, I understande,
  That brennes and slees° Goddes lande;°   *slays/nation, people*
240   Grete dole° it is to se.   *sorrow*

  The Turke his purpose is,
  I lete° you wete° withouten mys,°   *let/know/mistake*
      To wynne all Hungree.°   *Hungary*
  Therfore, fader, put thy holy hande[5]
245   And helpe to warre° Goddes lande,   *defend*
      His true vycar° yf thou be.   *vicar, deputy*
  He brenneth chirches in every place;
  Crysten men gothe° to deth apace—   *go*
      To beholde° is grete pyté.°   *behold (that)/pity*
250   Now, fader, helpe with thy socoure,° *succor, assistance*
  For Maryes love, that swete floure;[6]
      Our hope is moche° in the.   *much (placed)*

  With two hondred .m.° this same daye, *thousand*
  To Grecuswyssyngburgh[7] he toke the waye;
255   This is no scorne.°   *matter for derision*
  Many a thousande there shall dye;
  If he wynne that ryall° cytyé,°   *royal, noble/city*
      All Hungrye is forlorne.°   *lost*

---

the crusade throughout Europe. He was called to Buda [the capital of Hungary, now better known as Budapest] in 1455 by Cardinal Juan Carvajal, who had been appointed by Pope Calixtus III to preach the crusade in Hungary, Germany, Poland, and the surrounding nations. Capistrano was enjoined in Hungary to be Carvajal's spokesman [the subsequent descriptions in the poem of Capistrano's dealings with the Pope are thus conflated with recollections of Carvajal—though the Friar's actions stretched as far more dramatic than anything reported of Carvajal]. When Belgrade was besieged in 1456 [see l. 254, n.], Capistrano managed to rally a force [there are reports of as many as 60,000 men] to march on the city with John Hunyadi [about whom see l. 344, n.]; most, however, were poorly armed peasants, and many fewer probably showed up than had agreed to go. Capistano lived but a few months after the successful raising of the siege, during which most accounts agree he played an important part in motivating the troops; he died of plague on October 23. Though he was considered a saint in his own lifetime, he was not officially canonized until 1724.)

3. Cf. *The Sege off Melayne*, ll. 118–9.
4. I.e., father, for the sake of Christ's heavenly love.
5. I.e., give your holy blessing.
6. For the love of that sweet flower, Mary.
7. Belgrade (cf. a German name for the city, Kriechisch Weissenburg. At the time, the southern bounds of the kingdom of Hungary stretched as far as this city, which effectively stood as the gateway to the rest of the country. The city commands high ground overlooking the confluence of the Danube and Save rivers; it was defended all around by a strong wall, and a fortified citadel lay at the center of the town to which the only access was by a small wooden bridge.)

I am the messynger of Jhesus;
260 Truely, lorde, it wyll be thus,
    As I have sayd beforne.°   *before*
Therfore helpe with all thy myght
For Goddes love for to fyght,
    That was of Marye borne."[8]

265 Than the Pope sayd anone,
"Good broder, Frere John,
    As I understande,
Thou prechest° Goddes wordes wyde°   *preach / widely*
In the countree, on° every syde,°   *in / part*
270   In many a dyverse lande.
Thou knowest many a noble man;
Take° a capytayne° where thou can,   *Take on / captain, leader*
    Whyder that he be free or bonde,[9]
And, as I am Goddes vycar true,
275 This false Turke his rese° shall rue°—   *attack / rue, regret*
    And therto my holy hande.[1]

"Now, fader, I thanke the hartely.°   *heartily, earnestly*
To chese° a capytayne the bydde me,   *choose*
    Certayne, without ony mys;
280 Now holy fader, withouten layne,°   *concealing (the truth)*
This shall be my capytayne—"
    He sayd the° Pope, ywys—   *(to) the*

"A baner of Crystes Pyssyon,
That mannes soule dyde redempcyon[2]
285   And brought them from payne to lyght;
Holowe° it with thy hande.   *Hallow, Bless*
The people may the better stande°   *endure*
    That under it dooth° fyght.   *do*

This shall be my capytayne—
290 Another° wolde I have fayne:°   *Another (captain) / gladly*
    That is thy bull of leed,[3]
That° all that under it dooth fyght   *(Mandating) that*
For Goddes love moost of myght,[4]

8. To fight for the love of God, who was born of Mary.
9. (Regardless of) whether he is a nobleman or a servant.
1. Cf. l. 244, n.
2. A banner of Christ's Passion, which brought about the redemption of men's souls. (Presumably
   the Friar holds up a crucifix which is either to be illustrated on a banner or mounted on a
   standard pole—cf. l. 301. His choice is for both a substitute to the usual form of heraldic
   emblem taken into battle and, because the crucifix comprises a representation of a human
   figure, a substitute for a worldly commander.)
3. Your bull (written papal edict) of lead. (The most important bulls—from the Latin *bulla*,
   "seal"—would sometimes be given lead, as opposed to wax, seals; the seal assured the authenticity of the document.)
4. For the love of God, (who is) the greatest in power.

Ever in ony° stede°   *any/place*
295 If it happen them to be slayne,
That theyr soules come never in° payne°   *into/torment (of hell)*
    After that° they be deed."°   *(the time) that/dead*
The Pope sayd, "Blyssed° myght thou be—   *Blessed*
A holy man I holde° the;   *hold, esteem*
300   I wyll do after thy rede."[5]

Anone the baner was made and halowed,
The bull cealed° and up-folded,   *sealed*
    And the pardon of grace
Delyvered to the Frere truely.
305 The Pope blyssed hym tymes thre;
    And thus his leve° he taketh.   *leave*
Barefote,° he bare° out of the toune   *Barefoot/bore*
The baner of Crystes Passyoune.
    Towarde the Turke he hasteth,°   *hastened*
310 And preched Goddes lawe° as he yede;° *faith, religion/went*
And moche° people to hym gan° spede,° *many/did/hurry*
    To gete theyr soules solace.°   *salvation*

Grete° golde and sylver was hym gyven, *Great (quantities of)*
And ever he delte° it even°   *dealt/directly*
315   Tho° people that with him yede.   *(To) those*
So, certaynly, as I you saye,
All Romayne° for hym dyde praye—   *Romans*
    And so it was grete nede;
Suche Freres we have to fewe![6]
320 (Pray all we Cryste Jhesu
    To be his helpe and spede,
For of this I fynde a Fytte;[7]
Ferther and ye wyll sytte,[8]
    Herkyn° and take good hede.)°   *Hearken/heed*

[IV]

325 This Frere wente to Hungry,
And many men with hym truely,
    That for our Lorde dyde fyght.
To an unyversyté he toke the waye,
The gretest in Hungrye, I dare well saye;

5. I will act according to your advice. (The Pope thus agrees to offer a pardon from all their sins and the guarantee of God's grace to those who die fighting in the name of God; such is one of the most important components of a "legitimate" holy war.)
6. And it was very necessary to do so; we have too few such Friars! (Cf. *The Sege off Melayne*, ll. 767–68.)
7. For concerning this story I see that I have come to (the end of) a fit. (On fit divisions, see *The Sege off Melayne*, note to the heading after l. 384.)
8. If you will sit longer.

330   Gottauntas[9] it hyght.°   *was called*
       Out of the unyversyté there wente in-fere°   *altogether*
       Syxe and twenty .m. with the Frere
           Of relygyous men full ryght.
       The moost partye was preestes,[1] I saye;
335   Everyche° preved° hym that day   *Each one/proved, demonstrated*
           That he was Goddes knyght.

       The Frere with grete devocyon
       Bare the baner of Crystes Passyon
           Amonge the people all
340   Dysplayed abrode,° grete° joye to se;°   *abroad, openly/(a) great/see*
       Men of dyverse countré
           Fast to hym gan fall.[2]
       Thus passed forthe Capystranus
       And met with the good Erle Obedyanus,[3]
345   A capatyne pryncypall.
       Twenty thousande and mo,
       Amonge them was but knyghtes two;[4]
           And thus men dooth them call

       Rycharde Morpath,[5] a knyght of Englonde,
350   And Syr Johan Blacke,[6] I understonde,
           That° was a Turke before—   *Who*
       And now he is a curteys° knyght,   *courteous*
       I lete you wete, and a wyght,°   *valiant*
           And stedfast in our lore;°   *religion*
355   Many a Turke he hath greved° sore°—   *aggrieved, injured/sorely*

9. No such university existed in Hungary; but, as Petrovics and Szónyi observe, *untas* may
   represent the abbreviated form of Latin *universitas*, and *Gotta* may recall the university at
   Kraków, which Capistrano did visit in 1452.
1. The largest portion consisted of priests.
2. Men of diverse countries quickly joined in with him. (Though Capistrano's followers consisted
   mainly of local peasants, various historical accounts do mention the presence of fighting men
   from all over Europe—probably mercenaries—among the forces of John Hunyadi (about
   whom, see the next note).)
3. János (John) Hunyadi (c. 1407–56), the great Hungarian military leader and the true historical
   hero of the Belgrade campaign. He had distinguished himself in his youth with victories against
   small-scale Turkish incursions, and his successes brought him rapid promotion. As the chief
   military leader in the south of Hungary, he had by 1444 recovered from Turkish control the
   neighboring regions of Walachia, Albania, Bosnia, Hercegovina, Serbia, and Bulgaria. From
   1446 to 1452 he was appointed governor of the kingdom of Hungary during the minority of
   King László V. In 1448 he suffered a crushing defeat at Kosovo, after which he never quite
   recovered his previous influence in state affairs. Nevertheless, after his time as regent, he was
   appointed Captain General (cf. l. 345), and the Belgrade campaign of 1456 became one of
   his greatest and most extraordinary victories; the Turks would fail to gain a foothold in Hungary
   for another 65 years thereafter. Belgrade was also his last victory; he died of plague less than
   a month later, on August 11, reputedly in the arms of Giovani da Capistrano.
4. Among more than twenty thousand of them were but two knights.
5. The identity of this figure has yet to be established; English mercenaries are not known to
   have participated in the campaign.
6. The original print here reads "Johan Elacke," but "Blacke Johan" at ll. 405 and 447; both
   readings possibly represent misconstructions, via oral transmission, of some form of *Vlach*—
   that is, a native of Walachia, which region (to the southeast of Hungary) had until recently
   (see l. 344, n.) been under Turkish control since 1417.

Theyr lyves they lefte behynde:[7]
He hath made them hop heedles,°   *headless*
Many one, withouten les,[8]
    Where° he myght theym fynde!   *Wherever*

360   There .xx.° thousande met in-fere,   *twenty*
With Obedyauns and the Frere,
    In helme and hauberke° bryght.   *coat of mail*
To Grecuswyssynburgh he toke the waye;
There the Turke at syege° laye   *siege*
365   With many a knyght.
Fourtene wekes[9] the Turke had ben there,
And put the Crysten to° moche fere;°   *in / fear*
    To° hym they had no myght.°   *Against / strength*
Fyve .c. gonnes he lete shote at ones,
370   Brake doune the walles with stones;[1]
    The wylde° fyre lemed° lyght.°   *violent / glowed / brightly*

To here° it was grete° wonder   *hear / (a) great*
The noyse of gonnes moche lyke the thonder—
    That was a ferfull° dynn;°   *fearful / din, noise*
375   The noyse was herde many° a myle.   *(over) many*
Obedyaunce the meane whyle
    Entred the towne within[2]

At .vi.° of the clocke, the sothe° to saye,   *six / truth*
After noone on the Maudeleyne daye,[3]
380   And neyther lesse ne mo.[4]
And Capystranus, good Frere Jhon,
Assoyled° our men, everychone,°   *Gave absolution to / each one*
    To batayll or they dyde go,

And cryed loude, with voyce clere,
385   "Lete us fyght, for our soupere°   *supper*

7. I.e., they departed their lives (because of him).
8. Many a one, (I tell you) without lie.
9. Fourteen weeks. (The period of siege under bombardment has been rather exaggerated from the fourteen days mentioned by the historical sources; cf. ll. 58, n., and 379, n.)
1. He had five hundred guns shoot (all) at once, (and) broke down the walls with stones. (Some of the historical accounts report that, besides the usual artillery, the Turks brought with them large mortars capable of hurling huge round stones; the city walls were soon breached, leaving but trenches and fragmentary walls and towers for defense outside the citadel.)
2. The historical battle was first joined on water, as Hunyadi conveyed his troops down the Danube in a large flotilla; thus he first opposed the Turkish fleet instead of the larger land forces. The stratagem was assisted by the advance from the shore behind the Turkish fleet of forty vessels kept safe by the Christian garrison of the city. Within five hours the Turkish fleet was destroyed; only then did Hunyadi's forces make their way into the city to reinforce the garrison.
3. I.e., the feast day of Mary Magdalen, July 22. (This is in fact the date at which the raising of the Turkish siege was effectively completed; Hunyadi's incursion began at night on July 14, and, once he had gained the citadel, it was left to the Turks to mount a continual artillery bombardment of the city for another week before they attempted an assault with troops.)
4. I.e., and neither earlier nor later.

In heven is redy dyght!°   *prepared*
Our baner shall I bere todaye,
And to Jhesu fast shall praye
    To spede° us in our ryght."°   *help/just cause*
390 Anone they° togyder mette: *(the armies)*
Fyve .m. deed° withouten lette,°   *died/delay, hindrance*
    In helme and hauberke bryght.

Obedianus, that noble man,
Slewe them fast that served Sathan;°   *Satan*
395   Thorowe Cryst theyr crownes had care![5]
All that he with his faucon° hyt   *falchion, (broad)sword*
There was no salve,° I lette you wyt,°   *cure/know*
    That ever myght hele° that sare!°   *heal/wound*
There was no Turke that he with met
400 But he had° suche a buffet°   *received/blow*
    That he greved never Crysten man mare.°   *more, further*
He was a doughty knyght;
The fals° he felled for Goddes ryght—   *heathen*
    I praye God wele° myght he fare!°   *well/fare, get on*

405 Morpath and Blacke Johan
That daye kylled Turkes many one,°   *(a) one*
    Certayne, withouten lette;
There was none so good armoure
That theyr dyntes myght endure,[6]
410   Helme nor bryght basynet.°   *light helmet*
They hewe upon the hethen on° hye°—   *in/haste*
The fyre° out of every syde gan flye,   *i.e., sparks*
    So boldely on they bette.
Many a Turke there was cast,°   *thrown down*
415 Beten tyll the braynes° brast;°   *brains/burst out*
    Theyr maysters there they mette.[7]

Many a .m. of preestes there was;
The Turkes herde never suche a masse
    As they harde° that daye!   *heard*
420 Our preestes *Te Deum* songe;[8]
The hethen fast downe they donge°—   *struck*
    Then *pax*[9] was put awaye!
There was° scole° maystres of the best;°   *were/school/best (kind)*

5. I.e., through the power of Christ the crowns of their heads were troubled!
6. I.e., there was no armor so good that it could endure their blows.
7. Cf. l. 109.
8. Sang *Te Deum*. (A Latin hymn, beginning *Te Deum laudamus* ["We praise thee, O Lord"],
    sung as part of the Mass.)
9. Latin for "peace"; a reference to the Kiss of Peace conveyed in the high Mass, either through
    a formalized kiss between celebrants or through the kissing of a small portative plate usually
    bearing a depiction of the Crucifixion.

Many of them were brought to rest[1]

425   That wolde not lere° theyr laye!°   *learn / law, religion*

Thus our Crysten people dyde fyght,

From .v.° of the clocke on Maudeleyne nyght   *five*

  Tyll .x.° on the other° daye.   *ten / next*

Then came the Turkes with newe batayll,°   *army, division*

430 Clene° clad in plate and male,°   *Completely / (chain) mail*

  A .c. thousande and mo.

On dromydaryes° gan they ryde,   *dromedaries, camels*

And kylled our men on every syde:

  Two .m. were there sloo.°   *slain*

435 Our men to stande° they had no mayne,°   *endure / strength*

But fledde to the towne agayne

  With woundes wyde and bloo.°   *blue (i.e., bruised)*

Twenty thousande of our men

Were borne downe at the brydge ende,[2]

440   The Turkes were so thro;°   *fierce*

Dromydaryes over them ranne

And kylled downe bothe horse and man.

  In the felde° durst none abyde:°   *(battle)field / stay*

Obedianus had many a wounde

445 Or° he wolde flee the grounde,   *Before*

  For° all the Turkes pryde;   *Despite*

Morpath and Blacke Johan

Had woundes many one

  That blody were and wyde;

450 To the towne they fledde on fote—

They sawe it° was no better bote;°   *there / remedy*

  Theyr stedes° were slayne that tyde.°   *steeds, war-horses / time*

The Turkes folowed into the towne

And kylled all before them downe—[3]

455   Grete doyll° it was to see.   *sorrow*

Into the towne the grete Turke wanne,°   *went*

And kylled wyfe, chylde, and man;

  The innocentes thycke° gan dye.   *numerously*

Johan Capystranus se° that it was thus,   *saw*

460 And hent° a crucyfyxe of Cryst Jhesus,   *seized*

  Ranne up tyll° a toure° on hye.   *to / tower*

The halowed baner with hym he bare;

---

1. I.e., killed.
2. The historical accounts confirm that the fighting was most fierce on the narrow bridge leading to the citadel.
3. In fact, as the result of a ploy orchestrated by Hunyadi, the Turks met no resistance as they came within the outer walls; finding the town around the citadel abandoned, they became distracted with looting, at which point soldiers led by Capistrano set upon them from among the ruins of the walls where they had been hiding. At the same time Hunyadi led a force from the citadel to attack from the other side. The subsequent fight was desperate.

In the top of the toure he set it there,
 And cryed full pytefully—

465 He sayd, "Lorde God in heven on hyght,
 Where is become thyn olde myght
  That men were wonte to have?[4]
 O my Lord, Cryste Jhesus,
 Why hast thou forgoten us?[5]
470 Now helpe of° the° we crave.   *from / thee*
 Loke on thy people that do thus dye;
 Lorde, ones° cast downe thyn eye,   *once*
  And help thy men to save—
 Now! Lorde, sende downe thy moche° myght   *great*
475 Agaynst these fendes° for to fyght   *fiends*
  That so thy people dysprave°—   *harm*

 Thynke, Lorde, how I have preched° thy lawe,   *preached*
 Gone barefote bothe in frost and snawe,°   *snow*
  To please the to thy paye;°   *pleasure*
480 I have fasted and suffred dysease,
 Prayed all onely° the to please—   *only*
  The Psalmes ofte I saye.
 For all my servyse I have done the,
 I aske no more to° my fee°   *as / reward*
485 But helpe thy men today—
 For, and° thou lette them thus spyll,°   *if / die*
 I am ryght in good wyll
  Forever to forsake thy laye![6]

 Now! Mary, mayden, helpe me todaye,
490 Or elles thy matyns shall I never saye
  Dayes of all my lyve,[7]
 Ne° no prayer that the shall please   *Nor*
 But° yf thou helpe now our desease,°   *Except / distress*
  Ne menye thy Joyes fyve.[8]
495 Apoynt is for thy maydenhede[9]
 That all this° people suffreth dede;°   *these / death*

---

4. What has become of your ancient power which men were accustomed to receive? (Capstrano's angry complaint here seems to be a bellicose revision of an episode related in several of the historical accounts: the Friar is said to have climbed to the highest point of the surviving defenses, held out a crucifix, and called upon God's old *mercy* to deliver forthwith those whose souls He had already redeemed—lest the heathen say, "Where is their God?")
5. Cf. Matthew 27.46: ". . . Jesus cried with a loud voice, saying . . . My God, my God, why hast thou forsaken me?"
6. I.e., I have a good mind forever to abandon your faith!
7. Or else I shall never perform your matins (the early-morning liturgical office) all the days of my life.
8. Nor commemorate your five joys (the Five Joyful Mysteries mentioned in the first chaplet of the Rosary: the Annunciation [see Luke 1.26–38], the Visitation [Luke 1.39–56], the Nativity, the Purification [Luke 2.21–39], and the Finding of the Child Jesus in the Temple [Luke 2.41–47]).
9. It is because of your virginity.

Now helpe to stynte° our stryve°—   stop/strife
Now! lady, of thy men have pyté;°   pity
Praye for them to thy Sone° on hye,   Son
500   As thou arte mayden and wyfe.

O, Lorde, Fader omnypotent,
Thynke on the myracle that thou Charles° sent,   Charlemagne
    That for the dyde fyght;
Thrughe his prayer and grace
505   The sone shone styll thre dayes space,[1]
    And shone with beames bryght.
Pharao thou drowned in the see;[2]
Tho° that thou lete go free,   Those
    Awaye thou ledde them ryght—
510   This daye, Lorde, thou helpe thy men!
Thou art also° bygge° now as thou was then,   as/great
    And of as moche myght!"

The Frere loude on God cryed;
A longe myle on every syde
515   The people herde his voyse:
Twenty .m. dede for to see,
Within the twynclyn° of an eye,   twinkling
    To lyfe agayne they rose![3]
Echone° a wepyn° in hande hente,   Each one/weapon
520   And frely° began to fyght   freely
    And felde° downe fast theyr foes.   felled
The good Erle Obedianus
Faught frely for our Lorde Jhesus;
    On every syde spronge his lose.[4]

525   He drove the Turke out of the towne;
The Crysten felled the false° downe   heathen
    And drove them to the felde agayne.
Twenty .m. with them mette,°   joined (as reinforcements)
Or elles the Turke, withouten lette,°   delay, hindrance
530   Surely had ben slayne—
Than were they fayne° for to fyght   (more) pleased

---

1. The sun shone continuously for three days. (The miracle is reported in both the *Chanson de Roland*, ll. 2449–58, and the *Pseudo-Turpin Chronicle* [chapter 29 in the Latin original]: after returning to Roncevaux to find all his best knights slain in ambush, Charles declares his intention ceaselessly to seek revenge [and in the *Chanson* he asks directly that the sun be made to stand still to help him in his pursuit], at which point the miracle is wrought.)
2. Exodus 14.28–29: ". . . the waters returned, and covered the chariots, and the horsemen, and all the host of Pharaoh that came into the sea after them; there remained not so much as one of them. But the children of Israel walked upon dry land in the midst of the sea. . . ." Cf. l. 69.
3. Nothing like this is, of course, recorded in the historical accounts, but Capistrano's role in reviving the spirits of the weary troops is acknowledged, and his reputation as a worker of healing miracles no doubt contributed to the poem's affective fiction.
4. His valor was made known everywhere.

Than ever was foule° of daye-lyght,   *fowl*
  Certayne, withouten layne.°   *concealing (the truth)*

[V]

Now begynneth a newe batayll,
535 I let you wyt,° withouten fayle,   *know*
  Of myghty men of mayne:

Ychone° hewe° on other with ire°   *Each one/hewed/ire, anger*
That all the felde semed fyre[5]
Also lyght° as leme° of thonder.   *bright/flame (i.e., lightning)*
540 Every man hurte other in hast
And layde on basynettes to braynes brast;[6]
  And ever the false fell under.
The blode ranne all° the felde   *all (through)*
Of doughty men under schelde;[7]
545   To se it was grete wonder.

There was hewynge from the hals°   *neck*
The helmes and the hedes° als;°   *heads/also, together*
  Ryche knyghtes were unknytte°—   *undone, destroyed*
Many a Turke, withouten fayle,
550 Tombled top over tayle
  That never rose yet!°   *since*
So harde on helmes they hewe
That there were Turkes but fewe
  That in sadyll° coude° sytte.   *saddle/could*
555 There was no Turke there
But he myght tell of moche care,°   *trouble, distress*
  I lette you well wytte.

There was stycked° many a stede,   *stabbed*
Grete dromydaryes made blede;°   *(to) bleed*
560   Tho° they for faynt° fall.   *Those/weakness*
The Crysten men had quarelles good;
They dredde nothynge to shed theyr blode
  Whan Jhesu dyde them call.°   *call (upon)*
They hewed on with swerdes kene;°   *sharp*
565 Of° helmes, with the hedes bydene,°   *Off/together*
  Tumbled as a ball.
So delte they strokes on a brayde
That no Turke held hym apayde,
  The proudest of them all.[8]

5. So that the entire battlefield seemed a (burning) fire.
6. And laid blows on helmets to burst out brains.
7. I.e., from valiant armed men.
8. They dealt out strokes in such a rush that no Turk was pleased with himself, (not even) the most valiant of them all.

570 There was hurtelynge° in-fere,°   *hurtling, rushing / together*
    Broken many a sharpe spere,°   *spear, lance*
        And drawen many a knyfe;
    Stedes sterted out of stryfe,[9]
    And kest° theyr maystres in° the waye°   *cast / into / road*
575   Utterly belyve.[1]
    Many a hethen in theyr ghere°   *gear, armor*
    His felowe gan° downe bere,°   *did / bear, carry*
        And to the erthe hym dryve.

    The blode ranne thrughe the brest. . . .[2]

---

9. Steeds bolted away from the strife.
1. All at once.
2. Nothing more of the poem survives, but it is evident that the Christian victory is at hand. The historical accounts report that as the Christians neared exhaustion and as the influx of fresh Turkish forces began to seem interminable, the Christians hit upon the tactic of throwing from the walls all kinds of burning matter down upon the Turks. Thousands of Turks were burned alive, and others trapped by the fire within the walls were cut down; all others fled. On the next day (the 23rd), a foray by a few Christians into the Turkish camp escalated into a full-scale attack, during which the Turks appear to have lost their resolve; they fled, pursued for some way into the night by the Christians.

CRITICISM

ERICH AUERBACH

The Knight Sets Forth †

Near the beginning of Chrétien de Troyes' *Yvain*, a courtly romance of the second half of the twelfth century, one of the knights of King Arthur's court relates an adventure which once befell him. [The poem] begins as follows [cf. *Ywain and Gawain*, ll. 1–234]:[1]

Arthur, the good King of Britain, whose noble qualities teach us that we ourselves should be honourable and courtly, held a court of truly regal splendour for that most sumptuous festival that is properly called Pentecost. The court was at [Carduel] in Wales. After the meal, throughout the halls, the knights gathered where they were called by the ladies, damsels and maidens. Some related anecdotes, others spoke of love, of the torments and sorrows and of the great blessings that often come to the members of its order, which at that time was powerful and thriving. Nowadays, however, it has few adherents, since almost all have abandoned love, leaving it much debased. For those who used to love had a reputation for courtliness, integrity, generosity and honour; but now love is made a laughing-stock, because people who feel nothing of it lie by claiming to love; and they make a deceitful mockery of it when they boast of it without having the right. But let us leave those still alive to speak of those who once were! For, in my view, a courtly man who is dead is still worth more than a living churl. Therefore I am pleased to relate something worth hearing concerning the king who was of such repute that he is spoken of near and far; and I agree with the people of Britain that his name will live on for ever. And through him are remembered those fine chosen knights who devoted all their efforts to honour.

That day, however, they were quite astonished to find the king rise and leave their company; and some of them were very offended and did not spare their comments, having never before, on such an important feast-day, seen him retire to his room to sleep or rest. On this day, though, he came to be detained by the queen and happened to stay so long at her side that he forgot himself and fell asleep. Outside the door of his room were Dodinel and Sagremor, Kay and my lord Gawain and with them my lord Yvain; there too

1. The translation which follows is that of D. D. R. Owen (as identified in the leading footnote to the Sources and Backgrounds selections from *Yvain*, p. 334), reprinted by permission of David Campbell Publishers.

411

was Calogrenant,[2] a very good-looking knight, who had begun to tell them a story that was not to his honour but to his shame. As he was telling his tale, the queen could hear him; and she got up from the king's side and came upon them so stealthily that she had landed in their midst before anyone caught sight of her, except that Calogrenant alone jumped to his feet to greet her.

69   Then Kay, who was extremely abusive, wickedly sarcastic and sneering, said to him: "By God, Calogrenant, I see you're very gallant and sprightly now, and indeed I'm delighted you are the most courtly of us; and I know very well you think so—you're so completely devoid of sense. So it's only right for my lady to suppose that you possess more courtliness and gallantry than the rest of us. Perhaps it was out of laziness that we failed to rise, or else because we didn't deign to? I assure you, sir, that wasn't our reason, but the fact that we didn't see my lady until you had stood up first." —"Really, Kay, I do believe you'd burst", says the queen, "if you couldn't empty yourself of the venom you are full of. You're tiresome and churlish to insult your companions."—"My lady," says Kay, "if we don't gain from your company, take care we're not the worse for it! I don't think I said anything that should be counted against me, so I beg you to speak no more of it. It's neither courtly nor sensible to quarrel over a trifle. This argument should go no further, and no one should make any more of it. But have him carry on with the story he'd begun to tell us, for there shouldn't be any squabbling here."

105   At this Calogrenant speaks up in reply. "Sir," says he, "I'm not greatly worried by the quarrel: it's of small concern or importance to me. If you've wronged me, I'll never be harmed by that; for you, my lord Kay, have often insulted more worthy and wiser men than I, as indeed is your usual practice. The dung-heap will always stink, the gad-fly sting and the bee buzz, and a pest pester and plague. But, if my lady doesn't press me, I'll tell no more of my story today; and I beg her kindly to refrain from asking me to do anything I don't wish to."—"My lady," says Kay, "everybody here will be grateful if you do insist, as they will be glad to hear it. Don't do anything for my sake; but by the faith you owe the king, your lord and mine, you'll do well to tell him to go on."—"Calogrenant," says the queen, "take no notice of the attack of my lord Kay the seneschal! He's so used to uttering abuse that no one can talk him out of it. I would beg you urgently not to harbour any resentment on his account or to refrain because of him from telling us something we'd like to hear. So, if you want to enjoy my affection,

---

2. R.S. Loomis saw in Calogrenant (who appears as [Colgrevance in *Ywain and Gawain*]) a doubling of the figure of Kay (Cai-lo-grenant = "Kay the grumbler": see *Arthurian Tradition and Chrétien de Troyes*, p. 275). Kay's churlishness is emphasized by Chrétien in this opening scene, and his insults are used as a leitmotif in the first part of *Yvain*. . . . [D.D.R. Owen's note]

begin again from the beginning!"—"Really, my lady, I find what you ask me to do very irksome: I'd rather have one of my eyes plucked out than tell any more of my tale today, were I not afraid of annoying you. But I shall do as you please, however much it may hurt me. Listen, then, as this is what you wish!

150   "Lend me your hearts and your ears! For things one hears are lost unless they are understood by the heart. There are people who don't understand what they hear and yet commend it: they have nothing but the power of hearing. So long as the heart understands nothing of the words, they reach the ears like the blowing wind; but rather than stopping and lingering there, they very swiftly pass on, unless the heart is alert enough to be ready to receive them. The ears are the route and channel by which the voice reaches the heart, and the heart receives in the breast the voice that penetrates to it through the ear. Whoever, then, should wish to understand me now must lend his heart and ears; for I have no intention to speak of a fantasy, a fiction or a lie such as many others have served up to you, but shall instead tell you of what I've seen.

175   "It happened some seven years ago that, as solitary as a countryman, I was travelling in quest of adventures, fully equipped with arms as a knight should be, when on the right hand I found a way leading through a dense forest. It was a very difficult track, full of briars and thorns. Not without trouble and hardship I made my way by this path. Almost the whole day I rode on like that until I came out of the forest, which was in Broceliande,[3] I emerged from the forest on to a heath and saw a wooden tower half a Welsh league away: if it was as far as that, it was no further. I headed in that direction at more than a walking pace and saw the bailey and the deep, broad moat all round it. And standing on the bridge, with a moulted goshawk on his wrist, was the owner of the fortress. I had scarcely greeted him when he came up to take my stirrup and bade me dismount. I dismounted, there being no alternative, since I needed a lodging-place. Immediately, more than a hundred times in succession, he said to me that blessed was the road by which I had arrived there. With that, passing over the bridge and through the gate, we entered the courtyard. In the middle of the courtyard of this vavasour, to whom may God grant as much joy and honour as he bestowed on me that night, there hung a gong in which I think there was no iron or wood or anything but copper. The vavasour struck three times on the gong with a hammer that hung on a post. Those who were upstairs in the building heard the sound of its clanging and dashed from the house and down into

---

3. The Forest of Broceliande with its marvellous spring of Barenton is in Brittany, not in [Wales] as would appear from Chrétien's romance. For the Broceliande localisation Chrétien is probably indebted to Wace, who speaks of the spring in his *Roman de Rou* (ed. A. J. Holden, Paris, 1970–73, lines 6373–98). An earlier version of the story, however, may well have placed the spring in southern Scotland, where it appears in a related legend (see Loomis, *Arthurian Tradition . . .* , pp. 289–93). [D.D.R. Owen's note]

the yard, some taking charge of my horse, which the good vavasour was holding.

226 "I then saw a beautiful and attractive maiden coming towards me and looked at her with some attention: she was slender, tall and erect. She showed her skill in disarming me, which she did efficiently and well, and dressed me in a precious mantle of fine, peacock-blue cloth and trimmed with miniver. Then everyone left us alone, nobody staying either with me or with her; and that suited me well, for I wished to see no other. And she took me to sit on the prettiest lawn in the world, enclosed all around by a wall. There I found her so refined in behaviour and well informed in conversation, such delightful company and so well mannered, that to be there was a great pleasure for me, and I would never have wished to leave on any account. But that night the vavasour thwarted my wishes by coming to look for me when supper-time came round. Unable to linger there any longer, I at once did as he asked. Of the supper I will simply tell you that it was entirely to my liking once the maiden, when she sat down to it, was placed opposite me. After supper the vavasour admitted to me that he did not know how long it was since he had given lodging to a knight journeying in search of adventure, though he had been host to many. Afterwards he begged me to repay him by returning if possible by way of his home; and I replied: 'Gladly, sir!' since it would have been shameful to refuse him—not to grant that request would have been a poor return to my host.

269 "I was very well lodged that night; and as soon as daylight appeared my horse was saddled, as I had urgently asked the night before that it should be; so my request was properly carried out. I commended my good host and his dear daughter to the Holy Spirit, took leave of everyone, and left as quickly as I could.

Continuing his narrative * * * Calogrenant tells how he encounters a herd of bulls and how the herdsman, a grotesquely ugly and gigantic *vilain*, tells him of a magic spring not far away. It flows under a beautiful tree. A golden vessel hangs nearby, and when water from the spring is poured from the vessel over an emerald tablet which lies beside it, such a terrible storm arises in the forest that no one has ever lived through it. Calogrenant attempts the adventure. He withstands the storm and then enjoys the sunny calm which follows, enlivened by the song of many birds. But then a knight appears who, reproaching him with the damage the storm has caused to his property, defeats him, so that he has to return to his host on foot and weaponless. He is again very well received and is assured that he is indeed the first to have escaped from the adventure unscathed. Calogrenant's story makes a great impression on the knights at Arthur's court. The King decides to ride to the magic spring himself, with a large following. However, one of the knights,

Calogrenant's cousin Yvain, gets there before him, defeats and kills the knight of the spring, and, by means which are partly miraculous and partly very natural, wins the love of his widow.

Although only some seventy years separate this text from the *Chanson de Roland*, and although here too we are dealing with an epic work of the feudal age, a first glance suffices to show a complete change in stylistic movement. The narrative flows; it is light and almost easy. It is in no hurry to get on, but its progress is steady. Its parts are connected without any gaps. Here too, to be sure, there are no strictly organized periods; the advance from one part of the story to the next is loose and follows no set plan; nor are the values of the conjunctions yet clearly established—*que* especially has to fulfill far too many functions, so that many causal connections (e.g. ll. 231, 235, or 237) remain somewhat vague. But this does not harm the narrative continuity; on the contrary, the loose connections make for a very natural narrative style, and the rhyme—handled very freely and independently of the sense structure —never breaks in obtrusively. It permits the poet an occasional line of padding or a detailed circumlocution (e.g. l. 193 or ll. 211–216), which merge smoothly into the style and actually increase the impression of naive, fresh, and easy breadth. How much more elastic and mobile this language is than that of the *chanson de geste*, how much more adroitly it prattles on, conveying narrative movements which, though still naive enough, already have far freer play in their variety, can be observed in almost every sentence. Let us take lines 241 to 246 as an example: *La la trovai si afeitiee, si bien parlant et anseigniee, de tel sanblant et de tel estre, que mout m'i delitoit a estre, ne ja mes por nul estovoir ne m'an queïsse removoir.* ["There I found her so refined in behaviour and well informed in conversation, such delightful company and so well man-nered, that to be there was a great pleasure for me, and I would never have wished to leave on any account."] The sentence, linked by *la* to the preceding one, is a consecutive period. The ascending section has three steps, the third step contains an antithetically constructed summary (*sanblant-estre*) which reveals a high degree of analytical skill (already a matter of course) in the judgment of character. The descending section is bipartite, and the parts are carefully set off against each other: the first—stating the fact of delight—in the indicative mood; the second— hypothetical—in the subjunctive. Nothing so subtle in structure, and merging with the narrative as a whole so smoothly and without apparent effort, is likely to have occurred in vernacular literatures before the courtly romance. I take this opportunity to observe that in the slow growth of a hypotactically richer and more periodic syntax, a leading role seems to have been played (down to the time of Dante) by consec-utive constructions * * * * While other types of modal connection were still comparatively undeveloped, this one flourished and developed char-acteristic functions of expression which were later lost; the subject has recently been discussed in an interesting study by A. G. Hatcher (*Revue des Etudes Indo-européennes*, 2. 30).

Calogrenant tells King Arthur's Round Table that, seven years earlier, he had ridden away alone in quest of adventure, armed as befits a knight, and he had come upon a road leading to the right, straight through a dense forest. Here we stop and wonder. To the right? That is a strange indication of locality when, as in this case, it is used absolutely. In terms of terrestrial topography it makes sense only when used relatively. Hence it must here have an ethical signification. Apparently it is the "right way" which Calogrenant discovered. And that is confirmed immediately, for the road is arduous, as right ways are wont to be; all day long it leads through a dense forest full of brambles and thickets, and at night it reaches the right goal: a castle where Calogrenant is received with delight, as though he were a long-awaited guest. It is only at night, it seems, as he rides out of the forest, that he discovers where he is: on a heath in Broceliande. Broceliande in Armorica, on the continent, is a fairyland well known in Breton legend, with a magic spring and an enchanted forest. How Calogrenant—who presumably started out from King Arthur's court on the Island of Britain—managed to get to continental Brittany is not explained. We hear nothing of a crossing of the sea, as we hear nothing of it later (ll. 760ff.) in Yvain's case, who in turn undoubtedly sets out from Carduel in Wales although his journey to the "right road" in Broceliande is described in vague and legendary terms. No sooner does Calogrenant discover where he is, than he sees a hospitable castle. On the bridge stands the lord of the castle, with a hunting falcon on his fist, welcoming him with a delight which goes far beyond the expression of ready hospitality, and which once again assures us that we have been hearing about a "right way": *et il me dist tot maintenant plus de çant fois an un tenant, que beneoite fust la voie, par ou leanz venuz estoie.* ["Immediately, more than a hundred times in succession, he said to me that blessed was the road by which I had arrived there."] The subsequent phases of his welcome follow the knightly ceremonial whose graceful forms seem to have long been established; striking three times upon a copper plate, the host summons his servants; the traveler's horse is led away; a beautiful maiden appears, who is the daughter of the lord of the castle; it is her duty to relieve the guest of his armor, to replace it by a comfortable and beautiful coat, and then, alone with him in a charming garden, to keep him pleasant company until supper is ready. After the meal the lord of the castle informs his guest that he has been receiving knights errant in pursuit of adventure for a very long time; he urges him to visit the castle again on his way back; strangely enough he tells him nothing about the adventure of the spring, although he knows about it and although he is well aware that the dangers which await his guest there will in all probability prevent his contemplated return. But that seems to be quite as it should be; at any rate it in no wise reduces the meed of praise which Calogrenant and, later, Yvain bestow upon their host's hospitality and knightly virtues. So Calogrenant rides away in the morning, and it is not until he meets the satyrlike *vilain* that he hears of the magic spring. This *vilain* of course has no idea of what *avanture* is—how could he, not being a knight?—but he knows the magic qualities of the spring, and he makes no secret of his knowledge.

Obviously we are now deep in fairy tale and magic. The right road through the forest full of brambles, the castle which seems to have sprung out of the ground, the nature of the hero's reception, the beautiful maiden, the strange silence of the lord of the castle, the satyr, the magic spring—it is all in the atmosphere of fairy tale. And the indications of time are as reminiscent of fairy tale as the indications of place. Calogrenant has kept quiet about his adventure for seven years. Seven is a fairy-tale number, and the seven years mentioned at the beginning of the *Chanson de Roland* likewise impart a touch of the legendary: seven years—*set anz tuz pleins*—is the time the Emperor Charles had spent in Spain. However, in the *Chanson de Roland* they are really "full" years; they are *tuz pleins*, because the Emperor used them to subdue the entire land down to the sea and to take all its castles and cities except Saragossa. In the seven years between Calogrenant's adventure at the spring and the time of his narration, on the other hand, nothing seems to have happened or at least we are told nothing about it. When Yvain sets off on the same adventure he finds everything exactly as Calogrenant had described it: the lord of the castle, the maiden, the bulls with their horribly ugly giant of a herdsman, the magic spring, and the knight who defends it. Nothing has changed; the seven years have passed without leaving a trace, just as time usually does in a fairy tale. The landscape is the enchanted landscape of fairy tale; we are surrounded by mystery, by secret murmurings and whispers. All the numerous castles and palaces, the battles and adventures, of the courtly romances—especially of the Breton cycle—are things of fairyland: each time they appear before us as though sprung from the ground; their geographical relation to the known world, their sociological and economic foundations, remain unexplained. Even their ethical or symbolic significance can rarely be ascertained with anything approaching certainty. Has the adventure at the spring any hidden meaning? It is evidently one of those which the Knights of the Round Table are bound to undergo, yet an ethical justification for the combat with the knight of the magic spring is nowhere given. In other episodes of the courtly romances it is sometimes possible to make out symbolic, mythological, or religious motifs; for instance, the journey to the underworld in *Lancelot*, the motif of liberation and redemption in numerous instances, and especially the theme of Christian grace in the Grail legend—but it is rarely possible to define the meaning precisely, at least so long as the courtly romance remains true to type.

It is from Breton folklore that the courtly romance took its elements of mystery, of something sprung from the soil, concealing its roots, and inaccessible to rational explanation; it incorporated them and made use of them in its elaboration of the knightly ideal; the *matière de Bretagne*[4] apparently proved to be the most suitable medium for the cultivation of that ideal—more suitable even than the stuff of antiquity, which was taken up at about the same time but which soon lost ground.

A self-portrayal of feudal knighthood with its mores and ideals is the fundamental purpose of the courtly romance. Nor are its exterior forms of life neglected—they are portrayed in leisurely fashion, and on these occasions the portrayal abandons the nebulous distance of fairy tale and gives salient pictures of contemporary conditions. Other episodes in courtly romance convey much more colorful and detailed pictures of this sort than our passage does; but even our passage permits us to observe the essential features which indicate its realistic character. The lord of the castle with his falcon; the summoning of the servants by striking a copper plate; the beautiful young mistress of the castle, relieving the visitor of his armor, wrapping him in a comfortable cloak, and entertaining him most pleasantly until supper is served—all these are graceful vignettes of established custom, one might say of a ritual which shows us courtly society in its setting of highly developed conventionality. The setting is as fixed and isolating, as distinct from the mores of other strata of society, as is that of the *chanson de geste*, but it is much more refined and elegant. Women play an important part in it; the mannerly ease and comfort of the social life of a cultured class have been attained. And indeed it has assumed a nature which is long to remain one of the most distinctive characteristics of French taste: graceful amenity with almost an excess of subtlety. The scene with the young lady of the castle—her appearance, his way of looking at her, the removal of his armor, the conversation in the meadow—though it is not a particularly developed example, yet sufficiently conveys the impression of that delicately graceful, limpid and smiling, fresh and elegantly naive coquetry of which Chrétien in particular is a past master. Genre scenes of this sort are found in French literature very early—in the *chansons de toile* and once even in the *Chanson de Roland*, in the laisse which tells of Margariz of Seville (ll. 955ff.); but their full development was a contribution of courtly society, and Chrétien's great charm especially is in no small measure due to his gift for carrying on this tone in the most varied fashion. We find the style in its greatest brilliance where the subject matter is the dalliance of true love. Between these scenes of dalliance come antithetical reasonings over the emotions involved, seem-

4. The "Matter of Britain" (mostly tales of Arthur), as distinguished from the "Matter of France" (mostly tales of Charlemagne) and the "Matter of Rome" (tales of classical antiquity); the "Matters" of romance were first so named late in the 12th century by Jean Bodel, in his poem *Les Saisnes*. [Editor]

ingly naive yet of accomplished artistry and grace. The most celebrated example occurs at the beginning of the *Cligès*, where the budding love between Alixandre and Soredamors—with its initial reticence and mutual hide-and-seek and the ultimate welling up of emotions—is represented in a series of enchanting scenes and analytical soliloquies.

The grace and attractiveness of this style—whose charm is freshness and whose danger is silly coquetry, trifling, and coldness—can hardly be found in such purity anywhere in the literature of antiquity. Chrétien did not learn it from Ovid; it is a creation of the French Middle Ages. It must be noted, furthermore, that this style is by no means restricted to love episodes. In Chrétien, and also in the later romance of adventure and the shorter verse narrative, the entire portrayal of life within feudal society is tuned to the same note, not only in the twelfth but also in the thirteenth century. In charmingly graceful, delicately painted, and crystalline verses, knightly society offers its own presentment; thousands of little scenes and pictures describe its habits, its views, and its social tone for us. There is a great deal of brilliance, of realistic flavor, of psychological refinement, and also a great deal of humor in these pictures. It is a much richer, more varied, and more comprehensive world than the world of the *chansons de geste*, although it too is only the world of a single class. At times indeed Chrétien seems to break through this class confinement, as in the workroom of the three hundred women in the Chastel de Pesme Avanture (*Yvain*, 5107ff.) or in the description of the wealthy town whose citizens (*quemune*) attempt to storm the castle where Gauvain is quartered (*Perceval*, 5710ff.)—but such episodes are after all only a colorful setting for the life of the knight. Courtly realism offers a very rich and pungent picture of the life of a single class, a social stratum which remains aloof from the other strata of contemporary society, allowing them to appear as accessories, sometimes colorful but more usually comic or grotesque; so that the distinction in terms of class between the important, the meaningful, and the sublime on the one hand and the low-grotesque-comic on the other, remains strictly intact in regard to subject matter. The former realm is open only to members of the feudal class. Yet a real separation of styles is not in question here, for the simple reason that the courtly romance does not know an "elevated style," that is, a distinction between levels of expression. The easy-going, adroit, and elastic rhymed octosyllable effortlessly adapts itself to any subject and any level of emotion or thought. Did it not elsewhere serve the most varied ends, from farce to saint's legend? When it treats very serious or terrible themes, it is apt—at least to our way of feeling—to fall into a certain touching naïveté and childishness. And indeed, there is the courage of a child in the freshness of outlook which undertook—with the sole tool of a literary language so young that it had no ballast of theory, had not yet emerged from the confusion of dialectical forms—to master a life which had, after all, attained a considerable degree of differentiation. The problem of levels of style is not consciously conceived in the vernaculars until much later, that is, from the time of Dante.

But an even stronger limitation than that in terms of class results for the realism of the courtly romance from its legendary, fairy-tale atmosphere. It is this which makes all the colorful and vivid pictures of contemporary reality seem, as it were, to have sprung from the ground: the ground of legend and fairy tale, so that—as we said before—they are entirely without any basis in political reality. The geographical, economic, and social conditions on which they depend are never explained. They descend directly from fairy tale and adventure. The strikingly realistic workroom in *Yvain*, which I mentioned earlier, and in which we even find discussions of such things as working conditions and workers' compensation, was not established because of concrete economic conditions but because the young king of the Island of Maidens had fallen into the hands of two evil gnomelike brothers and ransomed himself by promising that once a year he would deliver to them thirty of his maidens to perform labor. The fairy-tale atmosphere is the true element of the courtly romance, which after all is not only interested in portraying external living conditions in the feudal society of the closing years of the twelfth century but also and especially in expressing its ideals. And with that we reach the very core of courtly romance, insofar as its particular ethos came to be important in the history of the literary treatment of reality.

Calogrenant sets out without mission or office; he seeks adventure, that is, perilous encounters by which he can prove his mettle. There is nothing like this in the *chanson de geste*. There a knight who sets off has an office and a place in a politico-historical context. It is doubtless simplified and distorted in the manner of legend, but it is maintained insofar as the characters who take part in the action have a function in the real world—for instance, the defense of Charles's realm against the infidels, their conquest and conversion, and so forth. Such are the political and historical purposes served by the feudal ethos, the warriors' ethos which the knights profess. Calogrenant, on the other hand, has no political or historical task, nor has any other knight of Arthur's court. Here the feudal ethos serves no political function; it serves no practical reality at all; it has become absolute. It no longer has any purpose but that of self-realization. This changes its nature completely. Even the term which we find for it in the *Chanson de Roland* most frequently and in the most general acceptation—the term *vasselage*—seems gradually to drop out of fashion. Chrétien uses it three times in *Erec*, in *Cligès* and *Lancelot* it occurs in one passage each, and after that not at all. The new term which he now prefers is *corteisie*, a word whose long and significant history supplies the most complete interpretation of the ideal concept of class and man in Europe. In the *Chanson de Roland* this word does not yet occur. Only the adjective *curteis* appears three times, twice in reference to Olivier in the combination *li proz e li curteis*. It would seem that *corteisie* achieved its synthetic meaning only in the age of chivalry or courtly culture, which indeed derives the latter name from it. The values expressed in it—refinement of the laws of combat, courteous social intercourse, service of women—have undergone a striking process of change and sublimation in comparison with the *chanson de geste* and are all directed toward a personal and absolute ideal— absolute both in reference to ideal realization and in reference to the absence of any earthly and practical purpose. The personal element in the courtly virtues is not simply a gift of nature; nor is it acquired by birth; to implant them now requires, besides birth, proper training too, as preserving them requires the unforced will to renew them by constant and tireless practice and proving.

The means by which they are proved and preserved is adventure, *avanture*, a very characteristic form of activity developed by courtly culture. Of course, fanciful depiction of the miracles and dangers awaiting those whom their destiny takes beyond the confines of the familiar world into distant and unexplored regions had long been known, as well as no less imaginative ideas and narratives about the mysterious perils which also threaten man within the geographically familiar world, from the influence of gods, spirits, demons, and other magic powers; so too the fearless hero who, by strength, virtue, cunning, and the help of God, overcomes such dangers and frees others from them was known long before the age of courtly culture. But that an entire class, in the heyday of its contemporary flowering, should regard the surmounting of such perils as its true mission—in the ideal conception of things as its exclusive mission; that the most various legendary traditions, especially but not only those of the Breton cycle, are taken over by it for the purpose of producing a chivalrous world of magic especially designed for the purpose, in which fantastic encounters and perils present themselves to the knight as if from the end of an assembly-line—this state of affairs is a new creation of the courtly romance. Although these perilous encounters called *avantures* now have no experiential basis whatever, although it is impossible to fit them into any actual or practically conceivable political system, although they commonly crop up without any rational connection, one after the other, in a long series, we must be careful not to be misled by the modern value of the term adventure, to think of them as purely "accidental." When we moderns speak of adventure, we mean something unstable, peripheral, disordered, or, as Simmel once put it, a something that stands outside the real meaning of existence. All this is precisely what the word does not mean in the courtly romance. On the contrary, trial through adventure is the real meaning of the knight's ideal existence. That the very essence of the knight's ideal of manhood is called forth by adventure, E. Eberwein undertook to show some years since with reference to the *Lais* of Marie de France (*Zur Deutung mittelalterlicher Existenz*, Bonn and Cologne, 1933, pp. 27ff.). It can also be demonstrated on the basis of the courtly romance.

Calogrenant seeks the right way and finds it, as we said before. It is the right way into adventure, and this very seeking and finding of it shows him to be one of the chosen, a true knight of King Arthur's Round Table. As a true knight worthy of adventure, he is received by his host—who is also a knight—with delight and with blessings for having found the right way. Host and guest both belong to one social group, a sort of order, admission into which is through a ceremonial election and all members of which are bound to help one another. The host's real calling, the only meaning of his living where he does, seems to be that he should offer knightly hospitality to knights in quest of adventure. But the help he gives his guest is made mysterious by his silence in regard to what lies ahead for Calogrenant. Apparently this secretiveness is one of his knightly duties, quite in contrast to the *vilain*, who withholds nothing of what he knows. What the *vilain* does know are the material circumstances of the adventure; but what "adventure" is, he does not know, for he is without knightly culture. Calogrenant, then, is a true knight, one of the elect. But there are many degrees of election. Not he, but only Yvain, proves capable of sustaining the adventure. The degrees of election, and specific election for a specific adventure, are sometimes more clearly emphasized in the *Lancelot* and the *Perceval* than in the *Yvain*; but the motif is unmistakable wherever we have to do with courtly literature. The series of adventures is thus raised to the status of a fated and graduated test of election; it becomes the basis of a doctrine of personal perfection through a development dictated by fate, a doctrine which was later to break through the class barriers of courtly culture. We must not overlook the fact, it is true, that, contemporaneously with courtly culture, there was another movement which gave expression to this graduated proving of election, as well as to the theory of love, with much greater rigor and clarity—namely, Victorine and Cistercian mysticism. This movement was not restricted to one class, and it did not require adventure.

The world of knightly proving is a world of adventure. It not only contains a practically uninterrupted series of adventures; more specifically, it contains nothing but the requisites of adventure. Nothing is found in it which is not either accessory or preparatory to an adventure. It is a world specifically created and designed to give the knight opportunity to prove himself. The scene of Calogrenant's departure shows this most clearly. He rides on all day and encounters nothing but the castle prepared to receive him. Nothing is said about all the practical conditions and circumstances necessary to render the existence of such a castle in absolute solitude both possible and compatible with ordinary experience.

Such idealization takes us very far from the imitation of reality. In the courtly romance the functional, the historically real aspects of class are passed over. Though it offers a great many culturally significant details concerning the customs of social intercourse and external social forms and conventions in general, we can get no penetrating view of contemporary reality from it, even in respect to the knightly class. Where it depicts reality, it depicts merely the colorful surface, and where it is not superficial, it has other subjects and other ends than contemporary reality. Yet it does contain a class ethics which as such claimed and indeed attained acceptance and validity in this real and earthly world. For it has a great power of attraction which, if I mistake not, is due especially to two characteristics which distinguish it: it is absolute, raised above all earthly contingencies, and it gives those who submit to its dictates the feeling that they belong to a community of the elect, a circle of solidarity (the term comes from Hellmut Ritter, the Orientalist) set apart from the common herd. The ethics of feudalism, the ideal conception of the perfect knight, thus attained a very considerable and very long-lived influence. Concepts associated with it—courage, honor, loyalty, mutual respect, refined manners, service to women—continued to cast their spell on the contemporaries of completely changed cultural periods. Social strata of later urban and bourgeois provenance adopted this ideal, although it is not only class-conditioned and exclusive but also completely devoid of reality. As soon as it transcends the sphere of mere conventions of intercourse and has to do with the practical business of the world, it proves inadequate and needs to be supplemented, often in a manner most unpleasantly in contrast to it. But precisely because it is so removed from reality, it could—as an ideal—adapt itself to any and every situation, at least as long as there were ruling classes at all.

So it came to pass that the knightly ideal survived all the catastrophes which befell feudalism in the course of the centuries. It survived even Cervantes' *Don Quixote*, in which the problem was interpreted in the most thorough manner. Don Quixote's first setting forth, with his arrival at nightfall at an inn which he takes to be a castle, is a perfect parody of Calogrenant's journey—precisely because the world which Don Quixote encounters is not one especially prepared for the proving of a knight but is a random, everyday, real world. By his detailed description of the circumstances of his hero's life, Cervantes makes it perfectly clear, at the very beginning of his book, where the root of Don Quixote's confusion lies: he is the victim of a social order in which he belongs to a class that has no function. He belongs to this class; he cannot emancipate himself from it; but as a mere member of it, without wealth and without high connections, he has no role and no mission. He feels his life running meaninglessly out, as though he were paralyzed. Only upon such a man, whose life is hardly better than a peasant's but who is educated and who is neither able nor permitted to labor as a peasant does, could romances of chivalry have such an unbalancing effect. His setting forth is a flight from a situation which is unbearable and which he has borne far too long. He wants to enforce his claim to the function proper to the class to which he belongs. It goes without saying that, three and a half centuries earlier, and in France, the situation is completely different. Feudal knighthood is still of crucial importance in military matters. The growth of an urban bourgeoisie and the growth of absolutism with its trend toward centralization are still in their earliest stages. But if Calogrenant had really set off on his quest as he describes it, he would even then have encountered things very different from those he reports. At the time of the second and third crusades, in the world of Henry II or Louis VII or Philip Augustus, things were hardly managed as they are in courtly romances. The courtly romance is not reality shaped and set forth by art, but an escape into fable and fairy tale. From the very beginning, at the height of its cultural florescence, this ruling class adopted an ethos and an ideal which concealed its real function. And it proceeded to describe its own life in extrahistorical terms, as an absolute aesthetic configuration without practical purpose. Certainly, one explanation of so strange a phenomenon lies in the surging imagination of that great century, in its spontaneous and soaring flight beyond reality into the absolute. But this explanation is too general to be adequate, especially since the courtly epic offers not only adventure and absolute idealization but also graceful manners and pompous ceremonies. One feels tempted to suggest that the long functional crisis of the feudal class had already begun to make itself felt—even at the time of the flowering of courtly literature. Chrétien de Troyes, who lived first in Champagne where, precisely during his lifetime, the great commercial fairs began to assume outstanding continental importance, then in Flanders where the burghers attained economic and political significance earlier than elsewhere north of the Alps, may well have begun to sense that the feudal class was no longer the only ruling class.

The widespread and long-enduring flowering of the courtly-chivalric romance exerted a significant and, more precisely, a restrictive influence upon literary realism, even before the antique doctrine of different levels of style began to be influential in the same restrictive direction. Finally the two were merged in the idea of an elevated style, as it gradually developed during the Renaissance. In a later chapter we shall return to this point. Here we shall discuss only the various influences which—as characteristics of the knightly ideal—were a hindrance to the full apprehension of reality as given. In this connection, as previously noted, we are not yet concerned with style in the strict sense. An elevated style of poetic expression had not yet been produced by the courtly epic. On the contrary, it did not even employ the elements of sublimity present in the paratactic form of the heroic epic. Its style is rather pleasantly narrative than sublime; it is suitable for any kind of subject matter. The later trend toward a linguistic separation of styles goes back entirely to the influence of antiquity, and not to that of courtly chivalry. Restrictions in terms of subject matter, however, are all the stronger.

They are class-determined. Only members of the chivalric-courtly society are worthy of adventure, hence they alone can undergo serious and significant experiences. Those outside this class cannot appear except as accessories, and even then generally in merely comic, grotesque, or despicable roles. This state of affairs is less apparent in antiquity and in the older heroic epic than here, where we are dealing with a conscious exclusiveness within a group characterized by class solidarity. Now it is true that before very long there were tendencies at work which sought to base the solidarity of the group not on descent but on personal factors, on noble behavior and refined manners. The beginning of this can already be discerned in the most important examples of the courtly epic itself, for in them the picture of the knightly individual, with increasing emphasis on inner values, is based on personal election and personal formation. Later, when—in Italy especially—social strata of urban background took over the courtly ideal and refashioned it, the concept of nobility became ever more personal, and as such it was actually often contrasted polemically with the other concept of nobility based solely on lineage. But all this did not render the ideal less exclusive. It continued to apply to a class of the elect, which at times indeed seemed to constitute a secret society. In the process, social, political, educational, mystical, and class motifs were interwoven in the most varied way. But the most important point is that this emphasis on inner values by no means brought a closer approach to earthly realities. On the contrary: in part at least it was precisely the emphasis laid on the inner values of the knightly ideal which caused the connection with the real things of this earth to become ever more fictitious and devoid of practical purpose. The relation of the courtly ideal to reality is determined by the fictitiousness and lack of practical purpose which, as we hope we have sufficiently shown, characterize it from the very first. Courtly culture gives rise to the idea, which long remained a factor of considerable importance in Europe, that nobility, greatness, and intrinsic values have nothing in common with everyday reality—an attitude of much greater emotional power and of much stronger hold on the minds of men than the classical forms of a turning away from reality, as we find them for example in the ethics of Stoicism. To be sure, antiquity offers one form of turning away from reality even more compelling in its hold on men's minds, and that is Platonism. There have been repeated attempts to show that Platonic elements were a contributing factor in the development of the courtly ideal. In later times Platonism and the courtly ideal complemented each other perfectly. The most famous illustration of this is probably Count Castiglione's *Il Cortegiano*. Yet the specific form which turning away from reality received from courtly culture—with the characteristic establishment of an illusory world of class (or half class, half personal) tests and ordeals—is still, despite its superficial Platonic varnish, a highly autonomous and essentially a medieval phenomenon.

All this has a bearing on the particular choice of subjects which characterizes the courtly epic—it is a choice which long exercised a decisive influence upon European literature. Only two themes are considered worthy of a knight: feats of arms, and love. Ariosto, who evolved from this illusory world a world of serene illusion, expressed the point perfectly in [the] opening lines [to *Orlando Furioso*]:

> Le donne, i cavalier, l'arme, gli amori,
> Le cortesie, l'audaci imprese io canto . . .
> [Of ladies, knights, of arms, of love's delight,
> Of courtesies, of brave deeds I sing . . .]

Except feats of arms and love, nothing can occur in the courtly world —and even these two are of a special sort: they are not occurrences or emotions which can be absent for a time; they are permanently connected with the person of the perfect knight, they are part of his definition, so that he cannot for one moment be without adventure in arms nor for one moment without amorous entanglement. If he could, he would lose himself and no longer be a knight. Once again it is in the serene metamorphosis or the parody, Ariosto or Cervantes, that this fictitious form of life finds its clearest interpretation. As for feats of arms, I have nothing more to add. The reader will understand why, following Ariosto, I have chosen this term rather than "war," for they are feats accomplished at random, in one place as well as another, which do not fit into any politically purposive pattern. As for courtly love, which is one of the most frequently treated themes of medieval literary history, I need also say only what is relevant to my purpose. The first thing to bear in mind is that the classical form of it, if I may use the expression, which instantly comes to mind when courtly love is mentioned—the beloved as the mistress whose favor the knight strives to deserve through valorous deeds and perfect, even slavish, devotion—is by no means the only, or even the predominant form of love to be found during the heyday of the courtly epic. We need but remember Tristan and Iseut, Erec and Enide, Alixandre and Soredamors, Perceval and Blancheflor, Aucassin and Nicolete—none of these examples taken at random from among the most famous pairs of lovers entirely fits into the conventional schema and some of them do not fit into it at all. As a matter of fact, the courtly epic displays at first glance an abundance of quite different, extremely concrete love stories, thoroughly impregnated with reality. Sometimes they permit the reader completely to forget the fictitiousness of the world in which they take place. The Platonizing schema of the unattainable, vainly wooed mistress who inspires the hero from afar—a schema stemming from Provençal poetry and reaching its perfection in the Italian "new style"—does not predominate in the courtly epic at first. Then too, although the descriptions of the amorous state, the conversations between the lovers, the portrayal of their beauty, and whatever else forms an essential part of the setting for these episodes of love, reveal—especially in Chrétien—a great deal of gracefully sensuous art, they yet have hardly any hyperbolic *galanterie*. For that, a very different level of style is required than what the courtly epic affords. The fictitious and unreal character of the love stories is as yet hardly a matter of the stories themselves. It rather lies in their function within the total structure of the poem. Love in the courtly romances is already not infrequently the immediate occasion for deeds of valor. There is nothing surprising in this if we consider the complete absence of practical motivation through a political and historical context. Love, being an essential and obligatory ingredient of knightly perfection, functions as a substitute for other possibilities of motivation which are here lacking. This implies, in general outline, the fictitious order of events in which the most significant actions are performed primarily for the sake of a lady's favor; it also implies the superior rank assigned to love as a poetic theme which came to be so important for European literature. The literature of the ancients did not rank love very high on the whole. It is a predominant subject neither in tragedy nor in the great epic. Its central position in courtly culture moulded the slowly emerging elevated style of the European vernaculars. Love became a theme for the elevated style (as Dante confirms in *De Vulgari Eloquentia*, 2, 2) and was often its most important theme. This was accomplished by a process of sublimation of love which led to mysticism or gallantry. And in both cases it led far from the concrete realities of this world. To this sublimation of love, the Provençals and the Italian "new style" contributed more decisively than did the courtly epic. But it too played a significant part in the elevated rank ascribed to love, for it introduced it into the realm of heroism and class principles and merged it with them.

So the result of our interpretation and the considerations which have accompanied it is that courtly culture was decidedly unfavorable to the development of a literary art which should apprehend reality in its full breadth and depth. Yet there were other forces at work in the twelfth and thirteenth centuries which were able to nourish and further such a development.

JOHN FINLAYSON

Definitions of Middle English Romance†

I

"No poet . . . has his complete meaning alone,"[1] and no work makes its meaning without to some extent depending upon the audience's recognition either that it belongs to a specific genre, or, more often, that it is composed in one imaginative mode rather than another. Even if we prudently resist the impulse to expect from various genres what they were never intended to give, we nevertheless arrive at any work with distinct preferences (which, in some cases, are rationalized into philosophies of literary value) and expect that, after a few pages or a hundred lines or so, certain directions will be given us, that we should be instructed or persuaded to shut out certain areas of expectation and to open up others. Our perceptions in the initial experiencing of the work of art are related, of course, to our previous literary experiences.

As students of medieval literature, however, our approach has to be less simple. We have to attempt to recreate in ourselves the probable experience and expectations of a medieval common reader. To perceive, for example, that in the *Knight's Tale* dramatic characterization does not exist is both to arrive at the work with certain expectations and to make a useful decision about what area of literary expectations one should not expect to satisfy. It is also, however, a perception which proceeds from a different cultural milieu from that in which the work was composed. The first forty lines of the poem set up a "realm of discourse" which would immediately define for even an unalert medieval reader "the range of experiences it will treat of and the structure of values that are to guide the reader's judgments."[2] The writer clearly works in relationship to an assumed range of literary experience in his audience which will allow it to perceive fairly quickly the kind of structure which is being initiated and hence the sorts of value and meaning which inhere in the "shape" of the presentation. The problem, then, is that in order to respond fully or even reasonably to a medieval writer, we have to carry around with us, not our contemporary cultural milieu, but some of the literary baggage of a man of the fourteenth century. The solution would appear simple: we should read some other Middle English romances, since the literary histories tell us that the *Knight's Tale* is a romance. But which romances? *The Destruction of Troy*, *Sir Perceval of Galles*, the *Franklin's Tale*, *Golagros and Gawane*, the alliterative *Morte*

---

† From *The Chaucer Review* 15 (1980–81), 44–62, 168–181. Copyright 1980 by The Pennsylvania State University. Reproduced by permission of The Pennsylvania State University Press.
1. T. S. Eliot, "Tradition and the Individual Talent," in *Selected Essays* (London: Faber, 1932), p. 15.
2. Trevor Whittock, *A Reading of the Canterbury Tales* (Cambridge: University Press), p. 58.

Arthure? These are all designated romances by the reputable histories, but it is very doubtful that a knowledge of them would illuminate for us the essential "shape" of the *Knight's Tale* or the prevailing mode of presenting experience, since their subject-matters, style, form, and preoccupations have nothing in common with it or with each other.

There exists in Middle English a large body of narrative poems, dealing in varied ways with a considerable range of subjects, which literary historians and their dependent critics have agreed to call *romances*. One of the greatest difficulties facing the student of Middle English narrative poetry lies in the ambiguity, or even vagueness, of this designation. By almost common consent, all narratives dealing with aristocratic *personae* and involving combat and/or love are called *romances*, if written after 1100. As a loose, deliberately inclusive way of categorizing narrative poems, this has some merit in distinguishing them from rustic tales, homilies, satires, histories, and allegories. However, the term *romance* is also used to indicate a system of values and, at the same time, a method of treatment. Thus, we find that a large, heterogeneous body of narrative poems which, as a recent writer on romance remarks, "nobody would think of classing together,"[3] is classified as "The Middle English Romances," and we make the assumption (I think the assumption follows the classification rather than generates it) that these narratives share common attitudes and attributes and can, therefore, be judged according to the same criteria.

The *romance* is conceived of as a genre and at the same time as a particular treatment of that genre.[4] Yet anyone reasonably familiar with Middle English fictitious narratives will be aware that the only thing which many of them have in common is the fact that the *personae* are aristocratic. Nor is the classification by *matières* much more useful. To begin with, Jean Bodel's three *matières*[5] obviously exclude many poems accepted as *romances* and in addition include poems which belong to the genre known as the *chanson-de-geste*. Moreover, to know that a poem is *about* Arthur, Charlemagne, or antiquity is to know only the subject, which is no more useful for critical purposes than to know that *Hamlet* is *about* a Danish prince of that name.[6] Yet, despite the number

---

3. Dieter Mehl, *The Middle English Romances of the Thirteenth and Fourteenth Centuries* (London: Routledge and Kegan Paul, 1969), p. 15.

4. See also Ojars Kratins, "The Middle English Romance *Amis and Amiloun*: Chivalric Romance or Secular Hagiography," *PMLA*, 81 (1966), 347, and A. C. Gibbs, ed., *Middle English Romances* (London: Edward Arnold, 1966), pp. 1–3. Gibbs' introduction contains many valuable remarks on the problem of definition of genre, though I disagree with many of its conclusions.

5. See p. 418 of the present volume, n. 4. [Editor]

6. Other classifications have been attempted on the basis of metre and area of composition: D. A. Pearsall, "The Development of Middle English Romance," *Mediaeval Studies*, 27 (1965), 91–116; of theme: A. II. Billings, *A Guide to the Middle English Metrical Romances*, Yale Studies in English, 9 (New York, 1901; rpt. New York: Haskel, 1965); and of length, Dieter Mehl, as above. Since the first two do not claim to define the genre and base their assumptions about romance on W. P. Ker and Dorothy Everett, I have seen no reason to consider their views here. My views on Mehl's thesis appear in a review, *Anglia*, 90 (1972),

of books and articles in English which have been written on the *ro-mances*, there are very few definitions of *romance*, and not even the best of these is free from the confusion indicated.

This confusion is due to a large extent to the history of the word *romance*. That there is a difference between what is meant by *romance* in the Middle Ages and what was meant in the nineteenth century has long been recognised,[7] though despite this one finds statements such as that of N. F. Griffin, who asserts that "the essential characteristic of the romance is that the story is incredible."[8] This is counterbalanced by Dorothy Everett, who states that the characteristic quality of the ro-mances was not an appeal to "the sort of imagination that possesses the mystery and spell of everything remote and unobtainable"[9] but lay rather in their modernity, and by George Kane, who describes the marvellous in the romances as an "accident" of the genre, rather than an essential,[1] though at the same time he values most highly those poems which employ the marvellous in a nineteenth-century Romantic way. Origi-nally, *romance* signified a language derived from popular Latin and also designated a translation from Latin into the vulgar tongue. Wace ex-tended this to include any work in the vernacular, whether a translation or not. A good example of this is his *Roman de Brut*, which is a chronicle, or the *Roman de la Rose*, which is an allegory of courtly love. In England the term was used to distinguish Anglo-Norman or French from the native language and literature. From the thirteenth century on, the sense "fictitious narrative" which the word has today predominated, and the word came to be applied to a particular type of fictitious narrative in which the writers in romance languages, particularly the French, chanced to excel. This type is defined by Faral as follows:

> Nous avons conservé, du XII° siècle, un certain nombre d'oeuvres écrites en vers de huit syllabes, généralement assez developpées (leur longueur varie de 8,000 à 30,000 vers), et qui ont pour sujet des histoires de chevalerie et d'amour: elles portent le titre de romans.[2]

220–24. The most recent study of the form of the romances, by Kathryn Hume, "The Formal Nature of Middle English Romance," *PQ*, 53 (1974), 158–80, accepts the existing biblio-graphical designations and categorizes "romances" according to "a spectrum of narrative types generated by varying the relation of hero to background" (p. 169), an approach which, though often leading to particular conclusions similar to those in the present study, is fundamentally different in its premises and general conclusions.

7. See Sir Walter Scott, "Essay on Romance," in *Miscellaneous Prose Works of Sir Walter Scott* (Edinburgh: Adam and Charles Black, 1852), VII, 130–33.

8. "The Definition of Romance," *PMLA*, 38 (1923), 57, n. 4.

9. "A Characterization of the English Romances," in *Essays on Middle English Literature* (Oxford: Clarendon, 1955), pp. 6–10. This essay contains many perceptive insights and has been extremely influential on subsequent commentaries on the romances. It is because her defi-nitions are both seminal and typical that I have chosen most frequently to refer to her work, rather than to that of her successors.

1. *Middle English Literature* (London: Methuen, 1951), p. 4.

2. Edmond Faral, *Recherches sur les sources latines des contes et romans courtois* (Paris: E. Champion, 1913), p. 391.

[We have preserved, from the 12th century, a certain number of works written in verse of eight syllables, generally rather protracted (their length varies from 8,000 to 30,000 lines), and which have for their subject stories of chivalry and love: they bear the title of romance.]

Quite obviously the seeds of the present confusion rest partly in the concurrent "specialization" and "generalization" of the word in Middle English.[3] Moreover, the medieval rhetoricians were little concerned with "kinds," so that we cannot look to them for clarification. There is, however, some indication that medieval authors did distinguish "kinds" in the various references we find to *gestes, romans, dits, contes,* and *lais,* and certainly by the late fourteenth century in England there seems to have been at least an implicit recognition of what a *romance* was, if we accept the evidence of the *Tale of Sir Thopas.* To be effective, or even exist, parody must depend on the audience's recognition of the standard elements of a convention. Chaucer's parody of the romance depends on the audience's recognition of the standard pattern of romance, "the knight rides forth to seek adventure," and of certain ubiquitous "characteristics," such as the love motif, the encounter with the supernatural, and the elaborate *descriptio personae* ["description of the person"]. The parody, however, is achieved, not by the simple mention of the stock elements (if this were true, then *The Rape of the Lock* would be a parody of epic, not mock-heroic), but by, first, their superfluity—in a short space Chaucer has crammed in almost more stock elements than are to be found in any but the worst Middle English romance—and, second, their lack of function. As in mock-heroic, it is the nonfunctional display of rituals which generates the parodic humour, not simply the rituals themselves. Thus, parody, because of its dependence on the recognition of conventions and their *appropriate* use, is a valuable witness to what a specific audience would have recognised as the characteristic features of a genre.

In addition, some evidence can be found in what, for the moment, I propose to call chivalric narratives. An examination of the use of the word "romance" in Middle English indicates that it develops a wide range of meanings, which has partly contributed to our present confusion. However, among its many uses, a careful attention to context indicates that a specialized connotation clearly existed alongside a generalization or "extension." In his valuable study of the meaning of romance, Hoops lists twenty-four poems which refer to themselves as romances.[4] If we took the claims of all these works at face value, and

3. I use these terms in the sense in which they are employed in semantics: see G. L. Brook, *A History of the English Language* (London: Andre Deutsch, 1958), pp. 178–79.

4. Reinald Hoops, "Der Begriff Romance in der mittelenglischen und frühneuenglischen Literatur," *Anglistische Forschungen,* Heft 68 (Heidelberg: Carl Winter, 1929), 34–37. The poems listed are *Sir Beues, Arthour and Merlin, Richard Coer de Lion, Sir Perceval of Gales,* Minot's

attempted a definition of romance based on all of them, we would find ourselves back in the position of proposing a "characterization" of rather disparate works as a definition of a genre and be forced to recognize certain inherent contradictions. However, a closer look at Hoops's list reveals that the majority of them conform to a basic paradigm, namely, that they are concerned with an individual knight who rides out to seek or achieve an adventure (feat of arms), and some of these also show a concern for *courtoisie* and have an amatory element: *Sir Beues, Arthur and Merlin, Richard Coer de Lion, Sir Perceval, Octavian, Sir Eglamour, Bone Florence of Rome, Sir Gowther, Torrent, Partenay, Partenope, Launcelot of the Laik.* Of the remainder, three (*Isumbras, Rowland and Otuel, Sowdone of Babylone*) are rough translations of late Old French *chansons de geste* which, though concerned overall with the national struggle against the Saracen, contain a number of more or less self-sufficient episodes involving individual adventures or feats of arms. There is also some amatory interest, though by no stretch of the imagination could it be called courtly. In other words, they are *chansons de geste* which, to a minor extent, may be said to show in their handling of episodes some influence from the more fashionable romances of adventure. What remain are four fabulous histories or "romanticized chronicles," a love allegory, a saint's life, a Passion poem, the "mirrour," and Minot's *Poems.* The majority of these works have certain essential elements in common: a type of subject matter and the concept of the hero. The others, while having certain elements in common with the paradigm provided by the majority, are only *superficially* or peripherally like the majority. The example of Minot here indicates what has happened: because of the dominance of "romance" in fashionable literature, some writers, on the basis of a peripheral resemblance or none at all, have attempted to attach a spurious glamour to their product. (The "romanticization" of history is clear enough in medieval contemporary history.) A kinder explanation is that the attribution in the minority may be due to a confusion caused by the concurrent specialization and generalization of the term. The claims of the religious examples are yet another instance of the tendency of religious writers to adopt and adapt fashionable genres for their less fashionable wares. I shall return to these claims later.

Though ambiguity in the meaning of "romance" is partly linguistic, literary studies of chivalric narratives have served to compound the confusion, rather than clarify it. Much of the present thinking on medieval

Poems, Octavian, Barbour's *Alexander* and *Bruce, Myrour of Lewed Men, St. Gregory, Sir Eglamour, Meditations on the Life and Passions of Christ, Laud Troy Book, Bone Florence, Rowland and Ottuel, Sir Gowther, Sowdone of Babylone, Romaunt of the Rose, Dyoclecyane, Sir Isumbras, Torrent of Portyngale, Partenay, Partenope,* and *Lancelot of the Laik.* A recent, more extensive and sophisticated study by Paul Strohm, "The Origin and Meaning of Middle English *Romaunce," Genre,* 10 (1977), 1–28, confirms the concurrent generalization and specialization of the word. He states that there seems to have been a generally shared concept of *romance,* but that the term is used in some strange ways and not with uniform precision. See Strohm, pp. 5, 7, 12–13.

narrative poetry in English has been conditioned by W. P. Ker's *Epic and Romance*. In his chapter on "Romance and the Old French Romantic Schools," he says:

> If Romance be the name for the sort of imagination that possesses the mystery and the spell of everything remote and unattainable, then Romance is to be found in the old Northern heroic poetry in larger measure than any epic or tragic solemnity. . . .[5]

And he goes on to recognize that "almost the last thing that is produced in a 'romantic' school is the infallible and indescribable touch of romance," while saying that "it is a disappointment to find that romance is rarely at its finest in the works that technically have the best right in the world to be called by that name" (pp. 325, 326). It is this curious mingling of a recognition of the difference between the actuality of medieval romance and the nineteenth century's vision and expectations of it and a regret that it is not something other than it is, which seems to have bedevilled discussion of the Middle English romance. Further confusion is added by such statements as "*Aucassin and Nicolette* . . . contains the quintessence of romantic imagination, but it is quite unlike the most fashionable and successful romances" p. 327). Here again we find the word "romance" and its derivative "romantic" used in a single sentence with two very different connotations, with the implication that the romances are to be evaluated, not according to what they consciously offered, but according to the extent to which one can read into them the preoccupations of a later age.

Though he was seeking something which in most cases it does not have to give, Ker also notes what seems to him the essential characteristics of the *medieval* romance. He remarks that "the value of the best works of the school consists in their representation of the passion of love. . . . In the twelfth-century narratives, besides the interest of the love-story and all its science, there was the interest of adventure, of strange things. . . . Courteous sentiment, running through a succession of wonderful adventures, is generally enough to make a romance" (p. 328). He says also, "it is plain enough both that the adventures are of secondary value as compared with the psychology, in the best romances, and that their value, though inferior, is still considerable, even in some of the best works of the 'courtly maker' " (pp. 333–34). Here at least we appear to have a workable definition of the romance, though it should be noted that it is, in fact, a description of what Ker takes to be the best works, which also illustrate his general thesis, and is, in effect, a definition of one *type* of romance, the most sophisticated, the *roman courtois*. If taken as a prescriptive definition of romance, then it automatically excludes a large number of chivalric narratives in which love is either

5. W. P. Ker, *Epic and Romance*, 2nd ed. (London: Macmillan, 1908), p. 321.

absent or purely nominal. In addition, his statement "that the sudden and exuberant growth and progress of a number of new poetical forms[,] particularly the courtly lyric" in the twelfth century implies "the failure of the older manner of thought . . . represented in the epic literature of France" (p. 322) seems to have been taken by some of his successors to mean that heroic poetry dies out completely and that every fictitious narrative poem after 1100 is a romance.[6]

In Ker's formative work the word "romance" is used in three distinct senses: to describe an attitude to, and a kind of, experience; to categorize post-heroic, chivalric narrative poetry; and to define a specific, narrowly prescribed genre, the *roman courtois*. The result, in commentary by Ker and his successors on Middle English chivalric poetry, has been that a large number of works which, as Mehl has recently pointed out,[7] frequently have nothing in common, have been classified as *romance*, and the assumption made that they were either more or less successful attempts to conform to the pattern and values of the *roman courtois*, or were deliberate, English modifications of this distinctive genre. The difficulties implicit in the ambiguity of the word "romance" and in the attempt to deal with the whole body of heterogeneous material called Middle English romances as a distinctive, monolithic genre have often led the critic to the paradoxical position of stating that the work under discussion as "romance" is not, in fact, a romance or "romantic."[8] The categorization "romance" originated in the enthusiastic work of early antiquarians and commentators, such as Hurd, Scott, and Ellis, whose Romantic background not only spurred their collecting, but also coloured their view of what they collected. It is clearly useful and meaningful only as a bibliographical classification, designating medieval, chivalric, fictitious narrative. To continue to take *romance* both as a comprehensive literary categorization *and* as a closely defined genre incorporating precise values and literary motifs is to invite continuing

6. A. E. Taylor, *Introduction to Medieval Romance* (London: Folcroft, 1930), devotes a chapter to the "Charlemagne romances," which are all little more than translations, with occasional abbreviation, of Old French *chansons de geste*: that is, they are of a kind of poetry recognized to be fundamentally different from romance. Similarly, George Kane refers to the English Charlemagne narratives as "romances" (pp. 15–16).

7. Mehl, p. 28: "It is practically impossible to generalize about the romances because there is so little they all have in common."

8. See, for example, Dorothy Everett: "The Charlemagne romances probably have least of the spirit of chivalry, being affected by their origin in the chansons de geste" (p. 5, n.1), and "One romance, the alliterative *Morte Arthure*, on a theme which roused more patriotic enthusiasm in an English poet than the doings of Charlemagne and his peers ever could, comes very near to claiming a place among heroic poems in English" (p. 21). See also George Kane, who recognizes that the alliterative *Morte Arthure* is "heroic not romantic" (p. 69), but later makes the paradoxical statement that "in the end the effect is heroic as it is in none of the other romances" (p. 73). The difficulty is most clearly faced by J. P. Oakden, *Alliterative Poetry in Middle English* (Manchester: University Press, 1935), p. 24, who classifies the *Destruction of Troy*, the alliterative *Morte Arthure*, and the three Alexander fragments as "chronicles in the epic manner" because "the alliterative poems dealing with the legends of Troy and of Alexander the Great are not romances in the ordinary sense of the word, and . . . the central figures are never mediaeval knights representative of the spirit of chivalry, but heroic supermen of the epic type."

confusion in critical discussion of Middle English chivalric narratives. It would seem better to define more exactly what one means by romance, to recognize clearly that romance probably is not a monolithic genre but, like the novel, is divisible into a number of largely different types, and to find another name or names for those poems which do not fit the proposed definitions.

Most of the works called *romance* in Middle English are based on French sources. The remainder are largely derived from Latin chronicles or saints' lives. While most of those works derived from French are based on French *romans*, a substantial number are adaptations of *chansons de geste*, which continued to be written in France during the thirteenth century, despite the dominance of the *romans* in courtly circles, and to be translated in England into the fifteenth century.[9] The distinctions between the two genres in French have, however, been urged as having no significance for Middle English. It has been urged that "English romance writers sometimes took French epics for their sources and dealt with them as far as possible as they did with other narrative material."[1] In fact, all the Middle English works based on Old French *chansons de gestes* are either faithful translations or hack abbreviations: none displays the sort of amplification or alteration which would allow us to claim that it had been consciously reworked. While recognizing that "there is never . . . the same sophistication as in the Arthurian romances" and that "the stories are mainly about fighting, and ladies and love-making mostly play a small part"—a dangerous understatement of the case— Miss Everett concludes that "apart from these things there is no difference between these romances and others."

These judgements reveal curious inconsistencies. It is recognized that the poems discussed, besides having their sources in French *chanson de geste*, are devoid of what she takes to be the essentials of *romance*, yet at the same time the critic wishes to claim them for the body of *romance* and also to assert that English poets dealt with all narratives in an identical fashion, even though she has already stated that they are quite different from the Arthurian romances. It is true that love-making plays a rather insignificant part in most English narratives. It is also true that physical activity, provided by military encounters, is probably the most important element in English "romances" and that because of this the distinctions between heroic and chivalric tend to be less easily discerned. I would

9. See Pamela Gradon, *Form and Style in Early English Literature* (London: Methuen, 1971), p. 217, who points out, in a wide-ranging and perceptive chapter on "the Romance Mode," that the *chansons de geste* continue to be translated into English in the fifteenth century. Note also the continued popularity of heroic chronicles in England and Scotland until much later; see Morton Bloomfield, "Episodic Motivation and Marvels in Epic and Romance," in *Essays and Explorations* (Cambridge, Mass.: Harvard Univ. Press), p. 117: "It (the epic) continued to flourish at the periphery . . . in Iceland, Scotland (whose *The Bruce* and *The Wallace* are really retarded epics) and possibly Ireland . . . and persisted in debased form in France and England and Germany themselves."

1. Everett, p. 20.

suggest, however, that this is not because the English view of romance was fundamentally different from that of the French, but because the differences which exist are in the first instance ones of quality and not of "kind."[2] Since French was still the language of secular culture and refinement in the fourteenth century, it would seem likely that those who had a taste for the sophisticated would read their romances in French. *Romances* of the quality of *Sir Gawain and the Green Knight* are extremely rare in English—in fact, one might easily assert that apart from the *Knight's Tale, Sir Gawain,* and a few others, the English achievement in the *romance* form is not of a very high order. Given that the *roman courtois* is a form peculiarly dependent on a largely artificial convention of manners and on a type of sophistication which could exist only in aristocratic, courtly circles, and that English was still often regarded in the fourteenth century (and later) as a language unsuited to the expression of refined sentiments, this is hardly surprising.

Most of the extant English romances would probably have been intended for an audience which did not read French at all or at least not with ease. In some cases, such as *King Horn, Havelok,* and *Rauf Coilyear,* the audience for whom the narratives were intended would seem to have been of a very popular sort. However, no matter what variety of audience the authors of the Middle English narratives, romantic or heroic, had in mind—ranging from aristocratic to popular—they must have had some idea of the type of poem they wished to compose. The very act of selecting a story to tell (or to retell, as is the case with most Middle English narratives) must have entailed choosing a theme, and this would imply the choice of treatment, whether or not this choice was a fully conscious one. Though it would not be true to say that there is no innovation in Middle English poetry, it cannot be doubted that imitation is dominant, partly due to medieval attitudes and partly no doubt to a desire to assimilate to English or the poet the prestige of a superior civilization through the imitation of its culture. Without ignoring the influence of Italian literature, it can still be asserted that French literature was undoubtedly the predominant influence on English secular literature throughout the Middle Ages. This being the case, it seems logical to assume that the models with which an English writer would be familiar and which he might wish to imitate would be French ones. The fact that most narratives have French sources or Latin ones, and only very rarely Italian, would seem to support this assumption.

If all these things are true (and most of them are commonplaces of Middle English studies), then it would seem to follow that far from being irrelevant to English studies, it is in fact highly relevant to distinguish between the *romance* and the *chanson-de-geste* on the basis of these

---

2. Mehl, pp. 4–6, more charitably suggests that they were aimed at a broader cross-section of society than Continental romances, which may explain their lack of art, but does not necessarily excuse it.

French works from which the Middle English writers borrowed and to have a clear idea of both so that we may judge whether or not they are usefully applicable to Middle English narrative. It is, in fact, highly probable that such distinctions do apply to Middle English and will allow us to avoid some of the confusions now apparent in studies of Middle English narrative poetry. In addition, by changing the range of our expectations, it may allow us to judge the worth of some poems more accurately; to see that a certain work may not be a very good *romance* simply because it was never intended to be; to realize that the absence of amatory or psychological material is not, in itself, a flaw in a particular work.

II

What, then, are the criteria by which we can distinguish between *romances* and narratives of the *chanson de geste* type?[3] It should be noted immediately that the *romance* and the *chanson de geste* would appear to have much in common. Both types of narrative are essentially aristocratic and deal with the qualities of the warrior class, such as courage, skill in arms, loyalty, and generosity. Both most frequently illustrate these virtues through the medium of combat. The difference lies in the emphases placed on these qualities, on the ends which they are made to serve, and on the contexts within which they operate. The following distinctions are necessarily of a general nature and are not intended as a complete description of the preoccupations and techniques of the two genres. Since no two works of art are exactly alike, and since the narratives under discussion catered for a wide variety of needs and tastes, it is more than likely that no one poem will be found to contain all of the features of any one of the divisions. It is, however, possible to claim that if a poem is found to contain most of the essentials of one division rather than of the other, then that poem can best be evaluated by considering it as belonging to that particular division. For example, it has often been pointed out that the thirteenth-century *chansons de geste* have assimilated certain features which belong more properly to the *roman courtois*, yet these poems are judged according to their predominant tone, which is still heroic, not romantic.

The *chanson de geste* is a type of heroic poem dependent on values

3. The following generalizations bear obvious relationships to the broad distinctions made by W. P. Ker in *Epic and Romance* and Eric Auerbach in *Mimesis*, but are also less specialized. The necessity of making such preliminary distinctions is also affirmed in three recent discussions of romance: Gradon, pp. 213–21; Gillian Beer, *Romance* (London: Methuen, 1970), pp. 24–26; and John E. Stevens, *Medieval Romance* (London: Hutchinson, 1973), pp. 76–77, 90–95. Some of the material in the next few pages has already been presented in my introduction to *Morte Arthure* (London: Edward Arnold, 1967) and in an article, "*Ywain and Gawain* and the Meaning of Adventure," *Anglia*, 87 (1969), 312–37. Strohm, p. 6, notes "the evidence for the emerging sense of difference between the typical content of the *chançon* and the *romans*" in the debate poem, "Les Deux Bourdeurs Ribauds," where the speaker distinguishes between *chançon de geste* and *romanz d'aventure*.

essentially associated with war. Valour is the main ingredient of a war-rior's character, but this valour need not be tempered by *mesure* or by *courtoisie* as it must be in a romance hero. At the same time, valour, to be admirable, must be employed in the defence of a worthy object, this generally being in the *chanson de geste* a combination of God and King. That is, the hero of a *chanson de geste* displays great, sometimes immoderate valour in the cause of his king or overlord, who is usually portrayed as the supreme champion of Christianity. W. P. Ker saw the essence of the *chansons de geste* as lying in their preoccupation with the problem of heroic character and in the dramatic variety with which this was expressed (pp. 292–95), and Dorothy Everett agrees with this: "The characters speak for themselves, whereas in the romances we are always conscious of the storyteller and his manipulation of episode and char-acter." Certainly, if we examine the Charlemagne poems in English, *The Destruction of Troy, The Wars of Alexander, Alexander A* and the alliterative *Morte Arthur, Sir Gawain,* and *Sir Perceval of Galles,* it will easily be observed that one of those groups makes far more use of direct speech and behaviouristic description than the other. It will also be observed that the concept of the hero differs widely between those groups: that in the first group the hero tends to fight in defence of his lord or society, or in the furtherance of political ends, whereas in the other the hero is conceived of basically as an individual, not as essentially a representative of his society, and that the combats in which he engages or the experiences he undergoes rarely have any direct relation to nation or church. Even such broad distinctions as the above clearly do have some relevance to Middle English narratives. The first group of narratives mentioned above evidently meets the loosest definition of *romance,* that is, a tale involving knights and combat, but bears no other significant resemblance to the second group. Each group manifests a very different attitude to experience—a difference sharply evident [between the allit-erative *Morte Arthur* and Malory's *Morte Darthur*]. To classify them together and define their common characteristics is an exercise of very limited usefulness. For example, to perceive that feasts, combats and the marvellous are "characteristics" of *romance* is of some interest, but cannot be taken as definitive of a genre, since these elements occur also in classical and feudal heroic literature. It is the function of these ele-ments and the author's way of presenting them that distinguishes *romance* from the heroic.

It is in the concept of the hero that the greatest and essential difference is to be found between the *chanson de geste* and the *romance.* In the *chanson de geste* the group is dominant. As C. B. West has observed of the French *chanson de geste,* "Roland and Oliver may and do stand out as distinct personalities, but they are first of all members of Charle-magne's *maisnie* ["retinue"], of the French *barnage* ["warrior class"], and of the Christian Church in the service of which they are ready to die against the infidels."[4] This is true also of the heroes of many Middle English poems, particularly, of course, the so-called "Charlemagne romances," but also of the heroes of *The Destruction of Troy*, the *Alexander* romances, the *Siege of Jerusalem*, and *The Sege of Troye*. At the same time, one will notice that there is another, more common attitude to the hero. In most of the [other] narratives the individual, as distinct from his social function, is of supreme importance. The sentiment of feudal loyalty will be found to play little part in those narratives. The emphasis will instead rest on the exploits of the hero, not insofar as they may relate to the furtherance of politico-religious ends, but as they win renown (*los et pris*) for the individual. As Gaston Paris noted, "Ce qui caractérise . . . le roman . . . en regard de l'épopée, c'est . . . que celle-ci subordonne les héros particuliers à l'ensemble dont ils font partie, et que celui-là met les individus au premier plan et se plaît au developpement nuancé de leur caractère et de leur façon de sentir."[5] [That which characterizes . . . the romance . . . in regard to the epic, is . . . that the one subordinates particular heroes to the group of which they are a part, and that the other places individuals in the foreground and delights in the graded development of their character and of their manner of feeling]. Both *chanson de geste* and *romance* heroes are known through their prowess, but while the former employs his skill in a public context, the latter does so solely or usually in pursuit of a private ideal.[6]

It is in this ideal that the *romance* hero differs so much from the hero of the *chanson de geste*. Whereas the character of the *chanson de geste* hero—indomitable courage in the face of danger and almost certain defeat—can be said to be no more than a heightening of reality, the character of the romance hero is largely an idealization which bears little relation to social reality and certainly did not spring from it.[7] The romance hero conforms to a code of behaviour which was largely a literary creation and convention, rarely observed in practice. As Painter points out,

4. C. B. West, *Courtoisie in Anglo-Norman Literature* (Oxford: Basil Blackwell, 1938), p. 2.
5. Gaston Paris, "Le roman d'aventure," *Cosmopolis*, 11 (Sept. 1898), 768–69. Although I later propose the term *romance of adventure*, it is not employed in the same way as Paris's *roman d'aventure*.
6. This is not to deny that romances occasionally provide some sort of extrapersonal motivation. Gawain, in theory, accepts the challenge in defense of Arthur and his society, but in practice it is Gawain's person that is at stake, not the court. Only indirectly, finally, and subtly is Gawain's adventure other than purely personal. In the Arthurian romances in particular knights go forth from Arthur's court and return to it, as they do from Charlemagne's, but there is a conspicuous difference between the defence of an ideal fantasy against dragons, witches, and wicked barons of varying hues and the defence of a realm against Saracen armies. Again, this is not to deny that feudal relationships and bonds exist in *romance* (as in the relation of Ywain and the lion, or in Horn's conflict with Saracens), but these are completely subordinated to the interest in the individual or the adventure.
7. See the analysis of the relation of ideal and practice in M. A. Gist, *Love and War in the Middle English Romances* (Philadelphia: Univ. of Pennsylvania Press, 1947), chapters 7 and 8; also K. Lippmann, *Das ritterliche Persönlichkeitsideal in der mittelenglischen Literatur des 13. and 14. Jahrhunderts* (Diss. Leipzig, Meerane, 1933).

The relation between ideas and practice in the period of decay was quite different from that which had prevailed in the period of growth. By the middle of the 14th century the noble class of France had accepted the ideas of feudal chivalry and was carrying them out in practice to a greater extent than at any earlier time. [8]

The attempted revival of chivalry in the fourteenth century, manifested in the creation of the Order of the Round Table by Edward III and by a similar move in France, seems to emphasize that where chivalry was practised in reality, it was in an attempt to emulate an already established and formulated idea, to conform to a code largely created by and disseminated through literature. To a large extent, the *chanson de geste* is closer to the "actualities" of the warrior class of the late Middle Ages than is the *romance*. The best romances and the greatest period of *romance*, of course, come in the twelfth and thirteenth centuries—that is, they precede considerably the period when chivalric ideas are most observed in practice. It is generally true to state that heroic literature *reflects* in a heightened manner rather than *creates* the system of values it expresses, whereas the *romance*, at least in its greatest period in France, creates a code and expresses values not generally current in society.

The basic paradigm of the *romance* is expressed in the formula, "The knight rides out alone to seek adventure":

Thane weendes° owtt the wardyne, Sir Wawayne°   *goes/Gawain*
    hym selfen,
Alls he that weysse° was and wyghte,° wondyrs   *wise/bold*
    to seke.

                 (*Morte Arthure*, 2513–14)

The lone knight rapidly finds himself in an unknown landscape (usually surprisingly close at hand and not requiring the strenuous journey Gawain undertakes), and encounters some perilous and often supernatural event. He resolves the problem presented by his skill in arms, and then rides on to yet another adventure. It is this formula which the alliterative *Morte Arthure* uses to point a contrast between the meaningful heroic struggle against the anti-Christian giant and the Roman invaders and the meaningless, purely personal glory-seeking of Gawain; this same formula is raised and rejected time and again in *Sir Gawain*, and parodied in *Sir Thopas*. This form, which stresses the sensational (and often tedious) succession of chivalric victories over ever-mounting odds, is the most common, particularly in England. The basic definition of *romance*, therefore, is that it is a tale in which a knight achieves great feats of arms, almost solely for his own *los et pris* in a series of adventures which have no social, political, or religious motivation and little or no connection with medieval actuality. At this level, it is not unlike the basic

8. *French Chivalry* (Baltimore: Johns Hopkins Press, 1940), p. 63.

cowboy film, or the simple novel of action in which the hero undergoes a series of adventures, which sometimes become a progressive sequence, and emerges victorious and unscathed at the end. A not inconsiderable number of the episodes in Malory clearly correspond to this pattern and level of significance. The basic romance is the *romance of adventure*.

The aristocratic or courtly romance, as perfected or created by Chrétien, takes this basic pattern and develops it, not by changing the form, but by giving the elements values and functions. In Chrétien the basic structure becomes the vehicle for a presentation and examination of the chivalric ethic. Where in the popular romance adventure exists purely for the demonstration of prowess, in Chrétien it exists as a test of more than the hero's martial skill. Motivation is provided by the presence of some amatory connection, direct or indirect. The meaningless (or purely glory-hunting) series of adventures becomes in Chrétien a progression: each adventure demonstrates different things about the hero, represents a stage in his journey towards internal harmony. Adventure becomes more than simply a chance encounter or a daring feat; it becomes something destined for the particular hero.[9] Where in earlier heroic literature Fate or chance had appeared accidental, though in its workings actively inimical to the individual, the new realization of Fate or chance is of something which is no longer accidental but rather "happens" to the individual in the sense of "destined for."[1] In *Ywain and Gawain*, for example, the adventure of the magic fountain is destined for Ywain.

Present in Chrétien's romances, therefore, is the idea of a personal, predestined office which is expressed by, and finds its proper manifestation in, chivalric adventure. Moreover, the locales and frames of each adventure become a meaningful part of the structure. When the hero encounters a castle or a person in Chrétien, such incidents are rarely purely decorative or circumstantial. Most frequently they are either related to the knight's moral progress or are expositions of the nature of aristocratic life. To some extent, sophisticated, courtly romance is educative: it proposes a model of fitting behaviour, *courtoisie*, which is expressed in three main areas of experience, combat, social intercourse, and the service of women. In *courtly romance*, these are vitally linked. The arrival at a castle during the quest for adventure and the giving or receiving of hospitality are significant in the scope they give for the display of *courtoisie*, as is the devotion which inspires the quest or the return of devotion which is the reward of success. The three main areas for the expression of *courtoisie* are united in the adventure which provides

---

9. For a full discussion of the concept of "adventure" see R. Bezzola, *Le sens de l'aventure et de l'amour* (Paris: La Jeune Parque, 1947), pp. 83ff.; E. Auerbach, *Mimesis*, trans. W. R. Trask (Princeton: Princeton Univ. Press, 1953), chapter 6 [reprinted in the present volume, pp. 411 ff.]; E. Köhler, *Ideal und Wirklichkeit in der höfischen Epik*, Beihefte zur *Zeitschrifte für Romanische Philologie*, 97 (Tübingen: Niemeyer, 1956), chapter 3; M. Wehrli, "Roman und Legende im deutschen Hochmittelalter," *Worte and Werte, Bruno Marckwardt zum 60 Geburtsiag*, ed. G. Erdmann and Alfons Eichstaedt (Berlin: 1961), pp. 428–43.

1. Bloomfield, p. 123.

the means of proving the hero and preserving or developing his chivalry. As Auerbach has remarked: "Trial through adventure is the real meaning of the knight's ideal existence. . . . The series of adventures is thus raised to the status of a fated and graduated test of election; it becomes the basis of a doctrine of personal perfection through a development dictated by fate."[2]

Adventure, then, is the real core of *romance*, whether it be popular or courtly. The manner of treating or seeing adventure, the context in which it is placed, the way it is related to the hero—these are what distinguish *courtly romance* from the simpler *romance of adventure*. They are also frequently concomitants of literary value. Most other elements which have been urged as essential features of *romance* are in fact less fundamental, and less preponderant, than the two essential elements defined above—the concept of the hero, and the nature and meaning of the episodic action.

Marvels or the supernatural have been urged, since the Renaissance, as the essence of *romance*.[3] While they are to be found in most of the works designated "romances," they are also to be found in classical and feudal epic literature and, indeed, throughout most medieval literature from folk tale to allegory. The supernatural, then, is not peculiar to *romance*, but it is clearly characteristic of it. What is notable is not its presence but its employment. It is, as Everett and Kane remark, a "property" rather than an essence,[4] and it is exploited in very many different ways, from the rather spare use in *Ywain and Gawain* where, although not essential to the *sans* ["sense, meaning"], it is structurally significant and the instrument of episodic progress, to the pure sensationalism of the superabundance of marvellous incidents in *Sir Perceval of Galles* and *Lybeaus Desconus*. While the marvelous is not the essence of *romance*, it is clearly more than an optional "property." In most *romances* it either initiates the action or defines the nature of the action. In its proper or best use it creates the special atmosphere of the *romance* world where elements of social reality and the unnatural commingle, not for the purpose of sensational contrast between the real and the unreal, but to provide "a balance between fiction and verisimilitude."[5] The marvellous, while not treated within the better *romances* in terms of wonder or awe, nevertheless contributes to a sense of mystery because it is frequently used to initiate the action or to introduce a new turn to events. That is, it motivates the action, but the very form of the "motivation" enhances the "irrational" quality of romance:[6] the "reasons" given for the actions of the hero have nothing to do with what we would recognize as reasons, and the marvellous seems almost always inseparable

2. Auerbach, pp. 135–36 [pp. 421–22, as reprinted in the present volume].
3. See Arthur Johnston, *Enchanted Ground* (London: Athlone, 1964), pp. 8ff.
4. See Everett, p. 13; Kane, p. 101.
5. Gradon, p. 235.
6. See Bloomfield's remarks on the "rational" epic and the "irrational" romance, pp. 106–07.

from, indispensable to, this atmosphere of unmotivated (or unrealisti-
cally motivated) action. To take an example: *romance* and heroic poems
frequently begin with a challenge. In the alliterative *Morte Arthure*, in
the midst of feasting, Roman senators arrive to demand tribute of Arthur;
in *Sir Gawain*, in the midst of festivities, the Green Knight arrives to
challenge Arthur. The pattern is identical, but the atmospheres and
results are quite different: in *Morte Arthure*, the challenge is issued in
terms of political or historical claims and the response is, first, a council
of state and then national warfare to defend political interests; in *Sir
Gawain*, the "causes" or terms of the challenge have nothing political,
social, or historical about them, and the response to the challenge is
individual and purely in terms of a special, and again personal, concept
of honour (that is, any challenge must be met, regardless of causes,
justification, or consequences): the response is a severing of a head, with
no observable or normal consequences, a tryst, and a quest. The nature
of the two actions here clearly differentiates the two genres, and high-
lights an important aspect of *romance*, namely that the nature of the
action (the whole action—response and activity) is dependent on the
initiating marvel: the fact that a challenge is issued by a *green* man with
a disposable head both permits and creates the type of response and
activity which follows. It is a world in which there may be *causes* for
events, but there are no *reasons*. The use of the marvellous can, of
course, and frequently does in works like Sir *Eglamour*, decline into the
sensational, but it still remains necessary to the kind of action. While
there are a few romances in which the incidents are not initiated or
"motivated" by marvels, the action is still of the same kind (lacking in
probability or reasonableness): where there is no marvel, the initiating
factor is generally love of the courtly kind, which, of course, suspends
all reason, as in the *Knight's Tale*:

Love is a gretter lawe, by my pan,°	*brain pan, skull*
Than may be yeve° to any erthely man; . . .	*given*
A man moot° nedes° love,	*must / necessarily*
maugree° his heed.°	*despite / intention (not to)*

The "modernity" of the romances is often noted as a definitive characteristic, and is undeniably present and noticeable from our historical
vantage point. However, it is also a general characteristic of medieval
histories, that is, of medieval man's way of regarding the past. Chaucer
alone among Middle English writers can be said to have much sense of
historic succession and cultural relativity,[7] and in his work there are
probably far more instances of historical errors and a contemporizing of
the past than of a realization of the historical differences.[8] "Modernity,"

7. Bloomfield, "Chaucer's Sense of History" in *Essays and Explorations*, p. 18.
8. C. S. Lewis, "What Chaucer Really Did to *Il Filostrato*," *Essays and Studies*, 17 (1932), 56–
57.

then, is as characteristic of medieval literature as the rhetorical *descriptio* of spring—a characteristic of an age rather than of a genre.

Paradoxically, in the *romance* there is little attempt to authenticate the story in terms of actual political, geographical, or economic conditions: the hero meets giants and encounters miracles without ever seeming to find them disturbing or unnatural, and time and place are of little importance. There is rarely an attempt to give the reader or audience a *reason* for what occurs, and if an explanation is offered, it is of the kind proposed to Gawain, an explanation which belongs to the closed, fictitious world of *romance*, not the world of nature and probability or history. The *romance* is contemporaneous in its manners, dress, and architecture, but totally outside of time and place in its actions. It may superficially contemporize, but it is not concerned to actualize.

Love, or, rather, courtly love is usually urged, from Ker onwards, as one of the chief distinguishing features of *romance*. For Ker the psychology of love is the centre of *romance*. Yet even in Chrétien, love is not the centre, but rather one of the two main components of the knight's persona. The search in Chrétien is not for the perfection of love, but for a harmonious balance between prowess and love. While most romances can be distinguished from the *chansons de geste* in containing some reference to sentimental love, it is by no means of the essence. While *courtly romances* make love an essential part of the character of the knight, and use it as a motivation for the plot, the trial by adventure still remains the core of the work: the lady, or love, is achieved through *prowess*, which may be enhanced by love, but nevertheless exists separate from it. When we turn to the Middle English romances, we find that only a few, such as the *Knight's Tale*, *Sir Gawain* (in a highly ambiguous fashion in both), *Ywain and Gawain*, *Sir Orfeo*, and *Sir Degrevant*, make courtly love in any way crucial to their plot. For the others, love is either simply one of the rewards of prowess (generally accompanied by a kingdom) or is used to motivate an episode and then casually abandoned. While it may be, therefore, a common characteristic, its treatment and importance vary widely. A possible explanation is that, since most Middle English romances are of a crude, popular nature, the absence of a full-fledged courtly love motif is due to a lack of understanding on the part of audience and composer. Whatever the reasons, the facts are clear enough: in most Middle English chivalric narratives love is peripheral or decorative, rather than central. Where love is central is, of course, in works like *Aucassin et Nicolette*, *Floris and Blancheflor*, and the *Franklin's Tale*, which are *romances* only in the catchall sense we noted at the beginning of this essay: the personages are aristocratic, and their love is subjected to a number of hazardous events. There is nothing here of the concept of the knight's search for self-fulfilment through adventure, of the necessity of proving personal, military prowess, of adventure as a special, fated task. In other words, the works mentioned may be romances in a modern sense, stories of love under trial, but they are probably best understood as quite different from chivalric romances, a genre of their own, the courtly love poem.

III

If any guiding principle emerges from the attempt to distinguish medieval heroic poetry from *romance*, it is this: that they are not distinguishable primarily by their subject matter and the larger elements of their composition, but by an attitude to that matter and these elements. The hero in both is a feudal, aristocratic chevalier, but they are distinguishable by the concept of the nature and function of the warrior. The differing concepts of the feudal warrior are controlled by a total attitude (in fiction at any rate) to the aristocratic world and its experiences.

What are some of the consequences of the definitions I have proposed? The first is that a number of Middle English narrative works can be disestablished from the canon of *romance*. Though most literary histories and general studies of Middle English *romance* tend to categorize narrative poems based on chronicles as *romance*, a number of critics have implicitly or explicitly recognized that they cannot usefully be described as *romance*, unless the word is to be taken in the loosest sense of "a narrative involving combat and aristocratic *personae*." Even the term "chronicle-romance" is misleading, since it suggests that the mode of these works is *romance*, whereas in the case of the alliterative *Morte Arthure* and *The Destruction of Troy* in particular the dominant mode is the heroic: in both, the pseudohistorical connection is of primary importance in giving shape and meaning to the sequence of episodes; in both the deeds of the heroes are to be understood in relation to the defence and destruction of a specific society which is conceived of as having a historical existence. This is very different from the mythical society of the Round Table in Arthurian romances, where the society or king provides a loose frame for event, but no attempt is made to suggest a historical reality, or, in most cases, to tie the individual achievement to the existence of that society.

* * *

Similarly, the amount of fabulous material in the *Alexander* narratives has led critics to call them *romances*, based on the assumption that the marvellous or exotic is a necessary and therefore definitive feature of the *romance*. However, the fabulous material in these works is drawn largely from their sources, occasionally augmented from Mandeville's *Travels*, which are not usually described as romances. Moreover, many of the exotic elements in the *Alexander* narratives are presented, not as deliberate departures from the natural world, but as testimonies to some of the curious things which are to be found in remote regions. The pres-

entation of a dragon in the Forest of Broceliande is a deliberate act of
fantasy, since the medieval audience *knew* that dragons no longer inhabited Europe; the statement that in India some men stand on one leg
with their heads under their shoulders is proposed, however, not as
fantasy but as fact. Mandeville may occasionally appear a little sceptical
about some exotic elements, just as William of Newburg casts a sceptical
eye on Geoffrey of Monmouth's history,[9] but these clearly do not represent conventional or influential views of the fabulous histories. What
is important in *romance* is not exotic material, but the attitude to it and
its function. Science fiction, for example, would once have been defin-
able as *romance*, because flights into space were an act of fantasy. We
cannot label something a fantasy because we no longer credit its existence: the Ptolemaic universe was "real" enough for some time. The
marvellous or supernatural, therefore, is not a thing but the product of
an attitude. Since the supernatural and the exotic occur quite promi-
nently in *Beowulf* (the indispensable dragon of romance as well), the
Iliad, and the *Aeneid*, its mere occurrence in a poem is clearly no
indication of genre or mode.

Similarly, the "Charlemagne romances" are best considered as largely
heroic works. It is a curious perversity to recognize that they differ little
from their sources, are quite different from Arthurian romances, and
display little interest in love or courtly behaviour, and yet to insist on
evaluating them as *romances*. Though in them individual combats and
assorted giants are a fairly prominent feature, these encounters are placed
in a larger context. Like the dream of the dragon and the fight with the
giant in *Morte Arthure,* or the individual victories of Hector and Achilles
in *The Destruction of Troy*, they have their meaning as elements in
either a continuing struggle of Christian against heathen or the defence
of a society. In no case are these encounters part of a process of self-
realization, the progress to the *mesure* ["measure, capacity"] of *romance*.
While individuals have and seek *los et pris* ["honour and esteem"], like
Roland and Beowulf, this is always motivated by reference to a socio-
political reality which may be considerably heightened in art but is not
a mythical ideal. Individual episodes in the Charlemagne poems may
be difficult to distinguish from episodes in the cruder Middle English
romances of adventure, if taken in isolation. However, placed in the
context of the whole work, the differences in kind are clear enough.
Where love enters these works (an element often cited as evidence of
the "romanticization" of the *chanson de geste*, as in the *Sowdone of
Babylone*), it is not love of the courtly type and the adventures are in
no way motivated by this love, though the hero may find his way out
of a tricky situation because of love ***. Social courtesy and refined
laws of combat have nothing to do with events in these works. Indeed,

9. Gradon, p. 230.

Froissart's *Chronicles* are frequently more "romantic" than the Charlemagne "romances."

Romance is not a monolithic genre,[1] but in its more sophisticated practitioners a mode which we can often characterize by isolation of elements such as the concept of the hero, the treatment of the marvellous, of time, and of place, the nature and function of adventure, and the episodic nature of structure. It is a genre, however, in that certain types of episode become the indispensable forms to express this attitude in the Middle Ages. A particular kind of activity becomes the vehicle for the presentation of an attitude to experience and comes to be representative of a whole system of values. It becomes a formula whose elements stand for the attitude to experience, so that in less talented hands they are repeated mechanically with little sense of the experience they were designed to release. At the same time they are so ritualized that even the worst exposition of them might be expected to evoke a generalized sense of the ethos which they represent.

The difficulty or danger for criticism arises if, in isolating elements which exhibit the attitude to experience of the writer, the mode of expression, we make of these elements the *essences* of the genre, rather as we mechanically define a pastoral elegy. If, however, we accept *romance* as essentially a way of presenting and an attitude to experience, then the distinction between the heroic and the *romance* becomes much clearer, despite the obvious overlap in matters of content and rhetorical expression. The way of seeing controls the nature of the action, so that it is the total action, not its parts, which is *romance*. At the same time, if we take certain "characterizing" elements, not as rigid essentials, but rather as indicators of the precise nature of the particular artifact, then it becomes evident that within the basic genre there are specific types. For example, the presence or absence of an erotic element is not an indicator of whether or not the work is *romance*, but an indicator of the particular area of experience the author proposes. In fact, only two elements are of sufficient weight to modify significantly the basic pattern or preoccupation of *romance*, the trial by destined adventure of the lone knight, without at the same time turning the genre into something else: these are courtly love and its related *courtoisie*, and the spiritual quest. The distinction between *romances* which are wholly or mainly concerned with adventure and those which deal with adventure in relation to love has been made earlier. It is a distinction which is partly the central *sans* of *Ywain and Gawain*,[2] and it is central in one way or another to the *Knight's Tale*, *Sir Gawain*, and Malory, as well as *Sir Degrevant*. There are, in fact, numerically few *courtly romances* in English, but they are usually regarded as the best, and most frequently for a modern reader

1. Bloomfield, "Sir Gawain and the Green Knight: an Appraisal," in *Essays and Explorations*, p. 152.
2. Finlayson, *"Ywain and Gawain* and the Meaning of Adventure," pp. 323–24.

they characterize the genre.[3] In those works, while the love interest is not the dominating element, it is nevertheless of at least equal importance with and is in fact inseparable from adventure, and from the meaning of the work. The type is to be defined, not simply by the presence of an element, but rather by the significance of its function.

There are comparatively few *courtly romances* in Middle English, and most of them (the *Knight's Tale*, *Sir Gawain*, Malory) are too well-known to need comment here. *Ywain and Gawain*, because it is a fairly close translation of Chrétien's *Yvain*, most closely exemplifies the paradigm suggested earlier in this paper, but since I have already written at length on it, I hope I may simply refer the reader to my article. Since the *Knight's Tale* and *Sir Gawain* can be interpreted as, to differing extents, critical examinations of the *romance* ethos, *Ywain* and certain parts of Malory are the only fully achieved *courtly romances* in English.

However, a small number of less well-known works exhibit attempts to emulate this particular type. *William of Palerne*, for example, though not as polished a work as its French source, nevertheless demonstrates a laudable ability to handle courtly material. As an early commentator notes, the Middle English writer does not simply translate, but rather renders his understanding of the *matter*.[4] My own comparison of this work with its source indicates that the English author very frequently expands or reexpresses the courtly material, and the combat descriptions are new creations, using Middle English formulaic diction. While the work as a whole is often repetitious and the plot too reliant on coincidental relationships badly handled, much of the author's (or paraphraser's) interest clearly lies, not in the magical occurrences or the obligatory battle scenes, but in the love element and in the physical settings. The inner dialogue of Melior on her love-pangs,[5] though derived in substance from the source, is reexpressed by the English poet in a manner which recalls the inner dialogues of Troilus [(see, for instance, lines 454–57, 471–72, and 567–68)]. *** [Such expressions,] while not as achieved as Chaucer's rendering of Petrarch's sonnet 88 in the *Canticus Troili*, are nevertheless not without merit. For the purposes of this paper, it is worth noting that the English poet has *not* excised the courtly matter or botched it; clearly, he understands the sentiments and the manner.

---

3. The latest study of medieval romance, Stevens's *Medieval Romance*, deals principally and perceptively with the types of experience which these acknowledged masterpieces "liberate." However, since his definitions are derived almost wholly from courtly romances, they do not hold true for the large body of Middle English romances.
4. M. Kaluza, "Das mittelenglische gedicht *William of Palerne* und seine französische Quelle," *Englische Studien*, 4 (1881), 197–98.
5. There is also considerable expansion of Melior's *complainte*, lines 433–570, in comparison with the source.

It is also worth noting that the English writer amplifies the *descriptio loci* [(formal "description of place")] he finds in his source. *** Passages such as [that found, for example, at lines 817–24] are more than competent translations of the source and indicate the writer's awareness of the "high" or courtly style necessary to the context. In a number of places, the English writer heightens his matter with rhetorical *descriptiones* not found in his source, and in one good passage makes the *descriptio* a necessary part of the action: the discovery of William is brought about in the Middle English version because the boy comes out of his cave attracted by the spring song of the birds—

What for melodye that thei made in the mey° sesoun,	*May, bloom*
That litel child listely° lorked° out of his cave,	*eagerly/started*
Faire floures for-to fecche. . . .	

(24–26)

The Squire of Low Degre is a much more sophisticated example of the courtly romance, and demonstrates a literary self-consciousness found in very few Middle English works. The author's references to other romances in lines 78–82, and his inclusion of a summary of an incident in *Lybeaus Desconus* in the speech of the King's daughter to the Squire (613–36), are valuable indications both of his literary self-consciousness and of medieval awareness of genre. It is a work packed with very elaborate *descriptiones* of people and things of the sort one expects of *romance*, but very rarely finds; a *romance* where attention is focused at least as much on the splendour of the created world and the rhetorical elegance of the sentiments as on the knightly adventures and the love story. Stylistically, in fact, it is a little overripe; the writer so clearly enjoys demonstrating his rhetorical ability to handle the various *figures* and *topoi* that one sometimes wishes he would get on with the story. This poem alone would be evidence enough that English writers were aware of the distinction between the simple *romance of adventure* and the *courtly romance*, and had the rhetorical skill to create in the courtly mode.[6]

Other romances such as *Sir Degrevant* demonstrate the same clear understanding of the nature of the *courtly romance*: the courtliness of the hero is established at length (st. 3), there are elaborate descriptions of hunts, castles, dress, heraldic devices and social rituals, and love and prowess are explicitly associated by the author (sts. 57 and 61), as well as providing the motivation and the central organization of the narrative.

The distinctions between these works and the *romance of adventure* are quite clear, even when the central story line is similar. *Sir Perceval*

---

6. Kane, p. 99.

of Galles is, like *William of Palerne*, basically a romance of "nurture,"
but the centre of the work has nothing to do with the *courtoisie* of *Sir
Degrevant*, nor with the love motifs of either *Palerne* or *The Squire of
Low Degre*. The first adventure maintains a ballad-like spell, the sense
of a wild naif let loose in a complex society and riding rough-shod, but
successfully, over its practices because of his innocence and innate nobility. The process of his adventures is the progress to his identity, that
is, to his name and his proper role. It is also one of the most coherent
examples in Middle English of the *entrelacement* ["interlacing"] which
Chrétien created as one of the most striking structural features of Old
French romance. As a whole, however, it is of uneven quality and too
frequently betrays an imperfect grasp of the essence of *romance*: there
is much carelessness about plot coherence, a considerable uncertainty
as to whether Perceval is sustained because of his basic innocence and
inherent (and inherited) nobility or simply because of the magic ring;
the uncertainty does not contribute to a sense of numinous, symbolic
action, but seems rather the product of an imperfect conception on the
author's part. It is, however, a fairly typical example of the Middle
English *romance of adventure* in that it sometimes creates its own meaning quite persuasively, but often depends on the formulaic value of
romance rituals.[7] It is also, of course, a typical example of how much
Middle English *romance* was generated, since it is clearly the result of
the reductive capacity of a far from sophisticated mind. *Perceval le
Gallois, ou le conte du Graal* becomes *Sir Perceval of Galles*, and the
reflective, symbolic aspects of the work are stripped away to reveal a
"rattling good adventure story" with lots of corpses, a certain amount of
primitive suspense, and a happy ending. Clearly, the English author's
intentions were vastly different from those of his possible source. It is
equally clear that he intends a *romance of adventure*, rather than anything religious or courtly. However, this difference of intention, which
is often stated in blanket fashion to be characteristic of Middle English
romance, should not be taken as an excuse for the avoidance of literary
evaluation. *Sir Perceval's* intentions are both different and imperfectly
executed; its artistic clumsiness and coarse sensibility are rather splendidly caught by lines such as

Percevell made the same othe
That he come never undir clothe
To do that lady no lothe.°   *harm*
(1933–35)

If we apply the same principle to "romances" which can be characterized by a religious element, we can make a significant distinction

7. D. M. Hill, "The Structure of Sir Orfeo," *Mediaeval Studies*, 23 (1961), 140: "Romance
writing . . . operates largely . . . through the employment of symbols whose meanings have
been established by continuous corporate use."

between works which exploit the *romance* genre without doing violence to its basic kind and those which speciously employ *romance* elements in a way which has got nothing to do with the essence of *romance*. The "religious romances" are a later development of the genre, although fairly early in the development of *romance* its symbolic and allegoric potentials, as well as its modishness, were recognized by the ever alert clergy. In English, the figure of the *chevalier errant* becomes a metaphor from the *Ancrene Wisse* onwards.[8]

The religious romances are of two basic types: those, like the Grail romances, in which the obvious allegorical and symbolic potential of the romance world is directed from secular to religious ends, in which the progress of the knight is turned from a socioethical self-examination to a narrower, or loftier, examination of the soul. Although in most cases the end of this "progress" is to reject the physical world and the original ideals of *romance*, nevertheless the nature of the whole action is not altered; its specific meaning is changed but its general imaginative impress has not. The examination of self through the demonstration of martial prowess in the encounter with fated adventure within an unreal world governed by chivalric modes of conduct still remains. The preoccupations may differ from those of the *courtly romance* and the *romance of adventure*, but the form and the kind of imaginative endeavour do not.

In English only Malory's Grail romances seem to use the central "experience" of *romance* to explore the search for spiritual illumination. They do so better than their source. The French *Queste* has a great tendency to turn the quest into a purely allegorical instrument, whereas Malory largely exploits its symbolic potential through deliberate counterpoint with its secular, physical nature. Works such as *The Siege of Jerusalem* and *Titus and Vespasian*, which are said to "place in an atmosphere of chivalry the life, passion and miracles of Christ, woven into stories of the cure of Vespasian and the destruction of Jerusalem,"[9] are clearly chivalric only in that the battles are described in terms of medieval warfare; they are legendary histories which have nothing in common with romance in the attitude to experience, in the concept of the hero, or in the nature and meaning of the narrative episodes. Even as religious narratives, they are religious more by virtue of the events described than by their attitude to these events and the meaning they draw from them. *Joseph of Arimathie*, which deals with the early, pre-Arthurian history of the grail, is largely no more than pious legend, but in the section dealing with the King of Babylon's invasion of Evalak's realm it is fitfully successful in uniting legendary history with the concepts and attitudes of the *romance of adventure*.

<hr>

8. See G. Shepherd, ed., *Ancrene Wisse* (London: Nelson, 1959), p. 55.
9. L. H. Hornstein, in *A Manual of the Writings in Middle English 1050–1500*, ed. J. Burke Severs (New Haven: Connecticut Academy of Arts and Sciences, 1967), I, 160.

There are, however, a number of works designated "religious romances" which, in my view, violate, rather than adapt, the *romance*.
These are largely the "homiletic" or "didactic romances." Clearly, the
impulse which generates the Grail romances is generally the same as
that of the homiletic *romances*, but the results are very different: in one,
the religious truth is reached *through* the quest, through the imaginative
world of romance; in the other, certain events have a romance dress
imposed on them, and the truths proposed are equally imposed. That
is, certain characteristic elements of *romance* are added to a story which
is told primarily for its moral significance. One of the best of these works,
in literary terms, is also one of the best examples of what I mean. *Amis
and Amiloun* is frequently cited as an example of the inextricable connection of saints' lives and romance. It contains, as its most persuasive
commentators have noted, many elements "characteristic" of *romance*:
aristocratic personages, individual combats, treacherous stewards, and
supernatural or marvelous events. Though these elements are all to be
found also in the *chanson de geste*, the relationship of the events of this
poem to the hero, and the absence of a broader social context, allow
these elements to be characterized as romantic. Yet I do not wish to
call this *romance*, because all these elements are in no way central or
essential to the "Truth" which is proposed. Amiloun's victory may demonstrate his prowess, but it is completely irrelevant to any concept of
his character; he is neither proving nor examining either himself or the
chivalric ethic in his martial feat, but is merely providing a way out of
a complicated physical problem. The combat is not functional except
in terms of plot. This fact alone, of course, is not sufficient to reject it
as *romance*; it could be seen merely as an artistic failure, that is, the
author was a hack writer whose sole interest lay in an improbable plot.
What I wish to stress here, however, is that, while the author reproduces
the stereotyped elements of *romance*, their function and meaning are
absent. The main reason, however, for rejecting this as romance lies in
the pattern of the plot, and the way in which meaning is made in the
work. The pattern is that of the saint's life: it is a story in which quite
horrendous things happen to the central character, partly as a punishment for transgression, partly as a test of faith. Through the hero's meek
acceptance of his lot and a supreme act of faith, he is relieved of his
suffering. None of this, of course, has any real resemblance to the trial
by adventure, the active confrontation with destined events and the
subsequent achievement of personal harmony which we have defined
as the core of *romance*. It is trial by ordeal, not adventure, and its end
is the granting of grace, not the achievement of self-knowledge. The
whole meaning of this story pattern depends, not on the process, but
on the end. In *romances* marvels are often instruments of plot progress,
or initiators of events, but they are not the definers of meaning, as the
miraculous cure of Amiloun and the resurrection of the sacrificed chil-

dren are. A miraculous story, in other words, does not become a *romance* simply by calling the characters knights and describing an individual combat.

Amis is certainly didactic, but it is *romance* only in that broadest of senses, "a narrative poem of the Middle Ages." The knightliness of Amiloun is not the subject, and it is in no way relevant to the conclusion. It is not even the story of the discovery of faith or acceptance of God's will through suffering, for "Amiloun never in all his wanderings as a beggar rebels against his lot, just as a saint never rebels against the suffering imposed on him for the sake of his faith."[1] *Amis* and many other "homiletic" or "religious romances" should, in fact, be seen as *exempla*, so that their true nature and, possibly, literary worth may better be appreciated.[2] While at the date of composition it may have served their interests to be considered as romances,[3] there is nothing to be gained in continuing to subject them to criticism as "poor romances," condemned for "many absurdities of subject and faults of construction."[4]

One other group of narratives seems to me to have been erroneously classified as "romances," due to an eagerness to label anything to do with knights and the supernatural as *romance*. It is prudent to remember that, for a medieval writer, the designation "knight" is initially one of social rank; it is not, as it clearly is for the Romantics and Victorians, immediately evocative of a handsome young man on horseback, clad in shining armour, galloping along to rescue a fair maiden from the unwelcome advances of the local dragon. It was also almost inescapable in medieval secular fiction, either courtly or popular, for different reasons, that the chief protagonists should be aristocratic; kitchen lads who achieve adventures must inevitably be of noble birth. The group to which I refer may best be termed "romanticized folktales." They are basically fairy tales overlaid with a few chivalric elements in what seems a quite deliberate intent to make them contemporary and modish. The hero is mechanically turned into a knight, and on occasion they [,like Chaucer's Prioress,] "countrefete cheere of court," [(*General Prologue*, 139–40)] but their plot material has not been reinterpreted in terms of the *romance*. In *Amadace* for example, the hero is a knight and the dead man who becomes his ghostly benefactor is also a knight; there are royal garments

---

1. Kratins, p. 353a; also, "Identifying it as a romance amounts to asking that it be regarded in the wrong perspective" (p. 154a).
2. Gibbs remarks that Amis's "quality as chivalric romance is not much more than top-dressing," although he also remarks "this poem represents the level of solid technical competence attained by the best of the English tail-rhyme romances" (pp. 34–35).
3. See Laura Hibbard, *Medieval Romance in England* (New York: Oxford Univ. Press, 1924), p. 65, and Gervase Matthew, "Ideals of Friendship," in *Patterns of Love and Courtesy*, ed. J. Lawlor (London: Edward Arnold, 1966), p. 45, for comments on its popularity.
4. The didactic intent of *Amis, Amadace, Robert of Cysylle*, and *Sir Cleges* is recognized by J. E. Wells, A *Manual of the Writings in Middle English* (New Haven: Yale Univ. Press, 1916), p. 157, who notes that "all depend on supernatural intervention in behalf of a pious hero." Other works which should probably be regarded as exempla are *Athelston, Emare, Isumbras*, the *Man of Law's Tale, The King of Tars*, and *The Seven Sages of Rome*.

and a kingdom to be had by marrying a king's daughter, but, apart from these two elements, there is nothing to distinguish it from folktale. Clearly, while it is possible that the author thought these "modern" touches would make his tale a romance, it is much more likely that he was simply making his tale more "contemporary" and that our literary historians have been too eager to identify anything that involves knights and the supernatural as *romance*.[5] Its main preoccupation is with the highly contrived ordeal in which the knight, in order to keep his word, must cut his own son in two. Like *Amis* it is a didactic tale of trial by ordeal, but unlike *Amis* its didacticism is not specifically religious.

If *Amadace* is not a deliberate attempt to add romantic glamour to a folktale, the *Wife of Bath's Tale* is. It fails to be a *romance*, but its failure is deliberate.[6] The basis of the story clearly belongs to the folk or fairy tale, but the material has been consciously reworked to transform it into an Arthurian *romance*. Where it fails is in its conception of the chivalric mode. It has the external features of the genre, a knight-hero, ladies of the court interceding, a marvel, a quest, and an erotic element of a sort; but the essential features of the knight's trial and discovery of self through prowess in adventure are absent. Instead, we have a dilemma which is resolved, not through chivalry, but through magic. The knight may learn something, but it is a knowledge which is imposed, not achieved. Finally, although there is an unexpected lecture on *gentilesse*, culled from Dante, the atmosphere is not that of *courtoisie*: the knight begins with a rape and clearly even by the end of the "adventure" hasn't learned good manners. His armour may shine, but his morals don't. In other words, although it has been tricked out in Arthurian clothes, it is still a folktale in preoccupations and sensibility. It admirably demonstrates, among many other things, an aspect of the Wife: her *bourgeoise* longing for the unreal world of *courtly romance* and high life, and her equally *bourgeoise* mistaking of the external characteristics for the essence. At the same time, it provides an admirable explanation of why so many Middle English romances fail as chivalric romances: they are clearly intended for a class unfamiliar except at a distance with *courtoisie*, a class whose social pretensions and desires impel them to imitate their social superiors; but, as with most social climbers, they mistake the manners of their superiors for what the manners are about. The Wife in her *Tale* betrays her kinship with the Prioresse and le Bourgeois Gentilhomme: they "countrefete cheere of courte," but to one who belonged to the court, even to a first-generation Knight of the Shire [i.e., Chaucer], they would appear ludicrously off centre in their imitation.

The criteria suggested here for defining the essence of medieval *romance* and for distinguishing its main types are presented mainly as ways

---

5. See again Lewis, "What Chaucer Really Did to *Il Filostrato*," on the tendency of medieval writers to medievalize (that is, to render "contemporary") all material.
6. Kane, pp. 24–25.

of discerning the intended or essential "shape" of a large number of Middle English narratives. Although I have not in this paper investigated the claims to be designated "romance" of all the works listed in Severs's *Manual of the Writings in Middle English* as romances, it should be clear that at least half of them do not in any way meet the paradigms proposed; that is, they are not romances in any meaningful sense, though this is not to deny that they occasionally exhibit characteristics which are to be found in the *romance*. This wholesale disenfranchising of familiar, if not beloved, works may not unduly distress the bibliographers, who so frequently are forced to note the "unromantic" or "unchivalric" nature of the works they describe. There is also a considerable benefit in that works as disparate as *The Destruction of Troy*, *Athelston*, and *Sir Amadace* need no longer be "yoked by violence together" under one rule, but can be allowed to reveal their own directions. Once freed of the *need* to be romances, they exhibit more artistic merit and coherence than has been allowed them. Of the works which to some reasonable extent survive judgement by the proposed criteria, it is clear that most are *romances of adventure*, not, as some earlier commentators have suggested, because the English writers deliberately rejected courtly love, but because this is the *basic* form of romance and the most "popular" in both senses of the word. That many Middle English romances conform only imperfectly to the suggested paradigm is due to a number of factors, sometimes in combination: the adaptation of what had been literary romances for a courtly French audience to suit either public delivery to a popular or socially mixed audience,[7] or a less sophisticated readership;[8] the artistic ineptness of individual romancers. The criteria of definition of genre also operate in the process of literary evaluation: it will be observed frequently that those romances we judge most deficient in overall literary merit are also those which have least conception of the essence of the "shape" they imitate. A fairly precise definition of the classical "shape" of the *romance* also enables the critic to judge whether apparent departures from the model are intended, and therefore part of the meaning, or are simply inept. It is, for example, often charged against the *romance* that it is shapeless, whereas, though romance is episodic, only the inartistic are shapeless. In the better works the episodes are part of a graded sequence leading to a final and resolving episode. Similarly, awareness of the characterizing features of the main *types* is often a key to the meaning of an individual work. We have already remarked that in *Ywain and Gawain* the change from *romance of ad-*

7. Gibbs, p. 21.
8. See L. H. Loomis, "The Auchinleck Manuscript and a Possible London Bookshop of 1330–40," *PMLA*, 57 (1942), 595–627. The main manuscript collections of romances, particularly the Auchinleck, Cambridge University Library Ff. II. 38, and British Museum Thornton, contain a very mixed bag of religious, didactic, devotional works as well as the "romances," and it is not unjust to assert that most of the works contained in them are of very limited artistic merit, especially if compared with fourteenth-century courtly literature.

venture to *courtly romance* is part of the *sans* of the work. This same manipulation of *types* can also be observed in *Sir Gawain*. The detailed "shapeliness" of *Sir Gawain* is, of course, unique to the author, but its essential form is typical: the knight rides forth to achieve an adventure and proceeds through a series of encounters to a final encounter which "resolves" the problem. An awareness of this basic pattern, and the legitimate expectations aroused in the audience by it, permits us to respond more alertly, as a contemporary audience probably did, to the manipulation of the pattern. We can see, for example, how the author, having raised expectations of feats of arms which are not satisfied—the encounter with wodwoes and warlocks is presented dismissively—diverts the reader's expectations into another channel by an "entrelacement" which suggests that the direction of this romance is to be that of the *courtly romance*. Having played with the reader, partly satisfying him, but not proceeding to the "expected" resolution (as Gawain and the lady "play" with each other), the narrative returns the expectations of the audience to *adventure*, only, of course, to disappoint them once more. The "game" in *Sir Gawain* is not simply in the episodes, but more in the virtuoso manipulation of genre. A knowledge of "characteristics" of *romance* can lead us only to the partly misleading conclusion that *Sir Gawain* contains most of the standard features of *romance*: adventure, the marvellous, courtly love; an awareness of the essentials of *romance* and the directions of its main *types* will lead us more surely to appreciate the very complex exploitation of literary form and the audience's literary experiences. [9]

ALBERT C. BAUGH

Improvisation in the Middle English Romance[†]

I

In trying to recapture the conditions under which the Greek epic and the Old French epopee were created and recited—conditions under which the conveyance of long narrative poems was oral—much use has been made in recent years of the presumably parallel conditions which exist in Jugoslavia and elsewhere. In Jugoslavia and other parts of the world long heroic poems are still recited or sung to the accompaniment of a musical instrument by singers who in many instances are unable

9. See J. Finlayson, "The Expectations of Romance in *Sir Gawain and the Green Knight*," *Genre*, 12 (Spring 1979), 1–24.
† Reprinted from *Proceedings of the American Philosophical Society*, 103 (1959), 418–454, with permission of the American Philosophical Society, Philadelphia. (To facilitate the reading of Baugh's many quotations of Middle English texts, þ and ʒ have been modernized, as has the use of *u* and *v*—Editor.)

to read and to an audience which is equally dependent upon the ear. While such conditions exist in parts of Russia, in Turkish areas, in Siberia, Crete, and elsewhere,[1] those in Jugoslavia have been the most studied and are the best known. A comparatively early study of Jugoslavic oral poetry was that of Mathias Murko,[2] but the most extensive studies have been those of Milman Parry and A. B. Lord.[3] The Jugoslavic evidence has been used especially for the elucidation of the Homeric poems, but recently Jean Rychner has used it to propound a theory of the composition of the early chansons de geste.[4]

There are several respects in which the Greek epic, the Old French chansons de geste, and the poems sung by Jugoslav *guslars* appear to be comparable. In subject matter they are essentially heroic narratives. They are sung to the accompaniment of a musical instrument. In Greece it appears to have been a lyre; when the celebrated minstrel Demodocus in the eighth book of the *Odyssey* relates the heroic deeds of the Achaeans he sings them to the accompaniment of the lyre. In the chansons de geste the instrument most frequently mentioned is the *viele* and the jongleur is said to "chanter et vieler ensemble" ["sing and play the hurdy gurdy together"]."[5] The Jugoslav instrument is a *gusle*, a primitive sort of violin of one string played with a crude bow. Most important, however, is the fact that all these heroic poems are at times very long. Milman Parry recorded the song of one *guslar* which ran to 13,331 lines,[6] which is longer by a thousand lines than the *Odyssey*, and a Kara-Kirghiz bard, shortly before his death in 1930 told the story of the Mohammedan hero, Manas, in some 40,000 lines.[7]

Now the thing to be noted in the practice of all singers of heroic songs in Jugoslavia and in other parts of Europe and Asia where their art has been studied is that the singing of these poems involves a considerable element of improvisation. For one thing, singers often sing the same story or instalment in versions of quite different length—in a version that takes twenty minutes or one that takes an hour or more. It is the same story but in different degrees of fullness. The shortening is not accomplished by skipping incidents or omitting passages. It is general condensation and each is a separate version. Yet it is not a matter of knowing a longer and a shorter song, both of which are in the singer's memory and from which he chooses one or the other as the time at his

---

1. See Radlov, V. V., *Proben der Volkslitteratur der türkischen Stämme Süd-Siberiens und der dsungarischen Steppe*, St. Petersburg, 1866–1907; *Trans. Amer Philol. Assoc.* 82:84; C. M. Bowra, *Heroic poetry*, chap. 6, London, 1952.
2. *La poésie populaire épique en Yougoslavie au début du xxe siècle*, Paris, 1929.
3. Most important in this connection is the article of Milman Parry, Studies in the epic technique of oral verse-making: I. Homer and Homeric style, *Harvard Stud. in Class. Philol.* 41:73–147, 1930.
4. *La chanson de geste: essai sur l'art épique des jongleurs*, Geneva and Lille, 1955.
5. *Le roman de la violette*, line 1402, describing Gerard the hero disguised as a jongleur and singing a passage from *Aliscans*.
6. *Trans. Amer. Philol. Assoc.* 52:42.
7. *Ibid.*, 86.

disposal requires. He can expand or contract at will and do it in the very act of singing. The result is that no two performances are exactly alike. Murko reports that on one occasion he had a singer dictate his song before singing it. The intention was to record any variants while listening to the song. Although only a few minutes intervened, the version which the singer sang was so different from the dictated copy that it was quite impossible to record the differences as variants. This is the situation which the editor of a medieval text sometimes finds himself in when he is dealing with more than one manuscript. Moreover, the theory of improvisation is supported by the testimony of singers themselves. A. B. Lord in his essay, "Compositon by Theme in Homer and South-slavic Epos"[8] says:

> A Yugoslav singer told me last year that when he learned a new song he made no attempt at word-for-word memorization but learned only the "plan" of the song, which he explained as "the arrangement of the events." This plan he then proceeded to fill in with the themes which he already knew.

In other words he partly improvised.

It is bound to cause some surprise to be told that an illiterate singer is able to compose his verses as he goes along. The secret of this apparently extraordinary ability lies in the fact that improvisation is not a sheer act of creative composition, but the adroit utilization and recombination of elements in a well-stocked memory. These elements are of two kinds: formulas and themes.

A *formula* in the definition of Milman Parry, based primarily on the Homeric poems but equally applicable to all epic poetry, is "a group of words which is regularly employed under the same metrical conditions to express a given essential idea." Everyone will recall "the blue-eyed goddess Athene" (θεά γλαυκῶπις 'Αθήνη) since the phrase occurs more than fifty times, or τὸν δ' αὐτεχροσέειπε (however, he said to him), which occurs nearly ninety times. There is no reason why the poet should so regularly use these stock expressions rather than seek greater variety except that they furnished ready-made phrases of a certain metrical pattern easily fitted into the line. In the same way, as Parry says, this is

> likewise true of the epithet ἄναξ ανδρῶν, "lord of men," which is used not only 48 times elsewhere in the *Iliad* and the *Odyssey* of Agamemnon, but also of Anchises, Aeneas, Augeias, Euphetes, and Eumelos, none of whom is any more a king of men than is any other of the chief heroes, but all of them have names of the same metrical value as that of Agamemnon.[9]

8. *Trans. Amer. Philol. Assoc.* 82: 73–74, 1951.
9. *Op. cit.*, 123.

Rychner finds a similar use of formulas in the early chansons de geste: for example in the nine chansons which he studied he found 39 instances of

Le° destrier° broiche°	*the / war-horse / (he) spurs*
Le cheval° broche	*horse*
Les destriers broichent	
Son° cheval brochet, etc.	*his*

at the beginning of the line, which was then completed with other formulas such as

des° esperons° tranchanz°	*with / spurs / sharp*
des esperuns d'or° fin°	*of gold / fine*
des esperons burnis°	*shining*
des esperons forbiz°	*polished*
des esperons d'or mier°	*pure*
des esperons des pies°	*feet*
des oriez° esperuns	*gilt*
des aguz° esperuns	*pointed*

* * * according to the requirement of the assonance. And he cites many other formulas similarly used.

The second of the traditional elements which the singer makes use of in telling his story is the *theme*. In his essay "Composition by Theme in Homer and Southslavic Epos," previously referred to, A. B. Lord defines the theme as "a recurrent element of narration or description in traditional oral poetry," and he adds:

> It is not restricted, as is the formula, by metrical considerations; hence, it should not be limited to exact word-for-word repetition. . . . Regular use, or repetition, is as much a part of the definition of the theme as it is of the definition of the formula, but the repetition need not be exact.

As examples of such recurring elements we may mention such stock situations as the boastful speech or taunt or challenge, the arming of the hero or the description of his arms, his mounting and spurring his horse to the fight, the description of the opposing army, description of a mêlée, the individual combat, injuries before, during, or after the fight, regret for a hero killed or seriously injured, prayers, greetings and leave takings, feasts, the dubbing of a new knight, and so on. In the chanson de geste Rychner finds that the theme often constitutes a laisse and that an entire laisse is sometimes repeated with only slight differences. Thus in the *Chanson de Guillaume* a sequence of three laisses totaling 42 lines describes the death of Girard and immediately afterwards the same three laisses are used with some omissions and additions to describe the death of Guichard.[1] Likewise in describing the arming of a knight, a theme that naturally occurs frequently, a stock sequence of ideas with a number of identical lines is used for Thibaut, Girard, and Guillaume at intervals of 400 to 900 lines [at lines 133–39, 1075–80, and 1498–1502].

* * *

The hypothesis of formulaic elements and oral improvisation has been proposed by Professor Magoun for the *Beowulf*.[2] I do not mean to imply that I consider the hypothesis proved either for the Homeric poems, the chansons de geste, or the Anglo-Saxon epic. In fact, I do not see that it is susceptible of proof in the absence of such direct evidence as we have for the contemporary practice of singers in Jugoslavia and other comparable areas. But since the practice of improvisation can be observed in our own day, since it results in the necessary use of formulaic elements, and since similar formulaic elements are found extensively in the epic poems of Greece, medieval France, and Anglo-Saxon England, the possibility cannot be denied that here also they have resulted from comparable circumstances of oral presentation. It would seem reasonable, therefore, to ask whether the Middle English romances as they have come down to us are to any extent the product of similar practices.[3]

II

Every one knows that the Middle English romances are honeycombed with stock phrases and verbal clichés, often trite and at times seemingly forced. A number of extensive collections of these commonplaces have been made.[4] They have generally been cited as parallels between different romances showing the conventional character of the ideas and expressions of the poets who wrote them. The attitude of modern critics toward this feature of romance style is on the whole unfavorable, al-

---

1. Rychner, 83–84.
2. Oral-formulaic character of Anglo-Saxon narrative poetry, *Speculum* 28: 446–467, 1953.
3. The present study is confined to those romances which make up the so-called Matter of England: *King Horn, Havelok, Beves of Hampton, Guy of Warwick, Richard the Lion-Hearted* [RLH], and *Athelston*.
4. So far as I know, the first to gather a large number of them together was Zupitza, in the notes to his edition of the Cambridge Univ. Library MS of *Guy of Warwick* (Early English Text Soc., Extra Ser. [EETS ES] xxv–xxvi, 1875–1876). In his inaugural dissertation of 1879 on *Sir Orfeo* Oscar Zielke assembled and roughly classified a representative selection of them. The material was incorporated in his edition of the poem the following year. Many were again cited by Kölbing in his editions of *Sir Tristrem* (Heilbronn, 1882), *Amis and Amiloun* (Heilbronn, 1884), *Beves of Hampton*, EETSES, xlvi, xlviii, lxv), *Athelston* (*Englische Studien* 13:331–414, 1889), *Ipomedon* (Breslau, 1889), and *Arthur and Merlin* (Leipzig, 1890). The third volume of the *Beves* contains an essay by Carl Schmirgel, typical expressions and repetitions in Sir Beves of Hampton, originally printed at Breslau in 1886. Repeated phrases of a more special type are catalogued and discussed by J. S. P. Tatlock in his: Epic formulas, especially in Lazamon, *Publ. Mod. Lang. Assoc.* 38: 494–529, 1923, a few of which are found in later romances. A. M. Trounce offers a classification of the uses to which they were put in the tail-rime romances (*Medium Ævum* 1: 168–182, 1932). Miss Ruth Crosby mentions many of the shorter and commoner clichés in her article: Oral delivery in the Middle Ages, *Speculum* 11: 88–110, 1936.

though there have been apologists. Saintsbury thought "that repetition, stock phrases, identity of scheme and form, which are apt to be felt as disagreeable in reading, are far less irksome, and even have a certain attraction, in matter orally delivered.[5] Tatlock suggested as a compensating virtue the fact that, "The well-tried phrase for what is usual leaves the full sharpness of the attention for what is fresh,"[6] and he elsewhere says, speaking of the epic formulas in Layamon, "Doubtless his auditors too found a pleasure in the repetition, as children feel in *The Three Bears* and *The House that Jack Built*, or even as we feel in recognizing a recurring *motif* in music."[7] There is doubtless an element of truth in all these observations, and if the use of conventional phrases had not so often made them into mere tags—a device for filling out the line or meeting the exigencies of rime—one might consider them a conscious artistic device, but as Tatlock observes, "they are apt to be brief, parenthetical and unessential, making little or no contribution to the narrative . . . a general stock of insignificant, shop-worn counters, the profusion of which suggests helplessness."

But are they mere clichés? We should perhaps not answer this question too hastily. By far the largest number occur at the end of a line, where their convenience for purposes of rime is obvious. Each fits into a given metrical situation—the last four syllables of a line, or the last three, or the last five. In other words, they meet the requirements of the formula. A few examples will make this apparent:

The king thar of	was glad & blithe	Beves	529
The king thar of	was glad & blithe		905
And Beves	was glad & blithe		2497
Tho was Beves	glad & blithe		3471
Of whom that he	was glad & blithe	Guy	1924*
As he that	was glad & blithe		6394
Evere he	was glad and blithe	Hav.	947
And maden hem	[ful] glad and blithe		1245
Bes of him	ful glad and blithe		2246

Other phrases such as *and was ful blithe, so was he blithe*, or, where a syllable less is needed, *swithe blithe* satisfy the metrical requirements in other thought contexts.

Adverbial phrases are particularly likely to become formulas because they may be so freely added to complete an idea:

Thai gonne schete	be ech a side	Beves	882
With gret joie	be ech a side		2162
The cri aros	be ech a side		4438

5. Saintsbury, George, *The flourishing of romance and the rise of allegory*, 49, New York, 1897; cited by Miss Crosby, *op. cit.*, 104.

6. *Op. cit.*, 528–529.

7. *Ibid.*, 513. The most enthusiastic defense of the device, in its extensive use in the tail-rime romances, is that of A. M. Trounce, in the article cited in note 14, above.

& mi lond destrud	in ich a side	Guy	2878
The messangers	by ylke a syde	RLH	147
And slowgh dounryght	on ylke a syde		5236
He sente aboute	on ylke a syde		6594
Out at is mouth	in aither side	Beves	809
Gret slaughter worth	in either side		4130
To hire godes thai bede	in either side		4144
Mani on ther dyed	in aither side	Guy	3025
Thar was joie	be everi side	Beves	3962
& ther-fore	on everich a side	Guy	969
Thus thai leide on	in bothe side	Beves	1755
He was be-set	in bothe side		4399
And smot him thourgh	out bothe side		1002
And hys hoostes	on bothe syde	RLH	1654

Here the variants *ech a, ylke a, either, bothë* are metrically equivalent, while a different requirement is met by *be his side*:

& fiftene Sarasins	be is side	Beves	588
& dede lede Arondel	be is side		1508
A swerd a tok	be his side		1599
& pyk and skrippe	be is side		2241
Ten thousand Sarezynes	by here side	RLH	7120

With a substitution of different prepositions the rime-word *cité* may enter into a variety of almost identical formulas:

At Warwike	in that cite	Guy	187
& al that weren	in that cite		2260
Worthschipliche	in that cite		5040
The noise aros	in that cite		6436
Off sylvyr & gold	in that cyte	RLH	4603
Noyse & cri he herd	in that cite	Guy	2897
We will abide	in this cite		5065

& gon again	to that cite		5372
Alle sori in	to that cite		6488
That hij come	to that cite		6514
Wel right he yede	to that cite		7023
Thus they come	to that cytee	RLH	4204

Thai wenten out	of that cite	Guy	2349
Alle that weren	of that cite		3867
& the citiseins	of that cite		5503
Tho ich went out	of that cite		5972
By that on syde	off that cytee	RLH	5406
At the sege	of that cytee		5424

Metrically equivalent but suiting a different construction is *that riche cite*:

Toward Acres	that riche cete	RLH	634
Jerusalem,	that ryche cyte		5898
To Arascoun,	that gode cite	Guy	1976*
To Espire	that riche cite		2794
& feffe the with mani	a riche cite		3352
Mombraunt is	a riche cite	Beves	2045
To London, to	that riche cite		4536

Contre may be substituted for *cité*:

Boute seve mile	of that contrei	Beves	1696
Ne com ther non	in that contre		2247
Boute fif mile	of that contray		3686
Ich was y-born	of that cuntre	Guy	938
Bot al the folk	of that cuntre		965
& al the folk	of that cuntre		1113
Ich was y-born	in that cuntre		1746

Other monosyllabic adjectives or pronouns may replace *that* without disturbing the metrical value of the formula:

Home te wende	to his contre	Beves	4023
What they dyde	in his countre	RLH	712
As thou hast folk	in this cuntree		6463
a knight icham	of fer cuntre	Guy	1635

There are, of course, many more.

One of the most useful formulas not so plainly used to fill out the line is the type which ends in a past participle. The verbs most frequently used are *y-brought* and *y-go(n)*, although the latter has substitutes available (*fare, ride,* etc.):

That neye he was	to deth y-brought	Guy	246
Ich wold ich were	to deth y-brought		336
That he is	to deth y-brought		1456
Hou mine men ben	to deth y-brought		3530
Who hath milyoun	to deth y-brought		4364
Have mi lyoun	to deth y-brought		4407
Alle he hath hem	to deth y-brought		4784
Hou god him hath	fram deth y-brought		5954
Hou Gij hem hath	fram deth y-brought		6582
Thy fayre sone	to dethe is brought	RLH	820
Whan the erle	to dethe was brought	Beves	2631
		(Chetham manuscript)	

A common variant is:

Whi that icham	in sorwe brought	Guy	286
Now is Gij	in sorwe ybrought		309
That hire haved	in sorwe brouht	Hav.	336
That haves him-self	in sorwe brouht		2811
That he ne weren	to sorwe brouht		57
And haveth me	to sorwe brouht		1372

Many other changes can be rung within the metrical pattern:

That wimen han	to gronde y-brought	Guy	1564
Now is Beves	to grounde brought	Beves	2783
That he was	to the erthe brouht	Hav.	248
Allas! to grounde	icham ybrought	Guy	486
And in this prisoun	icham y-brought		6198
Whan hii were eft	to gedre brought	Beves	1574

Even more prolific is *gon*. Out of nearly a hundred examples I quote five:

& in to an erber	he is y-go	Guy	565
To an ermite	he is y-go		1647
Toward Seynt Omer	he is y-go		1795
To his felawes	he is y-go		3063
Into the forest	thai ben y-go		4800

With very little change the infinitive may be substituted:

In to his chaumber	he gan gon	Beves	648
Into the castel	he gan to gon	Guy	678
Into that schyp	they gunne gone	RLH	94
To Horn	he gan gon	Horn	1351

Of this formula I count more than thirty examples in the six romances under consideration.

Although the demonstration—that what we have to do with here is the formula in the Milman Parry sense—carries conviction through the quantity of the evidence as well as its quality, there is not space to present the matter in greater detail. One could illustrate the point by citing examples under *in that bataile, that may betide, flesh and bone, that maiden bright, that was so bright, fair and bright, a good brond, sorrow and care, with glad (mild, laughing) cheer, night and day, when it was day, no longer dwell, word and end, well enough, withouten fable, withouten fail, saunfaile, mani and fale, that is so free, at the frome,* and so on through the alphabet.

While the formula finds its greatest use at the end of the line where the composer or reciter must face the requirement of rime, it is also useful in furnishing a ready-made opening for the verse, a general-purpose approach to the main predicate. Here the prepositional phrase with adverbial force has a high utility value. A few examples, taken from the narrator's general stock of such phrases, will illustrate the way they are used:

In the world	ne worth man of so gret might	Guy	4263
In the worlde	is not theyr pere	RLH	684
In the world	was non hym lyche	Ath.	57
In the world	was non here pere		69
In the world	is non hys pere		114
In this world	is better non at nede	Guy	6120
In al this werd	ne haves he per	Hav.	2241
In al this world	nis ther man	Beves	1101
In al this world	nis ther man		1113

Here the idea introduced is generally a comparison—there is no one the hero's equal. On the other hand, the phrase *in his heart* generally announces an emotional state or mood:

In is herte	swithe blithe	Beves	1078
In is hertte	him was ful wo		1712
In hys herte	he was ful glad, iwys	(Caius) p. 133	
In his hert	was sorwe anough	Guy	6866
In his hert	him was ful wo		2992
At his hert	him was ful wo		4496
At his hert	gret sorwe sat		6932
And in his herte	made glad chere	Ath.	120
In hert	he is me lef & dere	Guy	2278
In hert	y was glad & light		4640
In herte	he was ful woo	Ath.	81
In herte	he was ful woo		252

* * *

In many cases the conventional opening of the line is followed by an equally conventional close:

On the morowe,	whan it was daye	RLH	775
On the morwen,	hwan it was day	Hav.	811
On the morwen,	hwan it was day		1920
On the morwen,	hwan day was sprungen		1131
On the morwen,	hwan it was liht		2190
A morwe,	whan hit was dai cler	Beves	755
A morwe,	whan hit was dai cler		3521
A morwe,	so sone so it was day	Guy	4173
Amoreghe,	tho the day gan springe	Horn	645

| To morwe, | so sone so it is day | Guy   841 |
| Erliche a morwe, | when it was dai | Beves 1973 |

The descriptions of fighting naturally furnish many examples:

Thourgh is bodi	went the dent	Beves 4383
Thurch the bodi	the swerd gan gon	Guy 1372
Thurch the bodi	his swerd glod	1377
Thurch the bodi	he him smot	1431
Thurch the bodi	he him smot	4367
Thurch the bodi	knight he bar	5073
Thurch the bodi	he smot him anon	6427
Thurch the bodi	he him carf atuo	7283
Thurch his bodi	that swerd yede	1439
Thurch his bodi	the swerd he thriste	1463
Thurch his bodi	the brond went	5077
Thurch his bodi	the swerd is gon	6965
Thurch that bodi	that swerde bot	7282

and many more examples cited below in connection with the theme of battle.

The consequence of such an action is obvious and is expressed again and again in the same way. By the use of a few well-tried statements, such as *Dead he felled him*, the story-teller is able to give all his attention to the line ending and the necessary rime:

Ded he feld him	doun fot hot	Guy 2946
Ded he feld him	an hast tho	2994
Ded he feld him	adoun thar	5074
Ded he feld him	verrament	5078
Ded he feld him	of his stede	5132
Ded he feld him	in the feld	5218
That ded he feld him	in the mede	1368
That ded he feld him	in the way	1390
That ded he feld him	anon right	2400
& dede he feld him	on the grounde	2938
That ded he feld him	anon right	3516
That ded he feld him	on the ston	5122
That ded he feld him	anon right	5220
That ded he feld him	on the sond	5226
That ded he feld him	anon	5813
Ded a fel	on the paviment	Beves 4384
Ded he fel	with-outen abod	Guy 1378

Ded he fel	with-outen abod		2952
Ded he fel	to grounde tho		7284
That ded he fel	doun fot hot	Guy	1880
That ded he fel	anon right		2232
That ded he fel	withouten letting		3522
That ded thai fel	mani on		5088

After a dangerous or trying experience which has a happy outcome
the hero (or heroine) is naturally "blithe" and thanks God or his worldly
benefactor. For such a standard idea a formula is a convenient accessory:

He thankyd god	with devocyoun	Beves (Caius)
		p. 134
And thankyde hem	mani a sithe	Beves 530
And thankede him	ful mani a sithe	906
And thankede god	ful mani a sithe	3472
& thonked god	of that gras	Guy 1058
& thonked god	ful yern y-wis	4074
And thankyd god	fele sythe	Guy (Cbg.) 772
And thankyd god	fele sythe	5190
And thankyd god	fele sythe	6970
And thankyd god	oftesythe	11588
He thankyd god	in trynyte	11625
They thankyd god	on all manere	11966
And thankede God	ful fele sithe	Hav. 2189
She thanked God	[ful] fele sythe	2843
And thankyd God	off his myght	Ath. 590
And thankyd God	off his grace	614
They thankyd God	al so blyve	RLH 1249

Travel and movement make up a considerable part of the action of
medieval romance, and therefore an adverbial onset in a line is particularly common:

Into the cite	of Arrascoun him hath	Guy 1886
	y-dight	
Into the cite	he him dight	1992
Into the cite	thai ben y-gon	1995
Into the cite	thai gun it bring	4087
Into the cite	of Lorein . . .	5595
Into the cite	he is y-go	6343
Into the cite	of Pavie	6389

A variety of opening phrases can be constructed on this pattern—*And
to the cite, To the cite, Out of the cite,* all of which are common—and
of course one can enter or leave many other places:

Into the castel	he gan to gon	Guy	678
Into the court	he gan to gon		680
In to his chaumber	he gan gon	Beves	648
Out of that cuntre	he is sone y-go	Guy	6726
And to the castel	thai wente isame	Beves	3449
Into Almayne	ichil gon	Guy	3245
Into Inglond	he wald wende		1693
Into Cyprys	redy to fare	RLH	626
Into Denemark	for to fare	Hav.	2955
Unto Londone	wolde he fare	Ath.	89
And to the gate	Beves yode	Beves	2239
Into the forest	thai ben y-go	Guy	4800
Unto his in	he is y-go		2845

I have illustrated merely the variety of such phrases without attempting to indicate their frequency. Even so limited a phrase as *into the forest* occurs six times among the quotations I have gathered, and I have not tried to make my collection complete even for the six romances studied. As an exhibit of frequency I may cite:

Forth thai wente	with that child	Beves	509
Forth thai wente	al isame		705
Forth him wente	sire Bevoun		1133
Forth him wente	sire Bevoun		1347
Forth him wente	sire Bevoun		1947
Forth a wente	be the strem		1959
Forth a wente	in is wai		1974
Forth thai wenten	alle thre		2551
Forth a wente	to the castel gate		2977
Forth thai wente	& drowe saile		3026
Forth a wente	ase hot		3079
Forth a wente	also whate		3081
Forth thai wenten	ase snel		3353
Forth thai wente	bothe ifere		3635
Forth he went	into Speyne	Guy	1065
Forth thai yede	with gode welle		5115
Forth thai wenten	hastily		6598
Forth they wente	with glad chere	RLH	621
Forth they wenten	withouten ensoyne		1475

In view of the frequency of formulas at the beginning as well as at the end of the line it is not surprising to find that the formula sometimes extends to a whole line. Instances occur among the lines quoted in the previous discussion, but a few others may be offered here in evidence. It should be remembered that the substitution of a metrically equivalent word (*so, sone, that, tho*) is permitted in the formula:

(a) That with inne a lite stonde   Beves   733
    And tho in a lite stonde   885
    Sone with inne a lite stounde   1258
    So with inne a lite stounde   1409
    Tho with inne a lite stounde   3489
    So that in a lite stounde   4393
    Well sone in a lytull stounde   Guy (Cbg.)1250
    So that in a lytull stownde   3317
    That wythynne a lytull stownde   3363
    And ther wythynne a lytull stsownde   10757
    Sone withinne a lytyl stounde   RLH 4565
    So that withinne a lytyl stounde   6115
    So that on a litel stund   Hav. 1858

(b) Bothe in yrene and in stel   Beves 2728
    Bothe in yron and in stele   Guy (Cbg.) 960
    Bothe in yron and in stele   1548
    Bothe in yron and in stele   2398
    Bothe in yron and in stele   1644
    Bothe in yron and in stele   2816
    Bothe in yron and in stele   3388
    Bothe in yron and in stele   4976
    Bothe in yron and in stele   6048
    Odur in yron or in stele   8860
    Bothe in yryn and in steel   RLH 2544
    Bothe in yren and in steel   2788
    Bothe in yren & in steel   5658
    Bothe in yryn & in steel   6048

(c) With his swerd that wele bote   Guy   3562
    With her swerdes that wil wel bite   2934
    With swerdes that wil wele bite   5198
    With his fauchon that wele bote   3556
    With hys fawchoun that byttyr bot   RLH 4874
    Wyth a swerde that wolde wele byte   Guy 1056
                                                   (Cbg.)
    Wyth brondys that full wele cowde   7986
      byte
    Wyth ther swyrdys that well cowde   10960
      byte
    Wyth my swyrde that well can byte   11511
    With Morgelay, that wolde wel bite   Beves 3407

It is unnecessary to carry the matter further, although at times a couplet assumes the character of a formula, at least within a single romance. Thus in the Caius manuscript of the *Beves* (pp. 132–134) we find these three almost identical couplets:

A good swerd he gan out breyde,
And on the dragoun faste he leyde.   (23–4)

Hys swerd he gan out to breyde,
And on the dragoun faste he leyde.   (55–6)

Hys swerd he gan out for to breyde,
And on the dragoun faste he leyde.   (95–6)

Again, in the version of *Guy of Warwick* in the Cambridge University Library manuscript (sometimes called *Guy B*) the following couplets occur:

Nowe begynneth newe batayle:
Echon odur faste can assayle.   (1027–8)

Then began a grete batayle:
Echon odur faste can assayle.   (1825–6)

There beganne a grete batayle:
Every man odur faste can assayle.   (1939–40)

There beganne a stronge batayle:
Eyther other faste dud assayle.   (9347–8)

The second line also occurs without the first:

Ayther can odur faste assayle.   (5030)

Other instances of such repeated couplets are to be found, though they are naturally not common, and they may be due to the habit of the individual poet.

III

The use of *themes*—recurring features of the description of narrative which are treated according to an established pattern—is one of the characteristics of oral composition, and occurs also in the Middle English romances. Naturally, some of those that are common in the Old French epic have their equivalents in English. I have cited one of Rychner's examples above, the arming of a knight. Such descriptions in the English romances likewise follow a conventional pattern, although the knight is generally described as arming himself. It should be remembered that in the theme verbal identity is not expected. In English the knight girds on a sword, takes a spear in his hand, hangs a shield about his neck or at his side, and rides off:

A gerte him with a gode brond
And tok a spere in his hond,

A scheld a heng upon is side,
Toward the wode he gan ride.   Beves 759–62

And gerte him with a gode bronde
And tok a gode spere in is honde;
A scheld aboute is nekke he cast
And wente out of the chaumber in hast.   *Ibid*. 1667–70

And gerte him with a gode bronde
And tok a spere in is honde
Out ate gate he gan ride . . .   *Ibid*. 2729–31

And gerte him with a gode brond
And tok a spere in is honde,
Aboute his nekke a double scheld:
He was a knight stout and belde.
On Arondel a lep that tide,
In to the strete he gan ride.   *Ibid*. 4367–72

Sythen he gurde hym wyth hys bronde:
Hyt was worthe moche londe.
Hys schylde he caste abowte hys halse
And a spere he toke alse.
Hys gode stede he bestrode:
Forthe of the cyte sone he rode.   Guy B 3625–30

Sethe he gert him with a brond
That was y-made in elvene lond.
His scheld about his nek he tok,
On hors he lepe with-outen stirop,
On hond he nam a spere kerveinde,
Out of the cite he was rideinde.   Guy 3861–6

Another conventional theme involves the question "What is your name?" or "Where do you come from?" and the prompt answer, sometimes with the assurance that the person questioned will not lie or conceal his name. When Horn and his companions arrive on the western strand to which their small boat drifts, the king questions them:

Tho spac the gode kyng;
He nes never nythyng:
"Sey, child, whet is thy name?
Shal the tide bote game."
The child him onsuerede
So sone he hit yherde:
"Horn ycham yhote.
Ycome out of this bote
From the see side:
Kyng, wel the bitide!"   Horn 203–12

In a similar' situation Beves is questioned:

> "Child," a seide, "whar wer the bore?
> What is the name? telle me fore!
> Yif ich it wiste, hit were me lef."
> "For gode," a seide, "ich hatte Bef,
> Iboren ich was in Ingelonde,
> At Hamtoun, be the se stronde;
> Me fader was erl thar a while," etc.   Beves 539–45

In *Guy of Warwick*, the Cambridge version, we have:

> "Syr knyght, telle me beforne:
> What ys thy name? where were thou borne?"
> "Gye of Warwyk, for sothe, y hyght:
> In Ynglonde was y borne aryght."   Guy B629–32

and later he questions Herhaud in similar terms:

> "Gode man," he seyde, "what ys thy name?
> So god the schylde fro synne & schame."
> "Harrawde," he seyde, "men clepe me
> Of Ardurne in that cuntre."   *Ibid*. 1339–42

The knight often expresses his willingness to answer:

> "Sir knight," he seyd, "y prey the,
> Tel me thi name and whenne tow be."
>   Sir Gij answerd wel freliche,
> "Y schal the tel ful bletheliche:
> Gij of Warwike men clepeth me;
> Ich was y-born in that cuntre."   Guy 933–8

or says he will not conceal his name:

> Quath the soudan, "whennes artow,
> Into mi court comen art now,
> & misseysts me so schameliche,
> & thetest me so dedeliche?"
>   Gij answered, "ich-il the telle:
> Mi name for-hele y nille.
> Gij of Warwike mi name is;
> In that cuntre y was born y-wis."   *Ibid*. 3935–42

In *Richard the Lion-Hearted*, as a preliminary to a proposal of marriage Henry asks the lady her name:

> Thenne askyd he that lady bryght:
> "What hyghtest thou, my swete wyght?"
>   "Cassodorien, withouten lesyng,"
> Thus answeryd sche the kyng.   RLH 171–4

Such a conventional question and answer is of frequent occurrence in the romances and many other examples could be cited. When the poet or minstrel came to a point where an inquiry of this sort was appropriate he knew exactly what to do. In dealing with the theme the story teller follows an established pattern.

The most extended theme is the description of a fight, an encounter between two knights or a battle; the latter is generally a succession of such encounters. The frequency with which this theme occurs varies with the nature of the story. *Beves* and *Guy of Warwick* yield the most examples. In it there are certain recurring elements, not all of which are present in all examples, but all recur with sufficient frequency to indicate that they are part of the general stock upon which the narrator drew. They may be set down in a more or less logical order, as follows:

1. The opponent approaches
2. The hero takes note, or "stood and beheld"
3. He leaps into the saddle.
4. He spurs his horse
5. He shouts an angry defiance or orders his opponent to yield
6. He rides against the foe
7. The knights meet head-on; or
8. They strike each other
9. Fire flies
10. One strikes the other's shield
11. Part of the shield (helmet, hauberk) flies off
12. The hand goes too
13. He strikes the helmet
14. He strikes the head
15. He strikes the head off, or it flies off
16. He strikes the neck, shoulder, side, etc.
17. The spear breaks
18. He unhorses his opponent
19. He fells horse and man
20. Both are unhorsed
21. He draws his sword
22. The sword bites well
23. He strikes with sword
24. They lay on eagerly, fight "as they were [mad]," spare not
25. He cleaves opponent to the saddle, chin, etc.
26. He cuts the body, etc. in two
27. He kills opponent or gives a deadly wound
28. He pierces him through the body, heart, etc.
29. He fells him to the ground, or
30. The enemy falls to the ground (dead)
31. Armor availed not

32. He taunts the vanquished foe
33. "With that came . . ."
34. He smote him
35. The victor returns home, or departs, with or without prisoners

In addition to these rather specific details of the action there are certain
subsidiary features or types of general comment:

36. The knight is stung by injury or anger to retaliate
37. He is "full woe," "in heart wroth," etc.
38. The knight is named or characterized parenthetically
39. Size of host stated
40. How long they fought
41. Why tell a long story?
42. Summing things up
43. None could stand against him (them)
44. The hero slays many
45. Prisoners are taken
46. The enemy flees, or
47. None escaped alive
48. Never before was such a fight
49. The victors give thanks

* * * these are the keys which the narrator can press and receive from
his mental storehouse an idea suitable at the moment. Since it is an
idea or motif that he is summoning, he is not bound to express it always
in identical words but is free to vary it to suit the context, especially the
rime. It is interesting to note, nevertheless, how frequently the same
words are used. It is not necessary to point out that not all the forty-
nine elements are used in any one occurrence of the battle theme, nor
are those selected employed in a fixed sequence. Rather the story teller
may select freely from the stock and assemble the units in any way he
chooses.

* * *

IV

The formula and the theme are the features of improvisation upon
which most stress is laid in discussions of the Greek, Jugoslav, and Old
French epic. There is, however, in the English romances another which
seems to be somewhere between these two and to be of equal importance.
It is of very frequent occurrence and may be called the *predictable
complement*. Certain statements seem to call up automatically in the
mind of the poet or reciter a conventional way of completing the thought.
It is as though he were subject to a kind of conditioned reflex. Generally
the statement and its predictable complement form a couplet, and this

feature of the composition is the result of the fact that the couplet is the basic unit of most English romances, even the stanzaic romances. Here couplets are linked by tail lines, whether the stanza is the romance six or the twelve-line tail-rime stanza, a combination of two romance sixes. Considerations of rime are doubtless responsible for many a predictable complement, but are not the complete explanation. Such complements occur not only where rime words are not easy to find but in cases where there is a considerable range of choice. We may illustrate this, as well as the feature itself, by considering the word *knight*, which naturally occurs with great frequency in the romances.

The word *knight* is not a difficult rime word. It rimes with *dight*, *fight*, *hight*, *light*, *might*, *night*, *thight*, *right*, *sight*, *tight* (verb), and *wight* (noun and adjective), and all these rimes are actually found in the romances I am considering. But three of them occur with such frequency as to suggest that the narrator tends to fall into a few conventional thought patterns. For example, upon mention of a knight (or knights) it is very common to add that he was good in a fight:

On everyche lepte an Englysshe knyght,	
Stowte in armes, and stronge in fighte.	RLH 2275–6
And bad hym take with hym knyghtes,	
Stoute in armes, stronge in fyghtes.	RLH 5177–8
He made here warde of noble knyghtes,	
Stoute in armes, stronge in fyghtes.	RLH 5945
Thorwgh help off hys gode knyghtys,	
Stoute in arms and stronge in fyghtes.	RLH 6503–4
So that ichave fourti knightes,	
Stoute in armes & strong in fightes.	Beves 3605–6

It happens that in the five illustrations the second line of the couplet is practically the same throughout. But the idea can be expressed with variations in wording:

Afftyr comen barouns and knyghtes,	
An hundryd thousand stronge in fyghtes.	RLH 2979–80
Thai weren bothe strong knightes,	
Bold and hardi in ich fightes.	Guy 779–80
Of everich londe thider com knightes,	
That strong ben & bold in fightes.	Guy 813–4
Than com Torald, a gode knight,	
Swithe gode & hardi in fight.	Guy 1379–80
& with him other fifti knight,	
In feld the best that might fight.	Guy 1919–20

With fif hundred armed knightes,
Hardi & wele doand in fightes.   Guy 2323–4

Sir Gij toke an hundred of his knightes,
Strongest and best in fightes.   Guy 2861–2

With him he hath an hundred knightes
Of Almayne, the best in fightes.   Guy 3127–8

He was coraious & gode knight,
& michel adouted in everich fight.   Guy 3465–6

& with hem fif hundred knightes,
Orped men & gode in fightes.   Guy 6061–2

Many other changes are rung on the rime *knight-fight*, which would only serve to demonstrate the ingenuity of the poet or the variety of stock phrases available to carry out the same sequence of thought.

The adverbial phrase *anon riht* is a formula that serves as an easy rime in many couplets. In *Guy of Warwick* it is a favorite in couplets where in one line a knight is struck and in the next line falls dead:

Wel sternliche he smitt a knight,
That ded he fel anon right.   Guy 2231–2

Wel hardeliche he smot a knight,
That ded he felt him anon right.   Guy 2399–2400

He forth yede & smot a knight,
That ded he feld him anon right.   Guy 3515–6

His feren he rescoud as a gode knight,
Mani on he feld ded anon right.   Guy 5107–8

Anon he smot another knight
That ded he feld him anon right.   Guy 5219–20

The same sequence of ideas is apparent in

Wel heteliche he smot a knight,   Guy 5119–20
His bodi he clef adoun right.

Another he smot him as gode knight,   Guy 5133–4
Of his stede he feld him doun right.

As we have just seen, the hero sometimes takes a hundred or five hundred knights, hardy or strong in fights. But the second line may instead indicate that he sets out at once against the enemy, again with the rime *anon riht*:

He tok with him sex knights
And wente forth anon rightes.   Beves 4291–2

Nim we now an hundred knights,
& go asayl hem anon rightes.   Guy 2337–8

For ther were a thousand knyghtes   Guy 2109–10
With theim to mete anon Rightes.   (Caius)

& with him went alle the knightes,
Acord to make anon rightes.   Guy 6621–2

and with a slight variation of the adverbial phrase

Mani was the gentil knight
That with hem went tho right.   Guy 6695–6

But the rime *knight-anon right* lends itself to a variety of situations:

Whi slough ye that ich knight?
Alle ye schul die anon right.   Guy 4705–6

The bodi thai toke of that knight,
Opon a pal leyd it anon right.   Guy 4848–6

With fif hundred of gode knights:
An acumbraunce ous come anon rightes.   Guy 5165–6

When Gij him seye he knewe the knight,
He kist him ther anon right.   Guy 6041–2

With such a universally applicable adverbial phrase it is to be expected
that inversion would be easy and therefore common:

King Yvor grauntede anon rightes;
He let him chese fourti knightes.   Bees 3611–2

Josiane tho anon rightes
Clepede to hire twei knightes.   Beves 673–4

King Ermin tho anon righte
Dobbede Beves un-to-knighte.   Beves 969–70

And sai themperur anon right,
That i nam no Frensche knight.   Beves 3065–6

And armede ther anon rightes
Bothe he and is sex knightes.   Beves 4365–6

And kiste hire anon right
And sente after baroun & knight.   Beves 3171–2

With that stirt forth anon right
Otus cossyn, an unwrast knight.   Guy 5733–4

In all these cases it can hardly be doubted that the pattern in the narrator's mind is the rime *anon right-knight*, rather than any conventional sequence of ideas, and perhaps these cases should not be cited here. They represent, however, an associated phenomenon, and may have come about through the rime pattern in such cases of predictable complement as I have just cited.

Since strength and courage are such indispensable attributes of the knight, it was inevitable that the association of *wight* and *knight* should appeal to some poets. It was a favorite of the *Havelok* author:

> Thi-self shal dubben him to kniht,
> For-thi he is [man] so wiht.   Hav. 2042–3

> And so shaltu ben maked kniht
> With blisse, for thou art so wiht.   Hav. 2186–7

> In this middelerd nis no kniht
> Half so strong, ne half so wiht.   Hav. 2244–5

and with inversion of the rimes

> Bernard was trewe, and swithe wiht,
> In al the borw ne was no kniht. . . .   Hav. 1756–7

> For y se thu art so wiht,
> And of thi bodi so god kniht.   Hav. 2720–1

The prowess of a knight may also be symbolized by the word *might*:

> Now is sir Gij dobbed to knight;
> Feir he was and michel of might.   Guy 723–4

> He rode to him as a gode knight,
> He semed a man of miche might.   Guy 873–4

> Anon thai nomen an hundred knightes,
> Hardi & of most mightes.   Guy 2347–8

The following couplet shows inversion of the rimes, but the lines are the same syntactically in either order:

> So strong he is & of so gret might,
> In world y wene no better knight.   Guy 2907–8

But *might* may also be a verb:

> Of al the londe the stringeste knighte,
> That hii owhar finde mighte.   Beves 3309–10

> Never no was an-lepy knight
> That so mani stond might.   Guy 3991–2

Finally, the association of *knight*, *might*, and *fight* is neatly represented in the couplet

> A knight he was of gret might.
> Swithe gode & hardi in fight.   Guy 1419–20

There is not space to deal with all the conventional sequences of ideas in such couplets, but it may be noted in passing that in *Guy of Warwick* the author seems to like to open the second line with a phrase indicating nationality or geographical origin:

> Gauter come prikeing anon right,
> *Of Almayne* a wel gode knight.   Guy 2953–4

> & sethe he slough a Freyns knight,
> *In Bleyves* he was born aright.   Guy 2981–2

> With that come another knight
> *Of Fraunce y-bore*, Amori he hight.   Guy 5327–8

> With that com forth the steward light,
> *A Brabasone he was*, a wel god knight.   Guy 6899–6900

One of the predictable complements of greatest frequency is associated with the description of combats whether between individual adversaries or collective forces. A blow is delivered with sword or lance and the victim is felled by it in conventional phrasing. Instances occur among the illustrations already cited. But while I have given a number of examples involving the rime *knight-(anon) right*, the complement is not limited to this rime. Indeed, nowhere do we find better evidence that we are dealing not with a particular rime pair but with an almost inevitable sequence of ideas than in the great variety of rimes involved:

> With grete strengthe sir Gij him smot
> That he feld him anon fot hot.   Guy 3509–10

> To the douk Segyn he smot,
> & of his hors feld him fot hot.   Guy 2383–4

> Gij the steward so hard smot,
> Of his stede he feld him fot hot.   Guy 1957–8

> Gij to the steward hath y-smite,
> Of his hors he feld him with hete.   Guy 5147–8

> Sir Gij him smot to Gaier,
> & feld him doun of his destrer.   Guy 2355–6

> I smot hym that alle folk it seygh,
> Doun off hys hors almost he fleygh.   RLH 545–6

Ac a failede of his divis
And in the heved smot Trenchefis,
That ded to grounde fel the stede.   Beves 1887–9

With a dente amyd the shelde;
His horse he bare downe in the felde   RLH 291–2

& mani another he hath aqueld,
& adoun feld in the feld.   Guy 2995–6

Ermine he smot on thurch the scheld;
Almost he feld him in the feld.   Guy 3499–3500

The bodi atuo he hath to-deled,
That he fel doun in the feld.   Guy 2957–8

(where the consequence is not surprising)

Herhaud him hath ther afeld,
That dede he lay in the feld.   Guy 5229–30

Tirri another smite bigan,
That ded he feld bothe hors & man.   Guy 5479–80

& smot him so upon the croun,
That man and hors de clevede doun.   Beves 4513–4

And smot him so up-on the crune,
That Godrich fel to the erthe adune.   Hav. 2734–5

Upon is helm in that stounde,
That a felde him flat to grounde.   Beves 1039–40

Upon the helm in that stounde,
That man and hors fel to grounde.   Beves 3433–4

To a Lombard smot sir Gij,
& feld him & his fere him by.   Guy 5477–8

Thurch the bodi he him carf atuo:
Ded he fel to grounde tho.   Guy 7283–4

With his fest he him smot so,
That to grounde he dede him go.   Guy 5789–90

And on the geauntes brest a wonde,
That negh a felde him to the grounde.   Beves 1909–10

And smot ato his nekke bon:
The geaunt fel to grounde anon.   Beves 1919–20

In twoo he brak hys cheke-bon;
He fel doun ded as ony ston.   RLH 797–8

Rychard hym smot, forsothe to say,
Evene in twoo hys cheke-bon.
He fyl doun ded as ony ston.   RLH 866–8

Thourgh is bodi wente the dent,
Ded a fel on the paviment.   Beves 4383–4

And [the dragon] smot his hors with the taile
Right amideward the hed,
That he fel to grounde ded.   Beves 2780–2

That his heved he him to-clef:
Al to ded to ground he dref.   Guy 6905–6

Themperur he smot with is spere,
Out of is sadel he gan him bere
    And threw him to grounde.   Beves 232–4

Gij him smot ogain, no might he as naught,
That he hath the grounde y-raught.   Guy 6977–8

Ther-with he smot Ebban the king,
That ded he fel withouten letting.   Guy 3521–2

A little more novelty is introduced in *King Horn* when we are told

> The sarazyn he hitte so
> That is hed fel to ys to.   Horn 605–6

Although this list of examples is a long one, I have omitted more than I have included. Moreover, it could be greatly extended by instances from other romances. They would only prolong what has already reached wearisome length, the proof that given certain statements of frequent occurrence in the first half of the couplet, one can predict with reasonable assurance the idea of the second half. The narrator can complete the thought—one might almost say, without thinking—by drawing upon a stock of ready-made phrases which vary only enough to provide a choice of rimes.

V

In the foregoing discussion I have examined a small group of English romances from the point of view of the theory of oral composition as that theory has been developed in connection with the Homeric poems and recently applied to some early chansons de geste. That theory rests first of all upon the presence of stock expressions which fit a particular metrical need—the *formulas* in Milman Parry's terminology—and, secondly, the presence of certain descriptive or narrative elements, called *themes*, which in their repeated occurrences follow conventional patterns. I think it is beyond question that both of these features are present in the Middle English romances examined. Are we then to conclude that the same inference is to be drawn here as has been drawn by those who have developed the theory in connection with the Homeric poems and advanced it in connection with certain chansons de geste? Are we to believe that those English romances which meet the test of formulaic and thematic elements were composed in the act of oral delivery as are the heroic poems of Jugoslavia? In its full form I do not see how such a conclusion can be accepted.

I hold no brief for or against the theory of improvisation in the Homeric poems. We can never hope to know what lies back of these poems, what Homer or numerous Homers had to work with. But science proceeds by the constant testing of hypotheses, and the theory that certain features of the Homeric poems can be explained by the observed practices of Jugoslav singers of heroic poems at the present time may be rejected by the skeptical but cannot be disproved. Likewise when we turn to the origin of the chansons de geste we are in almost equal darkness. Whether we believe in the theory of cantilenae or epic lays or in the partnership of jongleur and cleric we do not know what lies behind the *Chanson de Guillaume* or *Raoul de Cambrai*. While the supreme art of the *Roland* (as of the *Iliad*) will prevent many from accepting the theory of oral composition, the theory cannot be disproved in the absence of any knowledge of the literary sources of the heroic poetry of medieval France. But for the Middle English romances the situation is quite different. Many of the Middle English romances are translations or else adaptations of French poems. In cases where the French original can be identified, at least as to its approximate form, the similarities are often such as to leave little doubt that the English poet was following his source with reasonable fidelity, such fidelity as to suggest that the source lay open in a manuscript before him.

The version of *Beves of Hampton* in the Auchinleck manuscript and its four congeners is an interesting text to study from the point of view of oral improvisation. It contains a considerable number of verbal clichés. If we could assume that the minstrel in reciting the story was also partially composing it as he went along, many of these clichés would qualify as formulaic elements. But there can be little doubt that we have to do here with a translation, an English rendering of a French text. There are first of all references to a source—"seith the bok" (844, 2468), "so hit is fonde in frensche tale" (888), "the romounce telleth" (1537), "So hit is in Frensch y-founde" (1782). There are still other allusions to the French source in the Cambridge manuscript. While such references could be conventional, I have found that in general when they occur in an English romance they are likely to be confirmed by other evidence. And that happens to be the case in the present instance. There are four versions of the *Beves* romance in Old French (disregarding the version in prose), differing so from one another that Stimming was compelled to publish them separately. One is Anglo-Norman, the other three Continental. (The A-N is in vol. 7 of the *Bibliotheca Normannica*; the others are in the series published by the Dresden Gesellschaft für romanische Literatur, vols. 25, 30, 34, 41–42.) A very little examination of these four texts suffices to establish the fact that the English version we are considering is based on the Anglo-Norman, which happens to be the earliest of the French versions. While the English is a free paraphrase, it follows the French text so closely as to leave no doubt of the relationship, and there are verbal correspondences which are con-clusive. The relationship may be indicated by a few stanzas at the beginning.

A-N *BOEVE DE HAUMTONE*
(ed. Stimming, Bibliotheca
Normannica, VII)

Seingnurs barons, ore entendez a
    mei,
si ws dirrai gestes, que jeo diverses
    sai,
de Boefs de Haumtone, li chevaler
    curtays,
ke par coup de espeie conquist tant
    bons reys.
Si vus volez oyer, jeo vus en dirrai;
unkes ne oistes meyllur, si com jeo
    crai.

Seingnurs, si de lui oyer desirez,
Jeo vus en dirrai, kar jeo sai asez;
primes vus en dirrai de soun
    parentez.
A Haumtone fu li quens plein de
    bontez,
il out a noun Guioun, chevaler fu
    prisez;
meilour de lui ne fust en son tens
    trovez.

Seignurs, iceo quens Guioun
    dount vus chaunt
estoit bon chavaler, pruz e
    combataunt;
mes de une chose lui alout home
    blamaunt,
k'ainz ne vout femme prendre en
    tot son vivaunt,

BEVES OF HAMPTON (AUCH. MS)
(ed. Kölbing, EETSES, XLVI)

Lordinges, herkneth to me tale!

Is merier than the nightingale,

    That y schel singe;

Of a knight ich wile ghow roune,

Beves a highte of Hamtoune,
    With outen lesing.

Ich wile yow tellen al to gadre
Of that kinght and of is fadre,
    Sire Gii:

Of Hamtoun he was sire

And of al that ilche schire,

    To wardi.

Lordinges, this, of whan y telle,

Never man of flesch ne felle

    Nas so strong,

And so he was in ech strive,

dunt pus se repenti par le men ascient.	And ever he levede with outen wive, Al to late and long.
Mes quant il fu veuz home e out long tens vescu,	Whan he was fallen in to elde,
donk prist il femme que de haute gent fu,	that he ne mighte him self welde,
file au roi de Escoce cele dame fu.	He wolde a wif take;
Guioun la prist a femme, lui chevaler membru.	Sone thar after, ich understonde,
Puis avint cel jour que mult iré en fu,	Him hadde be lever than al this londe,
ke il perdi le chef par desus le bu.	Hadde he hire forsake.

But there is still more interesting evidence. The English poem under-goes a change of metrical form at line 475 of the Auchinleck manuscript. At this point the meter changes from a six-line stanza ($aa^4b^3cc^4b^3$, oc-casionally $aa^4b^3aa^4b^3$) to four-stress couplets. Kölbing in editing the romance noted the change but confessed that he could not account for it, saying that there was nothing "to correspond with this change in the original French versions" (EETSES, LXV, p. xi). In this he appears to have been mistaken. The Anglo-Norman version does undergo a change in the versification. It is written in laisses like other chansons de geste. Of the 3,850 lines of which it consists the first 2,338 are in laisses in which the final syllables rime, but in the remaining 1,512 lines the laisses are bound together by assonance. But there is a more significant change. As Sarrazin, the editor, notes, the length of the laisses undergoes a very noticeable change after laisse 66 (which ends at line 415). Up to this point they have all been short, generally six lines, with an occasional divergence to five or seven. The effect is that of a poem written in six-line monorimed stanzas. From this point on the laisses are generally much longer, extending in an extreme instance to 187 lines (with as-sonance). Now the change from monorimed stanzas averaging six lines occurs at very nearly the same point in the story as that at which the English poem changes from six-line stanzas to couplets. While the English adapter's stanzas do not always stand in a one to one relation with the stanzas of the French, since the English poet occasionally omits a stanza, sometimes expands a stanza to two, or even interpolates a stanza of his own (which may, however, have been represented in the particular manuscript he was using), one cannot doubt that he was working with a written text before him. Oral composition would be conceivable only on the assumption that he was truly bi-lingual and could have sung or recited the story in French as well as English. This is conceivable but the less likely of the two possibilities.

It is equally possible to show the close dependence of *Guy of Warwick* upon the French, although the problem is more complicated. In one respect it is simpler. So far as we know there is only one version in French verse, and this has fortunately now been edited from all the manuscripts.[8] On the other hand there appear to be four versions, in whole or part, in Middle English. For my present purpose one of these will suffice; it is in couplets and is in many ways the best. We may call it the Caius-Auchinleck version.[9] It is so close to the French text that the two often correspond line for line. Although the relationship is beyond question, I quote for convenience a few lines. It is the passage in which Guy, having met Felice's requirement that he prove himself as a knight, returns to ask the fulfillment of her promise:

GUY OF WARWICK
French text, ll. 1039–54

Gui a Felice s'en est alé;
Mult ducement l'ad salué:
"Venuz sui, ma bele amie,
Par vus ai certes la vie;
Se ne fuissez, jo fuisse morz,   5
Destruiz e malbailliz del cors.
Les armes prendre me feistes,
Vostre pleisir puis me deistes:
Quant jo les armes pris avreie,
E la mer passé serreie,   10
E loinz en estrange regné
D'armes fuisse bien preisé,
Granté me serreit l'amur de vus,
Dunt ai esté tant desirus;
Ore sui venuz pur oir,   15
Bele amie, vostre plaisir."

---

8. *Gui de Warewik, roman du xiiie siècle*, ed. Alfred Ewert, 2v., Paris, 1933; *Classiques français du moyen âge* 74–75. The quotations from the English *Guy of Warwick* are from the Auchinleck MS unless otherwise noted. In Zupitza's edition. (EETSES, XLII, XLIX, LIX) the line numbers 1905–2006 are repeated. Numbers of the second sequence are here followed by an asterisk.

9. The Caius College MS is the most complete. It is paralleled by the Auchinleck MS as far as line 7306, and there is a fragment of one leaf in Sloane MS 1044. It is edited by Zupitza in EETSES, XLII, XLIX, LIX. The second text is in twelve-line tail-rime stanzas, also preserved in the Auchinleck MS, and begins where the couplet version in this manuscript stops. A third version, in couplets, is only known from three brief fragments. The fourth, likewise in couplets, is in a manuscript in the University Library, Cambridge. This is edited by Zupitza in EETSES, XXV-XXVI. However, two long passages totaling more than 2,000 lines in this otherwise independent version parallel the text in the Caius MS.

CAIUS MS, LL. 1115–30

On a daye he is to Felice goo,
And full lovyngly he seith hir too:
"I am comme as thou may see.
My lif y have, lemman, thurgh
    thee:
Ne were thou, lemman, dede y
    were,   5
My body destroied and leide on
    bere.
Armes y toke for love of the,
Thoo thy wille thou tolde me,
That, whan y had armes take,
Thou woldest not than me
    forsake.   10
And thou hast herde me preised
    bee
In many astraunge contree:
Thy love shuld not me bee
    werned,
For y have it, me thinketh,
    ayerned.
Sweting, nowe y am comme to
    the,   15
Thy wille therof thou telle me."

AUCHINLECK MS, LL. 1115–30

To Felice than sir Gij is go;
Sweteliche he seyd hir to:
"Leman," he seyd, "wele thou be,
Mi liif ichave for love of the;
Ded ich were yif thou nere,
Mi bodi destrud and leyd on bere.
When thou thi wille hadde seyd to
    me,
Armes y fenge for love of [the]
& when ich hadde armes take,
Thou seyd thou nolest me forsake,

Thou noldest thi love werne to me;
& nou ich am her comen to the:
Dere leman, y prey the
Thi wille thatow tel to me."

With respect to the other romances under consideration we are not
so fortunate. No source has been found for *Richard the Lion-Hearted*,
although there are many references in it to "the book," which the editor,
Karl Brunner, assumes to be a lost romance in French. The *Havelok*
story is known in two Anglo-Norman forms, but neither is the source
of the English romance. Nor is the Anglo-French *Horn et Rimenhild*
the source of *King Horn*. No other version of *Athelston* is known.

Thus of the six romances under consideration in this paper we are
able to study only two in relation to their source, but these two—*Beves
of Hampton* and *Guy of Warwick*—furnish convincing proof that they
were not originally the products of oral composition.

VI

Are we then to dismiss the whole question of improvisation from our
minds and to regard the presence of large numbers of formulas and
themes in English romances as proof only of the ineptness of the poets
who composed them? If this were the only conclusion to which the
present study leads, I am afraid I should have done no more than

convince you that Middle English poets had no monopoly on the in-significant. But it has not been my purpose to lead you by a circuitous route to so unrewarding a destination.

In seeking the answer to our question we must approach the problem from the point of view of medieval conditions and not those to which we are accustomed, and you must permit me a few platitudes. A basic feature of those conditions was a listening audience rather than one which took in the written word through the eye. While literacy outside the clerical class was doubtless spreading at the end of the Middle Ages, it was still quite limited, and anything that could be called the reading habit was nonexistent. Even if the ability to read were more general than it apparently was, the scarcity and expensiveness of books would have put a severe limitation upon its exercise. In other words, we must think of the purveying of literary entertainment as mainly oral—the singing, recitaiton, or reading aloud of a minstrel or some one performing his function. This is not the place to present the evidence for these three types of performance, but unless the words, *sing*, *tell*, and *read* have no meaning in Middle English I believe we must conclude that all three methods were on occasion employed. But once again we must be careful not to attribute modern meanings to medieval words. Anyone who has read the late Professor Chaytor's *From Script to Print* will be slow to think of the reading process in the Middle Ages as involving the easy and rapid transference of written symbol to word and idea that characterizes the modern educated person. In many cases a book would only have assisted the minstrel's memory.

Now if we start with the fact that the medieval minstrel singing or reciting the story of *Guy of Warwick* or *Beves of Hampton* must have been doing very much what the singer of a similar Jugoslav poem does, we may well inquire whether his performance involved a similar combination of memory and improvisation, including the use of stock formulas and themes. And if there is an *a priori* probability that this is so, is there any specific evidence that can be used to test this probability?

It is not uncommon in discussions of the Middle English romances to talk about *Guy of Warwick*, *Beves of Hampton*, or *Richard the Lion-Hearted* as we talk about other long poems like *The Owl and the Nightingale* or, let us say, the A-text of *Piers Plowman*, and thus give the impression that we have to do with a single literary composition which has undergone merely such alteration and corruption as results from the conscious tampering or unconscious lapses of medieval scribes—modernization of language or idea, modification of dialect, or mistakes of transcription, and the like. But with respect to romances I believe this is often not the case.

And here it is necessary to pause long enough to point out that the Matter of England romances, which we are here alone considering, fall into two quite distinct groups. There is the relatively short and fairly unified story like *Havelok* and *King Horn* and *Athelston*, and there is the long narrative made up of an endless succession of individual adventures in which the principal character or one of the main characters is involved. *Beves of Hampton*, *Guy of Warwick*, and *Richard the Lion-Hearted* are examples of the latter type. A characteristic of these romances of loosely strung adventures is their repetitiousness. The same situation—for example, the combat of the hero with an opponent, the free-for-all fighting of a battle in which the hero engages all comers— occurs over and over and lends itself to conventional narrative patterns. For some reason the shorter and more unified type has survived in fewer manuscripts and fewer "versions." *Havelok* and *Athelston* are known from only one manuscript each, and *King Horn* survives in only three. On the other hand there are seven manuscripts and one early printed text of *Beves*, six texts (counting fragments) of *Guy of Warwick*, and eight of *Richard the Lion-Hearted*. Moreover, the variations between the manuscripts containing these longer narratives are often quite striking, so great that it is generally impossible to establish a single critical text with the variants adequately reported in footnotes. Indeed, the attempt to do so has at times obscured the extent to which the different manuscripts differ from one another except where these differences are so extensive as to force the editor to print long passages independently in the notes. If it were not for certain bookish productions, one might venture the observation that the number of what are really separate versions of a story is in direct proportion to the length of the story.

As I see it, the answer to our question depends upon a study of all the versions of a given text, considering both the lines that are identical (which show that we are dealing with a single poetic composition) and the variations from manuscript to manuscript of that composition (which we must try to account for). If we find that many of these variations cannot be explained by scribal error, alterations such as scribes are known to introduce, or in short by any of the principles of text transmission, we are entitled to ask whether some other explanation accounts for the facts in a satisfactory way. And we must be prepared to do this without thinking in terms of a later time or a different set of conditions. Such a study must be based on romances which have come down to us in more than one manuscript—the more manuscripts the better. And this requirement is best fulfilled among the Matter of England romances by *Beves of Hampton*, *Guy of Warwick*, and *Richard the Lion-Hearted*. Such a study could embrace the whole of a romance, but fortunately the results can be presented rather briefly. If the evidence which I consider significant really exists, it can be seen as well in a hundred lines as in a thousand, often indeed in a relatively brief passage. I shall have to confine myself here to one exhibit, or at most two, from each of the romances just mentioned.

We may begin with *Beves of Hampton*. The romance is an excellent one for such an investigation since all the texts are clearly descended from a single original. I select a short episode which occurs in all seven texts. Beves and Josian are riding through the woods in France, accompanied by Beves's cousin Terri, when they have to stop in order that Josian may give birth to a child. They build her a lodge and then discreetly go some distance away "For hii ne mighte hire paines here." She is delivered of twins. Unluckily Beves has gone too far and Josian is almost immediately kidnapped and carried off. When Beves and Terri return they find only the two children. Wrapping them in ermine cloaks they ride until they meet with a forester, to whom they commit one of the infants. The passage as it appears in the Auchinleck manuscript is as follows (ll. 3723–40):

> Thar nolde hii no long abide,
> Thei lope to horse & gonne ride;
> In the wode a forster thai mette
> And swithe faire thai him grette:
> "God the blesse, sire!" Beves sede,
> "Sighe the eni levedi her forth lede
> Owhar be this ilche way?"
> "Sire, for gode," a seide, "nay!"
> "What dones man ertow, bacheler?"
> "Sire," a seide, "a forster!"
> "Forster, so Crist the be milde,
> Wiltow lete cristen this hethen childe?
> Right, lo, now hit was ibore
> And thong hit hath is moder for-lore:
> Wilt thow kep it for [to] min," a sede,
> "And i schel quite wel the mede?"
> The forster him grauntede ther,
> To kepe hit al the seven yer.

It is not possible to present the seven texts of this passage in parallel columns, and so I resort to the device of printing each line separately, followed by the corresponding line in the other manuscripts. The order of the manuscripts is always the same: Auchinleck (A), Cambridge (Cbg), Chetham Lbrary, Manchester (M), Caius College (Ca), Egerton (E), Naples (N), and the Pynson print (P). Since E and N are practically identical, wherever possible I print only E with the variants of N in parentheses:[1]

3723.	A.	Thar nolde hii no long abide,
	Cbg.	Wolde they no lenger byde,
	M.	No lengere they wold abide,
	Ca.	No lengere wolde they abide,

---

1. I have had to depend on Kölbing's notes for the variants and since he records only changes of wording, the spelling is not necessarily exact.

| E(N). | And no lengere nolde he (they) abide, |
| P. | No lenger there wolde he abyde, |

3724.
A.	Thei lope to horse & gonne ride;
Cbg.	But toke ther horsys & forthe can ride;
M.	But lope on horse & forthe can ride;
Ca.	But lope on horse & gonne to ride;
E(N).	But lept on horse for (& gonne) to ride;
P.	But toke his chyldren and forthe gan ryde.

3725.
A.	In the wode a forster thai mette
Cbg.	In the foreste a man thai mette
M.	In the wode a forster thai mette
Ca.	In the wode forster thai mette
E(N).	*like* A
P.	A foster in the wode he met,

3726.
A.	And swithe faire thai him grette:
Cbg.	And feyre sir Befus him grette:
M.	And Beves hym full feyre grette:
Ca.	*like* A
E.	And sir Beves feire him grette:
N.	Swithe sir Beves wel feire him grette:
P.	And syr Bevys fayre hym gret:

3727.
A.	"God the blesse, sire!" Beves sede,
Cbg.	"Crystys blessyng mote the betyde
M.	"Cryste must the blesse," he said
Ca.	And sayden to hym: "So god the spede
E(N).	"Crist the blesse," he seide than
P.	"Felawe," sayde he to hym than,

3728.
A	"Sighe the eni levedi her forth lede
Cbg.	"Sighe the eni wumman thys way ryde
M.	"Sighe the eni man a wumman lede
Ca.	"Sighe the owher a wumman lede
E(N).	"Sighe the eni wumman her forth gon
P.	"Sawest thou ought of suche a man

3729.
A.	Owhar be this ilche way?"
Cbg.	Or here about by any way?
M.	In this ilche derne way?
Ca.	Eythir be path eythir be way?
E(N).	Here about by any way?
P.	Lede a woman by any way?"

3730.
A.	"Sire, for gode," a seide, "nay!"
Cbg.	"Sire," he sayde, "for gode nay!"
M.	*like* A

	Ca.	"Sire," he sayde, "for gode nay!"
	E(N).	*like* A
	P.	"Syr," sayde the foster, "nay!"

3731.	A.	"What dones man ertow, bacheler?"
	Cbg.	What maner of man ertow here
	M.	What ertow, bacheler
	Ca.	What man ertow, he sayde, bacheler
	E(N).	What man ertow, beacheler
	P.	"What maner of man art thou, bach-elere?

3732.	A.	"Sire," a seide, "a forster!"
	Cbg.	"Sire, I am a forster!"
	M.	*like* A
	Ca.	Sire, a seide, "I am a forster!"
	E(N).	*like* A
	P.	"Syr," he sayde, "I am a foster!"

3733.	A.	"Forster, so Crist the be milde.
	Cbg.	Wylt thou, so Crist the be milde
	M.	Wylt thou, so Crist be thy shild
	Ca.	Wylt thou, he sayde, so Crist be the milde
	E(N).	So Crist the fro shame shilde
	P.	"Wylt thou," sayde Bevys, "so Cryst the shylde,

3734.	A.	Wiltow lete cristen this hethen childe?"
	Cbg.	Doo cristen this hethen childe
	M.	Lete cristen me this childe
	Ca.	Doo cristen here an hethen childe
	E(N).	Doo cristen this ilke hethen childe
	P.	Do crysten here an hethen chylde?

3735.	A	Right, lo, now hit was ibore
	Cbg.	Right, lo, now, hit was yn the wode ibore
	M.	This same day it was borne,
	Ca.	For ryght now hit was ibore
	E(N).	Right now ywys hit (he) was ibore
	P.	But ryght nowe was it borne,

3736.	A	And yong hit hath is moder for-lore
	Cbg.	To yong hit hath the moder lore
	M.	To yonge the moder hath it lorne.
	Ca.	The modyr it hath to yung forlore
	E(N).	And (*om.* N) yong he hath is moder lore
	P.	Ful erly it hathe the moder lorne,

| 3737. | A. | Wilt thow kep it for [to] min," a sede, |
| | Cbg. | *lacking* |

M.	And thow kep it to me, a sede
Ca.	And kepen it with mete and wede[2]
E(N).	And kepen it with mete and wede[2]
P.	*see footnote below*[3]

3738.	A.	"And i schel quite wel the mede?"
	Cbg.	*lacking*
	M.	I wyll the well yeld thy mede
	Ca.	And I schal quyte the weel thy mede
	E(N).	*lacking*
	P.	*see footnote below*[3]
3739.	A.	The forster him grauntede ther,
	Cbg.	The forster grauntyd hym ther
	M.	*like* A
	Ca.	The forster grauntyd Beves ryght ther
	E(N).	The forster him grauntede thore (ther)
	P.	*see footnote below*[3]

3740	A.	To kepe hit al the seven ther.
	Cbg.	For to kepe hit seven ther
	M.	For to kepe hit seven ther
	Ca.	To kepe the chyld fulle seven ther
	E(N).	For to kepe hem (him) seven ther
	P.	*see footnote below*[3]

Detailed comment on the variations which occur in the above lines is not necessary. The question which I think we must ask ourselves in examining them is, which are merely scribal and which are not? The changes in the couplet of lines 3737–8 can hardly be due to scribal inadvertence. And if not, then what possible motive could lead two scribes copying from a written exemplar to change their copy (either or both of them) so that in one case we get *"God the blesse, sire!" Beves sede* and in the other *"Crystys blessyng mote the betyde,"* especially as the change involves finding a new rime word? And the variant in the Pynson text not only makes use of a still different rime but so alters the idea that the thought of the couplet has to be completed in the subsequent line. All this seems to me to presuppose a scribe whose function is not to copy a text but to rewrite it, not in the interest of improving a line here and there but throughout the whole of a long poem, for the passage quoted can be matched almost anywhere in the romance. If, on the other hand, the various forms of the passage reflect the recitations of minstrels who substitute and improvise when the memory fails to produce

2. In the Caius MS this line and its complement are placed after line 3734.
3. For 3737–40 Pynson substitutes:

> And kepe it but this seven yere,
> For X marke, and have it here?"
> "Gladly!" sayde the foster tho;
> He toke the chylde & the golde also.

the exact words of a line or a couplet, and who for whatever reason are led to put down the story in writing, or assist in its recording, the differences in our existing texts are understandable.

What is true of the different manuscripts of *Beves of Hampton* is also true of *Guy of Warwick* and *Richard the Lion-Hearted*. But as I have explained above, the problem is complicated in the case of *Guy of Warwick* by the fact that the French original was turned into English, at least in part, four times, and in studying the variants we must be sure we are comparing passages of the same translation. I have already quoted a short passage from two manuscripts of one translation to illustrate the closeness of its dependence on the French. This passage would also serve my purpose here since it contains variations which do not seem to me to be scribal. But in order to present a further specimen for examination I select a passage from the second version in couplets, most completely preserved in the manuscript in the University Library, Cambridge, but some 2,000 lines of which are also represented in the Caius manuscript. And I also choose a short section which happens to be found as well in the brief fragment that has come down to us in Sloane MS 1044. In this way we may compare the readings of three manuscripts. Since the selection is quite short I include the French text and print the four passages in two sets of parallel columns:

GUY OF WARWICK

French ll, 7563 ff.	Caius MS ll. 7389 ff.
Ço fu en mai, el tens d'esté,	It was in may in somers tyde;
Que Gui ert en Warewic la cité.	Guy was at Warrewik in moche pride.
De berser est un jur repeiré,	From huntyng on a daye he is come,
Veneisun ad pris a grant plenté;	
Mult joius e lé se feseit; 5	Grete plente of venyson he hath nome.
A une vespree, que bele esteit.	
Gui en une tur munta,	Moche ioye he made and solas,
En halt as estres se pua;	So that in the evenyng so mery he was.
Le pais envirun ad esgardé,	
E le ciel, qui tant ert esteillé, 10	The Contree he behelde aboute farre,
E le tens, qui ert serré e cler.	And the skye thikke with sterre,
Gui comence dunc a penser	And the weder that was mery and bright.
Cum Deus li out fait grant honur, . . .	Guy bethoughte him anone right
	That god him had so moche honour doo

Sloane MS 1044 (Frag.)
ptd. Zupitza,
Wien. Sitzungs., 74: 629

Camb. Univ. Ms ll. 7119 ff.

It was in may in someres tyde,
Guy was at Warwik with pride.
From huntyng on a day was come,
Gode plente of venesoun had
    nome.
Muche joy he made and
    solace,   5
So that in an evenyng, that
    myry was,
Sir Guy to a toure steigh
And lened him to a corner an
    heigh.
He biheld the cuntre about ferre,
The welkne, that was wel thik of
    sterre,   10
And the weder was myry and
    bright;
And Guy thought him anon
    right . . .
[The fragment breaks off at this
    point.]

Hyt was in a somers tyde,
That Gye had moche pryde:
He came fro huntyng on a day
Wyth grete solace & mekyll play.
They toke plente of veneson
And broght hyt unto the towne.
At evyn he wente into a towre
Wyth moche yoye and honowre.
He behelde there the ayre
And the lande, that was so fayre.
The wedur was clere & sternes
    bryght.
Gye beganne to thynke ryght,
How god, that sate in trynyte,
Had made hym a man of grete poste

Here the Caius and the Sloane texts are fairly close to each other, and to the French; the differences can in most cases be explained as scribal variants. But the divergence of the Cambridge manuscript clearly goes beyond anything that we can attribute to scribal corruption. I have italicized the verses that are most conspicuously different, even where the rime words are the same. It will be noted that while the second line is basically the same in all three English texts it does not render *Warewic la cité* of the French.

In the case of *Richard the Lion-Hearted* the evidence of oral modification is not so frequent. The various manuscripts seem to reflect a written tradition to a greater degree than do the two romances previously examined. Nevertheless, oral modifications are at times evident. The manuscripts fall into two groups representing what the editor calls the *a* and the *b* tradition. Since we do not have the source of the romance for comparison, it is impossible to say whether or not the two traditions represent independent renderings of the assumed French original, but I have adopted the only safe procedure, that of examining the two as though they were independent versions. In his critical edition, Brunner prints as his basic text the Caius manuscript, representing the *a* tradition, supplying the gaps in this manuscript from the closely related text of

Wynkyn de Worde. The variant which I print from B.M. Add. MS 31,042 belongs to the same group, and these are the only texts which preserve the *a* tradition. The verses which I believe show more than scribal variation are again italicized:

Wynkyn de Worde	B.M. Add. MS. 31,042
The fyrste yere that he was kynge 251	In the fyrste yere that he was kynge
At Salysbury he made a justynge	At Salysbery he made a grete justynge
And comaunded every man to be there,	*And comanded that everilke knyghte* *that couthe hym were,*
Bothe with shelde and with spere,	Other with shelde or with spere,
Erles and barons every-chone; 253	Erlles, barouns everylkon
At home ne dwelled never one.	*Lukes that byhynd there byleve none*
On forfeyture, on lyfe and londe,	*For forfetoure of wyfe and lande*
For nothynge that they ne wonde:	And for nothynge that they ne wande.
This was cryed, I understonde,	*That was the crye I understande*
Thorughout all Englonde. 260	*That was cryed therowte all Yngland*
All was for to loke and se	And alle was to looke and to see
The knyghtes that best myght be.	*What knyghte beste doande myght bee*
There they came all at his wyll	*And thedir they come at the kynges wyll*
His comaundemente to fulfyll.	His commandement for to fulfyll.

The *b* tradition contains a 52-line passage not in *a*. Of this tradition the Auchinleck and the Douce manuscripts represent different branches, showing interesting divergences. The lines are inserted between 3346 and 3347 of the *a* tradition:

Auchinleck MS	Douce MS
For wrath worth sike the Kyng of Fraunce, 19	*Therfor evilyd the Kyng of Fraunce,*
His lechis seyde withoute distaunce 20	His leche seyde withowtyn distance
That he ne sholde never hol be	That he ne myth not hol bene
Bute he to Fraunce tourne aye.	But he turnyd home ageyne.
The Kyng of France tho understode	*The kynges councel understode*
That hure consail was trywe & goode	*& seyde the leche was trewe and goode*
	He tok leve at Kynge Richard
	& at the oder aftyrwarde.

His shippes he dighte more and
lasse   25
And wente hom atte Halwe-
Masse.
Kyng Richard on hym gan crie,
And seyde he dude vileynye,
That he wolde for any maladie
Wende of the lond of Surrye,   30
Er he hadde do Godes servyse
For lif or deth in any wise.
The Kyng of Fraunce wolde hym
noght here,
But wente forth on this manere.
For they departede thus,
for soth,   35
Evere after were they wroth.

*The Duke of Burgonye in his stede
he leet*
And of his folk a party gret.
Richard fast on hym gan crie,
And seyde he dede gret vileynye
That he wolde for maladie
Owte of the lond of Surrye
Wyl he wer in Godes servyse
For life or det or any wise.
Kyng Philip nolde hym not here
He partyde wrathe in his manere.
And after that partyng for soth,
Evere after that they were wroth.

Further comment on these passages is unnecessary.

I may close this discussion with a brief recapitulation of the argument and the conclusion to which I think it leads. The paper consists of six sections. In the first I outline the theory of oral composition, as it has been developed in connection with the Homeric poems and applied to the Old French chansons de geste. According to this theory two basic practices are all-important to the singer of heroic poems who partly improvises, party draws upon his memory: the extensive use (1) of *formulas* and (2) of *themes*. In the second and third sections I have shown that formulas and themes are present in certain Middle English romances to a degree fully as great as in the Greek epic and the French chanson de geste, and in the fourth section I have called attention to a feature of the Middle English romances—the predictable complement—which serves a similar purpose. Each poet or minstrel has to a certain extent his own favorite formulas and his own way of treating a theme, as would be expected, but many of these formulas and themes are the common property both of poets who compose in writing and (as I believe) of minstrels. Those who have developed the theory of oral composition have argued that the presence of these features in the *Iliad* or the *Chanson de Guillaume* justifies the conclusion that these poems were composed by those who recited them and in the process of recitation, just as the long narrative poems of Jugoslavia are composed by the *guslars* today. On this opinion I do not take a stand. I am inclined to think that it goes farther than is necessary, that it probably attaches too little importance to memory, and that, whatever changes a poem may undergo later, behind the poem stands the poet. This, I realize, would be criticized by proponents of the theory as begging the question, since in their view the reciter is the poet. However this may be, in the fifth section of my paper I show that the Middle English romances cannot in general have arisen in this way, since in so many cases they are translations of French romances, often so faithful to their source as to make it most likely that the English translator was working with his French original open before him. However, in the final section of my paper I have tried to show that improvisation has had a share in the production of the different versions of the same romance that have come down to us.

In examining the variations between manuscripts I do not suggest that we eliminate the scribe. Some manuscripts were copied and some copyists were careless. Not all the differences between one text and another reflect changes due to the reciter. I am only insisting that while some of these differences are such as can be accounted for by the familiar principles of hermeneutics, many others cannot. The variations when displayed in full, rather than obscured in a mass of textual notes, are seen to be of much the same kind as the variations between different versions of a ballad. As for the ballad, most of us I suppose have given up the romantic idea that *das Volk dichtet* ["the folk wrote"], but the late Professor Gerould once remarked that, if the people did not write the ballads, at least they rewrote them. I have elsewhere argued against the too easy acceptance of the view that the romances were written by minstrels, but in Professor Gerould's sense I believe they were rewritten by minstrels. Once we accept this possibility, many of the less admirable features of the romances—the many bad rimes, the clichés, the constant recurrence of ideas and expressions distinguished only by their lack of freshness, and the positive banalities—will appear not as an indictment of the poet but as the inevitable resort of one who in telling a story "cannot think without hurry about his next word, nor change what he has made, nor, before going on, read over what he has just written,"[4] but is under the immediate necessity of completing a verse, a couplet, or a rime. Whether the evidence which I have presented justifies this interpretation each one must decide for himself. If it does, then we may say that some of the Middle English romances owe their final form in part to improvisation.

* * *

4. Parry, *Harvard Stud. in Class. Philol.* 41: 77, 1930.

GISELA GUDDAT-FIGGE

The Audience of the Romances†

Social Standing

In a pioneer article published in 1961[1] Karl Brunner attempted to draw conclusions from the manuscripts about the kind of audience interested in Middle English romances—certainly a promising starting point. However, just as Brunner's previous paper on the transmission of Middle English verse romances,[2] this article suffers from the fact that Brunner evidently consulted library catalogues but not the manuscripts themselves. In addition, the article is hampered by a lack of clarity regarding the methods of analysis employed. Therefore, most of his results are, as Mehl remarks, "only guesswork and can hardly be proved."[3] A.C. Baugh sees a parallel between the social classes described in the romances and those interested in them[4]—a theory not altogether indisputable. There is, however, a safer way of arriving at a better description of the classes of people interested in Middle English romances: an examination of the language employed in the romance manuscripts. Again, the language used in texts surrounding the romances is not the only relevant aspect in a sociological assessment of their public—this would certainly not do justice to a poem like *Sir Gawain and the Green Knight*—but it will supply a sound basis for further argumentation. By far the largest number of extant romance manuscripts was written in the 14th and especially the 15th century, a period in which the English language was increasingly used by the higher social classes, while the command of French, which had become a foreign language and had its last stronghold in the law courts, was more and more a privilege of the well educated. Latin remained the language of science and the Church.[5] As a consequence of the increasing prosperity of the middle classes, the number of people able to read and write grew steadily in this period. To the "professional literacy" of the clergy and scholars in the earlier Middle

---

† From *Catalogue of Manuscripts Containing Middle English Romances* (München, 1976), 42–52. Reprinted by permission of Wilhelm Fink GmbH & Co., München. Guddat-Figge's parenthetical references to her catalogue numbers have been replaced with footnotes which identify the romances (though, it must be stressed, not other texts) found in the manuscripts under discussion; with the exception of those texts edited for the present volume, the titles of the romances cited are normalized. [Editor]

1. "Middle English Metrical Romances and their Audience", in *Studies in Medieval Literature in Honor of Professor Albert Croll Baugh*, ed. MacE. Leach (Philadelphia, 1961), pp. 219–27.
2. "Die Überlieferung der Mittelenglischen Versromanzen", *Anglia*, 76 (1958), 64–73.
3. Dieter Mehl, *The Middle English Romances of the Thirteenth and Fourteenth Centuries* (London, 1969), p. 265, note 31.
4. A.C. Baugh, "The Middle English Romance: Some Questions of Creation, Presentation, and Preservation", *Speculum*, 42 (1967), 17.
5. Cf. A.C. Baugh, A *History of the English Language*, 2nd ed. (London, 1959), pp. 243–44 *et passim*.

Ages was added the "literacy of the cultivated reader" who read for his own edification and entertainment, and finally the "literacy of the pragmatic reader"[6] who had to read and write for his business activities. Prospective apprentices in several trades had to prove that they had some formal education before they were accepted. Merchants owned books and bequeathed them in their wills—presumably they read them as well. After all, merchants at that time differed very little in their customs and the setting of their domestic life from members of the lower gentry; they could also afford the time spent on education and reading.[7]

The development of scripts ran parallel to the increase in the reading public: the complicated hierarchy of Latin book hands was increasingly replaced by the Anglicana and Secretary scripts. These new book hands were closely related to the cursive chancery scripts which were familiar to lay readers through official use and made the reading of manuscript books a less formidable task.[8]

This is the background against which the romance manuscripts have to be examined. Well over half of the ninety-nine manuscripts (including the fragments) are written entirely in English. A group of sixteen manuscripts with a few Latin titles and explicits will probably have to be added since the Latin tags at best prove some knowledge of Latin on behalf of the scribe, but hardly of the reader. Judging from the rather simple texts, the readers would seem to have been members of the less well educated middle classes, many of them probably women, although female names appear in only a few manuscripts.[9] Typical representatives of this group of manuscripts are Caius Coll. [manuscripts] (MSS.) 174 and 175,[1] British Library (B.L.) MSS. Additional 36523, 36983 and 37492,[2] and Boies Penrose [manuscript] (MS.) 6.[3]

B. L. MS. Cotton Nero A.X., art. 3[4] is also written entirely in English, but it is utterly beyond the scope sketched above. The manuscript is extraordinary in several respects: the four poems it contains are all unique. All four are alliterative poems; such consistency on the part of compilers is rare indeed. Finally, the dream allegory (*Pearl*), the two

6. See M.B. Parkes, "The Literacy of the Laity", in D. Daiches and A.K. Thorlby (eds), *Literature and Eastern Civilization* (London, 1973), II, 555–77.
7. See S. Thrupp, *The Merchant Class of Medieval London [1300–1500]* (Chicago, 1948), pp. 158–59 and 247.
8. Cf. M.B. Parkes, *English Cursive Book Hands* (Oxford, 1969, repr. Ilkley, 1979), pp. xiv–xvi, xix.
9. For example, Cambridge, King's Coll. MS. 13 [which includes *William of Palerne*]; U.L. MS. Ff. I.6 [see below, p. 501, n. 5]; National Libr. of Scotland MS. Adv. 19.3.1 [see below, p. 501, n. 5]; Glasgow U.L. MS. Hunterian V.2.8 [which comprises *The Geste Historiale of The Destruction of Troy*]; B.M. MS. Addit. 35288 [which includes *Partenope of Blois*]; Oxford, University Coll. MS. 142 [which includes *Isumbras*].
1. MS 174 includes *Robert of Sicily*; MS 175 includes *Richard Coeur de Lion, Sir Ysumbras, Athelston,* and *Bevis of Hampton*.
2. MS 36523 includes *Titus and Vespasian*; MS 36983 includes another version of *Titus and Vespasian*; MS 37492 (the "Fillingham MS") includes *Firumbras* and *Otuel and Roland*.
3. Boies Penrose Library MS 6 includes *Partenope of Blois*.
4. MS Cotton Nero A.X. (art. 3) includes *Sir Gawain and the Green Knight*.

Old Testament narratives (*Cleanness* and *Patience*), and the romance (*Sir Gawain and the Green Knight*) in the Cotton manuscript all maintain a literary standard well above the average romance manuscript. *Sir Gawain*, for instance, "is quite unique in its effortless combination of courtly, Arthurian knighthood, a tolerant and realistic sense of humour and uncompromising religious seriousness. . . . The poem is obviously addressed to an audience familiar with the aristocratic manners described."[5] An aristocratic background to these poems fits in well with the influence of French scribal traditions recognizable in the manuscript. The illuminations of this otherwise modest manuscript, which consist of several wholepage miniatures, are also unusual for a romance manuscript. Some of these coloured, artlessly painted pictures[6] seem to have been added later—as if in a not very successful attempt to decorate the manuscript in a manner suitable to its contents.

A number of manuscripts contain sporadic macaronic poems, mostly carols, in addition to Latin titles, or the widely known 51st Psalm in Latin together with an English metrical translation (B. L. MSS. Addit. 10036, 22283, 31042;[7] Bodleian Library MS. Eng. poet. a.1;[8] National Libr. of Wales Deposit MS. Porkington 10/II[9] or the English and Latin versions of the *Disticha Catonis* (Chetham's Library MS. 8009[1]. Several short, mostly religious, poems in Latin without an English paraphrase appear in Bodl. Libr. MSS. Ashmole 61, Rawlinson C. 86/IV and Douce 126.[2]

The only romance manuscript containing more extensive Latin items is Lincoln Cathedral Libr. MS. 91,[3] one of the Thornton MSS. After the romances, from [the eighteenth item] onwards, Thornton entered a group of Latin prayers, antiphones, collects, tracts (frequently by Rolle) and psalms. While laymen may well have been familiar with the religious Latin tags in the manuscripts mentioned above, the Lincoln manuscript makes considerable demands on the theological and, consequently, Latin education of its readers. Whereas in the other manuscripts religious

5. Mehl, pp. 200–201.
6. See Sir I. Gollancz (ed.), *Pearl, Cleanness, Patience and Sir Gawain. Reproduced in Facsimile from the Unique MS. Cotton Nero A.X in the British Museum*, Early English Text Society (EETS), Original Series (OS) 162 (1923, repr. 1955), pp. 7–9. Cf. also R.S. and L.H. Loomis, *Arthurian Legends in Medieval Art* (Oxford, 1959), pp. 138–39.
7. MS 10036 includes *Titus and Vespasian*; MS 22283 (the "Simeon MS") includes *Robert of Sicily* and *The King of Tars*; MS 31042 (the "London Thornton MS") includes *The Siege of Jerusalem, The Sege off Melayne, Duke Roland and Sir Otuel of Spain*, and *Richard Coeur de Lion*.
8. MS Eng. Poet. A.1 (the "Vernon MS") includes *Robert of Sicily* and *The King of Tars*.
9. MS Porkington 10/II includes *Sir Gawain and the Carl of Carlisle*.
1. MS 8009 includes *Sir Torrent of Portyngale, Bevis of Hampton*, and *Ipomadon* (Version A).
2. MS Ashmole 61 includes *Sir Isumbras, The Earl of Tolouse, Libeaus Desconus, Sir Cleges*, and a version of *Sir Orfeo*; MS Rawlinson C.86 includes *Sir Landevale* and *The Weddyng of Syr Gawen and Dame Ragnell*; MS Douce 126 includes *The Siege of Jerusalem*.
3. MS 91 (the "Lincoln Thornton MS") includes the *Prose Life of Alexander*, the alliteratuve *Morte Arthure, Octavian, Isumbras, The Earl of Tolouse, Sir Degrevant, Sir Elgamour of Artois*, a version of *The Awntyrs off Arthure at the Terne Watheleyne*, and *Sir Perceval of Galles*.

items are confined to moralizing and edifying material, the Lincoln manuscript goes beyond this limit by including strictly liturgical Latin texts—collects, antiphones, psalms and hymns.[4] More surprisingly, they are coupled with the romances in the first part and the medical matters at the end of the manuscript. *Miscere utile dulci* ["To mix utility with pleasure"] may have been Thornton's motto in compiling this manuscript. If he really wrote it for his own use and for his family, he proved himself an extraordinarily versatile compiler who had access to material usually beyond the reach of laymen.

A similarly varied but comparatively light mixture of Latin and English texts is offered by National Libr. of Scotland MS. Advocates' 19.3.1[5] in which legends, macaronic poems, romances, Latin mock homilies and carols, moralizing verse tracts, serious religious lyrics and Latin recipes follow each other in a colourful sequence of seriousness and mockery.

The owners of those romance manuscripts which contain Latin scientific, medical, astronomical and historical texts, such as Cambridge, Trinity College MS. 0.2.13;[6] National Libr. of Wales Deposit MS. Porkington 10;[7] Cambridge, University Library (U.L.) MS. Mm.V.14;[8] and B.M. MSS. Cotton Caligula A.II and Cotton Vespasian E.XVI[9] must also at the very least have been interested in secular education.

Bodl. Libr. MS. Greaves 60 began as a Latin exercise book; blanks were filled up later with fragments of the alliterative *Alexander.*[1] In view of the diverse interests of the owners of B.L. MS. Harley 2252[2] and Lambeth Palace Libr. MS. 306,[3] it is not surprising that these two commonplace books contain Latin items, too. The number of romance manuscripts indicating some knowledge of French on the part of their readers is even smaller than the number of those containing Latin items. The very early MS. Gg.IV.27(2)[4] in the Cambridge U.L. and the later Findern Anthology[5] can boast of a few French titles for

---

4. This could also be the case in Huntington Library MS. HM 128 [(which includes the *Siege of Jerusalem*)], unless the part of the manuscript containing the sequences was bound up with the volume at a later date, which seems to me rather likely.

5. MS Advocates' 19.3.1 (the "Auchinleck MS") includes *The King of Tars, Amis and Amiloun, Floris and Blancheflour, Guy of Warwick, Bevis of Hampton, Arthur and Merlin, Lay Le Freine, Roland and Vernagu, Otuel a Knight, King Alexander, Sir Tristrem, Sir Orfeo, Horn Child,* and *Richard Coeur de Lion.*

6. MS 0.2.13 includes *Bevis of Hampton.*

7. See above, p. 500, n. 9.

8. MS Mm.V.14. includes *The Siege of Jerusalem.*

9. MS Cotton Caligula A.II includes *Sir Elgamour of Artois, Octavian, Sir Launfal, Libeaus Desconus, Emaré, The Siege of Jerusalem, Chevelere Assigne,* and *Isumbras*; MS Cotton Vespasian E.XVI includes *The Siege of Jerusalem.*

1. Also known as *Alisaunder*; this is the only romance in the MS.

2. MS Harley 2252 (also known as "John Colyns's Commonplace Book") includes *Ipomadon* (Version B) and the stanzaic *Morte Arthur.*

3. MS 306 includes *Libeaus Desconus.*

4. MS Gg.IV.27 includes *Floris and Blancheflour* and *King Horn.*

5. Otherwise known as Cambridge University Library MS Ff.I.6; the MS includes *Sir Degrevant* and the so-called *Cambridge Alexander-Cassamus Fragment.*

items written in English, but these titles, like the Latin ones mentioned above, are of little consequence since at best they would testify only the scribe's knowledge of French. The Vernon and Simeon Manuscripts[6] contain two poems each where English, French, and Latin versions are given (Vernon: nos 349 and 350, no. 349 only English and French; Simeon: nos 27 and 28). Apart from these manuscripts only four more with French items remain, each of them unique.

Most widely known [of these] is the early anthology B.L. MS. Harley 2253[7] which contains poetry and prose of exceptional literary quality in English, Latin and French. "It is very fortunate for us that his [= the anthologist's] taste was so good, so catholic, and so unconventional, for he has left us a representative selection of a wide variety of different types of lyric, of whose existence we should, but for him, have been ignorant."[8] Prose writing, mostly religious in character, is accompanied by religious lyrics, some of the earliest historical poems extant and the famous love lyrics. MS. Harley 2253 is the most important collection of English secular lyrics of the late 13th and early 14th centuries. Nowhere else is the influence of French poetry manifested as clearly as here: in poems following the models of French *pastourelles* and *reverdies*, showing a deeper impression of the concept of courtly love than almost any other piece of Middle English literature. As detailed research has proved, no two poems were composed by the same author but they were collected from all parts of England and only superficially adapted to the West Midland dialect of the Hereford friar who is reputed to have compiled the anthology.[9] His extensive knowledge of languages and literature and his wide-spread interests which become evident here place him far above the average compiler of manuscripts.

Because of an error of a 15th century scribe we can list the magnificent Bodl. Libr. MS. Bodley 264[1] among the romance manuscripts containing French items. He considered the French *Romans du boin roi Alixandre* in Bodley 264 incomplete and added the episode he believed to be missing from a Middle English Alexander romance (*Alexander B*), with detailed directions for the reader where to insert it. As, however, can be proved by the French parallel versions available, the episode in question was out of place in the Bodley version of the *Alixandre*. The scribe's error signals the interest of an educated public of the early 15th century in Anglo-French poetry along with English literature. This audience was by then at least as familiar with English literature as with

---

6. See above, respectively, nn. 8 and 7, p. 500.
7. MS Harley 2253 includes *King Horn*.
8. G.L. Brook (ed.), *The Harley Lyrics. The Middle English Lyrics of MS. Harley 2253*, Old and Middle English Texts (Manchester, 31964), p. 26.
9. G.L. Brook, "The Original Dialects of the Harley Lyrics", *Leeds Studies in English* 2 (1933), 38–61.
1. MS Bodley 264 includes *Alexander and Dindimus*.

French—if not more so. The English episode is again followed by a French text, Marco Polo's prose *Liures du graunt Daam*.

The Red Book of Bath[2] also contains items in all three languages current in 15th century England, probably because this miscellany seems to have been intended for the official use of the Magistrate of Bath: traditionally, legal texts had to be in French,[3] historical texts and quotations from the Bible in Latin. The numerous English entries in this extraordinary collection clearly indicate that some knowledge of Latin and French could no longer be assumed as a matter of course by then.

Only poor quality fragments of the originally voluminous B.L. MS. Cotton Vitellius D.III[4] were saved from the fire in the Cotton Library in 1731, one each in English, French, and Latin. If the list of contents of the volume in the old catalogue[5] compiled by Cotton's librarian before the fire can be relied upon, MS. Cotton Vitellius D.III is the only known manuscript containing a Middle English as well as an Anglo-Norman romance (*Floris and Blauncheflour* and *Amis et Amiloun*). The possibility that originally independent manuscripts may have been bound together to form this volume cannot, however, be excluded.

A synopsis of the languages in the romance manuscripts, which also takes into consideration their contents, would thus permit the following conclusions as regards their public: most interest in the romances would have been found among the cultivated readers, members of the prospering middle classes, who could and did spend money and time acquiring and reading romances and other literature. The all-permeating influence of the Church and religion even in the 15th century is reflected in numerous Latin religious tags in the manuscripts. There is, however, only scanty evidence that members of the oldest literate public, the clergy, or "tradition", as Blake called it ("religious, particularly female religious in monastic and quasimonastic foundations . . .")[6] also read romances, as suggested by the Vernon and Simeon MSS.,[7] B.L. MS. Harley 2253[8] and perhaps also National Libr. of Scotland MS. Adv. 19.3.1.[9] It is difficult to decide whether the English and Latin texts seriously concerned with theological, historical or medical matters would have been understandable to an interested lay audience or must be seen as reading for professionals only, who would then also, presumably, have been readers of romances. The small number of French items in

---

2. Otherwise known as Longleat House MS 55; the MS includes *Arthur*.
3. Baugh, *History of the English Language*, p. 161 and pp. 177–78.
4. MS Cotton Vitellius D.III includes *Floris and Blancheflour*.
5. Thomas Smith, *Catalogus Librorum Manuscriptorum Bibliothecae Cottoniae* . . . (Oxford, 1696), p. 90.
6. N.F. Blake, "Middle English Prose and Its Audience", *Anglia*, 90 (1972), 446. Cf. also J.A. Burrow, "The Audience of Piers Plowman", *Anglia*, 75 (1957), 373–84.
7. See above, respectively, nn. 8 and 7, p. 500.
8. See above, p. 502, n. 7.
9. See above, p. 501, n. 5.

the present selection of manuscripts would seem to indicate that Middle English romances would not normally reach circles in which French still enjoyed great prestige as a language of literature,[1] i. e., the most educated classes, the nobility, and the court. Only Bodl. Libr. MS. Bodley 264[2] and B.M. MS. Cotton Nero A.X,[3] both containing alliterative romances, and possibly also the *Generides* MSS.[4] would indicate that these classes were to some extent familiar with romances. The lowest classes of society, being illiterate, had no part in the tradition of romances manifested in the manuscripts. They were almost certainly involved in the dissemination of romances in an oral tradition which existed side by side with its written counterpart but has left hardly any identifiable traces in the manuscripts.

Reading or Listening Audience

Through the consideration of the connection, which undoubtedly exists between the distribution of verse and prose in the manuscripts, on the one hand, and a listening or reading public on the other, we can again come to a more precise description of the audience of Middle English romances.

As is sufficiently well known, vernacular literature was delivered orally from the earliest times, by means of performing memorized or improvised texts or reading aloud from manuscripts.[5] Metrical language was particularly well suited for this purpose. "The physical circumstances determined that the form and content of most vernacular literature were popular, that is, potentially intelligible and interesting to members of all classes and capacities . . . It had to be read and heard in public and so was best when of clear metrical shape, repeatedly punctuated with appeals to the audience and summaries of the narrative and didactic burden."[6] The force of the traditional verse form was so strong that even in late Middle English times Latin and French prose works had to be translated into English verse if they were to become at all popular.[7] Versified theological, historical, medical or moralizing texts thus became edifying and pleasing "literature", which, as dull as it may seem to us,

---

1. A comparison of Middle English romance manuscripts with those of Anglo-Norman and French romances in England would be interesting.
2. See above, p. 502, n. 1.
3. See above, p. 499, n. 4.
4. Cambridge, Trinity College Cambridge MS 0.5.2 and Pierpont Morgan Library (New York) MS M 876.
5. See, for instance, R. Crosby, "Oral Delivery in the Middle Ages", *Speculum*, 11 (1936), 88–110; A.I. Doyle, "The Social Context of Medieval Literature", in *The Age of Chaucer*, The Pelican Guide to English Literature, I (Harmondsworth, 1954), 88; Mehl, p. 249.—The consequences of oral presentation of poetry have been especially emphasized in Chaucer scholarship; cf. R. Crosby, "Chaucer and the Custom of Oral Delivery", *Speculum*, 13 (1938), 413–33; B.H. Bronson, "Chaucer's art in relation to his audience", in *Five Studies in Literature* (Berkeley, 1940); J. Lawlor, *Chaucer*, Hutchinson University Library (London, 1968).
6. Doyle ["Social Context"], p. 89.
7. See R.M. Wilson, *Early Middle English Literature*, 3rd ed. (London, 1968), pp. 19–20.

appealed to the non-professional public.[8] Moreover, after the sudden decline of the late Old English literary prose the prose of the 12th to 14th centuries was a clumsy instrument, unfit to convey complicated matter in an attractive form. Extant Middle English saints' lives and homilies in prose may have been intended for oral delivery,[9] but generally prose was considered a "specialised medium,"[1] suitable for professional reference and studies. This can easily be proved by the numerous remarks on the texts which readers of Middle English prose scribbled on the margins of the manuscripts, which would be incompatible with an oral presentation. It is only in the 15th century that a general reading public grows in number, while the traditional oral performance even of verse loses importance.[2]

The largest group of romance manuscripts (29 manuscripts) contains exclusively English verse; ten more manuscripts contain sporadic prose items which, with the exception of a Latin chronicle in B.L. MS. Cotton Caligula A.II,[3] are all in English. In nine manuscripts English verse and prose items are equally balanced, three more contain additional Latin verse and prose. In twelve manuscripts prose clearly dominates. The first and last groups offer no great problems: the manuscripts containing only verse easily support the current assumption of an oral delivery of romances, religious and moralizing lyrics, historical poems and all other poetry. One can distinguish, according to subjects, among the prose manuscript groups: historical manuscripts (Cambridge, U.L. MS. Mm.V.14,[4] B.L. MS. Harley 4690,[5] College of Arms MSS. Arundel 22 and 58,[6] perhaps also Bodl. Libr. MSS. Digby 185 and Rawl. D.82[7]), rather late commonplace books (B.L. MS. Harley 2252,[8] Lambeth Palace Libr. MS. 306,[9] Bodl. Libr. MS. Ashmole 45[1] and scientific or medical manuscripts (National Libr. of Wales Deposit MS. Porkington 10/I,[2] Cambridge, Trinity Coll. MS. 0.2.13/IV[3] B.L. MS. Lansdowne 388[4] contains religious and medical prose. Longleat House MS. 55,[5]

---

8. Cf. D. Pearsall, *John Lydgate*, Medieval Authors (London, 1970), p. 10; Doyle ["Social Context"], pp. 89–90.
9. W. Matthews (ed.), *Later Medieval English Prose*, Goldentree Books (New York, 1963), p. 11.
1. Pearsall, *John Lydgate*, p. 10.
2. Pearsall, *John Lydgate*, p. 9; H.S. Bennett, "The Author and his Public in the 14th and 15th Centuries", *Essays and Studies*, 23 (1937), 18–21.
3. See above, p. 501, n. 9.
4. See above, p. 501, n. 8.
5. MS Harley 4690 includes *Richard Coeur de Lion*.
6. MS Arundel 22 includes *The Siege of Troy*; Arundel 58 includes *Richard Coeur de Lion*.
7. MS Digby 185 includes *King Ponthus*; MS Rawlinson D.82 includes *The Siege of Thebes* and the *Siege of Troy*.
8. See above, p. 501, n. 2.
9. See above, p. 501, n. 3.
1. MS Ashmole 45 includes *The Earl of Tolouse*.
2. See above, p. 500, n. 9.
3. See above, p. 501, n. 6.
4. MS Lansdowne 388 includes the fragment of *The Song of Roland*.
5. See above, p. 503, n. 2.

the "manual" of the Bath Magistrate, is again unique, but contains practical texts like the other prose manuscripts mentioned. Almost all these manuscripts, complete with the romances they contain, would have served as books for silent reading or studying for moderately educated members of the middle classes.

More difficult to interpret are the manuscripts containing verse and prose in varying proportions. The subject matter of the prose texts is similar to the manuscripts above, although religious items and medical recipes predominate. Whether a volume was used for oral presentation will probably have to be decided individually for each manuscript. Bodl. Libr. MS. Laud Misc. 656, containing the *Siege of Jerusalem* and *Piers Plowman* together with a prose homily and verses from the Bible—all very edifying—may well have been used for reading aloud. The case of Chetham's Libr. MS. 8009[6] with its two prose lives may be similar. But the classification of B.L. MS. Cotton Caligula A.II,[7] which contains a Latin chronicle, an English medical tract and a form of confession in prose besides the famous romances and religious poems, is more difficult. In the middle of the 15th century a Latin chronicle would hardly have been intelligible to lay listeners, a fact which may be indicated by the presence of most of the other items in the manuscript. Nor would the medical tract invite an oral performance. If these texts were not read to an audience but were studied silently, it seems just as likely that the religious lyrics and the romances were also enjoyed in this way.

For anthologies like [MS. Cotton Caligula A.II], Lambeth Palace Libr. MS. 491[8] or Dublin, Trinity Coll. MS. 432[9] the solution to the question of silent or public reading is probably to be found in deductions from their mixed contents: these corresponded to the needs of a mixed household and would have been intended for mixed use by readers and listeners, certainly from the 15th century onwards. Such manuscripts would have to serve as libraries for whole families. A non-clerical background would seem most appropriate for such miscellanies.

To sum up the results of the foregoing discussion in two points: firstly, the relationship of verse and prose deserves attention, especially in manuscripts of the 14th and 15th centuries, since it assists in a reconstruction of the nature of literature in that period. And secondly: the public interested in Middle English romances, which was once a purely listening audience, is at least partly a fiction in the 14th and 15th centuries—a fiction supported by the poems themselves with their ever recurring addresses to their "listeners" and kept alive even when the reading public had begun to increase.

6. See above, p. 500, n. 1.
7. See above, p. 501, n. 9.
8. MS 491 includes *The Siege of Jerusalem* and a version of *The Awntyrs off Arthure at the Terne Watheleyne.*
9. MS 432 includes *Robert of Sicily.*

Selected Bibliography

This bibliography does not include works excerpted in this volume.

BIBLIOGRAPHIES AND OTHER USEFUL WORKS OF REFERENCE

Annual Bibliography of English Language and Literature. published for the Modern Humanities Research Association, Cambridge.

International Medieval Bibliography. Published twice a year under the auspices of the University of Leeds.

Middle English Dictionary. Ann Arbor, Mich., 1952— [in progress].

MLA International Bibliography of Books and Articles on the Modern Languages and Litertures. Published annually by the Modern Language Association of America, New York.

The Oxford English Dictionary, 2nd ed. 20 vols. Oxford, 1989.

The Year's Work in English Studies. Published for the English Association, London.

Aarne, Antii. *The Types of the Folk-Tale.* Translated and enlarged by Stith Thompson. Folklore Fellows Communications, no. 184. Helsinki, 1961.

Bordman, Gerald. *Motif-Index of the English Metrical Romances.* Folklore Fellows Communications, no. 190. Helsinki, 1963.

Rice, Joanne A. *Middle English Romance: An Annotated Bibliography, 1955–1985.* New York, 1987.

Severs, J. Burke, ed. *A Manual of the Writings in Middle English.* Fascicule 1: *Romances 1050–1500.* New Haven, Conn., 1967.

Whiting, B. J. *Proverbs, Sentences, and Proverbial Phrases from English Writings Mainly Before 1500.* Cambridge, Mass., 1968.

GENERAL CRITICAL STUDIES

Amsler, Mark. "Literary Theory and the Genres of Middle English Literature." *Genre* 13 (1980), 389–96.

Barron, W. R. J. *English Medieval Romance.* London, 1987. [Includes a useful bibliography.]

Baugh, A. C. "The Authorship of the Middle English Romances." *Annual Bulletin of the Modern Humanities Research Association* 22 (1950), 1–28.

———. "The Middle English Romance: Some Questions of Creation, Presentation, and Preservation." *Speculum* 42 (1967), 1–31.

———. "Convention and Individuality in the Middle English Romance," *Medieval Literature and Folklore Studies: Essays in Honor of Francis Lee Utley,* ed. J. Mandel and B.A. Rosenberg, 123–46. New Jersey, 1970.

Beer, Gillian. *The Romance.* The Critical Idiom. London, 1970.

Bloomfield, Morton W. "Episodic Motivation and Marvels in Epic and Romance," *Essays and Explorations: Studies in Ideas, Language, and Literature.* Cambridge, Mass., 1970.

Brewer, Derek. "The Nature of Romance." *Poetica* 9 (1978), 9–48.

———, ed. *Studies in Medieval English Romances: Some New Approaches.* Cambridge, 1988.

Crane, Susan. *Insular Romance.* Berkeley and Los Angeles, 1986.

Doob, Penelope. *Nebuchadnezzar's Children: Conventions of Madness in Middle English Literature.* London, 1974.

Duggan, Hoyt N. "The Role of Formulas in the Dissemination of a Middle English Alliterative Romance." *Studies in Bibliography* 29 (1976), 265–88.

Dürmüller, U. *Narrative Possibilities of the Tail-Rhyme Romance.* Berne, 1975.

Everett, Dorothy. *Essays on Middle English Literature.* Ed. P. Kean. Oxford, 1955.

Fewster, Carol. *Traditionality and Genre in Middle English Romance*. Cambridge, 1987.
Gradon, Pamela. *Form and Style in Early English Literature*. London, 1971.
Green, D. H. *Irony in the Medieval Romance*. Cambridge, 1979.
Hill, D. M. "Romance as Epic." *English Studies* 44 (1963), 95–107.
Hume, Kathryn. "The Formal Nature of Middle English Romance." *Philological Quarterly* 53 (1974), 158–80.
Ker, W. P. *Epic and Romance: Essays on Medieval Literature*. London, 1896; reprinted New York, 1957.
Mehl, Dieter. *The Middle English Romances of the Thirteenth and Fourteenth Centuries*. London, 1968.
Pearsall, Derek. "The Development of Middle English Romance." *Mediæval Studies* 27 (1965), 91–116.
———. "Middle English Romance and its Audiences," Mary-Jo Arn and Hanneke Wirtjes, eds, *Historical and Editorial Studies in Medieval and Early Modern English for Johan Gerritsen*, 37–47. Groningen, 1985.
Schofield, W. H. *English Literature from the Norman Conquest to Chaucer*. New York, 1906; reprinted 1969.
Speirs, John. *Medieval English Poetry: The Non-Chaucerian Tradition*. London, 1957.
Stevens, John. *Medieval Romance: Themes and Approaches*. London, 1973.
Strohm, Paul. "The Origin and Meaning of Middle English 'Romaunce'." *Genre* 10 (1977), 1–28.
———, "Middle English Narrative Genres." *Genre* 13 (1980), 379–88.
Tuve, Rosemond. *Allegorical Imagery: Some Medieval Books and Their Posterity*. Princeton, 1966.
Vinaver, Eugène. *The Rise of Romance*. Oxford, 1971.
Wilson, R. M. *The Lost Literature of Medieval England*. New York, 1969.
Wittig, Susan. *Stylistic and Narrative Structures in the Middle English Romances*. Austin, Texas, 1978.

ANTHOLOGIES OF MIDDLE ENGLISH ROMANCES

Fellows, Jennifer, ed. *Of Love and Chivalry: An Anthology of Middle English Romance*. London, 1993.
French, W. H. and C. B. Hale, eds. *Middle English Metrical Romances*. New York, 1930.
Gibbs, A. C., ed. *Middle English Romances*. London, 1966.
Lupack, Alan. *Three Middle English Charlemagne Romances*. Kalamazoo, 1990.
Mills, Maldwyn, ed. *Six Middle English Romances*. London, 1973; revised 1992.
———. *Ywain and Gawain, Sir Percyvell of Gales, The Anturs of Arther*. London, 1992.
Rumble, T. C., ed. *The Breton Lays in Middle English*. Detroit, 1965.
Sands, Donald B., ed. *Middle English Verse Romances*. New York, 1966.
Schmidt, A. V. C. and Nicholas Jacobs, eds. *Medieval English Romances*. 2 vols. London, 1980.
Speed, D., ed. *Medieval English Romances*. 3rd ed. 2 vols. Durham, England, 1993.

HAVELOK
Separate Editions

Skeat, W. W. ed. *Havelok the Dane*. 2nd ed. Revised by K. Sisam. Oxford, 1915.
Smithers, G. V. *Havelok*. Oxford, 1987. [Includes transcriptions of the "Lambeth interpolation" (pp. xxii–xxiii), and previously unpublished portions of the Anglo-Norman prose *Brut* (pp. xxv–xxvi) and the *Petit Brut* (pp. xxvii–xxviii).]

Source and Background Texts and Studies

Bell, A., ed. *Le Lai d'Haveloc and Gaimar's Havelok Episode*. Manchester, 1925.
———. *L'Estoire des Engleis by Gaimar*. Anglo Norman Text Society nos. 14–16. Oxford, 1960.
Brie, F., ed. *The Brut, or The Chronicles of England*. Early English Text Society no. 131. London, 1906.
Foerster, W. *Richars li Baus*. Vienna, 1874.
Lollife, J. E. A. *The Constitutional History of Medieval England*. London, 1948.
Pollock and Maitland. *The History of English Law Before the Time of Edward I*. Cambridge, 1898.

Mannyng, Robert. *Chronicle.* In F. J. Furnivall, ed., *The Story of England by Robert Manning of Brunne*, vols. 1 and 2. Rolls Series. London, 1887.

Critical Studies

Biggs, Frederick M. Review of Smithers's 1987 edition. *Journal of English and Germanic Philology* 88 (1989), 87–89.
Bradbury, Nancy Mason. "The Traditional Origins of *Havelok the Dane.*" *Studies in Philology* 90 (1993), 115–42.
Delaney, Sheila, and Vahan Ishkanian. "Theocratic and Contractual Kingship in *Havelok the Dane.*" *Zeitschrift für Anglistik und Amerikanistik* 22 (1974), 290–302.
Finlayson, John. "*King Horn* and *Havelok the Dane*: A Case of Mistaken Identities." *Medievalia et Humanistica*, n. s., no. 18 (1992), 17–45.
Halverson, John. "*Havelok the Dane* and Society." *Chaucer Review* 6 (1971), 142–51.
Hanning, Robert W. "*Havelok the Dane*: Structure, Symbols, Meaning." *Studies in Philology* 64 (1967), 586–605
Hirsch, John C. "*Havelok* 2933: A Problem in Medieval Literary History." *Neuphilologische Mitteilungen* 78 (1979), 339–47.
Jacobs, Nicholas. Review of Smithers's 1987 edition. *Medium Ævum* 57 (1988), 303–7.
Levine, Robert. "Who Composed *Havelock* for Whom?" *Yearbook of English Studies* 22 (1992), 95–104.
Lindström, Bengt. "Eight Notes on *Havelok.*" *Notes and Queries* 239 (1994), 11–14.
Mills, Maldwyn. "Havelok and the Brutal Fisherman." *Medium Ævum* 36 (1967) , 219–30.
———. "Havelok's Return." *Medium Ævum* 45 (1976), 20–35.
Reiss, Edmund. "*Havelok the Dane* and Norse Mythology." *Modern Language Quarterly* 27 (1966), 115–24.
Scott, Anne. "Language as Convention, Language as Sociolect in *Havelok the Dane.*" *Studies in Philology* 89 (1992), 137–60.
Smithers, G. V. "The Style of *Hauelok.*" *Medium Ævum* 57 (1988), 190–218.
Staines, David. "*Havelok the Dane*: A Thirteenth-Century Handbook for Princes." *Speculum* 51 (1976), 602–23.
Weiss, Judith. "Structure and Characterisation in *Havelok the Dane.*" *Speculum* 44 (1969), 247–57.
Wilson, Edward. Review of Smithers's 1987 edition. *Notes and Queries* 233 (1988), 351–55.

YWAIN AND GAWAIN
General Arthurian and Celtic Backgrounds
(See also entries below for *Sir Orfeo.*)

Ackerman, Robert W. *An Index of the Arthurian Names in Middle English.* Stanford, 1952.
Bruce, J. D. *The Evolution of Arthurian Romance: From the Beginnings Down to the Year 1300.* 2 vols. 1923; reprinted Geneva, 1974.
Coghlan, Ronan. *The Encyclopaedia of Arthurian Legends.* London, 1991.
Darrah, J. *The Real Camelot: Paganism and the Arthurian Romances.* London, 1981.
Ellis, Peter Beresford. *A Dictionary of Irish Mythology.* London, 1987.
Geoffrey of Monmouth. *History of the Kings of Britian.* Trans. L. Thorpe. London, 1966.
Green, Miranda. *The Gods of the Celts.* Stroud, Gloucestershire, 1986.
Guyer, F. E. *Romance in the Making.* New York, 1954.
Lacy, Norris J., ed. *The Arthurian Encyclopoedia.* New York, 1986.
Loomis, R. S., ed. *Celtic Myth and Arthurian Romance.* New York, 1927.
———. *Arthurian Literature in the Middle Ages: A Collaborative History.* Oxford, 1959.
———. *The Development of Arthurian Romance.* London, 1963.
Nennius. "Historia Britonum," *British History and the Welsh Annals*, ed. J. Morris. Chichester, England, 1980.
Rees, Alwyn and Brinley. *Celtic Heritage.* London, 1961.
Wace and Layamon. *Arthurian Chronicles.* Trans. E. Mason. London, 1962; reprinted 1976.
Wilhelm, J. J., and L. Z. Gross, eds. *The Romance of Arthur: An Anthology.* New York, 1984.

Separate Edition

Friedman, Albert B., and Norman T. Harrington, eds. *Ywain and Gawain.* Early English Text Society no. 254. London, 1964.

Source and Background Texts

Jones, Gwyn, and Thomas Jones, eds. *The Mabinogion.* Rev. ed. London, 1989. [Includes *Culhwch and Olwen* and *The Lady of the Fountain.*]

de Troyes, Chrétien. *Arthurian Romances.* Trans. D. D. R. Owen. London, 1987. [Includes *Erec and Enide, Cligés, Lancelot, Yvain,* and *Perceval.*]

Critical Studies

Ackerman, Robert W. "Arthur's Wild Man Knight." *Romance Philology* 9 (1955), 115–19.

Busby, Keith. "Chrétien de Troyes English'd." *Neophilologus* 71 (1987), 596–613.

Britton, G. C. Review of the Friedman and Harrington edition. *Notes and Queries* 209 (1964), 478–79.

Finlayson, John. "*Ywain and Gawain* and the Meaning of Adventure." *Anglia* 87 (1969), 312–17.

Hamilton, Gayle K. "The Breaking of the Troth in *Ywain and Gawain.*" *Mediaevalia* 2 (1976), 111–35.

Harrington, N. T. "The Problem of the Lacunae in *Ywain and Gawain.*" *Journal of English and Germanic Philology* 69 (1970), 659–65.

Kratins, Ojars. "Love and Marriage in Three Versions of 'The Knight of the Lion.' " *Comparative Literature* 16 (1964), 29–39.

Matthews, David. "Translation and Ideology: The Case of *Ywain and Gawain.*" *Neophilologus* 76 (1992), 452–63.

Taglicht, J. Review of the Friedman and Harrington edition. *Medium Ævum* 34 (1965), 66–68.

———. "Notes on *Ywain and Gawain.*" *Neuphilologische Mitteilungen* 71 (1970), 641–47.

SIR ORFEO
Separate Edition

Bliss, A. J., ed. *Sir Orfeo.* 2nd ed. Oxford, 1966.

Facsimile

The Auchinleck Manuscript. National Library of Scotland Advocates' MS. 19.2.1. Introduced by Derek Pearsall and I. C. Cunningham. London, 1977.

Source and Background Texts and Studies
(For general Celtic backgrounds, see the entries for *Ywain and Gawain,* above.)

Beston, John B. "How Much Was Known of the Breton Lai in Fourteenth-Century England?" *The Lerned and the Lewed: Studies in Chaucer and Medieval Literature,* 319–36. Cambridge, Mass., 1974.

Bernheimer, R. *Wild Men in the Middle Ages.* Cambridge, Mass., 1952.

Boethius. *The Consolation of Philosophy.* Trans. V.E. Watts. London, 1969.

Damon, S. Foster. "Marie de France: Psychologist of Courtly Love." *Publications of the Modern Language Association of America* 44 (1929), 968–96.

Delaney, Frank, ed. and trans. *Legends of the Celts.* London, 1989. [Includes *The Wooing of Etain.*]

de France, Marie. *The Lais of Marie de France.* Ed. and trans. G. Burgess and K. Busby. London, 1986.

———. *Les Lais de Marie de France.* Ed. J. Rychner. Paris, 1966.

Dronke, Peter. "The Return of Eurydice." *Classica et Mediaevalia* 23 (1962), 198–215.

Du Méril, E. *Floire et Blanceflor.* Paris, 1856. [Esp. p. 231.]

Frey, John A. "Linguistic and Psychological Couplings in the Lais of Marie de France." *Studies in Philology* 61 (1964), 3–18.

Friedman, J. B. *Orpheus in the Middle Ages.* Cambridge, Mass., 1970.

Geoffrey of Monmouth. *Vita Merlini.* Ed. and trans. J.J. Parry. Urbana, 1925.

Hume, Kathryn. "Why Chaucer Calls the *Franklin's Tale* a Breton Lai." *Philological Quarterly* 53 (1974), 158–80.

Map, Walter. *De Nugis Curialium (Courtiers' Trifles).* Trans. Frederick Tupper and Marbury Bladen Ogle. London, 1924.

Loomis, Laura Hibbard. "Chaucer and the Breton Lays of the Auchinleck MS." *Studies in Philology* 38 (1941), 14–33.
Ovid. *The Metamorphoses*. Trans. Horace Gregory. London, 1960.
Sommer, H. O., ed. *Prose Lancelot, The Vulgate Version of the Arthurian Romances*, vols. 3–5. Washington, 1908–16. [Esp. iv, 290.]
Virgil. *The Aeneid*. Trans. W. F. Jackson. London, 1958.
———. *The Georgics*. Trans. L.P. Wilkinson. London, 1982.
Zenker, R., ed. *Lai de l'Espine. Zeitschrift für romanische Philologie* 17 (1893), 233–55.

Critical Studies

Allen, Dorena. "Orpheus and Orfeo: The Dead and the *Taken*." *Medium Ævum* 33 (1964), 102–11.
Friedman, J. B. "Eurydice, Heurodis, and the Noon-Day Demon." *Speculum* 41 (1966), 22–29.
Hynes-Berry, M. "Cohesion in *King Horn* and *Sir Orfeo*." *Speculum* 50 (1975), 652–70.
Lerer, Seth. "Artifice and Artistry in *Sir Orfeo*." *Speculum* 60 (1985), 92–109.
Lucas, P. J. "An Interpretation of *Sir Orfeo*." *Leeds Studies in English* 6 (1972), 1–9.
Olsen, A. H. "Loss and Recovery: A Morphological Reconsideration of *Sir Orfeo*." *Fabula* 23 (1982), 196–206.
Riddy, Felicity. "The Uses of the Past in *Sir Orfeo*." *Yearbook of English Studies* 6 (1976), 5–15.
Severs, J. Burke. "The Antecedents of *Sir Orfeo*," *Studies in Medieval Literature in Honor of Professor Albert Croll Baugh*, ed. M. Leach, 187–207. Philadelphia, 1961.
Smithers, G. V. "Story-Patterns in Some Breton Lays." *Medium Ævum* 22 (1953), 61–92.

SIR LAUNFAL

(For references to Marie de France and the Breton Lays, see the entries under *Sir Orfeo*, above.)

Separate Edition

Bliss, A. J., ed. *Sir Launfal*. London, 1960. [Includes editions of *Sir Landevale* and *Lanval*.]

Source and Background Texts and Studies

Bliss, A. J. "Thomas Chestre: A Speculation." *Litera* 5 (1958), 1–6.
Bullock-Davies, Constance. " 'Ympe tre' and 'nemeton'." *Notes and Queries*, n.s., 9 (1962), 6–9.
Mills, Maldwyn. "The Composition and Style of the 'Southern' *Octavian, Sir Launfal*, and *Libeaus Desconus*." *Medium Ævum* 31 (1962), 88–109.
———, ed. *Libeaus Desconus*. Early English Text Society no. 261. London, 1969.
Weingartner, Russell, ed. and trans. *"Graelent" and "Guingamor." Two Breton Lays*. New York, 1984.
Zupitza, J., ed. *Guy of Warwick*. Early English Text Society nos. 42, 49, 59. London, 1883, 1887, 1891; reprinted 1966 in one volume.

Critical Studies

Anderson, E. R. "The Structure of *Sir Launfal*." *Papers on Language and Literature* 13 (1977), 115–24.
Bradstock, E. M. " 'Honoure' in *Sir Launfal*." *Parergon* 24 (1979), 9–17.
Carlson, David. "The Middle English *Lanval*, the Corporal Works of Mercy, and Bibliothèque Nationale, nouv. acq. fr. 1104." *Neophilologus* 72 (1988), 97–106.
Edwards, A. S. G. "Unknightly Conduct in *Sir Launfal*." *Notes and Queries*, n. s., 15 (1968), 328–29.
Hirsch, John C. "Pride as Theme in *Sir Launfal*." *Notes and Queries*, n. s., 14 (1967), 288–91.
Lane, Daryl. "Conflict in *Sir Launfal*." *Neuphilologische Mitteilungen* 74 (1973), 283–87.
Martin, B. K. "*Sir Launfal* and the Folktale." *Medium Ævum* 35 (1966), 199–210.
Mills, Maldwyn. Review of Bliss's edition. *Medium Ævum* 31 (1962), 75–78.

————. "A Note on *Sir Launfal*, 733–744." *Medium Ævum* 35 (1966), 122–24.

Nappholz, Carol. J. "Launfal's 'Largesse': Word-Play in Thomas Chestre's *Sir Launfal*." *English Language Notes* (1988), 4–9.

Williams, Elizabeth. "*Lanval* and *Sir Landevale*: A Medieval Translator and His Methods." *Leeds Studies in English* 3 (1969), 85–99.

THE AWNTYRS OFF ARTHURE AT THE TERNE WATHELYNE
Separate Editions

Gates, Robert J. *The Awntyrs off Arthure at the Terne Wathelyne: A Critical Edition*. Philadelphia, 1969.

Hanna, Ralph III, ed. *The Awntyrs off Arthure at the Terne Wathelyn: An Edition Based on Bodleian Library MS Douce 324*. Manchester and New York, 1974.

Phillips, Helen, ed. *The Awntyrs off Arthure at the Terne Wathelyne: A Modern Spelling Edition*. Lancaster, 1988.

Source and Background Texts and Studies
(See also entries for *The Weddyng of Syr Gawen*, below.)

Armstrong, A. M., et al. *The Place-Names of Cumberland*. Cambridge, 1950.

Benson, Larry D. *King Arthur's Death: The Middle English Stanzaic Morte Arthur and Alliterative Morte Arthure*. Indianapolis, 1974.

Borroff, Marie, trans. *Sir Gawain and the Green Knight: A New Verse Translation*. New York, 1967.

Dahood, R., ed. *The Avowynge of King Arthur, Sir Gawan, Sir Kaye, and Sir Bawdewyn of Bretan*. New York, 1984.

Furnivall, F. J., and J. W. Hales, eds. *The Grene Knight, King Arthur and King Cornwall*, and *The Turke and Gowin*, in *Bishop Percy's Folio Manuscript: Ballads and Romances*. 4 vols. London, 1867–68; reprinted Detroit, 1968.

Hutchison, William. *The History of the County of Cumberland*. Carlisle, 1974.

Krishna, Valerie, ed. *The Alliterative Morte Arthure*. New York, 1976.

Kurvinen, A., ed. *Sir Gawain and the Carl of Carlisle in Two Versions*. Helsinki, 1951.

Madden, F., ed. [*The Jeaste of*] *Syr Gawayne*. London, 1839.

Medary, Margaret P. "Stanza-Linking in Middle English Verse." *Romanic Review* 7 (1916), 243–70.

Stevenson, G. S., ed. *Golagrus and Gawain*. Scottish Text Society no. 65. Edinburgh, 1918.

Tolkien, J. R. R., and E. V. Gordon, eds. *Sir Gawain and the Green Knight*. 2nd ed. Revised by Norman Davis. Oxford, 1967.

Turville-Petre, Thorlac. "*Summer Sunday, De Tribus Regibus Mortuis*, and *The Awntyrs off Arthure*: Three Poems in the Thirteen-Line Stanza." *Review of English Studies*, n. s., 25 (1974), 1–14.

————. *The Alliterative Revival*. Cambridge, 1977.

————, ed. *Somer Soneday* and *The Three Dead Kings*, *Alliterative Poetry of the Middle Ages*. London, 1989.

Critical Studies

Allen, Rosamund. "Some Sceptical Observations on the Editing of *The Awntyrs off Arthure*." *Manuscripts and Texts: Editorial Problems in Later Middle English Literature*, ed. Derek Pearsall, 5–25. Cambridge, 1987.

Hanna, Ralph, III. "*The Awntyrs off Arthure*: An Interpretation." *Modern Language Quarterly* 31 (1970), 275–97.

————. "A la recherche du temps bien perdu: The Text of *The Awntyrs off Arthure*." *Text* 4 (1988), 189–205.

Klausner, D. N. "Exempla and *The Awntyrs off Arthure*." *Mediæval Studies* 34 (1972), 317–25.

Phillips, Helen. "The Ghost's Baptism in *The Awntyrs off Arthure*." *Medium Ævum* 58 (1989), 49–58.

————. "*The Awntyrs off Arthure*: Structure and Meaning. A Reassessment," *Arthurian Literature* XII. Cambridge, 1993.

Spearing, A. C. *The Awntyrs off Arthure, The Alliterative Tradition in the Fourteenth Century*, ed. Bernard S. Levy and Paul E. Szarmach, 183–202. Kent, Ohio, 1981.

———. "Central and Displaced Sovereignty in Three Medieval Poems." *Review of English Studies*, n. s., 33 (1982), 247–61.
———. *Medieval to Renaissance in English Poetry*. Cambridge, 1985. [Esp. 121–42.]

THE WEDDYNG OF SYR GAWEN AND DAME RAGNELL
Separate Editions

Garbaty, T. J., ed. *The Wedding of Sir Gawain and Dame Ragnell, Medieval English Literature*, ed. T. J. Garbaty. Lexington and Toronto, 1984.
Sumner, Laura, ed. *The Weddynge of Sir Gawen and Dame Ragnell. Smith College Studies in Modern Languages* 5.4 (1924).
Whiting, B. J., ed. *The Weddynge of Sir Gawen and Dame Ragnell, Sources and Analogues of Chaucer's "Canterbury Tales,"* ed. W. F. Bryan and Germaine Dempster, 242–64. New York, 1941; reprinted 1958.
Wilhelm, J. J. *The Wedding of Sir Gawain and Dame Ragnell, The Romance of Arthur III*, ed. J.J. Wilhelm. New York, 1988.
Withrington, John. *The Wedding of Sir Gawain and Dame Ragnell: A Modern Spelling Edition*. Lancaster, 1991.

Source and Background Texts and Studies
(See also entries for *The Awntyrs off Arthure*, above.)

Cawley, A. C., and J. J. Anderson, eds. *Pearl, Cleanness, Patience, Sir Gawain and the Green Knight*. London, 1978.
Chaucer, Geoffrey. *The Wife of Bath's Prologue and Tale, The Riverside Chaucer*, ed. Larry D. Benson. Boston, 1987.
Child, F. J. *The English and Scottish Popular Ballads*. 5 vols. New York, 1882–98; reprinted 1965. [Includes *The Marriage of Sir Gawain* and the ballad *King Henry*.]
Eisner, Sigmund. *A Tale of Wonder*. Wexford, England, 1957.
Lumiansky, R. M., and David Mills, eds. *The Chester Mystery Cycle*. Early English Text Society, Supplementary Series 3 and 9. London, 1974 and 1986.
Maynadier, G. H. *The Wife of Bath's Tale: Its Sources and Analogues*. London, 1901.
Malory, Sir Thomas. *Works [Morte Darthur]*. Ed. Eugène Vinaver. Revised by P.J.C. Field. Oxford, 1990.
Matthews, William. "The Locale of *Le Morte Darthur*," *The Ill-Framed Knight: A Skeptical Inquiry into the Identity of Sir Thomas Malory*, 75–114. Berkeley, 1966.
Rogers, Gillian. "The Percy Folio Manuscript Revisited." In *Romance in Medieval England*, ed. M. Mills, J. Fellows, and C. M. Meale, 39–64. Cambridge, 1991.

Critical Studies

Field, P. J. C. "Malory and *The Wedding of Sir Gawain and Dame Ragnell*." *Archiv für das Studium der neueren Sprachen und Literaturen* 219 (1982), 374–81.
Glasser, Marc. " 'He Nedes Moste Hire Wedde': The Forced Marriage in the *Wife of Bath's Tale* and Its Middle English Analogues." *Neuphilologishe Mitteilungen* 85 (1984), 239–41.
Shenk, Robert. "The Liberation of the 'Loathly Lady' of Medieval Romance." *Journal of the Rocky Mountain Medieval and Renaissance Association* 2 (1981), 69–77.

THE SEGE OFF MELAYNE
Source and Background Texts and Studies

(This listing includes the standard edition of *Melayne*, by S. J. Herrtage; see also the revised modern editions in Lupack and Mills, as cited under Anthologies of Middle English Romances, above.)
Bain, R. Nisbett. "The Siege of Belgrade by Muhammad II, July 1–23, 1456." *English Historical Review* 7 (1892), 235–52.
Bédier, Joseph, ed. *La Chanson de Roland*. Paris, 1921. [For a translation, see that by D. D. R. Owen, cited below.]
Berners, Lord (Sir John Bourchier), trans. *Book of Duke Huon of Burdeux*. Ed. S. L. Lee. Early English Text Society, Extra Series nos. 40, 41, 43, and 50. London, 1882–87; reprinted in 2 vols, 1973.

Caxton, William, trans. *Charles the Grete*. Ed. Sidney J. Herrtage. Early English Text Society, Extra Series nos. 36 and 37. London, 1880–81.

———, trans. *The Foure Sonnes of Aymon*. Ed. O. Richardson. Early English Text Society, Extra Series nos. 44 and 45. London, 1884–85.

Finucane, R. C. *Soldiers of the Faith*. London, 1983.

Gray, Douglas, ed. *Capystranus* [*ll.* 360–521]. *The Oxford Book of Late Medieval Verse and Prose*, 199–203, and commentary, 459–60. Oxford, 1985.

Green, D. H. *The Millstätter Exodus: A Crusading Epic*. Cambridge, 1966.

Hausknecht, Emil, ed. *The Romaunce of The Sowdone of Babylone and of Ferumbras his Sone who conquerede Rome*. Early English Text Society, Extra Series no. 38. London, 1881.

Herrtage, Sidney J., ed. *"The Sege off Melayne" and "The Romance of Duke Rowland and Sir Otuell of Spayne"* . . . *Together with a Fragment of "The Song of Roland."* Early English Text Society, Extra Series no. 35. London, 1880.

———, ed. *"Sir Ferumbras" Edited from the Unique Manuscript Bodleian MS. Ashmole 33*. Early English Text Society, Extra Series no. 34. London, 1879.

———, ed. *"The Taill of Rauf Coilyear" with the Fragments of "Rouland and Vernagu" and "Otuel"*. Early English Text Society, Extra Series, no. 39. London, 1882.

Hodgkin, Thomas. *Italy and Her Invaders*. 2nd ed. 8 vols. Oxford, 1892.

Metlitzki, Dorothee. *The Matter of Araby in Medieval England*. New York, 1977.

Munro, D. C. "The Speech of Pope Urban II at Clermont, 1095." *American Historical Review* 11 (1906), 231–42.

O'Sullivan, M. I., ed. *"Firumbras" and "Otuel and Roland."* Early English Text Society, no. 198. London, 1935.

Owen, D. D. R., trans. *The Song of Roland*. Woodbridge, Suffolk, 1990.

Petrovics, István, and György E. Szónyi. "*Capystranus*: A Late Medieval English Romance on the 1456 Siege of Belgrade." *New Hungarian Quarterly* 27 (1986), 141–46. [Preceded by W.A. Ringler's regularized edition of the poem, pp. 131–40.]

Rauschen, Gerhard, ed. "Descriptio qualiter Karolus Magnus clavum et coronam Domini a Constantinopoli Aquis Grani detulerit, qualiterque Carolus Calvus hec ad sanctum Dyonisium retulerit." *Die Legende Karls des Grossen im 11. und 12. Jarhundert*. Leipzig, 1890. [Standard edition of the *Descriptio*.]

Ringler, W. A., Jr. "Charlemagne and the Relics of the Passion." *Notes and Queries* 222 (1977), 488–89. [On the *Capystranus*, although there misidentified.]

Róna, Éva. "Hungary in a Medieval Poem, *Capystranus*, a Metrical Romance." In *Studies in Honour of Margaret Schlauch*. Warsaw, 1966.

Runciman, Steven. *A History of the Crusades*. 3 vols. Cambridge, 1954.

Schwoebel, Robert. *The Shadow of the Crescent: The Renaissance Image of the Turk (1453–1517)*. Nieuwkoop, Belgium, 1967.

Smyser, H. M., ed. *The Pseudo-Turpin*. Cambridge, Mass., 1937. [Provides a useful English synopsis of the Latin chronicle.]

Trotter, D. A. "Judas Maccabaeus, Charlemagne and the 'Oriflamme.' " *Medium Ævum* 54 (1986), 127–31.

Critical Studies

Childress, Diana. "Between Romance and Legend: 'Secular Hagiography' in Middle English Literature." *Philological Quarterly* 57 (1978), 311–22.

Shepherd, S. H. A. " 'This grete journee': *The Sege of Melayne*," *Romance in Medieval England*, ed. M. Mills, J. Fellows, and C.M. Meale, 113–31. Cambridge, 1991.

Thompson, John J. *Robert Thornton and the London Thornton Manuscript*. Cambridge, 1987. [Esp. 48.]

Trounce, A. McI. "The English Tail-Rhyme Romances." *Medium Ævum* vol. 1 (1932), 87–108, 168–82; vol. 2 (1933), 34–57, 189–98; vol. 3 (1934), 30–50.

NORTON CRITICAL EDITIONS